FAMILY THEORIES TODAY

FAMILY THEORIES TODAY

A Critical Intersectional Approach

SECOND EDITION

Katherine R. Allen

Virginia Tech

Angela C. Henderson

University of Northern Colorado

SAN DIEGO

Bassim Hamadeh, CEO and Publisher
Amy Smith, Senior Project Editor
Jeanine Rees, Production Editor
Emely Villavicencio, Senior Graphic Designer
Kylie Bartolome, Licensing Associate
Natalie Piccotti, Director of Marketing
Kassie Graves, Senior Vice President of Editorial
Jamie Giganti, Director of Academic Publishing

3970 Sorrento Valley Blvd., Ste. 500, San Diego, CA 92121

To our families:

Jeff, Hank, and the memory of Matt.
Owen, Cameron, and Cora.

ACTIVE LEARNING

This book has interactive activities available to complement your reading.

Your instructor may have customized the selection of activities available for your unique course. Please check with your professor to verify whether your class will access this content through the Cognella Active Learning portal (http://active.cognella.com) or through your home learning management system.

Brief Contents

Detailed Contents

Preface

This book is about both foundational and emerging theories used to study and understand families. We take an exciting, creative, and scientific approach to the study of family theories that is grounded in real people's lives. As feminist, antiracist scholars and practitioners, our approach is critical, intersectional, interdisciplinary, and left of center. We are inclusive of a variety of family structures, processes, and contexts and the great diversity of how individuals live today. We include individual and family diversity as it appears across the multiplicity of lives, taking into account diversity by gender, race, social class, sexuality, ability, nationality, age, and relationship status. Our approach is informed by families as intimate settings for individual and relational development, where both care and compassion as well as conflict and trauma occur.

This is a transitional book, written with the contemporary challenges to pedagogy in mind in that the content we offer helps instructors pivot between the traditional classroom setting and the online learning environment. We also help instructors and students navigate the controversies that are now found in contemporary discourse about families, including how families are handling a global health pandemic, unprecedented technological changes, political polarization, and intensive activism for social justice. Grounded in our own decades of teaching about family and sociological theories, we have written this book for contemporary students at the undergraduate and graduate level as well as scholars and practitioners across multiple fields in the social and behavioral sciences, including family science, sociology, human services, psychology, communications, social work, nursing, education, recreation and leisure studies, counseling, disability studies, ethnic and racial studies, gerontology, sexuality, business, and health sciences. The writing style is accessible and engaging, and we rely on the latest research, personal experience, practitioner insight, reflexive exercises, and multimedia examples to make the theoretical concepts come alive.

Now in its second edition, we have completely updated every chapter to reflect the explosion of new knowledge about families, during a time of rapid social change. We have also added two completely new chapters (critical race theory and queer theory), for a total of 14 chapters, including an introductory chapter in which we define theory and the theorizing process, as well as a concluding chapter that ties together how theories are a necessary part of any professional's toolkit (building upon our theme: There's a theory app for that!). The foundational theories we cover are functionalist, conflict, symbolic interactionist, family developmental, family systems, social exchange, life course, family ecological, and family stress and resilience. The critical theories we cover are feminist, critical race, and queer. Each chapter includes the history and origins of the theory, its key concepts, its strengths and weaknesses, its contemporary use in theorizing, research, and practice, multimedia resources and examples, and many supplemental features, including questions and prompts for student engagement. Although every chapter includes the most recent theory and research citations, we have retained our rigorous approach to including classical writings about each theory. We also provide an extensive reference list for each of the theories, and each chapter offers five classic and engaging supplemental readings that are especially relevant for readers who wish to learn more.

Each of the 12 theory chapters include four in-depth boxes: (a) Theory at a Glance, (b) Theory in Modern Culture, (c) Global Comparisons, and (d) Voices From Lived Experience. Voices From Lived Experience is one of the new additions to the second edition, in which we analyze actual experiences from students, families, practitioners, or our own lives from a theoretical perspective. Given our commitment to a critical, intersectional approach by representing families across diverse ages, genders, races, classes, sexualities, nationalities, and abilities, we have saturated the second edition of *Family Theories Today* with additional antiracist content, trauma-informed approaches, and new technology sources. We have also updated the graphics and images to more fully represent diverse families and, especially, families of color. Each of the 14 chapters are introduced by a compelling case study, which we refer to throughout the chapter as a way to highlight definitions, theories, concepts, and applications in research and practice. The case studies give deliberate attention to race, class, gender, sexuality, ethnicity, and other systems of oppression and privilege in how individuals and families actually live.

The pedagogical aids we provide include a test bank we created, sample syllabi, and videos in which we introduce each of the theories. The book also includes an extensive glossary of key terms that have been highlighted throughout the text.

One of our goals in writing this book was to also bring the exciting realm of theorizing about families to disciplines beyond our own home fields of family science and family sociology, respectively. Our aim was to write a text for students and for instructors across a range of disciplines from the social and behavioral sciences. We envision this book as both a primary text and a supplemental text, appropriate for both graduate and undergraduate audiences. As the authors, we love theory and the theorizing process, and are very excited to share this worthy endeavor with students and instructors everywhere.

Acknowledgments

Writing this book together has been a great pleasure and a labor of love. Our shared passion for theory has developed into a seamless collaboration, where our strengths and interests enhance one another. As teachers and scholars, our goal is to reveal the possibilities in learning about and using theories to promote a life well lived and one that is informed by principles of social justice for all families. We have benefitted from the journey of theory and theorizing, especially from the voices that have come before us who have carried the weight of widespread injustice that have laid the groundwork for and inspired much of this book.

Speaking of our readers, we wrote this book by keeping in the forefront the thousands of students we have taught in our collective 40-plus years as educators. Our students have taught us many lessons about the value of theory in the scientific enterprise and the excitement in learning to understand and use it effectively. We have also kept in mind our peers who teach students about theory and theorizing. We love knowing so many other educators who share a passion for helping students appreciate the process of theorizing.

We are grateful to many individuals for their scholarly and editorial contributions to this book. We are thrilled to join the Cognella team. From the moment we signed our contract with the always-generous and effervescent Kassie Graves, we knew we would be in excellent hands with our new publisher. We are grateful for the steadfast support and outstanding expertise provided by Amy Smith, our project editor. In fact, all of the Cognella professionals we have worked with have been helpful and encouraging, including Ivey Preston, Emely Villavicencio, Stephanie Adams, Jeanine Rees, and Rachel Mann.

In writing the second edition, we benefited from Candy Beers, who read every chapter with great care and offered valuable insights. Erin Lavender-Stott, who read every chapter and all of the supplemental materials when we wrote the first edition, has returned to offer wise suggestions on several chapters for the second edition. Ezra Taylor and Bianca Ramos provided excellent support and editorial assistance. We thank all of the individuals who provided material for the voices from lived experience in the theories chapters. We also thank the anonymous reviewers secured by Cognella for their invaluable critiques and feedback on the first edition, and we took to heart all of their suggestions. Finally, we thank all of the instructors and students who read the first edition and gave suggestions along the way for making the content even more meaningful and relevant. We are so grateful for all of the insights and support of everyone who has engaged with our book, and we hope to continue to learn from you.

Finally, we thank the members of our own families and friendship networks, who enrich our lives and provide the private testing ground for theorizing about intimate life. We especially thank Jeff, Hank, Matt, Owen, Cameron, and Cora for walking with us on this journey every step of the way.

What Is Theory?

ou are probably familiar with Apple's popular phrase, "There's an app for that!" It is one we often use in modern society to refer to the ways in which our smartphones, tablets, and other electronic devices can help us be more efficient, more creative, and *better* at what we do. Apps help us problem-solve; they help us think in different ways about our everyday lives, friends, families, and social calendars. They help us put it all into a manageable, knowable format that provides a framework for understanding our daily lives.

You may ask yourself why we are beginning our theory text with a discussion of electronic applications. A **theory**—or a set of ideas—serves as a framework for understanding the world around us. The social science theories we describe in this text can be applied, tested, and even revised over time to fit the changing social world. This text presents you with 12 theories of family—12 unique ways to look at the world and to help you, as a student, better understand how to look at and solve problems that you will face in your profession someday. As a practitioner, how will you make sense of the dynamics of the families you are serving? How will you make an informed decision about how to provide services, inform policy, or conduct research on changing family dynamics? As an example, consider that you are charged with developing state policies to make the Family and Medical Leave Act of 1993 (2006) more accessible to very diverse working-class and middle-class families. As a policymaker, you will need to know the demographic trends that show just how diverse families are in modern society; there are blended families, single parent families, same-sex partnerships, grandparents raising grandchildren, adults living alone, polyamorous families, multigenerational households, and many more variations. Contemporary society tends to be **pluralistic**, which means we have a heterogeneous population made up of different genders, racial or ethnic groups, religions, sexual orientations, and social classes. You need to be aware of how each of these characteristics intersect to create advantage or disadvantage for your clients. You need to be aware of barriers that prevent working-class families from using family policies because they cannot afford to. You need to be aware of historical data, so you can consider what has and has not worked. You need to be able to think outside the box—question the status quo—so that you can develop new, innovative policies for today's changing families. In sum, you need an app for that.

Theory, as we present it in this text, is your app. Theories help you be a problem-solver, an informed researcher, an effective educator, a program director, a nurse, a social worker, or a therapist with a unique perspective to be able to work through problems and solve them with forethought that will set you apart. We want your theoretical mind to be actively engaged at all times, so when you are tasked with problem solving in your profession—whatever it may be—you are able to tackle the problem with the applicability that theory offers to your profession.

When it comes time for you to utilize your theoretical knowledge in the everyday world, we want you to be able to say "There's a theory for that!" A theory, which is a philosophical stance that underlies our approach to knowledge (Crotty, 2003), will help you look at the problem through a **critical lens**, which we define as an approach to challenging taken-for-granted assumptions, questioning the status quo, and trying to understand social life from the perspective of those who live it, rather than the dominant group (Agger, 2013; Allen & Henderson, 2022; Few-Demo & Allen, 2020). Knowing theory means you are able to access multiple data points, becoming familiar with larger trends and patterns that help explain social institutions and social injustice. Theoretical minds are also familiar with how the theory has informed research; for instance, we are able to study families on a **macro level** by analyzing larger patterns in society, such as rates of marriage, fertility, and divorce. Using macro-level analysis, we can examine patterns of behavior on a large scale; that is, how is socioeconomic status (SES) related to marital patterns, fertility, and divorce? Do middle- and upper-class individuals wait to get married until they are older when compared to working class individuals? In addition, studying families through a theoretical lens can also be done at the **micro level**, by analyzing phenomena more closely and in smaller doses. For example, a micro-level analysis would frame questions about social class and marriage much differently; instead of large-scale patterns, we would be interested in finding out what the meaning of marriage is for individuals from different social class backgrounds. We could also explore each partner's perceptions of what an "ideal" spouse is, based on their SES. Has the ideal changed over time? Does the description of an ideal spouse depend on gender? What about whether or not the partnership is lesbian, gay, heterosexual, or mixed orientation? Theories give us a framework for understanding each and every one of those intersecting factors—on multiple levels—as we work with and study families.

What Is a Critical Intersectional Approach?

The approach we take in this text is critical, intersectional, and left of center. We ground our writing in our own lived experience and the experiences of our students and practitioners in the field. As feminist antiracist scholars, we aim to be inclusive of all types of family structures, processes, and contexts, while highlighting structural inequalities that situate minoritized families and their members at disadvantages. Families continue to impact and be impacted by racist, heteropatriarchal societal norms. As such, we decenter the traditional approach to families by **queering family**—that is, challenging the binary notion that simplistically divides families into "normative" versus "nonnormative" (Acosta, 2018; Oswald et al., 2009). We wish to represent complexity and diversity, acknowledging that families are intimate settings for individual and relational development, where both care and trauma can occur in an endless array of structural configurations.

Throughout the book, we compare tenets of mainstream theory (i.e., normative family structures based on gender and generation divisions) and contrast them with critical, intersectional, and queer theory approaches. In doing so, we suggest ways in which mainstream theories can adapt to take into account a critical, intersectional lens (Allen & Henderson, 2022). We center minoritized families and their members by identifying their intersectionalities in each case study and examining privilege throughout each chapter, whether the theory is functionalist (Chapter 2), feminist (Chapter 8), or family stress and resilience (Chapter 11)—to name a few. Our hope is that this approach can fundamentally shift the ways students and scholars learn and apply these theories; there should always be room for both foundational and modern family theories to pivot and ask, "What assumptions are we making about families, modern race relations, invisible disabilities, or LGBTQ+ individuals?"

We take this approach to broaden the perspectives of students sitting in family science and related classrooms to consider lived experiences beyond their own (Allen & Henderson, 2018). This is not to say that one's own lived experience is invalid; in fact, we argue the opposite. Each student, each scholar, has a unique story that brings these theories to life. Our personal stories are valid (Allen, 2000, 2022; Langellier & Peterson, 2021). In social science, we often use those stories to help build theories. Theories become reliable when they are replicated time and time again and patterns emerge that help us frame the ways in which societies and families interact. Lived experience matters, and as critical intersectional feminist theorists, it is our job to raise up marginalized voices, so we can continually learn and grow from one another and fundamentally shift how we understand things *beyond* our own experience.

A Word About Terminology

We are committed to highlighting the intersections of identities throughout this textbook. We want to lay the groundwork for terms we will use in case studies and other parts of the text. Below, we present a table with a nonexhaustive list of terms that refer to aspects of identity that intersect in important sociological ways.

TABLE 1.1. Terms and Definitions Used for Identities

TERMS	DEFINITIONS
LGBTQ+	Lesbian, gay, bisexual, transgender, queer/questioning, and other sexual- and gender-minority identities
Cisgender/cis	Assigned sex at birth aligns with gender identity and expression
Transgender/trans	Assigned sex at birth does not align with gender identity and expression
Nonbinary	Subcategory of transgender that denotes a gender identity that does not align with man or woman
Gay	Someone who is not a woman that is attracted only to people who are not women; usually a man who is attracted to men, but there are nonbinary gays as well
Lesbian	Someone who is not a man who is attracted only to people who are not men; usually a woman who is attracted to a woman, but there are nonbinary lesbians as well
Bisexual	Attraction to two or more genders
Asexual	Lack of sexual attraction to others
Aromantic	Lack of romantic attraction to others
Pansexual	Attraction to multiple genders
Queer	An umbrella term historically used in academia and in certain communities to describe people who are not heterosexual/heteroromantic and/or cisgender
GNC	Gender nonconforming; someone whose gender presentation and expression does not align with their identity or the gender binary

(continued)

TABLE 1.1. *(continued)*

Polyamory/ polyamorous	A kind of relationship that rejects monogamy; an identity of someone who is willing to be romantically involved with multiple people at once
Intersex	A person born with a combination of sex traits that are typically presumed to be either exclusively male or female (e.g., physical genitalia or gonads incongruent with sex chromosomes)
Minoritized	A phrase intended to capture the ways in which powerful, dominant groups actively oppress others by capitalizing on power differentials, resulting in systemic injustice, disenfranchisement, stigma, invisibility, and other sometimes fatal consequences
POC	Person/people of color; a term used to refer to people who are non-White and have some shared experiences because of that
BIPOC	Black, Indigenous, and people of color; an alternate term to POC, used primarily in the United States, with a focus on the particular experiences of Black and Indigenous individuals
Indigenous peoples	Groups of people indigenous to their region with distinct cultures that predate colonialism
Latina/Latino	A person who is from Latin America or has Latin American heritage
Latinx/Latine	Gender-neutral alternatives to Latino or Latina

Case Study

Bo-Meh, the subject of our case study, is a cisgender, bisexual, able-bodied, first-generation college student, who has only been living in the United States for five years. She entered the country with refugee status, after living in a refugee camp in Thailand for eight years. After graduating from high school, she enrolled in college with the hopes of becoming a social worker, so she can someday pay back the many services she benefited from as a newcomer to the United States. She has three younger siblings, all of whom have depended on her for care, since her mother works 12-hour shifts at her job. Bo-Meh and her family belong to the American working class.

As Bo-Meh sits through her first Theories of Family course as a family science major, she wonders about her classmates. The professor put the students into groups of five for a class project, which requires them to work together to answer a research question using various theories of family. Her group members are very diverse. Maggie is a 41-year-old, U.S.-born citizen and mother of three, who put off college to raise her children, and she is majoring in nursing. Maggie identifies as a cisgender heterosexual Afro–Latina woman. Seneca is a 22-year-old naturalized U.S. citizen, majoring in media studies, who wants to develop more inclusive television programming for children. They identify as nonbinary and Latinx, and they belong to the American middle class. Natalie, a transgender lesbian with Japanese heritage, is a 20-year-old elementary education major. Curtis is a cisgender, heterosexual Black middle-aged war veteran, who wants to go into marriage and family therapy. Given how diverse the group members are, Bo-Meh wonders how well they will work together and how they will find anything in common to be able to accomplish the tasks for the semester. Will they be able to find times to meet outside of class, given their conflicting schedules and outside responsibilities? Will they be able to agree on a theoretical framework to answer the research questions, given how different their majors and career goals are?

Like other students taking a family theory course, these budding professionals (e.g., social worker, nurse, television programming developer, elementary school teacher, and family therapist) all have to take their intersecting identities and family dynamics into account as a part of their coursework. How do the systemic injustices they have faced in their own lives, coupled with their family's history, situate them as individual group members working together on a project? Undoubtedly, their interactions with and perceptions of families will differ greatly, possibly creating rough patches when it comes to completing their project. Finally, how will each classmate's own family upbringing affect how they view families? In this chapter, we explore **epistemologies**—or one's orientation to answering questions about the world—as they relate to the study of families (Bengtson et al., 2005). Your epistemology provides a framework for how you approach answering questions, such as, "Why do people get divorced?" Think about how different people may answer that question, depending on their life experiences and beliefs. If you have grown up in a family that has experienced divorce, you may feel like poor communication skills or financial strain lead to divorce. Another classmate may see divorce as a blessing, given how much his parents verbally abused one another. Yet another classmate may suggest that divorce is not even on his radar, since his two fathers fought most of his life for the right to be legally recognized as a married couple in his home state of Minnesota. Each of these different life experiences contribute to one's view of families. In addition, each student's major or career trajectory will influence how they perceive issues of the family as well. While Bo-Meh may see these differences as barriers to her group coming to consensus on a theory to explain family dynamics, it is important to instead consider them as valuable differences. With each person's experience and academic focus comes a new lens, or epistemology, that can help others in different professions view the family in a new way.

BOX 1.1. AT A GLANCE: THEORY IS ...

- The word *theory* sends a glaze over the eyes of most people. This is somewhat ironic because the word theory comes from the Greek *theoria*, which means "a looking at." ... A theory is simply one's understanding of how something works. (Shoemaker et al., 2004, pp. 5–6)
- Theorizing is like being presented with a puzzle where only some of the pieces are visible or seem to fit together. Fitting the pieces together is fun, though often frustrating particularly when the overall picture is vague or elusive. (Bengtson et al., 2005, p. 5)
- Good theories ... are internally consistent, useful, explanatory, evidence-based, falsifiable, broadly applicable, and consistent with other accepted theories. (Fine & Fincham, 2013, p. 1)
- In everyday family life, there are many activities that take up considerable time, energy, and attention but that are poorly represented in our theorizing about families ... The result is that family life tends to be viewed in terms of averages around measures of central tendency, rather than in the diversity and complexity of shared meanings and interrelated perceptions. (Daly, 2003, p. 772)
- The distinctions between social theory and theorizing as the process of generating social theory, the distinctions between social scientific and narrative approaches to theory and theorizing, and intersectionality's metaphoric, heuristic, and paradigmatic uses provide a vocabulary for intersectionality as a social theory in the making ... with aspirations for social transformation and social change. (Collins, 2019, p. 53)
- Creative ideas often happen randomly, spontaneously, and fortuitously. (Jaccard & Jacoby, 2010, p. 43)

Theory Building Blocks: Epistemologies, Assumptions, Concepts, and Propositions

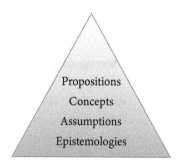

To understand theories, we first need to understand how they are used to explain ideas. Scientific theories consist of epistemologies, assumptions, concepts, and propositions. These building blocks of theory are important both to build *and* deconstruct theory. Figure 1.1 shows how to think of each layer of theory building as a pyramid; beginning with the bottom layer (epistemologies), each layer builds on the previous one. To understand how a theory explains families, we can remove the blocks and analyze each layer.

FIGURE 1.1. Building Blocks of Theory

Epistemologies

At the foundation of the pyramid are epistemologies. Epistemologies are the overall frame of reference that a theorist brings to the study of families. They answer the following questions:

- What is knowing?

- How do we know what we think we know?

- How useful is what we think we know? (Bengtson et al., 2005).

All theorists have an epistemology that guides their thinking.

For example, a **positivist epistemology** presumes that there is an objective truth we can discover about families through systematic research procedures. Positivism guides the scientific method and presents knowledge as value-neutral or value-free (Lincoln et al., 2018). When studying families, a positivist would approach the study of divorce by examining, perhaps, length of marriage, age at first marriage, and variables such as the race/ethnicity of the couple, the region of the country in which they married, and their religious identity. From a positivist view, a family researcher is able to explain the who, what, and where of divorce but not necessarily the why. Positivist theories are useful for predicting and explaining phenomena on a large scale.

On the other hand, an **interpretive epistemology** views knowledge as subjective, with the goal of understanding how families make meaning of their own experiences (Bengtson et al., 2005). Family scholars with this epistemological orientation differ from positivists in that they are interested more in the why of explaining family dynamics. That is, instead of being interested in facts and statistics about divorce, the interpretivist would want to know what divorce means to families. Divorce could mean very different things to families, depending on the situation. In some families, divorce could signify the end of an abusive and unhealthy relationship. In others, it could symbolize a mutually agreed upon move in a new direction for both partners. Therefore, an interpretive epistemology allows researchers and theorists a way to conceptualize "truth" as something that is changing, not the same for all parties, and dependent upon the lens of the theorist (Denzin & Lincoln, 2018). This orientation allows for multiple truths to hold for each family, and each family member, being studied. Interpretivist theories, aligned mostly with qualitative research methods, are useful for understanding multiple dimensions of family and being empathetic with different lived realities for each.

A **critical epistemology** is the primary one we take in this book (Allen & Henderson, 2018, 2022). This approach holds that what gets to count as knowledge is defined by those who are in power, and thus, the powerful members of society impose their definitions onto others (Bengtson et al., 2005; Collins, 2019). This orientation is critical of what we hold to be true about families—that is, the assumption that all families should procreate and that adult partners should be heterosexual and legally married. That perspective, however, is not a "truth" for all members of society wishing to call themselves families. Critical theorists also examine what are referred to as **social constructions of reality**. A social construction is something that was defined as important and valuable by powerful members of society, and over time, such shared knowledge becomes habituated and accepted by society as a whole (Berger & Luckmann, 1966). Often, socially constructed truths serve the purpose of reifying the social structure and inequality that exists. For example, if divorce rates increase, powerful members of that society may start disseminating **rhetoric**, which refers to messages that are aimed at persuading the audience. Anti-divorce rhetoric would suggest that the "American family is on the decline," and "the future of America is at stake," unless the increase in divorce rates stops. The rhetoric is based on a social construction that suggests divorce is always harmful—not only to the adults and children involved but to society as a whole. Critical theorists examine these messages as social constructions of reality that are not true for all families. Critical theory is useful for breaking down ideologies and suggesting it is important to raise up voices of those with marginalized power and status in society.

Assumptions

Given how different these epistemologies are, each theory will have certain assumptions about how the world works. **Assumptions** are the ideas that scholars believe to be true about families. They are the starting point for a theory—the taken-for-granted ideas that lay the groundwork for theory building. Assumptions are unique to each theory; they provide an orientation to studying the social world that is specific. For example, functionalist theory (Chapter 2) assumes that families are functional for all members. This assumption overlooks a stark reality for families—that some interactions are harmful for some family members. Other theories, such as conflict theory (Chapter 3), assume that conflict is an inherent part of both the social world we live in and inevitable within families as well. These two theories have very different assumptions about the nature of reality, which will shape how the theory is applied and how it is used to explain family forms and family dynamics.

The way social scientists view and theorize families inevitably changes over time as norms change and society evolves. How assumptions have shifted over time is evident when we examine perceptions of women in families and in the legal profession throughout the past century. For example, in the latter half of the 19th century, women tried to enter the legal profession, which prompted responses not only from law school administrators but also from state and Supreme Court justices in the United States. Women were denied both entrance into law school as well as licenses to practice law based on the dominant gender and family ideology of the time. Three concurring Supreme Court justices wrote in 1869:

> Man is, or should be, woman's protector and defender. The natural and proper timidity and delicacy which belongs to the female sex evidently unfits it for many of the occupations of civil life. The constitution of the family organization, which is founded in the divine ordinance, as well as in the nature of things, indicates the domestic sphere as that which properly belongs to the domain and

functions of womanhood. ... The paramount destiny and mission of woman are to fulfill the noble and benign offices of wife and mother. (Weisberg, 1977, p. 492)

In 1875, the Wisconsin Supreme Court agreed, writing that any woman who attempted to become a lawyer was "committing 'treason' against 'the order of nature'" (Weisberg, 1977, p. 493). This view of women was not only widely accepted in the legal profession but also among other professionals. A Harvard University physician argued that women should not even be allowed to study law, as it posed a threat to women's health (and, therefore, the future of America) because women would become unable to reproduce: "[It is] dangerous for women to engage in strenuous intellectual activity, [which would] divert energy from female reproductive organs to the brain, harming the health of women and their children" (Clarke, 1873, p. 126). Others argued that women should not be allowed to practice law because a beautiful woman might "make an impartial jury impossible if she appeared as counsel for a criminal" (Morello, 1986, p. 61). Clearly, these views are no longer a part of our orientation to studying families. Yet, perhaps, some of the views remain, such as the perception that women are better suited to care for children. This is called **cultural lag**, where society evolves, but facets of culture, such as beliefs and values, take longer to change. What do you think? Do we still view women differently than men when it comes to families? What are your own personal assumptions about studying gender and families?

One of the key aspects of learning to think theoretically and critically is to remember how your own epistemologies and assumptions evolve over time and intersect with important historical events. As an example, how has the recent COVID-19 pandemic differentially impacted you and your worldview, and your family? How have the recent protests against police brutality and supporting the Black Lives Matter (BLM) movement impacted your own worldview and discussions in your family? How have both events impacted families with marginalized identities? Consider how the recent pandemic exacerbated the inequality gap between families who occupy the top 1% of the income and wealth brackets around the world, compared to everyone else (the other 99%!). How did the widespread lockdowns make it possible for individuals to organize and protest following the murder of George Floyd? Individuals were forced to stay home from work, school, and other obligations, which, ironically, provided space for activists to come together online, organizing and protesting to increase racial awareness on a broader scale than ever before (Turner et al., 2022). Each of these historical shifts had indelible impacts on families, and we unpack them throughout this text.

Concepts

Concepts are terms and definitions used to explain the theory's framework based on the assumptions. Concepts are integral to explaining theories; they provide the building blocks used to create the theory. For example, structural-functionalist theorists use the term roles to describe a set of expectations associated with each family member. The head of household, typically assumed to be the husband in functionalist theory (Chapter 2), performs instrumental roles in the family, or the tasks needed to ensure the family's basic survival (Parsons, 1970). Based on the assumption that families are functional for all members, the husband makes important decisions, gives orders, and exerts power over other family members. The *concepts* used in this example are "role" and "instrumental." They are derived from the *assumptions* that functionalist theorists hold to be true about families.

There are many important concepts used in family theories. Sometimes the same term is defined in different ways by different theories. For example, the concept of "conflict" is defined as inevitable in conflict theory (Chapter 3) but as deviant in functionalist theory (Chapter 2). To understand how theorists "see" the world and explain family dynamics, we need to be familiar with the concepts and their definitions as they are used in various theories. Once we can explain the assumptions behind a theory and define the concepts, we can apply, test, and refine the theory in family practice and research.

Propositions

Propositions are statements based on both assumptions and concepts that we use when we "apply" theory to the study of families (Bengtson et al., 2005). For example, a proposition derived from social exchange theory (Chapter 7) is that a husband's income level is related to the probability of divorce. Propositions are operationalized as hypotheses; that is, hypotheses restate the proposition in a way that can be tested in research (Babbie, 2013). The proposition that a husband's income level is related to the probability of divorce can be restated to test in a research study as: Men with higher-than-average incomes have lower divorce rates than average (Nye, 1979). Hypotheses, which reformulate propositions into their empirical versions, specify the direction of change the researcher expects will occur. Propositions, then, can be upheld based on the findings in a research study, or they can be refuted or deemed inapplicable, depending on the family to which we are applying the propositions.

Propositions are the pinnacle of the theory; they allow us to tell whether the theory is still relevant 50 years after its creation, or perhaps, that it needs to be updated to reflect, for example, changing demographics and family patterns in society. Thus, theory informs research, and research informs theory (Klein, 2005; Wallace, 1971/2009). Science is a process of going from induction (beginning with observations and moving on to theory) to deduction (beginning with theory and moving on to observations) in repetitious fashion (see Figure 1.2 below). One way to think about this process of knowledge building is to imagine theory building as a cycle. Theoretical propositions contribute to scientific inquiry (hypotheses and data collection), and those results then contribute to a broader body of knowledge about the topic. Then, the theory is either confirmed or updated and modified, depending on the results.

Propositions make theories testable; what this means is that each theory has statements about how the world—or, in this case, families—work. When you are using the theory, whether it is for data collection as a researcher or interpreting a case as a social worker, you will be applying the propositions to the families you are working with or studying. Depending on the result of applying a proposition, you will either confirm or refute the proposition and, thus, further refine the theory. To build on our example using functionalist theory (Chapter 2), one of this theory's propositions is that when a family member deviates from their role expectations, dysfunction may occur. Then, for the family to properly function again as a whole, the family member must figure out a way to conform to the role expectations

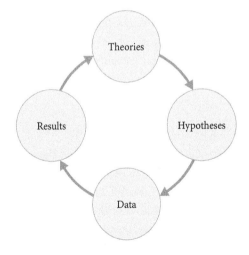

FIGURE 1.2. The Scientific Process and Theory Building

set forth by the family. Functionalists view the family as a human body; when the brain is compromised, so are other parts of the human body. The brain sends messages to the heart, lungs, and other vital organs. If the brain is injured, functionalists argue that for equilibrium to be reached, repairs need to be made to allow the brain to continue fulfilling its role expectations. Similarly, according to functionalist theory, a husband, or head of household, must fulfill instrumental role expectations for everyone else in the family to know what to do, when to do it, and how to do it.

What Is a *Family* Theory? Common Assumptions Across All Theories

Although this is a book about different types of family theories, there are several assumptions made about families that are embedded in all of the theories we cover in this book. These assumptions reveal what the community of scholars—the researchers, theorists, teachers, and practitioners—in the family field perceive about the inner workings of families and the broader structures that constrain their lives.

Developmental Assumption: Families Change Over Time

The incorporation of time into the family life course is one of the most important contributions of family theory. Families consist of interdependent lives that continually change over time. Conceptualizing both the individual life course and the family life cycle is critical to family theorizing. Your own life course, for example, begins with your birth and ends with your death. In that sense, the life course is linear. However, the life course of families is cyclical, in that family roles and relationships at each phase of life are eventually occupied by new members. As individuals move through time, they occupy various positions in the life course (e.g., child, sibling, partner, parent, and widow), but the cycle of the family spirals on, beyond any one person's life course. Think back to our case study; Bo-Meh is in the life course stage of young adulthood, and her group member Maggie is in the middle of her life course, having raised children before attending college. Each person has an individual life course (i.e., young adulthood versus midlife) as well as a family life cycle. Bo-Meh has cared for her younger siblings in the absence of her working mother, which situates her a little farther along in terms of the family life cycle than her peers. In fact, she and Maggie share child-rearing in common, even though they are at different stages of the life course. Each of these intersecting experiences is important to take into account when thinking about families and development.

Diversity Assumption: Families Vary in Their Composition and Structure

As we explain throughout this book, there is no singular type of family. Families differ in multiple ways, according to the intersections of each individual's race, class, gender, sexual orientation, age, nationality, and other characteristics. Families also differ across these divisions (e.g., Black families, LGBTQ-parent families, childless families, extended families, and single-adult families). There are many structural variations in families as well. For example, families include intragenerational relationships (e.g., cohabiting couples and adult–sibling relationships) and intergenerational relationships (e.g., parent–child, aunt–nephew, and grandparent–grandchild). Families also differ by household structure. Family members, even nuclear ones, can live in different households; examples include (a) a young adult who lives in an apartment away from home during college; (b) a married couple who "live together apart" by occupying two households, often due to working in separate locations; and (c) a binational family in which a mother goes to work in a country with greater economic opportunities, while her children stay back in the home country and are cared for by relatives.

This "diversity" assumption is an important one; before family theorists adopted the assumption that families were not "one-size-fits-all," theories were developed based on one standard model, which does not fit for most families in contemporary society. Instead, it is important to consider the relative privileges some individuals and families have compared to others. Privilege refers to a set of advantages that you have, which others do not, and these privileges are not typically due to your own efforts. Some privileges, especially those associated with being White, male, heterosexual, able-bodied, wealthy, and the like, are unearned or undeserved (McIntosh, 2020).

Olou (2018) recommends you take the time to think deeply about the privileges and advantages you have, compared to others, and then consider how these advantages have impacted your experiences and beliefs about life, society, and social justice. Understanding where you stand in relation to privilege will help you begin the process of dismantling those privileges and understanding the disadvantages dealt to others.

TABLE 1.2. Questions to Ask Yourself About Privilege and Advantage

1. Have you always had stable mental health?
2. Did you grow up middle class?
3. Are you White?
4. Are you male?
5. Are you able-bodied?
6. Are you neurotypical?
7. Are you a documented citizen of the country you live in?
8. Did you grow up in a stable home environment?
9. Do you have stable housing?
10. Do you have reliable transportation?
11. Are you cisgender?
12. Are you straight?
13. Are you thin, tall, or conventionally attractive?

Systemic Assumption: Families Are Systems

Families are more than a collection of individuals related to each other. Families consist of interrelated parts, in which lives are connected through communication (process) and composition (structure). When some event occurs in one person's life, all the members of the family system are impacted. If a father gets a new job, the whole family could move to a different state, possibly disrupting the children's lives by having to change schools and find new friends. The parents could experience stress at work, and that stress may spill over into family life. A global pandemic could occur (sound familiar?), impacting the communication and functioning among every member of the family and every member of society (Prime et al., 2020). What happens to one family member may affect the entire family system, and therefore, the whole of the family is greater than the sum of its parts (Lebow, 2020).

An example of this systemic assumption is Curtis, the middle-aged veteran from our case study. Curtis put off attending college until after he served in the military, including a two-year deployment in Afghanistan. During his time in Afghanistan, an explosion close to him injured Curtis and damaged his nervous system. Three years after the explosion, Curtis married his high school sweetheart, and they had a daughter within their first few years of marriage.

Unfortunately, the damage to his nervous system from the explosion started to cause seizures, one of which resulted in hospitalization and Curtis being unable to drive for six months (until he could be retested and evaluated). Therefore, every weekday morning at 5:00 a.m., his wife Donna has to wake up their infant daughter and drive Curtis to the train station for his commute into work and his night classes and then pick him up every night after his classes are done at 9:00 p.m. This is a perfect example of how one family member's well-being affects the entire family system.

Processual Assumption: Families Are Dynamic

At the micro level of analysis, families are an emotional domain (Daly, 2007). Family members constantly communicate with one another in visible and invisible ways. As feminist theorists emphasize, sometimes there is harmony, sometimes there is conflict, and sometimes both harmony and conflict are simultaneous (Allen, 2016). For example, families are often a site of tension between the dynamics of caring for one another and the competing needs that arise in fulfilling caregiving responsibilities, while also taking care of oneself (Dressel & Clark, 1990). Bo-Meh is a good example of completing the developmental tasks of emerging from adolescence to adulthood while, at the same time, filling in as a caregiver for younger siblings because her help is needed at home. At the macro level of analysis, families are dynamic in that they both affect and are affected by broader social systems. Families must deal with social and historical change—demographically, economically, and politically—as life course theory (Chapter 9) describes (Bernardi et al., 2019). Bo-Meh's family fled to the United States to escape war and persecution. Upon arriving to the United States, her family had to adapt in several ways, most notably to a new culture that was more individualized than collectivist. Refugees and immigrants alike still experience similar macro-level cultural adjustments after relocating to the United States.

It is also important to note that, from a macro perspective, legal barriers prevented certain immigrants from even entering the United States until the mid-20th century; the United States used the quota system, which limited the number of Asian, Latin and South American, African, and southern European immigrants from coming to the United States. In 1965, the Immigration and Nationality Act was passed, which opened the doors to others, regardless of race or nationality (History.com, 2019). Families need to be flexible and adaptable to cope with or thrive as broader social forces create new challenges and opportunities.

Popular media provide relevant examples to understand and critique the assumptions made by family theorists. As shown in the Box 1.2, we bring in examples of key figures in contemporary and popular culture to enhance the course material; in this case, internationally-recognized speaker Alok Vaid-Menon helps us frame our approach to this text by discussing compassion, which illustrates the importance of understanding one's own assumptions and epistemologies before we even begin to learn family theories.

BOX 1.2. FAMILY THEORY IN MODERN CULTURE: *QUEERING COMPASSION*

Alok Vaid-Menon is a writer, performer, activist, and public speaker known across the world for their powerful messages on gender, belonging, and queerness. Alok identifies as a gender nonconforming, transfeminine Indian-American. In a 2021 episode of *The Man Enough Podcast*, Alok discusses an urgent need for compassion. While on the surface, this does not seem like the kind of place we would find family theory in modern culture, it absolutely is. The approach we take in this book is critical, and the spirit of Alok's work, calling for all of us to queer compassion is how we want readers to approach the study of families and understand how queering family science is necessary to move the discipline forward.

Earlier in this chapter we discussed the importance of language and terminology. In this episode, cohost Justin Baldoni begins by authentically stating his anxiety about misusing Alok's pronouns, which are they/them. Alok's response captures the spirit of queering the ways that scholars have gone about studying families:

> Welcome to the awkward choreography of being a human. We're always gonna mess up because we are indoctrinated into a world that teaches us ideology, not compassion. So it's not you speaking when you misgender me, it's everyone that has spoken to you before and, in my life, what I always try to remind people is: I was not born with gender literacy, I was born hating myself and hunting myself and I had to learn too, so other people are gonna have to learn. And in that way, I think trans people can actually teach the world [that] transition is possible, not just between genders, but between paradigms. It's so possible to learn and constantly [be] learning. And in fact learning is the most delightful thing about being alive. So what I say is when you mess up, which is when you're alive, because being alive is about messing up gloriously, and I will fight for that ability to gloriously mess up because I don't believe that humans are statutes or sculptures, I believe that we're inconsistent and idiosyncratic and hairy and fat and unfurling and that's what's joyous about being alive. What we do then is say, "I'm sorry, I'm learning. It won't happen again." And then if it happens again, "I'm sorry, I'm gonna try even harder." And that's what love is for me: trying harder for each other.

What does this have to do with family theories? Everything. Because everything you know, everything you are bringing into this class on family theory, is predicated on your own experience as a member of your own family. What we encourage our readers to do is to step outside that box, be comfortable being uncomfortable, and do the hard work of unlearning what we know so we can truly learn anew and, as Alok says, "try harder for each other."

"The Family" vs. Families: The Normative Family and the Diversity of Families

From the beginning of theorizing about families, scholars were more concerned with similarities between all families, rather than with variation between families. The search for "what is normal" provided a starting point and a baseline for family theorists, researchers, and practitioners to understand how the typical family functions. Beginning with the "typical" family also gives scholars a shortcut to studying and understanding families. This shortcut allows us to focus only on **the Family**. Focusing on Family with a "capital F" makes it easier to theorize about families as a system that operates among many other macro systems in the social structure (e.g., the economic system, the religious system, the political system, and the criminal justice system).

Assumptions about the normative family are rooted in the 19th-century concept of separate spheres for women (inside the home, tending to family members' emotions) and men (outside the home, in the world of work and politics). In the language of functionalist theory (Chapter 2), which is one of the earliest family theories to dominate the field, women fulfilled the expressive roles within the families, and men fulfilled the instrumental roles, and this separation was deemed both efficient and natural. This normative model was based on what family researchers now refer to as the **Standard North American Family** (SNAF; Smith, 1993) and reflected the experiences of White, middle-class Americans with married, heterosexual parents. Assumptions about the family against which all other families should be judged included (a) families need a "head-of-household" with centralized power to function effectively, (b) males should fulfill that role, and (c) roles and expectations are static and unchanging over the life course.

As the saying goes, one size does not fit all. The SNAF model excluded variations, such as single-parent families, LGBTQ-parent families, families without children, grandparent-headed families, aging parents and their adult children, and families formed with chosen or fictive kin who are not biologically related to one another, among many other family forms (Allen, 2000). Coontz (2016) critiqued this model as being outdated and a product of what she refers to as the "nostalgia trap" that we fall into when we romanticize the 1950s as the "Golden Era". Her critique is based on the fact that during that time period, the post-World War II economy was booming. White families, in particular, had enough economic stability to only need one breadwinner (the male), enabling many mothers to stay at home. The Civil Rights Movement of mid-20th century America was still building steam, so women of color were overrepresented in domestic work, working for White families and excluded from Social Security and unemployment benefits. Federal assistance programs, such as the G.I. Bill and low-interest housing loans, were tailored to help young, White, middle-class families become home-owners (McGhee, 2021).

Today, in contrast, most families need two paychecks to maintain economic stability. In addition, the most common family "form" today is a **blended family**; one that includes children from a previous marriage (Raley & Sweeney, 2020; Sweeney, 2010). Today, scholars recognize that families are very diverse, and the roles of partners are not as strict as they once were (Cherlin, 2004; Demo et al., 2000; Smock & Schwartz, 2020). Therefore, families are inevitably affected by historical and social forces. When society changes, theories must also change to remain effective and timely. An example of such social change is legalizing same-sex civil unions (Knauer, 2019). When such a macro-level change occurs, it inevitably affects protections for and perceptions of LGBTQ+ individuals. It also affects micro-level factors, such as meanings associated with marriage, divorce, partnerships, and roles. Each of these dynamics affects the explanatory power theories have; a theory based on the SNAF model would not be appropriate in explaining family dynamics for all.

On balance, despite the fact that the normative model has been critiqued in recent decades (Allen, 2000; Bahr & Bahr, 2001; Cheal, 1991; Stacey, 1990), it is still very entrenched in family theory and research as well as popular culture (Cherlin, 2020). In other words, assumptions about what is normal, ideal, and how families should be, as opposed to how they really are, are very resistant to change. Social norms about the ideal that all families should strive for, and against which all families are judged, are still influential. As Pittman (1993) explains, the normative model may be down, but it certainly isn't out. It is important, then, to understand how this norm developed and why we cannot discount it altogether. Current trends reveal that the SNAF model does not fit all, or most, families, but its influence—and the holding on to family privilege—still lingers (Letiecq, 2019).

Although the SNAF model was useful for developing theories of family early on, its description is limited to individualistic cultures, such as in North America (e.g., the United States and Canada) and Northern Europe (e.g., England). However, as we emphasize in this book, social norms vary from culture to culture, and they also change over time, mostly because ideas and behaviors change. Another important concept related to SNAF is Beck and Beck-Gernsheim's (2001) idea of the "post-familial family" caused by, in part, the global transition from collectivist concerns of the responsibility to take care of others to individualist concerns, where personal freedoms take precedence in everyday life. That is, there is a major societal trend in which "living for others" has evolved into "living a life of one's own." This gradual process of **individualization** means that the decisions individuals make for themselves affect the possibilities of forming and maintaining families. What should come first: one's responsibility to oneself or one's responsibility to a spouse, children, aging parents, and others who have traditionally relied on family members for instrumental and expressive support? Thus, the critique of the nuclear family structure as the normative way in which people should live is a phenomenon that is occurring in North America, Western Europe, Australia, and, now, throughout the globe.

How Theory Informs Practice in Global Perspective

There are several ways in which educators, practitioners, and family policy makers can apply theory in their work with individuals and families. First and foremost, it is our hope that after reading this text and utilizing theory as your "app," you will view the world in a multidimensional way. That is, when you notice family dynamics in your own life, or in television and films, your "app" will automatically open, and you will better understand what you see because you have a trained theoretical mind. In this way, theory informs the practice of *every* professional; no matter where your studies or career take you, your theory app will be with you and will help you see the world and family issues from a variety of different theoretical perspectives. This is vital because one of the most important contributions you can make as a professional who works with and studies families is being flexible. By using your theoretical app, you will be able to think outside the box to tackle a problem by taking into account both historical data (e.g., what has and has not worked in particular contexts) as well as contemporary shifts in the changing family landscape.

Therefore, for each chapter in this book, we make specific suggestions for how each theory can be used in a practical setting. Some theories may be helpful for informing policy, such as feminist theory (Chapter 8), family ecological theory (Chapter 10), and family stress and resilience theory (Chapter 11). Others, like family systems theory (Chapter 6) and symbolic interactionist theory (Chapter 4), are especially useful for understanding how families communicate to help teachers, nurses, social workers, or therapists work more effectively with students, clients, and patients. Other theories, such as life course theory (Chapter 9) and family developmental theory (Chapter 5), are useful for understanding how families change over time through different life stages and structural variations, including the needs of caregivers or grandparents raising grandchildren.

In addition, theory frames problems we will encounter in our everyday lives and professions from both micro and macro perspectives. That is, we can understand family dynamics by gauging macro-level influences as well as micro-level interactions within the family. A good example of this is socioeconomic status; when a family's income situates them in the working class, the wage earners (i.e., parents) may not have access to a retirement plan because it is not likely to be included as a part of their benefits package at work. Therefore, they eventually realize the only stability they will have access to after a certain age is Social Security income. This could likely create strain among not only the wage earners but also among the children in the family because the children may be faced with supporting their parents in their later years. Over time, the power dynamic in the family shifts (micro-level interactions), and the parents, once in a powerful position in the family, are now depending on their children for financial support. These dynamics are influenced by larger forces at play—macro-level structures in society—that are often out of the family's control. Having a solid theoretical foundation—an "app" for problem-solving—will help you better serve the needs of your clients, students, and patients. Ideally, a strong theory app will also inform how policies are written and developed to meet the needs of modern families.

BOX 1.3. GLOBAL COMPARISONS ON THE LEGAL DEFINITIONS OF MARRIAGE AND FAMILY

There are variations from country to country about how marriage, divorce, parenthood, sex, and gender are defined. Consider these examples of current laws in five different countries:

- **Japan:** Japan's same-sex marriage ban has been ruled unconstitutional (www.npr.org).
- **Iceland:** In June 2019, official documents will include a third gender option ("X") for gender nonconforming individuals (www.theguardian.com).
- **Pakistan:** A man may be married to more than one woman (www.refworld.org).
- **Philippines:** Divorce is illegal (www.npr.org).
- **Spain:** As of 2021, same-sex couples are allowed to jointly adopt a child (www.ipsos.com).

Applying Theory: The Case of Transnational Care Work

One of the ways students learn theories is by applying each new theory to the same social issue. Below, we evaluate a contemporary family issue, transnational care work, using the theoretical concepts and assumptions for a few theories. This should provide you with a tangible, internationally relevant example that is applicable to several different theoretical perspectives.

Transnational care work is the term used to describe primarily migrant women working as live-in or live-out domestic workers for families in wealthy nations (Lutz, 2011). Domestic workers can be hired to care for children, older adults, housekeeping maintenance, or specific duties, such as cooking meals or running errands, and more recently, scholars have argued that transnational care work also includes the embodied, intimate labor of surrogate mothers (Gottfried & Chun, 2018). The reason this is a "transnational" issue is the majority of domestic workers are migrant women, which means that they come from developing nations, particularly the Philippines, Sri Lanka, India, and throughout the Caribbean and Africa, to live and work in more affluent nations, such as the United States, Hong Kong, Taiwan, Israel, and Middle Eastern nations (Mahalingam et al., 2009). Care workers leave their homes, their families of origin, and their spouses and children, to migrate to another country to work as a domestic servant, nanny, or elder caregiver. This creates complex new family forms that challenge Western ideas of what it means to be a mother, father, or, even, family (Mahalingam et al., 2009).

From a theoretical standpoint, how would we evaluate this issue? How would we begin to evaluate which theory would be a good fit for understanding transnational care work? First, we would have to decide whether we were going to examine the issue from a micro or macro perspective. If we are assessing the ways in which transnational care workers become so integrated into their employers' families that they are *considered* to be kin, we would be analyzing the issue from a micro-level perspective. From this perspective, we could examine how many hours a day the care worker spends with the family's children versus how many hours the parents, who are employing her, spend with their children and assess the strength and bonds of the different types of relationships. A family systems perspective (Chapter 6) would be an appropriate theory to use for this type of analysis. We could ask how care workers frame their domestic caring labor and how they maintain connections with their own children and family members in their home countries.

On the other hand, if we were to consider the macro-level processes that have led to this phenomenon of transnational care work, we would try to frame our analysis using conflict theory (Chapter 3). The second wave of feminism enabled more women (in wealthy countries) to be able to pursue professional careers that were previously unheard of. However, the capitalist nature of wealthy societies creates advantage for some and oppression for others. Feminist theorists (Chapter 8) critique care work for the disadvantage it creates for migrant women who work for wealthy families, sending home every paycheck to provide economically for their own children tens of thousands of miles away (Mahler et al., 2015; Ungerson, 2006).

Yet another macro-level perspective, functionalist theory (Chapter 2) might suggest that as long as care workers help family systems and social systems maintain equilibrium, scholars should not be concerned with transnational care work as a social problem. That is, each part of the system needs to contribute to the overall functioning of the whole; care workers fulfill the expressive duties within the employers' home, and they, in turn, have someone in their home countries caring for their own children and families. Every member of the system has a purpose, and each does their part to keep the system running smoothly.

You can see from the example of transnational care work how each theory applied above has a different epistemology (e.g., positivism, interpretivism, or critical), which leads to certain assumptions. A positivist epistemology, which undergirds functionalist theory (Chapter 2), would be interested in whether or not each part of the system worked—not necessarily what having a care worker *means* to the employer's family or the worker's well-being and impact on their family of origin. Therefore, a functionalist would make the assumption that if each role is fulfilled and the systems are working smoothly, the arrangement is functional for all members. This is very different from a conflict theory perspective (Chapter 3), which takes a critical epistemology and questions the dominant paradigm represented by a positivist epistemology. For example, conflict theorists would question the capitalist structure that necessitates the role of paid care workers in the first place. Feminist theorists (Chapter 8) and critical race theories (Chapter 12) would also examine how such arrangements can be harmful to societies and families, both the privileged and oppressed groups. For example, why is it assumed that care work should be performed by women? Does this social construction of gender roles prevent men from feeling as though they can fully participate in their children's caregiving? Furthermore, why is it that in some European countries (e.g., France), men's gender roles are more fluid and flexible than they are in other countries, such as the United States and Mexico? After reading this text, answering questions like these will come easier, using theory as your "app." Likewise, your eyes will be opened to the different epistemologies, concepts, assumptions, and propositions that make up family theories. You will also be able to see how theory can be used by a number of different professions that work with and study families, so like Bo-Meh and her group members, you can capitalize on differences and learn even more in the process of theorizing.

Our Definition of Theory

As we have shown in this chapter, we recognize there are many ways to define theory, and those definitions of what theory means change over time. Keeping that in mind, our definition of *theory* includes the following points: A theory is a strategy to describe, interpret, and/or explain a phenomenon (Bengtson et al., 2005). A theory helps us address questions that need answers, such as: Why do people do what they do under certain conditions? For example, researchers studying sibling relationships might use a theory to answer, "How do parents show favoritism to different children in their family?" Or they might try to reply to, "Why do parents show favoritism when they report that they do not?" (Suitor et al., 2013). To **theorize** is the process that we work through in creating or refining a theory.

Theory, in our view, must also be relevant to practice; that is, theory is a way of understanding the problems that people experience in daily life and offering relevant options for addressing those constraints (Allen & Henderson, 2022). A theory, then, offers a compelling storyline that helps us interpret the how and why of a situation or experience in which we need to know more. As we said at the beginning of the chapter, a theory is the "app" we use to help us organize, manage, and make sense of the people, processes, and relationships that comprise our social world.

Criteria for Evaluating Family Theories

Just as there are many ways to define theory, there are also many ways to evaluate the strengths and weaknesses of theory. Theory evaluation is a process; it must begin by situating the theory into the historical context in which it emerged and gained popularity in the field. Once the theory is placed in context, we can better understand its clarity, logic, relevance, and practical application. Below are some of the key criteria that we have found useful in evaluating theory (see also Bengtson et al., 2005; Charmaz, 2014; Doherty et al., 1993; Fine & Fincham, 2013; Gubrium & Holstein, 1990; Sprey, 1990, 2013; White, 2013). In evaluating a family theory, you can ask yourself questions, such as:

1. **Is the theory relevant?** This criterion refers to the applicability the theory has for the group(s) you are studying and/or serving. Is the theory adaptable to your population? Does the theory make assumptions about families that are not true for *your* family? Was this theory grounded in an epistemological orientation that is limiting (e.g., is it positivist in nature, when you need it to be interpretivist)?

2. **Is the theory practical?** Family theories must be able to be translated into practice. The scholarly, or academic, side of studying families must directly benefit families through policy, intervention, therapy, education, health care, or advocacy. Without practical implications, theories often are criticized for living only in the "ivory tower" of academia—far removed from families' every day realities.

3. **Is the theory logical?** Theories of family must be coherent. This means that the assumptions, concepts, and propositions must logically build on one another and fit together well into an explanatory model that makes sense.

4. **Is the theory explicit?** Components of a theory are explicit when they are stated clearly, specifically, and leaving nothing implied. When evaluating whether or not a theory is explicit, consider how thorough and detailed it is; are the concepts precisely defined? Or, on the contrary, are there implicit (underlying or unstated) components of the theory?

5. **Is the theory systematic?** Components of a theory need to be systematic, or formulated as a coherent set of assumptions, concepts, and propositions. This means that the theory can be applied repeatedly to the study of families with the reassurance that, because of the theory's systematic nature, application of the theory should produce reliable results.

6. **Is the theory contextual?** When evaluating this criterion, pay attention to the cultural context in which the theory was developed; not every theory fits every family. Can the theory be used in different contexts or adapted to fit a new context? For example, is the theory relevant to the study of native-born *and* immigrant families in the United States?

Text Organization

This textbook presents 12 theories of the family in the general chronological order in which they emerged within the disciplines of human development and family science, psychology, and sociology. Most of the theories were developed in social science disciplines before they were utilized to study the family, and we note this throughout the text.

Each chapter begins with a case study, which is designed to set the stage, so our readers can apply the theory in a meaningful way. The case study's characters are used to illustrate key concepts throughout each chapter. We also provide a brief history of each theory, so the theories are located in a sociohistorical context, which helps us understand why the assumptions of the theories are so important. For example, Parsons's (1970) structural functionalism was a very popular theoretical approach in sociology in the mid-20th century. It was based on assumptions that most families could conform to societal standards of the SNAF model. It is important to note that the 1950s was a unique period in American history (as we discussed earlier in this chapter), which contributed to structural functionalism's popularity. Later, this theory was criticized for its inability to deal with change during a time when the Civil Rights Movement and Women's Liberation Movement of the 1960s were gaining momentum. The history and origins section of each chapter details these types of sociohistorical shifts and how they contributed to each theory's assumptions and framework.

Each chapter also presents key concepts and assumptions and propositions, if applicable. A highlight of this text is the use of examples; we provide detailed descriptions of how family theories can be applied to modern culture as well as supplementary content designed to challenge students to think about how the theory is applicable to their own lives and the lives of the families they will eventually encounter in their professional roles. Each theory is also discussed with respect to its strengths, weaknesses, and alternate applications. Further, we provide global comparisons to illustrate that family theories are relevant beyond the United States.

Another highlight of this text is the inclusion of the "trifecta" (that is, attaining three important achievements) of detailed connections we draw among theorizing, research, and practice. Each chapter includes a section on current theorizing, which provides a cutting-edge look at how the theory is in the process of changing—formulating new ways of expanding the theory and applying it to changing demographics of individuals and families in society. This is followed by an example of an empirical study illustrating the theory to draw a closer link between theory and research. Each study included is given a detailed description, highlighting research terms and concepts and their usefulness in informing theoretical propositions. Finally, we draw links between the theory and its applicability to practice, encouraging practitioners who work with families to consider ways in which the theories can make them better human service workers, researchers, program directors, teachers, counselors, health care providers, and students of family science. We also highlight voices from lived experience to bring the theories to life for you by presenting examples of family theory in individuals' daily lives, whether they are from our experiences or those of our students, colleagues, family members, or professionals in the field. This decenters our academic voices and, instead, focuses on how family theory is actually applicable in the lives of real people in a variety of contexts. We end each chapter with several multimedia suggestions (e.g., websites, films, and television shows depicting family theories), suggestions for further reading, and questions and resources for students to reflect on the material and make it relevant to their lives.

Before you delve into this text on family theories, it is important to note that your "app" will take time and patience to develop. Unlike how applications work in modern technology, you will not become a seasoned family theorist overnight. Your theoretical mind will take time to develop, but once you get the hang of it, you will be well on your way to seeing family theories everywhere you look! This text will provide the groundwork for developing your "app," and by the time you reach the end, you will have a good understanding of how to navigate the "theory map" we present in Chapter 14. It is our hope that the way we have organized and presented material in this text will help you will be a strong theoretical thinker who is able to see theory as an exciting, applicable guide for understanding, serving, and studying families—no matter your profession.

Multimedia Suggestions

www.ncfr.org

This is the website for the premier professional association in family science, the National Council on Family Relations (NCFR), headquartered in Saint Paul, MN. NCFR publishes three major journals, all of which include the most current and rigorous ideas about family theory, research, and practice: (a) *Journal of Family Theory & Review*; (b) *Journal of Marriage and Family*; and (c) *Family Relations*. NCFR hosts an annual conference that includes the Theory Construction and Research Methodology (TCRM) workshop, certification in family life education, professional resources about jobs in family science, statewide and student chapters, and many other resources to theorize about and study families.

Activate your theory app: Look through the Professional Resources tab on the NCFR website, and familiarize yourself with the jobs center and career resources. Where are the majority of positions? What level of degree is required? How do these options match your own career interests? Add this website to your "favorites" list; you will need these resources before you know it!

www.everydayfeminism.com

This website covers issues related to gender, ability, sex, race, class, identity, and social justice. It is a great place to start for students who are just diving into a book that has a critical feminist lens. The vision statement of this popular site boasts:

> We want to live in a world where every person (and we mean every single person) is treated with respect, directs their own lives, and reaches their full potential. We want this to be true for every woman, man, adult, child, black, Asian, Latino, indigenous, white, gay, lesbian, transgender, straight, poor, rich, Muslim, Jewish, Christian, disabled, able bodied, immigrant, refugee, citizen, and every other group of people on this planet (www.everydayfeminism.com, n.d.).

Allow this site to serve as a guidepost for you as you navigate the way this book approaches our study of family theories.

Activate your theory app: Peruse this website, and consider which theoretical framework, aside from feminist theory, you might find here. Additionally, consider the target audience of this website. Is feminism just about women? Think about the intersection of all the identities highlighted here and how intersectionality impacts you in your life and your career aspirations.

Fatherhood (2021)

Fatherhood is an American-based comedy–drama, starring comedian Kevin Hart. His character's wife passes away shortly after giving birth to the couple's first child, Maddy. Though this film is fictional, it is based in an unfortunate reality that in the United States, Black mothers are three to four times more likely to die than their White counterparts during or shortly after giving birth (Louis et al., 2015). Sociologists and public health experts have documented a host of reasons that contribute to this health disparity (Admon et al., 2018). Though the film does not delve into such heavy issues, it does highlight the consequences of such tragedies in the lives of Matthew, as a

Image 1.2 A Scene From *Fatherhood*, 2021

single dad, and his daughter Maddy. Intersections of gender and race are woven throughout the film as Matthew navigates parenting as a minoritized father.

Activate your theory app: Consider ways this film could have tackled more serious issues that would help bring the reality of Black maternal mortality to light. What other aspects of the story could have been elaborated on? Could the inclusion of a few key scenes—perhaps conversations between Matthew and his daughter—have made a significant impact on raising awareness of Black maternal mortality in the United States? Reimagine the film with such scenes.

The Mandalorian (2019–2021)

Image 1.3 A Scene From *The Mandalorian*, 2019

The Mandalorian is a television show that premiered in 2019 on Disney+, based on the popular *Star Wars* drama. Throughout the two seasons, themes of parenting and fatherhood are evident, as Mando (the main character) develops a father–son relationship with "the Child" (Grogu). This approach, which highlights the softer side of fatherhood and parenting, is in stark contrast to many of the other *Star Wars* parent–child relationships, such as Darth Vader and Luke Skywalker and Han Solo and Kylo Ren, which are seemingly sidelined narratives, second to the drama and action typical of this collection of movies and animated television shows. Showcasing the tender side of parenting and fatherhood won over *Star Wars* fans and could signal a new frontier for how masculinity and parenting are portrayed in popular culture.

Activate your theory app: Identify the epistemologies of *The Mandalorian*, and contrast those with the way Mando approaches his work and his relationship with Grogu. How do their orientations for explaining the world around them compare and contrast, based on their unique perspectives?

Further Reading

Acosta, K. L. (2021). *Queer stepfamilies: The path to social and legal recognition*. New York University Press. Queer family theorist, Katie Acosta, takes on the growing complexity and diversity in families by studying how families with parents who are lesbian, bisexual, transgender, and queer define who is in their family and, hence, give new meaning to how they are "doing family." Using stories from 36 families with diverse racial, ethnic, gender, sexual orientation, marital, and parental backgrounds, Acosta reveals how families formed either after the dissolution of a heterosexual marriage or through queer parenting create new pathways toward plural parenting.

Adamsons, K., Few-Demo, A. L., Proulx, C., & Roy, K. (Eds.). (2022). *Sourcebook of family theories and methodologies*. Springer. About every 15 years, the National Council on Family Relations (described previously) updates and revises the authoritative reference work on family theories. This is a joint effort of NCFR's Theory Construction and Research Methodology Workshop and the Research and Theory Section. The latest *Sourcebook* volume takes a dynamic approach. Included are original descriptions of major theoretical approaches (e.g., family resilience theory, symbolic interactionism, family development theory, and family systems theory) and methodological advancements (e.g., family ethnography, grounded theory, dyadic data analysis, participatory action research, and mixed methods) in family science as well as specific applications to particular research settings (e.g., custodial grandfamilies, fatherhood as brotherhood, the military context, and relational injustice, among many other contexts).

Bengtson, V. L., Acock, A. C., Allen, K. R., Dilworth-Anderson, P., & Klein, D. M. (Eds.). (2005). *Sourcebook of family theory and research*. SAGE Publications. The 2005 version of the *Sourcebook* also takes a unique approach to family scholarship by demonstrating how theories are embedded in research studies and clinical practice. This edition offers chapters on substantive topics, such as "Theorizing about Marriage," "Theorizing about Aggression between Intimates," "Decentering Heteronormativity," and "Theorizing about Sibling Ties in Adulthood," and it demonstrates how theory, research, and practice work together to understand families from different perspectives. Innovative case studies and commentaries from established theorists round out the contributions.

Boss, P. G., Doherty, W. J., LaRossa, R., Schumm, W. R., & Steinmetz, S. K. (Eds.). (1993). *Sourcebook of family theories and methods: A contextual approach*. Plenum. Often referred to as "the green Bible," the 1993 version of the *Sourcebook* is an important resource that examines the classic and emerging theories used to explain family phenomena. Organized chronologically from when the various theories were first introduced in the family field, this edited collection allows readers to see the evolving nature of family theories and the building blocks that family scholars use to test and refine theories over time. Each chapter includes an application to how the theory is used in research or has been revised to reflect changing demographics and trends in families in modern day. The *Sourcebook* is an excellent reference for more in-depth coverage of family theories, and its chapters can be used to supplement the explanations supplied in our introductory text.

Sarkisian, N., & Gerstel, N. (2012). *Nuclear family values, extended family lives: The power of race, class and gender*. Routledge. In this brief text, the authors utilize both classic and current versions of family theory to describe how families actually live, communicate, and change in response to demographic developments, social problems, and cultural transformations. Sarkisian and Gerstel critique the Standard North American Family (SNAF) model that continues to permeate family research, and they show that families are much more varied than a nuclear structure of heterosexual marriage and parent–child relations. For most individuals, daily life is comprised of extended family relationships, including aging parents, adult children, siblings, aunts, uncles, cousins, grandparents, and fictive kin. Extended family and community ties are an essential survival strategy, especially for those families who face racial, class, gender, and sexual orientation prejudice. This book demonstrates how important it is to go beyond marriage and parenthood to examine the range of family structures and ties that proactively address social problems and help families survive and thrive.

Questions for Students

Discussion Questions

1. Why are theories important to individuals who work with, and study, families?

2. How have your views of theory changed after reading the first chapter?

3. Compare and contrast the different types of epistemologies described in this chapter: positivist, interpretive, and critical. Consider how research would be conducted using a theory "app." How would we devise research questions, or construct surveys to measure them, without guidance from a theory?

4. How does research inform theory? Do family scholars revise and develop new theories as a result of research? How do you think that process works?

5. Consider how practitioners use theory; is it realistic to think that theory better prepares us to understand our roles as practitioners serving families? Why, or why not?

6. How do *you* define "theory"? What definition would you add to the definitions included in this chapter?

Your Turn!

Find an article that has used *any* theory as a framework for their empirical research on families. What aspects of the theory did the research utilize? Now, reread the article, leaving theory out; just skip over it entirely whenever it is mentioned. Does the article make as much sense without it? Does the theory enhance the research? Why, or why not?

Personal Reflection Questions

1. Write down five reasons you think people get divorced. You can use personal experience or anecdotal insights for this. Save your five reasons, and return to them as you read through each chapter of this book. By the time you are finished, you will be able to attach a theory to your previous knowledge and experiences (because, yes, there's a theory for that!).

2. How does your family compare to the SNAF? What about families you know well? Compare and contrast your own experiences with the assumptions about SNAF and also about other forms and nationalities of families.

3. What assumptions do you personally hold about family? Based on those assumptions, how would you explain the way families interact and operate? Write down your orientation to the study of families, and like question #1, save it. Return to your assumptions about family as you read through each chapter of this book. By the time you are finished, you may be able to write your own theory of family!

4. Think about the family you have grown up in. Now, think about the family you have created or wish to create in the future (with a partner, with children, etc.). How does broader social change influence your perception of being in a family or origin, compared to a family of creation?

5. What is your favorite book, TV program, or movie? What theories have the writers used to explain the actions of the characters?

6. How do you use the word "theory" in your daily life?

References

Acosta, K. L. (2018). Queering family scholarship: Theorizing from the borderlands. *Journal of Family Theory & Review, 10*(2), 406–418. https://doi.org/10.1111/jftr.12263

Admon, L. K., Winkelman, T. N., Zivin, K., Terplan, M., Mhyre, J. M., & Dalton, V. K. (2018). Racial and ethnic disparities in the incidence of severe maternal morbidity in the United States, 2012–2015. *Obstetrics & Gynecology, 132*(5), 1158–1166. https://doi.org/10.1097/AOG.0000000000002937

Agger, B. (2013). *Critical social theories* (3rd ed.). Oxford University Press.

Allen, K. R. (2000). A conscious and inclusive family studies. *Journal of Marriage and the Family, 62*(1), 4–17. https://doi.org/10.1111/j.1741-3737.2000.00911.x

Allen, K. R. (2016). Feminist theory in family studies: History, biography, and critique. *Journal of Family Theory & Review, 8*(2), 207–224. https://doi.org/10.1111/jftr.12133

Allen, K. R. (2022). Feminist theory, method, and praxis: Toward a critical consciousness for family and close relationship scholars. *Journal of Social and Personal Relationships.* Advance online publication. https://doi.org/10.1177/02654075211065779

Allen, K. R., & Henderson, A. C. (2018). Writing a family theories textbook: A pedagogical praxis. *Journal of Family Theory & Review, 10*(4), 814–820. https://doi.org/10.1111/jftr.12292

Allen, K. R., & Henderson, A. C. (2022). Family theorizing for social justice: A critical praxis. *Journal of Family Theory & Review.* Advance online publication. https://doi.org/10.1111/jftr.12450

Babbie, E. (2013). *The practice of social research* (13th ed.). Wadsworth.

Bahr, H., & Bahr, K. S. (2001). Families and self-sacrifice: Alternative models and meanings for family theory. *Social Forces, 79*(4), 1231–1258. https://doi.org/10.1353/sof.2001.0030

Beck, U., & Beck-Gernsheim, E. (2001). *Individualization: Institutionalized individualism and its social and political consequences.* SAGE Publications.

Bengtson, V. L., Acock, A. C., Allen, K. R., Dilworth-Anderson, P., & Klein, D. M. (2005). Theory and theorizing in family research: Puzzle building and puzzle solving. In V. L. Bengtson, A. C. Acock, K. R. Allen, P. Dilworth-Anderson, & D. M. Klein (Eds.), *Sourcebook of family theory and research* (pp. 3–33). SAGE Publications.

Bernardi, L., Huinink, J., & Settersten, R. A., Jr. (Eds.). (2019). The life course cube: A tool for studying lives. *Advances in Life Course Research, 41,* Article e100258. https://doi.org/10.1016/j.alcr.2018.11.004

Berger, P. L., & Luckmann, T. (1966). *The social construction of reality: A treatise in the sociology of knowledge.* Anchor Books.

Charmaz, K. (2014). *Constructing grounded theory* (2nd ed.). SAGE Publications.

Cheal, D. (1991). *Family and the state of theory.* University of Toronto Press.

Cherlin, A. J. (2004). The deinstitutionalization of American marriage. *Journal of Marriage and Family, 66*(4), 848–861. https://doi.org/10.1111/j.1741-3737.2010.00710

Cherlin, A. J. (2020). Degrees of change: An assessment of the deinstitutionalization of marriage thesis. *Journal of Marriage and Family, 82*(1), 62–80. https://doi.org/10.1111/jomf.12605

Clarke, E. H. (1873). *Sex in education: Or a fair chance for the girls.* Houghton Mifflin.

Collins, P. H. (2019). *Intersectionality as critical social theory.* Duke University Press.

Coontz, S. (2016). *The way we never were: American families and the nostalgia trap* (Rev. ed.). Basic Books.

Crotty, M. (2003). *The foundations of social research: Meaning and perspective in the research process.* SAGE Publications.

Daly, K. J. (2003). Family theory versus the theories families live by. *Journal of Marriage and Family, 65*(4), 771–784. https://doi.org/10.1111/j.1741-3737.2003.00771.x

Daly, K. J. (2007). *Qualitative methods for family studies & human development.* SAGE Publications.

Demo, D. H., Allen, K. R., & Fine, M. A. (Eds.). (2000). *Handbook of family diversity.* Oxford University Press.

Denzin, N. K., & Lincoln, Y. S. (2018). Introduction: The discipline and practice of qualitative research. In N. K. Denzin & Y. S. Lincoln (Eds.), *The SAGE handbook of qualitative research* (5th ed., pp. 1–26). SAGE Publications.

Doherty, W. J., Boss, P. G., LaRossa, R., Schumm, W. R., & Steinmetz, S. K. (1993). Family theories and methods: A contextual approach. In P. Boss, W. Doherty, R. LaRossa, W. Schumm, & S. Steinmetz (Eds.), *Sourcebook of family theories and methods: A contextual approach* (pp. 3–30). Plenum Press.

Dressel, P., & Clark, A. (1990). A critical look at family care. *Journal of Marriage and the Family, 52*(3), 769–782. https//doi.org/10.2307/352941

Family and Medical Leave Act of 1993, 29 U.S.C. § 2601-2654 (2006).

Few-Demo, A. L., & Allen, K. R. (2020). Gender, feminist, and intersectional perspectives on families: A decade in review. *Journal of Marriage and Family, 82*(1), 326–345. https://doi.org/10.1111/jomf.12638

Fine, M. A., & Fincham, F. D. (2013). Introduction: The role of theory in family science. In M. A. Fine & F. D. Fincham (Eds.), *Handbook of family theories: A content-based approach* (pp. 1–7). Routledge.

Gottfried, H., & Chun, J. J. (2018). Care work in transition: Transnational circuits of gender, migration, and care. *Critical Sociology, 44*(7–8), 997–1012. https://doi.org/10.1177/0896920518765931

Gubrium, J. F., & Holstein, J. A. (1990). *What is family?* Mayfield.

History.com Editors. (2019, June 7). *U.S. Immigration Since 1965.* History.com. www.history.com/topics/us-immigration-since-1965

Jaccard, J., & Jacoby, J. (2010). *Theory construction and model-building skills: A practical guide for social scientists.* Guilford.

Klein, D. M. (2005). The cyclical process of science. In V. L. Bengtson, A. C. Acock, K. R. Allen, P. Dilworth-Anderson, & D. M. Klein (Eds.), *Sourcebook of family theory and research* (pp. 17–18). SAGE Publications.

Knauer, N. (2019). Implications of *Obergefell* for same-sex marriage, divorce, and parental rights. In A. E. Goldberg & A. P. Romero (Eds.), *LGBTQ divorce and relational dissolution* (pp. 7–30). Oxford University Press.

Langellier, K. M., & Peterson, E. E. (2021). Narrative performance theory: Making stories, doing family. In D. O. Braithwaite & P. Schrodt (Eds.), *Engaging theories in interpersonal communication: Multiple perspectives* (pp. 210–220). Routledge.

Lebow, J. (2020). The challenges of COVID-19 for divorcing and post-divorce families. *Family Process, 59*(3), 967–973. https://doi.org/10.1111/famp.12574

Letiecq, B. L. (2019). Surfacing family privilege and supremacy in family science: Toward justice for all. *Journal of Family Theory & Review, 11*(3), 398–411. https://doi.org/10.1111/jftr.12338

Lincoln, Y. S., Lynham, S. A., & Guba, E. G. (2018). Paradigmatic controversies, contradictions, and emerging confluences, revisited. In N. K. Denzin & Y. S. Lincoln (Eds.), *The SAGE handbook of qualitative research* (5th ed., pp. 108–150). SAGE Publications.

Louis, J. M., Menard, M. K., & Gee, R. E. (2015). Racial and ethnic disparities in maternal morbidity and mortality. *Obstetrics & Gynecology, 125*(3), 690–694. https://doi.org/10.1097/AOG.0000000000000704

Lutz, H. (2011). *The new maids: Transnational women and the care economy.* Zed Books.

Mahalingam, R., Balan, S., & Molina, K. M. (2009). Transnational intersectionality: A critical framework for theorizing motherhood. In S. A. Lloyd, A. L. Few, & K. R. Allen (Eds.), *Handbook of feminist family studies* (pp. 69–80). SAGE Publications.

Mahler, S. J., Chaudhuri, M., & Patil, V. (2015). Scaling intersectionality: Advancing feminist analysis of transnational families. *Sex Roles, 73*(3/4), 100–112. https://doi.org/10.1007/s11199-015-0506-9

McGhee, H. (2021). *The sum of us: What racism costs everyone and how we can prosper together.* One World.

McIntosh, P. (2020). *On privilege, fraudulence, and teaching as learning: Selected essays 1981–2019.* Taylor & Francis.

Morello, K. B. (1986). *The invisible bar: The woman lawyer in America 1683 to the present.* Random House.

Nye, F. I. (1979). Choice, exchange, and the family. In W. R. Burr, R. Hill, F. I. Nye, & I. L. Reiss (Eds.), *Contemporary theories about the family: General theories/theoretical orientations* (pp. 1–41). Free Press.

Olou, I. (2018). *So you want to talk about race.* Seal Press.

Oswald, R. F., Kuvalanka, K. A., Blume, L. B., & Berkowitz, D. (2009). Queering "The Family". In S. L. Lloyd, A. L. Few, & K. R. Allen (Eds.), *Handbook of feminist family studies* (pp. 43–55). SAGE Publications.

Parsons, T. (1970). *Social structure and personality.* Free Press.

Pittman, J. F. (1993). Functionalism may be down, but it surely is not out: Another point of view for family therapists and policy analysts. In P. Boss, W. Doherty, R. LaRossa, W. Schumm, & S. Steinmetz (Eds.), *Sourcebook of family theories and methods: A contextual approach* (pp. 218–221). Plenum Press.

Prime, H., Wade, M., & Browne, D. T. (2020). Risk and resilience in family well-being during the COVID-19 pandemic. *American Psychologist, 75*(5), 631–643. http://dx.doi.org/10.1037/amp0000660

Raley, R. K., & Sweeney, M. M. (2020). Divorce, repartnering, and stepfamilies: A decade in review. *Journal of Marriage and Family, 82*(1), 81–89. https://doi.org/10.1111/jomf.12651

Schoemaker, P. J., Tankard, J. W., Jr., & Lasorsa, D. L. (2004). *How to build social science theories.* SAGE Publications.

Smith, D. E. (1993). The standard North American family: SNAF as an ideological code. *Journal of Family Issues, 14*(1), 50–65. https://doi.org/10.1177/0192513X93014001005

Smock, P. J., & Schwartz, C. R. (2020). The demography of families: A review of patterns and change. *Journal of Marriage and Family, 82*(1), 9–34. https://doi.org/10.1111/jomf.12612

Sprey, J. (Ed.). (1990). *Fashioning family theory: New approaches.* SAGE Publications.

Sprey, J. (2013). Extending the range of questioning in family studies through ideas from the exact sciences. *Journal of Family Theory & Review, 5*(1), 51–61. https://doi.org/10.1111/jftr.12002

Stacey, J. (1990). *Brave new families: Stories of domestic upheaval in late twentieth century America.* Basic Books.

Suitor, J. J., Gilligan, M., & Pillemer, K. (2013). Continuity and change in mothers' favoritism toward offspring in adulthood. *Journal of Marriage and Family, 75*(5), 1229–1247. https://doi.org/10.1111/jomf.12067

Sweeney, M. M. (2010). Remarriage and stepfamilies: Strategic sites for family scholarship in the 21st century. *Journal of Marriage and Family, 72*(3), 667–684. https://doi.org/10.1111/j.1741-3737.2010.00724.x

Turner, E. A., Jernigan-Noesi, M., & Metzger, I. (2022). Confronting anti-Black racism and promoting social justice. In K. Cokley (Ed.), *Making Black lives matter: Confronting anti-Black racism* (pp. 55–69). Cognella Academic Publishing.

Ungerson, C. (2006). Gender, care, and the welfare state. In K. Davis, M. Evans, & J. Lorber (Eds.), *Handbook of gender and women's studies* (pp. 272–286). SAGE Publications.

Wallace, W. L. (2009). *The logic of science in sociology.* Aldine Transaction. (Original work published 1971)

Weisberg, D. K. (1977). Barred from the bar: Women and legal education in the United States 1870–1890. *Journal of Legal Education, 28*(4), 485–507. https://www.jstor.org/stable/42897011

White, J. M. (2013). The current status of theorizing about families. In G. W. Peterson & K. R. Bush (Eds.), *Handbook of marriage and the family* (3rd ed.; pp. 11–37). Springer.

Image Credits

Functionalist Theory

ave you ever had to go a day, or even a few hours, without your mobile phone? Perhaps, you dropped it in the tub, cracked the screen to the point of no repair, or maybe it just refuses to turn on. What are the consequences when you are without your mobile phone? Think about your close friends or family, who may have sent you important text messages that you do not have access to. How will you stay in touch with them? How long could you really stand to be without your phone? Imagine the updates, photos, and events you might miss if you had to go—shudders at the thought—one week without your phone. What other options do you have for contacting someone? How would you stay integrated, or connected, into your social circles?

Functionalist theory, as it is often called, helps us understand what happens when one part of a larger whole or system stops working. Functionalism, one of the founding theories in social science, is based on the biological analogy that society is like a living organism, and when one part of it stops working, other parts are affected. If your lungs do not receive enough oxygen, your body reacts, and you might feel lightheaded, dizzy, or nauseous. The entire system is affected by the functionality of just one piece of the whole. In addition, functionalism helps us understand how healthy levels of social integration are important to normal functioning in society. This theory considers how individuals within families need to maintain healthy levels of social integration, promoting and reinforcing societal norms for "citizens in training." This theory highlights the interplay between social norms, family functions, and how family members contribute to the equilibrium (or not) of the entire family. In addition, this perspective sheds light on the purpose the family serves beyond the four walls of the home; as a social institution, families are vital to the overall functioning of the greater society.

In this chapter, we discuss the history of functionalist theory and how the key concepts can be used to understand how families function in society. As one of the earliest theories applied to family science, functionalist theory has been widely influential yet also widely critiqued (Kingsbury & Scanzoni, 1993). Functionalist theory seems to be the family theory we love to hate, despite the fact that it still used, even without identifying our debt to some of its key concepts. We will address both aspects of the theory (its strengths and its limitations) as it has developed over time. Our treatment of functionalist theory is designed to show the continuing influence and potential utility of this theory, despite claims that it is not relevant to the study of the diverse and complex families in our world today. To gain a fuller understanding of how functionalism works, we start with a case study that illustrates how families adapt to change and how overall system functionality is affected by each contributing member.

Case Study

Casbah identifies as a transgender, bisexual boy (natal sex female) born two years after his parents had their first child, Shaila, a cisgender heterosexual girl. Before Casbah transitioned, his parents treated him like a little girl. Shaila was so excited to have a little sister—someone to play dolls and dress up with and someone to teach new things to. Throughout their childhood, Shaila and Casbah became very close, and their parents joked that they were attached at the hip. They rarely fought because their personalities complemented one another so well. Shaila was very emotionally mature for a young child and was able to help Casbah understand his own emotions early on. Their parents were often impressed when they overheard Shaila explaining in detail how they would play dolls for 30 minutes and then go outside and play soccer for 30 minutes, so each of them got to do what they wanted. Casbah usually agreed with most of Shaila's plans because, most of the time, they ended with his favorite activity—playing soccer.

Thinking back to his childhood, Casbah knew the whole time how different he was from his sister, despite their closeness. Casbah felt like a boy trapped in a girl's body, and the way his sister insisted he "perform" his gender was the exact opposite from how he felt inside. Casbah felt like a boy. He knew he was transgender the minute he learned as an adolescent what transgender meant. He waited until he was 15 to talk to his parents and sister about it, and to Casbah's relief, they were very supportive. His third-generation Pakistani American parents helped support him through psychological therapy and assisted in his transition from she to he with hormone replacement therapy and a legal name change. Shaila was sad to "lose" her sister, and she struggled with the transition internally. The family sought support from a family counselor referred to them by good friends. Over time, Shaila became more accepting of Casbah, excited to have a brother and even more thankful that it was someone she knew all along. Their parents also learned valuable communication skills in therapy—skills that carried over into their marriage and other family relationships.

Think about Shaila and Casbah's childhood, and how Shaila helped their relationship function smoothly by fairly distributing their playtime between two very different tasks. This also contributed to a smooth daily life for their parents—mom and dad rarely had to intervene in their children's play time, helping the family maintain overall system functionality. Moreover, consider how valuable it was for the family to receive help from an external, trained professional and licensed counselor. How would the family have dealt with this issue without this resource?

Additionally, consider Casbah's life as a boy in high school: What are the consequences of him identifying as a boy? Casbah was a star player on the girls' soccer team and still wants to play the sport. Many may still debate whether or not he should be allowed to participate on the boys' soccer team and use the locker rooms. Think even more broadly about this situation: Would this transition from being born female but identifying as male have been accepted even 20 years ago? Functionalism helps us understand how societies and social institutions change over time, reacting to difference and adapting to maintain stability. From a functionalist perspective, families both interact with larger social norms and also serve functions inside the family for their members. Functionalists would argue that it is impossible to understand society without taking into account the functionality of all parts of a social system, and families, as one of the most important social institutions in society, are no exception.

What Is Functionalist Theory?

Functionalist theory is used by researchers to help explain processes, both within families as well as how families operate in and contribute to society at large. Functionalism has a long history in the social sciences, beginning with the French scholar Émile Durkheim, considered to be the father of sociology, who identified problems associated with the rise of the modern world during the Industrial Revolution (Appelrouth & Edles, 2021). Later, American sociologist Talcott Parsons (1951), also discussed in Chapter 1, developed a model for studying society during a time of economic prosperity and conservative values, which included taking large and complex social processes into account, including how families **function**, or serve a purpose, as social institutions in society and how they react to change at the macro level. Finally, Robert Merton (1957), who was Parsons's student, extended functionalism by taking deviance and reactions to cultural goals into account, which are useful when trying to understand how families react to difference *within* and *outside* of their families.

History and Origins

To understand any theory, it is vital to situate it into the proper historical context. Durkheim (1893/1984) first introduced functionalist concepts into the study of society during the Industrial Revolution, which began in the 18th century, when major social upheaval and economic change occurred in Western Europe. Before the Industrial Revolution, most people lived in villages and small towns, relying on the local community to provide for them. Food was produced locally, and agriculture sustained only the surrounding communities. When industrialization replaced agricultural production, people flocked to cities as a result of the changing economy; families now had to find employment to sell their labor for a wage to provide for their family's basic needs. Therefore, most families that were once self-sufficient, relying on agricultural production for sustenance, had to give up agriculture as a way of life and instead move into large cities to find jobs (Giddens, 2002). This had consequences not only for social life but also for how families functioned both inside and outside the home. Families often tried to have fewer children because the shift from an agriculture-based economy to a market-based economy meant that families no longer needed more "workers" (i.e., children) at home, tending to the land and livestock. Instead, in the new economy, families often *all* went to work in factories, until compulsory education and child labor laws were passed in industrializing countries. An example in the United States was the Fair Labor Standards Act, which set minimum ages for child laborers (16 for boys and 18 for girls; U.S. Senate, 1937). These macro-level historical changes undoubtedly affected families' structure and functionality in society.

You will read about the Industrial Revolution in other chapters because it was such a major event in our world's history in terms of the way it shaped social interactions and families. However, you will probably notice right away how differently each theorist interprets the Industrial Revolution. Karl Marx (Chapter 3) and Durkheim defined the problems associated with Industrialization very differently. Below, we start our discussion of the key concepts of functionalist theory by first outlining Durkheim's perspective of how society works.

Key Concepts

Durkheim's View: Functionalism

Émile Durkheim (1893/1984) was concerned with the increasing **dynamic density** that occurred following the Industrial Revolution, defined as the number of people living in any given place as well as the number of people interacting. The reason this was problematic for Durkheim was that the accompanying shift from mechanical solidarity to organic solidarity. Solidarity is a term functionalists used to describe the processes by which societies or groups, such as families, are "held together," or, put another way, what unifies members of a group into a functioning unit. **Mechanical solidarity** is found in more primitive societies, such as those that existed before the Industrial Revolution. Members of these societies were generalists, performing similar tasks with similar responsibilities. Family members could carry out nearly any task necessary for the survival not only of the family but of the larger community as a whole. It was common for the patriarch—or father—to provide education inside the home with a family Bible, educating his wife and children on morality and other religious teachings. He also contributed to farming his land (and, most likely, also that of his landowner, from whom he rented farmland) and probably also helped with the construction of buildings in the community as well as on his own property. Most women and children also worked at home but not in the sense we think of today. Before Industrialization, women and children had contributed to the overall functioning of the family unit by farming the land, gathering water and firewood, and tending to livestock (Appelrouth & Edles, 2021). Most members of these societies were what we could call jacks-of-all-trades. Societies had a repressive law in place, which meant lawbreakers were held accountable to the entire society because any deviation from the law was a threat to group cohesiveness or solidarity. Punishment for deviants was swift and harsh. At the same time, members of societies like this contributed to a **collective conscience**, which is a common sense of morality that all community members believed in and upheld (Durkheim, 1893/1984). This kept members of a society accountable and provided a set of rules and regulations, guided by morality, for all to follow.

After the Industrial Revolution, societies were characterized by **organic solidarity**, a term used to describe societies with a well-specified division of labor. This meant that people went from being generalists to specialists, responsible for a very specific aspect of work both within the family as well as outside of it, in the larger community (Durkheim, 1893/1984). This shift occurred in sync with the increase in dynamic density. With a very large number of individuals interacting, there was a major social shift away from similar people having shared experiences to people with different tasks, more isolated from one another, having very different experiences. In contrast to mechanical solidarity, where societal members were cooperative for the benefit of the greater good, these more industrialized societies were more competitive in nature. Competition increased because of the sheer number of people in any given society or city. Additionally, competition increased because there was not a shared sense of morality among all members of the group; it was virtually impossible for all residents of a city, for example, to subscribe to the same worldview or religion. Therefore, the collectivist aspects of society that characterized pre-Industrialized societies were replaced by competition and difference. People depended on one another because they did need each other; a machinist did not do the job of a transporter or a miner. Their jobs were very specialized, which, according to Durkheim, was part of what held this new type of society together.

Consider the structure of a family in either type of society: In an agriculture-based society, family members are likely focused on the needs of the entire family, working toward providing for siblings, helping parents, and caring for their land. In an industrialized society, family members are much more scattered in terms of where they likely spend their waking hours; the father is at work as a manufacturer, the mother is at work as a weaver, and the children as chimneysweeps or domestic workers (most children did not attend elementary school until after child labor laws were passed). This type of familial structure, inevitably, has an impact on the functionality of the home and family. Each family member is likely concerned with their wages making a meaningful contribution to the family, but their daily lived experiences are vastly different from one another, compared to pre-Industrialized family life.

This macro-level shift in how society and families operated altered the social norms and social integration of all members of society. Instead of being held together by a common sense of morality like in agricultural societies, Durkheim suggested that **moral individualism**—an outlook on life based on what is good for oneself—replaced collective consciousness. That is, when dynamic density and the division of labor both increased, no solidifying conscience increased along with it. This, in turn, affected levels of **social integration**, or the degree to which people are tied to their social groups. According to functionalism, you can experience normal levels of social integration, levels that are too high, or levels that are too low. Social integration is best described using a continuum (see Figure 2.1).

Normal social integration for everyone is ideal, but sometimes, individuals become too highly integrated into a group, losing sight of the norms of the greater society that govern behavior. An example of this would be a religious cult; cult members might idealize their cult leader as a "god," putting the needs of the group ahead of their own individual needs and definitely ahead of the goals of greater society. On the other hand, individuals who are not members of any social groups and live in a secluded area, removed from society, are at danger of

FIGURE 2.1. A Continuum of Social Integration

experiencing extremely low levels of social integration and vulnerable to acting on human impulses or violence against others. Unfortunately, there are examples of this type of behavior in our society when we consider those who perform mass shootings. Often, we wonder about the shooter's background, how their family could have overlooked the heavy weaponry hidden under their bed, or the painful experiences the shooter had being bullied in school. In asking these questions, we are inadvertently using functionalist theory because we are trying to identify the **dysfunction**, or the part of the whole that broke down. What happened in the shooter's life that led to this event? We hypothesize about the level of social integration, by asking if the student was a "loner," without proper guidance or healthy social ties. We ask about their family upbringing, church family, and extended family, which are some of the details that Sue Klebold (2016) describes in the aftermath of coming to terms with her own experience as the mother of Dylan, one of the young men responsible for the Columbine shootings. Most of us, without even knowing it, then, already view the world from a functionalist perspective. While Durkheim is considered to be the father of functionalist theory, other theorists who came after him adapted his theoretical framework to apply to a more modernized society (i.e., long after the Industrial Revolution had occurred). Next, we discuss two more modern theorists, Talcott Parsons and Robert Merton, and their adaptations of functionalist theory, the new concepts they introduced, and how each perspective shaped theorizing about the family.

Parsons's View: Structural Functionalism

In contrast to Durkheim's level of analysis, which often included functions inside the family, Parsons (1951) based much of his theoretical ideas on how society functioned at the macro level. That is, his model of functionalism took into account both societal *structure* and function, or how social systems produced shared moral codes and norms and how those trickled down to social actors. In this way, he extended Durkheim's model by suggesting that several large-scale systems—the cultural, social, and personality systems—are interdependent and help to maintain stability. Therefore, his model is best known as **structural functionalism**. However, before we discuss those systems in detail, it is important to provide historical context to help understand how these theoretical ideas emerged.

From the 1930s through the 1970s, structural functionalism was a very popular theoretical perspective in American social sciences (Appelrouth & Edles, 2021) and had a significant impact on the field of family science. You might remember from Chapter 1 that this time period, specifically the 1950s, was often referred to as the "Golden Era," when the post-World War II economy was booming, and most White families only needed one breadwinner (Coontz, 2016). The cultural norm in America was for mothers to stay at home with children, and federal assistance programs, such as low-interest housing loans, significantly helped young families maintain economic stability. Therefore, Parsons's model was situated in a historical time and place in which social institutions seemingly functioned "well" for the White, middle-class American family, or what we referred to in Chapter 1 as the Standard North American Family (SNAF; Smith, 1993). The Civil Rights Movement for Black Americans to ensure equity in housing, employment, education, voting, and other key legal rights was ongoing throughout this era (McGhee, 2021), but for the mostly White families that Parsons wrote about, adhering to the "norm" was still achievable.

Therefore, it is not surprising that Parsons's (1951) model is based on the idea that shared norms and values are the key to a smoothly functioning society. However, in contrast to Durkheim, who described what holds societies together before, during, and after rapid social change, Parsons instead attempted to explain how individuals "fit" within larger social systems (in abstract terms) and how those systems are interdependent. Parsons identified how individuals fit within preexisting systems and how, by fitting in, society functions in an orderly way. Let's analyze each of those systems in turn.

The first, and arguably the most overarching system, is the cultural system. The **cultural system** is made up of the "values, norms, and symbols which guide the choices made by actors and which limit the type of interaction which may occur among actors" (Parsons & Shils, 1951, p. 55). Think of this system as the taken-for-granted norms and ideas about how things work in the world; this includes the range of acceptable behaviors, ideas, and beliefs that govern society (Shils et al., 1965). According to Parsons, our culture determines every social institution that exists in our society, every role we are allowed to fulfill, the choices we are allowed to make, and even the preferences and tastes we have! Think about your own decisions—what you decide to wear every day, what kind of mobile phone you buy, or where you chose to go to college. All of these are part of the cultural system, which suggests that we should dress fashionably (according to whichever subculture you identify with), that we should each have our own mobile phones, and that we assume most young adults will go to college. Each of these norms is often taken for granted and assumed to be the way of life for most people in our culture. It is those norms that make up our cultural system, and as long as we "fit" into these ideals and conform to the preexisting system, society functions in a predictable and orderly way. The cultural system, then, works down on the other two systems: the personality and social systems. To show the relationships among the three systems, see Figure 2.2 below.

It is important to point out here that Parsons's framework is often critiqued for suggesting that the goal of society is complete institutionalization of and conformity to norms and values (Appelrouth & Edles, 2021). Though Parsons did argue that following rules benefited each system and maintained equilibrium, his model did not ignore the possibility of social change (as it is often criticized for doing) or environmental conditions adapting and producing subsequent changes in his three systems. In fact, Parsons's model suggests that society is like a living organism, and systems are continuously in flux, adjusting and changing over time: "Complete and perfect institutionalization is an ideal; it refers to when role demands from the social system complement cultural ideals and when both, in turn, meet the needs of the personality system" (Appelrouth & Edles, 2021, p. 353).

Parsons wrote about generation gaps to illustrate this point. Often, younger generations' views and outlooks on life clash with the views and outlooks of older generations, which can create conflict within systems. These conflicts can be functional for one part of the system but not another. Because each of the systems is comprised of various **subsystems** (e.g., larger American culture includes a sport subculture and a hunting subculture), disagreements between subsystems is inevitable, but that does not mean they cannot be managed. Indeed, one of the functions of youth culture is to "[ease] the difficult process of adjustment from childhood emotional dependency to full 'maturity'" (Parsons, 1943, p. 189). Therefore, these disagreements can, and do, slowly lead to social change over time, which will affect the cultural system as well. Though Parsons did not fully develop

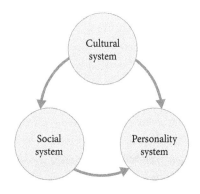

FIGURE 2.2. Parsons's Systems

how divergences from the norm can also contribute to functionality of society, his student, Robert Merton, did. We will discuss Merton in more detail later in this chapter.

In a broad sense, then, we can apply Parsons's systems to Casbah from our case study. The cultural system during Casbah's youth is vastly different from the one his grandparents and great-grandparents experienced. Casbah is coming of age in a culture that is becoming increasingly aware and accepting of LGBTQ+ persons. Until the 1970s, the American cultural system defined homosexual persons as having a diagnosable illness or disorder (Silverstein, 1991). In more contemporary societies, however, the cultural system has adapted to change, which trickles down to the other system levels. Transgender persons are, for the most part, no longer considered to be mentally ill or disordered. Today, you probably know someone who is transgender. It is a part of our larger culture; Hollywood films and television shows are increasingly portraying and celebrating transgender characters, in films like *Transamerica* (Tucker, 2005) and in the television series *Pose* (Murphy et al., 2021). All of these indicators suggest that the cultural system does adapt to social change, which, in effect, dictates both the social and personality systems.

The social system is directly influenced by the cultural system. To understand what Parsons meant by "social system," let's start with what it is *not*. Social systems do not refer to tangible, material structures or social institutions, such as churches or educational systems. The idea is more abstract and has to be considered by imagining how we interact with one another. Parsons defined the **social system** as the level of interaction between two or more actors, where actors are aware of one another's ideas and intentions, and their interactions are governed by shared norms or expectations (Parsons & Shils, 1951). In other words, the behaviors we carry out on a daily basis are part of the social system. We understand what to do when we enter a bank, for example; we approach a bank representative, conduct our banking business, and leave. We do not go behind the counter to make our own withdrawals, start helping other customers, or ask the bank teller to dance while being waited on at the counter. The social interactions are predictable, and orderly, and are part of a larger social system, or set of social interaction expectations, that we adhere to, consciously or not.

The reason these interactions are considered part of a system is because they are made up of roles (Parsons & Shils, 1951). **Roles** are complementary, detailed sets of obligations for interaction. For example, there are expectations associated with the role of professor. Consider your professor for this course; they have a higher degree; they most likely have areas of expertise in the family and theory; and their behavior is predictable because you know they fulfill a specific role. You likely do not invite your professor on vacations with your family or ask your professor to pick up your dry cleaning. Those interactions are not part of a professor's role, and are, therefore, not part of the social system (we hope!).

The third system Parsons wrote about is the **personality system**, which takes individual characteristics into account. However, the personality system is still embedded in the social structure, which means individuals' unique and distinctive sense of self is limited by the choices they are given by both the cultural and social systems. Therefore, the personality system is organized by what Parsons refers to as **need-dispositions**, which are types of action guided by emotion and individual drive or representations of individuals' personal uniqueness. Our daily decisions—our tastes, preferences, and drives—are limited by what is available. To help us understand what that means for families, we return to Casbah.

As mentioned earlier, the cultural system makes it possible for Casbah to come out to his family in contemporary society. The social system is also undoubtedly affected by this larger norm. Consider how social interactions have changed since LGBTQ+ persons have been afforded more rights and respect. First and foremost, a word, transgender, exists for how Casbah identifies, and now, scholarly research and popular literature are growing about transgender lives (Goldberg & Beemyn, 2021). The case study suggested that Casbah knew he was different from a very young age, and when he learned during adolescence what transgender meant, he knew that label correctly identified him. He was then able to research support groups online for others who were similar to him and feel a sense of belonging with a community of people, instead of feeling alone and as if there was something wrong with him. This helped make coming out easier for him, as did his parents' willingness to assist him in transitioning with hormone therapy as well as individual psychological therapy and group therapy for the family. The existence of these resources shows evidence that the cultural system has adapted to broader social change. Following the various civil rights movements of the 1960s, society began to react to and absorb new subsystems, which redefined patterns of interaction at the social and personality levels. Again, while Parsons was not writing specifically about material spaces and places, it is still worth noting that the processes that led to the establishment of transgender as an identity, hormone therapy as a possibility, and individual and group therapy as a solution for dealing with adjustments to family and individual identity were all part of a set of integrated interactions. This means that as society absorbed new subcultures as an acceptable part of the cultural system, conversations and concerted efforts were made to include and support LGBTQ+ persons in the social system. This opened up new possibilities for inclusivity for people who were once considered to be on the margins of society and not acceptable to the larger cultural system.

In sum, we can see how each system worked together as Casbah moved through the next stage in his life. Eventually, his need-dispositions were met, even though his family's subsystem was disrupted in the short-term. Parents, friends, and faculty and staff in Casbah's school have likely been exposed to Safe Zone training, which was created to "develop, enhance and maintain environments in workplaces, schools and other social settings that are culturally competent and supportive to LGBTQ individuals" (Safe Zone Project, 2021). Casbah, when deciding where he will go to college, will most definitely take into account which campuses are considered to be trans-friendly and inclusive. His personal choices of what to major in, what clubs he will be a part of, and which dorm he feels most comfortable in are all determined by the cultural system. The social system—the interactions he hopes he will experience, when the time comes—should be somewhat predictable based on his knowledge of the campus culture. Then, the personality system, or the unique way he will go about his daily life, who he is attracted to, and who he dates, are all dependent on what is available. He is still unique, but the culture and social systems definitely affect his personality. He could not truly "be" Casbah had he been born 50 years earlier to different parents in a different time and place. Each of the systems has worked together to function and impact his life.

Part of what contributes to the change we see in systems is institutionalization. **Institutionalization** occurs when a part of the larger cultural system becomes part of a standard in society—a long-standing tradition that is embedded and identifiable. As an example, consider the cultural norm that exists in most of American society that two people who choose to marry can go through the legal process of becoming legally recognized as a married couple. We can see institutionalization when the cultural system works down on the social system.

Internalization, on the other hand, is when individuals adhere to the cultural norms in such a way that they become part of need-dispositions and our patterns of communication and ways of thinking. Because of the overarching cultural system, we may all adhere to the norms that guide behavior (e.g., the expectation that you should marry), but we do so differently. We make different choices based on the subculture we identify with, and soon the signs, symbols, and interactions with others in subsystems become second nature, or taken for granted, because we have internalized the cultural norms. We can see internalization when the cultural system works down on the personality system. Consider the contemporary options for marriage; some couples are choosing to integrate a flash mob type of dance choreography into either their wedding ceremony or reception. Couples who have participated in this new practice are still conforming to cultural norms, but they choose their own song, dance moves, and setting to fulfill their need-dispositions of being unique.

One of the reasons having a flash mob at a wedding ceremony is acceptable is how we are socialized. **Socialization** occurs when individuals come to regard specific norms as binding. It occurs during the interaction of the personality and social systems. How we are raised by our parents or loved ones determines our socialization; in contemporary cultures, there are several choices parents can make when it comes to raising their children. Some parents may choose to hover over their children, a practice referred to as "helicopter parenting," where parents pay extremely close attention to their teenage and young adult children's lives, often stepping in to solve problems for their children. Researchers and other experts have criticized this model of parenting because it prevents children from ever experiencing disappointment, leading to higher rates of anxiety and depression among children of helicopter parents (LeMoyne & Buchanan, 2011; Nomaguchi & Milkie, 2020; Schiffrin et al., 2014). This approach to parenting, which is part of the contemporary cultural system, is a choice for parents. Parents in contemporary culture, particularly mothers, are socialized to be "perfect" parents (Hays, 1996; Henderson et al., 2016), which, in turn, determines how their children will be socialized.

Now that we have described some of Parsons's general concepts as they relate to family, we can turn to one of his most notable articles: "The Kinship System of the Contemporary United States." In this work, Parsons (1943) reiterates that all systems have functions, and the family's main function is to procreate and socialize children. This work is highly criticized for dictating to families that there is only one family form, and any deviation from the SNAF is dysfunctional. This work is also criticized for suggesting the ideal way families can serve positive functions in society is by reinforcing traditional gender roles. That is, Parsons suggested that women are better suited for **expressive roles**, which include showing love, care, concern, and support for the system. Therefore, men are better suited to perform **instrumental roles**, which include being a leader, making important decisions, and providing material needs for the system. Essentially, if families are to function appropriately, then the family structure needs to be divided along traditional gender lines. This makes sense, given Parsons's assertion that the need-dispositions of individuals in the personality system are met within the social and cultural systems. If an individual has a need, they should turn to the social and cultural systems to make a choice about how to fulfill that need. That choice should stay within acceptable, established cultural norms in order to strive for equilibrium between and within all systems and subsystems.

Parsons's model of structural functionalism did not account for deviance, or difference. If a family did not fit an established model within the preexisting cultural system (e.g., the SNAF), then it was deemed dysfunctional. The only way for system equilibrium to be reached is for everyone to stay within acceptable boundaries that are already established by the culture. The reason for this is because Parsons believed that changes in one system (e.g., mothers leaving the home to enter the paid workforce) would inevitably affect other systems, creating dysfunction. In the example of two working parents, which other systems might be affected? From Parsons's structural-functionalist perspective, we would need to examine how childcare facilities would need to adapt to meet the need-dispositions of the mother who wants to work outside the home for pay. If a vast majority of mothers decided to enter the paid labor force, a major shift in other systems would need to occur to maintain equilibrium between systems.

Considering the historical context in which Parsons formulated his theoretical framework, his assertions make sense. Dual-earner households did not conform to the cultural system of the 1940s and 1950s, when Parsons conceptualized his theoretical framework. It was not until later, after the cultural system adapted to economic and social change, that dual-earner households became part of a cultural norm with accompanying support from external social institutions. To better understand how society shifted over time to allow for different family forms to still "fit" within the larger culture, even though they are different from the mainstream, we now turn to Merton's theory of structural functionalism.

Merton's View of Structural Functionalism

Merton (1957) was studying sociology at Harvard University during Parsons's early years as a faculty member there. Because of this, Merton has been noted for directly expanding Parsons's abstract structural functionalism to be a more useful and applicable framework to explaining action (Appelrouth & Edles, 2021). Merton disagreed with Parsons's view that changes that are functional for one part of a system will produce changes that are dysfunctional for other parts of a system. In fact, Merton is best known for his theory of deviance, which suggests that when there is a disconnect between the cultural goals of a society and the means available for individuals to achieve cultural goals, the natural result is strain. From Merton's perspective, not all members of society have the means to achieve, for example, the "ideal family." Therefore, the systems and subsystems that Parsons identified do more than simply fulfill functions and maintain equilibrium; they often produce unintended consequences that contribute to moving society forward in a positive way.

Though Merton did not write specifically about the family like Parsons did, his theoretical contributions can most definitely be applied to the study of families. Merton suggested that each system, or social institution in society (including families), has both manifest and latent functions. **Manifest functions** describe the intended purpose of the system; as an example, the criminal justice system exists to deter crime. However, Merton acknowledged that, sometimes, there are latent functions embedded into our social interactions and structures as well, and these unintended consequences, or **latent functions**, still contribute to the functionality of systems. The latent function of the criminal justice system is that it creates jobs. Police officers, judges, lawyers, prison guards, parole officers, and court reporters, among others, all depend on individuals committing crime, so they can remain employed. Have you ever thought about what might happen if all of a sudden, one day, everyone stopped committing crime? Imagine the effect that would have on the economy!

To bring an example a little closer to the study of families, think back to Casbah. When he decided to come out to his family, his parents sought help to support their child. They discussed psychological therapy with Casbah, and together, they decided that was something they wanted to pursue. The manifest function of therapy was to help the family address and adapt to changes. The latent function was that the therapy sessions taught Casbah's parents (a married couple) many tools they could use for communication in other parts of their lives. For example, they became more emotionally intelligent at work and in their interactions with friends and loved ones. The latent functions of Casbah's transformation and therapy led to *positive* change in other systems connected to his family.

Another one of Merton's theoretical contributions to structural functionalism is strain theory. **Strain theory** posits that societies have a set of cultural goals that all societal members are pressured to achieve or live up to; this results in strain. However, not all members of society follow the norm when it comes to achieving those cultural goals. Merton defined these individuals as deviant and came up with four categories that describe the nonconforming ways in which people react to cultural goals. The first category, innovators, are individuals who accept cultural goals but use innovative and sometimes illegal means to achieve them. An example would be a single woman who wants to have children and decides to have them on her own by using a sperm donor.

The second category, ritualists, are those who accept cultural goals but simply "go through the motions" of achieving them. A ritualist may seem apathetic or dispassionate. An example of this would be a parent who is married and has children but does not *really* enjoy those roles. They may just go through life, day by day, trying to get through. Their nature is not to leave the family but to do "what's right"—even if it means not truly being involved or 100% invested. Merton (1938) used the example of someone "being in a rut" to illustrate a ritualist.

Third, retreaters are individuals who reject cultural goals of a society as well as the means of achieving them. The Amish would fall under this category; they subscribe to traditionalist Christian church teachings and generally reject modern technology for simple living and self-sufficiency. They typically seek to remain separate from mainstream culture, operating their own schools and living a rural lifestyle characterized by manual labor and humility (Amish People and Amish Culture, n.d.).

Fourth, rebels are similar to retreatists, but they are active in trying to create a new social structure. This category represents a "transitional response seeking to *institutionalize* new goals and new procedures to be shared by other members of the society" (Merton, 1938, p. 44, italics in original). Therefore, rebels reject prevailing cultural goals in an attempt to substitute new values. This concept is a major point of divergence from Parsons's theoretical framework. While Parsons would have suggested that systems do adapt to environmental change over time, Merton details and defines the process, using strain theory and, in particular, the case of rebels. Indeed, consider this: Would the Civil Rights Movement have moved forward without "rebels" like Rosa Parks, Martin Luther King, Jr., or Malcolm X?

Although Merton does not view a final category—conformists—as deviant, we still need to mention that individuals in society do accept cultural goals and use institutionalized means to achieve them. While values do vary within cultural systems and subsystems, we could suggest that conformists are individuals who try to marry around the ages of the "average" couple, have children around the ages of the "average" family, and follow the

BOX 2.2. FUNCTIONALIST THEORY IN MODERN CULTURE: *WANDAVISION*

Based on Marvel Comics characters Wanda Maximoff and Vision, this television series premiered in 2021 and explored the ideas of the "ideal family" and the grieving process. The main character, Wanda, is an Avenger whose superpowers include altering reality. Wanda uses this superpower to avoid dealing with the overwhelming grief after her brother (Pietro) and partner (Vision) die in other *Avengers* films. Wanda constructs a false reality and is able to bring Vision back to life in an unrealistically perfect family setting. They live in an idyllic suburban neighborhood with two children and have seemingly no issues.

Over the course of the show, Vision slowly begins to realize that the world around them is being manipulated and that Wanda is the one behind it. From a functionalist perspective, consider how strain theory could apply to this situation. Strain theory suggests that society creates deviance because not all societal members are able to achieve success using legitimate means. Wanda could not, in reality, bring her partner or brother back to life, so she used her superpowers to manufacture an alternate reality, so she did not have to live without Vision. As such, she reacted to the cultural goal of having a Standard North American Family (SNAF; Smith, 1993) with a perfect life. Because she could not conform to that ideal, she *innovated*, or designed her own ways to achieve the perfect family. Without spoiling the series, we can imagine that it did not turn out so well for Wanda in the end.

norms of parenting that "average" families do. Despite an increasing recognition of diversity, individuals in this category are the ruler against which all other families are measured (Allen, 2016; Ganong et al., 1990; Sassler & Lichter, 2020).

Evaluating Functionalist Theory

Strengths of Functionalist Theory

Although functionalist theory is the most widely criticized of all the family theories today, it has served as the foundation for many, if not most, of the other theories, and it is still in use, whether scholars acknowledge it or not (Allen & Henderson, 2022; Few-Demo & Allen, 2020). Indeed, functionalist theory has proven to be remarkably adaptable even to current family circumstances (Hughes et al., 2003; White, 2013). A recent analysis of kinship practices in contemporary societies reveals that concepts, such as the "functional importance" of the ceremonial family are still highly useful for examining nuclear and extended kin relationships (Furstenberg, 2020).

Families Are Part of a Global System

Functionalist theory provides the basis for understanding how families work at the macro level. In examining the functions of family as an all-encompassing social system, the theory provides an umbrella under which family systems around the world may be analyzed. For example, every society and culture has some form of family system to specify how individuals depend upon one another for nurturance, sustenance, social support, and the regulation of sexual and reproductive behaviors. In this way, functionalism provides a common language for comparing family systems as a global structure and, therefore, at the broadest level of social organization.

The Institution of the Family Persists Through Major Social Changes

Functionalist theory assumes that "the family" is one of the major institutions around which societies are organized. Other major institutions are the economic system, the political system, and the legal system. That is, every society has ways of organizing that are the most efficient way to keep that society going. Every society must also deal with sweeping changes that transform the functioning of institutions. For example, the technological revolution has created a social order in which national boundaries break down and time becomes compressed (Zuboff, 2019). Family members can stay connected through the internet, even if they are living in different countries (Fingerman et al., 2020). Television shows made in the United States are broadcast all over the world, and vice versa. The nightly news brings family life styles and intra-societal conflicts into our homes, blurring the lines between diverse cultures. Functionalist theory allows us to examine the ways in which intimate lives are organized and operate in unique ways from other institutional systems and assess the relevance and enduring functions of family as an institution, despite global transformations. Is the family still the primary institution for regulating individual decisions around reproduction, sexuality, marriage, and care of children and elders? Global communications reveal that, yes, families are still vitally important, and the disruption or loss of family ties is traumatic in the face of war and other international conflicts.

Modern Adaptations of Functionalism Account for Different Family Forms

Modern adaptations of functionalist theory suggest that various family structures can be functional for society, accounting for changes in the sociohistorical context that lead to significant changes in the cultural system. Indeed, Merton adapted the original model to include deviant family forms and suggested that different structures can still contribute to overall function and positive change in society. For example, the social upheaval surrounding World War II produced a need for women to leave their posts at home and enter the workforce to "fill in" for men who had been deployed abroad. The cultural system redefined, for a short time, what the normative roles were for women; day care centers emerged to care for working mothers' children; and following the war, women realized they had other options than just being a stay-at-home mother. Adapting to meet the needs of major systems (e.g., the American military and manufacturing workforce) led to positive social change for families and women over time.

Weaknesses of Functionalist Theory

Many scholars have critiqued functionalist theory. Conflict theorists (Chapter 3) and feminist theorists (Chapter 8), in particular, have challenged the relevance of a theory that describes families as having a universal, normative structure that divides family roles according a strict interpretation of gender differences as the naturalized social order, and that posits the most functional version of family as two generational and headed by a heterosexual married couple. These critiques can be organized in the ways discussed in the following sections.

Outdated and Limited in Scope

In general, functionalist theory, regardless of its evolving nature, has been criticized as being "old-fashioned" for imposing a way of explaining family structures and functions as a "one-size-fits-all" model (Cheal, 1991, p. 6). The functionalist view does a disservice to the vast diversity of how we actually enact family life; it idealizes and oversimplifies gender roles and enforces a rigid view of how men and women interact in marriage and family relationships. The basis of the functionalist view of families that was common in mid-20th-century America cannot adequately account for the variations in how families live today. Indeed, the search for a universal definition of family is not relevant when we consider the infinite ways individuals couple, uncouple, raise children, and care for the old throughout the world. In their version of "new action theory," Scanzoni and Marsiglio (1993) identified the weaknesses of traditional functionalist theory and expanded the theory to the inclusion of diverse structures. That is, it is not the "structure" of blood ties and legal marriage that make individuals a family. Instead, families are a social form of organization in which blood and marriage are only two of the ways that interpersonal commitments and caring responsibilities are expressed. Recently, Sanner and Jensen (2021) expanded the traditional conceptualization of family structure to account for the complexity in diverse sibling compositions in families.

Overlooks Inequalities Built Into Social Structure

Functionalist theory has tended to downplay the ways that individuals are treated differently and unequally on the basis of gender, race, class, sexual orientation, and other forms of social stratification. In her critique of functionalism, feminist sociologist Barrie Thorne (1982) challenged three of the major assumptions of functionalist theory: "The ideology of the monolithic family, beliefs that the family is natural or biological, and analyses that freeze present family ideals in a language of function and roles" (p. 3). That is, the functionalist view of the family blames mothers for child problems, assigns higher status to men as the major breadwinner, and treats families from ethnic minority groups as deviant to the White, nuclear, middle-class family form. In his classic analysis of how Black families are treated as cultural systems, Walter Allen (1978) proposed that, instead of viewing Black families as culturally deviant and dysfunctional or viewed only in relation to cultural equivalency with White families, scholars need to take a culturally variant approach, which views Black families in the framework of their own distinctive cultural form, thus allowing for an understanding of the unique constraints and adaptations they develop.

Ignores Extended Family Systems

Family scholars who study multiple generations and intergenerational relationships have challenged Parson's view of structure functionalism on the basis of its exclusive view of the nuclear family (e.g., two generations). As we show in the example of Vern Bengtson and his colleagues (2002), generations matter in families. That is, families consist of more than parents and their children. Sibling ties remain important throughout life, and the parent–child relationship continues with intensity after children leave (and sometimes return) home (Connidis

& Barnett, 2019). Increasingly, families are characterized by multiple generations, and kin ties are an important source of social support (Bengtson, 2001; Furstenberg, 2020; Sarkisian & Gerstel, 2012).

An Alternative Theory App: Critical Race Theory

In this chapter, we have laid out the key concepts, origins and background, and modern applications as well as the strengths and weaknesses of functionalist theory. Sometimes, when learning a new theory, it is useful to compare it to another one to more easily pinpoint the differences between the two. Therefore, in each chapter we show you how to switch your "app" at any time by offering up an additional theory that contrasts to the one you just learned.

Critical race theory (Chapter 12) stands in sharp contrast to functionalist theory. Critical race theory rejects the notion of deviance and, thus, is in opposition to the normative ideas promoted by functionalism. To illustrate the differences, consider how we could analyze the case study (Casbah) from a critical race perspective. We would take into account the formative realities of Casbah's ethnic heritage as a Pakistani American and how issues such as white privilege, colorism, and antiracism have impacted the treatment his ancestors received as well as

---

BOX 2.3. GLOBAL COMPARISONS OF MATERNITY AND PATERNITY LEAVE POLICIES

There are variations from country to country when it comes to how much time new parents are given to take care of children (www.pewresearch.org/fact-tank/2019/12/16/u-s-lacks-mandated-paid-parental-leave). Consider these examples:

- **United States:** Mothers are guaranteed 12 weeks of unpaid family leave according to the Family & Medical Leave Act (FMLA) of 1994, which includes maternity leave.
- **Estonia:** Estonian parents receive more than a year and half of paid leave (86 weeks total), by far the more expansive parental leave policy in the world.
- **Norway:** Norwegian parents receive 59 weeks of parental leave, earning 80% of their pay while gone. Alternatively, they can take 49 weeks off at full pay. Fathers can take up to 10 weeks, depending on income (www.businessinsider.com).
- **Canada:** Canadian parents (including adoptive) receive up to 35 weeks of paid parental leave, which can be used by either parent or shared within the first year. Canadian parents are paid 55% of their regular earnings while on leave. Extended parental benefits can be paid up to 61 weeks at 33% pay (www.canada.ca).
- **Japan:** Japan recently updated their parental leave policy to include fathers, allowing them to take up to four weeks off after the birth of a child with up to 80% pay. Mothers are granted up to 58 weeks (including 26 weeks of paid leave and 32 weeks of unpaid leave; www.japantimes.co.jp).
- **Poland:** Mothers are guaranteed full pay for 20 weeks of maternity leave for the first child, 31 weeks for subsequent births, 34 weeks for multiple births. Parents can split additional "parental" leave for up to 32 weeks (www.ec.europa.eu).

lingering generational effects on his own life. We would focus on within-family conflicts, as well, in terms of how Casbah's transition from female to male was handled by family members in terms of their religious and cultural beliefs and practices. Critical race theory would thus allow us to consider sociohistorical factors, macro-level structures, and micro-level (face-to-face) interactions Casbah had with his family before and after transitioning to identifying as male, including the issues of power associated with the male and female labels in modern society. Where functionalism focuses on how institutions change over time to help society function smoothly, critical race theorists focus more closely on issues, such as how power and policies impact the opportunities individuals and families have to create and recreate lives of their own making.

Next, we highlight how functionalist theory is applicable to the study of families across the globe. Because access to paid or unpaid maternity and paternity leave is an important consideration for functionalist theorists and family scholars, we highlight how parental leave is encouraged and economically supported in some nations but not others.

Working With Functionalist Theory: Integrating Research and Practice

Now that we have described the historical origins, key concepts, and strengths and weaknesses of functionalist theory, we turn to how the theory can be used in research and practice. We then analyze an empirical study that was rooted in functionalist theory to see how scholars put the theory to work in a research project. Finally, we present ideas about how the theory informs the practice of developing policies on a college campus.

Functionalist Theory Today

In their pioneering longitudinal research on intergenerational transmission of values, social gerontologists Bengtson, Biblarz, and Roberts (2002) examine the concept of how (and if) families are important in the lives of individuals. Their research, The Longitudinal Study of Generations (LSOG), began in 1970–1971 as a way to examine the linkages between the quality of intergenerational family relationships and a person's psychosocial development over time. Initially, they surveyed more than 300 families, consisting of a total 2,044 individuals and representing three generations from each family. Thus, the study initially mirrored a structural-functionalist perspective on the family as a macro system that is charged with meeting the social-psychological needs of its members. One of the most important early contributions of the LSOG was that they did not stop at Parsons's notion of the two-generation nuclear family but added a third generation (e.g., grandparents) to consider how social-historical events across the life course impacted each subsequent generation and, thus, affected the transmission of family values. The framing of the study is an early exemplar of how older functionalist ideas and newer ideas about the life course (Chapter 9) can be integrated to study generations.

Over time, great-grandchildren were added to the mix of family members studied. The four generations studied were the following:

- **G1:** Grandparents, born 1896 to 1911
- **G2:** Their children, born 1916 to 1931

- **G3:** Their grandchildren, born 1945 to 1955

- **G4:** Their great-grandchildren, born 1978 to 1983

Individuals were asked to report on many issues. The researchers gathered extensive demographic data over time, particularly on education, occupation, residence, income, ethnicity, marital status, and number of children. These data helped them to understand how families transmit aspirations, such as economic achievement over time. They also assessed many aspects of social-psychological health. Self-esteem, for example, was measured by questions such as, "I feel that I'm a person of worth, at least on an equal basis with others." Finally, participants were also asked to rank order their values in life, including social justice, financial security, friendship, patriotism, personal freedom, and family loyalty.

After assessing all of these areas of intergenerational transmission, Bengtson et al. (2002) found the remarkable persistence of values across the generations. Contrary to reports in the popular media, members of Generation X (G4) were not disengaged from their families. Indeed, they found tremendous support for the belief in family solidarity. And although major demographic shifts were transforming families over time (e.g., the increase in the divorce rate), families were able to deal with conflict and remain connected to one another. This study shows the importance of measuring family change over time, so what endures about families (that is, what is functional) can be uncovered. Two decades later, in their analysis of recent research on intergenerational relationships, Fingerman et al. (2020) concluded that the prevalence and importance of ties across the generations are stronger than ever.

Functionalist Theory in Research

Modern family scholars have built on the original principles of functionalist theory to gain a fuller understanding of how families have adapted to cultural norms over time. Sociologists Kathryn Edin and Maria Kefalas (2005) investigated the norms of motherhood for poor women in the inner city. While not overtly stated as using functionalist theory, these researchers investigate the ways in which women conform to cultural goals (having children), using innovative means to reach them (foregoing marriage for motherhood).

In their book, *Promises I Can Keep: Why Poor Women Put Motherhood Before Marriage*, Edin and Kefalas (2005) spent five years living with, working with, and interviewing poor women from various racial and ethnic backgrounds in the inner city of Philadelphia. The authors present data from 162 single mothers, illustrating how social class affects women's expectations about marriage and the importance of having children. Merton's (1938) strain theory is evident in this study because the overarching cultural goal—to have children—is accepted and sought after among women in the inner city. Indeed, many of the women readily admitted that they wanted children and were happy when they found out they were pregnant. They also reported fearing being "owned" by an authoritarian man, and some said they did not believe in divorce, which is why they were not married. The women also reported accepting the cultural goal of wanting a successful career, but they were not interested in waiting until after their career was established to have children. This pattern is in contrast to how many middle-class individuals approach family, where people are more likely to marry to have children (Cherlin, 2014; Coontz, 2016). The cultural goals are the same, but women in the inner city are more likely to reorder establishing a family with children, then career, then marriage. This study is a good example of how women can be innovative to achieve cultural goals even in the face of obstacles. Family educators, practitioners, and policymakers should study this text as a way to access why poor women choose motherhood above all else.

Functionalist Theory in Practice

Researchers are increasingly called upon to step up their contributions to translational science and connect with policymaking and policy makers (Day et al., 2019). One of the most important places family scholars can utilize concepts associated with functionalist theory is in the development of workplace policy (Pittman, 1993). Human resource (HR) offices exist in a multitude of settings, such as hospitals, universities, private for-profit companies, nongovernmental organizations, and the military, to name a few. All HR professionals have to adapt policies to protect their employees. Given the shift in cultural awareness about LGBTQ+ rights, it should be no surprise that some institutions offer training to help all employees maintain respect for others in the workplace.

An example of a program that has become part of the cultural mainstream is the Safe Zone program. In 1992, the Lesbian, Bisexual, and Gay Student Association at Ball State University (now, the LGBTQA community) developed a "safe program" to help eradicate homophobia and discrimination against LGBTQ+ people on college campuses (Safezone, n.d.).

The program is designed as a bridge between the LGBTQ+ community and the heterosexual community via "allies," a term used to describe heterosexual people who are supportive of inclusion and equality. Since 1992, the program spread across the United States and is best known for its symbol of an inverted pink triangle, which stands for alliance with gay rights and promoting a safe, open, and respectful dialogue free from homophobia. On college campuses, HR professionals, faculty, staff, administrators, and students are educated and exposed to the symbolism of the "safe zone," or "safe space." Campus community members are encouraged to participate in the Safe Zone training sessions, which usually last a few hours and include eye-opening activities designed to let attendees walk awhile in an LGBTQ person's shoes. One such activity, a heterosexist guided imagery, was introduced to the higher education community as a tool for using in college classrooms across multiple disciplines (Henderson & Murdock, 2012).

Several aspects of this evolving set of practices surrounding the rights and respect of LGBTQ+ persons are applicable using functionalist theory. As previously mentioned, the cultural system has absorbed LGBTQ+ rights as part of the mainstream dialogue on human rights. This trickles down to the social system, redefining interactions between people (e.g., being introduced to guided imagery activities and reminded of homophobic language in the college classroom). It also opens up opportunities for individuals' need-dispositions to be met at the personality level because, ideally, one's awareness of LGBTQ issues is raised, which provides a safe space for individuals to come out. Indeed, National Coming Out Day (October 11) was established in 1988 as an internationally-observed civil awareness day to celebrate individuals who publicly identify as members of the LGBTQ+ community (Stein, 2004). Individuals who pioneered these causes could definitely be considered "rebels" according to Merton's Strain Theory because they actively rejected old (homophobic and heterosexist) cultural norms and sought to create new social norms. The result was, and continues to be, change at the cultural level in society.

BOX 2.4. VOICES FROM LIVED EXPERIENCE

When it comes to how Parsons's systems can be interpreted, it is important to think critically about how the cultural system includes often harmful—and sometimes fatal—ideas about how gender and sex should operate in society and how these messages are perpetuated in the family social system and internalized by its members. Staysha is a sex trafficking survivor, who reflects on the ways in which the broader cultural norms, as well as her family, normalized the objectification of women's bodies, which she feels contributed to the vulnerability that preceded her exploitation:

> I was taught that [my body] was where my value was. I was also taught because I grew up in a very strict Christian non-denominational home where the Bible was used against me in my abuse, that that I was to be the baby factory. That was my worth, which then also tied into the sexuality piece. My body is where my worth is placed.

These feelings about women's bodies as objects for reproduction and sexual objectification were perpetuated at home, which planted the seed that her trafficker watered as he groomed her into believing that was *all* she was worth. Staysha also reflected on the larger cultural system, in which men are taught they are entitled to women's bodies and to sex:

> We also live in a society where once you turn 18, as a man, it's a rite of passage to go to a strip club and buy a girl off the internet. That is your rite of passage, you turned 18, good for you, let's take you to the club and put you in this situation and then it becomes normal, it becomes part of growing up as an adult and so then when you're no longer around your friends and it's like oh like this is fun, this is stimulating, this gave me some kind of excitement, I want to do this again.

The cultural system perpetuates the ideas that women and girls are for men's enjoyment and servitude, and girls and women internalize these ideas. Subsequently, traffickers perpetuate message rooted in the cultural system and institutionalized in social (and family) systems. These messages are an effective means of control and manipulation because they are not uncommon and only need to be strengthened as part of the grooming process. Unfortunately, this also means they are difficult to deprogram as sex trafficking victims attempt to exit their exploitation; as a result, many victims suffer severe abuse, sometimes fatal, at the hands of their traffickers (Henderson & Rhodes, 2022).

Conclusion

Functionalist theory has provided important ideas that allow researchers and practitioners to put the theory to use beyond the conceptual level. Highly critiqued as an outdated theory, and limited in application, there are many ways in which functionalist theory can still be applied to the study of families. Indeed, it is often considered to be foundational to all of the major family theories. We challenge you to consider these applications of the theory as you move on to the discussion questions, reflection questions, and areas for further study in the concluding pages of this chapter.

Multimedia Suggestions

www.feministmormonhousewives.org

This website houses a blog that covers various social issues, and the contributors to the blog all self-identify as "feminist Mormon housewives." Both the contributors to the blog and their readers find a sense of community and solidarity by discussing how their feminist views can both conflict with and complement their religion. This site is a great example of how the need-dispositions of feminist Mormon housewives are met through an online community. In addition, this site is also an example of how a typically conservative, patriarchal culture can adapt to social change over time.

Activate your theory app: After browsing through this website, compare and contrast how Durkheim, Parsons, and Merton would each explain the presence of this group. Would they agree or disagree, and why?

www.bountifulbaskets.org

This is the website for Bountiful Baskets (BB), a food cooperative, which provides families with a low-cost alternative to shopping in big-box grocery stories for healthy foods. This cooperative operates weekly, and families can choose to give around $20 to the pool of money (depending on the geographical location), which the BB volunteers use to purchase produce and bread directly from producers. This co-op is just one of many that families are joining to be a part of the movement to eat healthy and save money. From a functionalist perspective, shopping for food is beginning to look and function differently. Individuals who participate in this (and other) co-ops are, in Merton's terms, innovators, responding to the relatively recent cultural message to eat healthy, organic food, but not conforming to the "norm" of shopping in a chain grocery store to do it.

Activate your theory app: Find another website (or product) that offers a new way of fulfilling some of the family's main functions. How will this affect overall cultural change and family expectations? Will it shift gender norms, or intensify them?

Babies (2009)

This documentary simultaneously follows four babies around the world and illustrates cultural differences in childrearing during the first year of the babies' lives. Mari is raised in Tokyo, Japan, by her two parents in a very busy metropolitan area. Hattie lives in San Francisco and is raised by two very ecologically-conscious, egalitarian parents. Ponijao lives in Namibia with her parents and eight older siblings. She is part of the Himba tribe and lives in a small village with other families. Bayar is raised in

Image 2.2 A Scene From *Babies*, 2010

Mongolia on a small family farm with his brother and parents. The documentary illustrates the differences in how families "function" in varying cultural systems, from Westernized cultures like Japan and the United States to developing countries like Namibia and Mongolia.

Activate your theory app: Compare and contrast Parsons's cultural, social, and personality systems amongst the four different countries. How does each system affect how babies are raised around the world?

Breaking Bad (2008–2013)

Image 2.3 A Scene From *Breaking Bad*, 2008

This American television series, one of the highest-rated television shows of all time, features a high school chemistry teacher, Walter White, who is diagnosed with inoperable lung cancer. To make sure his family is provided for after he dies, he turns to a life of crime by producing and selling crystallized meth. This series illustrates several functionalist concepts, one of the most obvious being Walter's endeavors as an innovator. Also evident in this series is the idea of moral individualism; Walter's very specific job of making and selling meth may have honorable roots (providing for his family in the long term), but he continually operates on morally shaky ground—not necessarily always doing what is good for greater society.

Activate your theory app: See if you can find additional evidence of Merton's strain theory in this program. In addition to Walter White's clear portrayal of an "innovator," do you see examples of ritualists, rebels, retreatists, and conformists?

Further Reading

Bernard, J. (1981). The good provider role: Its rise and fall. *American Psychologist, 36*(1), 1–12. https://doi.org/10.1037/0003-066X.36.1.1 Jessie Bernard, one of the leading figures in sociology, analyzed how the gendered nature of marriage makes it a very different institution for men and women. Men have experienced more economic, emotional, and health benefits from marriage, given their historically elevated position as breadwinners. Yet with dramatic macro-level economic and global changes that have eroded manufacturing and industrial jobs employing a large number of men, men's opportunities to live up to the ideal of "the good provider" role have drastically reduced. In this classic article, Bernard analyzes the trends that have led to the undoing of the expectation that men can continue to enjoy this privileged status in families.

Cherlin, A. J. (2009). *The marriage-go-round: The state of marriage and the family in America today*. Vintage. In this book, Cherlin explains the enduring importance of marriage in U.S. society, even in the face of major demographic changes in the way that individuals partner and raise families. Despite high rates of cohabitation, divorce, and remarriage in the American context, marriage is still the idealized social status, prized by most Americans as the ultimate goal. Yet social change has also led to restrictions in who is able or allowed to marry. Marriage is readily available to members of the middle class, who are able to delay it until they have completed education and established careers. To poor individuals, on the other hand, marriage is often not feasible, given the lack of available partners and the lack of economic resources. And, until recently, gay and lesbian couples have been legally barred from marriage in the United States. Despite these practical and legal barriers, marriage is seen as the ultimate path to adult status and retains its importance as one of the primary functions of the family.

Durkheim, E. (1951). *Suicide: A study in sociology* (J. A. Spaulding & G. Simpson, Trans.). Free Press. In this classic work, originally conducted in the late 19th century, Durkheim analyzed the occurrence of suicide as a social phenomenon. He critiqued the individualistic perspective that suicide is linked only to psychopathology (e.g., mental illness, such as depression and anxiety) and, instead, revealed its roots in how a society is organized. He conducted a cross-cultural analysis of suicide rates (from 1841–1878) in the major European countries at the time (e.g., France, Prussia, England, Denmark, Saxony, and Bavaria). He found three different types of suicide, all of which are linked to social events and/or cultural factors. Anomic suicide was prevalent when a major event, such as war, occurred and disrupted the social fabric of individuals' lives. Egoistic suicide occurred more often in different types of family and cultural patterns. For example, he found that Protestants more likely to take their own lives than Catholics. Finally, altruistic suicide occurred in situations in which individuals were (too) strongly tied to their families and communities, as in the case in which women might take their own lives upon the death of their husbands.

Hawkins, A. J., Amato, P. R., & Kinghorn, A. (2013). Are government-supported healthy marriage initiatives affecting family demographics? A state-level analysis. *Family Relations, 62*(3), 501–513. https://doi.org/10.1111/fare.12009 Following changes in the federal welfare system, the U.S. government provided funding streams under the umbrella of the Healthy Marriage Initiative to encourage marriage for economically needy couples and to reduce the rise in nonmarital pregnancies among women living in poverty. This effort has been controversial because it involves the federal government's intrusion in people's private lives by taking away economic assistance and trying to reestablish the nuclear, two-generation family ideal among those in economic need. The study reported on in this article is the first experimental evaluation of federal programs designed to create and sustain healthy heterosexual marriages. Although inconclusive, the findings reveal the potential positive effects of marriage enrichment programs. This article also provides a way to systematically assess how well governmental funding is conducted.

Pruett, K. D. (2000). *Fatherneed: Why father care is as essential as mother care for your child.* Broadway Books. Renowned child psychiatrist Kyle Pruett addresses the importance of father engagement in children's lives. He claims that fathers and mothers have different roles to play in the family. The role of the father is necessary to positive child development, even if fathers still believe that mothers are most important. He explains how fatherhood also contributes to the well-being of men. Although Pruett emphasizes that fathers are essential in fulfilling one of the defining functions of the family, he also recognizes that the role of father may differ from culture to culture. For example, he has criticized the misuse of his perspective about the importance of fatherhood by those who argue against gay marriage.

Questions for Students

Discussion Questions

1. Parsons's model of structural functionalism was developed in the United States during a time of economic prosperity (the 1950s). Consider applying his model to contemporary Chinese culture. Would it fit? Why or why not?

2. Compare and contrast how Merton and his mentor, Parsons, would view the issue of same-sex marriage. How would Parsons's explanation of gay marriage differ from Merton's? Use at least two terms from each theorist.

3. Many behaviors are defined as social problems, even deviant, including drug abuse, prostitution, and theft. In what ways would a functionalist theorist suggest that any of these behaviors could be "functional" for society?

4. We presented several examples of how countries other than the United States offer maternity and paternity leave for workers. Choose a South American country to compare their policies to those we have described.

5. In recent years, the definition of heterosexual marriage as the most functional family form for raising children has changed to include other forms, such as cohabiting and single-parent families. Are there additional forms that you think should also be included as functional?

6. Which other theory from this text is most similar to functionalist theory? Which is most different? Explain.

Your Turn!

Many schools across the country are now addressing the needs of transgender students. Your job, as school board president of a public school in a small rural community in Wisconsin, is to consider all aspects of the debate and decide on a policy to bring to the school board for a vote. What are the cultural, social, and personality systems you should consider as you draft your policy? How do you deal with the fact that the school board and parents are divided on the rights and protections of transgender students? At issue are whether or not they can use the restroom and locker rooms of the gender with which they identify and whether or not male-gendered students can participate on male sports teams and female-gendered students on female sports teams. Find information on what other schools are doing, so you are well-informed.

Personal Reflection Questions

1. How did gender roles operate in your household? Were they traditionally divided, or did your family adapt to maintain equilibrium?

2. Think about times in your family when equilibrium was disrupted. What happened? Who and how was the dysfunction managed?

3. Did you grow up in a society more characterized by organic or mechanical solidarity? In what ways?

4. Describe a time when either you or someone you know has experienced low or high levels of social integration.

5. How has the cultural system you've grown up in differed from that of your parent(s) or grandparents?

6. Have you ever travelled to another country or had a cross-cultural relationship with a friend or classmate? How did you rely on your own cultural knowledge to help you understand and appreciate the other?

References

Allen, K. R. (2016). Feminist theory in family studies: History, biography, and critique. *Journal of Family Theory & Review, 8*(2), 207–224. https://doi.org/10.1111/jftr.12133

Allen, K. R., & Henderson, A. C. (2022). Family theorizing for social justice: A critical praxis. *Journal of Family Theory & Review*. Advance online publication. https://doi.org/10.1111/jftr.12450

Allen, W. R. (1978). The search for applicable theories of black family life. *Journal of Marriage and the Family, 40*(1), 117–131. https://doi.org/10.2307/350613

Appelrouth, S., & Edles, L. D. (2021). *Classical and contemporary sociological theory: Text and readings* (4th ed.). SAGE Publications.

Bengtson, V. L. (2001). Beyond the nuclear family: The increasing importance of multigenerational bonds (The Burgess Award lecture). *Journal of Marriage and Family, 63*(1), 1–16. https://doi.org/10.1111/j.1741-3737.2001.00001.x

Bengtson, V. L., Biblarz, T. J., & Roberts, R. E. L. (2002). *How families still matter: A longitudinal study of youth in two generations.* Cambridge University Press.

Cheal, D. (1991). *Family and the state of theory.* University of Toronto Press.

Cherlin, A. J. (2014). *Labor's love lost: The rise and fall of the working-class family in America.* Russell Sage.

Connidis, I. A., & Barnett, A. E. (2019). *Family ties & aging* (3rd ed.). SAGE Publications.

Coontz, S. (2016). *The way we never were: American families and the nostalgia trap* (Rev. ed.). Basic Books.

Day, E., MacDermid Wadsworth, S., Bogenschneider, K., & Thomas-Miller, J. (2019). When university researchers connect with policy: A framework for whether, when, and how to engage. *Journal of Family Theory & Review, 11*(1), 165–180. https://doi.org/10.1111/jftr.12306

Durkheim, E. (1984). *The division of labor in society.* Free Press. (Original work published 1893).

Edin, K., & Kefalas, M. (2005). *Promises I can keep: Why poor women put motherhood before marriage.* University of California Press.

Fair Labor Standards Act of 1937, S. 2475, H.R. 7200 (1937).

Few-Demo, A. L., & Allen, K. R. (2020). Gender, feminist, and intersectional perspectives on families: A decade in review. *Journal of Marriage and Family, 82*(1), 326–345. https://doi.org/10.1111/jomf.12638

Fingerman, K. L., Huo, M., & Birditt, K. S. (2020). A decade of research on intergenerational ties: Technological, economic, political, and demographic changes. *Journal of Marriage and Family, 82*(1), 383–403. https://doi.org/10.1111/jomf.12604

Furstenberg, F. F. (2020). Kinship reconsidered: Research on a neglected topic. *Journal of Marriage and Family, 82*(1), 3640382. https://doi.org/10.1111/jomf.12628

Ganong, L. H., Coleman, M., & Mapes, D. (1990). A meta-analytic review of family structure stereotypes. *Journal of Marriage and the Family, 52*(2), 387–297. https://doi.org/10.2307/353026

Giddens, A. (2002). *Capitalism and modern social theory: An analysis of the writings of Marx, Durkheim and Max Weber.* Cambridge University Press.

Goldberg, A. E., & Beemyn, G. (Eds.). (2021). *The SAGE encyclopedia of trans studies.* SAGE Publications.

Hays, S. (1996). *The cultural contradictions of motherhood.* Yale University Press.

Henderson, A., Harmon, S., & Newman, H. (2016). The price mothers pay, even when they are not buying it: Mental health consequences of idealized motherhood. *Sex Roles: A Journal of Research, 74*(11–12), 512–526. https://doi.org/10.1007/s11199-015-0534-5

Henderson, A. & Rhodes, S. M. (2022). "Got sold a dream and it turned into a nightmare": The victim-offender overlap in commercial sexual exploitation. *Journal of Human Trafficking, 8*(1), 33–48. https://doi.org/10.1080/23322705.2021.2019530

Henderson, A. C., & Murdock, J. L. (2012). Getting students beyond ideologies: Using heterosexist guided imagery in the classroom. *Innovative Higher Education, 37*(3), 185–198. https://doi.org/10.1007/s10755-011-9198-4

Hughes, J. A., Sharrock, W. W., & Martin, P. J. (2003). *Understanding classical sociology: Marx, Weber, Durkheim* (2nd ed.). SAGE Publications.

Kingsbury, N., & Scanzoni, J. (1993). Structural-functionalism. In P. G. Boss, W. J. Doherty, R. LaRossa, W. R. Schumm, & S. K. Steinmetz (Eds.), *Sourcebook of family theories and methods: A contextual approach* (pp. 195–217). Plenum Press.

Klebold, S. (2016). *A mother's reckoning: Living in the aftermath of tragedy.* Broadway Books.

LancasterPA.com. (n.d.). *Amish people and Amish culture.* www.LancasterPA.com/amish/

LeMoyne, T., & Buchanan, T. (2011). Does "hovering" matter? Helicopter parenting and its effect on well-being. *Sociological Spectrum, 31*(4), 399–418. https://doi.org/10.1080/02732173.2011.574038

McGhee, H. (2021). *The sum of us: What racism costs everyone and how we can prosper together.* One World.

Merton, R. K. (1938). Social structure and anomie. *American Sociological Review, 3*(5), 672–682. https://doi.org/10.2307/2084686

Merton, R. K. (Ed.). (1957). *Social theory and social structure.* Simon & Schuster.

Murphy, R., Falchuk, B., Jacobson, N., Mock, J., Simpson, B., Woodall, A., Marsh, S., & Canals, S. (Executive Producers). (2018–2021). *Pose* [TV series]. Color Force, Touchstone Television, 20th Television; FX.

Nomaguchi, K., & Milkie, M. A. (2020). Parenthood and well-being: A decade in review. *Journal of Marriage and Family, 82*(1), 198–223. https://doi.org/10.1111/jomf.12646

Parsons, T. (1943). The kinship system of the contemporary United States. *American Anthropologist, 45*(1), 22–38. https://doi.org/10.1525/aa.1943.45.1.02a00030

Parsons, T. (1951). *The social system.* Free Press.

Parsons, T. E., & Shils, E. A. (Eds.). (1951). *Toward a general theory of action.* Harvard University Press.

Pittman, J. F. (1993). Functionalism may be down, but it surely is not out: Another point of view for family therapists and policy analysts. In P. G. Boss, W. J. Doherty, R. LaRossa, W. R. Schumm, & S. K. Steinmetz (Eds.), *Sourcebook of family theories and methods: A contextual approach* (pp. 218–221). Plenum Press.

Safezone: Projects in support of the LGBTQA community. (n.d.). Ball State University. cms.bsu.edu/campuslife/counseling-center/additional services/safezone

Sarkisian, N., & Gerstel, N. (2012). *Nuclear family values, extended family lives: The power of race, class, and gender.* Routledge.

Sanner, C., & Jensen, T. M. (2021). Toward more accurate measures of family structure: Accounting for sibling complexity. *Journal of Family Theory & Review, 13*(1), 110–127. https://doi.org/10.1111/jftr.12406

Sassler, S., & Lichter, D. T. (2020). Cohabitation and marriage: Complexity and diversity in union-formation patterns. *Journal of Marriage and Family, 82*(1), 35–61. https://doi.org/10.1111/jomf.12617

Scanzoni, J., & Marsiglio, W. (1993). New action theory and contemporary families. *Journal of Family Issues, 14*(1), 105–132. https://doi.org/10.1177/0192513X93014001009

Schiffrin, H. H., Liss, M., Miles-McLean, H., Geary, K. A., Erchull, M. J., & Tashner, T. (2014). Helping or hovering? The effects of helicopter parenting on college students' well-being. *Journal of Child and Family Studies, 23*(3), 548–557. https://doi.org/10.1007/210826-013-9716-3

Shils, E., Naegele, K. D., & Pitts, J. R. (Eds.). (1965). *Theories of society: Foundations of modern sociological theory.* Free Press.

Silverstein, C. (1991). Psychological and medical treatments of homosexuality. In J. C. Gonsiorek & J. D. Weinrich (Eds.), *Homosexuality: Research implications for public policy* (pp. 101–114). SAGE Publications.

Smith, D. E. (1993). The Standard North American Family: SNAF as an ideological code. *Journal of Family Issues, 14*(1), 50–65. https://doi.org/10.1177/0192513X93014001005

Stein, M. (Ed.). (2004). *Encyclopedia of lesbian, gay, bisexual, and transgender history in America* (Vol. 2). Gale/Cengage Learning.

Thorne, B. (1982). Feminist rethinking of the family: An overview. In B. Thorne & M. Yalom (Eds.), *Rethinking the family: Some feminist questions* (pp. 1–24). Longman.

Tucker, D. (Director). (2005). *Transamerica* [Film]. Belladonna Productions.

White, J. M. (2013). The current status of theorizing about families. In G. W. Peterson & K. R. Bush (Eds.), *Handbook of marriage and the family* (3rd ed., pp. 11–37). Springer.

Zuboff, S. (2019). *The age of surveillance capitalism: The fight for a human future at the new frontier of power.* PublicAffairs.

Image Credits

Conflict Theory

hink about when you were a child—what you wanted to be when you grew up. What did you dream of, who did you dress up as for career day at your elementary school? Most children have unlimited imaginations when it comes to this question. A child may want to grow up to be a professional football player or maybe even the president of the United States. Why is it improbable that these dreams will come true for most children? Can all children achieve the dream of being president of the United States someday? Does social class have anything to do with where we start, where we see ourselves, and where we end up? How are our childhood dreams affected by social stratification?

Conflict theory, which is one of the foundational and most influential theories in the social sciences, provides family scholars with a powerful framework for understanding and measuring how social stratification affects families. Like functionalist theory (Chapter 2), conflict theory is one of the grandparents of many theoretical concepts and models in use today, and thus, it is important to understand how it was originally proposed and how it has evolved over time. In this chapter, we discuss the history of conflict theory and how the principles and key concepts can be used to understand challenges families face. Conflict theory helps us answer questions about how families' access to limited (or unlimited) resources can affect their ability to cope with day-to-day struggles. To gain a fuller understanding of how conflict theory works, we start with a case study that illustrates how a family's access to resources is important to all members of the family.

Case Study

Marie, the subject of our case study, was no different than most children with big hopes and dreams. Marie is a cisgender, able-bodied girl, who grew up lower-middle class. During career day in fifth grade, Marie dressed up as Neil Armstrong because she wanted to be an astronaut. Marie was fascinated by the fact that we were able to send humans into outer space, and she fantasized about how cool it would be to be floating around in space, looking back at the earth from so far away. Marie honestly thought that someday she could be an astronaut just like Neil Armstrong.

Throughout high school, Marie did not fully understand that having the dream of wanting to be an astronaut was so far-fetched. She spent her entire life in a very small town in rural South Dakota, where her parents owned the local hardware store. They worked 10-hour days six or seven days a week, just to provide for Marie and her two brothers. On Thursday nights, when the freight truck would bring the weekly shipment of merchandise to her parents' store, Marie's family had to meet the truck driver at the store to unload everything. Since they did not know exactly when the truck would arrive, Marie's parents asked the truck driver to honk his horn when he drove by their house (which was on the outskirts of town), so they knew to get up out of bed—no matter how late it was—to come unload that week's shipment of merchandise. When the truck driver honked, Marie and her brothers climbed into their parents' old pickup truck and went up to the store to unload the truck. Marie's childhood memories are built around helping in the store; she loaded cases of oil onto a dolly from the truck and wheeled them into the warehouse when she was eight years old. For her whole life, Marie thought that it was normal for kids to do these things; it was what she had to do to support her parents' hardware store.

Contrast the realities of Marie's childhood with her dream of wanting to be an astronaut. Why was that dream probably not going to come to fruition? Why is it not possible for "just anyone" to be what they want to be when they grow up? Conflict theory helps us understand differences between classes in society in competition for scarce resources, including wealth, power, and prestige. Conflict theorists argue that the way society is structured benefits a few at the expense of many and, consequently, for most of us, it is very difficult to escape the social class into which we are born.

BOX 3.1. AT A GLANCE: CONFLICT THEORY

Members of society and families are in competition over scarce resources.

Macro-Level Competition

- Haves (capitalists) versus have nots (workers) struggle for power.
- Workers sell labor to capitalists in return for a wage.
- Workers become alienated from their labor.

Types of Capital Families Produce for Members

- **Economic:** Wealth, land, and income
- **Cultural:** Education level, tastes and preferences, and verbal skills
- **Social:** Network of contacts
- **Symbolic:** Prestige, reputation, and charisma

Micro-Level Competition

- Conflict within families is inevitable but can be positive.
- Family dynamics are a zero-sum game; one family member wins, and another loses.

Handling Conflict

- **Conflict management:** Addressing conflict directly
- **Conflict resolution:** Conflict ends; solution reached
- **Consensus:** A state of stability (or balance between competing needs) necessary to reach resolution or management

What Is Conflict Theory?

Conflict theory is used by researchers to help explain competition between the "haves" and the "have nots" in society. At its core, this theory addresses conflict between these two groups over scarce resources, which can range from families' access to wealth, power, and privilege to the conflict within families over inheritance rights and caregiving duties. Therefore, in this chapter, we will present both micro and macro approaches to using conflict theory as it relates to differences between families, based on social structure and access to resources as well as differences within families when it comes to power and decision-making. Additionally, we will consider how conflict at the macro-level (i.e., structured inequalities) is reinforced by interactions at the micro level (i.e., parenting approaches) through the transmission of different types of capital.

History and Origins

Although it might be fairly easy to see conflict between the rich and the poor in modern society, conflict theory is rooted in a different time and place, arising from the Industrial Revolution when major social upheaval and economic change occurred in Western Europe (see functionalist theory, Chapter 2). Karl Marx, writing in the mid-19th century and considered to be the father of conflict theory, saw firsthand the effects industrialization had on the workers (Marx, 1977). Families had to send men, women, and children to work long hours (sometimes between 50 and 70 hours per week) to make ends meet. Most families lived in makeshift housing in dismal sanitary conditions, without heat or light, because the population growth in cities was too rapid for the infrastructure to sustain. It was during these economic times that Marx and his collaborator Friedrich Engels developed conflict theory's theoretical model for understanding the social and economic conditions of the time. Not surprisingly, the model, published by Marx and Engels in 1848, is based on economic classes and the struggle for resources.

While the conflict approach to understanding society was clearly grounded in real experiences of inequality and access to resources, conflict theory was not commonly used as a framework for understanding society, much less families, until long after Marx was gone. Sociologists who did utilize Marx's theories—referred to as **Marxists**—critiqued the effects of capitalism on racial minorities (Blank et al., 1970), the criminal justice system (Quinney, 1970), and families in poverty (Piven & Cloward, 1971). Marxists were deemed radical by many during the 1950s and 1960s because the post-World War II economy was booming, and a critique of capitalism also brought with it a critique of the revered "American social institutions and core cultural values" (Farrington & Chertok, 1993, p. 364). Because conflict theory was not widely used in the United States— and arguably did not have scientifically testable propositions—most family scholars did not utilize conflict theory until the late 1960s (Farrington & Chertok, 1993). At that point, family scholars like Jetse Sprey (1969) argued that conflict theory is a useful framework for understanding families because conflict within families is inevitable. Applying Marx's proposition that social structure causes conflict, Sprey argued that the family itself causes conflict. Family members have different, often competing, interests, which cannot be satisfied for every member of the group, and family conflict inevitably arises due to inequality between men and women (Bernard, 1982; Osmond, 1987). Additionally, conflict arises when family members want the *same* things, but there is only a limited supply. Family scientists adapted a macro-level theory, often critiqued for being a grand theory—too big to actually apply to real, scientific study and analysis—and began applying it on a micro level to the study of families.

Key Concepts

According to conflict theory, society is composed of groups in competition for scarce resources. These groups, or **classes,** are defined by their relationship to the means of production. The ruling class, or **bourgeoisie** (e.g., landowners and capitalists), own the means of production, and the working class, or **proletariat,** only own their labor, which they sell to the capitalist class in return for a wage (Appelrouth & Edles, 2021). In the example of a factory, the owner profits from it, and the laborer earns a wage from selling their labor to it. According to conflict theorists, this two-sided relationship to the means of production inherently creates oppression because the two sides are interdependent with one another. **Capitalists** need workers to sell their labor to turn a profit, and laborers have very few other choices than joining the masses working in factories to provide for their families.

While it may seem like both sides benefit from this relationship because laborers need wages and capitalists need workers, conflict theorists find it troubling. This is because the dichotomy of the capitalist system creates two—and only two—classes: property-owners and propertyless workers (Marx, 1977). Therefore, workers sell their labor to the factory owner and receive only a wage in return. They do not have the opportunity to build capital, buy property, or "move up" the social class ladder. The worker, according to Marx, is a slave to the system of capitalism. They only make enough to sustain the bare minimum standard of living.

Because of the way the capitalist system works, only one side of the relationship can benefit (see Figure 3.1). The owners profit directly from the labor that the workers sell (e.g., an increase in wages decreases profit and a decrease in wages increases profits). This invisible, yet powerful, force characterizes conflict theory. Conflict between groups is dependent on one side profiting and the other being exploited.

Because of workers' dependence on wage labor, Marx argued that alienation was inevitable. Workers become alienated from the product of their labor; they are no longer in control of the products they produce. Put this

Upper class (owners) profit

Working class (proletariats) sell their labor, see no profit

FIGURE 3.1. Two Sides of Oppression

concept into historical context; Marx studied economic and social change during a time when people were leaving agricultural ways of life and moving into mass-producing goods in factories. As explained in Chapter 2, before industrialization, farmers were much more likely to feel closely tied to what they were producing—crops. They were involved in every aspect of growing corn, for instance. They planted the seeds, watered and weeded, and harvested the corn when it was ready. After industrialization, these same farmers, who likely took great joy in producing food for their loved ones and community members, were not only producing something that they might not see completed, but they were only a minor part of the overall production (Ritzer, 2010).

Let's go back to Marie's childhood. After she was old enough to get a job on her own, outside of her parents' store, she worked at a local factory for minimum wage. The summer Marie turned 13, she awoke every morning at 6:45 a.m. and rode her bike to the factory and worked for five hours on the production line. The factory made leather jackets for welders, and Marie's job was to cut 1-inch strips to reinforce the buttons that the next person on the line would put in the jackets. That is all that her job entailed—cutting 1-inch canvas strips for the jackets with a pair of metal scissors. If the factory had a big order to fulfill, Marie and her coworkers had to work harder. Marie's minimum wage did not increase because she cut more strips; the wage stayed the same. In fact, if there was a big order to fulfill in a short time, the workers all worked harder. The workers did not profit; the owner of the factory profited from their labor. The owner bought their labor for a wage, and Marie only went to work to earn that wage. She never made the jacket from start to finish by herself; she never wore one, used one, or saw one being used. Marie was alienated from her labor; she was merely an appendage of the machine, according to Marx (1977). **Alienation** occurs when workers are removed from the product of their labor—that is, when workers complete tasks devoid of any redeeming human qualities. Conflict theorists are concerned with alienation because they are optimistic about human nature. They want human beings to realize their full human potential—whatever that may be. However, capitalism prevents us from doing what we are meant to do and being what we "want to be when we grow up." Because the structure of the economy requires us to earn money by selling our labor to capitalists, we are not only unable to realize our full human potential, but we are also inevitably alienated from the products we make. The alienation that workers feel from their labor and the items they are helping to produce, as well as the lack of social solidarity, is even more pronounced today—a time in which technological transformation from the digital age has radically altered the relationship among workers, corporations, and communities on a global scale (Harari, 2019; Smith & Browne, 2019). This current zeitgeist threatens the very social, political, and economic foundations of our society (Zuboff, 2019).

What does this have to do with families? Families are dependent on the economy to sustain a basic standard of living. Additionally, family membership is involuntary; we do not choose our parents or our siblings, and we certainly do not choose which social class we are born into. Therefore, family conflict is something every individual will experience; society is comprised of members of different social classes with different upbringings, different family dynamics, and differential access to power and resources both inside and outside of our families. Conflict, at both the micro level and the macro level, is inevitable and affects all families across the board (Farrington & Chertok, 1993; Saxbe et al., 2013).

Consider the illustration in Figure 3.2—the "inequality track." Using a macro-level of analysis, we can see how social phenomena are related to other larger social forces, such as the interaction of education, race, ethnicity, and social class (and we further address these ideas through our discussion of intersectionality in Chapter 8 on feminist theory and Chapter 12 on critical race theory). Using this lens, the four lanes each represent a different rung on the social class ladder. In the image, the runner on the inside track has the advantage. Lane 1 portrays an "insider" with access to Ivy League schools and distinct economic advantages that the other participants do not; in conflict theory terms, the "competition for scarce resources" will be more or less challenging, depending on which lane you are in. The lanes represent the different social classes; there is a direct relationship between their capital, or resources, and their ability to win the race.

The individual in lane 1 comes from a wealthy family. He is dressed nicely and has access to a tailor, who custom makes his suits. His parents both went to Ivy League schools and own real estate throughout the Northeast. He, too, graduated from an Ivy League school with a degree in business administration, and after graduation, he took a position as a manager in his father's investment firm. In the illustration, we can see that he does not even have

FIGURE 3.2. Inequality Track

Source: The African American Policy Institute

to walk in his lane—he is on a "people mover" that moves forward for him, and he even has a place to rest his left hand while he is moving. He is probably a member of the bourgeoisie (capitalist) class.

The individual in lane 2 is dressed in casual business attire. He probably has a bachelor's degree—perhaps working toward a master's degree—and he is engaged in a slight jog to keep his position in second place. His lane is free of obstacles, but he is carrying his briefcase with him during the race. He is probably a mid-level manager at a bank branch, hoping to someday move up the social class ladder.

The individual in lane 3 has quite a few obstacles in his lane. He is sweating, trying to dodge large rocks and holes in his lane. He has to work very hard just to make sure he does not trip and get hurt, disqualifying him from the race. He is wearing a tank top and shorts and has darker hair than the two men in lanes 1 and 2, which could signify that he belongs to a minoritized group with even less privilege than the dominant (White) group. His workbag is bigger than the person's in lane 2, so he may be an electrician or part of a specific trade. He is probably a member of the proletariat (working class) or lower-middle class.

The individual in lane 4 has the most obstacles to get over to stay in the race. This person has darker skin, no briefcase or workbag at all, and has to get around barbed wire, barricades, potholes, and boulders. There is no room in this lane to jog without having to navigate an obstacle. This person has by far the most difficult time reaching the finish line, much less staying injury-free during the race. They could be a seasonal worker, hired to pick grapes or other produce in the fields. At best, they have a job as a maid, nanny, or domestic worker (the gendered nature of these types of jobs is discussed in detail in Chapter 8 on feminist theory). This individual is definitely a member of the proletariat (working class).

As we can see, the four lanes are separated in distinct ways by social class, and their access to resources either helps or harms them in the race to the finish line. However, it is also important to look at how all four lanes are related to one another. Not only are the individuals in each lane stratified, but they are also dependent on one another. The individual in lane 1 would not be successful without the person in lane 2, who manages his bank accounts. The individual in lane 3 services lane 1's "people mover." The individual in lane 4 takes care of lane l's children, which makes it possible for lane 1's wife to be actively involved in charity events. Therefore, the inside lanes depend on the lanes farther out (2, 3, and 4) to maintain the inside track. The individual in lane 1 directly benefits from the other three individuals selling their labor to him. He becomes wealthier, better dressed, and more effective at work because of the structure of society. He does not have to depend on wages to stay ahead; he is a capitalist. If he became unemployed suddenly, his investments and his wealthy family would be his safety net. The other three individuals are dependent on employment—an hourly wage—to stay afloat. They become alienated from the product of their labor because it does not directly benefit them; it benefits only the individual in lane 1.

Thus far, we have been discussing conflict theory as it relates to families, using a macro perspective. Before we shift our focus to using a micro perspective, we need to look a little more closely at the lanes and how they are maintained by taking a look at what is going on inside families on the track. Sometimes it is just as important to understand how privilege is reproduced by analyzing the intangible ways in which inequality is transmitted within families. While at first glance, we would describe inequality using only economic means, sociologist Pierre Bourdieu (1990) suggested that sometimes the forces that reproduce inequality are invisible. According to Bourdieu, individuals in each lane have access to different types of capital that families produce for their members, which creates advantages that can be transmitted from generation to generation. These advantages can range from simply having the same family name to learning proper etiquette for formal dinner parties. The four types of capital Bourdieu outlines are economic capital, cultural capital, social capital, and symbolic capital. Each is described with respect to families in the following paragraphs.

Economic capital refers to the material resources—wealth, land, and money—that one controls or possesses (Appelrouth & Edles, 2021). This is the only type of capital that Bourdieu refers to that is tangible, or something that can be seen or touched. Economic capital is the basis for determining access to the other types of capital. As an example, money makes it possible to travel. Traveling allows one to see the world and take in diverse cultures, thereby developing one's tastes for upper-class living. Economic capital directly translates into privileges that are closely related to the other types of capital that also set people apart on the inequality track.

Cultural capital is nonmaterial—it cannot be "seen"—and it refers to aesthetic preferences, verbal skills, and levels of knowledge, expertise, and education. This is just another way of indicating what one's tastes are and can refer to food, music, and art. Consider Marie's cultural capital, or her tastes; growing up in a lower middle-class family, she developed expertise on how to catch her own food. She remembers taking great pride in catching a big catfish for the family to fry on the weekends. An interesting way to think about social class and cultural capital is to consider what types of fish people eat; there are vast differences depending on social class. For Marie, the only fish she is exposed to is catfish (or walleye if she gets lucky!) that her family catches in the river near her house. Catfish are clearly not a high-class food; they are readily available in rivers and are consumed mostly by individuals from families in the working and lower middle classes. Bluefin tuna, on the other hand, is not readily available in rivers and lakes. This type of fish is rare compared to catfish and cannot be caught by the "average" American; the fish are caught by professional fishermen and sold in stores for a very high price. Because of this, bluefin tuna is consumed by individuals in higher social classes; the only tuna Marie had as a child came from a can, mixed into tuna casserole. As another example, think about Marie's exposure to music; growing up, she only heard country music on the radio. She never attended symphonies, knew what a viola was, or knew why anyone would want to listen to opera. Her tastes—her cultural capital—are vastly different from those in the inside track, or upper class. Her expertise on how to bait a hook, clean a catfish, and fry it for dinner is a far cry from those on the inside track, who eat bluefin tuna prepared by gourmet chefs in high-end restaurants.

Another type of capital Bourdieu describes is social capital. **Social capital** refers to an individual or family's network of contacts and acquaintances that can be used to secure or advance one's position (Appelrouth & Edles, 2021). While we all know friends or acquaintances who may help us out on occasion, Bourdieu argued that social capital circulates within defined boundaries that reproduce the existing social structure. That is, Marie's parents' contacts would likely not be able to help her achieve the dream of becoming an astronaut. Her parents' contacts would at best help her secure her own small business or, perhaps, help her become a teacher or a secretary. Had she been a member of a family with a history of engineers, public figures, or scientists, it would be much more likely that she could also follow that trajectory.

Symbolic capital refers to prestige, honor, reputation, or charisma. Individuals with symbolic capital might have credentials that make them "experts" or help them to command an audience to exert power. Something as simple as a family's last name (e.g., Kennedy or Rockefeller) can insinuate power and the ability to command an audience. Symbolic capital is key when discussing families' access to power because children often inherit reputations that are not of their own making, such as the propensity to pick up golf as a pastime or fluency in foreign languages. Marie had no access to upper-class symbolic capital growing up, even though her parents did own their own business, albeit in a small, rather isolated rural area. Therefore, unless she breaks out of her social class category, the chances that she will gain access to symbolic capital are slim.

As we have described in this section, families are affected by the economic structure in major ways. This is painfully evident during the COVID-19 pandemic, which is difficult and challenging for all families but especially for those in low-wage positions or families in which the breadwinner has lost a job. In contrast, middle- and upper-class families have been able to navigate the unprecedented demands of work stress, school closings, and homeschooling with greater financial resources than those who live paycheck to paycheck or who live in states with limited public childcare availability (Goldberg et al., 2021; Scarborough et al., 2021).

In addition, families are affected by the fact that individuals are born into a social class that is not of their own choosing. Marie did not "choose" to grow up in a lower middle-class family. Yet, Marie's family's wealth (or lack of it) has a direct effect on her opportunities. Could she have gotten into Harvard? Probably not; Ivy League schools tend to weigh alumni status heavily when considering admissions (Kahlenberg, 2010). That is—if your relatives graduated from Harvard, you are more likely to be admitted. Utilizing conflict theory in this way is macrosociological; this means that we are conceptualizing conflict theory in relation to greater social structures in society. Families have differential access to power, resources, and property as well as access to varying levels of social, cultural, and symbolic capital (Adams & Sydie, 2002; Appelrouth & Edles, 2021). Where a family is situated on the inequality track limits its opportunities.

Not only does social stratification limit the choices family members have, but it also has an influence on the struggle for resources *within* the family (Saxbe et al., 2013). This is where conflict theory can be applied using a micro level of analysis. That is, conflict theory takes into account forces both external to as well as within families and how they might influence competition for resources. As a budding family theorist, it is important to know how conflict relates to both contexts of studying family dynamics. Therefore, theorists using conflict theory to study dynamics within families ask: Who has access to resources *inside* the family? Who has power, and who does not? While the gendered struggle for power and resources will be addressed in more detail in Chapter 8 on feminist theory, it is worth mentioning here that conflict theory helps us understand that husbands typically have more power in a heterosexual marriage, which is related to differences in husbands' and wives' marital happiness, the marital division of labor, and ownership (Bernard, 1982; Gilman, 1998/1898; Jackson et al., 2014; Sassler, 2010). Indeed, research across 20 European countries reveals that, despite women's progress in the paid labor force, overall, compared to men, women still shoulder the burden of a disproportionate share of household labor, which further reinforces their disadvantage and dissatisfaction (Treas & Tai, 2016). Additionally, research on same-sex couples reveals that it is the higher-earning partner in a coupled relationship who typically has more power (Goldberg, 2013; Solomon et al., 2005). In trans families, normative gender roles in the division of family labor do not always disappear, either (Pfeffer, 2017). These examples illustrate that the link between macro-level and micro-level issues of inequality is clearly related to conflict within partnerships and families as well.

Family researchers have also built on the conflict theory framework by arguing that conflict within families is inevitable; most notable among these scholars is Jetse Sprey. Sprey (1999) applies conflict theory to families by suggesting that, as is true in the greater society, family conflict occurs because of differential access to resources and power and a lack of alternatives throughout family members' lives. Those family members with the power to make decisions generally are able to maintain the social order within the family. Children do not choose their parents; the stratification within families is inevitable. In addition, membership in families is generally involuntary. Yet, children (for the most part) have to adhere to the social order of the family to be cared for. Think about Marie's life: Did she have a choice when it came to helping to unload the freight truck every Thursday night? No, she did not; her parents needed her help, along with her brothers, to support the family business. Once she was old enough, she was able to get a job at the factory, which increased her power in small ways. She had some economic freedom, which meant she was able to make decisions about spending money, so she was less dependent on having to work at her family's business. However, given that they still provided food and shelter to her, the obligation toward maintaining the family business was still present.

Family conflict is the "state of negative interdependence between the elements of a social system" (Sprey, 1979, p. 134). At the micro level, family dynamics, then, are dependent on one another and are a **zero-sum game**; when one member of the family gains, other family members lose. It is not possible for all members of the family to have equal access to resources, nor is it true that family members have access to resources and power consistently over the course of their life cycles. In the early stage of the family life cycle, parents have access to power; in the later stages, parents tend to lose power as they age, and the power shift may create conflict across the generations. The key is to remember that, even as the power dynamic shifts, conflict will remain, and family studies scholars are interested in how conflict is managed or resolved.

Conflict management is one way of responding to the existence of competition within the family. **Conflict management** occurs when the conflict is addressed, but it does not disappear. It acknowledges that there is conflict over access to scarce resources, and competitors should have equal access to those resources (Sprey, 1969). However, since equal access is not possible, competitors have to concede to manage the situation. As an example, since both of Marie's parents had to be at the hardware store on Thursday nights to unload the truck, Marie and her brothers also had to be there. They were not old enough to be left home alone so late at night. The children knew that when their oldest brother turned 12, their parents felt comfortable leaving the younger siblings under his supervision. The conflict—work–family struggle—did not disappear, as both parents still had to work. However, it was managed by bringing the entire family to the store to help unload the freight truck. The competitors (all members of the family) had to concede to this arrangement until the conflict could be directly resolved by letting them stay at home late at night once the eldest child was old enough to be trusted with that responsibility.

Conflict resolution, then, is when the conflict ends because a solution has been reached (Sprey, 1969). This is different from conflict management because in the former, the conflict does not end; it is merely managed in an ongoing way. With conflict resolution, the issue creating conflict gets resolved, and there is an end point. For example, Marie's mother could decide to stay at home full-time to relieve the stress (conflict) of having to bring young children to the hardware store when the freight truck comes in. Because of the stress that everyone in the family was experiencing, Marie's mother's decision would shift the breadwinner responsibility to her husband.

Consensus refers to a stable state needed to reach either conflict resolution or management (Sprey, 1969). Conflict affects all members of a family in different ways because each family member has differential access to power within the family. However, for consensus to occur, a common awareness or, at the very least, the ability to think in the role of the "other" is necessary given the inequitable distribution of power within families. Marie has to put on several hats for the sake of the family: She is a worker, a peacemaker, and a caregiver for her younger brother. To be able to come to consensus as a family, Marie had to take the role of the "other" (her mother and father) by understanding that the family business needs her parents, and the care of her younger brother could be reallocated. Marie was responsible for him from sunup to sundown. She got him ready for school, she made his lunch, and she helped him with homework after school. She also vacuumed, dusted, and made dinner. She did not have a choice; there was a void in the family, and because the family relied on her, she filled that role. This is a good example of conflict from both outside the family and also within the family pressuring her to be the caregiver. Marie learned at a young age (by reaching a mutual consensus with the entire family) that she needed to step in because her family lived in the third lane; she also knew she had no other choice than to take care of her younger brother. If she did not, no one would.

It is important to note here that the micro-level of analysis through a conflict lens can be and *often is* positive. Conflict management, resolution, and consensus are all ways in which families address inevitable disagreements, struggles, or problems. Conflict is a process; it is not inherently negative because it brings about change and adaptation that families and relationships need to survive and thrive (Saxbe et al., 2013; Sprey, 1979). The results of conflict—addressing needs, barriers, and improved communication—promote progress and change. Indeed, the research on apology, forgiveness, and repair in marriage and other close relationships reveals that conflict can promote healing processes in families (Lewis et al., 2015). Further, conflict often reinforces solidarity and unity within groups. At the same time, it also challenges norms at the structural level. An example of conflict, both within families as well as at the structural level, is a University of Iowa student named Zach Wahls, who spoke about the strength of his family during a 2011 public forum on House Joint Resolution 6 in the Iowa House of Representatives (Iowa House Democrats, 2011; see multimedia suggestions at the end of the chapter). Zach has two mothers, and testified to oppose House Joint Resolution 6, which would end civil unions in Iowa (this occurred a few years before same-sex marriage was legal in the United States). Zach's story is an example of conflict on both the micro- and the macro-levels; his grandparents would not acknowledge that his mother was pregnant with him because of their opposition to homosexuality.

These tensions undoubtedly created conflict between Zach's mother and her parents, which was resolved after he was born. In another example, Zach discussed how he managed conflict within the classroom at the University of Iowa when the issue of gay marriage came up. He emphasizes in his testimony how he is no different from anyone else in the room:

> My family really isn't so different from yours. After all, your family doesn't derive its sense of worth from being told by the state, "You're married, congratulations!" The sense of family comes with the commitment we make to each other to work through the hard times so we can enjoy the good ones. (Iowa House Democrats, 2011)

Zach manages the potential conflict by emphasizing how similar he is to other college students, raised by heterosexual parents. He uses this sameness (on a micro level) to broaden the discussion to equal and fair treatment from the Iowa state government (on a macro level). Additionally, as Zach acknowledges that conflict exists for his family on a macro level. The very reason he testified is because his family's rights to marriage were threatened; the conflict in this case is between two groups in society: lesbian, gay, bisexual, transgender, or queer (LGBTQ+) persons and those who oppose marriage equality. Those who oppose marriage equality have power and access to resources (legal protections) that, until very recently, LGBTQ+ persons did not. This discrimination on a macro level creates conflict between two groups in society. He ends his testimony by again managing the conflict on a macro level, using emotions that originate from a micro level, saying, "Not once have I ever been confronted by an individual who realized independently that I was raised by a gay couple. And you know why? Because the sexual orientation of my parents has had zero impact on the content of my character" (Iowa House Democrats, 2011).

This case is also an example of the positive aspects of conflict. Without individuals or groups challenging social norms and advocating for their rights, social change would not occur. When groups in society have different values, conflict is inevitable. But as history has shown, fighting for equal rights eventually leads to social change and consensus, which results in conflict resolution. In this sense, individuals and families demonstrate their empowerment (see Chapter 8 on feminist theory for further ideas about empowerment).

To summarize, conflict theory can be applied to families in various ways with both positive and negative outcomes. Thinking about Marie, we can see how the family's position in the lower middle class inevitably affects conflict over resources within the family as well. Marie could not escape the obligation to help the family; the obligation existed because of structural barriers that were out of her control as a child in this working-class family. She could not move "up" a lane because she was too busy overcoming the obstacles in her own lane. Her childhood was spent helping her family dodge roadblocks, such as spending Thursday nights unloading the freight truck. Marie did not have the time to put in long hours to prepare for an engineering degree, researching schools, making connections with faculty at prestigious universities; she was responsible for her younger brother, and his well-being came first. Additionally, Marie did not have access to the cultural or social capital she needed to make her dreams a reality. Her social capital consisted of her parents' contacts, who were also working- or middle-class contacts as small business owners, at best. These external barriers created conflict within the family that had to be managed, or resolved, if possible.

BOX 3.2. CONFLICT THEORY IN MODERN CULTURE: *SCHITT'S CREEK*

Image 3.1 A Scene From *Schitt's Creek*, 2015–2C20

Schitt's Creek is a comedy show that chronicles the lives of the Rose family (Johnny, Moira, David, and Alexis) as they face the harsh reality of losing their immense wealth all at once. The one asset that remains is a town Johnny bought David as a joke for his birthday: Schitt's Creek, a rural community in upstate New York. The Roses move into the roadside motel and navigate small-town, modest living over the course of six seasons.

Though, at first glance, this show appears to be fraught with surface-level, irritating-to-watch fights between siblings, as the characters develop, viewers are exposed to more depth and nuance of the family members and townspeople. One example that is particularly relevant for conflict theory is a scene in which Johnny and Moira go out on a double date with the town mayor and his wife (Roland and Jocelyn). While at the restaurant, they run into a couple from their past (wealthier) life, and the scene quickly becomes uncomfortable as the old friends put down the area and the town where the Roses now live. This old social capital quickly fades for the Roses, as Roland and Jocelyn step in and stand up for Johnny and Moira. Their new cultural capital may be different, and less affluent, but the strong friendships they develop in the small town are worth far more than the superficial relationships from their wealthy past.

Evaluating Conflict Theory

Strengths of Conflict Theory

Conflict theory is one of the earliest and most influential of all the theories applied to families. Family scholars find it useful in dealing with how individuals and families distribute power and deal with change. Conflict theory helps us appreciate that all families have challenges and problems, and the important issue is not the fact of having problems but how families manage and resolve the inevitable conflicts that arise. Thus, conflict theory has many strengths in terms of helping us understand the positive and negative dimensions of power.

Conflict Can Lead to Positive Change

As conflict theory is presented in this text, it is diverse in its scope, allowing researchers to understand structural barriers families face on a macro level as well as power dynamics and access to resources *within* the family on a micro level. Conflict theory frames the study of family dynamics in terms of access to resources and the struggle for equal access. Yet it also often results in positive outcomes: marriage equality for same-sex couples and family members facing tough problems that result in management, consensus, or resolution on issues they face every day are just two examples. A major strength of conflict theory is that it addresses injustices and problems directly, which is necessary for positive social changes to occur.

Examines "Invisible" Processes

Contemporary conflict theorists help us understand intangible processes—those we cannot easily see—in families. Intangible dynamics, such as parenting strategies that are passed down from generation to generation, can actually work to reproduce inequality at the structural level. For instance, through the process of interaction, cultural, social, and symbolic capital are invisibly transmitted to children, helping secure their place in their parents' social class. This is vital to understanding why certain policies or programs designed to help level the playing field for families may not be effective. A parent's level of education will likely predict how they interact with authority figures in society. As an example, if a child needs to be placed in a special needs program in elementary school, parents may not know how important it is to reach out and advocate for their child, they may not know exactly what to say or who to ask or have the ability to persist in making sure their child's needs are met. Alternatively, parents may not have time to take out of their workday to take on such time-intensive tasks. Therefore, another strength of conflict theory is that it takes both tangible and intangible processes into account.

Practical Tools for Managing and Resolving Conflicts

Conflict theory is not simply a way to theorize about or explain social processes. It offers practitioners practical tools to lead families in conflict to management, consensus, and resolution. Practitioners are able to draw from the "big picture" that conflict theory provides by taking into account structural barriers families face based on social stratification. At the same time, conflict theory provides useful ways to help families work through and address conflict on the family level. This combination of both a macro and micro perspective in the study of families allows us to understand how those external forces create limitations *within* the family and how families may adapt to such challenges. For example, a working-class family faces significant economic barriers when it comes to caring for older family members. They may not be able to afford the best assisted living facility for their loved ones; yet, given their extensive kin network of aunts, uncles, and cousins who live nearby, they may be able to come to consensus about sharing caregiving duties. Thus, a macro-level barrier (low economic capital) is addressed at the micro level using social capital resources, illustrating how the family can reach consensus to manage the conflict.

Weaknesses of Conflict Theory

As we have established throughout this text, every theory has strengths as well as weaknesses. Conflict theory is no exception; here we discuss the weaknesses of using this approach when studying family dynamics.

Overlooks Diverse Family Resources and Strengths

One of the criticisms of conflict theory is the assumption that it places family dynamics in negative terms, assuming that conflict is destructive. Many family scholars and practitioners may argue that, on a macro level, families are not as restricted by the "inequality track" as conflict theorists would suggest. As an example, while families in the outermost lanes of the track experience structural barriers that may lead to additional family conflict, they may also have access to resources and adaptations that are atypical in upper middle-class White families, who have not had to contend with class and race discrimination and who have benefitted from unearned privileges, as we exemplify throughout this book. Families of color, specifically African American families, tend to have stronger kinship ties (e.g., joint residency, visiting, the exchange of mutual aid among kin, and caring for older relatives; Lareau, 2003; Liu et al., 2021; Stack, 1974; Taylor et al., 2021; Wilson, 1989). In addition, families of color are traditionally more likely than White families to feel that children should help their older parents, and reciprocal obligations of help from kin are more salient among diverse racial and ethnic groups, including African American families, Latinx families, and families from India (AARP, 2001; Dilworth-Anderson et al., 2002; Murthy, 2016; Taylor et al., 2013). Therefore, structural barriers may be mitigated by extended family networks and a culturally embedded tendency to foster and experience closer kinship relationships. Family systems theory (Chapter 6) and family stress and resilience theory (Chapter 11) may be better equipped to handle family resources and strengths.

Overlooks Intersectionalities

Another weakness of conflict theory is that it oversimplifies the complex social dynamics that also contribute to inequality, such as the *intersections* of race, gender, and sexual orientation. As an example, how might a child in the outermost lane experience discrimination for being transgender? Are there social class differences in how families would perceive trans issues? What if they were from diverse racial and ethnic backgrounds? Conflict theory tends to focus mainly on class consciousness and economic stratification and, thus, does not readily allow for an examination of these intersecting statuses. Therefore, it is arguably more limited in scope. We turn to contemporary feminist theory (Chapter 8) and critical race theory (Chapter 12) for understanding intersectionality across multiple dimensions.

Is Conflict Theory Relevant to Modern Social Class Distinctions?

A third weakness of conflict theory is that it oversimplifies social class distinctions present in modern society. The father of conflict theory, Karl Marx, is often criticized by modern scholars for formulating a two-class system of only the owners and workers, when in contemporary society, there is undoubtedly a middle class and more distinctions between owners and workers. The same analysis goes for applying conflict theory to families; conflict present within a family could have several layers, origins, and ambiguities, which can be overlooked, using the dichotomy of the powerless versus the powerful.

An Alternative Theory App: Social Exchange Theory

In this chapter, we have laid out the origins and background, key concepts, and modern applications as well as the strengths and weaknesses of conflict theory. As we illustrated in Chapter 2 on functionalist theory, it is useful to compare theories to more easily identify the differences between the two. In addition, it is interesting to consider that, even though several theories focus on the concept of power, their interpretations of power relations are very different. Don't worry; even though you have not read about social exchange theory yet, we will compare it to the case study from this chapter (Marie) to continue to build on your ability to switch your theory "app" at any time.

BOX 3.3. GLOBAL COMPARISONS OF SAME-SEX MARRIAGE

There are variations from country to country when it comes to legalizing same-sex marriage (www.pewresearch.org/fact-tank/2019/10/29/global-snapshot-same-sex-marriage/). Consider these examples:

- **Argentina, Canada, Netherlands, Spain, and United Kingdom:** Universal same-sex marriage is allowed.
- **Mexico:** Same-sex marriage is allowed in some jurisdictions.
- **Armenia, Italy, and Nepal:** Same-sex marriage is pending or under consideration.
- **Cuba, Gambia, Saudi Arabia, and South Korea:** Same-sex marriage is illegal.

As you just learned in this chapter, conflict theory can take into account power relations on both the micro and the macro levels. Social exchange theory (Chapter 7), on the other hand, uses the *individual* as the unit of analysis, assuming that individual family members are interested in and capable of negotiating for the "best" deal in exchanges with other family members. The exchange that takes place within families is based on both parties' desires for power and rewards that guide their decision-making. This theory assumes that individuals within families have the ability to negotiate the "best deal" for themselves and often focuses on micro-level interactions and exchanges to better understand family dynamics. How would we explain Marie's family life using social exchange theory? First, we would most likely disregard the structural inequality that situates Marie's family lower on the social class ladder. In contrast, we would hone in on the actual exchange of resources between Marie and her family or even between Marie's mother and her father. Social exchange theorists would ask how Marie and her parents engage in "bargaining" interactions to make sure they are individually getting the best deal. We would focus on what resources, power, and rewards are available within the family and analyze how individual family members negotiate for these things, weighing costs against the potential benefits. The major commonality between these two theories is the assumption that conflict over resources is inevitable within families and that negotiations are a zero-sum game, in which one family member wins and another one loses.

Next, we apply conflict theory to families across the globe. Access to legal protections is an important consideration for conflict theorists and family scholars, and Box 3.3 highlights how same-sex marriage is protected in some nations but not others. Why do you think this is? How would conflict theorists explain the differences between the countries we highlight?

Working With Conflict Theory: Integrating Research and Practice

Now that we have described the historical origins, key concepts, and strengths and weaknesses of conflict theory, we turn our attention to how the theory can be used in research and practice. We then analyze an empirical study that was rooted in conflict theory to see how scholars put the theory to work in a research project. Finally, we present ideas about how the theory informs the practice of family policy.

Conflict Theory Today

As we have discussed throughout this chapter, researchers using conflict theory can apply it to families in a number of ways, addressing power struggles both within and outside of families that create conflict. In Chapter 1, we described the changing demographics of society, such as the rising costs of health care, increased life expectancy, changes in the levels and timing of fertility, and the increase in women's labor force participation. These demographic shifts mean there are more generations of one family alive at any given time, and each generation might be in very distinct and conflicting life course stages, which creates unprecedented demands on family caregivers (Allen et al., 2011; Cherlin, 2010; Silverstein & Giarrusso, 2010; Smock & Schwartz, 2020). It is important to understand how these factors impacting the population generate conflict and burden within families at the same time that love and solidarity co-occur (Connidis & Barnett, 2019).

The current approach to generational relations within families builds on conflict theory. Intergenerational ambivalence theory (IGA) suggests that family members can feel hate and love for another family member at the same time, especially in a caregiving relationship (Luescher & Pillemer, 1998). Thus, simultaneous feelings of duty, love, and obligation toward caring for older adults can exist in caregiving relationships. This theory considers both the individual-level and the structural-level feelings of ambivalence, suggesting that family members experience contradictions in relationships that cannot be reconciled (Connidis, 2015). This may include personal feelings of love and concern that occur on the individual level and the obligations of a career and other nuclear family duties that occur on a social-structural level. Demographically, a couple may have started their family in their mid- to late-thirties, which situates them on a trajectory in which they could be well into their fifties when their children are graduating from high school. At the same time, their own parents could be in their seventies or eighties, needing help driving to and from doctor's appointments and dealing with chronic or serious illness and a general loss of independence. Individuals caught between caring for their children and their parents have been referred to as members of the "sandwich generation." This group of individuals is at risk of experiencing ambivalent feelings toward the care receiver simply because the stress of managing the conflicting duties and responsibilities lends itself to simultaneous feelings of love, duty, and frustration and anger because of the additional responsibilities of caregiving (Henderson, 2013). Additionally, given a family's position on the inequality track, they may or may not have access to economic resources that would help pay for in-home health care to help alleviate the strains associated with caregiving. However, families in the outside lane may not only have an extended family depending on them, but they also are likely to have low-wage jobs with no paid time off to care for a family member. This limits their ability to access needed resources, which exacerbates the feelings of ambivalence within the family. At the same time, during the COVID-19 pandemic, when caregivers have reported even less social support from formal services, relationships with other family members may be a hidden and valuable source of well-being, despite the potential for increased family conflict (Gilligan et al., 2020). In all of these ways, IGA is a useful contemporary use of conflict theory at both the structural and individual levels.

Conflict Theory in Research

Modern family scholars have built on the original principles of conflict theory to gain a fuller understanding of how inequality persists both outside of and within families. In her study, Annette Lareau (2003) suggests that societal inequalities we see between families emanate from invisible parenting styles occurring within families from different social class backgrounds. Therefore, Lareau's work is an ideal example of how to link the macro-level forces to the micro-level interactions that occur within families' everyday lives. Lareau interviewed and observed 12 families and their children from middle-class, working-class, and poor families. About half of the people in her sample were Black, and the other half were White.

Lareau's methodology involved three phases of research. In phase 1, she and her research assistants conducted participant observation of two third-grade classrooms in a public school in the Midwest. After two months of observation, Lareau grouped the families of the third graders into separate racial and social class categories and requested interviews with the mothers and fathers of the children. Ninety percent of the parents agreed to be interviewed, which is what social scientists refer to as a response rate—the percentage of participants who agree to take part in the study after being asked.

The second phase of Lareau's study involved a different data collection site to broaden the scope of the study. For this phase, Lareau and her research assistants conducted participant observation over a 15-month period in two third-grade classrooms in the northeast region of the United States. They then interviewed 17 more families of those third graders. In the third phase of the study, the researchers conducted home observations of 12 children and their families, who had been previously interviewed. This meant that over the course of the three weeks, one fieldworker from the research team spent a few hours with the families, participating in their normal routines. This included at least one overnight visit and attending events, such as baseball games, church services, and taking part in the normal activities of everyday life. The researchers observed, audio recorded, and took notes, which they later used to help frame their analysis. They also utilized interviews with the family members over the three weeks as well. It is important to note that the researchers took steps to match fieldworkers with the families they were observing. For Black families with male children, the team included a Black male graduate student fieldworker, and a White male fieldworker observed the poor family with a White son. Throughout the week, the research teams met and compared notes to review the emerging analytic themes (Lareau, 2003).

The goals of this research were to produce a realistic picture of the day-to-day rhythms of families with children of elementary school age, paying special attention to what differences could be attributed to social class. The results of the study revealed two distinct approaches to parenting, coined by Lareau as concerted cultivation and the natural growth model. Concerted cultivation is promoted by middle-class parents, who enroll their children in numerous age-specific activities that dominate family life. The parents believe the activities foster children's talents, opinions, and skills and provide important life skills as well. These life skills include the development of reasoning and language (i.e., answering questions with questions) and encouraging children to think and talk for themselves. The natural growth model, on the other hand, is emphasized by working-class and poor families. This model is based on the idea that as long as the child's basic needs are provided for, the children will grow and thrive. These children participate in few organized activities and have more free time as well as "deeper, richer ties with their extended families" (Lareau, 2003, p. 749).

What Lareau discovered in her study is that in the middle-class parents' approach of concerted cultivation, the children developed an emerging sense of entitlement. This conclusion was reached through a qualitative research method called triangulation. That is, the researchers used multiple sources of data and multiple researchers analyzing the data to interpret the results. Teams of three researchers (including Lareau) observed every family, and they also gathered data in different ways, including both interviews and participant observation. Without the observation piece, the researchers might not have come to the conclusion that the parenting approaches were leading to entitlement. Researchers observed the children's entitled behaviors in doctors' offices and classrooms and were able to infer from the other data points, including parental interviews, that the concerted cultivation approach leads to child entitlement.

On the flip side, Lareau also concluded that the natural growth model resulted in a growing sense of constraint among working-class and poor children. This is characterized by being cautious, only speaking when being spoken to, and distrusting authority figures like school officials. Again, while one of the children indicated that he knew his mother mistrusted school officials in an interview, the researchers were also able to validate this while observing the mother interact with teachers during the parent–teacher conferences. Here we can see conflict theory in action on many levels; working-class and poor parents are structurally disadvantaged in society, and the constraints of social class are recreated within the family on the individual level for children. Within this one study, we can see conflict theory on both the micro and macro levels, and we can also see how researchers invoke theory, using research methods designed to capture the theoretical complexities with multiple data sources and techniques.

Conflict Theory in Practice

There are several ways in which educators, practitioners, and family policy makers can apply conflict theory in their work with individuals and families. One of the most important places family scholars can utilize conflict theory is in the development of policy. As we outlined in Chapter 1, the demographic landscape of American families is changing. Right now, the Family and Medical Leave Act (FMLA) of 1993 (2006) mandates that businesses with over 50 employees offer 12 weeks of unpaid leave for employees to care for loved ones (e.g., a newborn, a family member with dementia). From a conflict perspective, we need to ask several questions about this policy, such as who it benefits, who it includes, and who it leaves out. Particularly in light of the COVID-19 pandemic, in which so many families have fallen through the social safety net, reconsideration of the FMLA is increasingly called upon by practitioners and families themselves.

First, the policy does not include employees working for businesses with fewer than 50 employees. This means that small businesses are exempt from offering family leave to their employees. Also, when considering a life event like the birth of a baby, FMLA allows for 12 weeks of *unpaid* leave. In an economy in which most families are dependent on two incomes to sustain a basic standard of living, could they truly sustain three months without a second pay check? If they can, the next thing to consider is who will leave work to take care of the newborn. Traditional notions of gender would suggest that the mother should stay home with the baby, but this is also supported by the economic realities of employment as well. Women still only make about 82% of what men make (U.S. Bureau of Labor Statistics, 2020); therefore, it would make the most economic sense to lose the income from the parent who brings home the lower salary. That way, the family keeps the main breadwinner's salary for the duration of the maternity leave.

Applying conflict theory to practice—or in this case, policy development—allows us to see clearly how macro-level structures affect families on the micro level. Policies that are supposed to support families when they need it the most could actually be creating intrafamily conflict. Not only does FMLA particularly disadvantage single-parent families that simply cannot afford to go three months without pay, it also has the potential to create

BOX 3.4. VOICES FROM LIVED EXPERIENCE

While it may seem daunting to try to understand conflict theory within the context of families, when you think about your own experiences in a class system, the theory can really come to life for you.

As part of a class activity, Angie asked her theory students when they first recalled being aware of which social class they were born into. Though Marx originally defined this **class consciousness** as it related to the working class only, it is relevant for modern society as well. Marx originally defined class consciousness as "an awareness on the part of the working class of its common relationship to the means of production and common source of the workers' oppressive conditions" (Appelrouth & Edles, 2021, p. 46). Students in Angie's theory class shared a variety of examples describing when they first understood they came from less privilege than other children.

Cara, a White, Jewish, nonbinary, bisexual college student shared:

I remember figuring out we were in the lower class because my parents got divorced between the ages of 4 and 5. My dad just left, so my mom kept all us kids. I remember that first summer, she got two additional side jobs to make up for the lost income. We had to move to the other side of town and live in a much smaller house. It was literally that experience when I knew what social class was.

Jaron, a cisgender heterosexual biracial male college student shared:

I was an army brat and in that hierarchy there are sergeants at the top, down to privates, so when you go to school with other army kids, you notice the difference between what the kids wore at school and what kind of cars they drove, and houses they lived in. I also noticed how other kids would be able to have the newest, coolest toy right when it came out, and my mom always told me when I asked at the store that that "wasn't a need, it was a want," so that solidified in my head that we were less than.

Once students are able to identify how conflict theory and awareness of social class impacts them individually, it is much easier to get a grasp on how it impacts all families differentially.

conflict within the family if and when the couple disagrees over who should stay home with the newborn. Over time, women typically expect, and are assumed, to be the caregivers not only for children but also for parents who need help or caregiving as they age (Ridgeway, 2011). This pattern of gendered expectations not only has the potential to create strain within couples and families, but it also recreates disadvantage on the macro level (Henderson et al., 2016). Women are more likely to leave the workforce to care for family members, which limits their earning potential, including access to promotions as well as social security and retirement. Over time, women who leave the workforce for caregiving accumulate disadvantage because they lose out on earnings, pension, and other wealth that accumulates for those who are able to persist in the workforce (Gibb et al., 2014). The invisible, uncompensated, gendered, lifelong, and essential nature of care work was especially revealed during the COVID-19 pandemic (Kemp, 2021).

Conclusion

Conflict theory has provided important ideas that allow researchers and practitioners to put the theory to use beyond the conceptual level. Once critiqued as a grand theory, limited in empirical and practical application, family scientists have developed ways in which conflict theory can be applied to multiple levels of family conflict. We challenge you to consider these applications of the theory as you move on to the discussion questions, reflection questions, and areas for further study in the concluding pages of this chapter.

Multimedia Suggestions

www.zachwahlsforiowa.com

This is the homepage of Zach Wahls, who testified before the Iowa House Judiciary Committee in 2011, as described earlier in this chapter. Now an Iowa State Senator himself, his webpage contains links to see the issues he takes a strong stance on, read his latest blogs and his interviews, and find information on his book, *My Two Moms* (Wahls, 2012).

Activate your theory app: Can you find examples of Bourdieu's different types of capital in Wahls's materials (i.e., his speaking engagements, his blog posts, or in his bio)?

www.epi.org/resources/budget/

This is the website for the Economic Policy Institute's family budget calculator. This budget calculator is updated annually and allows users to enter their family type (i.e., one parent, one child) and the city and state where they live. Based on those demographics, the budget provides estimated monthly expenses for housing, food, child care, transportation, health care, taxes, and other necessities. This website is useful to help you understand the costs associated with raising children, which are often underestimated. You can also compare your own budget results to the federal poverty line and average salaries and wages in your geographical area.

Activate your theory app: Calculate your budget, based on your current family status. Add up all of your current expenses (including education) on top of what is listed for you, and compare the two figures (what you live on now and what is needed to maintain a basic standard of living calculated by the website). How do the two compare? Run other numbers, for single parents or two-parent families with two children. Are you surprised by the results?

Image 3.2 A Scene From *Arrested Development*, 2003

Arrested Development (2003–2006 and 2013)

In this comedic television series, a dysfunctional wealthy family is in desperate need of the show's main character, Michael Bluth, to pull them out of impending financial ruin. This show illustrates micro-level conflict, as the family members compete for resources within the family. The show also provides examples of cultural and symbolic capital via the patriarch George Bluth's past abilities to talk his way out of illegal business practices. The family's capital contrasts with the career aspirations of their son-in-law Tobias, which include being an actor. Throughout the series, Michael is forced to bring the family together, illustrating conflict management, and, sometimes, conflict resolution and consensus.

Activate your theory app: See if you can find examples of Bourdieu's concepts of economic, cultural, and social capital in this series as well. How does the family protect its members due to their different types of capital? How does that compare to your own family?

Fleabag (2016–2019)

This British comedy–drama follows the life of protagonist Fleabag and her adult life, including sexual escapades, a relationship with a priest, and her relationship with her family of origin. Throughout the entire series, Fleabag navigates relationships with her to-be stepmother, which illustrates conflict management on a micro scale. The audience also gets a taste of conflict resolution with episodes centered on her relationship with the priest, her sister's confession, and her father's wedding.

Image 3.3 A Scene From *Fleabag*, 2019

Activate your theory app: Are there examples in this series of symbolic, cultural, economic, and social capital? Think about examples of each as they relate not only to Fleabag but the characters throughout both seasons.

Further Reading

Ehrenreich, B. (2010). *Nickel and dimed: On (not) getting by in America*. Macmillan. Barbara Ehrenreich writes about her experience as an undercover journalist working in low wage jobs across the country to investigate the repercussions of the 1996 Welfare Reform Act. She posed as a waitress, hotel maid, house cleaner, nursing home aide, and Walmart salesperson and found that the lived realities of low-wage workers include needing two low-wage jobs just to afford basic necessities of food, shelter, and transportation to and from work. Readers should be able to identify conflict theory on both macro and micro levels because the author delves into the realities of her own as well as her coworkers' lives, while they face issues related to employment, child care, chronic illness, and domestic violence.

Hochschild, A. R. (2016). *Strangers in their own land: Anger and mourning on the American right*. The New Press. Sociologist Arlie Hochschild exposes a source of conflict that working families face, and it is played out in the rhetoric of the liberal left and the conservative right. She interviewed working class families in rural Louisiana, many of whom live in poverty and are in very poor health as a result of economic decline, environmental disasters, and government inattention to their needs. Yet rather than direct their anger at the powerful institutions that have devastated their communities and families, from corporations to politics, many directed their ire toward liberal elites. Hochschild uses the concept of "deep story" to enable their emotional, economic, and political realities to come alive. A deep story is "the story feelings tell" (p. 135), and in this book, Hochschild offers a bridge between the polarization on the left and the right to help readers understand the individuals and families caught in the center of the conflict.

Jaramillo-Sierra, A. L., Kaestle, C. E., & Allen, K. R. (2016). Daughters' anger towards mothers and fathers in emerging adulthood. *Sex Roles, 75*(1/2), 28–42. https://doi.org/10.1007/s11199-016-0599-9. Anger is a taboo topic, especially for women. Yet as we have described throughout this chapter, having conflictual feelings is part of being in a family, and anger is an emotion we all share. Gender shapes how anger is experienced and expressed in families, with girls, in particular, being taught to control or suppress their anger. In this qualitative study, Jaramillo-Sierra et al. found that there were a variety of ways in which young women expressed their anger toward their parents, depending upon the relational context. Although the young women tended to experience more warmth and responsiveness from their mothers, they conceded more of their power and privilege to their fathers. They also tended to indirectly express their anger, or hold it in, and, thus, avoid any direct confrontation. Of note is that the young women tended to give their fathers a "pass" and not hold them accountable, whereas they had higher expectations, and, thus, somewhat more anger, toward their mothers.

Kozol, J. (2006). *Rachel and her children: Homeless families in America.* Random House. (Original work published 1988) Jonathan Kozol tells Rachel's story of homelessness in an attempt to critique New York's welfare policy during the 1980s. While this book is not a scientific study of families, it is a nonfiction piece that helps readers understand how families are affected by public policies, bureaucracy, and homelessness. Kozol tells the story of real people, like Rachel and her family, who are not lazy, crazy, or misfits. Rather, they suffer from inefficient, inappropriate policies that are supposed to help them.

Mills, C. W. (1956). *The power elite.* Oxford University Press. This book, one of the most important sociological texts, explains how the interests of the military, corporations, and political realms of society determine social reality. C. Wright Mills also examines how wealthy families contribute to the power elite's domination of most of the free world. This text is useful for scholars in family science, sociology, and related disciplines because it debunks taken for granted ideas when thinking about families, including how powerful affluent families truly are when they transmit wealth from generation to generation, thereby reproducing the class structure on a global scale.

Questions for Students

Discussion Questions

1. Why is it important to understand both the external and internal causes of conflict over resources? How do both interplay to create advantage or disadvantage within and outside of families?

2. Do families on the inside track experience conflict, given their access to almost unlimited resources? On the flip side, is it possible to experience very little within-family conflict in lane 4 (structurally, the most disadvantaged lane)? Explain and provide support for your answer.

3. Using conflict theory, explain how each of the lanes on the inequality track are dependent on one another. Could the inside lane function without the other lanes? What about the outside lane—are families in the working poor dependent on the three inside lanes? Why, or why not?

4. Describe the types of capital. How do they change over time? That is, in what ways do different social institutions, besides the family, give individuals access to different types of capital?

5. Describe what would happen if we were to apply Marx's original conflict theory to modern society. Does the theory work for today's society?

6. In light of the COVID-19 pandemic, what is the current economic disparity between the rich and the poor?

Your Turn!

Imagine that you were charged with determining the strengths and weaknesses of the Family and Medical Leave Act of 1993 using conflict theory. Your employers want a solid theoretical analysis of the act as well as suggestions for change based on the strengths and weaknesses. Using terms from this chapter, describe the policy, and make suggestions based on both external and internal sources of conflict.

Personal Reflection Questions

1. Consider where you might be situated on the inequality track presented in this chapter. Who is in the other lanes? Can you think of examples from your own life of either access to privilege or barriers that caused disadvantage for you and your family? How did those external forces influence the struggle over resources within your family?

2. Consider how much different your life might be if you moved up or down a lane. What influence would that have on your possible pathways? Is it possible for large numbers of people to move up a lane? What about down? How are all of the lanes dependent on one another?

3. Give an example of how your family has experienced internal conflict and how you managed or resolved the conflict.

4. Thinking about your own family, describe what types of economic, social, cultural, and symbolic capital you have. How does your capital help or harm your chances of moving up a lane?

5. Consider Lareau's conceptualization of parenting approaches: concerted cultivation and natural growth. Which one most closely resembles how you were raised? If you plan to have children, which approach will you most likely use? Why?

6. Conflict theory can be used to study families on very different levels, ranging from analyzing structural-level inequalities to conflict between siblings over resources. What aspect of conflict do you find most interesting? Micro or macro? In what ways?

References

AARP (American Association of Retired Persons). (2001). *In the middle: A report on multicultural boomers coping with family and aging issues.* Belden Russonello & Stewart.

Adams, B. N., & Sydie, R. A. (2002). *Classical sociological theory.* SAGE Publications.

Allen, K. R., Blieszner, R., & Roberto, K. A. (2011). Perspectives on extended family and fictive kin in the later years: Strategies and meanings of kin reinterpretation. *Journal of Family Issues, 32*(9), 1156–1177. https://doi.org/10.1177/0192513X11404335

Appelrouth, S., & Edles, L. D. (2021). *Classical and contemporary sociological theory: Text and readings* (4th ed.). SAGE Publications.

Bernard, J. (1982). *The future of marriage.* Yale University Press.

Blank, O., Knowles, L. L., & Prewitt, K. (1970). *Institutional racism in America*. Prentice Hall.

Bourdieu, P. (1990). *In other words: Essays towards a reflexive sociology*. Stanford University Press.

Cherlin, A. J. (2010). Demographic trends in the United States: A review of research in the 2000s. *Journal of Marriage and Family, 72*(3), 403–419. https://doi.org/10.1111/j.1741-3737.2010.00710.x

Connidis, I. A. (2015). Exploring ambivalence in family ties: Progress and prospects. *Journal of Marriage and Family, 77*(1), 77–95. https://doi.org/10.1111.jomf.12150

Connidis, I. A., & Barnett, A. E. (2019). *Family ties & aging* (3rd ed.). SAGE Publications.

Dilworth-Anderson, P., Williams, I. C., & Gibson, B. E. (2002). Issues of race, ethnicity, and culture in caregiving research: A 20-year review (1980–2000). *The Gerontologist, 42*(2), 237–272. https://doi.org/10.1093/geront/42.2.237

Family and Medical Leave Act of 1993, 29 U.S.C. § 2601–2654 (2006).

Farrington, K., & Chertok, E. (1993). Social conflict theories of the family. In P. G. Boss, W. J. Doherty, R. LaRossa, W. R. Schumm, & S. K. Steinmetz (Eds.), *Sourcebook of family theories and methods: A contextual approach* (pp. 357–384). Plenum.

Gibb, S. J., Fergusson, D. M., Horwood, L. J., & Boden, J. M. (2014). The effects of parenthood on workforce participation and income for men and women. *Journal of Family and Economic Issues, 35*(1), 14–26. https://doi.org/10.1007/sl0834-013-9353-4

Gilligan, M., Suitor, J. J., Rurka, M., & Silverstein, M. (2020). Multigenerational social support in the face of the COVID-19 pandemic. *Journal of Family Theory & Review, 12*(4), 431–447. https://doi.org/10.1111/jftr.12397

Gilman, C. P. (1998). *Women and economics: A study of the economic relation between men and women as a factor in social evolution*. Dover. (Original work published 1898)

Goldberg, A. E. (2013). "Doing" and "undoing" gender: The meaning and division of housework in same-sex couples. *Journal of Family Theory & Review, 5*(2), 85–104. https://doi.org/10.1111/jftr.12009

Goldberg, A. E., McCormick, N., & Virginia, H. (2021). Parenting in a pandemic: Work–family arrangements, well-being, and intimate relationships among adoptive parents. *Family Relations, 70*(1), 7–25. https:/doi.org/10.1111/fare.12528

Harari, Y. N. (2018). *21 lessons for the 21st century*. Jonathan Cape.

Henderson, A., Harmon, S., & Newman, H. (2016). The price mothers pay, even when they are not buying it: Mental health consequences of idealized motherhood. *Sex Roles: A Journal of Research, 74*(11–12), 512–526. https://doi.org/10.1007/s11199-015-0534-5

Henderson, A. C. (2013). Defining caregiving relationships: Using intergenerational ambivalence theory to explain burden among racial and ethnic groups. In S. Marrow & D. Leoutsakas (Eds.), *More than blood: Today's reality and tomorrow's vision of family* (pp. 289–303). Kendall Hunt.

Iowa House Democrats. (2011, February 1). *What makes a family* [Video]. YouTube. https://www.youtube.com/watch?v=FSQQK2Vuf9Q&ab_channel=IowaHouseDemocrats

Jackson, J. B., Miller, R. B., Oka, M., & Henry, R. G. (2014). Gender differences in marital satisfaction: A meta-analysis. *Journal of Marriage and Family, 76*(1), 105–129. https://doi.org/10.1111/jomf.l2077

Kahlenberg, R. D. (Ed.). (2010). *Affirmative action for the rich: Legacy preferences in college admissions*. Century Foundation Press.

Kemp, C. L. (2021). #Morethanavisitor: Families as "essential" care partners during COVID-19. *The Gerontologist, 61*(2), 145–151. https://doi.org/10.1093/geront/gnaa161

Lareau, A. (2003). *Unequal childhoods: Class, race, and family life*. University of California Press.

Lewis, J. T., Parra, G. R., & Cohen, R. (2015). Apologies in close relationships: A review of theory and research. *Journal of Family Theory & Review, 7*(1), 47–61. https://doi.org/10.1111/jftr.12060

Liu, C., Badana, A. N. S., Burgdorf, J., Fabius, C. D., Roth, D. L., & Haley, W. E. (2021). Systematic review and meta-analysis of racial and ethnic differences in dementia caregivers' well-being. *The Gerontologist, 61*(5), 228–243. https://doi.org/10.1093/geront/gnaa028

Luescher, K., & Pillemer, K. (1998). Intergenerational ambivalence: A new approach to the study of parent–child relations in later life. *Journal of Marriage and the Family, 60*(2), 413–425. https://doi.org/10.2307/353858

Marx, K., & Engels, F. (1977). *The economic and philosophic manuscripts of 1844 and the communist manifesto* (D. J. Struik, Trans.). Martin Milligan International. (Original work published 1844 and 1848)

Murthy, R. S. (2016). Caregiving and caregivers: Challenges and opportunities in India. *Indian Journal of Social Psychiatry, 32*(1), 10–18. https://doi.org/10.4103/0971-9962.176761

Osmond, M. W. (1987). Radical-critical theories. In M. B. Sussman & S. K. Steinmetz (Eds.), *Handbook of marriage and the family* (pp. 103–124). Plenum.

Pfeffer, C. A. (2017). *Queering families: The postmodern partnerships of cisgender women and transgender men.* Oxford University Press.

Piven, F. F., & Cloward, R. A. (1971). *Regulating the poor: The functions of public welfare.* Random House.

Quinney, R. (1970). *The social reality of crime.* Little, Brown.

Ridgeway, C. L. (2011). *Framed by gender: How gender inequality persists in the modern world.* Oxford University Press.

Ritzer, G. (2010). *Sociological theory* (8th ed.). McGraw-Hill.

Sassler, S. (2010). Partnering across the life course: Sex, relationships, and mate selection. *Journal of Marriage and Family, 72*(3), 557–575. https://doi.org/10.1111/j.1741-3737.2010. 00718.x

Saxbe, D. E., Rodriguez, A. J., & Margolin, G. (2013). Understanding conflict in families: Theoretical frameworks and future directions. In M. A. Fine & F. D. Fincham (Eds.), *Handbook of family theories: A content-based approach* (pp. 169–189). Routledge.

Scarborough, W. J., Collins, C., Ruppanner, L., & Landivar, L. C. (2021). Head start and families' recovery from economic recession: Policy recommendations for COVID-19. *Family Relations, 70*(1), 26–42. https://doi.org/10.1111/fare.12519

Silverstein, M., & Giarrusso, R. (2010). Aging and family life: A decade review. *Journal of Marriage and Family, 72*(5), 1039–1058. https://doi.org/10.1111/j.1741-3737.2010.00749.x

Smith, B., & Browne, C. A. (2019). *Tools and weapons: The promise and the peril of the digital age.* Penguin.

Smock, P. J., & Schwartz, C. R. (2020). The demography of families: A review of patterns and change. *Journal of Marriage and Family, 82*(1), 9–34. https://doi.org/10.1111/jomf.12612

Solomon, S. E., Rothblum, E. D., & Balsam, K. F. (2005). Money, housework, sex, and conflict: Same-sex couples in civil unions, those not in civil unions, and heterosexual married siblings. *Sex Roles, 52*(9/10), 561–575. https://doi.org/10.1007/si1199-005-3725-7

Sprey, J. (1969). The family as a system in conflict. *Journal of Marriage and the Family, 31*(4), 699–706. https://doi.org/10.2307/349311

Sprey, J. (1979). Conflict theory and the study of marriage and the family. In W R. Burr, R. Hill, F. I. Nye, & I. L. Reiss (Eds.), *Contemporary theories about the family: General theories/theoretical orientations* (Vol. 2, pp. 130–159). Free Press.

Sprey, J. (1999). Family dynamics: An essay on conflict and power. In M. Sussman, S. K. Steinmetz, & G. W. Peterson (Eds.), *Handbook of marriage and the family* (pp. 667–685). Plenum Press.

Stack, C. B. (1974). *All our kin: Strategies for survival in a Black community.* Harper & Row.

Taylor, R. J., Chatters, L. M., Woodward, A. T., & Brown, E. (2013). Racial and ethnic differences in extended family, friendship, fictive kin, and congregational informal support networks. *Family Relations, 62*(4), 609–624. https://doi.org/10.1111/fare.l2030

Taylor, R. J., Chatters, L. M., & Cross, C. J. (2021). Taking diversity seriously: Within-group heterogeneity in African American extended family support networks. *Journal of Marriage and Family, 83*(5), 1349–1372. https://doi.org/10.1111/jomf.12783

Treas, J., & Tai, T. (2016). Gender inequality in housework across 20 European nations: Lessons from gender stratification theories. *Sex Roles, 74*(1/2), 495–511. https://doi.org/10.1007/s11199-015-0575-9

U. S. Bureau of Labor Statistics. (2020). *Women in the labor force: A databook*. U.S. Department of Labor. https://www.bls.gov/opub/reports/womens-databook/2020/home.htm

Wahls, Z. (2012). *My two moms: Lessons of love, strength, and what makes a family*. Penguin.

Wilson, M. N. (1989). Child development in the context of the Black extended family. *American Psychologist, 44*(2), 380–385. https://doi.org/10.1037/0003-066X.44.2.380.

Zuboff, S. (2019). *The age of surveillance capitalism: The fight for a human future at the new frontier of power*. PublicAffairs.

Image Credits

Fig. 3.2: Copyright © by African American Policy Forum.

IMG 3.1: Copyright © 2020 by CBC/Radio-Canada.

IMG 3.2: Copyright © 2003 by Netflix.

IMG 3.3: Copyright © 2019 by BBC.

CHAPTER

4

Symbolic Interactionist Theory

Think about a celebrity you like—maybe it's your favorite actor, professional athlete, comedian, or musician. You may follow their career as it develops over time, and you may also notice news articles about their personal life. Oftentimes, celebrities get married and/or divorced for very different reasons when compared to the general population. Why is that? What does marriage mean to a celebrity couple that differentiates it from what it means to the rest of us? Finally, even while we know that celebrity marriages typically do not last long, why do we sometimes truly feel surprised when we learn that our favorite celebrity couple is splitting up?

Symbolic interactionist theory is considered to be one of the most influential theories in family science, as it provides scholars with a useful framework for understanding how symbols, interactions, and social context explain marriage and family dynamics. In this chapter, we discuss the history of symbolic interactionist theory and how the principles and key concepts can be used to understand individuals, families, and the meanings associated with both. Symbolic interactionism, as it is also called, helps us answer questions about how we create meaning in our everyday lives and how those social constructions contribute to our views of families. To gain a fuller understanding of how symbolic interactionism works, we start with a case study that illustrates how individual definitions of family can carry very different meanings, depending on one's particular perspective and experience.

Case Study

Jeremy is a 32-year-old cisgender heterosexual man, who has just started graduate school after taking some time in his twenties to explore what he truly wanted to do. He has had several romantic relationships—one in particular that was serious and ended after a year-long engagement. He has dated on and off but hasn't found anyone he really clicks with.

Jeremy is Armenian and was raised by his father after his mother split from the family and moved hundreds of miles away. He and his brother grew very close with his father, but Jeremy still has not found a way to truly trust a romantic partner. He always thought he would love to get married and have children, but at this stage in his life, he is not sure if it will happen. His experience as a child to a single father has undoubtedly impacted his views of parenting and fatherhood. He has several wonderful friendships—one in particular with a woman who is in a similar situation. Ana, a 34-year-old single cisgender asexual woman with a very successful career, has also dated off and on but has decided to forego marriage and, instead, have a child on her own. After spending thousands of dollars at a sperm bank, Ana began to feel frustrated and hopeless. Ana and Jeremy did try dating once but felt more comfortable remaining as friends.

Ana finally built up enough courage to ask Jeremy if he would consider being her sperm donor. This would save her thousands of dollars because his donation would come at no financial risk to her. Jeremy immediately agreed to do it; he told Ana he was flattered that she would ask him to be a donor, and he would be honored knowing that even if he did not end up starting his own family someday, he had helped contribute to the creation of a life so that Ana could have a family. He also felt secure knowing that this child would be raised by a responsible, intelligent, caring, and loving parent. Ana had a legal contract drawn up that released Jeremy from any financial or parental obligation. The two agreed to the legal terms—bound by the fact that they do not and will probably never have a sexual relationship—and embarked on the journey of intrauterine insemination.

Contrast the realities of this scenario with how we view love, family, and marriage. What can we glean from this case study about Jeremy's view of family, parenting, and fatherhood? How have his experiences, both as a child and now as an adult, contributed to his feeling of honor at having been asked to contribute to creating Ana's family? What will Ana's child symbolize to the two of them? How will Jeremy, in particular, navigate his identity as a parent? Symbolic interactionism helps us understand how we construct meanings that are always changing based on our interactions with one another. Symbolic interactionists argue that objects do not have meaning outside of themselves; instead, they arise out of social interactions and are highly dependent on context. Think about how "pregnancy" can mean very different things to different people, depending on the situation. We could hypothesize that pregnancy to a 13-year-old girl in Sudan, Africa means something vastly different than it does to a married couple in Chicago, Illinois, who have been trying to conceive for 10 years. Symbolic interactionists examine these

BOX 4.1. AT A GLANCE: SYMBOLIC INTERACTIONIST THEORY

- **Symbolic interaction:** People act toward things based on the meaning those things have for them, and these meanings are derived from social interaction and modified through interpretation.
- **Self:** Our "social" self is created by going through the sequential stages of (a) imitation, (b) play, and (c) the game.
- **Roles:** Behavioral expectations and meanings attached to positions in the social structure.
- **Identity:** Self-meanings in a role; internalized role expectations and meanings.
- **Significant others:** Humans give greater weight to the perspectives of certain others.
- **Generalized other:** An organized set of attitudes that are common in the group to which an individual belongs.
- **Looking-glass self:** A person's beliefs about how they are perceived by significant others.
- **Dramaturgy:** Social life is like a drama or stage play.
- **Impression management:** The process by which we attempt to manage others' perceptions of our social performances.
- **Emotion work:** Unpaid emotional work that one undertakes in relationships with loved ones.
- **Emotional labor:** Managing emotions in a paid work environment.

differences, which processes we go through to create meanings and labels, why they differ from culture to culture, and how they change over time. Given how diverse families are and how adaptable this theory is, it should be no surprise that it is one of the most popular and enduring theories used for studying families across the globe.

What Is Symbolic Interactionist Theory?

Symbolic interactionist theory is used by researchers in sociology, family science, social psychology, and other areas to explain how processes of interaction produce meanings. This theory examines how humans define objects but not in the typical sense you would think about "objects." For social scientists and theorists, an **object** can refer to ideas, roles, social norms, behaviors, or actions (Blumer, 1969). This means that whatever we do, we are constantly in the process of creating and recreating meaning through interactions. Therefore, nothing has meaning without human interaction—not even human beings! George Herbert Mead (1934), one of the founding theorists, argued that infants are blank slates when they are born, and without socialization, they would not become "human". The **self** develops through social interaction:

> The self is something which has a development; it is not initially there, at birth, but arises in the process of social experience and activity, that is, develops in the given individual as a result of his relations to that process as a whole and to other individuals within that process. (Mead, 1934, p. 135)

Therefore, we define reality based on the personal meanings things have for us. These meanings can be based on something we already deem to be true about an object because it is what we were told or what we learned through interactions with others. Let's contrast how each theory you have read about so far—functionalist theory (Chapter 2) and conflict theory (Chapter 3)—would view the social issue of divorce. For functionalists, reality is defined by preexisting systems that are interdependent. Divorce, then, signifies that one part of a system became dysfunctional, which led to the divorce. Conflict theorists argue that reality is best understood by examining who has access to power and who does not. Therefore, conflict theorists would analyze divorce in relation to the power dynamic between spouses—between those with greater financial security (e.g., the breadwinner in the family) and those who have no financial support should they choose to end a marriage (e.g., the caregiver in the family). According to these two macro-level theories, our realities are predetermined; we cannot escape the boundaries of social class and overarching social systems that structure our lives.

Symbolic interactionists, on the other hand, argue that *we*—individuals—define reality. **Symbolic interactionism** is a micro-level theory, which, as outlined in Chapter 1, considers processes at the individual level. Symbolic interactionists start from the assumption that *we* create boundaries that exist in society—not some external system or social institution that is separate from us. Instead, cultural realities, including symbols, language, meaning, identities, and expectations, are all created from the "bottom up." In this way, using symbolic interactionism as a theoretical framework gives individuals substantial influence and flexibility, or agency, over how reality is constructed (Adamsons & Carter, 2022). Here, we outline the history of symbolic interactionist theory, including the many theorists who have contributed to its development over the past century.

History and Origins

Symbolic interactionism is a unique theory in that it consists of the perspectives of many different theorists and has been in use since the 19th century. The underpinnings of this theory are drawn from **pragmatism**, which argues that the meaning of objects lies in their practical use (Appelrouth & Edles, 2021). Noted pragmatists, such as Charles S. Peirce (1839–1914), William James (1842–1910), and John Dewey (1859–1952), were interested not in fixed ideals but in how objects, ideas, and behaviors depend on how the *individual* defines them (Appelrouth & Edles, 2021; LaRossa & Reitzes, 1993). While this may seem like a minor switch in orientation from studying macro- to micro-level processes of social phenomena, it represented a major shift in the social sciences. Symbolic interactionist theory is interested in local definitions, or the ones that we immediately assign to things, instead of prescribed definitions of reality, which can be found in a theory such as functionalism (Chapter 2). This shift in focus meant that objects, interactions, events, and situations are essentially devoid of meaning without someone perceiving them.

For example, imagine showing your grandfather how to set up a Snapchat account for the first time. It may be difficult for you to remember your very first time using the website or application, so you have a hard time explaining to him what it "is" without inadvertently telling him what it means to you. How do you explain what Snapchat "is" to someone unfamiliar with it? You might say that it is a medium through which you can post pictures of yourself to share with friends and see pictures of them as well. You might cautiously explain what a selfie is and how to share your location with people in your circle. Your grandfather might wonder why on Earth he would be interested in posting pictures of himself doing regular things in his daily life. Sensing his resistance, you switch your description to something he might find useful. You suggest that maybe he would like to at least have a Snapchat account, so he can keep up on popular current events, see pictures of all of his grandchildren (your siblings and cousins), and keep abreast of what they are doing on a daily basis, even though they live hundreds of miles away. You, on the other hand, have little interest in seeing the loads (too many, in your opinion) of pictures your uncle and his wife post of their children losing their first teeth, winning a trophy in soccer, or singing in a school concert. Instead, you are much more interested in your friends' snaps, pictures of people you find attractive and are interested in dating, and funny videos and pop culture updates. Snapchat, then, does not have objective meaning as an "object" out in cyberspace. Instead, it depends on how people use it. And just like you and your grandfather, different people use it for very different reasons. This suggests that it is not objective truths that symbolic interactionists are after; instead, they are much more interested in the **subjective** experiences we have with objects and how we make meaning of those experiences through social interaction.

Once pragmatists laid the groundwork for a new orientation to explaining the social world, symbolic interactionism flourished and is still widely used today. In the following sections, we outline the theorists whose work falls under the umbrella of symbolic interactionism as well as the key concepts that are foundational for understanding how this theory can be used to study individuals and families.

Key Concepts

Looking-Glass Self

As one of the earliest symbolic interactionists whose work built directly on William James's idea of the self, Charles Horton Cooley is best known for his theory of the **looking-glass self**. This concept describes how an individual's sense of self develops, based on beliefs about how they are perceived by significant others (Cooley, 1902). The looking-glass self involves three steps. First, we imagine how we appear to others. This involves an internal thought process, whereby we think first about what others might think about us, before the interaction occurs. Essentially, this is the first step in getting ready for the day. We try on clothing, style our hair, and look in the mirror while doing so. We choose clothing to wear based on where we are going and who we will see. We imagine how our clothing will be perceived; we might change clothes several times before stepping out for the day because we know certain clothes give off a certain look. The second step occurs when the interaction actually takes place—when we interpret others' reactions. When we interact, we take in facial expressions, gestures, and communication about our appearance and overall presentation. The third and final step in this process occurs when we use those interpretations to develop a self-concept. Perhaps, someone looked surprised at your appearance or at something you did or said in a social interaction. This third step can occur both during and after the interaction, where we process what others' reactions were and use them to adjust or modify our self-concept. Based on signals we received during interaction, we internalize the views of others, and these shape our future behavior.

This process undoubtedly occurs within families. As the primary socializing unit, the family responds to our presentation of self before any other group. Negative, positive, and ambivalent self-concepts are built starting as early as infancy, where parents and family members express both approval and disapproval of our actions, behaviors, and words, and babies begin to internalize the reactions of those around them. Parents and their children co-construct such internalized meanings based on their private interactions as well as on the metanarratives about child developmental and parental behavior they derive from the broader social context (Bell, 2019; Daly et al., 2012; Kerrick & Henry, 2017; Scheibling, 2020). As we develop, our sense of self is highly dependent on this social mirroring. Consider Jeremy from our case study. He told Ana that he felt honored that she asked him to be a donor. His perception of merely being asked to help her start a family was meaningful for him because it meant he would have a chance at contributing to the creation of a life with someone he respected and admired. For Jeremy, the interaction and meaning associated with it was very influential in developing his sense of self. His interactions with Ana as well as others led him to feel flattered to be asked; his "social mirror" reflected back to him that Ana thought he was a great person and that she would be thrilled to carry his child. This is separate and distinct from his views of fatherhood and parenting; he does not want to have his own children, so he is happy to contribute to his friend's dream of parenting instead. These interactions invariably tell us a lot about meanings and symbols that operate at the societal level. By analyzing the process of the looking-glass self, Cooley argued that we can glean quite a bit about how society works on a broader level.

Stages of Developing Self-Consciousness

Considered to be one of the founders of social psychology, George Herbert Mead contributed significantly to the development of symbolic interactionism during the 20th century (Morris, 1962/1934). His contributions were arguably more complex than that of Cooley (1902), conceptualizing a more detailed examination of how the individual mind and self both arise out of the social process. According to Mead, the **mind**, or individual psychology (how the mind works), is intelligible only in terms of social processes (Appelrouth & Edles, 2021). The mind develops by using symbols and language, deriving meaning from interactions, which includes an internal conversation of gestures or considering alternative lines of conduct based on past interactions. Inherent in this process, then, is the ability to be self-conscious, or reflexive, and consider how one's actions are affected by others and how those actions may be altered in the future.

Contrary to Cooley, Mead outlined the specific stages humans go through to arrive at the pinnacle of self-development, referred to by Mead as taking the role of the "other." There are three stages of intersubjective activity that we go through to get to this phase: (a) we learn language as early as infancy, based on interactions with our caretakers, (b) we imitate others in the play stage, and (c) we truly become self-aware as a member of an organized community in the game stage. Going through each of these stages is crucial to developing a "self" and becoming self-conscious. Humans enter the play stage typically during childhood, when children are able to take on a role they observe in those around them. An example would be a child pretending to be a superhero; as a result of playing this role, children are able to learn that they are both subject and object. This means the child understands the difference between their true "self" and the role they are acting out. They have specific gestures, language, and maybe even a costume that they use to "act out" the role of superhero. In the play stage, the child can only take on and understand one role at a time; it is merely play.

The game stage, on the other hand, is referred to as such because it is best understood in the context of a game. This phase of development occurs when children are able to more fully understand their sense of self in the context of others. That is, Mead explained the roles of others as part of a larger set of interactions, offering the example of a baseball game to illustrate this stage:

> But in a game where a number of individuals are involved, then the child taking one role must be ready to take the role of everyone else. ... He must know what everyone else is going to do in order to carry out his own play. He has to take all of these roles. ... In the game, then, there is a set of responses of such others so organized that the attitude of one calls out the appropriate attitudes of the other. (Morris, 1962/1934, p. 151)

Therefore, the game stage is a much more sophisticated and mature understanding of group roles and dynamics than the play stage. During early socialization, children enrolled in organized sport learn not only their own place in the game, but they also learn the roles of all others who are involved with them in the game. They also need to comprehend the rules of the game, which condition the various roles. Granted, this analysis does not apply to very young children who, for example, play soccer and chase the ball around like a swarm of bees, each of them trying to kick the ball at once. Instead, the game stage involves a more mature understanding of positioning and each individual player's role and expectations. Once humans are able to truly understand their role, the roles of their teammates, and the purpose of the game, they become much closer to understanding the generalized other.

The **generalized other** refers to an organized set of attitudes that are common in the group to which an individual belongs. According to Mead, when the individual can view herself from the standpoint of the generalized other, "self-consciousness in the full sense of the term" is attained (Morris, 1962/1934, p. 195). Of course, it is important to note here that the fact that children are enrolled in a sports team, doesn't mean they are truly "done" developing. We are constantly exposed to the attitudes of the generalized other throughout our lives.

There are multiple generalized others that are specific to different contexts; think of it as a set of expectations associated with different groups. For example, we have a general idea of what the expectations of parents are in any given society. At the most basic level, parents are supposed to care for their children, provide basic necessities, and help socialize them to become full members of society. However, those expectations vary from culture to culture and have definitely changed over time. For example, Ana, from our case study, has experienced some pushback from her grandparents for choosing to start a family on her own. The generalized other that her parents experienced growing up in a traditional, Catholic family in Brazil suggests that getting pregnant out of wedlock is frowned upon. Ana's grandmother has told her more than once that she disapproves of her decisions "because a child needs a father." However, this view is becoming outdated, as society evolves and we redefine what it means to be a family. For example, Sanner et al. (2019) used the lens of symbolic interaction theory to examine how young adults constructed kinship relationships with their "inherited" stepgrandparents—that is, the parents of their stepparents. They found that young adults were able to put aside biological definitions of family and emphasize co-constructed meanings, especially when the older adults made explicit efforts to develop close, affectionate relationships with them that revealed the "symbols" of family ties.

FIGURE 4.1. Generalized Other

The generalized other changes over time as social norms change. Figure 4.1 depicts how the generalized other evolves over time. The widespread use of social media has played a major role in helping individuals explore aspects of their gender identity. Today, nonbinary individuals are able to access the generalized other like never before and compare their own internal experiences via social media threads, crowdsourcing, and hashtags, which expand their frame of reference significantly. In another example, think about how access to birth control, adoption, artificial insemination, and sperm banks has changed the way we view families over time. Before these resources were available, individuals were limited in how they were able to start (or prevent) having a family. But now, access to different technologies and second-parent adoption opens up possibilities for individuals to define and redefine "family." Symbolic interactionism is unique compared to the other theories presented in this book because it allows family researchers, practitioners, and policymakers to focus on how our interactions with these "objects" (e.g., laws, policies, and technologies) change over time, making room for new realities and meanings for individuals and families.

As you are probably starting to see by reading through different theorists' approaches and contributions to symbolic interactionism, this framework represents a variety of theoretical ideas about families (see

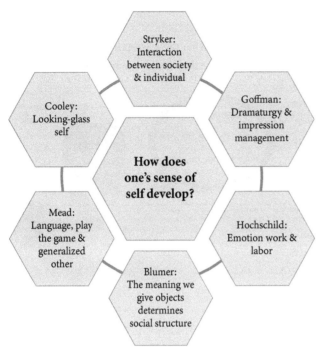

FIGURE 4.2. Comparison of Symbolic Interactionists' View of Self

Figure 4.2). While it would be impossible to cover every theorist and concept in this chapter, we do present six key theorists important to the application of symbolic interactionism to the family. While Cooley and Mead are considered classical symbolic interactionists, Blumer, Goffman, Hochschild, and Stryker, covered below, are more contemporary theorists, who drew on the work of earlier scholars.

Naming Symbolic Interactionism

Though Mead and Cooley contributed to the broad framework we now know as symbolic interactionist theory, it was not until the latter half of the 20th century that Herbert Blumer (1969) officially coined the phrase "symbolic interactionism." As a student of Mead, Blumer based most of his theoretical insights on Mead's work. Like Mead, Blumer argued that social structure does not determine individual action; instead, humans engage in interaction to make sense of the world around them, thereby creating a **conversation of gestures**. The social structures that are external to humans are significant "only as they enter into the process of interpretation and definition out of which joint actions are formed" (Blumer, 1969, p. 75). What this means is that rules, laws, regulations, and social institutions are only effective in guiding our behavior if they are relevant to us. Consider laws that exist "on the books" but do not affect how we go about our daily lives. In Connecticut, it is illegal to walk across the street on your hands, and it is also illegal for anyone to try to stop a child from playfully jumping over puddles of water (Brandeslaw.com, 2016). In Nebraska, a parent may be arrested if their child cannot hold back a burp during a church service. There are dozens more examples of these types of laws that are still in existence but likely not enforced or prosecuted. This reinforces Blumer's assertion that "it is the social process in group life that creates and upholds the rules, not the rules that create and uphold group life" (p. 19). While parents may be embarrassed if their children burp in church, it is likely not because they fear arrest, but instead, they fear social judgment from their peers.

Impression Management and Dramaturgy

Erving Goffman contributed much to the study of symbolic interactionist theory, even though he did not see himself as a symbolic interactionist (Appelrouth & Edles, 2021). He drew heavily from many social theorists but derived his most famous concepts from Mead's assertion that we "divide ourselves up in all sorts of different selves with a reference to our acquaintances. ... There are all sorts of different selves answering to all sorts of different social creations" (Morris, 1962/1934, p. 142). In this excerpt, Mead hinted at the possibility that we actively present a different "self" to significant others, depending on the situation. Goffman (1959) elaborated on this in one of his most famous works, *The Presentation of Self in Everyday Life,* which describes how face-to-face interactions can be likened to theatrical performances.

Inherent in Goffman's conceptualization of symbolic interactionism is the presence of motivation. By suggesting that "all the world is a stage," Goffman (1959) argues that social actors try to control or guide the impression others form of them, which is referred to as **impression management**. We manipulate performances based on who is in the "audience" and what kind of impression we are trying to achieve. Goffman also identified a **front stage**, where we tailor a performance for an audience, and a **backstage**, where we retreat from the performance. Socialization, then, consists of learning to perform on the stages of life.

As you read this and consider Goffman's conceptualization of **dramaturgy**, or the idea that life is acted out like a stage drama or play, you can probably identify times in your own life where you attempted to control others' impressions. Let's revisit the example of Snapchat from earlier in this chapter. Have you ever *not* posted a photo to Snapchat because it would give off an impression to your Snapchat audience you are not comfortable with? Maybe your grandfather (who is now on Snapchat, thanks to you!) would not approve of the photos of you partying with your friends, so maybe you share them only with a specific audience. Indeed, researchers from several different disciplines in countries, such as the United States and Norway, have delved into the world of social media analysis to investigate how impression management occurs in an online setting, such as Facebook (Chou & Edge, 2012; Rosenberg & Egbert, 2011) or Snapchat (Carlquist et al., 2019). This line of research indicates that Snapchat users tend to present themselves in a favorable way, which gives the impression they are happy. As a result, individuals who utilize Snapchat, Facebook, and other image-based social media applications frequently come to have the impression that others have better lives than they do. Though Goffman did not analyze social media as a "stage" where people manage impressions, it fits well for the purposes of studying his concepts. Can you think of other examples from the social media you use today that illustrate how Goffman's concept of dramaturgy, with front and backstage behavior, works in your own experiences?

When it comes to everyday interaction among family members and loved ones, Goffman's concepts offer valuable insight as well. For instance, consider the "stage" you perform on as part of your interactions with your immediate family. It is likely that you find yourself in the backstage, where you can retreat from acting out a concerted performance, more often than the front stage, because at home we are able to truly be ourselves. Indeed, Goffman (1959) argues that in the backstage, "the performer can relax; he can drop his front, forego speaking his lines, and step out of character" (p. 112). You may have seen your family members stepping out of character at home as well; perhaps, your parents show anger, resentment, and disappointment at home when only the nuclear family is present but put on a "face" when there are guests in the home. Viewing these exchanges within the context of a performance adds a level of complexity to understanding what meaning we derive from interaction. Goffman's theory helps us imagine not only how we and others *should* appear in social situations but also how self-interest and preservation motivates our presentation of self. If you want to borrow the car to take your friends to a party, you have most likely learned over time which "self" to present to your parents when you ask for the car. This skill is learned and honed over time and is undoubtedly salient for families, couples, and children as they interact over the life course.

Emotions

Arlie Russell Hochschild (1979; 1983) has published extensively on issues of the family, and you will read about her work in other chapters, such as conflict theory (Chapter 3). In this chapter, we present some of her earlier theorizing, which focused on "feeling work," or the management of emotions and nicely complements Goffman's interactional model. To Hochschild (1983), emotions are "biologically driven" (p. 219) as well as interactional—directly tied to behavior as we engage in interaction. We perform **emotion work** when we attempt to change a feeling so that it is appropriate for the situation. Social guidelines dictate what emotions are appropriate and when, which means we have to actively produce and manage them. Hochschild notes the gendered difference in emotion work, pointing out that men and women often "do" emotions much differently and for different reasons. Women, who in general have far less access to power, wealth, and authority, turn their emotions into a resource and offer it to men as a gift in return for the resources they lack (Hochschild, 1983). Particularly among middle-class families, women tend to engage in "emotion work that affirms, enhances, and celebrates the well-being and status of others" (Hochschild, 1983, p. 165). Men, on the other hand, have the "socially assigned task of aggressing against those that break rules of various sorts, which creates the private task of mastering fear and vulnerability" (Hochschild, 1983, p. 163). Have you ever heard the infamous words, "Wait until your father gets home!" uttered in frustration by someone's mother? Emotion work can manifest itself in various ways, so when you really think about it, chances are you can identify it in many different types of family communication.

Hochschild (1983) extends the idea of emotion work into the paid labor force, suggesting that **emotional labor** also exists to "sell" emotions to customers. Emotional labor is increasingly common in the service industry and is regularly used by restaurant servers, flight attendants, and retail salespeople, among others. Individuals working in such roles have to sell emotion as part of their service in order to increase tips or have satisfactory performance evaluations. This includes smiling, being courteous and pleasant, and other methods of what Hochschild refers to as surface acting, which is when individuals alter their displayed emotions but not their private emotions (e.g., having a terrible day but not letting it show to your customers). Deep acting occurs when both the inner and outer feelings are altered because of the pressure to perform emotional labor. Finally, genuine acting refers to when our felt emotions are already congruent with expressed emotions. In her description of genuine acting, Hochschild references the global trend of transnational care work we discussed in Chapter 1. Referring to this type of global emotional labor as a heart transplant, Ehrenreich and Hochschild (2003) describe how women from less developed countries leave their own young families and older family members to work as nannies or caregivers in affluent countries such as the United States, Israel, and Taiwan. By transplanting their love and care from their own family to a new family they now work for, women have to manage their own grief and anguish from leaving their families behind in their home countries.

Roles and Identity

Sheldon Stryker (1959; 1964) is best known for his work on identity theory, which draws on Mead and actually counters the work of Blumer. Stryker introduced a social-structural view of symbolic interactionism, centered on the reciprocal relationship between self and society. That is, Stryker argued that a theoretical framework must be able to move from the level of the person to that of large-scale social structure and back again (Stryker, 1964). This is in opposition to earlier symbolic interactionist work that suggested that interactions determined social structure—not the other way around. Stryker, on the other hand, believed that society and the individual are integral to one another; understanding one is impossible without taking the other into account.

Stryker's most famous concepts, then, make up the middle ground that earlier symbolic interactionist work was arguably missing: roles and identities. Individuals fulfill roles, or behavioral expectations and meanings that are attached to positions located in the social structure (Appelrouth & Edles, 2021). Roles are structural in nature but are filled by individuals, who, in turn, internalize those roles and build the concept of the "self." Thinking back to Ana from our case study, we can see that she wants to someday soon fulfill the role of mother. To her, this role in society carries weight and importance. In addition, Ana specifically wants to be able to carry her own biological child. She could have chosen to adopt or to become a foster parent, but those roles carry different meanings and are situated differently in the social structure. For example, as Willis Hepp et al. (2019) revealed in their analysis of adoptive parenthood using symbolic interactionist theory, nonbiological parenting includes additional experiences and interactions with broader social systems that affect both the transition to adoptive parenthood as well as its later adjustment.

Taking these factors into account, we are analyzing Stryker's (1980) structural side of identity. At the same time, we must analyze the micro-level processes that are impossible to untangle from Ana's decisions. Ana's sense of identity as a biological mother to her child is part of the sense of "self" she wants to achieve. Of the roles she could choose to fulfill on her journey to becoming a mother, being a biological mother carries more meaning for her. Using this example, we can see how **identity** (internalized expectations and meaning) and roles (structure) are inevitably both responsible for contributing to the complexity of the "self." The number of identities a person possesses corresponds to the number of structured role relationships in which they participate (Appelrouth & Edles, 2021).

Stryker's (1980) theoretical contributions to symbolic interactionist theory also include the concept of **identity salience,** which suggests that our identities are arranged in a hierarchy. This means that your identities, as a student, child, sibling, parent, worker, or best friend, are all arranged in order of importance in the construction of your identity. Identity salience is evident in the concept of a **significant other** (Stryker, 1964), in that greater priority is given to the perspectives of certain individuals over others. Depending on the situation you find yourself in, you are most likely to invoke an identity that is more important to you. As an example, let's imagine you and your significant other are having a heated fight that may end the relationship. The problem is you also have an important exam the next day, so you are thinking about how to best handle this situation. According to Stryker, you will make a choice based on which identity is most salient to you at that time. Which would you choose?

BOX 4.2. SYMBOLIC INTERACTIONIST THEORY IN MODERN CULTURE: *SOUL*

Image 4.1 A Scene From *Soul*, 2020

Soul, an academy-award winning animated film that features the first Black protagonist in a Pixar movie, follows a jazz musician who has a near-death experience and gets stuck in "The Great Before," where souls exist before they inhabit bodies and are sent to earth. Throughout the film, Joe wrestles with regret, disappointment, and the meaning of his own life. Because of this narrative, examples of Cooley's looking-glass self are evident throughout the film. As he processes his own life and what he feels he missed out on by "dying," he thinks through what he has

meant to everyone in his life and comes to realize at the end of the film just how important it is to be mindful, present, and grateful.

Film critics and philosophers alike appreciated the psychological underpinnings of this animated film as they delved into issues surrounding how our individual personalities develop. Sociologists and symbolic interactionists would likely argue that much of our personality development stems from our social interactions, and without other humans, we would not fully develop as complete human beings. Yet in this film, personalities are developed in the "Great Before" and then sent to earth to inhabit a body. One of the main characters, 22, played by Tina Fey, had inhabited the bodies of Gandhi, Abraham Lincoln, and Mother Teresa. Because of those experiences, they are very hesitant to return to Earth. Sociologically speaking, those experiences likely shaped their view of earth and humanity in a very unique way, leaving them fairly pessimistic as a result. This is just one (of many) examples of symbolic interactionist theoretical concepts throughout the film.

Evaluating Symbolic Interactionist Theory

Strengths of Symbolic Interactionist Theory

As you are noticing throughout this book, all theories have strengths and weaknesses. Symbolic interactionist theory is a very popular family theory because its tenets can be easily applied from one research setting to another. Unlike functionalist theory (see Chapter 2), symbolic interactionist theory is not a "grand theory" that purports to explain "the facts." Rather, this theory is applicable to multiple ways in which human beings and their circumstances change over time.

One of the Most Influential of All the Family Theories

Symbolic interactionist theory has a long history in the family science field, and it is considered one of the "classical" theories in sociology. Yet at the same time, the theory remains relevant to contemporary applications and has stood the test of time, as illustrated in Walters's (2021) recent use of the theory to understand the meanings individuals ascribe to their experience of sex. Although functionalism has had many critics, symbolic interactionism has never gone out of style. In fact, LaRossa and Reitzes (1993) claim that this theory has had the greatest impact on the study of families since its original application. Symbolic interactionist concepts such as "significant other" have made their way into popular culture and everyday speech. The theory provides an excellent way to utilize concepts about how family members develop a shared sense, or symbolic reality, of the world.

Easy to Integrate With Other Theories

Symbolic interactionist theory is often combined with other perspectives because no other theory does a better job of understanding how human beings are socialized and interact with one another on a micro level of analysis. Early family theorists combined symbolic interactionism, as a micro perspective, and structural functionalism (Chapter 2), as a macro perspective, that led to the creation of family developmental theory (Rodgers, 1973), which we discuss in Chapter 5. More recently, Garrett-Peters and Burton (2015) combine symbolic interactionist theory principles about dramaturgy, self-conceptions, identities, and motive talk, with critical perspectives on the social worlds of poverty and uncertainty to offer an alternative explanation of low-income single mothers' approaches to both marital delay and intention to marry. Glass and Few-Demo (2013), which we discuss below, combined symbolic interactionist theory with Black feminist theory. These innovative theoretical pairings deepen our understanding of family process because symbolic interactionist theory so richly describes the complex and diverse ways humans learn how to be members of families through social interaction.

Highly Compatible With Qualitative Research Methods

Many family theories are rich with ideas and explanations but do not translate well into the practice of guiding a research study. For example, in Chapter 5, we will find that family developmental theory is considered conceptually rich but methodologically poor. That is, many theories in the field are very useful in organizing concepts and providing an explanation of family process and structure, but when scholars try to put the theory into research practice, it is difficult to create hypotheses and research questions that are easily answered through empirical methods. Unlike other theories that are difficult to operationalize, symbolic interactionism goes hand in hand with qualitative research methods (Bogdan & Biklen, 2007). Symbolic interactionist theory provides the foundation for research studies that explore how human beings interact and make meaning in the world.

Symbolic interactionist ideas undergird the qualitative research practice of grounded theory methodology (Charmaz, 2014; Daly, 2007; Gilgun, 2013; LaRossa, 2005). This method provides a set of rules, or guidance, for helping researchers generate theory from the ground up. That is, this theory presumes that more relevant and accurate depictions of the lives of real people can only be generated from the actual observation and interviewing of people in their own social context. In their classic study of staff–parent communication on neonatal units, Bogdan et al. (1982) presented a grounded theory they called "Be honest but not cruel" to explain how doctors and nurses in an intensive neonatal care unit temper the information they share about an infant's chances of survival with the infant's parents. It would be difficult to obtain such a complex understanding of family trauma unless we saw it firsthand and generated theory from those observations.

Through the process of telling our stories, we help others get a glimpse into our worldview, which may include harsh realities. Telling our stories to a trusted person is a way to build bridges that allow us to co-construct meaning, helping others understand what we are going through, especially if they haven't walked in our shoes. In a recent example, Ashbourne et al. (2020) make this connection between symbolic interactionist concepts, such as the social construction of reality and the use of qualitative in-depth interviews with mothers and fathers from Syria and Iraq who have settled in Canada. In this study, Muslim parents, who have been displaced by war and have migrated as refugees to a new country, tell their stories alongside service providers who are helping them with the resettlement process. This analysis allows concepts of identity, context, and culture to come to life as families and practitioners tell their stories of trauma, survival, and empowerment. Thus, researchers ground their practices of data collection and analysis in everyday life experience and allow a theoretical explanation to emerge inductively (see Figure 1.2 in Chapter 1).

Weaknesses of Symbolic Interactionist Theory

Despite its popularity and usefulness, symbolic interactionist theory is not without its critics. Primarily, critics have charged that in promoting Burgess's (1926) idea of the "family as a unity of interacting personalities" the individuality, interpersonal conflicts, and social structural inequalities that challenge family unity are obscured (Cheal, 1991). Next, we examine three critiques that have been directed at symbolic interactionist theory. We also note that many of the limitations of this theory have been addressed by recent scholars, and it is, in the long run, maintaining its reputation as a central family theory.

Overestimates the Role of Human Agency

One of the main critiques of symbolic interactionist theory is the emphasis on human agency. The controlling nature of macrosystems are downplayed in this theory, which gives individual actors more power in determining their reality (also called the subjective fallacy) than external forces allow (LaRossa & Reitzes, 1993). In this sense, symbolic interactionist theory does not give as much weight to the conflict and inequality created by the economy, social institutions, and embedded stereotypes and systematic discrimination that conflict theory (Chapter 3), feminist theory (Chapter 8), and critical race theory (Chapter 12) address more directly and that theories that combine symbolic interactionism with other critical theories can address (e.g., Garrett-Peters & Burton, 2015; Glass & Few-Demo, 2013).

As an example of overestimating the role of human agency, symbolic interactionists would be interested in Ana and Jeremy's story and how they come to define their own situations and definitions of family. A macro-level theorist would criticize this perspective for not taking into account the forces outside of Ana and Jeremy that directly affect their choices. For instance, Ana is undoubtedly affected by our pronatalist society, which highly values having children. This is not the case around the world. Indeed, in some countries like India, governments have enacted policies aimed at reducing the number of births. At one point, the Indian government offered new cars for both men and women who volunteered for sterilization (BBC News, 2011). In addition, macro-level theorists would ask what other forces led to Ana's choice not to adopt: Was adoption too expensive? As you can see, critics of symbolic interactionism argue that by focusing on the dyad as the primary unit of analysis, the issue of power as an objective reality is obscured. Families differ in their ability to define what is real in their lives. In another example, minority group families and immigrants still must contend with the objective reality of prejudice and discrimination against their families that are imposed by external laws and structures outside of their control. Ana and her child will undoubtedly face questions about where the child's father is and why Ana and Jeremy did not get married because they do not fit the "ideal" that is defined at the structural level of society. In addition, imagine Ana as a Black woman; would she be perceived differently for being a single mother, based on her race? Or what if Ana is White and Jeremy is Black, and the child they create is biracial? An example like this demonstrates how symbolic interactionism can be critiqued for not focusing on such larger, macro-level factors as racism, classism, and heterosexism.

Not a Unified Theory

Another major critique of symbolic interactionist theory is that it is more of a loose collection of concepts than a formal, or grand, theory that attempts to explain human actors in families and society (Adamsons & Carter, 2022; Hill & Hansen, 1960; LaRossa & Reitzes, 1993). Although the very notion that it is even possible or necessary to have a grand theory, such as Sigmund Freud's theory of psychosexual development (Gay, 1995) or Talcott Parsons's (1951) theory of structural functionalism, to explain individual and family development has been widely criticized, most theorists from the symbolic interactionist tradition have not been willing or successful at developing the concepts into a formal and systematic theory. Consider the long history of symbolic interactionism, and the many versions that contributing theorists have added to the framework. Because the theory has been so adaptable, it is criticized for being too flexible and offering only a "mixed bag" of concepts (LaRossa & Reitzes, 1993, p. 154).

Downplays the Role of Emotion in Human Behavior

As a theory of social interaction, symbolic interactionism has been criticized for not being sensitive enough to the irrational, unconscious, and biological mechanisms that also control human behavior (LaRossa & Reitzes, 1993). In some ways, this criticism is unfounded because earlier theorists, such as Cooley in his notion of the looking-glass self, did suggest that emotions provide the motivation for individuals to engage in social relationships. As is often the case with theories that have stood the test of time, new theorists have built upon the criticisms by addressing the neglected aspects of the original theory. As noted above, Hochschild (1979, 1983) developed a theory of emotion work that explains how men and women learn to consciously manage their emotions in dealing with culturally appropriate gender identities (e.g., women as responsible for family work and men as responsible for breadwinning) when both spouses work outside the home (Erickson, 2005).

An Alternative Theory App: Family Systems Theory

In this chapter, we have presented the key concepts, historical origins, modern applications, and strengths and weaknesses of symbolic interactionist theory. It is both useful and interesting to compare theories to more easily pinpoint the differences between them, so in this chapter, we will compare symbolic interactionist theory to family systems theory, which we cover in more detail in Chapter 6.

Symbolic interactionist theory takes into account micro-level social relations to help us understand how individuals within families are socialized and develop identities as well as how they communicate and go about their daily lives. Family systems theory, on the other hand, gives us a panoramic view of all the subsystems that both influence and are influenced by families. A subsystem within a family can consist of dyads or triads; the dyad could be the two parents, and a triad could be three children. For each subsystem within the family unit, the pathways of communication are endless: The parents may argue over a child's behavior, which affects the child as well as their siblings. Family systems theory also takes into account hierarchies that exist within families, allowing researchers to analyze who in a family has the most and least amount of power and how that influences family communication. This theoretical perspective allows for an analysis of interaction and symbols but approaches the study of families from a more holistic perspective while doing so.

Next, we highlight how symbolic interactionist theory is applicable to the study of families across the globe. Marriage patterns and wedding rituals differ vastly, depending on the country's culture and history. Why do you think this is? How would symbolic interactionists explain the differences between the countries we highlight in Box 4.3?

Working With Symbolic Interactionist Theory: Integrating Research and Practice

Now that we have described the historical origins, key concepts, and strengths and weaknesses of symbolic interactionist theory, we turn our attention to how the theory can be used in practice. We then analyze an empirical study that was rooted in this theory to see how scholars put the theory to work in a research project. Finally, we present ideas about how the theory informs policies associated with race, adoption, and families.

Symbolic Interactionist Theory Today

Kerry Daly (2003) utilizes and expands ideas associated with symbolic interactionist theory to distinguish between the ways that families actually live day-to-day and the ways that scholars theorize about how families live their lives. Using the concept of **negative spaces**, Daly says that there are many aspects of everyday family activities that we have not seen or given a name to, as we attempt to explain how family members interact with one another. He theorizes that **culture** is an important way to understand the inner workings of families because cultural categories reveal what we value, as evidenced through how we dress and speak, what we believe, and how we make meaning of family experience. Culture provides us with a tool kit that guides us toward meaning and action (Swidler, 2001). In contrast to looking at the spaces of family life that are elusive, or hidden from view, many scholars have theorized about families as if cultural context does not matter. Daly (2003) proposes that we need to make visible the varied and unique ways that families construct meaning as they interpret cultural codes and beliefs.

Daly (2003) suggests three negative spaces that are important for understanding the meaning-making process in families. The first negative space concerns the realm of belief, feeling, and intuition. Here, Daly

BOX 4.3. GLOBAL COMPARISONS OF WEDDING RITUALS

Weddings are a major cultural event in which community values and meanings are revealed. Many Western countries tend to place more focus on the two partners. But in traditional cultures, families and entire communities are more central. At the same time, wedding ceremonies and celebrations combine elements of old and new customs. The following examples reveal that each society demonstrates what is important to them through the rituals associated with major life events. Although particular practices may vary, the elaborate nature of weddings, in terms of adornment, food, celebration, and the like, are evidence that these events are festive occasions that are meant to include the couple, their families, and their community. Here, we examine wedding traditions from around the world:

- **China:** One of the new customs to emerge in contemporary China is the wedding album. The bride and groom hire a professional photographer to pose them in different locations and outfits prior to their wedding. The highly stylized album does not contain pictures of the wedding ceremony itself.
- **Greece:** Most wedding customs feature the bride, but a tradition for Greek weddings involve the groom. The best man, or "koumparos," shaves the groom's face. Then, his new mother-in-law feeds him honey and almonds.
- **India:** Although there are many celebrations and rituals before, during, and after the traditional Hindu wedding ceremony, one of the most elaborate rituals is the Mehndi ceremony. Mehndi is an art form using henna dye, in which the bride's palms, wrists, arms, legs, and feet are decorated in elaborate and colorful designs.
- **Jamaica:** Weddings in Jamaica involve the entire community. Receptions have traditionally been held in the groom's home. They are lavish celebrations with flowers, food, games, dancing, and music, and often last for days.
- **Sami:** Lapland weddings of the Sami people include the entire community (from 600 to 2,000 guests). The bride and groom wear elaborate decorations in the form of traditional footwear made of reindeer skin and silver jewelry historic to their community.
- **United States:** A long-standing tradition in the United States is for the father to "give away" the bride to her new husband. More recently, both parents have walked their daughter down the aisle. Receptions often vary by how much money the couple, or their parents, can afford to spend.

Sources: https://sites.google.com/site/worldweddingtraditionsnet/home/international-wedding-traditions
https://www.brides.com/gallery/wedding-traditions-around-the-world

(2003) gives attention to the less rational and logical aspects of our lives. Although scholars typically study attitudes and activities, much of family life, in contrast, is characterized by very charged feelings, such as love, care, envy, anger, hurt, and disappointment. As Hochschild (1979) found, the family's emotional climate is highly charged, and families operate by unspoken feeling rules. For example, in some families, crying and feelings of sadness are frowned upon. Yet these negative spaces are important to explore for how feelings are allowed to be expressed. Feelings are often ambivalent, or comprised of both positive and negative emotions (Boss, 2016). Dahl and Boss (2020) discuss what Daly would likely call the negative space of being physically present but psychologically absent and the ambiguity that results. Other aspects of the feeling side of families are expressed through spirituality, religion, and how a family interprets the realm of the sacred. We can gain deeper insight into family interactions by examining their rituals. Further, the stories, or myths, that families tell about themselves are one of the chief ways they reveal what they believe is important. By understanding how emotions, spirituality, and the inherited myths are passed down through the generations, we can gain a deeper insight into their inner workings. Returning to our case study, how do you think the family culture in which Ana grew up differed from Jeremy's family culture? Ana was raised in a two-parent nuclear family and has a sister who is married with a son. Jeremy, on the other hand, grew up in a one-parent household after being abandoned by his mother. What stories and myths about the way families are supposed to be and look like were probably passed down to these two individuals? How have they affected their desires for having a biological child that one raises on a daily basis (Ana) or contributing to the creation of a life but not being involved in the child's daily life (Jeremy)?

The second of these negative spaces concerns consumption and the meaning that things reveal about family life (Daly, 2003). Families are constantly exposed to messages that promote the motivation to accumulate things. The objects we buy are an expression to others about what we value and what we can afford; these expressions of consumption are often invisible but very present within families. As an example, think about your own family's consumption patterns. Did your parent(s) buy generic brands of food at the grocery store, or was everything organic or name brand? Have you ever noticed how other families "do" food consumption? Some families eat out five times a week, and other families eat home-cooked meals every night. What we eat and what we are exposed to within our families says a lot about how we value brands, types of consumption (restaurant prepared or pre-pared at home by a parent or the entire family), and the image we are trying to give off. Going a step further, how have your own family rituals around food, mealtimes, and consumption been challenged by living through the COVID-19 pandemic?

The things that we buy also divide a family. Consumption is a negative space in which individuals in families communicate facts about their social class, gender, age, occupation, educational level, and the like. Think about the cars people buy and the number of cars owned by a family. What does it communicate about an individual and a family to drive a sedan, a Jeep, a luxury car, a smart car, a used car, or a minivan? Each of these vehicles conveys a message about its owner and occupants.

Finally, the third negative space concerns the location of family members in time and space. Daly (2003) describes how the relation between home and work or home and community create "territories of self" and boundaries within and between families. For example, what happens to family time when a parent has a long commute to work? How does a couple's ability to be emotionally close differ when they live in the same home, or when they live apart and have a "commuter" marriage (Murray et al., 2019)? How much time in housework is spent when one owns a large house or rents a small apartment? Technology, as well, is a major influence on time and space in family life. Today, many family members communicate primarily through texting or video calls (Hertlein & Twist, 2019). Even the concept of "picking up the phone" is outdated, as stationary telephones have all but been replaced by cell phones that can be kept on one's person at all times. Time and space are, thus, examples of negative spaces that new theoretical perspectives on symbolic interactionist theory suggest we should consider when studying the complex meaning-making process in families.

In a contemporary example, the experiences, behaviors, and meanings associated with fatherhood are especially relevant to contemporary uses of symbolic interaction theory because the study of families has largely been associated with mothers' and wives' perspectives (Allen et al., 2009), as we describe in Chapter 8 on feminist theory. Thus, many fatherhood researchers utilize variations of symbolic interactionist theory to examine conceptual issues about a father's identity and roles (Adamsons & Pasley, 2013). Examples include the meanings Canadian men ascribed to their sense of identity as both a man and a father in response to the influence of their children (Daly et al., 2012) and how incarcerated fathers involved in the illegal drug economy in Norway struggled with their paternal identity, especially in terms of their absence from their children (Grundetjern et al., 2021). Other contemporary contexts in which fatherhood researchers utilize symbolic interactionist theory include the relational dynamics of cooperation (rather than the stereotype of competitive masculinity) between stepfathers and their stepchildren's biological fathers (Marsiglio & Hinojosa, 2007) and the development of fathering identities across social media platforms, such as "dad blogs" (Scheibling, 2020; Scheibling & Marsiglio, 2021). As a result of these emerging trends in the literature, it could be argued that what Daly (2003) referred to as negative spaces are, nearly two decades later, becoming more prominent in research and theorizing on families.

Symbolic Interactionist Theory in Research

In their qualitative study of 11 Black lesbian couples, Valerie Glass and April Few-Demo (2013) ground their analysis in symbolic interactionist theory but also integrate how Black feminist theory (Few, 2007) is useful to address the issue of power. This study is an example of how well symbolic interactionism blends with other theories, especially critical perspectives that challenge the status quo (Allen & Henderson, 2022). By combining these theories, the authors were able to show that Black lesbian couples had unique sources of support and constraint from their various communities. For example, extended family members were more likely to accept their daughter's lesbian partner as a friend, rather than seeing the two women as a couple. Although they downplayed the lesbian relationship by desexualizing it, they did not reject their daughter or her "friend." Given the great importance of family and kinship ties in the Black community, families were able to deal with the contradiction of keeping a lesbian daughter close without having to approve of the lesbian relationship. Further, given the significance of religion in the Black community, many of the couples still participated in religious services but did so as individuals, not as a couple.

Symbolic interactionist theory allowed Glass and Few-Demo (2013) to interpret the cultural contradictions of being a lesbian and being a Black woman whose family traditions value kinship and church communities. At the same time, the lesbian couples had to deal with subtle racism in the lesbian, gay, bisexual, transgender, or queer (LGBTQ+) community and a bias against parenthood (10 of the 11 couples had children living in their home). It was hard to find family-friendly spaces for lesbian parents in their communities, as most of the women lived in rural locations outside of the urban areas that have large and diverse LGBTQ+ members. Still, the constraints of race, gender, sexual orientation, geography, and maternal status did not stand in the way of creating a "homeplace" that honored their lesbian and family identities. As Glass and Few-Demo (2013) explain, Black feminist theory defines **homeplace** as a self-supporting safe space where minority individuals can experience the safety, affection, and full acceptance not available in the wider society (hooks, 1997). Thus, the integration of symbolic interactionism and Black feminist theory allowed the authors to uncover how women with racial and sexual minority status interpreted and enacted contradictory cultural values, symbols, and roles in self-supporting ways.

Symbolic Interactionist Theory in Practice

There are many ways educators, practitioners, and policymakers can apply symbolic interactionism in their work with individuals and families. Though symbolic interactionism has been critiqued for not being applicable to studying macro-level phenomena, one of the areas this theory is relevant is in the study of racially stratified adoption fees. As a family practitioner or researcher, you will likely confront the issues of adoption or racial discrimination, either separately or perhaps together. The two issues are important to consider together because transracial adoptions are increasing annually in the United States (Goldberg, 2019; Lee, 2003) and how much a family will pay to adopt is directly related to the race of the child. Why is such a macro-level system important to the application of symbolic interactionism? It is important because the ways in which we make meaning of race varies from person to person and culture to culture. In the United States, adoption agencies are able to charge significantly higher for a healthy White baby than they are a baby of any other race or ethnicity, a trend that has been documented in research for decades (Sokoloff, 1993). In a recent book, Raleigh (2018) critiqued the ways in which adoption agencies reinforced the global racial hierarchy in their work:

> Adoption workers played up these distinctions by differentially pricing, labeling, and allocating biracial Black children. Likewise, adoption agencies also perpetuated the idea that the placement of foreign born Black children would be different from adopting a native-born Black child, permitting White parents to characterize their African children as 'not Black.' Taken together, these racialized policies and practices actively bolstered the delineation between children who are full African American and those who are not. (p. 5)

While this may seem on the surface to be a macro-level issue, it is important to note that from a symbolic interactionist perspective, there is much to be said about perceptions of race and individual and family identity. Indeed, sociological researchers have found that prospective adoptive parents prefer a child who shares similar traits with them, such as race or ethnicity, so they may better resemble a biologically formed family (Ishizawa & Kubo, 2014). In addition, families with biological children have pursued international adoptions, so the adopted child would not look different from the siblings (Kubo, 2010). The family in these cases prefers to have a racially matched family, hesitating to adopt transracially because of the fear that they would be criticized, for instance, by the Black community for not being culturally equipped to raise Black children (Brooks et al., 2002). Therefore, from a symbolic interactionist standpoint, we can see evidence of the looking-glass self, the importance of the family identity, and how the meaning we assign to individuals based on race are key to understanding racially stratified adoption fees.

BOX 4.4. VOICES FROM LIVED EXPERIENCE

Katherine is a bereaved mother who lost her son when he was 23 years old to suicide. Never a big Facebook user, she now finds Facebook very difficult to even look at. She reflects on how social media is often used to present idealized images of ourselves:

> Like many people, I have often found myself putting my best foot forward in the public eye and sharing the joys and successes of my life, especially when it involves my loved ones. Then tragedy struck and my beloved son died by suicide. Gone were the opportunities to write the holiday letters about his latest accomplishment or to post on social media how he was graduating from college or getting a new job or becoming engaged. Losing a child in such a devastating way is not the content of the social media posts I often read that are full of elation, accomplishment, and celebration. Now, I am at a loss. How do I share this devastating experience and its aftermath with others on social media platforms? The answer is, I don't. Social media is very limited when it comes to sharing about the ways that our own families don't live up to the idealized images. There is always another side to what and how we present our intimate lives and experiences. For example, one of the most taboo topics to discuss is death, and this is not something that will get a lot of likes or hearts on social media. In the Parent Bereavement Support Group that I co-facilitate with a friend who lost her son to a drug overdose, we parents often talk about the painful experience of family and friends sharing only about "when things go right" or the positive side of their family experiences, as if they were oblivious to the things that happen in almost every family, for which there are "no words." Social media provides a snapshot—not the realities and complexities of family life that we discuss in this book.

Conclusion

Symbolic interactionism has provided important ideas that allow researchers and practitioners to put the theory to use beyond the conceptual level. From its earliest days as a theory of self and mind to its current uses as a theory that helps us understand emotions and diverse social contexts, symbolic interactionist theory covers a wide range of territory regarding the microprocesses in families. We encourage you to consider these varied applications of the theory as you move on to the discussion questions, reflection questions, and areas for further study in the concluding pages of this chapter.

Multimedia Suggestions

www.symbolicinteraction.org

The Society for the Study of Symbolic Interaction (SSSI) is an international professional organization of scholars and researchers who study issues such as identity, language, and everyday life. SSSI publishes the journal *Symbolic Interaction*, hosts an annual conference where scholars present their latest work, and offers a number of honors and awards, including the George Herbert Mead Award for Lifetime Achievement, the Charles Horton Cooley Award for Recent Book or Article, and the Herbert Blumer Graduate Student Paper Award.

Activate your theory app: Browse through the website, and see if you can find other examples of current theorizing and/or contemporary research studies, using this theory in the conference program and recent journal issues.

www.youtube.com/watch?v=mTKv8AhH1Xc

This video, *Black Doll White Doll The Story*, was created by U.S. high school student Kiri Davis in 2006 as a follow-up to Kenneth and Mamie Clark's famous doll study from the 1930s and 1940s. In the video, Kiri shows 21 young Black American children either a White or Black doll with the exact same features, except for skin color. Kiri asked the children similar questions to the ones the Clarks asked: which doll they would prefer to play with, which one was nice, and which one was bad. The final question asked the children which doll was most similar to them. Fifteen of the children chose the White dolls over the Black dolls, giving reasons similar to the ones the Clarks heard. These results indicate that, even among very young children, individuals' self-concept and identities are very important to understanding structural issues of racism.

Activate your theory app: How can we explain the interactions in the video, using symbolic interactionist concepts? Consider how individuals' self-concepts and identities develop when it comes to experiencing structural (albeit invisible) issues of racism.

Trigonometry (2020–present)

Image 4.2 AA Scene From *Trigonometry*, 2020

Symbolic interactionist theory is evident in nearly every film and television show because the theory is so adaptable and applicable, which makes it hard to narrow down the focus to just one example. British Broadcasting System's (BBC's) original series *Trigonometry* explores the meaning of relationships as main characters Gemma and Kieran take on a roommate, Ray. This show bravely navigates the complexities of this budding "thrupple," a colloquialism used to describe an intimate, romantic relationship among three people. Throughout the series, the main characters deal with their own families of origin, relationships with parents, and how those foundational experiences impact the ways in which they show up as adults. This show undoubtedly illustrates symbolic interactionist concepts surrounding emotion work, conversation of gestures, and identity, to name a few.

Activate your theory app: How does this show disrupt the dominant narrative of the "typical" relationship and family? Do we see examples of chosen family in this show?

Euphoria (2019–present)

Euphoria is an American television show based loosely on an Israeli show created by Ron Leshem and Daphna Levin. The show centers the voices of adolescents as they deal with difficult issues, like drug addiction, mental health, sexual relationships, identity, and significant trauma. This show is full of incredibly tough scenes, in which young people are forced to grapple with intense situations that illustrate how difficult it is to come of age in a highly sexualized, drug-infused, and traumatic world.

Image 4.3 A scene from *Euphoria*, 2019

Much of the present trauma these teenagers deal with stems from early childhood experiences and unresolved relationship strain.

Activate your theory app: Which symbolic interactionist concepts can you see in this television show? Do any parts of the show resonate with your own coming-of-age experiences?

Further Reading

Blakely, K. (2008). Busy brides and the business of family life: The wedding-planning industry and the commodity frontier. *Journal of Family Issues, 29*(5), 639–662. https://doi.org/10.1177/0192513X07309453 Kristin Blakely built upon Ehrenreich and Hochschild's (2003) ideas about the commercialization of intimate life to examine how families now "outsource" work that has traditionally been done within the home. Such work includes takeout meals as a substitute for home cooking, the use of nannies to care for children as a substitute for maternal care, dry-cleaning as a substitute for doing the family's laundry, maid services, dog walking services, birthday party planning services, and a host of other activities that were once the primary responsibility of women. To this list, Blakely added the role of wedding planning as a new "commodity frontier," in which domestic work has expanded into the paid labor market. She suggested that this increasing outsourcing of family work may allow for women to work outside the home, but it is not without its costs. As we become more and more detached from the actual work of caring for self and family, we may experience greater disenchantment and isolation from the very emotions and activities that keep us tied to one another.

Burr, W. R., Leigh, G. K., Day, R. A., & Constantine, J. (1979). Symbolic interaction and the family. In W. R. Burr, R. Hill, F. I. Nye, & I. L. Reiss (Eds.), *Contemporary theories about the family: General theories/Theoretical orientations* (Vol. 2, pp. 42–111). Free Press. In this classic chapter, Wesley Burr and colleagues describe the history of the application of symbolic interactionism to the study of families. They attempt to integrate the concepts associated with symbolic interactionist theory into a formal theoretical framework from which propositions can be used to guide research. This work provides a comprehensive review and comparison of the various schools of thought associated with the theory, such as the Chicago School, which emphasized the subjective development of self through interaction, and the school of thought that emphasized the objective roles and structures that are more deterministic in guiding human behavior in families.

Hochschild, A. R. (2013). *So how's the family? And other essays.* University of California Press. This book is a collection of some of Arlie Russell Hochschild's prolific work on contemporary family life. She addresses her current work on issues such as the use of surrogate mothers (e.g., wombs) to provide wealthy families with children they could not otherwise have. She also elaborates upon her ongoing work on how emotional labor is managed in families and other institutional settings, such as the workforce. The essay on "the two-way global traffic in care" applies an analysis of Goffman's (1959) concept of "back-stage behavior" to how migrant care workers come to work for wealthy families in developed countries. Their work is both necessary to support their own families back home but also poorly paid and devalued in their host countries.

Killoren, S. E., Updegraff, K. A., Christopher, F. S., & Umana-Taylor, A. J. (2011). Mothers, fathers, peers, and Mexican-origin adolescents' sexual intentions. *Journal of Marriage and Family, 73*(1), 209–220. https://doi.org/10.1111/j.1741-3737.2010,00799.x In this study of 246 families, the authors used a symbolic interaction perspective to address the serious sexual risks of Latino adolescents, who have the highest teen birthrates compared to any other ethnic background and higher rates of sexually transmitted infections than non-Latino Whites. They examined the interrelated roles of mothers, fathers, and deviant peer affiliations (with deviance being measured as the likelihood to use drugs, lying about one's age to buy or do things, etc.) in the choices Mexican immigrant youth and U.S.-born Latino youth make about their sexual activity. Contrary to expectations, they found that levels of parental acceptance and disclosure to parents did not differ across the two groups. A major factor, however, was that being born in the U.S. increased the likelihood that Latino youth would be influenced by the negative behaviors of their peers.

Leveto, J. A. (2018). Toward a sociology of autism and neurodiversity. *Sociology Compass, 12*(12), e12636. https://doi.org/10.1111/soc4.12636 In this interdisciplinary analysis of multiple literatures in the humanities and social sciences addressing the lives of individuals and families impacted by autism and neurodiversity, Leveto reviews the history of autism studies and juxtaposes the contributions of critically informed social justice work on behalf of those who live with neurodiversity. She brings a sociological perspective to this analysis by incorporating symbolic interaction principles, such as mind, self, meaning, and stigma. This both informs the current contentious debates around autism studies as well as shifts the cultural narratives about testing, diagnosis, and treatment of individuals with autism away from deviance and disordered to acceptance, understanding, and transformation.

Questions for Students

Discussion Questions

1. Generate a list of all of the types of family labor you can think of. Which family members tend to perform each task?

2. How does gender affect the way that emotions are managed in families and at work? Where do you see evidence of differences in how "emotional labor" is performed?

3. Considering that symbolic interactionism is easy to pair with other family theories, can you think of one that has very different assumptions and is not easily paired with this theory?

4. How would you use symbolic interactionist theory to guide a quantitative research study? Locate a recent quantitative study in the literature to see how symbolic interactionist ideas (e.g., stigma, self, mind, or gestures) are operationalized.

5. How is backstage behavior expressed on the internet? What about in other electronic communication?

6. In what ways do you think families are "a unity of interacting personalities"? In what ways does the concept of family conflict (Chapter 3) challenge this view?

Your Turn!

You are a school counselor and happen to overhear some middle schoolers' conversation as you are walking down the hall one day. They are joking and laughing about classmates they have found on OnlyFans, a website on which content creators sell provocative (and often pornographic) content of themselves. This website is supposed to verify that content creators are over the age of 18, so you immediately become concerned for a host of reasons. Once you get back to your office, you come up with a game plan on how to address this issue and how to carefully bring it to the attention of authorities. What do you decide is the best approach? How can the theories you have read about in this chapter inform your conversation with other school administrators about how to handle this? Come up with a communication plan, and base it on at least one of the theorists' concepts and theoretical framework.

Personal Reflection Questions

1. Give an example of how you may have experienced the looking-glass self as you grew up. How did family members or loved ones contribute to your self-perception?

2. How would you define your "self"? How has your sense of self been shaped by the ways you and your family members interact with one another?

3. Describe a situation in your family in which it was very important to *manage* your emotions. Now, find examples in other societies around the globe in which the cultural context dictates a different form of emotion management. What do you notice in this cultural comparison of emotions?

4. Who are the significant others in your own life? How long have these relationships lasted? How have they changed over time?

5. Give an example of "taking the role of the other" in your own life.

6. What are the metaphors and negative spaces that describe the kind of family in which you grew up?

References

Adamsons, K., & Carter, M. (2022). Symbolic interactionism. In K. Adamsons, A. L. Few-Demo, C. Proulx, & K. Roy (Eds.), *Sourcebook of family theories and methodologies*. Springer.

Adamsons, K., & Pasley, K. (2013). Refining identity theory to better account for context: Applications to fathering. *Journal of Family Theory & Review, 5*(3), 159–175. https://doi.org/10.1111/jftr.12014

Allen, K. R., & Henderson, A. C. (2022). Family theorizing for social justice: A critical praxis. *Journal of Family Theory & Review*. Advance online publication. https://doi.org/10.1111/jftr.12450

Allen, K. R., Lloyd, S. A., & Few, A. L. (2009). Reclaiming feminist theory, method, and praxis for family studies. In S. A. Lloyd, A. L. Few, & K. R. Allen (Eds.), *Handbook of feminist family studies* (pp. 3–17). SAGE Publications.

Appelrouth, S., & Edles, L. D. (2021). *Classical and contemporary sociological theory: Text and readings* (4th ed.). SAGE Publications.

Ashbourne, L. M., Atalla, S., Al Jamal, A., & Baobaid, M. (2020). Understanding the effects of involuntary migration on family relationships: Meaning construction by parents and service providers. *Journal of Constructivist Psychology, 34*(1), 36–55. https://doi.org/10.1080/10720537.2019.1700852

BBC News. (2011, July 1). *India: Rajasthan in 'cars for sterilisation' drive.* http://www.bbc.co.uk/news/world-south-asia-13982031

Bell, N. J. (2019). Relational developmental systems and family research: Considering qualitative applications. *Journal of Family Theory & Review, 11*(2), 230–242. https://doi.org/10.1111/jftr.12305

Blumer, H. (1969). *Symbolic interactionism: Perspective and method.* Prentice Hall.

Bogdan, R. C., & Biklen, S. K. (2007). *Qualitative research for education: An introduction to theories and methods* (5th ed.). Pearson.

Bogdan, R., Brown, M. A., & Foster, S. (1982). Be honest but not cruel: Staff/parent communication on neonatal units. *Human Organization, 41*(1), 6–16. https://doi.org/10.17730/humo.41.1.03x7x4214201v7p2

Boss, P. (2016). The context and process of theory development: The story of ambiguous loss. *Journal of Family Theory & Review, 8*(3), 269–286. https://doi.org/10.1111/jftr.12152

Brandeslaw.com. (2016). *Strange laws still on the books.* http://www.brandeslaw.com/Lighter/lawsob.htm.

Brooks, D., James, S., & Barth, R. P. (2002). Preferred characteristics of children in need of adoption: Is there a demand for available foster children? *Social Service Review, 76*(4), 575–602. https://doi.org/10.1086/342996

Burgess, E. W. (1926). The family as a unity of interacting personalities. *The Family, 7*(1), 3–9. https://doi.org/10.1177/104438942600700101

Carlquist, E., Proitz, L., & Roen, K. (2019). Streams of fun and cringe: Talking about Snapchat as mediated affective practice. *Subjectivity, 12*(3), 228–246. https://doi.org/10.1057/s41286-019-00074-9

Charmaz, K. (2014). *Constructing grounded theory* (2nd ed.). SAGE Publications.

Cheal, D. (1991). *Family and the state of theory.* University of Toronto Press.

Chou, H.-T. G., & Edge, N. (2012). "They are happier and having better lives than I am": The impact of using Facebook on perceptions of others' lives. *Cyberpsychology, Behavior, and Social Networking, 15*(2), 117–121. https://doi.org/10.1089/cyber.2011.0324

Cooley, C. H. (1902). *Human nature and the social order.* Schocken.

Dahl, C. M., & Boss, P. (2020). Ambiguous loss: Theory-based guidelines for therapy with individuals, families, and communities. In K. S. Wampler (Ed.), *The handbook of systemic family therapy* (Vol. 4, pp. 127–151). Wiley.

Daly, K. J. (2003). Family theories versus the theories families live by. *Journal of Marriage and Family, 65*(4), 771–784. https://doi.org/l0.1111/j.l741-3737.2003.00771.x

Daly, K. J. (2007). *Qualitative methods for family studies and human development.* SAGE Publications.

Daly, K. J., Ashbourne, L., & Brown, J. L. (2012). A reorientation of worldview: Children's influence on fathers. *Journal of Family Issues, 34*(10), 1401–1424 https://doi.org/10.11770192513X12459016

Ehrenreich, B., & Hochschild, A. (Eds.). (2003). *Global woman: Nannies, maids, and sex workers in the new economy.* Metropolitan Books.

Erickson, R. (2005). Why emotion work matters: Sex, gender, and the division of household labor. *Journal of Marriage and Family, 67*(2), 337–351. https://doi.org/10.1111/j.0022-2445.2005.00120.x

Few, A. L. (2007). Integrating Black consciousness and critical race feminism into family studies research. *Journal of Family Issues, 28*(4), 452–473. https://doi.org/10.1177/0192513X06297330.

Garrett-Peters, R., & Burton, L. M. (2015). Reframing marriage and marital delay among low-income mothers: An interactionist perspective. *Journal of Family Theory & Review, 7*(3), 242–264. https://doi.org/10.1111/jftr.12089

Gay, P. (Ed.). (1995). *The Freud reader.* W. W. Norton.

Gilgun, J. F. (2013). Qualitative family research: Enduring themes and contemporary variations. In G. W. Peterson & K. R. Bush (Eds.), *Handbook of marriage and the family* (pp. 91–119). Springer.

Glass, V. Q., & Few-Demo, A. L. (2013). Complexities of informal social support arrangements for Black lesbian couples. *Family Relations, 62*(5), 714–726. https://doi.org/10.111/fare.12036

Goffman, E. (1959). *The presentation of self in everyday life.* Doubleday.

Goldberg, A. E. (2019). *Open adoption and diverse families: Complex relationships in the digital age.* Oxford University Press.

Grundetjern, H., Copes, H., & Sandberg, S. (2021). Dealing with fatherhood: Paternal identities among men in the illegal drug economy. *European Journal of Criminology, 18*(5), 643–659. https://doi.org/10.1177/1477370819874429

Hertlein, K. M., & Twist, M. L. C. (2019). *The Internet family: Technology in couple and family relationships.* Routledge.

Hill, R., & Hansen, D. A. (1960). The identification of conceptual frameworks utilized in family study. *Marriage and Family Living, 22*(4), 299–311. https://doi.org/10.2307/347242

Hochschild, A. R. (1979). Emotion work, feeling rules, and social structure. *American Journal of Sociology, 85*(3), 551–575. https://doi.org/10.1086/227049

Hochschild, A. R. (1983). *The managed heart: Commercialization of human feeling.* University of California Press.

hooks, b. (1997). Homeplace (a site of resistance). In D. S. Madison (Ed.), *The woman that I am: The literature and culture of contemporary women of color* (pp. 448–454). St. Martin's Press.

Ishizawa, H., & Kubo, K. (2014). Factors affecting adoption decisions: Child and parental characteristics. *Journal of Family Issues, 35*(5), 627–653. https://doi.org/10.1177/0192513X13514408

Kerrick, M. P., & Henry, R. L. (2017). "Totally in love": Evidence of a master narrative for how new mothers should feel about their babies. *Sex Roles, 76*(1/2), 1–16. https://doi.org/10.1007/s11199-016-0666-2

Kubo, K. (2010). Desirable difference: The shadow of racial stereotypes in creating transracial families through transnational adoption. *Sociology Compass, 4*(4), 263–282. https://doi.org/10.1111/j.1751-9020.2010.00274.x

LaRossa, R. (2005). Grounded theory methods and qualitative family research. *Journal of Marriage and Family, 67*(4), 837–857. https://doi.org/10.111 l/j, 1741-3737.2005.00179.x

LaRossa, R., & Reitzes, D. C. (1993). Symbolic interactionism and family studies. In P. G. Boss, W. J. Doherty, R. LaRossa, W. R. Schumm, & S. K. Steinmetz (Eds.), *Sourcebook of family theories and methods: A contextual approach* (pp. 135–163). Plenum.

Lee, R. M. (2003). The transracial adoption paradox: History, research, and counseling implications of cultural socialization. *Counseling Psychologist, 31*(6), 711–744. https://doi.org/10.1177/0011000003258087

Marsiglio, W., & Hinojosa, R. (2007). Managing the multifather family: Stepfathers as father allies. *Journal of Marriage and Family, 69*(3), 845–862. https://doi.org/10.1111/j.1741-3737.2007.00409.x

Mead, G. H. (1934). *Mind, self, and society.* University of Chicago Press.

Morris, C. W. (Ed.). (1962). *Mind, self, and society. Vol. 1 of Works of George Herbert Mead.* University of Chicago Press. (Original work published 1934)

Murray, L., McDonnell, L., Hinton-Smith, T., Ferreira, N., & Walsh, K. (Eds.). (2019). *Families in motion: Ebbing and flowing through space and time.* Emerald.

Parsons, T. (1951). *The social system*. Free Press.

Raleigh, E. (2018). *Selling transracial adoption: Families, markets, and the color line*. Temple University Press.

Rodgers, R. H. (1973). *Family interaction and transaction: The developmental approach*. Prentice Hall.

Rosenberg, J., & Egbert, N. (2011). Online impression management: Personality traits and concerns for secondary goals as predictors of self-presentation tactics on Facebook. *Journal of Computer-Mediated Communication, 17*(1), 1–18. https://doi.org/10.1111/j.l083-6101.2011.01560.x

Sanner, C., Ganong, L., Coleman, M. Chapman, A., & Kang, Y. (2019). Building family relationships with inherited stepgrandparents. *Family Relations, 68*(4), 484–499. https://doi.org/10.1111/fare.12381

Scheibling, C. (2020). Doing fatherhood online: Men's parental identities, experiences and ideologies on social media. *Symbolic Interaction, 43*(3), 472–492. https://doi.org/10.1002/symb.459

Scheibling, C., & Marsiglio, W. (2021). #healthy dads: "Fit fathering" discourse and digital health promotion in dad blogs. *Journal of Marriage and Family, 83*(4), 1227–1242. https://doi.org/10.1111/jomf.12743

Sokoloff, B. Z. (1993). Antecedents of American adoption. *The Future of Children, 3*(1), 17–25. https://doi.org/10.2307/1602399

Stryker, S. (1959). Symbolic interaction as an approach to family research. *Marriage and Family Living, 21*(2), 111–119. https://doi.org/10.2307/348099

Stryker, S. (1964). The interactional and situational approaches. In H. T. Christensen (Ed.), *Handbook of marriage and the family* (pp. 125–170). Rand McNally.

Stryker, S. (1980). *Symbolic interactionism: A social structural version*. Benjamin/Cummings.

Swidler, A. (2001). *Talk of love: How culture matters*. University of Chicago Press.

Walters, T. L. (2021). Socialized sexual values and meanings ascribed to sex as predictors of the experience of sex: A theoretical model. *Journal of Family Theory & Review*. Advance online publication. https://doi.org/10.1111/jftr.12439

Willis Hepp, B., Hrapczynski, K., & Fortner-Wood, C. (2019). Using symbolic interactionism to model transitions to adoptive parenthood. *Journal of Family Theory & Review, 11*(2), 262–276. https://doi.org/10.1111/jftr.12326

Image Credits

Family Developmental Theory

ave your family members ever given you a hard time about when you are going to get married? Or if you're already married, maybe they ask when you are going to have kids. Or if you already have one child, why don't you have another? Family members, usually older than you, are notorious for trying to push young adults through the family life cycle stages, giving out cautionary advice that always starts with, "Wait until you … [fill in the blank]!" Maybe they have tried to tell you what it's like to move from being a couple to being married for three, seven, or even forty years. Young parents are often forewarned of what the transition is like going from two to three children or from having babies to having teenage children. Or maybe even farther down the road, you hear your retired grandparents talking about how wonderful retirement is and how you need to keep working hard now, so you can enjoy it later! It might be difficult to imagine that far into the future, but given how central the family life cycle is to how we see the world, it should be no surprise that family members who have "been there, done that" are trying to give us advice (wanted or unwanted!) about what to expect.

Family developmental theory considers each of these "stages" as part of the family life cycle, which is the central concept in this theory. Unlike other theories that focus on individual development you may have read about in a psychology or child development class, such as Sigmund Freud's model of psychosexual development (Gay, 1995), Erik Erikson's (1968) eight-stage model of human development, or Jean Piaget's (1952) four-stage model of cognitive development, family developmental theory does not begin with the individual. It begins with the creation of a family—the family of procreation. Because it was first developed in the 1940s–1950s, family developmental theory reflected the type of family that scholars envisioned back then: First, a man and a woman marry; then their first child is born, and they transition from being a couple to being parents; and then they go through the stages of expanding and contracting their family. The family life cycle begins with a marriage and ends with the death of both spouses. For each stage in the life cycle, there are expectations and developmental tasks assigned to individuals in those stages. Think about the rituals we enact in modern society associated with "entering" these stages of the family life cycle. For example, we give baby showers for mothers-to-be, filled with advice from women who have been through the stage the pregnant woman is about to enter. We usually have an idea of what to expect in each stage (based on the generalized other concept that you read about in Chapter 4 on symbolic interactionism), but for the most part, we learn and develop as we go through the family life cycle.

Given how we've described family developmental theory so far, you may already be noticing that this theory has roots in both functionalist theory (Chapter 2) and symbolic interactionist theory (Chapter 4). This is because family developmental theory is the result of merging the macroanalyses of structural functionalism and the microanalyses of interactionism with the innovative inclusion of the multiple dimensions of time. Thus, family developmental theory deals with the structural level (major social institutions), the interactional level (family dynamics and processes), and the individual level (personality variables) as they progress through sequential stages over time (Hill & Rodgers, 1964). Family developmental theory is about the very nature of change and development: how individuals in families interact at the micro level with each other and transact at the macro level with societal institutions across time (Rodgers, 1973). Other disciplines also recognize the utility of a family developmental perspective. For example, business management scholars utilized the transactional strength of family development theory to explain how family roles, relationships, and developmental tasks impact a family business developmental model for the enterprising family, defined as "a family that runs one or more businesses, and that has an intent to grow these businesses with the family as the foundation" (Minola et al., 2016, p. 296). These scholars posit that family development theory is appropriate for helping to understand how family businesses go through sequential life cycles that correspond with individual roles and responsibilities as generations age, die, and pass on businesses to younger generations in the family.

When first proposed, family developmental theory was hailed as the first major conceptual framework with a focus on the family. Specifically, it was created to place marriage and family in the center of how we study and understand the ever evolving nature of family interaction across the life of a family (Hill & Hansen, 1960). At the time when it was first conceptualized, this theory positioned the social group of the nuclear family as the key starting point for theorizing about and studying individual personality, family dynamics, and social institutions as they intersect over time (Mattessich & Hill, 1987). One of the major areas of study that this theory helps scholars understand is how families accomplish the tasks and milestones that are necessary for families to fulfill their prescribed normative roles in society at each stage of family life cycle (Aldous, 1978). Further, as the first family theory to factor in the temporal dimension (time), family developmental theory came before and influenced both life course theory (Chapter 9) and family ecological theory (Chapter 10). To gain a fuller understanding of how this theory works, we start with a case study that illustrates how members of the same family experience different stages of the family life cycle and how their interactions with each other contribute to varying developmental outcomes.

Case Study

The subject of our case study, Margo, was very sheltered by her parents, and learned very early to rely on her mother, Karen, for emotional support. Margo was handled with "kid gloves" her entire life; when she married an underemployed drifter, her parents pretended he was a good guy and spent thousands of dollars on a lavish wedding. Their marriage was rocky, to say the least. Margo, a bisexual, cisgender, White woman, situated squarely in the working class, had to work two jobs to support her husband because he could not hold down a steady job. Because of this, she struggled to find a way to manage her stress and strain. Her mother secretly intervened in Margo's life every step of the way, saving her from declaring bankruptcy and buying her a home to live in when she and her husband were forced out of their own home. Karen also paid for Margo's moving expenses when she finally filed for divorce from her husband after three years and moved back home with her parents.

After a few years, Margo moved out of her parents' home, remarried, and she and her new husband gave birth to a son. On the surface, their family appeared happy, healthy, and normal. However, Margo never learned how to cope with anger, frustration, or sadness. She sank into a deep depression after giving birth and asked Karen to move in with her, so she could help her take care of her newborn son. Having just retired herself, Karen was having a difficult time adjusting to being home with her husband all the time. He was verbally abusive and controlling, making him very unpleasant to be around. Though Karen suffered from disabling chronic pain, she loved being needed and welcomed the distraction of her daughter and grandson as a way to help her avoid her own relationship strain and the uncertainties associated with retirement.

Contrast this family scenario with how we envision love, marriage, and raising children before we enter these family life cycle stages. How is it that what we envision sometimes does not turn out to be true, when we eventually go through certain stages of the life cycle? Further, did Margo go through the appropriate

BOX 5.1. AT A GLANCE: FAMILY DEVELOPMENTAL THEORY

- **Family development:** The family is a social group in which growth occurs through the unfolding of predictable stages.
- **Family life cycle:** Families progress through a series of normative stages that begin with marriage, expand with adding children, contract with launching children, and end with the death of both spouses.
- **Family stage:** Families can best be studied by dividing up the structural changes in marriage and parenthood into model segments that all families experience.
- **Family time:** Families are long-lived groups with a history that incorporates three elements: individual time, social process time, and historical time.
- **Family developmental tasks:** Society assigns certain activities, or tasks, which families are expected to perform in order to ensure the survival of the family unit and the socialization of its members.
- **Societal-institutional dimension:** The family is charged with the responsibility of regulating reproductive roles of marriage and parenthood. As one of the key social institutions, families are influenced by broader cultural values and goals that dictate what is normal and valued.
- **Group-interactional dimension:** Families are a semi-closed system of interaction, where each individual family unit varies in the ways in which it enacts the societal-institutional expectations for family life.
- **Individual-psychological dimension:** The individual is the basic unit of the family, and each individual has a unique genetic makeup and unique family roles.

developmental stages at the normative time, or was she protected too much, never learning coping skills or strategies? And how was Karen transmitting values to Margo by avoiding conflict in her own marriage? Family developmental theory helps us understand how families move through developmental stages as they age, beginning with marriage, raising and launching children, having grandchildren, retirement, and death. This theory was developed to specifically analyze families, so it gives great insight into the stages both Margo and her mother have gone through thus far, including the developmental issues encountered along the way. This theory also helps us see how families deal with change, transitions, and timing of events across their lives and how they affect other family members along the way. Here we present the concepts of family developmental theory as well as important theorists who contributed to this perspective, including modern adaptations that make it applicable to today's changing families.

What Is Family Developmental Theory?

Family developmental theory is used to explain the unique functions, processes, and mechanisms for change associated with the family unit. The family unit is unique in that it is the social institution charged with the responsibility of regulating human reproduction, socialization, and survival. As we mentioned earlier, this theory was introduced to study families specifically, which makes it unique when compared to other theories that were borrowed from other social or psychological sciences and applied to families.

One of the biggest draws of using family developmental theory is that it helps scholars understand how families expand, contract, and change over time. Think about your own family and how it has changed since you were a toddler. Think about how you have changed—how your parents, siblings, grandparents, and even your extended family have changed! One of the most important concepts to consider when using this theory is the concept of **family development**. Family development is a longitudinal process of going through a hierarchical system of age and stage related changes. All families experience the processes of expansion and contraction throughout the family's history due to a multitude of changes, including birth, death, marriage, divorce, graduation, retirement, and any other developmental milestone. Family development can also involve a family crisis, like the one Margo from our case study experienced when she divorced her first husband and needed to move back home to reestablish financial and emotional security. Family crises will be discussed in more detail in Chapter 11 when we introduce family stress and resilience theory, but for now it is important to know that crises can and do often propel the family unit into the next phase of development. Theorizing about family crises first occurred under the rubric of family developmental theory, when Reuben Hill (1949), one of the architects of this theory, proposed the ABC-X model. The notion of both normative and stressful family transitions grew out of the experiences of the second World War, when families were in disarray and dealing with the stress and trauma of social change (Martin, 2018). Yet scholars also wanted to define the normative transitions families experienced, originally proposing that families progressed through eight stages that are marked by different family configurations, roles, relationships, and tasks, as explained by another architect of family developmental theory, Evelyn Duvall (1988). Because the family unit is a unique structure in society, all families are obligated to perform common functions. Thus, we often conceptualize a normative structure to families that we use to compare across all families. In the 21st century, however, and as we describe in Chapter 1, it is increasingly clear that family variation, not universality or uniformity, characterizes how families are structured and interact (Coontz, 2016; Goldberg & Allen, 2020; Jensen & Sanner, 2021; Laszloffy, 2002).

Given that this theory was developed specifically to analyze families, it assumes that "the typical family" is defined as a nuclear or conjugal unit that begins with the wedding of two young adults and continues until the death of the last spouse. This theory also suggests that each family begins the **family life cycle** with marriage, which signals the start of a new **family of procreation**, when partners start a new family of their own. Moving into the stage of procreation propels the family forward to new roles associated with parenthood. Then, once children leave the family nest, the family contracts back to the married couple. In its original conceptualization, the family created by the original married partners ends when both of them die.

At face value, family developmental theory argues that moving through these **family stages** is predictable across all families. Yet because society has changed significantly since this theory was first proposed, the nature of families as the unit for carrying out the reproductive function has changed as well. Just how rigidly family developmental theory is tied to normative stages, primarily associated only with the nuclear family of the parent and child generation, has always been a source of contention and continues to threaten the relevance of this important theory (Laszlolly, 2002; Martin, 2018). In the early years of the theory, Rodgers (1973) attempted to downplay the "stage" concept, and instead introduced "categories", but this way of framing the inevitability of family diversity across the generations can be clumsy and difficult to quantify. Recently, Crapo and Bradshaw (2021) proposed the multidimensional concept of "developmental space," with four dimensions (personal, vocational, couple, and generative) to move away from the conceptual problems associated with a rigid stage model and provide a more flexible, comprehensive approach to family change over time.

Other scholars have also altered the original concepts to include variations linked to additional aspects of marriage and parenthood. For example, not all family life cycles begin with marriage. Some families form when one person has a child and is not married to the child's other parent; this disentangling of marriage and parenthood is a key feature of family life today (Smock & Schwartz, 2020). The concept of monogamous marriage is challenged in many parts of the world, such as some sub-Saharan African nations, in which the practice of polygyny (a man having multiple wives) is common (Agadjanian, 2020). Some families are polyamorous and include multiple adult partners (Pallotta-Chiarolli et al., 2020). Further, unlike the original formulation of family developmental theory, many marriages do not end with the death of a spouse but, instead, end through desertion, permanent separation, or divorce. Although Hill (1986) did try to account for the rise of single-parent families in an earlier adaption to the theory, the variations in family structure are far too complex (Jensen & Sanner, 2021) to be captured in a simple amendment to the theory that still leaves the concept of a "normative" family intact. The experiences of cohabitation, relational dissolution, and repartnering—in any form—are likely to characterize the complexity of families who often experience this process of transition through multiple adult relationships (Berger & Carlson, 2020; Lichter et al., 2020), rather than a smooth ride through the uniform stages of marriage, parenting, retirement, and, ultimately, death.

Families are not limited to the nuclear, two-generational unit of parent and child. Families may be headed by intergenerational adults, as in families headed by a grandmother and a mother (Burton, 1996; Nelson, 2006) or families in which the parent generation is completely absent and children are only being raised by their grandparents—a situation linked to the drug use or incarceration of young nonresident parents (Pilkauskas

& Dunifon, 2016). In some rural Native American or Alaska Native families not only are grandparents raising their grandchildren, but the entire community is involved in maintaining cultural and family environments for the children (Henderson et al., 2017). Some families also incorporate the sibling relationship as part of the family cycle (Aldous, 1978), especially among childless older adults (Connidis & Barnett, 2019), thereby extending the two-generational model laterally. Still other families are headed by one or more lesbian, gay, bisexual, or transgender parents (Goldberg, 2010; Goldberg & Allen, 2020). Thus, what began as the family life cycle concept of normative stages of heterosexual marriage and biological parenthood (Glick, 1947; 1988) has evolved to accommodate an infinite variety of diverse family structures, roles, and processes that inevitably change over time.

History and Origins

As we have pointed out throughout this book, it is important to examine the historical context in which a theory was developed to fully understand how the theory was originally meant to be applied. Family developmental theory was developed in the mid-20th century, specifically for studying families' unique structural and dynamic qualities as a social group. As noted above, family developmental theory borrowed from functionalist theory (Chapter 2) and symbolic interactionist theory (Chapter 4) and added the concept of multiple dimensions of time, which are individual time, social process time, and historical time (Rodgers, 1973). By borrowing from functionalist theory, family developmental theory added structural concepts, such as **position** (i.e., the location of a family member in the family system), **role** (i.e., the dynamic aspect of a position), and **norms** (i.e., societal expectations). By borrowing from symbolic interactionist theory, the developmental approach incorporated Burgess's (1926) concept of the family as a unity of interacting personalities.

In addition, family developmental theory borrowed the concept of **ontogenic change** from individual theories of human development (e.g., Erikson and Piaget) to explain how growth occurs through hierarchical stages (Bengtson & Allen, 1993). Ontogenic change refers to how an organism—in this case, a family and/or individual family members—changes and matures over time. Since the day you were born, you have gone through several stages of development that are necessary for maturation; your caregivers taught you how to walk and talk, and you were potty trained. You went through puberty and adolescence and now are likely to be in the stage of young adulthood or older. Families, by definition, are supposed to contain necessary elements that assist in moving their members through these changes, with one stage building upon the previous stage. One of the things that makes this theory unique is its emphasis on how the family is the guiding force behind moving members through these changes; no other social institution can perform these same tasks. Think about your own life; you likely did not go to preschool to learn what it means to love your family. You learned what family means and what roles certain family members play by watching, and modeling, your own family members. More than any other theory, family developmental theory championed how important families are as temporal, interactional, and institutional entities with a very unique purpose.

Because of families' unique characteristics, as a social institution, families are supposed to be pre-programmed to develop through stages that typically correspond to the age structure of parents and children over time. At each stage of the family life cycle, families are destined to perform unique developmental tasks associated with sexuality, reproduction, caregiving, and intimacy that no other system in the social structure can do.

Given that family developmental theory was conceptualized using the 20th-century nuclear, heteronormative, and pronatalist family unit as the model for its stages, a strong debate has emerged on the relevance of this theory to explain family growth and change in the face of major demographic and historical shifts. As a result, life course theory (Chapter 9) emerged as a new paradigm to liberate the family life cycle from the gridlock of rigid stages and roles and to take into account the dynamic interplay among individual, family, and sociohistorical time (Bengtson & Allen, 1993; Rodgers & White, 1993). Further, James White and David Klein (2008) have updated the work of earlier family developmental theorists and combined their ideas with the life course approach (Martin, 2018). White and Klein's family life course development framework, further refined in White et al. (2019), is a modern update of the three original perspectives that went into making family developmental theory: the individual life span, family process and structure, and social-historical context.

Assumptions of Family Developmental Theory

You may already be picking up on some of the assumptions of this theory, but let's take a closer look at how the earliest framers of family developmental theory (e.g., Duvall, 1957; Hill & Hansen, 1960; Hill & Rodgers, 1964) have identified the taken-for-granted assumptions of this theory. Aldous (1978) consolidated these ideas into five underlying assumptions. The first assumption is that "family behavior is the sum of past experience of family members as incorporated in the present as well as in their goals and expectations for the future" (Aldous, 1978, p. 15). This means that understanding a family's history is important to be able to understand current and future behavior. Think about Margo from our case study; based on how she was raised, it should be no surprise that her mother would do whatever it takes to step in and rescue her from experiencing both the ups and downs of adult life. Her mother sheltered her during childhood and continues to do so, even as an adult.

The second assumption builds off of this idea and posits that "families develop and change over time in similar and consistent ways" (Aldous, 1978, p. 15). This assumption presumes that family behavior and change are fairly predictable by stage and age structure. Therefore, all new parents, regardless of their circumstances, can expect to go through a major transition period when the family composition changes from two to three members or from one generation (e.g., parent) to two generations (e.g., parent and child). Becoming parents is a predictable pattern in the life of a family and will be experienced in similar ways across all families. That's why expectant parents are warned about "never getting a full night's sleep again!" after a baby is born. Indeed, this is one of the reasons that pregnancy preparation books and parenting advice are so popular: People want to know how others got through similar life cycle stages without pulling their hair out!

The third assumption is that "humans not only initiate actions as they mature and interact with others but also they react to environmental pressures" (Aldous, 1978, p. 15). This means human beings both shape and are shaped by the behavior of other family members as well as by the broader social system. Families are interdependent units; they must accommodate the individual needs of members as well as the norms and expectations of society. An example of the third assumption is what happens when a child "fails to launch." In contemporary society, young adults' transition from the family home to their own independent lives can be compromised by the lack of guaranteed and plentiful employment opportunities (Arnett,

2000). Although many young adults now go to college, they may have to move back home for a time until they can secure employment (Sironi & Billari, 2019). The family must readjust to economic realities and make room, once again, for their adult children in the home. Another example of this can be seen in the extension of U.S. health insurance laws, where parents may now carry their adult children on their policies until the child is 26.

The fourth assumption is that "the family and its members must perform certain time-specific tasks set by themselves and by persons in the broader society" (Aldous, 1978, p. 15). This assumption refers to the concept of individual and **family developmental tasks** that are associated with each time of life. An individual and a family unit have normative goals that they must accomplish to move forward to the next level of development. A developmental task requires coming to terms with reality, or taking responsibility for work life, family life, community life, and the like. Have you ever heard someone joke that, "You know you're an adult when you get excited about getting a vacuum as a gift" or "you spend your Saturdays at Home Depot." These examples illustrate how with each new stage in the life cycle, we fulfill roles and engage in behavior that can be vastly different from the preceding life cycle stage. Your "ideal Saturday night" in your twenties probably looks pretty different when compared to your thirties or forties. As we age and move through life cycle stages, our developmental tasks change, and we adapt accordingly. This is necessary for individual fulfillment, family functioning, and societal well-being.

Finally, Aldous's (1978) fifth assumption is that "in a social setting, the individual is the basic autonomous unit" (p. 15). This assumption means that the family system, as a whole, is dependent on the actions and reactions of its individual members. An example of the fifth assumption is when a stay-at-home parent decides to get a job outside the home; all of the individuals in the whole family system must make adjustments in response to the actions of one member. Teenage children will, no doubt, have new chores to do; the other parent may have to take on more housework or spend less time on the job; and caring for aging parents may become more difficult and stressful. Families are systems in which the individual members are interdependent. What happens to one person has implications for the others.

Key Concepts

Family developmental theory offers a wealth of concepts that are appealing to multiple audiences and easy to apply in education and practice. Many of the concepts derived from family developmental theory have become part of our everyday language, so we often just assume we know their meaning. This is also the case with concepts from other theories we describe in this book. For example, in Chapter 4, we pointed out that the concept of "significant other," taken from symbolic interactionist theory, has become an everyday phrase. And in Chapter 2 regarding functionalist theory, we described the concepts of "instrumental and expressive roles" that are gender related. These concepts, too, have entered the popular vernacular. Similarly, as you read on in this chapter, you will discover that concepts derived from family developmental theory are also part of our common vocabulary.

The Family Life Cycle

This concept is the most enduring contribution of family developmental theory because it offers a way to logically segment the shared experiences in families as they progress over time. Embedded in this concept are the normative stages associated with the initiation, expansion, contraction, and dissolution of a marriage. Marriages and other intimate partnerships are expanded with the addition of children, and as the children leave home, families contract. Marriage typically ends with the death of the first spouse (or through divorce, as family development theorists now recognize), and the family life cycle eventually dissolves upon the death of the surviving spouse. This concept provides an index of how roles are allocated in families over time. According to Mattessich and Hill (1987), there are three key components—persons, roles, and role patterns—of family structural organization that appear and disappear over the life cycle of a family of procreation. Persons refers to individuals who enter or leave the family life cycle through transitions, such as birth, marriage, launching, and death. Roles refers to the family activities associated with each family position that must be enacted. Patterns of roles are interactive or transactive behaviors that are "adjusted to meet the changing demands of family members and society, in accordance with the resources available to the family at any point in its career" (Mattessich & Hill, 1987, p. 443).

The family life cycle, as originally proposed by Duvall (1957), consists of eight stages. Family stages are determined by the number of roles or positions in the family (e.g., stage 1 and stage 7 consist only of the married couple) and by the age and role of the oldest child (e.g., stages 2 to 5). Figure 5.1 depicts the *original* normative model of the eight stages.

Here we describe each of the stages, role positions, and family goals (i.e., developmental tasks) that are associated with each phase of the family life cycle as originally conceptualized (Hill & Rodgers, 1964). Again, we note that both the language and the time frame used for the stages, to be of contemporary relevance, must be updated and made more inclusive of the great variety of ways that individuals partner, parent, and separate in their family units. Still, we believe it is important to present the architecture of the original theorizing that went into family developmental theory to guide theoretical changes and revisions:

- **Stage 1—establishment and expectant:** Stage 1 starts the family life cycle with the marriage of a man and a woman, both of whom are conceptualized as young adults. In this stage, there are only two members in the family, and they fulfill the traditional roles of husband and wife. This stage lasts about one year. The primary task of this stage is for the young couple to adjust to living as a married pair. As they adjust to marriage, the wife becomes pregnant, and the couple must adjust to pregnancy and planning for the transition to parenthood when they will add a child to their family constellation.

- **Stage 2—childbearing:** Stage 2 changes the family structure from that of a husband and a wife to the parental roles of mother and father and adds the third role of child. This stage lasts about two years. The developmental task of stage 2 is to reorganize the family unit around the needs of infants and begin to add additional children to the family.

- **Stage 3—preschool family:** Stage 3 includes the husband/father, wife/mother, son/brother, and daughter/sister in various combinations, depending on the number and gender of the children born. Stage 3 lasts about four years. The developmental tasks of stage 3 continue with the family reorganizing around the needs of infants and, now, preschool children.

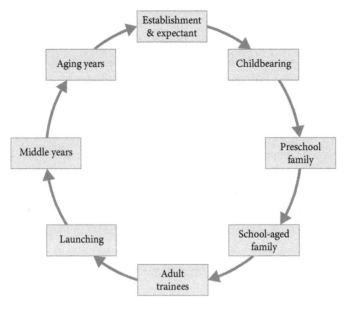

FIGURE 5.1. The Normative Family Life Cycle

- **Stage 4—school-aged family:** Stage 4 is identified as a stage that lasts about seven years. It consists of the parents and approximately three children. Note that three children was the average number of children per family in the 1950s and 1960s (Glick, 1988). These children probably range in age from very young to preadolescent. The developmental task of this stage is the reorganization of the family to fit into the expanding world of school-aged children.

- **Stage 5—adult trainees:** Stage 5 now includes the parents and up to four of their children, where the oldest child is a teenager, and the youngest child is a preadolescent. This stage lasts about seven years, and the developmental tasks include allowing the children to have greater freedom in terms of taking on responsibility for their own lives.

- **Stage 6—young adult launching:** Stage 6 now adds a third generation: grandparents. By this stage, young adult children marry and start their own nuclear families, and their parents become grandparents. The developmental tasks of stage 6 include parents returning to a more egalitarian relationship now that their children are launched (note that the assumption of traditional gender roles was very evident in the original statement of this theory). This stage lasts about eight years.

- **Stage 7—middle years:** Stage 7 returns the family life cycle to just two members, the postparental older adults. Here the family consists of a husband/grandfather and a wife/grandmother. This stage lasts about 14 years. The family has now reorganized around the marital pair. As parents disengage from their roles as caregivers for dependent children and enter into the last half of life, they may experience loneliness and even a crisis of meaning. This has been referred to as "the empty nest syndrome," though currently, it is associated with an adjustment phase instead of a problem. The major developmental task of stage 7, then, is for the married couple to reengage in new social roles that bring meaning and fulfillment in the absence of caring for and supporting children.

- **Stage 8—aging years:** Stage 8 takes the married couple up to the loss of one then both spouses. This stage lasts anywhere from 7 to 13 years. It is important to note that when Hill and Rodgers (1964) first conceptualized this stage of the family life cycle, the average life expectancies for men (age 74) and for women (age 77) were much younger than they are today in most developed countries. Indeed, the average life expectancy at birth in Japan in 2019 was 81 for men and 87 for women (World Bank, 2021); in the United States in 2019, it was 76 for men and 81 for women (Arias et al., 2021). The major developmental tasks of this stage are for adjusting to a narrower type of life and then adjusting to widowhood. Younger generations must also cope with the death of the oldest generation once their family life cycle ends.

It should be obvious by now that the original model of the family life cycle needed to be revised and updated as scholars recognized that it was idealizing only one type of family: the so-called "normative" marriage of two heterosexual parents and their own children. As noted before, Hill's (1986) recognition that many families only include one parent led to an updated model of the family headed by a single parent.

Another major revision of the family life cycle concept addresses the increasingly common stepfamily form with its "out-of-sequence" family development patterns (Adler-Baeder & Higginbotham, 2020, p. 561) and the vulnerabilities, stigma, and other constraints faced by complex stepfamilies that lack the services provided to other families that conform to the normative structure (Ganong & Coleman, 2017; Russell et al., 2018). As Stewart (2007) explained, Papernow's (1993) adaptation of the family life cycle to "the step-family cycle" provides a very concrete model for educators, therapists, and other professionals in their work guiding stepfamilies through the reconstitution phase of family life. Papernow proposed three stages of the life cycle and seven components. In the early stage, stepparents must address the developmental tasks of "fantasy," "immersion," and "awareness." In the middle stage, the developmental tasks are "mobilization and "action." Finally, in the later stage, stepparents and stepchildren experience the developmental tasks of "contact" and "resolution." Papernow's stepfamily life cycle model builds upon the normative model of the family life cycle by taking a longitudinal perspective and segmenting critical transitions into stages. On the other hand, Papernow's model recognizes far more conflict and difficulty among family members than the more rosy view of family development characterized in the original model. This more realistic view of the inevitability of conflict and the need for its resolution in the family (as discussed in Chapter 3) suggests a departure from the original structural functionalist roots (Chapter 2) of family developmental theory, which are far less relevant to contemporary families.

Crapo and Bradford (2021) have gone much farther than the founders of this theory to liberate the family development model from the stage concept altogether. As noted above, in their revision each family member can experience events and trajectories within at least four dimensions, roughly linked to individual development, including spirituality (personal), learning and work (vocational), intimacy and relational (couple), and caring for others (generativity). This multidimensional revision also leaves room for additional dimensions to be added in terms of cultural and societal influences, keeping in mind the importance of taking into account historical and macro-level contexts for understanding family development.

Family Developmental Tasks

For each stage of the life cycle, there are major goals that family members must accomplish. Rodgers (1973) defined a developmental task as the following:

> A set of norms (role expectations) arising at a particular point in the career of a position in a social system [e.g., father], which, if incorporated by the occupant of the position as a role or part of a role cluster, brings about integration and temporary equilibrium in the system. (p. 51)

As an example, there are several tasks that accompany the life cycle stage of adolescence:

> (a) The alteration of the parent–adolescent relationship in order to allow the adolescent to move more freely out of and back into the family environs; (b) a renewed focus on marital issues and parental career interests; and (c) taking on a greater role in caregiving for older family members. (Gavazzi, 2013, p. 306)

Developmental tasks must be accomplished in an orderly fashion for the family to successfully reorganize to the next level of family structure and interaction. Failure to accomplish these normative goals at each stage in the life cycle can lead to individual unhappiness, family stress, disapproval by society, and difficulty in accomplishing the goals of future stages (Havighurst, 1972/1948).

Family developmental tasks have many features. First, there are developmental tasks associated with each one of the family life cycle stages, and family members are simultaneously at different stages of development when they are required to meet them. In Gavazzi's (2013) example of families with adolescents, the adolescent's developmental tasks include becoming independent from their parents, but the parents' developmental tasks include an increasing focus on caring for aging parents. Accomplishing developmental tasks can be very complex, especially when there are multiple family members. Imagine the developmental tasks associated with adjusting to marriage that involve only two people, compared to adjusting to having adolescents in a family.

Second, there are more general developmental tasks that are ever changing and span the entire family life cycle (Rowe, 1966). Duvall (1957) described these as the need to establish and maintain: (a) an independent home; (b) satisfactory ways of getting and spending money; (c) mutually acceptable patterns in the division of labor; (d) continuity of mutually satisfying sex relationships; (e) an open system of intellectual and emotional communication; (f) workable relationships with relatives; (g) ways of interacting with associates and community organizations; (h) competency in bearing and rearing children; and (i) a workable philosophy of life. Chances are you have not spent a lot of time thinking about each of these tasks unless you have had to address them firsthand in the midst of a relationship. It would be interesting to see how your list of developmental tasks would change from age 20 to age 30, 40, 50, and beyond. What kind of sex life do you expect to maintain as a 20 year old thinking forward to marriage? What types of household tasks did you have to do growing up, compared to what your spouse or partner will expect of you if and when you marry or cohabitate? You might be surprised if you write down your developmental tasks for the stage you are in and the stages you will enter and observe how they stay the same or change over time.

It is important to note that the accomplishment of developmental tasks is more of an ideal than a reality (Rowe, 1966). Family members have rarely "caught up" with themselves and with the normative expectations. Some developmental tasks inevitably carry over to the next stage, as we have seen in the example of young adults' "failure" to launch and become completely independent of their parents' financial support. Although developmental tasks are essential features of how families change and grow, they are not an "all or nothing" proposition. For example, do you ever completely transition to adulthood or adjust to the loss of a loved one? Perhaps, it is better to think of developmental tasks as guideposts, rather than endpoints. Still, as normative expectations, we can all identify what we are "supposed" to do. We are supposed to get a high school diploma, a job, a spouse, children, our own home, and so on. The order in which we do these things and the people we do them with, however, are much more variable than the developmental task concept implies.

Family Career

Several scholars have expanded the concept of the family life cycle to include the **family career**. Rodgers (1973) defined the family career as "the most general statement of the dynamics of the family over time" (p. 19). This concept allows us to concurrently examine the life of the family as a social group that includes individual members, the family as a whole system, and the family in transaction with the broader society. Aldous (1978), however, suggested that the concepts of family career and family life cycle are synonymous.

In an innovative revision of the family life cycle concept, Harold and Margaret Feldman (1975) addressed the critiques of family developmental theory. They suggested a new schema for "recycling" it, proposing that there are actually two types of family "histories" (see Figure 5.2). The first is the **lifetime family**, or the family of ego, which consists of four subcareers: the sex experience career, the marital career, the parent–child career, and the adult–parent career. Although "ego" (i.e., a person) can be in several of these careers simultaneously, the person's family career is linear and spans their lifetime. The other concept for "recycling" the family life cycle is the **lineage family,** which lasts through time over generations.

The lineage family is actually cyclical, in that at any given time there is a different role occupant in each position of the family, but the same positions always exist—no matter who fills them. Thus, in our case study Margo has been in the position of child and mother. Karen has occupied the same positions, with the addition of grandmother, though at different points in time. The two dimensions of lifetime family and lineage family allow us to understand families from the perspective of those who do marry and have children and

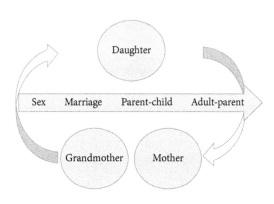

FIGURE 5.2. The Lifetime Family and the Lineage Family

those who do not. For example, a woman will be a daughter throughout her life but may not be a wife, mother, and grandmother (Allen & Pickett, 1987).

BOX 5.2. FAMILY DEVELOPMENTAL THEORY IN MODERN CULTURE: *THE LION KING*

Image 5.1 A Scene From *The Lion King*, 1994

The Lion King franchise includes an original animated Disney movie first released in 1994, recreated for Broadway in 1997, and then remade in 2019. This story centers on the lion family of King Mufasa, Queen Sarabi, and their newborn male cub, Simba. This film has several examples of family developmental theory throughout the story. As male heir, Simba is now destined to inherit the throne from his father, which makes Mufasa's brother, Scar, incredibly jealous. Scar goes on a mission to destroy both Simba and Mufasa because of this, which demonstrates his difficulty in dealing with the expectations of "middle age." Having never started a family of his own, we cannot analyze Scar's movement through the family life cycle as a father, but we can see how he covets power because of the norms associated with the development of a family. He most likely resents the norms associated with inheritance because if Mufasa (assumed to be the eldest male) had not started a family of his own, Scar would have inherited the throne when Mufasa died. However, because of the norms associated with royalty and inheritance, it is assumed that Mufasa had to select a mate and procreate in order to keep the throne in his family line.

One of the most famous songs from this film, "Circle of Life" illustrates family developmental theory as well. The song, with music composed by Elton John and lyrics written by Time Rice (John & Rice, 1994), describes moving through the circle of life, as depicted in this stanza:

> It's the wheel of fortune
> It's the leap of faith
> It's the band of hope
> In the circle of life

The lyrics address the phases of the life cycle, including both happy and sad times. The song accompanies the scene when Mufasa is giving Simba a tour of the Pride Lands, teaching him the responsibilities that come with inheriting the animal kingdom and becoming a leader. While human families do not typically train children to inherit wealth, property, or prestige until much later in life, the analogy of moving through family life cycle stages is still relevant.

Related to that, we can see examples of the various generations in this film, as Simba and Nala are the replacement generation for Mufasa and Sarabi. After Mufasa dies in a stampede orchestrated by Scar, Simba and Nala become the king and queen and have a lion cub themselves. The film ends with the pride's elder, Rafiki, holding up the baby cub to all the lions in the pride below, and everyone sings the "Circle of Life."

Source: John, E., & Rice, T. (1994). Circle of life [Song]. On *The Lion King: Original motion picture soundtrack*. Walt Disney.

Evaluating Family Developmental Theory

Strengths of Family Developmental Theory

Like all of the theories we describe in this book, family developmental theory has both strengths and weaknesses. Family developmental theory is the first of its kind to be created by scholars with a unique focus on families, and it is the first to integrate multiple conceptions of time. This theory also integrates both micro and macro perspectives. Further, family developmental theory captures the popular imagination, given the fact that it is the human condition to be born, develop, and, eventually, die. Many of its concepts, including family life cycle and family developmental tasks, are common in our everyday language and shared understanding of families.

Incorporation of Multiple Dimensions of Time

A very important contribution of family developmental theory has been the conceptualization of families through the perspective of time. This is the first theory to analyze family process and structure across time. This allows researchers to measure family dynamics and structural shifts in roles, positions, and norms at both short-term (e.g., cross-sectional) and long-term (e.g., longitudinal and historical) levels. By taking time into account, family change can be measured within each stage and across the stages that comprise the entire life cycle of the family. The perspective of time helps researchers understand the immediate impact of having a baby on a marriage, as well as the long-term consequences of raising children to adulthood and launching them out into the world.

General Framework for Understanding the Family Life Cycle

The family life cycle concept has broad appeal because it is intuitively helpful in characterizing the fact that we are born, we couple, we reproduce, we change, and we die. We do this not simply as individuals but as individuals who associate with others and help one another fulfill the mandates of society. The family life cycle concept is so engrained in the very fabric of society, including religion, myth, literature, economics, politics, and education, that it provides a useful model for communication. Try to think of a context in which the family is not the major institution to accomplish the developmental task of raising children to a healthy adulthood. There are only rare exceptions to this idea, and even then, the thought of them is discordant to how we are taught, throughout the world, to partner and raise our children.

Applicable to Family Life Education

Family developmental theory is one of the most effective conceptual frameworks for applying concepts to family life education (Darling et al., 2020). Over the decades, this theory has served as the basis for community programs designed to help families accomplish the developmental tasks associated with the family life cycle (Duvall, 1988; Crapo & Bradford, 2021). Programs include marriage preparation classes; marriage enrichment classes for mid-life married couples; support groups for new mothers and their babies; transitioning to retirement for older family members; families in the military; and dealing with loss and bereavement. Rather than taking an individualistic approach that is common in psychotherapy, family life education focuses on the family as the target of support, intervention, and change (Ballard, 2020; Mattessich & Hill, 1987). For example, a family life educator assigned to Margo's case would identify stages in the life cycle where Margo or her mother need to work on accomplishing the appropriate developmental tasks. Instead of leaning so heavily on her mother for rescue, should Margo instead try to push her own boundaries of development and work together with her new husband to grow stronger as a couple and parents? A family life educator could suggest several routes Margo and her mother could take to get their families back on track developmentally.

Weaknesses of Family Developmental Theory

Despite its strengths, family developmental theory also has several weaknesses. Although many scholars have updated the theory, it is still critiqued for oversimplifying and universalizing family stages, ages, and cycles. On balance, however, family developmental theory has been incorporated into other theories, and in that sense, it still remains relevant today. Next, we consider the primary weaknesses of this perspective.

Too Static

Family developmental theory was very innovative and useful in the early years of merging individual psychosocial theories with family roles and careers. However, it soon became apparent that the equating of family roles with static positions did not allow scholars to consider family diversity and variation. By static, we mean that the theory put too much emphasis on the actual "faces" of the occupants of normative roles by characterizing unchanging definitions of the positions of husband/wife, father/mother, and child/sibling. As we have noted throughout this book, however, families come in a wide variety of forms, and family members do not have to be related by blood or marriage; thus, the theory's assumption of universality is a major stumbling block (Laszloffy, 2002). Because of the many ways families are organized and change over time, both within and across societies, the original static proposal of common stages, roles, and positions gave way to the individual variations that can be captured by a life course perspective (Bengtson & Allen, 1993). Although family developmental theory has continued to evolve in order to accommodate the criticisms, the main result is that family developmental theory has been overshadowed by life course theory (Chapter 9) or by a combination of the individual life course and the family cycle models, as shown in White et al.'s (2019) revision of the approach, entitled "[t]he family life course developmental framework" (p. 103).

More Conceptually Useful Than Empirically Useful

In a critique of the family life cycle concept, Nock (1979) assessed the usefulness of family developmental theory as stronger in terms of identifying concepts than in actually operationalizing those concepts in research. The family life cycle concept has wide popular appeal as a metaphor for the stages of birth, life, and death that all humans, indeed all living things, experience. Yet it is very hard to measure a stage, let alone measure it in terms of the age span of its multiple occupants. How do we compare families in the preschool-age stage when there is so much variation across family types and sizes? Further, the cross-cultural comparisons are very difficult, depending on demographic factors, such as the average life span, the birthrate, the interactions across the generations, among others, that occur within and between different societies (Crapo & Bradford, 2021). With such endless variations, you can see that although the concept is intuitively appealing, utilizing it in scientific research is still quite a challenge.

Ignores Family Problems

Another major critique of family developmental theory is that it ignores some of the most problematic aspects of family life. The theory assumes that families will adjust positively to the major events and transitions of the family life cycle (Cheal, 1991). After all, these events and transitions are normative and expected. But what about the all-too-common problems that occur in families due to violence, substance abuse, job loss, and the like? The theory cannot adequately address these issues because, like functionalist theory (Chapter 2), it defines them as deviant and abnormal. A related issue is that this theory assumes that families proceed through the life cycle in an orderly manner and that they adhere to a socially structured time frame. But family events and transitions do not occur at the same time and in the same order for everyone. Parents are not always in their early twenties when they have their first child. Many families never experience an "empty nest" because it is increasingly common for adult children to not leave home. In the case of childlessness, some family roles and transitions are never experienced. Yet the theory promotes the idea that families develop on the same schedule, that they complete each stage of the family life cycle, and that they accomplish their developmental tasks in a positive manner.

An Alternative Theory App: Feminist Theory

In this chapter, we have presented the origins, key concepts, and modern applications as well as the strengths and weaknesses of family developmental theory. In earlier chapters, we have mostly compared theories that have had both similarities as well as differences. In this chapter, however, we take a different approach. Family developmental theory and feminist theory (Chapter 8) definitely have more differences than similarities, as we outline next.

To start, consider your own desires and dreams about family. Do you want to get married or have children? Do you think every one of your classmates has the same dreams and desires? Feminist theory contrasts sharply with family developmental theory in that it does not assume that all individuals want the same things in life. Some individuals do not want to marry or have children, or perhaps, they want to cohabit or have children as single parents. These models do not fit into the framework of family developmental theory because they do not fit into the linear stages of the family life cycle. The heart of feminist theory is the emphasis on differences, whether they emerge out of socially constructed ideas about gender or intersections of race, class, gender, and other systems of privilege and oppression. Not all individuals want the same things in life, and even more important is the fact that not everyone has *equal access* to the same goals and dreams. Feminist theory emphasizes each of these factors in turn in Chapter 8.

Next, we highlight how family developmental theory is applicable to families around the globe. We consider when adolescents are identified as legal adults. In Box 5.3, we compare the age of majority in several cultures. How would family developmental theorists explain the differences between the countries we highlight?

BOX 5.3. GLOBAL COMPARISONS OF AGE OF MAJORITY (LEGAL ADULT STATUS)

Societies differ in the age at which a child is recognized or declared as an adult in law. According to the Organisation for Economic Co-operation and Development (2016), age of majority is the "age at which minors cease to legally be considered as children and assume control and full responsibility over their persons, actions and decisions, thereby terminating the legal control and legal responsibilities of their parents or guardian over and for them" (p. 1). Depending on the society, adult status can confer certain rights: to marry, to vote, to drive a car, to move out of the parental home, to have sexual intercourse, to drink alcohol, to get a bank account or credit card, to serve in the armed forces, and the like. Consider how various jurisdictions and countries confer the age of majority:

- **United States:** The age of majority is 18 and is consistent across all states except for three. The exceptions are age 19 in Alabama and Nebraska and age 21 in Mississippi.
- **Indonesia:** The age of majority is 15.
- **Scotland:** The age of majority is 16.
- **Brazil:** The age of majority is 18, with the exception of the right to vote (age 16) and consent to sexual intercourse (14).
- **Canada:** The age of majority varies (18 or 19) by provincial and territorial jurisdiction.
- **Senegal:** The age of majority is 18 for men and women, but the minimum age for marriage is 18 for men and 16 for women. The age at which you can be held criminally liable as an adult is 13.

Source: https://www.oecd.org/els/family/PF_1_8_Age_threshold_Childhood_to_Adulthood.pdf

Working With Family Developmental Theory: Integrating Research and Practice

Now that we have defined family developmental theory, described the historical origins and key concepts, and pointed out its strengths and weaknesses, we turn to how the theory can be used in research and practice today. We provide an example of current theorizing, analyze an empirical study that was guided by family developmental theory and describe how the theory informs the practice of family policy.

Family Developmental Theory Today

Many contemporary family scholars have provided alternative models to the family life cycle concept. One area in which such alternative theorizing has occurred is in the family therapy field. Notably, Monica McGoldrick and her colleagues (McGoldrick et al., 2015; McGoldrick & Hardy, 2019) have provided a corrective to the ways the original version of the family life cycle reflects the standard nuclear family arrangement and, thus, minimizes and ignores differences in family experience by race, class, gender, sexual orientation, ethnicity, and religion. Their recent work in expanding the family life cycle is much more inclusive of the diverse ways individuals experience families, including family households, communities, and cultural groups.

Also a family therapist, Suzanne Slater (1999) revised the family life cycle concept and applied it to the lesbian couple's family experience. She proposed that there are five stages in the lesbian family life cycle, and that these stages are predictable and normative for lesbian couples. The stages put forth by Slater encompass couple formation, couplehood, the middle years, generativity, and old age. Each stage takes into account how lesbian couples deal with the structural inequalities and social prejudices of homophobia that can accumulate in the later years. The lesbian family life cycle model is aimed at helping women understand that the transitions they are experiencing as they age are not deviant or unique but, rather, common to other lesbian families. Criticisms of Slater's model include that it presents only a positive perspective on lesbian couple family life, and it focuses on White, middle-class lesbians in committed relationships—thus, mirroring the heterosexist notions of families (Lev & Sennott, 2020). In spite of these drawbacks, Slater's model has also been hailed as an important step in updating the family life cycle concept to more realistically reflect diverse family structures.

More recent research has also built on the original family developmental model, adapted for more family diversity. Rubio et al. (2021) conducted research in three European countries (Netherlands, United Kingdom, and France) that investigated heterosexual, gay, and lesbian couples' experiences with the transition to first-time parenthood. The researchers found strikingly few differences between each type of couple as they transitioned from end of pregnancy into parenting an infant. This study is important for decentering what "normal" looks like, suggesting that humans experience similar emotions moving through the developmental stage of becoming a parent, regardless of their sexual orientation and gender identity.

Family Developmental Theory in Research

John Davies and Douglas Gentile (2012) utilized a family developmental perspective to examine media use and effects in their study of families consisting of one child, as compared to families consisting of several children. They address the impact on families of living in a media-saturated environment. They cite research on family media habits, and note that children use, on average, 7.5 hours of media a day, with media use measured by screen time (e.g., television, movies, video games, and computers). It is interesting to note that these figures do not include the amount of media use per day in school or cell phone use. Thus, children spend more than half of their waking hours engaging in "screen time." The concern over screen time is especially acute for "digitods," who are the first generation of very young children exposed to digital media since birth, often prematurely, as Dias and Brito (2020) found in their study of Portuguese families and digital media use. According to Davies and Gentile, parental monitoring of children's media time use varies by child age. For example, young children (approximately three to five years old) watch more educational programming than school-aged children (approximately 6 to 12 years old). By the time children are in elementary school, they are spending more time with their peers than their parents, typically on videogame devices in their bedrooms.

Building upon Duvall's (1957) eight-stage model of family developmental theory, Davies and Gentile (2012) selected the three stages in the family life cycle that include children: (a) families with preschool children, ages 2 to 6 years; (b) families with school-age children, ages 6 to 13 years; and (c) families with adolescent children, ages 13 to 20 years. Importantly, the authors updated the social context in which families develop to include the technological revolution that has taken over in families. The major research question they asked was how the media habits of families differ according to the three family developmental stages with children. They were especially interested in the influence that *siblings* have on children's media use. They wanted to know in what ways it might matter if children viewed television with a sibling or a parent. To test their hypotheses, they used two independent samples: (a) a nationally representative sample consisting of 527 parents with children living at home and between the ages of 2 and 17; and (b) a convenience sample consisting of 1,257 families who attended a MediaWise parent education program created by the National Institute on Media and the Family (2012).

As expected, the authors found that families with adolescent children had less healthy media viewing habits than families with younger children. Parents of teenagers provided significantly less monitoring of their children's media use, reported that their teens were participating in fewer alternatives to screen time than younger children, and reported that they themselves were less consistent about enforcing family rules that restricted media use. The authors interpreted these findings in light *of* family developmental theory: They suggested that what counts as normative media use has escalated in our media-saturated society today. Media use now peaks in the adolescent years. Because parents have come to expect that their adolescents will engage in less healthy media habits, they have relaxed their standards for controlling their children's access. The importance of siblings for media use was more equivocal. On the one hand, families with siblings showed more healthy media habits than families with only children. On the other hand, having only one child tends to make parents more anxious about that child and, thus, motivates them to develop positive interactions that will foster healthier media habits. What is interesting to consider here is how this issue would differ depending on the cultural context; how do children in developing countries experience the media? Are parents socialized to be aware of and care about media consumption in all countries and cultures around the world? As a family theorist, it's important to take these global considerations into account.

In addition, in the 10 years since Davies and Gentile (2012) published their study, the isolating effects of individualized media use among teens has increased (Dworkin et al., 2019; Manago et al., 2020). A newer development is associated with parents' overuse of smart phones in the presence of their children. The quality of the parent–child relationship suffers when parents are overfocused on their smart phone, thereby distracting them from paying attention to their children (McDaniel et al., 2018; Meeus et al., 2021; Wong et al., 2020).

Family Developmental Theory in Practice

There are several ways in which educators, practitioners, and family policy makers can apply family developmental theory in their work with individuals and families. One of the most important places this theory can be applied is in working with young adults who are making decisions about reproduction and family.

You may be familiar with the phrase "childless by choice"—it represents a fairly recent movement among individuals who reject the pronatalist ideology that values childbearing. In fact, both mainstream and social media has featured young women and nonbinary individuals' stories of frustration with being counseled out of and even denied sterilization procedures by their medical providers because they are too young (Demopoulos 2020; Pearson, 2014). Given that family developmental theory outlines childbearing as a natural and essential stage of the family life cycle, it is important to consider the potential challenges this might create for individuals who do not want to have children. This issue is particularly salient for women who prefer to be childless because their options for permanent sterilization are limited until they reach a certain age. The official stance of the American College of Obstetricians and Gynecologists (ACOG) is that "women who have completed their childbearing are candidates for sterilization" (Pearson, 2014). Each provider may interpret this statement differently: Does it mean that women have to have had a child to be eligible? Or does it mean women have to be over age 35 to be considered eligible? As a practitioner, you may very well confront this issue as, perhaps, a nurse, family life educator, therapist, policymaker, or health care worker. How would you help your clients with this issue and navigate available options?

While the official statement of the ACOG may seem arbitrary, it is important to understand that researchers in obstetrics and gynecology have reason to be concerned with women choosing permanent sterilization in their twenties. Research has shown that up to 26% of women regret their decision to undergo sterilization (Bartz & Greenburg, 2008; Curtis et al., 2006). In addition, this research also indicates that the factor most strongly associated with regret is age; women under the age of 30 are much more likely to regret the decision when compared to older women (Bartz & Greenburg, 2008). More recent work on this topic has questioned the underlying racist and classist ideologies that may impact a health care provider's advice or willingness to assist patients with permanent sterilization (Davis & Dubisar, 2019). The concern here is that tubal ligation (TL) may be offered to women of color or poor women repeatedly and eagerly without reflecting on how medical training influences a pattern of seeing some women as eager for TL and others as eager to become pregnant, implicitly enacting sterilization's oppressive history (Davis & Dubisar, 2019, p. 8).

Given what we know about family developmental theory, including its strengths and weaknesses, how can we evaluate this issue? Should the ACOG's stance on permanent sterilization change, according to this theory? How does the theory's history and origins help us understand its applicability to issues of reproductive rights and family planning in an ever-changing world?

BOX 5.4. VOICES FROM LIVED EXPERIENCE

How can individuals and beloved communities be the change they wish to see in the world? Karen Beiber, executive director of Oasis Village, tells her story about transforming family to include a pregnant woman who was incarcerated and her child (now almost 16) and the communities that surrounded them. Karen and her partner, Jeanine, answered a call put forth by their faith community if they would assist a woman who was to deliver a baby in prison but had a year left on her sentence and no family support. Karen, Jeanine, and another congregant agreed to care for the child until the mom was released. Here is her story:

> The child was born 10 weeks early, weighing 2½ pounds, due to her Mom having preeclampsia (though she was still brought to the hospital in leg irons and handcuffs). After a C-section, the baby spent a month in NICU & step-down unit, but was very strong and determined to move on with her life and was called by the hospital staff the "1,200 gram wonder."

> Since the premature birth did not enable us to meet prior to the baby arriving, we met with the mom after she was back at the prison prior to her daughter's release from the hospital. When we were at the prison, the mom was asked if she had any questions of us, she stated: "Just one— why? Why would you do this when you don't know me or anything about me?" My memory of our response was simply that we thought we'd be able to do this, and we were concerned that women who were locked up were relatively ignored by society. Especially at risk were those

(continued)

with no family or outside support—no one visiting or putting money into their accounts for food, supplies, and phone calls.

Once out of the hospital, the now 4-pound baby came home with us, and for the next year, she went to visit her mom in prison every weekend—either taken by us or other members of our church. During the week, while my partner and I went to our jobs, the baby stayed in the homes of those who volunteered to provide care for a day or more during the week. After the mom's release date, for the next few years, Mom and child both lived with us while Mom got herself in a more stable position to care for them both.

Jeanine and I have always been, and always will be, this child's nanas, being intentional from the start about not being referred to as her moms because she has a mom. We have seven other grandchildren, and this child made eight, and she was/is involved in our lives continually as another one of our grandchildren. Since she is actually the only grandchild (now along with her brother) who lives in the same community as us, she actually has had the most time and relationship of presence with "the nanas." Ours is a community of care.

What I learned through this experience is that as you offer support for others, you learn and grow in your own life as well. It does, indeed, take a village—and when all join in, there is also a connection with the villagers, inside and outside. For the baby's first birthday, we held a spaghetti lunch after church and asked for donations to help cover the cost of daycare for two days a week to help in the upcoming transition when her mom was released. To make that happen, some people offered to cook and many attended and were happy to give a donation for the daycare cost. I learned over and over again, if you ask, people will step up and help.

After being involved in this life-changing experience, I was inspired to start a nonprofit organization named Oasis Village (www.oasis-village.org) to create an intergenerational residential community for single moms coming out of incarceration who have little to no family support. It is one of the many ways I do the work of ending the impact of mass incarceration, especially for women, who are the fastest growing population of those incarcerated.

Conclusion

Family developmental theory has provided important ideas that allow researchers and practitioners to understand the predictable stages that guide families through the events and transitions associated with marriage and reproduction. Once championed as the first theory to place the family unit in the center of analysis, family developmental theory has been challenged by the vast diversity that characterizes families nationally and internationally. However, the theory has proven to be remarkably useful in terms of a general understanding of how humans conduct their intimate lives and care for the young. The life cycle concept is a powerful metaphor for family growth and change, and no other theory has done better at highlighting what is unique and enduring about families everywhere. We challenge you to consider these applications of the theory as you move on to the areas for further study and the discussion and reflection questions in the concluding pages of this chapter.

Multimedia Suggestions

www.ted.com/talks

Search Jennifer Senior's TED Talk, which touches on the stages of the life cycle that involve parenting. She refers to a "parenthood crisis" that characterizes modern parenting. Senior's talk is based on her 2014 book *All Joy and No Fun,* which explores how children reshape their parents' lives. She describes how "we got here," pointing out that the word "parent" was not widely used as a verb until the 1970s. Senior uses this idea to show that modern parenthood is riddled with anxiety and suggests that we rethink how we raise our children.

Activate your theory app: After watching this clip, can you think of examples you have witnessed or heard about in your own life of this parenting challenge? Consider the type of parents affected by this challenge—does it include every demographic or just a specific group?

www.advocatesforyouth.org

This website serves as a resource for anyone working with young adults as they navigate the life cycle and make decisions about their reproductive and sexual health. It includes resources, links to partner organizations, and information for activists who seek to influence public policy in this area.

Activate your theory app: Consider the issues facing today's youth on this website: How could family developmental theory be used to help practitioners address these concerns?

Coco (2017)

This animated Disney film follows a young boy, Miguel, as he learns about his ancestors and family secrets that have been hidden for generations. The idea for this film emerged out of the Mexican holiday, Día de Muertos (Day of the Dead). Because Miguel's great-great grandmother was deserted by her husband and the father of her children to pursue a musical career, the family all but banned music from their daily lives. The story follows the journey of Miguel to discover his musical lineage and offers a glimpse into the life cycle of multiple generations in their family as a result. This film illustrates several concepts from family developmental theory as the family members confront generational trauma, honoring the stages of the life cycle and traditions grounded in ethnic heritage and associated norms that emphasize the importance of honoring deceased family members.

Image 5.2 A Scene From *Coco,* 2017

Activate your theory app: Have norms associated with death and the life cycle celebrated among diverse ethnic groups become more mainstream? What can all cultures learn from celebrating and honoring the dead in the same ways that Mexican tradition does?

Image 5.3 A Scene From *Minari*, 2020

Minari (2020)

This Oscar-nominated film tells the story of a Korean American family adjusting to a new, rural life in Arkansas in the 1980s. As the family adapts to their new surroundings and the associated challenges, the story follows the multi-generational household's traditions. The grandmother, Soon-Ja, takes a central role in the film as she steps in to help with childrearing before she suffers a stroke. The film shows glimpses of what it's like to be at varying stages of the life cycle and the importance of family connectedness in troubled times.

Activate your theory app: As we pointed out earlier in this chapter, one of the weaknesses of family developmental theory is that it ignores family problems. How were the problems facing this family solved in this film?

Further Reading

Bélanger, M., & Ward, M. (2019). *The family dynamic: Canadian perspectives* (7th ed.). Nelson. This book highlights the pluralism of family forms and dynamics among 21st-century families in Canada, including how families move through the life cycle. This text provides insight into how a nation's laws and policies affect families' access to marriage, child care, and assisted reproduction. In addition, some interesting comparisons included in this book emerge when considering Canadians' experiences of immigration, transnational marriages, adoption, and grandparents raising grandchildren. As an example, the Canadian census includes grandparents raising grandchildren (with no parents present) in their legal definition of family.

Cicirelli, V. G. (2010). Attachment relationships in old age. *Journal of Social and Personal Relationships, 27*(2), 191–199. https://doi.org/10.1177/0265407509360984. This research emphasizes attachment patterns in old age, a stage in the life cycle that does not receive quite as much attention when it comes to attachment and relationships. Victor Cicirelli sheds light on this process, taking into account how deceased family members, the onset of disability, or experiencing widowhood may affect older adults' attachment patterns. Based on Bowlby's (1988) assertion that individuals are dependent on others throughout the life span, this work highlights one stage of the life cycle, helping us understand how attachment and relationships inevitably change over time.

Furstenberg, F. F., Jr. (2010). On a new schedule: Transitions to adulthood and family change. *The Future of Children, 20*(1), 67–87. https://doi.org/10.1353/foc.0.0038. Frank Furstenberg discusses the major changes that have occurred in marriage and family patterns within the context of global and economic changes. These changes have affected the way that young people experience the transition to adulthood. Unlike other Western nations, the United States does not invest heavily in education, health care, and job benefits for young adults. As a result, dependency on parents continues into the third decade of life, delaying the start of the family life cycle for current youth. Moreover, youth who come from economically disadvantaged families have a more difficult time attaining independence from their family of origin than youth from families with more ample support. Now, youth operate on a newly extended timetable in terms of being launched from the parental home and transitioning to adulthood. They can no longer expect the type of predictable schedule posited by family developmental theory.

Murkoff, H. (2016). *What to expect when you're expecting* (5th ed.). Workman. Hailed as America's "pregnancy Bible," this is often the first book read by pregnant individuals and their partners when they discover they are expecting a baby. Updated for current family life, this popular "how to" manual addresses everything from getting pregnant to keeping healthy during pregnancy to adjusting to having a newborn baby to getting back in shape. Although mostly written from the perspective of the positive side of pregnancy and childbirth, this book also addresses pregnancy loss. It provides an accessible and authoritative voice to help expecting parents anticipate this key part of the family life cycle.

Murray, C. I., & Reuter, J. C. (2021). Death, dying, and grief in families. In K. R. Bush & C. A. Price (Eds.), *Families & change: Coping with stressful events and transitions* (6th ed., pp. 481–506). SAGE Publications. Death is a crisis experienced by all families; yet by the 20th century, death had become, as Murray and Reuter noted, sequestered, privatized, and invisible. The authors describe several theoretical frameworks used to explain the complexities of dealing with death, dying, and bereavement and apply a developmental model that takes into account individual, familial, cultural, and temporal dimensions simultaneously. Such a comprehensive perspective is needed because the way that most industrialized societies deal with death tends to sensationalize the public nature of death (e.g., death by murder, death by war, death by natural disaster), splashing such deaths across the news and on social media on a daily basis. There is a major difference between the public events and the private nature of death in families, with the public nature sensationalized, and the private experience of death and mourning treated as a taboo topic. Death is often an invisible process with little anticipatory socialization in how to deal with it. Family developmental theory proposes that the end of the family life cycle includes the experience of coping with the loss of a spouse and the ultimate death of both married partners, but very little support is given for the grief process. It is, therefore, important to take into account how death affects individual family members, the family unit as a whole, and the social context in which it occurs.

Questions for Students

Discussion Questions

1. In what ways is the concept of the family life cycle still relevant for families in the 21st century? In what ways is it not?

2. Considering the cultural differences of families around the world, how might family developmental theory be applied in different economies or countries?

3. How do family developmental tasks cause conflict in families, depending upon the person's position in the hierarchical structure?

4. Like some other theories you have read about in this book, family developmental theory was proposed in the United States during a time of economic prosperity. Does this model fit for minoritized individuals, living in varying conditions throughout the world?

5. Consider the developmental tasks associated with the different stages of the family life cycle. Are there some that can be accomplished in alternative ways (i.e., outside the family unit)?

6. Compare and contrast family developmental theory with conflict theory (Chapter 3). What do they have in common? How do they differ?

Your Turn!

Most individuals do not necessarily "map out" how they expect to move through stages of the life cycle; instead, we typically daydream or imagine ourselves in the future. For this activity, we ask you to put pen to paper and draw or write out what you envision is your next stage in the life cycle. Write your career goals, where you will live, and how much you expect to earn. Then, envision the next stage of your life cycle, drawing where you are currently, according to Figure 5.1 in this chapter, and where you are headed next. Answer the basic questions of "who, what, where, when, how, and why," regarding the next stage in your life cycle. Be specific, detailing even the small things, like if or how the household labor will be divided, who will do the care work (if applicable), and how you will maintain any individual interests, hobbies, or activities in the face of new changes.

Personal Reflection Questions

1. What family developmental tasks did you and your parents struggle with the most and at what ages?

2. Meet with one or more of your older relatives, and talk about their experience of the family life cycle. How does their experience differ from your own?

3. If you plan to marry, do you intend to go through a marriage preparation class? If so, what do you hope to learn as you prepare for this major change?

4. Are there films other than the ones discussed in which the circle of family life is evident? Name one of your favorites, and explain why it fits with family developmental theory.

5. Thinking about your own progression in the family life cycle, are there any developmental tasks you have accomplished outside of your family? Or are there any developmental tasks not listed as part of family developmental theory that your family *did* help you achieve?

6. Meet with a classmate, either virtually or in person, and discuss differences and similarities you've each experienced thus far in the family life cycle. Are there cultural or religious differences you can identify? What similarities exist, and why?

References

Adler-Baeder, F., & Higginbotham, B. (2020). Efforts to design, implement, and evaluate community-based education for stepfamilies: Current knowledge and future directions. *Family Relations, 69*(3), 559–576. https://doi.org/10.1111/fare.12427

Agadjanian, V. (2020). Condemned and condoned: Polygynous marriage in Christian Africa. *Journal of Marriage and Family, 82*(2), 751–768. https://doi.org/10.1111/jomf.12624

Aldous, J. (1978). *Family careers: Developmental change in families.* Wiley.

Allen, K. R., & Pickett, R. S. (1987). Forgotten streams in the family life course: Utilization of qualitative retrospective interviews in the analysis of lifelong single women's family careers. *Journal of Marriage and the Family, 49*(3), 517–526. https://doi.org/10.2307/352197

Arias, E., Tejada-Vera, B., & Ahmad, F. (2021, February). *Provisional life expectancy estimates for January through June, 2020.* National Center for Health Statistics. https://dx.doi.org/10.15620/cdc:100392

Arnett, J. J. (2000). Emerging adulthood: A theory of development from the late teens through the twenties. *American Psychologist, 55*(5), 469–480. https://doi.org/10:1037/0003-066X.55.5.469

Ballard, S. M. (2020). The practice of family life education: Toward an implementation framework. *Family Relations, 69*(3), 461–478. https://doi.org/10.1111/fare.12443

Bartz, D., & Greenberg, J. A. (2008). Sterilization in the United States. *Reviews in Obstetrics and Gynecology, 1*(1), 23–32.

Bengtson, V. L., & Allen, K. R. (1993). The life course perspective applied to families over time. In P. Boss, W. Doherty, R. LaRossa, W. Schumm, & S. Steinmetz (Eds.), *Sourcebook of family theories and methods: A contextual approach* (pp. 469–499). Plenum.

Berger, L. M., & Carlson, M. J. (2020). Family policy and complex contemporary families: A decade in review and implications for the next decade of research and policy practice. *Journal of Marriage and Family, 82*(1), 478–507. https://doi.org/10.1111.jomf.12650

Bowlby, J. (1988). *A secure base: Parent–child attachment and healthy human development.* Basic Books.

Burgess, E. W. (1926). The family as a unity of interacting personalities. *The Family, 7*(1), 3–9. https://doi.org/10.1177/104438942600700101

Burton, L. M. (1996). Age norms, the timing of family role transitions, and intergenerational caregiving among aging African American women. *Gerontologist, 36*(2), 199–208. https://doi.org/10.1093/geront/36.2.199

Cheal, D. (1991). *Family and the state of theory.* University of Toronto Press.

Connidis, I. A., & Barnett, A. E. (2019). *Family ties & aging* (3rd ed.). SAGE Publications.

Coontz, S. (2016). The way we never were: *American families and the nostalgia trap* (Rev. ed.). Basic Books.

Crapo, J. S., & Bradford, K. (2021). Multidimensional family development theory: A reconceptualization of family development. *Journal of Family Theory & Review, 13*(2), 202–223. https://doi.org/10.1111/jftr.12414

Curtis, K. M., Mohllajee, A. P., & Peterson, H. B. (2006). Regret following female sterilization at a young age: A systematic review. *Contraception, 73*(2), 205–210. https://doi.org/ 10.1016/j.contraception.2005.08.006

Darling, C. A., Cassidy, D., & Rehm, M. (2020). The foundations of family life education model: Understanding the field. *Family Relations,* 69(3), 427–441. https://doi.org/10.1111/fare.12372

Davies, J. J., & Gentile, D. A. (2012). Responses to children's media use in families with and without siblings: A family development perspective. *Family Relations, 61*(3), 410–425. https://doi.org/10.1111/j.1741-3729.2012.00703.x

Davis, S., & Dubisar, A. M. (2019). Communicating elective sterilization: A feminist perspective. *Rhetoric of Health & Medicine,* 2(1), 88–113. https://doi.org/10.5744/rhm.2019.1004

Demopoulos, A. (2020, December 4). *Women and non-binary people tired of getting turned down by doctors for sterilization are talking to TikTok to express their frustration—and also their joy at being child-free. The Daily Beast.* https://www.thedailybeast.com/meet-the-women-telling-their-sterilization-stories-on-tiktok

Dias, P., & Brito, R. (2020). How families with young children are solving the dilemma between privacy and protection by building trust—A portrait from Portugal. *Journal of Children and Media, 14*(1), 56–73. https://doi.org/10.1080/17482798.2019.1694552

Dworkin, J., Hessel, H., & LeBouef, S. (2019). The use of communication technology in the context of adolescent and family development: An integration of family and media theories. *Journal of Family Theory & Review, 11*(4), 510–523. https://doi.org/10.1111/jftr.12350

Duvall, E. M. (1957). *Family development.* Lippincott.

Duvall, E. M. (1988). Family development's first forty years. *Family Relations, 37*(2), 127–134. https://doi.org/10.2307/584309

Erikson, E. H. (1968). *Childhood and society* (2nd ed.). W. W. Norton.

Feldman, H., & Feldman, M. (1975). The family life cycle: Some suggestions for recycling. *Journal of Marriage and the Family, 37*(2), 277–284. https://doi.org/10.2307/350961

Ganong, L. H., & Coleman, M. (2017). Studying stepfamilies: Four eras of family scholarship: *Family Process, 57*(1), 7–24. https://doi.org/10.1111/famp.12307

Gavazzi, S. (2013). Theory and research pertaining to families with adolescents. In G. W. Peterson & K. R. Bush (Eds.), *Handbook of marriage and the family* (3rd ed., pp. 303–327). Springer.

Gay, P. (Ed.). (1995). *The Freud reader.* W. W. Norton.

Glick, P. C. (1947). The family cycle. *American Sociological Review, 12*(2), 164–174. https://doi.org/10.2307/346771

Glick, P. C. (1988). Fifty years of family demography: A record of social change. *Journal of Marriage and the Family, 50*(4), 861–873. https://doi.org/10.2307/352100.

Goldberg, A. E. (2010). *Lesbian and gay parents and their children: Research on the family life cycle.* American Psychological Association.

Goldberg, A. E., & Allen, K. R. (Eds.). (2020). LGBTQ-parent families: *Innovations in research and implications for practice* (2nd ed.). Springer.

Havighurst, R. J. (1972). *Developmental tasks and education* (3rd ed.). David McKay. (Original work published 1948)

Henderson, T. L., Dinh, M., Morgan, K., & Lewis, J. (2017). Alaska native grandparents rearing grandchildren: A rural community story. *Journal of Family Issues, 38*(4), 547–572. https://doi.org/10.1177/0192513X15597292

Hill, R. (1949). Families under stress: *Adjustment to the crises of war separation and reunion.* Harper.

Hill, R. (1986). Life cycle stages for types of single parent families: Of family development theory. *Family Relations, 35*(1), 19–29. https://doi.org/10.2307/584278

Hill, R., & Hansen, D. A. (1960). The identification of conceptual frameworks utilized in family study. *Marriage and Family Living, 22*(4), 299–311. https://doi.org/10.2307/347242

Hill, R., & Rodgers, R. H. (1964). The developmental approach. In H. Christensen (Ed.), *Handbook of marriage and the family* (pp. 171–211). Rand McNally.

Jensen, T. M., & Sanner, C. (2021). A scoping review of research on well-being across diverse family structures: Rethinking approaches for understanding contemporary families. *Journal of Family Theory & Review, 13*(4), 463-495. https://doi.org/10.1111/jftr.12437

Laszloffy, T. A. (2002). Rethinking family development theory: Teaching with the systemic family development (SFD) model. *Family Relations, 51*(3), 206–214. https://doi.org/10.1111/j.1741-3729.2002.206098.x

Lev, A. I., & Sennott, S. L. (2020). Clinical work with LGBTQ parents and prospective parents. In A. E. Goldberg & K. R. Allen (Eds.), *LGBTQ-parent families: Innovations in research and implications for practice* (pp. 383–403). Springer.

Lichter, D. T., Price, J. P., & Swigert, J. M. (2020). Mismatches in the marriage market. *Journal of Marriage and Family, 82*(2), 796–809. https://doi.org/10.1111/jomf.12603

Manago, A. M., Brown, G., Lawley, K. A., & Anderson, G. (2020). Adolescents' daily face-to-face and computer-mediated communication: Associations with autonomy and closeness to parents and friends. *Developmental Psychology, 56*(1), 153–164. https://doi.org/10.1037/dev0000851

Martin, T. F. (2018). Family development theory 30 years later. *Journal of Family Theory & Review, 10*(1), 49–69. https://doi.org/10.1111/jftr.12237

Mattessich, P., & Hill, R. (1987). Life cycle and family development. In M. B. Sussman & S. K. Steinmetz (Eds.), *Handbook of marriage and the family* (pp. 437–469). Plenum.

McDaniel, B. T., & Radesky, J. S. (2018). Technoference: Longitudinal associations between parent technology use, parenting stress, and child behavior problems. *Pediatric Research*, 84, 210–218. https://doi.org/10.1038/s41390-018-0052-6

McGoldrick, M., & Hardy, K. V. (Eds.). (2019). *Re-visioning family therapy: Addressing diversity in clinical practice*. Guilford Press.

McGoldrick, M., Garcia-Preto, N., & Carter, B. (2015). *The expanding family life cycle: Individual, family, and social perspectives* (5th ed.). Pearson.

Meeus, A., Coenen, L., Eggermont, S., & Beullens, K. (2021). Family technoference: Exploring parent mobile device distraction from children's perspectives. *Mobile Media & Communication*, 9(3), 584–604. https://doi.org/10.1177/2050157921991602

Minola, T., Brumana, M., Campopiano, G. Garrett, R. P., & Cassia, L. (2016). Corporate venturing in family business: A developmental approach of the enterprising family. *Strategic Entrepreneurship Journal, 10*(4), 395–412. https://doi.org/10.1002/sej

Nelson, M. K. (2006). Single mothers "do" family. *Journal of Marriage and Family, 68*(4), 781–795. https:doi.org/10.1111/j.l741–3737.2006.00292.x

Nock, S. L. (1979). The family life cycle: Empirical or conceptual tool? *Journal of Marriage and the Family, 41*(1), 15–26. https://doi.org/10.2307/351727

Pallotta-Chiarolli, M., Sheff, E., & Mountford, R. (2020). Polyamorous parenting in contemporary research: Developments and future directions. In A. E. Goldberg & K. R. Allen (Eds.), *LGBTQ-parent families: Innovations in research and implications for practice* (pp. 171–183). Springer.

Papernow, P. (1993). *Becoming a stepfamily*. Jossey-Bass.

Pearson, C. (2014, October 28). *Meet the 20-somethings who want to be sterilized*. HuffPost Women. http://www.huffingtonpost.com/2014/10/24/female-sterilization-young-women_n_5882000.html

Piaget, J. (1952). *The origins of intelligence in children* (M. Cook, Trans.). W. W. Norton.

Pilkauskas, N. V., & Dunifon, R. E. (2016). Understanding grandfamilies: Characteristics of grandparents, nonresident parents, and children. *Journal of Marriage and Family, 78*(3), 62–633. https://doi.org/10.1111/jomf.12291

Rodgers, R. H. (1973). *Family interaction and transaction: The developmental approach*. Prentice Hall.

Rodgers, R. H., & White, J. M. (1993). Family developmental theory. In P. G. Boss, W. J. Doherty, R. LaRossa, W. R. Schumm, & S. K. Steinmetz (Eds.), *Sourcebook of family theories and methods: A contextual approach* (pp. 225–254). Plenum.

Rowe, G. P. (1966). The developmental conceptual framework to the study of the family. In F. I. Nye & F. M. Berardo (Eds.), *Emerging conceptual frameworks in family analysis* (pp. 198–222). Macmillan.

Rubio, B., Vecho, O., Gross, M., van Rijn-van Gelderen, L., Bos, H., Ellis-Davies, K., Winstanley, A., Golombok, S., & Lamb, M. E. (2020). Transition to parenthood and quality of parenting among gay, lesbian and heterosexual couples who conceived through assisted reproduction. *Journal of Family Studies*, 26(3), 422–440. https://doi.org//10.1080/13229400.2017.1413005

Russell, L. T., Coleman, M., & Ganong, L. (2018). Conceptualizing family structure in a social determinants of health framework. *Journal of Family Theory & Review, 10*(4), 735–748. https://doi.org/10.1111/jftr.12296

Senior, J. (2014). *All joy and no fun: The paradox of modern parenthood*. HarperCollins.

Sironi, M., & Billari, F. C. (2019). Leaving home, moving to college, and returning home: Economic outcomes in the United States. *Population, Space and Place, 26*(4), 32302. https://doi.org/10.1002/psp.2302

Slater, S. (1999). *The lesbian family life cycle*. University of Illinois Press.

Smock, P. J., & Schwartz, C. R. (2020). The demography of families: A review of patterns and change. *Journal of Marriage and Family 82*(1), 9–34. https://doi.org/10.1111/jomf.12612

Stewart, S. D. (2007). *Brave new stepfamilies: Diverse paths toward stepfamily living.* SAGE Publications.

White, J. M., & Klein, D. M. (2008). *Family theories* (3rd ed.). SAGE Publications.

White, J. M., Martin, T. F., & Adamsons, K. (2019). *Family theories: An introduction* (5th ed.). SAGE Publications.

World Bank. (2021). *Life expectancy at birth, total (years)—Japan.* https://data.worldbank.org/indicator/SP.DYN.LE00.MA.IN?locations=JP&most_recent_value_desc=true

Wong, R. S., Tung, K. T. S., Rao, N., Leung, C., Hui, A. N. N., Tso, W. W. Y., Fu, K. W., Jiang, F., Zhao, J., & Ip, P. (2020). Parent technology use, parent–child interaction, child screen time, and child psychosocial problems among disadvantaged families. *The Journal of Pediatrics, 226,* 258–265. https://doi.org/10.1016/j.jpeds.2020.07.006

Image Credits

Family Systems Theory

Have you ever had a roommate whose housekeeping quirks really made you wonder? Did they leave piles and piles of dirty dishes in the sink? Over time, some people might come to the conclusion that the roommate was just unclean or, perhaps, lazy—or one might even go so far as to say simply disgusting. However, as a family theorist, it is important to take a look at the bigger picture to understand behavior. It is easy to use a simple individualist viewpoint, in which we focus on the individual and assume that the problem is unique to that person. Most likely there are other contributing factors we need to consider before seeing the behavior as innate and unchangeable. Perhaps, the roommate is rebelling from having a very strict upbringing in which they were harshly punished for not doing their chores. Or maybe their parents did all the chores, so they did not know where to start, or they just assumed someone else will do them, which is what they have expected and experienced for nearly 20 years of life. In any case, systems theorists look at the *whole*—not just the parts—of the system before interpreting behavior. Family systems theorists wonder what else is going on in the family to help understand issues and conflicts. Family systems theorists ask: How is the problem related to other processes, such as parenting styles, expectations for siblings, and how well members of a family communicate? With family systems theory, every contributing factor is taken into account because we cannot understand any part of the system without looking at the whole picture.

One way to envision how family systems theory works is to think about a family portrait you have seen. With that image in your mind, look at the subjects in the photo and the landscape behind and next to the subjects, and take in each aspect of the picture. Family systems theory gives us this type of panoramic, 3D view of family; no aspect can be taken for granted, ignored, or left unexamined. Consider, when imagining the portrait, what the weather is like that day, what the family members are wearing, whether a family member is in a wheelchair, how close it is to meal time, whether there is a barking dog nearby, and whether anyone either in the photo or even behind the lens was having a bad day or had a misunderstanding with someone else before or while the photo was taken. You can also think about who is missing from the photo—whether they are emotionally estranged, living in another country, deceased, or simply away at college. When you think about it, the possibilities are endless! Family systems theorists take into account all of the interrelated parts when examining family dynamics and issues. Our case study gives us a closer look at family.

Case Study

When Jackson's mother married her second husband, Jackson not only gained a new father, but he also became a sibling for the first time. His stepfather's son, Dustin, just a year younger, came to live with them. The new brothers couldn't be more different. Jackson, a cisgender able-bodied Latino boy, was an introvert, who liked anything to do with science fiction. He was especially into the Harry Potter books and films. In addition, Jackson and his mother were very close during his childhood. Jackson's biological father died when he was only four, so for the past 10 years, it was just the two of them. At bedtime, he and his mother would take turns reading chapters from the Harry Potter books out loud to one another. Jackson was a good student in school and an avid reader. For a 14 year old boy, he was uniquely emotionally tuned in to those around him. He was also quiet and shy.

Dustin, on the other hand, was much more outgoing than Jackson. The main reason he came to live with his dad was because his mother said she could not control him. Going to live with his father, stepmother, and stepbrother also meant that he was moving up in the world. His father lived in an exclusive suburb with excellent schools and safe neighborhoods. This was very different for Dustin, who had grown up in an apartment in inner-city Boston.

Since Dustin was so outgoing, he immediately made friends with the cool kids at Jackson's school. Dustin was also taller and tougher than Jackson, a difference that only exaggerated Jackson's difficulties fitting in with his peers. Jackson became increasingly withdrawn and now spent most of his time alone in his room. Formerly an A student, his grades began to drop. He became more and more belligerent toward his mother and would barely speak to his stepfather. His stepfather tried to use the same discipline techniques on both boys, but Jackson resented the fact that he was no longer treated as special. Jackson's mother worried about his adjustment to his new family situation and felt torn in her loyalties to her old family, consisting of her first husband and Jackson, and to her new family that also included her second husband and his son.

When she got a call from Jackson's teacher that he was no longer turning in his assignments, she knew he needed help. Her new husband was furious and suggested disciplining Jackson at home, but she was able to convince him that Jackson needed to see a therapist first. She contacted a therapist, so Jackson could get the individual attention and help he needed. When she explained Jackson's problems to the therapist, the therapist said the whole family needed to come to the session. Jackson's mother was stunned: Why did they all have to go when it was Jackson who was acting out?

Why was Jackson's mom so shocked that the therapist wanted to see the whole family? Why would there be a difference between addressing Jackson's behavior from an individual perspective, compared to a family perspective? What could be learned from focusing on family dynamics, loyalties, and the introduction of new "parts" into the family system? Family systems theorists would argue that individuals do not function in isolation: Family members are interdependent. Their behaviors are best understood in terms of the interrelatedness of all of the parts of a system, including the history of all members, the backstory of the family unit, and the interplay of family dynamics as a result. Therefore, when we use family systems theory, we are equipped to look beyond the problem—we take a panoramic, 3D view—to help frame the underlying issues contributing to the system as a whole.

- A family consists of interdependent individuals.
- The family system consists of interdependent subsystems.
- The family system, subsystems, and individual members seek to maintain equilibrium.
- The whole (family) is greater than the sum of its parts (individuals and subsystems).
- The whole family has to be examined in order to understand family dynamics.
- Families differ in the degree to which they are cohesive or disengaged.
- Families are organized by open and closed boundaries.

What Is Family Systems Theory?

Family systems theory is concerned with the ways parents and children, spouses, and extended family members mutually influence and communicate with one another. This theory focuses on the relationships that make up a system, rather than just the system as a whole. This theoretical lens allows for a closer examination of the "inner workings" of systems, such as rules that govern the behaviors of individuals in the family as well as within the subsystems that comprise the family unit. A **family system** is defined as a unit of interdependent individuals. **Subsystems** are units within the family that can be examined on their own in relation to the larger unit (Whitchurch & Constantine, 1993). Examples include a parental subsystem, sibling subsystem, aunt–nephew subsystem, and grandparent–grandchild subsystem. Families, as systems, seek to maintain their existing boundaries and patterns. Understanding each of these dynamics as part of the larger whole—including patterns of interaction, communication, and resistance to change—is the key to applying family systems theory (Anderson et al., 2013; Broderick & Smith, 1979; Galovan et al., 2017; Holmes & Huston, 2010).

Family systems theory emerged from general systems theory (GST), a perspective that explains the wholeness and the interconnection among all parts in the system. Systems theory was developed to identify how all types of systems—especially those that are mechanical or inanimate—function in universal ways (von Bertalanffy, 1973). Some scholars have argued that general systems theory contains universal principles that can be applied to any context, whether inanimate or living. For example, an information system, a weaponry system, a governmental system, and a family system, all share the same characteristics according to systems theory. They are composed of interconnected parts that affect and are affected by their environments. To understand how any of these systems operate, you have to understand the system as a whole (White et al., 2019).

Other scholars, however, have argued that applying general systems concepts to families requires some adjustment. As living systems, families must be understood differently than inanimate systems. Human beings are unpredictable. We are motivated by different things, and our choices and preferences even change over time—as do the social forces surrounding us. Because of a family's ever changing dynamics, family systems theory as we know it today was developed by scholars and therapists in psychology, sociology, social work, and family science, who studied and worked with families, particularly in addressing their emotional and behavioral problems (e.g., Ackerman, 1984; Beavers & Hampson, 2000; Cowan et al., 1996; Minuchin, 1985; Olson, 2000; Satir, 1988). This perspective is concerned with the ways interrelated individuals in families are affected whenever a change is introduced into any one part of the family system; that change will affect all other members in the system (e.g., a parent gets a new job, and the family must relocate; a new baby is born, and the older children have to adjust to another family member). Family systems theorists address the interactions and emotional issues that arise in every-day life, whether they are in the **family of origin**, which is the family one is born into, or the family of procreation, which, as we learned in Chapter 5 on family developmental theory, is the family one establishes in adulthood by marriage or other type of intimate partnership. These interactional patterns and processes occur among spouses or partners, between parents and children, and they echo across the generations in the extended family. As we explained in the case study involving Jackson and his family, family systems theory helps us to uncover patterns that are often unseen and unspoken, as in the case of how a child's "acting out" behaviors are a clue to broader tensions in the family system (Cowan et al., 1996; O'Gorman, 2012) and helps practitioners develop theoretically informed interventions that promote interconnectedness (Cowan & Cowan, 2019).

A family system also must be understood in social context, and family systems theory can and should incorporate ethnic and racial diversity to a much greater extent than has occurred in the past (Baptist & Hamon, 2022; James 2020). In understanding family dynamics among Asian American families, for example, Baptist and Hamon (2022) highlight the role of filial piety, which refers to the sense of deference and obligation to care for parents and grandparents. They also point out the importance of loyalty, harmony, and conformity as part of the collectivist family values among Asian American families. Further, we need to understand the risk associated with the generational trauma experienced by Asian Americans, due to the history of exclusionary laws against Asian families from entering the United States to the internment of Japanese Americans during World War II. This generational trauma has been exacerbated during the COVID-19 pandemic with the rise of hate crimes against Asian Americans (Baptist & Hamon). In a study of 12 Asian American young adults that was guided by family systems theory, Young et al. (2021) found that their families were relatively silent when it came to preparing youth for understanding their own racial identity or the history of trauma their parents may have experienced, particularly as immigrants. Racial socialization for young Asian Americans is vital in the current cultural context, which is marred by racism, anti-Asian sentiment, and the prevalence of verbal harassment and physical assaults.

Similarly, James et al. (2018) point out ways in which family systems theorizing, when it has been decontextualized from the history of race and racism in the United States or used in a color blind fashion, has not been able to "capture the culturally relevant and existing strengths of Black families often exhibited through their organizational structure and interactive processes" (p. 420). Instead, systemic theorizing about Black families must include an understanding of how Black parents need to socialize their children by preparing them for racial bias as well as promoting positive messages about self-acceptance and equality in society (Dotterer & Skinner, 2020). It is important to explicitly center race and racism, so the experiences of families of color can be examined from a historicized and contextualized per-spective (James et al., 2018). Given the historic focus on White family structures and processes, we still have a long way to go in developing more comprehensive research about the variations within Black communities, particularly in terms of diverse structures associated with cohabiting, remarriage, and stepfamily relationships (Russell, 2020a).

History and Origins

There are many variations to systems theory, and it has developed, as both a theoretical framework and a diverse array of clinical practices, over the past several decades (Priest, 2021). Family systems theory is one of the most relevant approaches for "identifying and understanding how individuals, couples, and families experience reciprocal interactions with their environment" (Gale et al., 2020, p. 86). Systems thinking offers a useful framework for conceptualizing the individual and relational processes occurring in families with adolescents, integrating attachment theory and accounting for the experiences of separateness and connection that impact parents and children in the family constellation (Bortz et al., 2019). In this section, we examine the emergence of the theory as it was first developed in the mid-20th century and then address how systems thinking was applied to the study of families. Although we emphasize systems theory in the context of families, we also point out that, like other theories, family systems theory is interdisciplinary in its roots and very diverse in its current applications.

General Systems Theory

Compared to conflict theory (Chapter 3) and symbolic interactionist theory (Chapter 4), general systems theory (GST) is a relatively new perspective. It is a perspective that crosses scientific disciplines, with roots in biology, engineering, mathematics, physics, statistics, and other sciences. Whitchurch and Constantine (1993) explain that GST was developed during World War II out of desperation because more sophisticated weaponry was needed in combat with enemy forces:

> [E]xtensive use of airplanes in warfare during World War II necessitated intensive research on antiaircraft gunnery to improve accuracy of aiming at moving targets from ships rolling on ocean waves. Therefore, mathematical theory of prediction was developed to calculate the positions of enemy aircraft ahead of their current positions to enable ammunition to meet airplane targets in mid-air. Of course, accurate tracking of the target required constant comparison of the aim of the antiaircraft gun with the movements of the target and tracking the gun's own position. This was a self-monitoring process by the antiaircraft gun that became known as *cybernetic feedback*. (pp. 326–327)

A key feature of GST is the ability to look inside of a system to examine what processes keep it functioning. This notion is based on the science of **cybernetics**, developed by mathematician Norbert Wiener (1967). Cybernetics provides a model for understanding the forms and patterns that steer a system and allow that system to self-regulate. While this process seems macro level in nature by examining overall functioning of a system, what is unique about cybernetics is the ability to explore the patterns of communication and control that a system develops to maintain stability. Systemic patterns change when confronted with the new information and constraints that are constantly bombarding the system. This process of change is similar to how families operate on a daily basis and over time. Cybernetics deals with the internal rules that govern a system to keep it functioning. For example, cybernetics explains how a thermostat adjusts itself to maintain the desired temperature or how the circuits in the brain control behavior in animal systems (Broderick, 1993). Therefore, GST takes into account both the functioning of the overall unit as well as how the unit reacts to and adapts to changes, new information, constraints, and roadblocks over time. This allows researchers to really understand how units function on a much deeper level than, for example, a more macro theory like functionalism (see Chapter 2).

The Emergence of Family Systems Theory

Following World War II, psychiatrists and sociologists who studied families started to think about families as systems. This development led to the growth of family therapy (a departure from the biologically and individually oriented field of Freudian psychoanalysis that dominated psychiatry). Family systems theory was used to explain how a young person might develop schizophrenia by positing that the mother's influence was the most important in creating the conditions under which this psychiatric disorder developed (Bateson et al., 1956). The argument was based on the idea that mothers created a **double bind** situation, which occurs when a person is given two commands that contradict each other. For example, a double bind is created when the parent repeatedly asks for more affection from the child and, at the same time, shows through their body language (e.g., stiffens when they touch) they are rejecting that affection. The double bind is said to create a paradoxical straightjacket, maintained with unspoken rules that family members must uphold this "crazy-making situation" (Broderick, 1993, p. 34). Although the concept of double bind was eventually critiqued by feminist family therapists as mother blaming, sexist, and male-centered (Luepnitz, 1988/2002), the application of GST to family social science had begun.

Family systems theory, then, is built on the idea of **holism**—that the whole family should be studied. The subsystems within families need to be understood as part of a larger hierarchy, defined by internal boundaries. The parent–child relationship is the prototypical hierarchical subsystem, with coparents viewed as the leaders and managers of the family system (Petren & Puhlman, 2021). Hierarchy explains the distribution of power and shows how one or more family subsystems can have more power than others. Gender is a primary way in which hierarchy functions in family subsystems, and gender shapes and organizes social life "from the cradle to the grave" (Endendijk et al., 2018). For instance, a father–son subsystem may have access to more resources within the family because they are considered important in decision-making processes. A father may place more trust in his son to manage his estate instead of his wife or daughter after he dies. These subsystem dynamics and boundaries that are created within families need to be understood in terms of a hierarchy that carries theoretical significance when studying families. In Box 6.3 later in this chapter, we provide examples of how this gendered hierarchy persists and is reflected in different forms around the globe.

Family scholars have also examined how broader social systems, cultural experiences, and external boundaries, including race, class, gender, sexuality, religion, national origin, and the like, affect individual and family relationships (Grych et al., 2013; McDowell et al., 2018). In one of the classic studies of societal level influences, Bowen (1985) studied societal functioning around the issues associated with juvenile delinquency. Many societal subsystems are engaged when youth are involved in criminal acts. Bowen's study showed the interconnectedness of law enforcement agencies, the legal and judicial systems, public schools, and social service agencies in addressing this social problem (Cornelia, 2011). Further, family systems theory is helpful for understanding the links between how families operate in the home and how families operate in contexts related to but outside the home, such as family businesses (Norton, 2011) and religious institutions (Brown & Errington, 2019; Crimone & Hester, 2011; Pinkus, 2006). Family systems has also been a useful framework for helping family members in their struggles with money (and who among us does not have a conflicted relationship with money?), particularly in terms of providing financial therapy from a systems perspective (Gale et al., 2020).

Like many other theories we cover in this book, family systems theory has evolved over time. One of the major applications of family systems theory is in the area of family therapy, and there are many variations that characterize this clinical field. Some family systems models emphasize intergenerational relationships (e.g., Bowen, 1985).

Other models emphasize experiential communication patterns (e.g., Satir, 1988). The circumplex model (Olson et al., 1979) provides a way to study and assess the insider's view of a family, where each member provides a perspective of the family's flexibility (i.e., balance) and cohesion (i.e., closeness). Still other family systems models are emotionally focused and emphasize attachment relationships in adulthood (Johnson, 2019). A structural version of family systems theory uses techniques, such as reframing in order to restructure family rules and boundaries. Reframing involves relabeling an event or problem and putting it in an entirely different context, so it alters the way family members view it (Goldenberg et al., 2016). Social constructionist models of family systems theory rework the metaphor of systems and focus on the way we weave the stories of our lives into a coherent narrative; therapists try to intervene in self-defeating narratives and help people to rewrite their past, present, and future story lines to actively change their lives (White & Epston, 1990). Taken together, family systems theory can be applied to the study of families in various ways, taking into account multiple points of conflict, difference, communication patterns, cultural and structural diversity, and many other contributing factors (McDowell et al., 2018). Again, this perspective allows for a panoramic view, where we are able to focus on any one variable or facet of a family to paint a more accurate picture of the often confounding complexity of family dynamics.

Key Concepts

There are several main concepts that characterize family systems theory, all of which are useful as a "map for understanding everyday and erratic family behavior" (Galvin et al., 2006, p. 320). Family scholars and practitioners have taken general systems theory concepts and adapted them to the particular context of the family.

Family System

A family system refers to the overarching entity that contains individuals who are related to one another by birth, marriage, adoption, and choice. Family systems are multigenerational. They include nuclear arrangements of two generations, in which much of family drama unfolds; multigenerational relationships, in which the carryover of family of origin dynamics across the generations are visible; and connections with the wider society, which push and pull family members together and apart. Within a family unit, members' emotional functioning is established, perfected, and challenged (Broderick, 1993; Johnson, 2019; Rothbaum et al., 2002; Whitchurch & Constantine, 1993). In one of the classic statements of family systems theory, Virginia Satir (1988), who has been called "the mother of family systems theory," described families as "peoplemaking" organizations where our sense of self-worth and our ability to communicate with one another are first formed and developed. Rather than emphasize their problems, Satir focused on the good intentions of families to create authentic and sensitive relationships with one another, while still valuing the individual self. In addition, Satir furthered family systems theory by emphasizing the developing self in the context of the family. One of the goals of healthy development is to have an individual sense of oneself and to be able to share oneself with others.

Like a theatrical performance, each family member knows the part they have to play to keep the system running smoothly. As interactional patterns are rehearsed over and over again, the players repeat their parts, sometimes not even aware of what they are doing. Family roles are often assumed; each system is governed by a set of invisible rules that everyone seems to understand but are often subconscious in nature. As an example, in many families, it is assumed that when a child is ill, the mother will stay at home and care for the child. This is not typically stated in a family handbook or part of a larger set of family rules that are formally discussed. Instead, most families run on assumptions about the roles each family member fulfills. It is important to examine these assumptions because some families may operate with traditional family roles, and others may decidedly try to share household duties and caretaking more equally. Part of what makes family systems theory so useful to family therapists and other practitioners is that it attempts to take into account the "bigger picture"—starting from square one, how does the couple subsystem feel about enacting specific roles in the family? How do the children interpret their parents' fulfillment of these roles?

Going back to our case study, Jackson's family consists of both biological and stepfamily relationships. There seems to be an unstated assumption that Jackson's new stepfather will be the disciplinarian of the children in the home; after all, one of the primary functions of fathers has been to fulfill that role. Jackson resents the authority his stepfather is trying to impose on him. Instead of addressing the parenting issues that arise when a new family system is formed, as in the case of remarriage, the tendency is to blame, or scapegoat, one person as the problem, while ignoring ways in which the whole family contributes to the problem. Families have unwritten rules that can become problematic under stress and during transitions, such as when a parent remarries. In Jackson's family, he has become the scapegoat.

Related to the idea of performance and roles is the idea of subsystems within families. Subsystems exist as part of the larger family unit and usually consist of one of three primary relationships in families: marital (or adult partnership), parental (parent–child relationships), and sibling subsystems (brothers, sisters, half-siblings, stepsiblings, etc.). As family structures become increasingly complex, new subsystems emerge, such as the sibling ties and parent–child ties in repartnered families, where the parents have a shared child, but that child has older half-siblings from a parent's previous relationship (Sanner et al., 2020). Each of these dyads or triads has specific patterns of communication and could be hierarchically situated above or below any of the other dyads or triads. For example, in a one-parent household, the eldest male child may be seen as a partial breadwinner or adult partner because both his financial help and his leadership are needed to run the household. Younger siblings may both defer to him and also resent him for exerting power over them. We elaborate on this process in the following sections.

Family Communication Styles

Satir (1988) suggested that there is a typology of basic family communication styles that are particularly evident when families are under stress. This typology is based on her many years of therapeutic practice with families all over the globe, where she came to view and intervene in problematic behaviors based on the roles family members play. The first type is the *placater*. This person tries to please, probably based on feelings of worthlessness. The placater might say, "Whatever you want is okay. I'm just here to make you happy." The second type of family member is the *blamer*. This person wields the power in families and communicates to others through finger pointing and saying, "You never do anything right" or by redirecting attention away from self by shirking responsibility. A third type is the *super-reasonable person*, who tries to be logical and distanced from any emotionality at all costs. This person masks their vulnerability by maintaining a cool and calm demeanor—thus, keeping others at bay. A fourth type is the *irrelevant person*, who tries to distract others in the family from any intense interaction. Let's say that the family members are having an argument. Rather than addressing the conflict directly, the irrelevant person might try to make a joke about something related to the discussion but ultimately distract attention away from the conflict. Finally, a fifth type is the *congruent communicator*, who is the only person willing to be authentic and honest in family interactions. Satir and other systems theorists have emphasized that these types can be found in any family or in any combination. As Goldenberg et al. (2016) observed, if a "blamer" is married to a "super-reasonable" person, communication is hampered when the wife, for example, complains bitterly, "We hardly ever make love anymore; don't you have any feelings for me?" and the husband responds coldly, "Of course I do, or I wouldn't be married to you. Perhaps we define the word love differently". By being super reasonable, the husband is not addressing the wife's feelings of hurt that he might not love her anymore. Similarly, an irrelevant spouse would probably hear the complaint and either brush it off with a joke or offhand remark and then maybe change their behavior slightly in the future. The possibilities for communication according to family systems theory are endless; no one is functioning independently of one another. We turn next to the concept of influence and interdependence.

Mutual Influence

As is true in any system, individuals, relationships, and subsystems that comprise the family system are interdependent, or mutually influential. This means that what happens in any one part of the family system affects every other component (Grych et al., 2013). That is, if we were to dissect the communication patterns of each member of a family of five, several pathways would emerge. First, there is the dyad of the partner or spouse relationship. The couple that originally fell in love and decided they wanted to have children has their own relationship that needs time, energy, and emotion separate from that of the rest of the family. However, when that relationship is not tended to, it can deteriorate over time. If the quality of the partner or spouse relationship declines, it will undoubtedly affect the emotional well-being of others living in the house. The parents may take out frustrations with their spouse on the child or children, creating a negative communication pathway that emanates from outside of the child–parent relationship. This misplaced emotional expression could create strain among siblings, echoing all across each and every member of the household. What is important to understand is that, for every shift between a subsystem in a family, other family members will inevitably be affected by it—negatively or positively.

The same systemic process is found with external causes of strain; if a child or parent has a bad day at school or work, the ripples of that external interaction will be felt inside the rest of the family in one way or another. This ripple effect also applies to family members who do not communicate or show strain or stress to the rest of the family. Even if a family member is either incapable of communicating or withholds emotions and attitudes from other members of the family, this action will still affect the other family members in the overall system. Indeed, the components of the family system are organized into a whole that transcends the sum of its individual parts (Goldenberg et al., 2016). That is, even if we only have five people in a family, the pathways of communication and influence are infinite. See Figure 6.1 for an illustration of mutual influence in family relationships.

In this figure, we see that the entire family is greater than the sum of its parts. This means that, although there are only five people in the family, there are many pathways for influence and communication. The eldest child may feel the brunt of the argument between the parents; this, in turn, leads to jealousy of the youngest child, who is too young to process the weight of the emotions. The middle child tries to keep peace and resolve the conflict, leading to more communication between child and parent. Each of these parties to the functioning of the overall system can play a vital role in reaching or preventing equilibrium in the family as a whole.

Hierarchy

Family subsystems are arranged hierarchically. As we discuss throughout this chapter, this layering is related to the power structures in families (Whitchurch & Constantine, 1993). Traditionally, husbands have had more

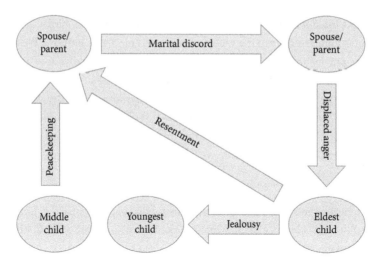

FIGURE 6.1. Pathways of Communication Using Family Systems Theory

power than wives. Parents are above young children in the family hierarchy and, thus, have more power than their offspring (Petren & Puhlman, 2021). Older siblings can function as pseudo parents, expected to take on the caregiving for younger siblings. Hierarchies are not necessarily problematic, unless unhappiness or dissatisfaction develops within the family (Benson et al., 1995). For example, if an older sibling has to quit school to care for his younger siblings while the parents work, that sacrifice can have serious consequences for the child who is unable to finish school. The eldest child both carries more power than the younger two and can also take on more unnecessary burden when there is conflict because of his place in the family hierarchy. The unspoken rules about hierarchy can also work in the opposite direction. In our case study, Jackson had been his mother's closest confidant for 10 years, following the death of his biological father and before his mother married his stepfather. Now, his place in the family hierarchy is threatened by his mother gaining a new partner. Further, Jackson is no longer the only child in the family. All of a sudden, he has to share his home with an unwelcomed stepbrother. Stepfamily researchers have found that these feelings require overt attention in the reconstituted family, so parents, new partners, and children can form close bonds and build strong attachments with one another (Ganong et al., 2020).

Boundaries

To conceptualize families as a "system," it is important to be able to draw boundaries, so we can separate out and filter what is included and what is not. Therefore, family systems theory requires us to visualize the various parts of a system in discrete units; in short, to draw a **boundary** (Whitchurch & Constantine, 1993). In family systems theory, boundaries can be permeable or impermeable. A permeable boundary is open to interchange from outside the system. An impermeable boundary, by contrast, is closed to the outside. By their very nature, families are open systems because there is always some interaction with the environment, but families differ in the degree to which they are bounded. Boundaries with age-appropriate limits and consequences are important for developing a strong sense of self as well as the ability to be close to another person, as therapists who work with adult attachment relationships point out (Heller, 2019). Families with flexible boundaries are more likely to be engaged with the outside world, whereas families with inflexible boundaries are more likely to be tightly knit and withdrawn from external social contact. A family system that places a premium on privacy, for example, would be less likely to seek family therapy when experiencing a major shift (e.g., transitioning to parenthood; having a child acting out in school; forming a stepfamily; coping with a chronic illness) than a family system that valued the expertise and assistance of outside professionals. As we can see in our case study example, although Jackson's mother was open to finding help for Jackson's so-called behavioral problems, her initial instinct was to locate an individual therapist to deal with Jackson one on one. A family with more flexible boundaries, on the other hand, would be more open to seeking professional help for the entire family.

Feedback

Given its roots in cybernetics and technology, feedback is probably a concept unique to family systems theory. **Feedback** is a way of capturing the interdependence function of systems—that individuals in family systems influence one another. Feedback can be either negative or positive. Negative feedback puts a stop to communication or behavior to bring the system back to equilibrium. Positive feedback, on the other hand, responds to the stimulus by allowing change in the overall functioning of the system. An example of positive feedback could be one of the spouses suggesting the couple attend therapy to address the mix-up in communication that occurred to cause the discord in the first place. Negative feedback, on the other hand, would prevent such change from happening. The spouses would continue in their pattern of communication, and the negative emotions would trickle down to the children and back up to the parents like they always do when that situation occurs. In sum, positive feedback helps the system to innovate and change, while negative feedback dampens efforts to change by helping the system achieve and maintain stability. A healthy family system needs a balance of both positive and negative feedback loops. That is, families need enough flexibility to allow change but enough restraint to keep change from getting out of control (Whitchurch & Constantine, 1993). You can see the challenge of balancing flexibility and restraint in families, particularly when they undergo many major changes at once. Jackson's family, for example, was dealing with remarriage, stepparent–stepchild relationships, the introduction of a new sibling into the family system, ongoing grief from the death of a parent, and the normal developmental challenges associated with adolescence.

Equilibrium

Seeking a balance between change (positive feedback loops) and stability (negative feedback loops) is referred to as **equilibrium**. In the face of change, all systems seek to return to the status quo, or homeostasis. Families are no exception in their efforts to stabilize themselves. Equilibrium does not mean, however, that there is some universal harmonious state that all systems seek. Rather, each family operates according to rules that they have developed in order to protect their own survival. Because families are diverse in structure, process, and context, the balance that families seek does not look the same across families. The key to equilibrium is that families seek to stabilize according to their own internal rules. Each family has its own blueprint for reaching equilibrium, and equilibrium can look different in open or closed family systems. What works to create balance for some families may not work for others.

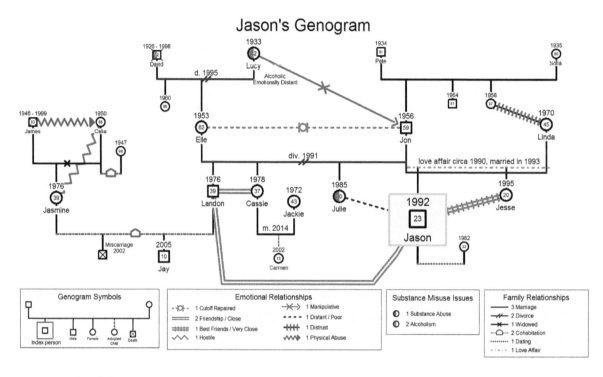

FIGURE 6.2. Jason's Genogram

Intergenerational Family Patterns

A hallmark of family systems theory is that family problems and recommendations for change can be uncovered by studying family patterns from an intergenerational perspective. One of the primary techniques for uncovering intergenerational family patterns is the **genogram**. Based in Bowen's (1985) family systems theory, the genogram protocol was further developed by McGoldrick and colleagues (2020) as a clinical technique to use in helping individuals understand the intergenerational context of family dynamics and problems. The genogram is highly useful for mapping the complexity of family relationships and dynamics in research practices as well, providing researchers with a conversational and visual tool with which to help develop trust and interest among participants (Potter et al., 2019; Russell, 2020b).

The genogram consists of structural and emotional systems used to represent one's family. Structural symbols include boxes for males, circles for females, diamonds for pets, and a double square for the **index person** (e.g., the person whose life is featured in the genogram). In our example in Figure 6.2, the index person is Jason. Emotional symbols include a double line indicating a strong or special relationship between two people, a wavy line indicating a conflictual relationship, a double slash for a divorce, and a shaded symbol indicating substance abuse problems. It is most helpful to go back at least three generations to get more factual information and then to interview older family members about their emotional journeys. Figure 6.2 depicts a rendering of how a genogram can be used to understand family dynamics.

Family Cohesion: Enmeshment vs. Disengagement

Family systems theory is concerned with the degree to which family members feel close to one another. This idea reflects the concept of family cohesion, which refers to a continuum between the extremes of high cohesion to low cohesion. High cohesion is characterized by **enmeshment**, wherein family members are highly dependent upon one another and closed off to others external to the family system. Enmeshed families have a high sense of "we-ness" and a low sense of "I-ness." On the other hand, low cohesion is characterized by **disengagement**, wherein family members tend to operate independently of one another. Extreme forms of disengagement can challenge the loyalty that family members feel toward one another. At the same time, families may also contain elements of both enmeshment and engagement. The classic example of enmeshment and disengagement in a family can be found in the middle-class, two-parent home that has been idealized in Western society as superior to all others. In such a family, fathers are highly disengaged because they are expected to work long hours and support the family financially, and mothers are highly enmeshed because their primary role is to take care of children and tend to the nurturance of the family (Goldenberg et al., 2016).

BOX 6.2. FAMILY SYSTEMS THEORY IN MODERN CULTURE: *ENCANTO*

Image 6.1 A Scene From *Encanto*, 2021

Encanto is an animated film featuring the Madrigal family in rural Colombia. At the helm of the family is Abuela Alma, who possesses a magical candle that not only houses the family in a casita to protect them from their enemies, but it also protects the entire mountain town in which they live. Each family member for three generations holds a special magical gift as a result—all except one granddaughter, Mirabel. The story follows the family as each member navigates their special gifts, and Mirabel struggles with what her role in the family is without one.

Family systems theory helps us understand how each family member's "gift" contributes to the overall functioning not only of the family but of the village in which they reside. One line in particular depicts family systems theory well; Mirabel is asked what her gift is, and she replies, "I can't just talk about myself. I'm only part of the amazing Madrigals." Here, she is acknowledging she is simply part of a family system that is greater than the sum of its parts. The film also features the ways in which each family member interacts with the larger system individually as well as in dyads and triads. Maribel's relationship with certain family members seems strained but warm with others.

Maribel struggles to find her way, overcompensating for not having a magical gift like all the others. To a stranger, it would be impossible to understand Maribel's struggles without understanding the family as a whole. Further, it would be difficult to understand the family dynamics without examining the importance of the Madrigal family to the villagers. Their magical abilities play a huge role—with open boundaries—to their immediate community. This presents an added layer of pressure to the family to maintain stability, so the village is not negatively impacted.

Because flexibility is seen as a goal, according to family systems theory, neither of these extremes is considered to be healthy. Families can also vacillate between these poles. In our case study, Jackson's experience in a single-mother family, where it was just Jackson and his mom, reveals enmeshment. They did everything together and were bonded by the death of Jackson's dad. When his mother remarried, the old pattern of enmeshment was challenged. Change can be very unsettling to individuals and, thus, destabilize the family system as a whole.

Evaluating Family Systems Theory

Strengths of Family Systems Theory

Family systems theory has many strengths. It is rooted in the application of theory to examine how families interact, allowing theorists to look at very complex processes that affect family members, both individually and as a whole, and it is applicable beyond studying the family as a stand-alone unit. Here we elaborate on these strengths.

Highly Practical

Family systems theory is a very practical theory that is easy to apply to everyday life. Systems concepts can be easily translated into common sense language that is accessible to a wide variety of individuals and families. One of the most helpful tenets of family systems theory can be captured in the idea that "if something isn't working, more of the same won't work." For example, if your car does not start, continuing to try to start it by turning the ignition is not going to make it start. Perhaps, you should check the battery! In family systems terms, if your mom continually tells you to clean your room, and you do not clean your room, then her repeated reminders to clean your room are not likely to be successful. Some other intervention is needed. In another example, as a practical theory, family systems concepts resonate with real people's lives. The work of social worker and therapist Brené Brown (2012, 2021) on the power of vulnerability and creating meaningful connections with "self" and "other" have reached millions via her internet videos and TED Talks. Brown's ideas about positive energy and the courage to change one's life are grounded in family systems theory.

Useful for Family Interventions

Because of its emphasis on understanding family communication patterns and relationship processes, family systems theory is also very useful for developing intervention programs to help families, especially when they are under stress and experiencing troubles (Olson et al., 2019). For example, Gottman and Gottman (2017) detail the history of nearly five decades of research on what leads marriages to succeed or fail. They have uncovered physiological, psychological, and interpersonal signs that predict relational conflict and divorce. Rooted in their years of clinical research, they developed the "sound relationship house theory," which translates into interventions that couples can apply in their own relationships and educators and clinicians can employ in intervention programs. They use the concepts of love maps and friendship, fondness, and turning toward connection (rather than away or against) to help couples create shared meaning and build trust, loyalty, and commitment. Recent research on the dynamics of marital uncertainty, even among couples whose marriages endure, is helpful for marital intervention because it is grounded in the lived experiences of people actually struggling with the future of their marriage. Sarah Allen and colleagues (2022) found that a process-oriented systemic approach, rather than one focused simply on the outcome of staying married or getting divorced, better explains marital commitment over time, wherein couples engage in a process of leaning in, leaning out, and holding onto their marriage.

In another example, interventions with military families is a major area in which family systems theory is applicable (Drummet et al., 2003; Faber et al., 2008; Monk et al., 2018; Paley et al., 2013). Research on military families has shown that children whose parents are in service experience greater loneliness and depression when their parents are deployed and, thus, away from home for months at a time. An effective intervention has been to use technology, such as email and digital video calls, to keep parents and children in touch and communicating with each other (Blaisure et al., 2016). Interventions that use a family-centered care and prevention approach treat the service member, their children, and their partner as interdependent members of the family system (MacDermid Wadsworth et al., 2013). Treatments found to be effective include brief, but intensive, retreats for veterans, their partners, and their families, where distress and trauma can be assessed, and positive interventions can be made (Monk et al., 2017).

Applicable to Aspects of Family Research Beyond the Nuclear Family

In addition to its cybernetic and clinical roots, family systems theory can be used to study relationships beyond the nuclear family. To extend individual and family development beyond marriage and parent–child relationships, Cox (2010) applied systems theory to sibling relationships and showed that the sibling subsystem is often more influential than the parental subsystem. Further, the sibling subsystem is the longest lasting tie. An application of this finding is that sibling relationships are very important for members of the baby boom generation, as described in Chapter 9 on life course theory. As life expectancy is increasing and members of the baby boom generation are aging, they are more likely to have a sibling than a spouse in old age (Connidis & Barnett, 2019). Systems theory has also been used to examine the inclusion of pets as members of families and, thus, address the therapeutic value of pets (Walsh, 2009). Indeed, the majority of Americans (60%) have pets, and they are considered part of the family (Adams et al., 2021). Another key research topic is how role reversals between parent and child can be handed down through the generations (Macfie et al., 2007). Role reversals often occur in families in which parents have alcohol or drug addictions or are unable to function as responsible parents due to incarceration or severe illness. In such cases, children are subject to "adultification," wherein they are required to function as a substitute parent or partner, thereby crossing hierarchical family boundaries (Burton, 2007).

Weaknesses of Family Systems Theory

No theory holds all the keys. Despite the numerous strengths of systems theory and its adaptability to practice and multiple empirical contexts, there are some challenges in applying this perspective to families.

Possibility of Stereotyping

Just as family systems theory is very applicable to many different contexts, it is also very easy to apply it in superficial and stereotyped ways. Considered from a feminist perspective, for example, the systemic concepts of "overfunctioning" and "underfunctioning" can be seen as disrespectful to families, particularly if a family member is gravely ill and requires a great deal of care. Such concepts are typically based on gender stereotypes, in which women are said to overfunction, and men are said to underfunction, without recognizing that the reverse is often true as well. Satir's (1988) work, for example, can be criticized for being acontextual and not sensitive to structural issues, such as gender stereotyping. By recognizing the limitations of the era in which theorizing was originally conceptualized, it is possible to retain the vitality of the intellectual and practical ideas that Satir promoted and update them in an "evolving" context that will be "more galvanizing" for "the creativity of a new generation of scholars, clinicians, and researchers" (Lee & Rovers, 2016, p. 273).

Simplifies the Complexity of Sibling Roles and Relationships

Another area in which systems theory is often uncritically applied concerns sibling birth order and relationships. Assumptions about the sibling subsystem can be alluring but inaccurate. It is tempting to reduce sibling personalities to birth order characteristics (e.g., only children are selfish; eldest children are high achievers; middle children are scapegoats or the family clown; youngest children are pampered) because there can be a grain of truth in any stereotype (Bradshaw, 1988; Conley, 2004). However, sibling relationships are complex, multifaceted, and vary by cultural context. For example, in China, parents often favor oldest sons over daughters and younger sons. Yet in the United States, older women tend to favor their youngest daughters when relying upon adult children for care and support (Suitor et al., 2013). One of the recent advances in family science is the use of dyadic data analyses, so we no longer just rely on individual perspectives, which have resulted in uncritically simplifying complex subsystem relationships like the sibling–sibling tie (Galovan et al., 2017; Umberson & Thomeer, 2020).

Minimizes Power Dynamics in Families

One of the strongest critiques of family systems theory is that it minimizes, and even ignores, the power differences in families. By proposing that a family's problems arise only from dysfunctional interpersonal relationships, family systems theory ignores not only the racial, ethnic, and cultural contexts we discussed previously (e.g., Baptist & Hamon, 2022; James et al., 2018) but also how gender and generation ascribe different and unequal power to family members. A critique of family systems theory is thus a critique about how power is distributed unevenly in families. As feminists have observed (see Chapter 8), power differences in families reflect the broader social and political context (Silverstein & Goodrich, 2003). By assuming that each member of the family has an equal responsibility and vested interest in family dynamics, family systems theory hides that some members of families are more "equal" than others (Leslie & Southard, 2009). For these reasons, intersectional feminist scholars, in particular, have revised and updated many existing therapeutic models, so they can be more attuned to the great diversity in terms of how family values and family social locations shape our lives across intimate, local, national, and global levels (Brown, 2018; McDowell et al., 2018).

An Alternative Theory App: Family Ecological Theory

In this chapter, we have explained the key concepts, origins, and modern applications as well as the strengths and weaknesses of family systems theory. In Chapter 5, we compared two very different theories (family developmental theory and feminist theory) to activate your theory "app." In this chapter, we compare two theories that are fairly similar to emphasize how, over time, theories build on one another to adapt to new considerations in family theory.

Family systems theory is considered a foundational theory in family science because it allows practitioners and researchers to take the "whole family" into account. Family ecological theory (Chapter 10) takes this perspective as well but broadens the lens of analysis to include the environment and institutions that exist surrounding families. According to family ecological theory, humans directly modify their environments and are influenced by external forces as well. Consider Jackson from this chapter's case study. If we were using family ecological theory to study Jackson's experience, we would take a much closer look at the external environment in which his family interacted. Jackson had access to excellent schools and lived in a safe neighborhood, so we could determine that his family had tangible privileges compared to other families. Because of this, his mother was able to afford to go to therapy with him and other family members. At the same time, we need to note that family ecological theory would consider the historical reality that psychological services might

BOX 6.3. GLOBAL COMPARISONS: PUBLIC HEALTH, DOMESTIC WORK, AND GENDER-BASED VIOLENCE

Though of course there are exceptions everywhere, most countries still value men's lives over women's. The United Nations (2020) report *The World's Women 2020: Trends and Statistics* provides demographics from various countries regarding gender traditions practiced in countries around the world. From the UN's analysis, it is clear that women have less power than men in terms of all major indicators of well-being, including that they are more likely to live in poverty; they are more likely to be subjected to violence both in and outside their home; they have less access to education and employment; and they are overwhelmingly responsible for child care. Further, since the COVID-19 pandemic shook the foundations of society beginning in early 2020, researchers have determined that unpaid domestic and care work continues to fall on women, disproportionately and negatively impacting their employment and livelihoods outside the home. Consider the various practices around the globe in which male dominance in families (e.g., family hierarchy) is reproduced and put into action:

- **Unpaid domestic work:** Rates of unpaid domestic work have increased for all during the COVID-19 pandemic, yet women are shouldering the brunt of the labor in this sphere of family life. Across the globe, women are estimated to spend roughly three times as much time on unpaid domestic work as men—a difference even more pronounced in Northern Africa and Western Asia.
- **Public health:** Around the world, women make up the majority of health care workers, including nurses, which means shouldering the burden of care professionally while also personally putting themselves at risk for being infected and being expected to care for loved ones at home who fall ill or are quarantined. Research has shown the widespread psychological toll the pandemic has had on health care workers, and coupled with the additional burden of caring for loved ones on a personal level, long-term emotional consequences are inevitable for women on a massive scale.
- **Gender-based violence (GBV):** The COVID-19 lockdowns have put women and girls at even higher risk of experiencing GBV in the home. Around one-third of all women have experienced GBV by an intimate partner, and it is estimated that over 100 women are killed by their intimate partner or a family member every day.

not even exist to benefit Jackson and his family. Fifty years ago, sending a child (particularly a male child) to counseling would have been unheard of. In this way, we can see how family ecological theory broadened the lens through which family theorists could analyze behavior by taking into account even larger macro-level forces than family systems. In comparison, family systems theory seems like a fairly micro-level theory, even though it is not!

Next, it is important to understand how family systems theory is applicable to the study of families across the globe. Earlier in this chapter, you read about hierarchies within families. How families are structured as a system will affect the type of communication, established boundaries, and feedback loops. In Box 6.3, we consider how concepts associated with family hierarchies are represented in different countries and regions of the world. We challenge you to consider these global applications of the theory as you move on to the areas for further study and the discussion and reflection questions in the concluding pages of this chapter.

Working With Family Systems Theory: Integrating Research and Practice

Now that we have described the historical origins, key concepts, and strengths and weaknesses of family systems theory, we turn our attention to how the theory can be used in practice. We then analyze an empirical study that was rooted in family systems theory to examine how scholars put the theory to work in a research project. Finally, we present ideas about how the theory informs the practice of family policy.

Family Systems Theory Today

Paul Rosenblatt (2013), a family scholar and therapist, contends that family systems theory offers rich metaphors that are useful in understanding both family functioning and family change. Key metaphors of family systems theory include the family as a machine, prison, container, river, house, and more. A metaphor is a figure of speech or analogy in which "words or actions that literally denote one kind of object or idea are used in place of another" (Rosenblatt, 1997, p. 1). Metaphors are evocative and can help trigger emotions and ideas that need to be dislodged to facilitate growth or resolution. In today's multicultural society in which we recognize that no single metaphor can capture so many types and dimensions of family, we need diverse metaphors to characterize the multiple realities of families.

Family systems metaphors are particularly useful in understanding how families deal with loss, trauma, death, and grief. Consider Rosenblatt's (2013) example of the death of a child. First, even though family members are connected to one another, grief over the death of a child can make individuals less available or less tuned in to one another. In the face of such tragedy, the family system can cease communicating and "shut down" altogether. Second, because families seek to maintain the system as it was, after a child dies, family members may still act and think in ways that keep the child "alive" in the system. It is not uncommon for parents to "talk to" their deceased child. Or they may begin to focus all of their attention on how a surviving child is faring. Third, because a family is a system of rules that are typically unspoken, if a family member tries to grieve in ways that violate the family rules, it could make others uncomfortable and push the griever to "change back" to the ways that are expected. Some families allow intense emotion to be expressed, but other families may try to shut it down. These metaphors of connection, maintenance, and rules help us understand how processes of change, such as grief and loss, operate in families. Because families are systems that are more than the sum of their parts, how families cope with loss, and change of all kinds, is a family affair—not just an individual one.

Family Systems Theory in Research

In a rare longitudinal study that incorporated both mothers' and fathers' perspectives, Holmes et al. (2013) examined changes in the family system when young married couples experience the transition to parenthood. In most studies, only mothers have been asked to report on family transitions—a practice that family systems theorists criticize. Instead, a family systems perspective says that all of the individuals in the family have a unique, though interdependent, experience to avoid the downfall of only individualized perspectives (Galovan et al., 2017). The authors used quantitative research methods to study 125 married couples by giving them a series of measurements at three points in time: prenatal, eight months after birth, and when the child was two years old.

Many subsystems are disrupted or created during the transition to parenthood due to the introduction of a new family member. In addition to the individual level issues (e.g., whether a parent experiences depression during the adjustment to having a child), there are relationship-level components to consider, such as the parental marriage, particularly in terms of how contradictory emotions are experienced (e.g., how love and conflict are both present in a marriage). The transition to parenthood, then, is a hotbed of new challenges because several individuals and subsystems are being disrupted as the family system attempts to reestablish equilibrium after the addition of a new member. As a rule, family systems seek balance and resist change, making them vulnerable to stress when change does occur. The husband–wife relationship, the mother–child relationship, the father–child relationship, and the eventual sibling–sibling relationship are just a few of the subsystems that are put on high alert upon the birth of a child. Further, given the interrelatedness of all members in the system, how each member is affected and responds impacts everyone else. According to family systems theory, there is pressure to restabilize. Some parental subsystems have a smoother transition than others.

When a major milestone, such as the birth of a new baby, occurs, family systems theory predicts that family relationships and patterns become unstable. The resulting disequilibrium can intensify existing family problems (e.g., conflict between spouses) and also allow positive adjustments as the family seeks homeostasis to rebalance in light of the new disruptions to the system. Holmes et al. (2013) sought to understand why some of these heterosexual couples are able to navigate the transition to parenthood more easily than others. They hypothesized that parental gender (i.e., being a mother or father), infant gender (i.e., whether the first child is a boy or a girl), infant temperament (i.e., whether the infant is fussy and reactive, or calm and easily soothed), the emotional climate in the family (i.e., whether individuals are depressed), how realistic the parents' expectations are about having a new baby, and the presence of both love and conflict between husbands and wives will affect the transition to parenthood for both men and women. Ultimately the authors asked: What is it about variations among mothers, fathers, infants, marriages, and families that facilitates a smooth or rocky adjustment to parenthood?

One of the main findings had to do with fathers, which is an important development, given the lack of representation of father's emotions and voices in family research until recently (Schoppe-Sullivan & Fagan,

2020). Holmes et al. (2013) found that the baby's reactivity and gender were factors in fathers' adjustment. Fathers' marital conflict increased if they had a fussy baby or if they had a daughter—a finding that corresponds to the worldwide preference for boys, or at least for the firstborn to be a boy. Incorporating the diversity of fathering experiences into family research is a positive trend, particularly in terms of new theorizing about foster fathering (Mallette et al., 2021), masculinity and fathering experiences among Chinese fathers (Li et al., 2021), and Latino fathers' emotional engagement in families, despite being separated by national borders (e.g., Roy & Yumiseva, 2021).

Family Systems Theory in Practice

Over the course of 40 years, Murray Bowen (1985) developed a version of general systems theory that he applied to the study and treatment of emotional processes in families. Like Bateson et al. (1956), Bowen originally used family systems theory in relation to families who had a member diagnosed with schizophrenia. Over time, Bowen and colleagues developed a version of family systems theory that included society's role in contributing to dysfunctional or toxic family interactions and demonstrated that problems with emotional functioning occur in all families, including those that we think of as "normal" (Broderick, 1993; Kerr & Bowen, 1988). His theory is helpful for understanding issues as complex as the bidirectional transmission process of how anxiety, depression, and other patterns can be passed from parent to child, down the generations (Reed-Fitzke et al., 2021). Bowen's family systems theory is very appealing for family scholars and practitioners because it recognizes that to understand emotional functioning in family relationships, one must become an expert in one's own emotional functioning in relationships. This theory teaches that we are all susceptible to observational blindness and that becoming adept at recognizing the "triggers" that cause you to react in certain ways is a helpful skill in human services and other helping professions (Cornelia, 2011).

Bowen (1985) proposed several interrelated ideas that are very influential in how scholars and clinicians think about internal family dynamics, particularly in the therapeutic setting. For example, **differentiation of self** refers to one's sense of being an individual compared to being related to others. This concept captures a person's ability to distinguish what they think from what they feel and to respond appropriately to anxiety and stress (Baucom & Atkins, 2013; Kerr & Bowen, 1988). Another key idea is **triangulation**, when a three-person relationship occurs, and two of the members of the relationship exclude the third. A triangle is formed to stabilize the family unit (Titelman, 2008). The classic example is when the parental interaction becomes overly stressful, a child is pulled in ("triangulated") to smooth things over between the parents (McGoldrick et al., 2020; Taylor et al., 2013). Emotional units, in Bowenian theory, refer to the system of interlocking triangles that help to maintain the family system in the face of chronic anxiety, conflict, and other intense emotions (Cornelia, 2011). **Emotional cut-off** refers to the extreme distancing family members can experience to cope with heightened anxiety. When such intensity is activated, an "emotional divorce" may be a way of coping with the swell of emotions that occur. Family transitions (e.g., the birth of a new child; when parents separate or divorce; when a young adult moves out of the parental home; the death of an aging parent) are crucial times when emotional cut-off often occurs. In this way, a major jolt to family equilibrium that triggers stress and emotional withdrawal may also be seen as an adaptive reaction.

BOX 6.4. VOICES FROM LIVED EXPERIENCE

Family systems theory asserts that gender transition for one individual family member challenges the entire system (Katz-Wise et al., 2016). Walter Cardona, a licensed mental health counselor and systems theorist, shares his experience in learning to support his child through gender transition, claiming the change his child has undergone has not only impacted his life, but everyone else, including immediate and extended family members as well as neighbors. He shares his own experience with his child's transitioning process:

Mid-pandemic, my then 11-year-old daughter announced she was identifying as gender nonbinary/nonconforming and that her pronouns would be "they/them." She said she wanted to change her name to something more gender-neutral. Outwardly, I was supportive and committed to processing this with her at a later time. Inwardly, I was aware of my shock and dismay. "What do we do?" and "How did this happen?" were just a couple of the hundreds of questions that had raced thought my mind. Simultaneously, I watched as her mother balked, withholding her immediate support as she tried to understand what was happening and weighed the pros and cons of support versus rejection. Ultimately, her mother paid a price for that hesitation, as our daughter felt hurt, rejected, and unsupported.

Her mother and I engaged in multiple conversations, in one of which I explained my full throated support. In reference to our relationship with our daughter and the possible effects to her development, I said, "We have nothing to lose by offering our support … it costs us nothing. But to reject this process might cost us severely." Her mother came down on the side of supporting her fully. Prior to her 12th birthday and her summer visit with me in the Pacific Northwest, my then daughter stated her pronouns would be "he/him" and rejected any female descriptors: no more daughter, no more sister. I now have a son.

It took me some time to adjust. I took a few helpful trainings, including What Does It Mean to Identify as Transgender or Gender Nonconforming (TGNC)? and a webinar on the importance of pronouns. I heard a variety of responses from friends and family ranging from all out rejection and pathologizing this new identification with statements like, "They're learning this from the internet/friends" and "This is a trend/phase" to questions like, "Don't you think this is a result of the mother's bad parenting?" I encountered many wary of the "affirmative" model of care, assuming there was harm in a child's development if a transgender identity was accepted. There was literature alluding to the "condition" of rapid-onset gender dysphoria (ROGD), which serves as a "maladaptive coping mechanism"—a controversial diagnosis that also persists on pathologizing this transition.

One time, my son surfaced from his room, wearing full makeup, loop earrings, blouse, and miniskirt, letting me know he needed to go to the grocery store to pick up tampons. We stood in the kitchen, both amused by the atmosphere and by the seeming contradiction of the moment, that my son was starting his menstrual cycle. This moment broke the ice and allowed us to discuss the awkwardness and nuances of conversing about gender and gender identity.

(continued)

What I never expected to experience was grief. I once said his former name in his presence, and he referred to it as his deadname. I was astonished and instantly saddened by my son's willingness to forsake any memory of his former identity. I did not anticipate the grief associated with this change and instantly realized I would have to "bury" my daughter to make space for my son. I immediately called upon my training and understanding of change and transition meaning the same thing and that death is a part of life.

Conclusion

Family systems theory has provided important ideas that allow family researchers and practitioners to put the theory to use beyond the conceptual level. Stemming from general systems theory and cybernetics, scholars have developed ways in which systems theory can be applied to the study of families as a unit, using multiple levels of analysis and analyzing both internal and external shifts in systems. Family systems theory helps us understand the interacting dynamics of the entire family, providing a more comprehensive view that moves beyond the perspective of individual family members. One of the most important parts of family systems theory is helping us understand that we are all responsible for our own part in any interaction, and what we do impacts the whole system. Understanding how a system operates helps each one of us to initiate changes that are needed for healthy family interaction.

Multimedia Suggestions

www.gottman.com

As previously noted, John Gottman's (1994) research has become well known for predicting whether or not a married couple is likely to get divorced. Over his career, Dr. Gottman and his wife Dr. Julie Gottman (2017) have been able to successfully predict and explain factors leading to divorce with an over 85% accuracy rate. The Gottman Institute's website provides links to research articles, relationship help, educator training, parenting advice, and clinical training for family practitioners and individuals.

Activate your theory app: There is a strong emphasis on research throughout this website. Where can you see evidence of theory? Can you see evidence of other theories, besides family systems theory, on this website?

www.thebowencenter.org

This website, that of the Bowen Center for the Study of the Family, is dedicated to the work of Dr. Murray Bowen, who developed a theory of human functioning that views the family as an emotional unit. The website provides information on family systems theory as well as recent research using the theory. The website also provides links to information on clinical services for families, upcoming meetings, training materials, and other publications that are helpful for family therapists, teachers, and other practitioners.

Activate your theory app: How could this website resource be used for practitioners, researchers, and teachers who are not going into the field of family and marriage therapy?

Ted Lasso (2021)

Ted Lasso follows a former college football coach as he becomes the manager of Richmond Football Club, a professional soccer team in England. Throughout the first season, the audience learns very little about Ted Lasso himself, except that he is going through a divorce and has a young son back in the United States. In season two, his own family of origin story becomes clear and helps put his approach to life, including his

Image 6.2 A Scene From *Ted Lasso*, 2021

present struggles, into context. The same is true for many of the other main characters, including Sam Obisanya's and Jamie Tartt's relationships with their fathers; Roy Kent's relationship with his niece, Phoebe; and Rebecca's relationship with her ex-husband, Rupert. From a family systems perspective, the importance of understanding how each part influences the whole is evident in each of these underlying storylines and is also important when considering how the football club as a whole interacts as a family system.

Activate your theory app: Consider any nonbiological family systems you have been a part of; have you experienced dynamics similar to the ones presented in this show? What are some examples in the show of enmeshment and closed boundaries?

The Blind Side (2009)

Family systems theory is illustrated throughout the movie *The Blind Side,* which is based on a true story and novel written by Michael Lewis (2006). The main character, Michael, is an African American youth who had been in foster care with different families throughout his childhood because of his mother's drug addiction. As he is "taken in" by the Tuohy family, the family as a unit has to adjust to the new member in order to maintain equilibrium. A major controversy erupts in the film when the

Image 6.3 A Scene From *The Blind Side*, 2009

National Collegiate Athletic Association (NCAA) investigates the family for academic misconduct. This illustrates the concepts of boundaries, in which external forces permeate the open boundaries of the family and disrupt the system. The processes of reconnecting and establishing healthy communication patterns between all members of the family unit is well illustrated throughout this film.

Activate your theory app: What examples of boundaries and positive and negative feedback loops do you see in the film? How does the system adapt to both internal and external issues over time?

Further Reading

Boss, P. (2021). *The myth of closure: Ambiguous loss in a time of pandemic and change.* W. W. Norton. Pauline Boss applies her theory of ambiguous loss to the current pandemic crisis. The theory of ambiguous loss has shaped the way many of us understand how stress and trauma affect our lives and can be treated in clinical practice to enhance family coping, resiliency, and health. Ambiguous loss deals with both absence and presence in families. A family member could be psychologically absent but physically present, as in the case of a parent with dementia. A family member could also be physically absent but psychologically present, as in the case of a son missing in action during a war. These experiences of ambiguous loss can keep family members frozen in grief. Now, with a global pandemic that has led to great uncertainty and rendered children, adults, and families feeling hopeless, in despair, and angry, Boss brings her characteristic wisdom about trauma in the family system to help us understand and build resilience in the midst of an unprecedented crisis.

Journal of Feminist Family Therapy (JFFT). https://www.tandfonline.com/toc/wfft20/current. This journal is devoted to exploring the relationship between feminist theory and family therapy theory and practice. *JFFT* offers a comprehensive resource for theoretical, applied, and empirical readings for those interested in the intersection of family systems theory and feminist theory and practice, dealing with issues related to gender, culture, power, and oppression. Check the journal website for articles regarding the treatment of mental health issues, trauma, intimate partner violence, relational problems as well as media reviews and cultural critiques.

Kantor, D., & Lehr, W. (1975). *Inside the family: Toward a theory of family process.* Jossey-Bass. In this highly influential text, David Kantor and William Lehr provide one of the classic revisions of general systems theory by applying systems concepts to the micro level of family interaction. They propose that the family system is composed of three subsystems: the family-unit subsystem, the interpersonal subsystem, and the personal subsystem. This book was one of the first to show that seemingly simple family processes are actually very complex rules for governing and regulating family members' behaviors.

Lerner, H. G. (2013). *Marriage rules: A manual for the married and the coupled up.* Penguin. Harriet Lerner writes widely popular and readable books about women's emotional lives and their interpersonal relationships. She applies Bowen's family systems theory to marriage, family, and friendship ties. In *Marriage Rules*, Lerner provides suggestions that hit the "hot spots" in marriage and other long-term relationships, including how to fight fair, listen well, avoid overtalking and defensiveness, establish boundaries, deal with difficult family members, and handle your partner's relationship with technology.

Regalia, C., Manzi, C., & Scabini, E. (2013). Individuation and differentiation in families across cultures. In M. A. Fine & F. D. Fincham (Eds.), *Handbook of family theories: A content-based approach* (pp. 437–455). Routledge. The authors examine the dual concepts of individuation (i.e., how individuals develop their identity) and differentiation (i.e., how parents and families either support or hinder the individuation process) in cultural context. They give examples of how the development of the self is reflective of different cultural norms and practices. For example, collectivist cultures, often found in Asian countries, differ from Western societies, such as those in North America and the United Kingdom, by emphasizing the greater influence of the extended family and wider community in how a person becomes "a social being" (p. 442). In India, for example, individual identity is best seen as a "familial self" because of the emphasis on respect for the authority of older generations.

Questions for Students

Discussion Questions

1. Do you think the general systems metaphor can be applied in a universal way? That is, do family systems resemble inanimate systems, or are there aspects of living systems (e.g., families) that are unique and not reducible to the metaphor of a machine?

2. Which metaphor of family systems theory most appeals to you?

3. Systems theory in family science has been very effective in terms of family therapy and marital communication research. What are other areas where you might apply "systemic thinking"?

4. How is family systems theory different from functionalist theory (Chapter 2)? How is it similar?

5. Describe how family systems theory would apply to the study of a Mexican American family newly immigrated to the United States. Does family systems theory take into account issues such as culture shock, generational change, and assimilation?

6. In what ways do the new technologies and social media options facilitate family interaction and cohesion when family members are living in separate cities, nations, or continents? How can technology be used to strengthen families and intervene in problems of loneliness, isolation, and other associated stressors? Are there particular strategies that are useful for children who are separated from their parents?

Your Turn!

Construct a family genogram by going back as many generations as you know, using the concepts and symbols in the McGoldrick et al. (2020) book and Figure 6.2 as a resource. Locate an older relative (e.g., a grandparent, a great aunt, or a third cousin) to help you fill in the gaps of key genogram components, such as birth, death, marriage, and divorce dates, and other key patterns that have happened in the past several generations. What are the patterns you notice across the generations? How have they affected your life?

Personal Reflection Questions

1. Use a family systems perspective to analyze and describe a family whose origin is very different from your own. Are there meaningful ways to understand such differences, using family systems theory?

2. Consider your parents' and grandparents' generations and what was thought to be normal communication for them growing up. Has "normal" shifted over time? How are hierarchies and subsystems related to communication styles across these generations?

3. How do you understand sibling relationships? Where are you in the birth order of your family: an only child, a youngest, an oldest, or somewhere in the middle? How do your gender, sexual orientation, race, and other characteristics affect your sibling relationships? What kind of siblings do you have (e.g., biological, half-siblings, or step-siblings)?

4. Think about an experience in your family in which there is an emotional cutoff. How did this family process begin? Who is helping to maintain it? What need does it serve? What are ways you could intervene to help your family become "unstuck"?

5. Are there other systems to which we can apply concepts of family systems theory? What about your "fictive kin"—or nonblood-related friends you consider family?

6. What is an example in your own life of the systems notion that "if something isn't working, more of the same won't work"? Have you ever found yourself caught in such a cycle of resistance to change? What helped you break the pattern and try a new strategy?

References

Ackerman, N. J. (1984). *A theory of family systems*. Gardner.

Adams, B. L., Applebaum, J. W., Eliasson, M. N., McDonald, S. E., & Zsembik, B. A. (2021). Child and pet care-planning during COVID-19: Considerations for the evolving family unit. *Family Relations, 70*(3), 705–716. https://doi.org/10.1111/fare.12542

Allen, S., Hawkins, A. J., Harris, S. M., Roberts, K., Hubbard, A., & Doman, M. (2022). Day-to-day changes and longer-term adjustments to divorce ideation: Marital commitment uncertainty processes over time. *Family Relations, 71*(2), 611–629. https://doi.org/10.1111/fare.12599

Anderson, S. A., Sabatelli, R. M., & Kosutic, I. (2013). Systemic and ecological qualities of families. In G. W. Peterson & K. R. Bush (Eds.), *Handbook of marriage and the family* (3rd ed., pp. 121–138). Springer.

Baptist, J., & Hamon, R. (2022). Family systems theory. In K. Adamsons, A. L. Few-Demo, C. Proulx, & K. Roy (Eds.). *Sourcebook of family theories and methodologies*. Springer.

Bateson, G., Jackson, D. D., Haley, J., & Weakland, J. (1956). Toward a theory of schizophrenia. *Behavioral Science, 1*(4), 251–263. https://doi.org/10.1002/bs.3830010402

Baucom, B. R., & Atkins, D. C. (2013). Understanding marital distress: Polarization processes. In M. A. Fine & F. D. Fincham (Eds.), *Handbook of family theories: A content-based approach* (pp. 145–166). Routledge.

Beavers, W. R., & Hampson, R. B. (2000). The Beavers systems model of family functioning. *Journal of Family Therapy, 22*(2), 128–143. https://doi.org/10.1111/1467-6427.00143

Benson, M. J., Curtner-Smith, M. E., Collins, W. A., & Keith, T. Z. (1995). The structure of family perceptions among adolescents and their parents: Individual satisfaction factors and family system factors. *Family Process, 34*(3), 323–336. https://doi.org/10.1111/j.1545-5300.1995.00323.x

Blaisure, K. R., Saathoff-Wells, T., Pereira, A., MacDermid Wadsworth, S., & Dombro, A. L. (2016). *Serving military families: Theories, research, and application* (2nd ed.). Routledge.

Bortz, P., Berrigan, M., VanBergen, A., & Gavazzi, S. M. (2019). Family systems thinking as a guide for theory integration: Conceptual overlaps of differentiation, attachment, parenting style, and identity development in families with adolescents. *Journal of Family Theory & Review, 11*(4), 544–560. https://doi.org/10.1111/jftr.12354

Bowen, M. (1985). *Family therapy in clinical practice*. Jason Aronson.

Bradshaw, J. (1988). *Healing the shame that binds you*. Health Communications.

Broderick, C. B. (1993). *Understanding family process: Basics of family systems theory*. SAGE Publications.

Broderick, C., & Smith, J. (1979). The general systems approach to the family. In W. R. Burr, R. Hill, F. I. Nye, & I. L. Reiss (Eds.), *Contemporary theories about the family* (Vol. 2, pp. 112–129). Free Press.

Brown, B. (2012). *Daring greatly: How the courage to be vulnerable transforms the way we live, love, parent, and lead*. Gotham.

Brown, B. (2021). *Atlas of the heart: Mapping meaningful connection and the language of human experience*. Random House.

Brown, J., & Errington, L. (Eds.). (2019). *Bowen family systems theory in Christian ministry: Grappling with theory and its application through a biblical lens*. The Family Systems Practice & Institute.

Brown, L. S. (2018). *Feminist therapy* (2nd ed.). American Psychological Association.

Burton, L. (2007). Childhood adultification in economically disadvantaged families: A conceptual model. *Family Relations, 56*(4), 329–345. https://doi.org/10.1111/j.l741-3729.2007.00463.x

Conley, D. (2004). *The pecking order: Which siblings succeed and why*. Pantheon.

Connidis, I. A., & Barnett, A. E. (2019). *Family ties & aging* (3rd ed.). SAGE Publications.

Cornelia, P. A. (2011). Observing emotional functioning in human relationship systems: Lessons from Murray Bowen's writings. In O. C. Bregman & C. M. White (Eds.), *Bringing systems thinking to life: Expanding the horizons for Bowen family systems theory* (pp. 3–30). Routledge.

Cowan, C. P., & Cowan, P. A. (2019). Enhancing parent effectiveness, fathers' involvement, couple relationship quality, and children's development: Breaking down silos in family policy making and service delivery. *Journal of Family Theory & Review, 11*(1), 92–111. https://doi.org/10.1111/jftr.12301

Cowan, P. A., Cohn, D. A., Cowan, C. P., & Pearson, J. L. (1996). Parents' attachment histories and children's externalizing and internalizing behaviors: Exploring family systems models of linkage. *Journal of Consulting and Clinical Psychology, 64(1)*, 53–63. https://doi.org/10.1037/0022-006X.64.1.53

Cox, M. J. (2010). Family systems and sibling relationships. *Child Development Perspectives, 4*(2), 95–96. https://doi.org/10.1111/j.1750-8606.2010.00124.x

Crimone, M. W., & Hester, D. (2011). Across the generations: The training of clergy and congregations. In O. C. Bregman & C. M. White (Eds.), *Bringing systems thinking to life: Expanding the horizons for Bowen family systems theory* (pp. 197–207). Routledge.

Dotterer, A. M., & Skinner, O. D. (2020). Racial socialization in black families. In A. G. James, Jr. (Ed.), *Black families: A systems approach* (pp. 114–123). Cognella Academic Publishing.

Drummet, A. R., Coleman, M., & Cable, S. (2003). Military families under stress: Implications for family life education. *Family Relations, 52*(3), 279–287. https://doi.org/10.1111/j.l741-3729.2003.00279.x

Endendijk, J. J., Groeneveld, M. G., & Mesman, J. (2018). The gendered family process model: An integrative framework of gender in the family. *Archives of Sexual Behavior, 47*(4), 877–904. https://doi.org/10.1007/s10508-018-1185-8

Faber, A. J., Willerton, E., Clymer, S. R., MacDermid, S. M., & Weiss, H. M. (2008). Ambiguous absence, ambiguous presence: A qualitative study of military reserve families in-wartime. *Journal of Family Psychology, 22*(2), 222–230. https://doi.org/10.1037/0893-3200.22.2.222

Gale, J., Ross, D. B., Thomas, M. G., Jr., & Boe, J. (2020). Considerations, benefits and cautions integrating systems theory with financial therapy. *Contemporary Family Therapy, 42*(1), 84–94. https://doi.org/10.1007/s10591-019-09518-5

Galovan, A. M., Holmes, E. K., & Proulx, C. M. (2017). Theoretical and methodological issues in relationship research: Considering the common fate model. *Journal of Social and Personal Relationships, 34*(1), 44–68. https://doi.org/10.1177/0265407515621179

Galvin, K. M., Dickson, F. C., & Marrow, S. R. (2006). *Systems theory: Patterns and (w)holes in family communication*. Sage.

Ganong, L., Jensen, T., Sanner, C., Chapman, A., & Coleman, M. (2020). Stepparents' attachment orientation, parental gatekeeping, and stepparents' affinity-seeking with stepchildren. *Family Process, 59*(2), 756–771. https://doi.org/10.1111/famp.12448

Goldenberg, I., Stanton, M., & Goldenberg, H. (2016). *Family therapy: An overview* (9th ed.). Cengage Learning.

Gottman, J. M. (1994). *What predicts divorce: The relationship between marital processes and marital outcomes*. Lawrence Erlbaum Associates.

Gottman, J., & Gottman, J. (2017). The natural principles of love. *Journal of Family Theory & Review, 9*(1), 7–26. https://doi.org/10.1111/jftr.12182

Grych, J., Oxtoby, C., & Lynn, M. (2013). The effects of interparental conflict on children. In M. A. Fine & F. D. Fincham (Eds.), *Handbook of family theories: A content-based approach* (pp. 228–245). Routledge.

Heller, D. P. (2019). *The power of attachment: How to create deep and lasting intimate relationships.* Sounds True.

Holmes, E. K., & Huston, A. C. (2010). Understanding positive father–child interaction: Children's, fathers', and mothers' contributions. *Fathering: A Journal of Research, Theory, and Practice about Men as Fathers, 8*(2), 203–225. https://doi.org/10.3149/fth.l802.203

Holmes, E. K., Sasaki, T., & Hazen, N. L. (2013). Smooth versus rocky transitions to parenthood: Family systems in developmental context. *Family Relations, 62*(5), 824–837. https://doi.org/10.1111/fare.12041

James, A. G., Jr. (Ed.). (2020). *Black families: A systems approach.* Cognella Academic Publishing.

James, A. G., Coard, S. I., Fine, M. A., & Rudy, D. (2018). The central roles of race and racism in reframing family systems theory: A consideration of choice and time. *Journal of Family Theory & Review, 10*(2), 419–433. https://doi.org/10.1111/jftr.12262

Johnson, S. M. (2019). *Attachment theory in practice: Emotionally focused therapy (EFT) with individuals, couples, and families.* Guilford Press.

Katz-Wise, S. L., Rosario, M., & Tsappis, M. (2016). Lesbian, gay, bisexual, and transgender youth and family acceptance. *Pediatric Clinics, 63*(6), 1011–1025. https://doi.org/10.1016/j.pcl.2016.07.005

Kerr, M. E., & Bowen, M. (1988). *Family evaluation: An approach based on Bowen theory.* W. W. Norton.

Lee, B. K., & Rovers, M. (2016). From "saving Satir" to "evolving Satir." *Social Work, 61*(4), 372–374. https://doi.org/10.1093/sw/sww056

Leslie, L. A., & Southard, A. L. (2009). Thirty years of feminist family therapy: Moving into the mainstream. In S. A. Lloyd, A. L. Few, & K. R. Allen (Eds.), *Handbook of feminist family studies* (pp. 328–339). SAGE Publications.

Lewis, M. (2006). *The blind side: Evolution of a game.* W. W. Norton.

Li, X., Hu, Y., Huang, C.-Y. S., & Chuang, S. S. (2021). Beyond W.E.I.R.D. (Western, educated, industrial, rich, democratic)-centric theories and perspectives: Masculinity and fathering in Chinese societies. *Journal of Family Theory & Review, 13*(3), 317–333. https://doi.org/10.1111/jftr.12403

Luepnitz, D. (2002). *The family interpreted: Psychoanalysis, feminism, and family therapy.* Basic. (Original work published 1988)

MacDermid Wadsworth, S., Lester, P., Marini, C., Cozza, S., Sornborger, J., Strouse, T., & Beardslee, W. (2013). Approaching family-focused systems of care for military and veteran families. *Military Behavioral Health, 1*(1), 31–40. https://doi.org/10.1080/21635781.2012.721062

Macfie, J., Mcelwain, N. L., Houts, R. M., & Cox, M. J. (2007). Intergenerational transmission of role reversal between parent and child: Dyadic and family systems internal working models. *Attachment and Human Development, 7*(1), 51–65. https://doi.org/10.1080/14616730500039663

Mallette, J. K., Richardson, E. W., & Futris, T. G. (2021). Foster father identity: A theoretical framework. *Journal of Family Theory & Review, 13*(3), 300–316. https://doi.org/10.1111/jftr.12391

McDowell, T., Knudson-Martin, C., & Bermudez, J. M. (2018). *Socioculturally attuned family therapy: Guidelines for equitable theory and practice.* Routledge.

McGoldrick, M., Gerson, R., & Petry, S. (2020). *Genograms: Assessment and intervention* (4th ed.). W. W. Norton.

Minuchin, P. (1985). Families and individual development: Provocations from the field of family therapy. *Child Development, 56*(2), 289–302. https://doi.org/10.1111/j.l467-8624.1985.tb00106.x

Monk, J. K., Oseland, L. M. O., Nelson Goff, B. S., Ogolsky, B. G., & Summers, K. (2017). Integrative intensive retreats for veteran couples and families: A pilot study assessing change in relationship adjustment, posttraumatic growth, and trauma symptoms. *Journal of Marital and Family Therapy, 43*(3), 448–462. https://doi.org/10.1111/jmft.12230

Monk, J. K., Ruhlmann, L. M., Nelson Goff, B. S., & Ogolsky, B. G. (2018). Brief-systemic programs for promoting mental health and relationship functioning in military couples and families. *Journal of Family Theory & Review, 10*(3), 566–586. https://doi.org/10.1111/jftr.12280

Norton, J. (2011). Bringing Bowen theory to family business. In O. C. Bregman & C. M. White (Eds.), *Bringing systems thinking to life: Expanding the horizons for Bowen family systems theory* (pp. 219–227). Routledge.

O'Gorman, S. (2012). Attachment theory, family system theory, and the child presenting with significant behavioral concerns. *Journal of Systemic Therapies, 31*(3), 1–16. https://doi.org/10.1521/jsyt.2012.31.3.1

Olson, D. H. (2000). Circumplex model of marital and family systems. *Journal of Family Therapy, 22*(2), 144–167. https://doi.org/10.1111/1467-6427.00144

Olson, D. H., Sprenkle, D. H., & Russell, C. S. (1979). Circumplex model of marital and family systems: I. Cohesion and adaptability dimensions, family types, and clinical applications. *Family Process, 18*(1), 3–28. https://doi.org/10.1111/j.1545-5300.1979.00003.x

Olson, D. H., Waldvogel, L., & Schlieff, M. (2019). Circumplex model of marital and family systems: An update. *Journal of Family Theory & Review, 11*(2), 199–211. https://doi.org/10.1111/jftr.12331

Paley, B., Lester, P., & Mogil, C. (2013). Family systems and ecological perspectives on the impact of deployment on military families. *Clinical Child and Family Psychology Review, 16*(3), 245–265. https://doi.org/10.1007/sl0567-013-0138-y

Petren, R. E., & Puhlman, D. J. (2021). Routines and coparenting as interrelated family management systems. *Journal of Family Theory & Review, 13*(2), 164–180. https://doi.org/10.1111/jftr.12422

Pinkus, S. (2006). Family systems: Applying a family systems perspective for understanding parent-professional relationships: A study of families located in the Anglo-Jewish community. *Support for Learning, 21*(3), 156–161. https://doi.org/10.111l/j.1467-9604.2006.00422.x

Potter, E. C., Allen, K. R., & Roberto, K. A. (2019). Agency and fatalism in older Appalachian women's information seeking about gynecological cancer. *Journal of Women & Aging, 31*(3), 192–212. https://doi.org/10.1080/08952841.2018.1434951

Priest, J. B. (2021). *The science of family systems theory.* Routledge.

Reed-Fitzke, K., Withers, M. C., & Watters, E. R. (2021). Longitudinal connections of self-esteem and depression among adult children and their parents. *Journal of Adult Development, 28*(3), 237–250. https://doi.org/10.1007/s10804-021-09371-7

Rosenblatt, P. C. (1997). *Metaphors of family systems theory: Toward new constructions.* Guilford Press.

Rosenblatt, P. C. (2013). Family systems theory as a tool for anyone dealing with personal or family loss. *The Forum: Quarterly Publication of the Association for Death Education and Counseling, 39*(1), 12–13.

Rothbaum, F., Rosen, K., Ujiie, T., & Uchida, N. (2002). Family systems theory, attachment theory, and culture. *Family Process, 41*(3), 328–350. https://doi.org/10.1111/j.l545-5300.2002.41305.x

Roy, K., & Yumiseva, M. (2021). Family separation and transnational fathering practices for immigrant Northern Triangle families. *Journal of Family Theory & Review, 13*(3), 283–200. https://doi.org/10.1111/jftr.12404

Russell, L. T. (2020a). Cohabitation, remarriage, and step-relationships in Black families. In A. G. James, Jr. (Ed.), *Black families: A systems approach* (pp. 156–167). Cognella Academic Publishing.

Russell, L. T. (2020b). Capturing family complexity in family nursing research and practice. *Journal of Family Nursing, 26*(4), 287–293. https:doi.org/10.1177/1074840720965396

Sanner, C., Ganong, L., & Coleman, M. (2020). Shared children in stepfamilies: Experiences living in a hybrid family structure. *Journal of Marriage and Family, 82*(2), 605–621. https://doi.org/10.1111/jomf.12631

Satir, V. (1988). *The new peoplemaking.* Science and Behavior Books.

Schoppe-Sullivan, S. J., & Fagan, J, (2020). The evolution of fathering research in the 21st century: Persistent challenges, new directions. *Journal of Marriage and Family, 82*(1), 175–197. https://doi.org/10.1111/jomf.12645

Silverstein, L. B., & Goodrich, T. J. (Eds.). (2003). *Feminist family therapy: Empowerment in social context.* American Psychological Association.

Suitor, J. J., Gilligan, M., & Pillemer, K. (2013). Continuity and change in mothers' favoritism toward offspring in adulthood. *Journal of Marriage and Family, 75*(5), 1229–1247. https://doi.org/10.1111/jomf.l2067

Taylor, A. C., Robila, M., & Fisackerly, B. (2013). Theory use in stepfamily research. In M. A. Fine & F. D. Fincham (Eds.), *Handbook of family theories: A content-based approach* (pp. 280–297). Routledge.

Titelman, P. (Ed.) (2008). *Triangles: Bowen family systems theory perspectives.* Haworth.

Umberson, D., & Thomeer, M. B. (2020). Family matters: Research on family ties and health, 2010 to 2020. *Journal of Marriage and Family, 82*(1), 404–419. https://doi.org/10.1111/jomf.12640

United Nations. (2020). *The world's women 2020: Trends and statistics.* https://www.un.org/en/desa/world%E2%80%99s-women-2020

von Bertalanffy, L. (1973). *General system theory: Foundations, development, applications* (rev. ed.). George Braziller.

Walsh, F. (2009). Human–animal bonds II: The role of pets in family systems and family therapy. *Family Process, 48*(4), 481–499. https://doi.org/10.1111/j.1545-5300.2009.01297.x

Whitchurch, G. G., & Constantine, L. L. (1993). Systems theory. In P. Boss, W. J. Doherty, R. LaRossa, W. Schumm, & S. K. Steinmetz (Eds.), *Sourcebook of family theories and methods: A contextual approach* (pp. 325–352). Plenum.

White, J. M., Martin, T. F., & Adamsons, K. (2019). *Family theories: An introduction* (5th ed.). SAGE Publications.

White, M., & Epston, D. (1990). *Narrative means to therapeutic ends.* W. W. Norton.

Wiener, N. (1967). *The human use of human beings: Cybernetics and society.* Avon.

Young, J. L., Kim, H., & Golojuch, L. (2021). "Race was something we didn't talk about": Racial socialization in Asian American Families. *Family Relations, 70*(4), 1027–1039. https://doi.org/10.1111/fare.12495

Image Credits

Social Exchange Theory

I n a world where sitcoms have increasingly been replaced by reality television, it is interesting to consider just how real reality shows truly are. Is it possible that producers are puppeteering the reality characters from behind the scenes? Further, is it possible that when romantic relationships occur on reality television, they are predetermined and maybe not based on what many of us consider to be "true" love? As much as we would like to believe the contrary, the truth is that most of these shows are actually scripted, and the "romance" we see, even when it is supposed to be real, is created and sold to us for other reasons. The same goes for shows that depict families and their daily lives as reality television.

Imagine being privy to conversations that occur around the proverbial "board room" table between television producers and actors' agents. Producers are fishing for a romance to sell, and agents know that even staged on-air romances boost the familiarity of and likability of their clients. Perhaps, what occurs behind these closed doors is similar to a draft for sports teams. The typecast heartthrob character is sought after for the romance, as is the shy, girl-next-door character. In exchange for their agreeing to be a part of an on-screen romance, they are promised more air time, appearances on talk shows to promote the show, and other endorsement deals. The romance we see on television, then, is hardly what it is in reality. Each of these deals is struck behind the scenes—perhaps, before filming even begins—and is based on a pragmatic cost–benefit analysis. Further, think about the power relations that are present during the discussion of the "plot" of the show. Who holds the power, and who wants it? Is the exchange that occurs between the actors, agents, and producers balanced, or imbalanced? Are there intrinsic (e.g., internal) or extrinsic (e.g., external) rewards to anyone involved by striking a deal to create a romance for the show? What happens if one of the actors develops feelings for someone else on the set or, even more complicated, if they already have a partner off-screen? When it comes to love and relationship negotiation, the costs, benefits, and intrinsic and extrinsic rewards for behavior have real consequences for individuals and families.

Social exchange theory provides family researchers and practitioners with a useful way to understand how dating, marriage, and family relationships are often based on the use of exchange in decision-making. In this chapter, we discuss the history of social exchange theory and how the principles and key concepts apply to the study of families and individual relationships. Social exchange theory helps us answer questions about how individuals within families and other relationships negotiate the "best deal" for themselves, based on the availability of power, rewards, and costs. To gain a fuller understanding of how this theory works, we start with a case study that illustrates how romantic relationships and families can be understood, using the concepts of social exchange.

Case Study

Stefan and Christina, both White, cisgendered, Jewish, and heterosexual, have been married for over 10 years and have three children. Both parents work outside the home and have negotiated the roles inside the household to be fairly equitable. For example, Christina loves to cook, so Stefan does the dishes. They take turns driving the children to and from school and soccer, helping the 7 and 9 year olds with homework, volunteering in the children's classrooms, and doing other activities. Their youngest is only 18 months old, so they even take turns changing dirty diapers and preparing her for bedtime. They each get time to themselves as well: Christina exercises four days a week, and Stefan plays in a recreational softball league. Their family life is busy, with most weekdays and weekends scheduled down to the hour because of all they have going on. The five of them are satisfied with the arrangements and are a very close-knit family that works together well as a unit. Their roles have each been negotiated so that Stefan and Christina feel like they spend quality time alone, with each other, as well as with each of the children, thanks to their distribution of household labor.

One aspect of the couple's lives that is still relatively unbalanced is Stefan and Christina's work lives. Christina has a prestigious job that offers her flexibility, travel, and contract work that supplements the family's income, so they can take family vacations together, renovate their home, and still have money left over for savings. Stefan, on the other hand, is at a standstill in his career. He has hit the earning ceiling in his occupation—making 40% less than Christina—and has recently started looking for other jobs in his field. The problem is, his area of expertise is so specific that a promotion would mean the family would need to relocate. He spent years working on his specialized graduate degree, and his only jobs have been in a specific area within higher education. Stefan has really struggled with feelings of depression and despair, constantly comparing himself to his wife in terms of salary, flexibility, and overall happiness because Christina is arguably at the peak of her career.

Ten years into their marriage, Stefan has a meltdown and admits to Christina that he cannot do it anymore. Though it goes against the way he has approached his career his entire adult life, he decides to leave his position and seek out a job in a different field. He loves his family and his children and does not want the family to relocate because, financially, it would not make sense to move everyone for his lower-paying job. Instead, Stefan tells Christina that he has "come to terms" with his career being secondary to hers. It took 10 years and extensive thought, but he tells her he is okay with not being the main breadwinner. He starts stepping aside for Christina to excel in her career by fulfilling the "traditional" roles of taking time off work to care for sick children and doing more at home, so Christina has less to worry about and can focus more time and energy on her career. This decision did not come without costs; Stefan struggled with feeling emasculated, disappointed professionally, and resentful toward his wife. However, in the end, Stefan told Christina he does not want to be on his deathbed and be known for being a great employee; he wants to be known for being a good father and husband. He truly embraces his new perspective of his identity, and the family is stronger because of it.

Think about the complexities associated with both Stefan and Christina's relationship as well as their family life as a whole. Throughout the time they have been together, they have had to negotiate the costs and benefits of each step of their relationship. The first two times they relocated, it was for Stefan's career. It was not until the last eight years that Christina's career really took off, which both contributed to the financial security of the family as well as the overall family functioning because her schedule was much more flexible than Stefan's. In fact, her security and flexibility contributed to the couple's decision to have a third child. For each step in their lives, Stefan and Christina had to consider the available resources, rewards, costs, and commitment as they moved forward. Some marriages dissolve when the couple faces a crossroads like this; why did that not happen for Stefan and Christina? In addition, what might have happened if Stefan and Christina had not had children? Would the relationship be more fickle and subject to dissolution? Social exchange theory helps researchers and practitioners frame family issues in terms of the balance between individuals' self-interest, norms of reciprocity, and available alternatives.

This theoretical framework focuses on how dependence in a relationship can lead to commitment and persistence. Social exchange theorists might suggest Christina's level of financial dependence on Stefan is relatively low, but at the same time, she relies heavily on him to perform the unpaid tasks of childrearing and household management. His devotion to their family is vital to her success. In addition, until Stefan came to terms with his

BOX 7.1. AT A GLANCE: SOCIAL EXCHANGE THEORY

- **Rational choice:** The assumption that individuals make decisions about their relationships by trying to maximize benefits and minimize costs.
- **Power:** The ability of one person in a social relationship to get their own way despite resistance from the other.
- **Rewards:** Any satisfaction, gratification, status, or relationship that one enjoys and, therefore, would like to experience with greater frequency.
- **Costs:** Any factor that would deter an activity, such as a punishment, that results from engaging in one behavior over another. There are three types: investment costs (time and effort), direct costs (resources given to another in an exchange), and opportunity costs (rewards available in other exchanges that were foregone as a result of participating in a particular relationship).
- **Norm of reciprocity:** Social expectations or rules that dictate that people should help those who have helped them and that they should not harm those who have helped them.
- **Comparison level:** The evaluation of the profitability of a relationship against what we feel we deserve.
- **Comparison level for alternatives:** The lowest level or relationship rewards a person is willing to accept in light of rewards that are available from alternative relationships or being alone.
- **Profit:** What is left after reward minus cost is calculated.
- **Self-interest:** The motivation to act in ways that yield the most beneficial outcome (to maximize one's profit) in a social exchange.

place in the family as the secondary breadwinner, he struggled with his self-interested desire to continue moving up in his career at the cost of his family's stability and security. Although these issues appear, on the surface, to be at the level of the individual, social exchange theory suggests that these decisions are not made in a vacuum. At the core of these seemingly individualistic decisions, there is—at a minimum—the presence of at least one other person; thus, the name social "exchange" theory! The exchange framework allows us to see the interdependence in relationships, as individuals move from an "I" and "me" perspective to an "us" and "we" perspective through their interactions and investments in each other (Ogolsky et al., 2017). This perspective gives researchers and practitioners unique insight into how relationships are formed, maintained, and dissolved and how they are affected by family growth and change.

What Is Social Exchange Theory?

Social exchange theory posits that all human relationships can be understood in terms of a cost–benefit analysis and the exchange of resources available to participants. When it comes to families, this theory is useful for examining relationships at their inception—sometimes before they are even formed! Why did you enter into your current relationship? Or, why are you not currently in a relationship? This theory's applicability does not stop at the onset of a relationship; it also can be used to understand how relationships shift, grow, and change over time, as well as why they end.

One of the major assumptions of this theory is the idea that people act out of **self-interest** and are interdependent on one another (Lawler & Thye, 1999). This means individuals have something of value to bring to a relationship, and during interaction they decide whether or not to exchange those "goods" and in what amounts (Lawler, 2001). Self-interest provides the motivation for people to take action in deciding to exchange resources (Stafford & Kuiper, 2021). It is important to remember that self-interest does not need to always be conceptualized as a negative, greed-driven act. In fact, it could be argued that most people are involved in relationships to achieve a sense of fulfillment, which is a guiding force of human interaction (Roloff, 1981). Therefore, whether they are willing or even able to admit it, people often form relationships based on the consideration of "What's in it for me?" while also considering possible alternatives because the goal is to try to get the most beneficial outcomes.

While this might seem harsh when applied to loved ones, think about your own selection of a significant other. In response to the questions raised earlier about your past and current relationship status, make a list of three to five reasons you answered the way that you did. Are you single by choice? If so, what is the driving force behind that preference? Chances are, your reasons for whatever your relationship status is have roots in social exchange theory. Maybe you prefer to not be controlled by a significant other. Maybe you no longer felt attracted to the other person you were last in a relationship with. On the contrary, if you are in a relationship, examine why that is the case. Does the other person build up your self-confidence? Do they support you when you need it? Really consider the heart (no pun intended) of the relationship and whether or not self-interest plays a role. Also consider what you depend on the other person for, and vice versa. Maybe what we define as "love" is in reality just an exchange of feelings that we experience when we are around the other person. Maybe we feel inseparable or so compatible that we cannot imagine a day without that person. Is interdependence at the heart of that feeling? Is it in our best interest to build a life with the person we most enjoy spending our time with because it is fulfilling? At the core of these considerations is social exchange; emotional support, connections, trust, and obligations are all elements in a relationship that can be exchanged between two people.

Considering relationships in that way, hopefully it can become easier to see beyond the quantitative, economics-based cost–benefit analysis and apply this theory to love and relationships as well as to your own individual preferences. In fact, most of the other theories you have read about in this book have focused on the family as the unit of analysis. By contrast, social exchange theory begins with the individual as the unit of analysis. As originally proposed by George Homans (1958), any social entity (e.g., a person, a family, or a social structure such as work) can be understood at the level of the individual. The "self-interested" individual is in the center of an exchange analysis. As such, "the needs, wants, and desires of an individual account for his or her actions" (Perry-Jenkins & MacDermid, 2013, p. 386). Therefore, it may be useful to consider your own preferences, needs, and experiences in any relationship and how they have influenced the outcome. If you have heard (or given) the excuse "it's not you, it's me" when a relationship is ending, you probably already understand the basis of this theoretical framework. When we hear that phrase, we often consider it to be a clichéd excuse for ending a relationship—a "cop-out" of sorts. In reality, the person using that phrase may actually be telling the truth because their self-interest is at risk. In most relationships, we do try to do what is best for ourselves, and we do often put ourselves first, knowingly or not. Below, we go into more detail about the historical underpinnings of this theory that contribute to where this framework is today, including its usefulness and applicability to individuals, relationships, and families.

History and Origins

As with all theories, it is important to examine the historical context in which the theory was developed. Social exchange as a theoretical framework is derived from many disciplines and has a rich history across a range of academic fields, such as cultural anthropology, economics, behavioral psychology, sociology, communication studies, and relationship science (Sabatelli et al., 2018; Stafford & Kuiper, 2021). Over time, the theory has been adapted to a number of other contexts and is especially relevant in the study of interpersonal relationships and families today (Sharkey et al., 2022). The origins of the theory are rooted in two basic philosophical principles: utilitarianism and behaviorism. Utilitarianism refers to a view held by early economists, such as Jeremy Bentham and John Stuart Mill, that humans are rational and self-interested, and they try to maximize the "benefits or utility from transactions or exchanges with others in a free and competitive marketplace" (Sabatelli & Shehan, 1993, p. 387). Essentially, when people make "utilitarian" decisions, they are doing what is best for themselves.

Another key influence on the origins of social exchange theory can be found in the work of cultural anthropologists, particularly Claude Lévi-Strauss, who went beyond the individual level of rational exchange, and conceptualized exchange as collectivist, whereby social norms and institutions regulate interpersonal exchanges (Sabatelli & Shehan, 1993). This means cultural expectations dictate what types of exchanges we participate in and are decided at the societal level as opposed to the individual level. For example, arranged marriages are a type of collectivist social exchange.

Behaviorism, on the other hand, focuses on how individuals participate in behavior based on operant learning theory and reinforcement. This concept was developed by B. F. Skinner and attempted to explain the persistence of exchange relations (Appelrouth & Edles, 2021). Behaviorists examine why people engage in behaviors time and time again. This aspect of social exchange theory helps us understand why some individuals, for example, are attracted to a certain type of significant other, even if that relationship does not on the surface appear to be in the person's best interest. For instance, consistently dating the "rebel" type fulfills a need, and after dating several rebels over a period of time, the behavior becomes a pattern. Something about that type of significant other elicits a profit and payoff. Indeed, Cook et al. (2013) explain that behavior is related to the payoffs that can be found in the exchange of activity between at least two individuals.

One of the early theorists who developed the **behavioral psychological approach** to exchange was Homans (1958). Not only was he interested in exchange as an interaction of activity, but he was also influential in proposing that reinforcement principles keep an exchange going over time. Homans's early work on exchange theory focused mostly on the psychological aspects of exchange as it occurred between a dyad, or two individuals. Homans believed that social exchange was based on three reinforcement principles: (a) success proposition; (b) stimulus proposition; and (c) deprivation–satiation proposition. **Success proposition** provides the basis for social exchange in that it supposes that when individuals are rewarded for their actions, they repeat them. Then, a **stimulus proposition** leads the individual to respond to a stimulus that provided a reward in the past. Finally, **deprivation–satiation** refers to when the reward itself loses value after it has been given too often in the recent past to hold high value.

Essentially, this early model specifically investigated why individuals would engage in exchange as well as why the exchange might cease to exist. In Homans's (1958) view, humans continue to participate in an exchange (or relationship) until participation ceases to be rewarding. An example of this would be the beginning stages of romantic relationships. Early on, partners often engage in romantic gestures, like showering their love interest with flowers, compliments, and gifts. Initially, these acts might elicit excitement and appreciation of the newness of the relationship. However, over time, if the gifts and attention continue, their power to reward wears off. At this point, deprivation–saturation is reached, and therefore, the reward loses value. The receiver may even start to get sick of all the attention. Feeling so saturated with such attention, according to Homans's early conceptualization of social exchange, could end the relationship.

Peter Blau (1964) was another early social exchange theorist who contributed to this theoretical perspective with his sociological background. Blau moved beyond analyzing the reinforcement principles of the dyad and of instrumental (i.e., learned) behavior. Building upon an **economic–utilitarian framework**, Blau extended the theory to include an understanding of the institutions and organizations that emerge out of social exchange. In doing so, Blau abandoned Homans's behavioral psychological analysis and, instead, focused on sociological issues, such as power, inequality, and norms of legitimation (Appelrouth & Edles, 2021).

Blau (1964) focused on **power**, which he defined in a similar way to sociologist Max Weber as "the probability that one actor within a social relationship will be in a position to carry out his own will despite resistance" (p. 115). By stepping back to analyze not only the exchange but also the power dynamics involved in the exchange, Blau added a level of complexity to the theoretical framework. Essentially, Blau conceptualized social life as a "marketplace in which participants negotiate with each other in an effort to make a profit" (Sabatelli & Shehan,

1993, p. 391). Conceptualizing the exchange process in this way insinuates there are alternative courses of action individuals can pursue, and the decision process itself involves considering one alternative over the other as part of the exchange. Individuals competing for power in the marketplace seek rewards that can fall into four general classes: social approval, money, esteem or respect, or compliance (Sabatelli & Shehan, 1993). Of course, the dominant social norms will dictate what is valued more (or less) in an exchange. In this way, we can see how Blau's model of social exchange extends beyond just the individual-level decision; it also takes into account how dominant ideals and norms play a part in the exchange. Indeed, Blau defined **norms of reciprocity** and **norms of fairness** to account for the social history of the exchange. The more individuals engage in exchange, the more trust is built and feelings of reciprocity are strengthened. At the same time, both parties need to perceive the exchange as fair and equitable for it to continue, and these perceptions are often defined at the cultural or social level, though they are experienced at the emotional level. For example, if a person views an exchange as unfair or unjust, they could react with anger or guilt, depending on whether they were benefitting from the unfair exchange (Cook et al., 2013).

Think back to the case study: Had Stefan and Christina built their lives together in a different era, gendered cultural expectations might have made their particular exchange impossible. It has not always been expected that (White) women should work outside the home, much less earn more than their husbands. Even today, with the presence of more progressive gender role attitudes, most young women still expect to have a double burden of housework and childcare, in addition to being in the paid labor force, with only some "helping" from their husbands (McConnon et al., 2021). Similarly, Stefan may also experience derogatory jokes from his male peers for taking on much of the housework and childcare responsibilities to make it possible for his wife to become more successful in her career. The interplay of cultural norms and the availability of power both affect the exchange in Stefan and Christina's relationship.

Blau (1964) also introduced the influence of viable alternatives to the analysis of exchange: If individuals in the exchange have alternatives to receive benefits outside of the relationship, they have more power than someone who does not have viable alternatives. This leads to **imbalanced exchange**, where one individual becomes dependent on the person with more power because they have few rewards to offer and no alternatives to turn to besides the more powerful individual in the exchange. What are the rewards Stefan could access if he ended the relationship? If he felt emasculated by Christina, he might have chosen to file for divorce and find a partner who made less money than he did, so he could regain some relative power. On the flip side, the financial obligation he would have by paying child support to Christina may be too costly and, essentially, outweigh the benefit of finding a new partner. Therefore, given the alternatives, the relationship remains stable.

While sociologists Homans and Blau laid the groundwork for exchange theory, social psychologists John Thibaut and Harold Kelley (1959) elaborated on the theory to include relationship stability and satisfaction. That is, while Stefan and Christina's relationship may persist, how can we explain their relationship satisfaction in terms of the exchange? Thibaut and Kelley suggest that it is important to consider the partners' perceptions of the comparison level (CL) and the comparison level for alternatives (CLalt). According to Thibaut and Kelley, the **comparison level** (CL) is a standard by which people evaluate the rewards and costs of a given relationship in terms of what they feel is deserved or realistically obtainable (Sabatelli & Shehan, 1993). In other words, individuals compare their own situations to the societal norms for people in similar situations. If

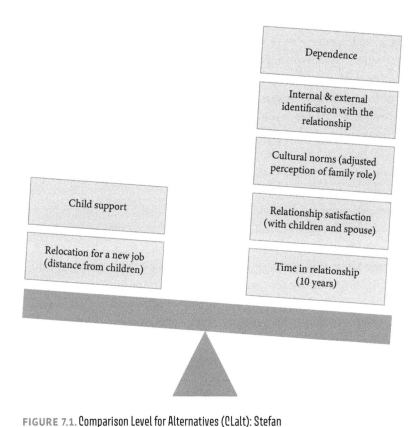

FIGURE 7.1. Comparison Level for Alternatives (CLalt): Stefan

they perceive that aspects of their relationship fail to meet their expectations, their global assessments of the relationship will be low. On the flip side, if someone feels they "have it made" in their relationship, their relationship satisfaction is high. Christina, from our case study, may feel especially satisfied in the relationship, depending on what she values out of the exchange. If she values freedom and independence from the "apron strings" of home and children and prefers to spend energy on work, then the sacrifices Stefan is making for their family likely lead to her relationship satisfaction. She may see her colleagues at work struggle with work–family balance, which gives her a comparison standard by which to judge her own situation, making her feel lucky to have the balance she has.

At the same time, Thibaut and Kelley suggest it is important to consider the available alternatives, if there are any. The **comparison level for alternatives** (CLalt) refers to "the lowest level of relational rewards a person is willing to accept given available rewards from alternative relationships or being alone" (Sabatelli & Shehan, 1993, p. 398). In other words, individuals may consider whether or not alternatives would bring more rewards and fewer costs than their current situation. In this way, CLalt provides a measure of stability, rather than satisfaction. Figure 7.1 provides an illustration of CLalt, using Stefan from our case study.

As you can see, the right side of the scale is tipped in favor of Stefan staying in the relationship because the alternatives (on the left) are too costly and serve as barriers to relationship dissolution. At the same time, the right side of the scale represents several aspects of CLalt: (a) Stefan's dependence on the relationship; (b) his internal identification with the relationship (beliefs about divorce) and external factors (i.e., economic considerations); (c) cultural norms (i.e., it is acceptable for men to take on a more expressive role in the family); (d) relationship satisfaction (i.e., love, fulfillment, and meaning); and (e) time in the relationship. It is important to note here that CLalt is a subjective assessment, and it is dependent on an individual's perception that better alternatives exist, regardless of whether they are actually better. In addition, this model is more complex than it may appear as applied to Stefan; it predicts stability, while taking satisfaction into account. That means unstable relationships may persist for lack of a better alternative. At the same time, relationships may become unstable in spite of high levels of satisfaction and may remain stable in spite of low levels of satisfaction.

Key Concepts

Now that we have examined the history of social exchange theory, we will define some of the key concepts that are used in this theory. From its origins in the broader fields of economics, psychology, and sociology, among others, it is clear that social exchange theory has a rich history in the family related disciplines (e.g., Edwards, 1969; Nye, 1979; Scanzoni, 1979). For example, because social exchange theory is concerned with the costs and rewards of work and family life for individual actors and intimate partners, exchange principles enter into couples' and families' decision-making "about where to work, how much to work, whether and when to marry, when to have children, and even when to divorce" (Perry-Jenkins & MacDermid, 2013, p. 386).

Rational Choice

The concept of **rational choice**, primarily articulated by James Coleman (1990), represents a theory in and of itself; it is important to social exchange theory because it provides the basis from which we conceptualize human interaction. Social exchange theory assumes that humans will make decisions based on a rational cost–benefit analysis of any situation. Note that the word "rational" has colloquial meanings that we should not confuse with the meaning we intend to explain here. Typically, we associate the word "rational" with "sane" or "sensible"; someone is making a decision with a clear head. Instead, from a theoretical standpoint, rational choice means that no matter what the mental state of the actor, they will act based on the aim to maximize their own personal advantage (Friedman, 1953). As we have pointed out thus far in the chapter, this type of orientation to decision-making can also be applied to issues of love, romantic relationships, marriage, and families (Nye, 1979; Sabatelli & Shehan, 1993; Karney & Bradbury, 2020).

Resources

In addition, according to rational choice theorist James Coleman, humans have several types of **resources,** or capital, to exchange (Adams & Sydie, 2002). The first kind is **physical capital**, which is tangible and observable. An example would be a farmer's tractors and equipment, land, and other assets that help run the farm. A second kind of capital is **human capital**, which is less tangible than physical capital and refers to the knowledge and skills a person acquires. Individuals acquire human capital through furthering their education, acquiring wealth, and "moving up" in society. A third kind of capital is **social capital**, which is the least tangible form because it is embodied in social relationships. A good example of this type of capital is the old adage, "I'll scratch your back if you scratch mine." When it comes to social relationships, these mutual expectations operate on two conditions: (a) a level of trustworthiness to be able to believe that the obligation will be met; and (b) the individuals interacting in the exchange need to understand the extent of the obligations (Coleman, 1994).

It is important to point out that social capital is not easily exchanged, however. First, individuals need to have access to investing in social capital, which often occurs within "'closed' social networks in which most individuals either directly or indirectly (as in a friend of a friend) know one another" (Appelrouth & Edles, 2021, p. 522). This prerequisite of network access is not easily overcome. To access a network to which we do not belong, sometimes we have to take a chance in investing in a social structure we are not yet a part of. An example would be volunteering or interning at a company before becoming employed there. The investment of time and resources into the social structure is high, and the risk that it might not pay off is also high. However, once an individual has access to social capital, the more likely they can benefit from social exchange and reciprocity. At its core, Coleman's conceptualization of social capital champions the ideas of fairness and commitment, both essential for establishing and maintaining healthy family relationships. Note that we present a somewhat different view of capital in Chapter 3, when we describe conflict theory; another form of capital is symbolic, as developed by Bourdieu (1990).

Norms of Reciprocity

Reciprocity occurs when individuals return one exchange for another of equal value. These exchanges can be positive (e.g., sharing carpooling duties with other parents) or negative (e.g., saying no to a request for help to "pay back" an individual for refusing to do the same thing for you previously). In his examination of social exchange and power in families, Scanzoni (1979) has studied norms of reciprocity in marriage, focusing specifically on how it influences marital role consensus, marital conflict, and marital stability. For the most part, norms of reciprocity serve to stabilize marital relationships because, over time, reciprocity becomes patterned behavior. This tends to be stabilizing because at the beginning of relationships, individuals can feel indebted or obligated to participate in reciprocal exchange. In a marriage, however, these exchanges become part of the established partnership and are expected. Recent research has found that reciprocity norms in marital interaction—in the form of listening well, which is a form of nonverbal affection exchange—helps couples deal with difficult conversations. That is, the reciprocal ability to listen and to feel listened to in marital discussions around issues as challenging as the #MeToo movement is reflective of heterosexual couples who are comfortable with communication and self-disclosure (Coduto & Eveland, 2022).

Cost–Benefit Analysis

A **cost–benefit analysis** is usually carried out at the beginning of a relationship to help us decide whether or not a relationship is worth investing in. It involves a process for calculating the value of a relationship in terms of potential rewards and costs. The potential **costs** of a relationship are those things that we see as negative: giving up freedom or settling for a partner who does not have the most desirable qualities. The **rewards** or benefits of a relationship are those things that we see as positive: desirable personality traits, physical attractiveness, positive emotions, and so on. This type of cost–benefit analysis follows an economic model that can predict the overall value of the relationship as well as net profits to those involved.

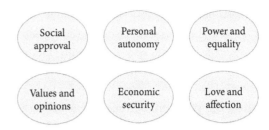

FIGURE 7.2. General Sources of Rewards and Costs

Intrinsic and Extrinsic Rewards

Blau differentiated between two different types of rewards (intrinsic and extrinsic) because "linking intimate relations to exchange processes runs counter to our conventional understanding of such relations" (Appelrouth & Edles, 2021, p. 503). Thus, Blau added these two concepts to aid in our understanding of how rewards could be perceived by the receiver. **Intrinsic rewards** are both tangible and intangible things "we find pleasurable in and of themselves, not because they provide the means for obtaining other benefits" (Appelrouth & Edles, 2021, p. 502). An example would be going on a walk with loved ones on a beautiful hiking trail. **Extrinsic rewards**, on the other hand, are things that are detached from the actual relationship one is involved in. That is, the relationship may be a means to an end; the "end" is the extrinsic reward. As an example, someone who just wishes to get married and have children as soon as possible may settle for a partner who is not their "ideal" type. The end goal—getting married and having kids before age 40—is more important than the actual emotional value placed on the relationship.

Figure 7.2 depicts some of the considerations individuals use when evaluating the best ways to maximize their rewards, reduce their costs, and secure the most profits (or least losses). Nye (1979) explained that the process of weighing alternatives to make the best choices is a critical part of social exchange. There are several generalized sources of rewards and costs that are at the heart of social exchanges. For example, social approval is a major source of exchange. To gain social approval is to maximize one's ability to receive respect, admiration, and prestige and to minimize social disapproval and rejection. Security, as well, is a generalized source of rewards and costs, in that security can entail having a home, health insurance, and an income, but without those commodities, life can be very insecure.

Bargaining

The concept of **bargaining**, which refers to the ways that couples distribute resources, derives from Gary Becker's (1981) classic exchange/economic model of marriage, which is based on rational choice theory. Becker, a political conservative, was an economist who studied marital relationships and family economics. He was awarded the Nobel Prize in 1992 for extending the domain of microeconomic analysis to a wide range of human behavior and interaction, including nonmarket human behavior. In the family field, Becker's work has been applied to an array of topics including marriage, divorce, fertility, and the work–family interface (Becker, 1992).

Using microexchange principles, Becker (1981) hypothesized that men and women seek to maximize the utility of their marriage by comparing benefits and costs and that they may choose divorce if they expect it to increase their own welfare (Braver & Lamb, 2013). Bargaining is based on the proposition that men and women compete as they seek mates, which creates a marriage market. According to Becker, this explains not only why most adults are married but also why potential mates are hierarchically arranged, compared, and evaluated according to their wealth, education, and other valuable characteristics. In essence, the courting process involves a form of economic bargaining for the best deal on a partner within the restrictions "imposed" by market availability. To further complicate this, demographers help us understand that marriage, as a social institution, requires money, and cohabitation "continues to provide a kind of 'poor man's' marriage, a temporary arrangement or a holding station for the 'real thing'" (Sassler & Lichter, 2020, p. 42).

Power

Social exchange theory posits that marriage and family relationships are microstructures in which power—and compliance—are exercised and experienced (Scanzoni, 1979). As we discuss in Chapter 8 on feminist theory, gender is a primary way through which power operates in families, and partners must constantly negotiate their own perceptions of fairness in terms of contributions to childcare, housework, and paid labor (Thompson, 1991)—a trend that continues even for more egalitarian youth and adults today in the United States (McConnon et al., 2022; Pepin & Cotter, 2018) and Europe (Grunow et al., 2018). From a utilitarian perspective, marriage is basically an economic arrangement where "money talks." And money often talks in different ways for men and women, depending on their experiences with privilege and oppression. In a study comparing how couples from the United States, Germany, and the United Kingdom experience post-birth earnings decline, Musick et al. (2020) found that women experienced steep declines in their share of the couple's earnings following first birth—a result that persisted across the three countries and over several years of follow-up. This research is pivotal when it comes to social exchange theory because of how much parenting impacts the gendered division of labor in the household. Over time, men's and women's earnings diverge, which reduces women's access to power in any exchange inside the marriage. Less access to financial security and resources limits options and alternatives should one partner desire to end the marriage. Using exchange theory, Bittman et al. (2003) found that women were able to decrease their time spent in housework but only if their earnings did not exceed their husbands' income. Conversely, for men, they found that gender is more important than money; men did not increase their share of housework even if they earned less. For men, their gender allows them the privilege of doing less housework than their wives, but for women, their options are to either allow some housework to stay undone or to purchase household services (e.g., housecleaning). Thus, these findings are a useful example of social exchange theory when it comes to understanding how power (and gendered expectations) influence marital exchange.

Equity Theory

Equity theory is a type of social exchange theory that emphasizes the principle of **distributive justice**. Homans (1961) explained distributive justice as the expectation that each person in an exchange relation will expect that their rewards will be proportional to their costs. That is, the greater the rewards are, the greater the costs will be, and the greater the investments are, the greater the profit will be (Ekeh, 1974). In equity theory, a relationship can be considered equitable if the ratio of benefits to contributions is the same for both partners. An inequitable relationship is one in which one partner is overbenefitting from the

BOX 7.2. SOCIAL EXCHANGE THEORY IN MODERN CULTURE: *YELLOWSTONE*

Image 7.1 A Scene From *Yellowstone*, 2021

Yellowstone is an American drama that follows the Dutton family: patriarch, John; daughter, Beth; and sons, Kayce and Jamie. They own the largest amount of land in the United States in rural Bozeman, Montana and raise cattle. As adult children, each individual has a role to play to win favor with their father. It is clear throughout the show that there was very little in the way of emotional exchange and nurturing throughout the children's upbringing; their adult attachment to the family ranges from chaotic (Beth) to anxious (Jamie) to avoidant (Kayce).

Beth has a tumultuous relationship with her father and her brother Jamie. Retrospective scenes throughout the show reveal significant childhood trauma for Beth; the show makes clear that none of that trauma was ever discussed in the family—much less addressed in therapy. Jamie consistently feels like an outsider, always on a mission to please his father and "fit in"—and in season three, viewers find out why (no spoilers!). Because of their significant unaddressed trauma and the pressure on the family from their father to maintain the ranch and its way of life, adulthood relationships are built solely on exchange; in many ways, the children are simply employees of the wealthy estate.

Jamie is the attorney of the family and plays a major role in season one as the attorney for the family business and estate. Beth works in the financial industry and helps her father maintain control over the competition eager to buy up his adjoining land to build casinos, golf resorts, and second homes. Kayce is a bit of a black sheep of the family; a former Navy SEAL, his expertise comes in handy when his father needs him to help take care of business.

Because their mother and John's wife died when the children were young, and the fact that the family has not fully processed that trauma, their adult relationships are mostly transactional. Additionally, the wranglers they "hire" to work at the Dutton ranch have very few (if any) alternatives and, thus, provide their labor in exchange for room and board and the occasional feeling of belonging to a family—no matter how toxic.

relationship, and the other partner is underbenefitting. To underbenefit in a relationship means that you are giving more to the relationship than you are receiving. Although the partner who is overbenefitting from the relationship can also feel negative emotions like stress and guilt, the inequity of the relationship bears a greater cost to the underbenefitted, who may experience even more intense feelings of anger, depression, and the like because their contributions may be unacknowledged or devalued (Dainton & Zelley, 2006). As an example, think about who provides most of the care for older relatives in families. Typically, caregiving for older men is provided by daughters, wives, and daughters-in-law. Sons may provide instrumental support, in the form of financial assistance, but the lion's share of the work is provided by close female kin. Thus, men tend to overbenefit in family relationships, and women tend to underbenefit. Nowhere is this more apparent than in the relationships between adult brothers and sisters. Sisters tend to provide much more care for their parents than do brothers, and yet brothers get more credit for the (more limited) work they perform (Connidis & Barnett, 2019).

Evaluating Social Exchange Theory

Strengths of Social Exchange Theory

Like all theories, social exchange theory has both strengths and weaknesses. The strengths include its widespread popularity and usefulness as a comprehensive theory of humans, couples, and families in their social and economic contexts.

The Economic Metaphor Is Highly Adaptable to Multiple Contexts

One reason social exchange theory is very versatile and applicable to many areas of study is the succinct nature of the economic metaphor. When reduced to the calculus of reciprocally trading resources in the marketplace to maximize profits, it is easy to see how this metaphor is as applicable to the international stock market as to the interpersonal exchanges of love, social approval, and power. The elegance of the simple mathematical equation of rewards minus costs equal outcome (e.g., Rewards − Costs = Outcome) offers a shorthand way to understand rational human action and transaction (Dilworth-Anderson et al., 2005; Stafford & Kuiper, 2021). And when examining family relationships, the economic metaphor helps to explain the investments parents and children make to one another over time (Silverstein, 2005).

Social Exchange Concepts Bridge the Gap Between Research and Practice

Social exchange theory is easy to put into practice (Roloff, 1981). How many times, when facing a difficult decision, have you pulled out a pen and paper and drawn two columns, with pros on the one side and cons on the other? This very effective problem-solving strategy shows just how intuitive and useful social exchange principles are for everyday life. For example, theoretical concepts, such as rewards, costs, bargaining, and comparison level, have often been applied in clinical practice (Bagarozzi, 1993; Nakonezny & Denton, 2008). Therapists try to help individuals and couples bring to light the underlying rules and values they use to negotiate with one another and make mutually beneficial decisions. Therapists also know that human behavior that seems illogical on the outside does have some underlying rationality that reflects a person's way of assessing information and investments to lead to the most satisfactory outcome.

Social Exchange Theory Is Highly Testable in Research

One of the major hallmarks of social exchange theory is that it is easily translatable into testable hypotheses. The simple elegance of its theoretical propositions are parsimonious and fit the requirements of experimental quantitative research (Nye, 1978). (Also, see Chapter 1, Figure 1.2 for an explanation of the scientific process as it relates to theory building.) Because the theory translates so well into research, a systematic, incremental approach, rather than a haphazard approach, has been used to refine and expand the theory (Collett, 2010; Stafford & Kuiper,

2021). Further, many of the complicated relationships that comprise the family can be put to a test. Nye (1979) describes an array of family contexts that can be proposed and then tested in research. In Nye's description of social exchange theories, a few of the more than 120 testable propositions (e.g., hypotheses) include (a) middle-class employed mothers are more likely to have more "disposable time" than lower-class employed mothers; (b) the more highly educated a woman is, the more nonmonetary rewards will be obtained from employment; (c) the more highly educated a woman is, the less physically tiring the work will be (Nye, 1979, p. 14). In addition to these hypotheses about social class and education in families with employed mothers, Nye also proposes hypotheses about topics including ages and number of children, race and employment of mothers, timing of marriage and parenthood, sexual behavior, social networks, divorce, family violence, and communication.

Weaknesses of Social Exchange Theory

Despite its strengths, social exchange theory is not without its weaknesses. As we have found with other family theories, some of its strengths are also some of its weaknesses.

Assumes Individuals Rationally and Accurately Calculate Costs and Benefits

One of the major limitations of exchange theory is that it presumes that individuals are rational and act out of self-interest. But humans are not always rational and are not always able to weigh rewards and costs accurately (Ogolsky & Monk, 2019). Further, what about behavior that is motivated by emotionality or altruism? That is, not all people are motivated by maintaining complete equity in their relationship, where they closely keep score about each other's cost–benefit ratios (Jarvis et al., 2019). This theory even presumes that altruism is rational because "the person will predictably be rewarded by approval both by the person helped and by others who are aware of the act" (Nye, 1979, p. 8). Viewing even altruism as strictly rational and self-interested seems to trivialize the importance of moral principles that dictate values, such as kindness, forgiveness, and self-sacrifice. For example, would you say that Mother Teresa's work on behalf of the poor is motivated by self-interest? Fortunately, recent research on the role of emotions in personal relationships is beginning to address the purely rationalistic, instrumental understanding of social exchange to include more of its intangible qualities as well as aspects of socioeconomic, racial, or gender inequality (Cho et al., 2020; Landor & Barr, 2018; Stafford & Kuiper, 2021).

Studies of Family Relationships Have Not Kept Pace With New Exchange Concepts

In spite of the simple elegance and appeal of the language of costs, rewards, and outcomes, more recent research shows that family scholarship has been slow in moving beyond these key ideas and has taken advantage of new developments in the sociological study of exchange theory. Collett (2010) charges that the new research now allows us to go past the earlier ideas about how individuals participate in exchange relationships by examining the role of the social relationship itself—and not the individual—as the mechanism of exchange. Indeed, relationship science research (Sharkey et al., 2022) and the growth of dyadic data analysis (Kenny et al., 2006) offer theoretical and empirical tools, respectively, to advance the understanding of the social aspect of exchange. Further, by studying the relationship, there are new possibilities for examining the importance of trust, commitment, perceptions of fairness, and positive emotions in how marital and family relationships are developed and maintained.

Oversimplifies the Influence of Power at the Macrostructural Level

Feminist scholars (see Chapter 8) argue that the individual level is not sufficient to understand how bargaining occurs in marriage, basically because it minimizes the complex role of gender and power in intimate relationships (Komter, 1989; Micdema et al., 2016). Bargaining, at the microstructural level, is influenced by how power is distributed at the macrostructural level in the ways that law, politics, and social structures inequitably shape opportunities and access to resources. For example, gender norms that provide men with greater earning power enter into their private relationships with their wives by the expectation that men do not have to share equally in housework. Only interpreting behavior as a function of personal preferences and resources, and not acknowledging that gender privilege is derived from social institutions, is, thus, a major limitation of exchange theory.

An Alternative Theory App: Queer Theory

In this chapter, we have laid out the origins, key concepts, and modern applications as well as the strengths and weaknesses of social exchange theory. Although social exchange theory primarily uses a micro level of analysis, it is useful to think about how it compares to queer theory, which you will learn about in Chapter 13. Queer theory provides a critical analysis of families and couples, and especially society, when it comes to understanding power dynamics, alternatives, exchange, and inequity. Consider how one's sexual and gender identity develops over time; what options are available in the larger society determines how much power one has in an exchange. Additionally, consider polyamorous relationships. When a family unit consists of more than one adult partner, how is the power distributed? Is it possible to be more equitable in an "alternative" version of family? What about when parents provide the support and resources to a child who identifies as nonbinary or transgender? Do the static, rigid gender roles that social exchange theory is founded on become dismantled? How can queer theory be used to improve and update a social exchange framework?

Next, it is important to understand how social exchange theory is applicable to the study of families across the globe. Box 7.3 considers information from four different countries to highlight the cultural differences that exist when it comes to caring for older adults.

Working With Social Exchange Theory: Integrating Research and Practice

Now that we have defined social exchange theory, described its historical origins and key concepts, and pointed out its strengths and weaknesses, we turn to how it can be used in theory, research, and practice. We provide an example of current theorizing, analyze an empirical study that was guided by social exchange theory, and describe how the theory has been applied to understanding the very important issue of family financial management.

Social Exchange Theory Today

Social exchange theory has come a long way since its founders—Homans (1958), Blau (1964), Thibaut and Kelly (1959), and Emerson (1976)—first conceptualized the role of rewards, costs, resources, alternatives, and opportunities as a set of principles and propositions, rooted in behaviorism and utilitarian economics. Today,

BOX 7.3. GLOBAL COMPARISONS: CAREGIVING FOR OLDER ADULTS

Countries around the world have different ways of addressing the needs of the older adult population, depending on their customs and norms of intergenerational exchange. In the following list, we highlight four countries' approaches to caring for older adults:

- **Australia:** Caregivers are officially recognized in Australia, and the government pays each caregiver a "carer's allowance" for providing daily care in a private home. Social services funds nongovernmental organizations to provide respite care for caregivers in Australia as well.
- **France:** In 2015, France passed the Law on the Adaptation of Society to Aging, which officially recognizes unpaid carers as those individuals providing caregiving to frail elderly individual(s). These individuals are allowed to claim a personalized independence allowance and are also provided access, under certain circumstances, to benefits from the carer's old-age insurance as well as respite.
- **China:** The Confucian ideal of filial piety toward family elders has traditionally meant that older parents and grandparents are cared for by family in the home. However, recent demographic shifts have made it difficult for families to fulfill this traditionally held value. Chinese young adults are migrating from rural to urban areas, a demographic shift that increases the geographical distance between children and parents. In addition, until its abolishment in 2015, the one-child policy had created the "4:2:1 problem," which refers to the typical four grandparents and two parents for every one working Chinese person. Analysts suggest that perceptions of "value" by both those involved in the exchange—those paying for the care (potentially the Chinese government) as well as those receiving the care—are of utmost importance.
- **Italy:** Italians had previously favored norms of reciprocity and caring for older adult family members at home, but that was before a major demographic shift occurred that has put Italians in a tight spot. Historically, large Italian families meant built-in caregivers, but family sizes have been steadily shrinking over the past several decades. Italians generally still prefer to be cared for at home, so they have begun to rely on foreign caregivers to take the place of family. Older adults do have access to a program that provides help to subsidize the costs of hiring a caregiver, but currently, there is a waiting list.

As we can see, the choices available to families are dependent on the cultural expectations and the institutional support (or not) given to caregivers and their families. Caregivers must weigh the costs and benefits by examining the options available to them, especially when it comes to norms of reciprocity and the comparison level for alternatives of care.

Source: www.embracingcarers.com

however, new scholarship calls into question the utility of such a theory, as it was "never applied to families of color" (Landor & Barr, 2018, p. 331). Below, we highlight this work, as it brings new light to the ways in which social exchange theory can incorporate critical race and intersectionality into its framework.

To begin, Landor and Barr (2018) critique the assumptions on which social exchange theory is built. The ideal "Standard North American Family" (Smith, 1993), they argue, is the assumption on which this theory was built, and yet it has never been a reality for African American families. On the contrary, African American families are known to experience more egalitarian relationships, as "women have generally always participated in the labor force" (p. 332), and African American men have certainly not experienced marriage in the same way that White men have, due to historical barriers, disadvantage in the labor market, systemic racism, and over-incarceration of Black men in the United States. This reality calls into question the foundational view that marriage is a "reward" for all parties, especially African American women. Landor and Barr (2018) suggest that African American women view marriage as a "tax" because of these systemic disadvantages and, instead, must weigh the costs and risks associated with marriage against the benefits of single parenthood.

As a result, Landor and Barr suggest centering the "material and cultural realities of those at the margins, often people and families of color" (p. 341) by considering that all actors involved in exchange are, perhaps, not self-interested in the same ways:

> Failing to situate the motivations for social exchange within the broader sociohistorical context of intersecting race, gender, and class inequalities, like those inherent in and perpetuated by the symbolic violence of respectability politics, fails to see individuals as differentially situated and intersectionally interested actors and closes off inquiries into understanding when, in what contexts, for whom, and at what cost self-interest drives intimate exchanges. (p. 342)

Sabatelli et al. (2018) echo these sentiments by suggesting that family theorists utilize social ecological theory as a complement to social exchange theory. This, they argue, could help researchers, theorists and practitioners more fully understand how exchanges in intimate relationships and families are better understood by taking macro-level forces, such as structural inequalities and the like, into account.

Social Exchange Theory in Research

As we have shown, social exchange theory is very useful across many fields of study and also provides a common language for discussing how different cultures around the world engage in marital bargaining. In a growing body of work examining the collectivist-oriented society, Nepal, in rural South Asia, Jennings (2014) sought to understand marital conflict and divorce by using a cost-benefit approach, and Zhang and Axinn (2021) further investigated arranged marriages by examining the role depression plays in an exchange that is out of the hands of the two parties involved. Investigations like this have, until recently, been fairly uncommon, and both studies revealed the importance of conducting research on what is considered a Western topic in a society very unlike the United States.

Jennings (2014) conducted a quantitative study using a sample of 674 couples from the Chitwan Valley Family Study in Nepal. Results revealed that, although divorce is still uncommon and stigmatized in this traditional society, the author found that individualist factors, such as marital discord, were more important predictors of divorce than cultural dictates to remain married. Even though women have little household power and few opportunities to support themselves, they still would prefer to get out of marriages for their own emotional wellbeing and physical safety. Thus, marital quality was still highly valued by these wives—so much so that they were willing to risk financial insecurity to leave a marriage characterized by conflict and unhappiness. Further, the women found alternatives to living in a harsh marriage. Some planned to move back in with their parents, others chose separation and living in separate households, and still others found a new partner and remarried soon after they divorced their previous husband. Of interest, then, is that "both spouses' perceptions of discord are important for marital outcomes, even in settings where the costs of marital dissolution are relatively high" (Jennings, 2014, p. 476).

Zhang and Axinn (2021) investigated the existence of depressive symptoms and intimate partner violence (IPV) in arranged marriages in Nepal. They used longitudinal data from the Chitwin Valley Family Study (N = 3,912) and found that among women whose marriages were entirely arranged outside of their control, both partners experience an increase in depression, but it was more notable for women. Additionally, regardless of the level of involvement in the "choice" for women in who they will marry, getting married at all significantly increases the likelihood of depression for women, but not for men, and women who experience IPV are at even greater risk for depression. These findings are key not only because there is such limited data on this taboo topic among Nepalese women but also because it demonstrates how important it is for individuals to have a balanced exchange inside a marriage. With no alternatives, very little (if any) power, and no rewards, women are left to suffer from a lifetime of gender-based violence and significant mental illness.

Social Exchange Theory in Practice

There are several areas in which social exchange theory can be applied in practice. Next, we elaborate on how social exchange theory has been applied to understanding ways that families manage their finances. Family financial management, which is the allocation of income and material resources, is one of the crucial functions of family life (Bennett, 2015), especially in family-run businesses (Waldkirch et al., 2018). In the typical model of how family financial management operates, the family is seen as a singular unit. Husbands are seen as the primary breadwinner, wives work only for extras (if at all), and children are dependent on parental support. More recent insights into family financial management, however, reveal that the accumulation and distribution of finances are subjected to gendered and economic power structures and roles. The economic history of the family is anything but equal; it is very important to consider not only who earns money but also who controls how it is spent. As we have learned in other chapters, one of the major concerns of family life is who has control over money and wealth. Just like in conflict theory (Chapter 3), conflict over where resources go can be managed and overcome by the ability of family members to cooperate with one another, regardless of who holds more power.

Another consideration for understanding how families negotiate the utilization of financial and material resources is that families are very diverse. Rather than assuming that the economic processes in families are alike, despite differences in family structure, age, gender, and income, among others, it is important to consider the unique ways that social class, race, gender, and other important circumstances impinge on family relationships and individual members' ability to participate in family financial decision-making, pooling resources, engaging in paid work, and living under the same roof. Thus, in trying to work with families regarding their finances, practitioners must consider an array of different situations, including working families; couples in retirement; remarried families in which biological or stepchildren may or may not live in the couple's household; and unemployment.

Consider all the scenarios in which understanding family finances in light of social exchange theory is important. As noted in the case study, a marriage and family therapist would benefit from knowing that Stefan and Christina have struggled with meaning associated with financial power in the past. Though it seems like the couple has worked out many of the issues associated with their exchange, it may inevitably arise in both small and big ways

BOX 7.4. VOICES FROM LIVED EXPERIENCE

Angela Clark is a survivor leader, speaker, and teacher of mindfulness tools. As a survivor of sexual abuse and trafficking, specifically, she offers reflections here about transactional love, a concept that considers how love is something to be earned or exchanged, as opposed to something given unconditionally. Trigger warning: This excerpt includes discussion of rape and sexual violence:

> I saw cash change hands over my head at the age of 5 for sexual access to my body. I'd already been raped by the grandfather that sold me. He'd been grooming and sexually abusing me for 3 years. I'm in my fifties now and still dealing with the ramifications. How that's carried over into my life is rather sickening to me.
>
> I have unconsciously been in constant assessment of "What are the risks with this friendship?" versus the benefits. Earlier in life, I always had a strong need to be needed and valuable. If I wasn't needed to babysit the kids, the dogs, drive someone to appointments—essentially fill someone's needs (thank God not with sex anymore)—then I might cease to exist. I had generational training in this neediness too. The women in my family also lived in the shadows of men. And if they found themselves single (divorced/widowed), then they felt unprotected and constantly shopping for a knight in shining armor. Gender roles were very clearly laid out for me. It makes sense that I defaulted into the shadows when I entered a relationship in recent years; it was my old training kicking in. My partner's old training kicked in too, which complicates trust and vulnerable exchanges.
>
> Because of my past, my current relationship is defined by transactional love. My complex posttraumatic stress is activated in this exchange-based type of love, and I've experienced claustrophobia for the first time ever—not specific to a small dark place but during an ongoing argument and general life circumstances. I didn't know situational claustrophobia existed. There are many times that I want to run or fight, which is an improvement over pleasing (which I still do too!). I look back at who I was at the beginning of the relationship, and I see how I lived in his shadow. Each year I've found courage to step out more.
>
> My friendships (with all genders) are hard won; we've cried together, apologized, and boldly stayed committed to friendship. My whole adult life I've worked to view love and relationship, and even friendship in a healthier way. First, I had to learn to separate myself from those around me. Who was I, and what did I want? I'd learned to intuit what was wanted and needed in a situation, which is a great skill to have, but it's problematic when I found myself unconsciously manipulating others in ways that I thought were good for me. No doubt that saved my life, but it's not the kind of behavior that I want in my adult life. It's been an ongoing struggle to speak up for myself and take up space in this world.
>
> I have focused much of the last several years of life on healing. For me, intimacy means reaching out to trusted people that I've invested time and energy into having an equitable friendship with. Choosing to be vulnerable with a friend is my default now, even when fetal position in my bed seems safest. That is what healing from transactional love looks like, and it is ongoing.

in their future. How does "flex" or "fun" money get allotted in their household? Does Christina get more because she brings in more? What about family wealth and inheritance? Depending on the financial status of each of their parents, Christina and Stefan may subconsciously consider who may inherit more money or which parent will require caregiving or long-term care as they near the end of life. Since Stefan is taking on more "traditional" roles in his family so Christina can work more, does that mean he would also assume caregiving responsibilities for their parents? Clearly, the breakdown of gendered earning norms, along with familial wealth, inheritance, and financial planning, have real consequences. Each of these issues can contribute to relationship quality, which undoubtedly affects not only the couple's relationship but the relationship with their children and extended family as well.

Conclusion

Since its origination in economics and its elaboration in the fields of psychology and sociology, social exchange theory continues to be applicable to the study of personal relationships and families today. This theory has been used extensively to study issues of aging and family as well, particularly when it comes to norms of reciprocity and caregiving. Social norms of exchange differ significantly around the world, depending on the economic, cultural, and religious expectations that surround intergenerational exchange. Social exchange theory is, thus, essential to understanding how diverse individuals and changing societies view the costs, rewards, and outcomes associated with human interaction in relationships.

Multimedia Suggestions

www.npr.org/2020/01/10/795246685/emotional-currency-how-money-shapes-human-relationships

Hidden Brain is a podcast sponsored by National Public Radio. The "Emotional currency: How money shapes human relationships" episode from January 13, 2020 discusses how the exchange of money and, in other parts of the world—goods—fundamentally changes the way people interact with one another. The host interviews notable anthropologist Bill Maurer about his research on civilizations that are over 5,000 years old, where individuals kept track of obligations they owed one another. They contrast this with the modern relationship we have with obligations, including the one to care for our aging parents and how we place value on intangible (and tangible) goods.

   Activate your theory app: Think about this episode in the context of the things you buy and the things you "provide" for free. How do we determine value as a society? Do we value intangible (unpaid) exchanges? Why, or why not?

www.gerontology.vt.edu

Many older adults, regardless of age, race, social class, gender, or health status, can be exploited financially by a loved one or caregiver. A comprehensive report on this topic, *The Metlife Study of Elder Financial Abuse: Crimes of Occasion, Desperation, and Predation Against America's Elders* (2011), was commissioned by the Metlife Mature Market Institute and completed by Karen Roberto and Pamela Teaster from the Center for Gerontology at Virginia Polytechnic Institute and State University and the National Committee for the Prevention of Elder Abuse (www.preventelderabuse.org). The report offers many helpful suggestions to both seniors and their caregivers for preventing elder financial abuse (Teaster et al., 2012). Advice for seniors includes: (a) stay active and avoid isolation; (b) monitor your own financial affairs; (c) keep legal documents in a safe, secure location; (d) protect your passwords; (e) beware of telephone solicitations; and (f) know what to do if you believe you are a victim of financial abuse. On the website, look for the brochure "Helpful Hints—Preventing Elder Financial Abuse for Family Caregivers."

Activate your theory app: Consider how social exchange theory could help explain issues like elder financial abuse. How do power relations change over the life course and provide opportunities for exploitation between family members?

Arranged (2007)

Image 7.2 A Scene From *Arranged*, 2007

This film follows the story of two young schoolteachers—one an Orthodox Jewish woman and the other a devout Muslim woman. It is based loosely on a true story told to the filmmaker and has won multiple independent film awards. Both of these young women are going through the process of having their marriages arranged. In addition to examining their relationship, the film also contains latent messages about cultural ignorance, religion, and friendship and how these issues reflect micro- and macro-level social exchanges. The film explores the benefits of a deep friendship but in the context of its costs at micro and macro levels.

Activate your theory app: How do the two main characters in this film weigh the benefits against the costs associated with traditional cultural norms that discourage their friendship? What do they each have to "give up" to maintain their friendship?

The Bachelor (2002–present)

Image 7.3 A Scene From *The Bachelor*, 2021

This American reality television show is set up to help an eligible man choose from a pool of 25 women to find a woman he wants to propose to on the show's finale. The show features the bachelor getting to know the women, going on dates, and, ultimately, presenting roses each week to only the women he wishes to see remain on the show as a possible mate. Inevitably, contestants are criticized for being on the show only to increase publicity for their own careers, as opposed to being truly interested in finding a spouse. The same could be said for the bachelor, as only one of the couples actually gets married after the on-air proposal. After 19 seasons of the show, it is clear that the show does not actually lead to love and marriage; instead, several of the contestants and bachelors have been offered roles in other television shows and have increased their celebrity status as a result of appearing in *The Bachelor*.

Activate your theory app: Are there other popular reality television shows we could apply social exchange theory to? How often do you think the reality behind the production of these shows is really producers, agents, and writers making the "best deal" instead of what we see on television?

Further Reading

Hirshman, L. R., & Larson, J. E. (1998). *Hard bargains: The politics of sex*. Oxford University Press. The authors, both legal scholars, posit that heterosexual relationships are ones in which couples must bargain about their sexuality. This bargaining is not just a matter of private negotiations between a man and a woman. Rather, sex is political, and private negotiations about what, where, when, and how to be sexual take place under increasingly public scrutiny. The sexual landscape is always in flux. What was considered scandalous in previous eras (e.g., showing skin in the Victorian era) may be taken for granted today. What is considered illegal in some cultures (e.g., wives' adultery is punishable by death) is considered with more neutrality in others. Further, regardless of advances women have made in their economic lives, sexual politics still require hard bargains in navigating sexual access, sexual cooperation, and sexual practices. Hard bargains mean we must negotiate the costs and benefits of sexual interaction and consider the empowerment and disempowerment of partners in sexual relationships. Ultimately, sexuality is of the body, mind, heart, and spirit, but all of these are grounded in broader issues of cultural beliefs and practices associated with law, politics, and religion.

Horan, S. M. (2016). Further understanding sexual communication: Honesty, deception, safety, and risk. *Journal of Social and Personal Relationships, 33*(4), 449–468. https://doi.org/10.1177/0265407515578821 In this study of 183 young adults with an average age of 22 years, Horan used affection exchange theory, a variation of social exchange theory, to examine the role of honesty and dishonesty in disclosing one's sexual history to new partners. Although benefits of disclosing one's sexual history include having accurate information that can affect whether one wants to take health risks with a new partner, there are also costs, such as possible rejection or judgment. Horan found that individuals who tended to omit the number of their previous partners (e.g., practiced dishonesty) were also uncomfortable with other aspects of safer sex communication (e.g., decisions about condom use). Further, the more informal the relationship is (e.g., friends with benefits, compared to committed partners), the less likely the individuals were to communicate about sexual topics at all. Interestingly, about 60% of the participants reported that, in the past, they had been deceptive in disclosing the number of previous sex partners, with 20% of those saying they never disclosed this information. Implications of this study suggest that young people should be provided with health education that moves beyond simply stressing condom use and focuses on the role of communication and sexual safety during any type of sexual activity.

LeBaron, A. B., & Kelley, H. H. (2021). Financial socialization: A decade in review. *Journal of Family and Economic Issues, 42*(Suppl. 1), S195–S206. https://doi.org/10.1007/s10834-020-09736-2 Becoming financially independent is one of the critical goals of adulthood, yet in contemporary life, young adults increasingly struggle with financial vulnerability, leading to prolonged dependence on their families. Basic knowledge of money, inflation, debt, credit scores, risk diversification, and saving for retirement may be lacking, leading to undue economic, academic, and health stressors at a time of life when individuals are trying to live on their own and start their lives apart from their parents and caregivers. Interpersonal relationships suffer as well, affecting the ability to initiate and maintain a romantic relationship. LeBaron and Kelley argue for purposive, explicit financial socialization during childhood, so parents teach their children about money management and financial goal setting for the future, all in the service of developing positive approaches to healthy financial behaviors. Social institutions play a key role in financial socialization, as well, including educational programming and government policies that, for example, place restrictions on credit cards for minors and other questionable practices.

Having confidence in one's ability to earn a living, manage money, and accumulate wealth is essential for individual, relational, familial, and societal well-being.

Schwartz, P. (1994). *Peer marriage: How love between equals really works.* Free Press. Pepper Schwartz is a professor of sociology at the University of Washington, a popular relationship and sex columnist for the *New York Times* and *Glamour Magazine* (among other publications), a radio personality, and a consultant for organizations, such as AARP, Perfectmatch.com, and WebMD. In *Peer Marriage,* she analyzes interviews with egalitarian couples who are consciously trying to undo traditional gender norms in their families. Schwartz found four general characteristics of peer marriages: First, couples had no more than a 60/40 split in terms of doing housework and childcare. That is, couples did not achieve an equal share of 50% each. Second, partners believed that each person in the relationship had equal influence and decision-making power. Third, both partners felt they had equal control over the family economy. Finally, each partner's work had equal weight in the marriage. As in our case study of Stefan and Christina, regardless of earning ability, peer couples shared money, decision-making, childcare, and housework. There was no hidden hierarchy. Schwartz concluded that a relationship based on "deep friendship" is much more realistic than a marriage rooted in the romantic ideals of gender differences. Yet peer marriage also has its costs because the process of negotiating and reshuffling power and equity in a relationship can be physically and emotionally draining. On balance, Schwartz shows how relationships that are based on equality, intimacy, and friendship can lead to a deeply rewarding and long-lasting partnership.

Sprecher, S., Wenzel, A., & Harvey, J. (2008). *Handbook of relationship initiation.* Psychology Press. In this comprehensive volume, Susan Sprecher and her colleagues address many topics regarding how relationships are formed, maintained, experienced, and dissolved. Although multiple theories are used by the various authors in the book, exchange and equity theories are present in many of the chapters. In addition to the topics we would expect to find in a scholarly resource on attraction, self-disclosure, relationship processes and structures, and when relationships dissolve, there are chapters on more modern ways of starting and pursuing relationships, such as speed dating, hookups, and internet matchmaking services.

Questions for Students

Discussion Questions

1. Compare and contrast social exchange theory with family stress and resilience theory (Chapter 11). Are these two theories similar in any ways? How are they different?

2. Although social exchange theory has primarily been applied at the micro level of analysis (e.g., the individual), describe ways it is also useful at the macro level (e.g., how social institutions and unequal power structures impact individual choices).

3. Critique the popular belief that men offer their wealth, and women offer their beauty when entering a relationship. Do you think this idea is still prevalent today? If not, how do you think ideas about this gender stereotype are changing?

4. What other family relationships, other than romantic or parent–child, can be studied using social exchange theory? How would you apply social exchange to the diversity of family (and family-like) relationships in your own life?

5. How might social exchange theory be used to study LGBTQ+ relationships? If you were to update the theory to provide a broader applicability to *all* families and relationships, what would need to be added or reconsidered?

6. Provide examples of the different types of capital that individuals have and how each type can be used in an exchange relationship.

Your Turn!

When you plan to enter an intimate partnership—either in terms of a cohabiting or married relationship—how do you think you will distribute (or pool) your money? Do you plan to set up separate bank accounts, a joint account, or have a "yours, mine, and ours" system, where you both pool resources and also maintain your own control over a separate account? What are the rewards and costs of the particular financial arrangement you set up?

Personal Reflection Questions

1. Have you ever known someone who repeats the same pattern again and again in relationships? Consider how those choices may be a result of reinforcement, deprivation-satiation, and the comparison level for alternatives.

2. Make a list of "ideal" qualities you find desirable in a partner and another list of what you feel you bring to relationships. Consider your lists in light of social exchange theory and reward, cost, profit, and comparison level.

3. Do you think it is possible for individuals to act in altruistic ways, without expecting something in return? If so, describe the altruistic actions of someone you admire and assess these qualities in relation to the concept of rational choice.

4. Think about power dynamics in the relationships you, or someone close to you, have been involved in. Is it truly possible to have an equal share of power in a dyadic relationship? Why, or why not?

5. How do you "rationalize" your choices to put your own needs ahead of the needs of someone you love? Under what conditions do you think it is okay to act solely in self-interest?

6. What is the most "irrational" thing you ever did? As you reflect on it, do you think there are some rational aspects to this as well?

References

Adams, B. N., & Sydie, R. A. (2002). *Contemporary sociological theory.* Pine Forge Press.

Appelrouth, S., & Edles, L. D. (2021). *Classical and contemporary sociological theory: Text and readings* (4th ed.). SAGE Publications.

Bagarozzi, D. A. (1993). Clinical uses of social exchange principles. In P. Boss, W. Doherty, R. LaRossa, W. Schumm, & S. Steinmetz (Eds.), *Sourcebook of family theories and methods: A contextual approach* (pp. 412–417). Plenum.

Becker, G. S. (1981). *A treatise on the family.* Harvard University Press.

Becker, G. S. (1992). *Gary S. Becker—biographical.* www.nobelprize.org/nobel_prizes/economic-sciences/laureates/1992/becker-bio.html.

Bennett, F. (2015). Opening up the black box: Researching the distribution of resources within the household. *NCFR Report: Family Resource Management, FF63,* Fl–F3.

Bittman, M., England, P., Sayer, L., Folbre, N., & Matheson, G. (2003). When does gender trump money? Bargaining and time in household work. *American Journal of Sociology, 109*(1), 186–214. https://doi.org/10.1086/378341

Blau, P. M. (1964). *Exchange and power in social life.* Wiley.

Bourdieu, P. (1990). *In other words: Essays towards a reflexive sociology.* Stanford University Press.

Braver, S. L., & Lamb, M. E. (2013). Marital dissolution. In G. W. Peterson & K. R. Bush (Eds.), *Handbook of marriage and the family* (3rd ed., pp. 487–516). Springer.

Cho, M., Impett, E. A., Campos, B., Chen, S., & Keltner, D. (2020). Socioeconomic inequality undermines relationship quality in romantic relationships. *Journal of Social and Personal Relationships, 37*(5), 1722–1742. https://doi.org/10.1177/0265407520907969

Coduto, K. D., & Eveland, W. P. (2022). Listening and being listened to as affection exchange in marital discussions about the #MeToo movement. *Journal of Social and Personal Relationships* 39(5), 1460–1481. https://doi.org/10.1177/02654075211058402

Coleman, J. S. (1990). Rational organization. *Rationality and Society, 2*(1), 94–105. https://doi.org/10.1177/1043463190002001005

Coleman, J. S. (1994). *Foundations of social theory.* Harvard University Press.

Collett, J. L. (2010). Integrating theory, enhancing understanding: The potential contributions of recent experimental research in social exchange for studying intimate relationships. *Journal of Family Theory & Review, 2*(4), 280–298. https://doi.org/10.1111/j.1756-2589.2010.00062.x

Connidis, I. A., & Barnett, A. E. (2019). *Family ties and aging* (3rd ed.). SAGE Publications.

Cook, K. S., Cheshire, C., Rice, E. R. W., & Nakagawa, S. (2013). Social exchange theory. In J. Delamater & A. Ward (Eds.), *Handbook of social psychology* (pp. 61–88). Springer.

Dainton, M., & Zelley, E. D. (2006). Social exchange theories: Interdependence and equity. In D. O. Braithwaite & L. A. Baxter (Eds.), *Engaging theories in family communication: Multiple perspectives* (pp. 243–259). SAGE Publications.

Dilworth-Anderson, P., Burton, L. M., & Klein, D. M. (2005). Contemporary and emerging theories in studying families. In V. L. Bengtson, A. C. Acock, K. R. Allen, P. Dilworth-Anderson, & D. M. Klein (Eds.), *Sourcebook of family theory and research* (pp. 35–57). SAGE Publications.

Edwards, J. N. (1969). Familial behavior as social exchange. *Journal of Marriage and the Family, 31*(3), 518–526. https://doi.org/10.2307/349775

Ekeh, P. P. (1974). *Social exchange theory: The two traditions.* Harvard University Press.

Emerson, R. M. (1976). Social exchange theory. *Annual Review of Sociology, 2*(1), 335–362. https://doi.org/10.1146/annurev.so.02.080176.002003

Friedman, M. (1953). *Essays in positive economics.* University of Chicago Press.

Grunow, D., Begall, K., & Buchler, S. (2018). Gender ideologies in Europe: A multidimensional framework. *Journal of Marriage and Family, 80*(1), 42–60. https://doi.org/10.1111/jomf.12453

Homans, G. C. (1958). Social behavior as exchange. *American Journal of Sociology, 63*(6), 597–606. https://doi.org/10.1086/222355

Homans, G. C. (1961). *Social behavior: Its elementary forms.* Harcourt, Brace & World.

Jarvis, S. N., McClure, M. J., & Bolger, N. (2019). Exploring how exchange orientation affects conflict and intimacy in the daily life of romantic couples. *Journal of Social and Personal Relationships, 36*(11–12), 3575–3587. https://doi.org/10.1177/0265407519826743

Jennings, E. (2014). Marital discord and subsequent dissolution: Perceptions of Nepalese wives and husbands. *Journal of Marriage and Family, 76*(3), 476–488. https://doi.org/10.1111/jomf.12104

Karney, B. R., & Bradbury, T. N. (2020). Research on marital satisfaction and stability in the 2010s: Challenging conventional wisdom. *Journal of Marriage and Family, 82*(1), 100–116. https://doi.org/10.1111/jomf.12635

Kenny, D. A., Kashy, D., & Cook, W. L. (2006). *Dyadic data analysis.* Guilford.

Komter, A. (1989). Hidden power in marriage. *Gender & Society, 3*(2), 187–216. https://doi.org/10.1177/089124389003002003

Landor, A., & Barr, A. (2018). Politics of respectability, colorism, and the terms of social exchange in family research. *Journal of Family Theory & Review, 10*(2), 330–347. https://doi.org/10.1111/jftr.12264

Lawler, E. J. (2001). An affect theory of social exchange. *American Journal of Sociology, 107*(2), 321–352. https://doi.org/10.1086/324071

Lawler, E. J., & Thye, S. R. (1999). Bringing emotions into social exchange theory. *Annual Review of Sociology, 25*(1), 217–244. https://doi.org/10.1146/annurev.soc.25.1.217

McConnon, A., Midgette, A. J., & Conry-Murray, C. (2022). Mother like mothers and work like fathers: U.S. heterosexual college students' assumptions about who should meet childcare and housework demands. *Sex Roles, 86*(1), 49–66. https://doi.org/10.1007/s11199-021-01252-3

Miedema, S. S., Shwe, S., & Kyaw, A. T. (2016). Social inequalities, empowerment, and women's transitions into abusive marriages: A case study from Myanmar. *Gender & Society, 30*(4), 670–694. https://doi.org/10.1177/0891243216642394

Musick, K., Bea, M. D., & Gonalons-Pons, P. (2020). His and her earnings following parenthood in the United States, Germany, and the United Kingdom. *American Sociological Review, 85*(4), 639–674. https://doi.org/10.1177/0003122420934430

Nakonezny, P. A., & Denton, W. H. (2008). Marital relationships: A social exchange theory perspectives. *The American Journal of Family Therapy, 36*(5), 402–412. https://doi.org/10.1080/01926180701647264

Nye, F. I. (1978). Is choice and exchange theory the key? *Journal of Marriage and the Family, 40*(2), 219–233. https://doi.org/10.2307/350754

Nye, F. I. (1979). Choice, exchange, and the family. In W. R. Burr, R. Hill, F. I. Nye, & I. L. Reiss (Eds.), *Contemporary theories about the family: General theories/theoretical orientations* (Vol. II, pp. 1–41). Free Press.

Ogolsky, B. G., & Monk, J. K. (2019). Dating and couple formation. In B. H. Fiese (Ed.), *APA Handbook of contemporary family psychology: Vol.1. Foundations, methods, and contemporary issues across the lifespan* (pp. 427–443). American Psychological Association.

Ogolsky, B. G., Monk, J. K., Rice, T. M., Theisen, J. C., & Maniotes, C. R. (2017). Relationship maintenance: A review of research on romantic relationships. *Journal of Family Theory & Review, 9*(3), 275–306. https://doi.org/10.1111/jftr.12205

Pepin, J. R., & Cotter, D. A. (2018). Separating spheres? Diverging trends in youth's gender attitudes about work and family. *Journal of Marriage and Family, 80*(1), 7–24. https://doi.org/10.1111/jomf.12434

Perry-Jenkins, M., & MacDermid, S. M. (2013). The state of theory in work and family research at the turn of the twenty-first century. In M. A. Fine & F. D. Fincham (Eds.), *Handbook of family theories: A content-based approach* (pp. 381–397). Routledge.

Roloff, M. E. (1981). *Interpersonal communication: The social exchange approach*. SAGE Publications.

Sabatelli, R. M., Lee, H., & Ripoll-Nunez, K. (2018). Placing the social exchange framework in an ecological context. *Journal of Family Theory & Review, 10*(1), 32–48. https://doi.org/10.1111/jftr.12254

Sabatelli, R. M., & Shehan, C. L. (1993). Exchange and resource theories. In P. Boss, W. Doherty, R. LaRossa, W. Schumm, & S. Steinmetz (Eds.), *Sourcebook of family theories and methods: A contextual approach* (pp. 385–411). Plenum Press.

Sassler, S., & Lichter, D. T. (2020). Cohabitation and marriage: Complexity and diversity in union-formation patterns. *Journal of Marriage and Family, 82*(1), 35–61. https://doi.org/10.1111/jomf.12617

Scanzoni, J. (1979). Social processes and power in families. In W. R. Burr, R. Hill, F. I. Nye, & I. L. Reiss (Eds.), *Contemporary theories about the family: Research-based theories* (Vol. I, pp. 295–316). Free Press.

Sharkey, J. A., Feather, J. S., & Goedeke, S. (2022). The current state of relationship science: A cross-disciplines review of key themes, theories, researchers and journals. *Journal of Social and Personal Relationships, 39*(4), 864–885. https://doi.org/10.1177/02654075211047638

Silverstein, M. (2005). Testing theories about intergenerational exchanges. In V. L. Bengtson, A. C. Acock, K. R. Allen, P. Dilworth-Anderson, & D. M. Klein (Eds.), *Sourcebook of family theory and research* (pp. 407–410). SAGE Publications.

Smith, D. E. (1993). The Standard North American Family: SNAF as an ideological code. *Journal of Family Issues, 14*(1), 50–65. https://doi.org/10.1177/0192513X93014001005

Stafford, L., & Kuiper, K. (2021). Social exchange theories: Calculating the rewards and costs of personal relationships. In D. O. Braithwaite & P. Schrodt (Eds.), *Engaging theories in interpersonal communication: Multiple perspectives* (pp. 379–390). Routledge.

Teaster, P. B., Roberto, K. A., Migliaccio, J. N., Timmerman, S., & Blancato, R. B. (2012). Elder financial abuse in the news. *Public Policy & Aging Report, 22*(1), 33–36. https://doi.org/10.1093/ppar/22.1.33

Thibaut, J. W., & Kelley, H. H. (1959). *The social psychology of groups.* Wiley.

Thompson, L. (1991). Family work: Women's sense of fairness in marriage. *Journal of Family Issues, 12*(2), 181–196. https://doi.org/10.1177/019251391012002003

Waldkirch, M., Nordqvist, M., & Melin, L. (2018). CEO turnover in family firms: How social exchange relationships influence whether a non-family CEO stays or leaves. *Human Resource Management Review, 28*(1), 56–67. https://doi.org/10.1016/j.hrmr.2017.05.006

Zhang, Y., & Axinn, W. G. (2021). Marital experiences and depression in an arranged marriage setting. *American Journal of Sociology, 126*(6), 1439–1486. https://doi.org/10.1086/714272

Image Credits

Feminist Theory

W hy is it that when parents are expecting a child, they typically want to know the sex of the baby before they are born? Why has sex at birth continued to be so important for many expectant parents, when later in life, individuals may not identify with their natal sex? Why do we as a society make so many assumptions about the relationship between sex and gender? Even more importantly, are these assumptions harmful to individuals and their families?

Questions about power, oppression, social change, gender relations, and intersectionality are addressed in a feminist perspective. Like family science overall, feminist theory has a broad, interdisciplinary background. In this chapter, we focus on the ways in which scholars typically use feminist approaches to study individual experience and family relationships within a social context. We take a critical, intersectional, and queer approach to feminist theorizing. Although feminist theory was initially concerned with gender as a personal experience and system of social stratification, calling into question the inherent right and necessity of men to serve as the head of families, nations, and society, it has evolved in at least two additional ways: to accommodate both intersectional and queer perspectives. Feminist theory now considers how issues of gender, race, class, sexual orientation, age, nationality, and disability, among others, intersect to create different experiences of privilege and oppression—a topic we address further in Chapter 12 on critical race theory. Feminist theory is also evident in studies that queer the family. In Chapter 13, we examine queer theory, which further deconstructs and reimagines gender, calling attention to the normative theorizing associated with cisgenderism and the emergence of transgenderism. Ultimately, feminist theory critiques the status quo and generates suggestions for transformative social change. We turn to a story about intersectionality and identity to set the stage for how this theory is used to explain family issues.

Case Study

Jules is a Hispanic, cisgender, bisexual 14-year-old boy. When Jules was 11, he attended an overnight soccer camp with his older brother and felt overwhelmed with emotion. His brother was staying in a different dorm room, so he felt isolated and alone even though he was surrounded by peers. Jules begged his brother to call their mother, so she would come and pick him up from

BOX 8.1. AT A GLANCE: FEMINIST THEORY

- **Feminism:** An evolving, transdisciplinary worldview of theory and political action with the goal of dismantling patriarchy, racism, heteronormativity, and other forms of oppression.
- **Gender equality:** The original concern of feminists—to ensure gender equality for all.
- **Intersectionality:** How multiple systems of oppression, such as race, class, gender, sexuality, religion, age, ability, and nationality, intersect to create advantage or disadvantage.
- **Praxis:** Putting theory into practice by working for social change, both locally and globally.
- **Patriarchy:** A system of male dominance in which most cisgender men have more privilege, power, and worth than women and other less-dominant men.
- **Reflexivity:** The conscious practice of applying feminist knowledge to one's life and work.
- **Doing gender:** Gender is a social construction and performance, not a biological given.
- **Privilege and oppression:** Power differences in society create social institutions and interactions that value the elite group and create disadvantages for minoritized groups.
- **Misogynoir:** An anti-Black form of misogyny at the intersection of racialized and sexualized oppression experienced by Black women and girls.
- **Womanism:** Feminist theory that acknowledges and champions the experiences and contributions of primarily Black women and women of color.
- **Hegemonic masculinity:** Men's roles, expectations, and identities are defined as superior to women's.

---

camp early; he did not know what to do with the feelings he was having. His brother was having a great time and kept telling Jules to "just get over it"—though neither boy could really put a finger on what the issue was that had Jules so upset.

On the call to his parents, Jules still could not describe what was wrong. His mother and father were concerned about him but could not figure out how to help, and they struggled to see how picking him up early would benefit him if he was just homesick. Jules stayed at the camp the two nights he had planned and seemed fine at pick up.

Two months later, Jules came out to his mother as queer (and later bisexual). He revealed that he had met a boy he was attracted to at camp and was very confused about it because he did not realize he was not attracted to girls like everyone else his age seemed to be. Jules's mother was very supportive, caring, and loving when he shared this. Jules's behavior during camp made so much more sense now. Jules and his mom talked for a long time, and she helped him navigate how to tell his father and his siblings and, later, his friends.

This case study brings to light many questions about Jules's intersecting identities and how his fear and anxiety—especially at a soccer camp—made it difficult for him to identify his emotions to be able to communicate them effectively when he was struggling. Was it his Hispanic heritage, or the **machismo** (exaggerated male pride prevalent in some Hispanic cultures) in particular, that made it difficult to tell his mother what was wrong? Was it his gender or his age? What about the setting—being at a soccer camp populated with other boys who appeared to fit neatly into the gender roles that society prescribes for male athletes? Or was it a combination of all of the above? Intersectional feminism helps us better understand how each of these factors plays a role in individual experiences, and feminism, in general, lays the groundwork for critiquing how society at large dictates how men and boys should behave and any deviation from that is stigmatized. We unpack these ideas throughout the rest of this chapter.

What Is Feminist Theory?

Feminist theory is a complex and contentious form of theorizing that is constantly evolving, which makes it both exciting and difficult to wrap our arms around (Allen, 2022). Feminist theory in family science was initially grounded in the struggle for gender equality because women—as students, scholars, and family members—were relegated to second class status. Feminist scholars pointed out that this struggle for recognition and equality was caused by the belief that women's lives are perceived as less important than men's lives and that men are the standard against which women are compared and rendered "less than," as French feminist philosopher Simone de Beauvoir (1949/2011) so famously observed in her book, *The Second Sex.* Yet as we explain in this chapter, it soon became apparent that gender is not the only axis of difference that creates inequality in lived experience and social structure. Feminists of color and of diverse sexualities, among feminists of many other social locations and stratifications, address the importance of intersectionality (which we also discuss in Chapter 12 on critical race theory). Intersectionality includes the multiple axes upon which our lives are structured through various degrees of privilege and oppression, reproduced in both intimate and institutional ways (Anzaldua, 1990; Collins, 1990, 2019; Crenshaw, 1989; Lorde, 1984). In addition to intersectional analyses of gender, race, class, sexuality, ability, and the like, feminist family science is now highly influenced by queer theory (see Chapter 13) and the ways in which feminists have queered the family (Acosta, 2018; Oswald et al., 2009). Feminist theory also guides the practical or activist part of feminism, which is called **praxis.** Thus, feminist theory and feminist activism are highly valuable to family scholars for uncovering gender prejudice, intersections with other social stratification systems, demystifying power dynamics and working toward transformative social change (Allen & Henderson, 2022; Bermudez et al., 2016; Few-Demo & Allen, 2020).

Given its many variations, feminists believe the inability to capture feminism in one single perspective is its very strength (Elam & Wiegman, 1995; Lorber, 2012). Yet there are several common themes regarding individuals and their experiences in families and in society that motivate praxis, which is, as we noted, the integration of feminist theory and feminist activism (Baber & Allen, 1992). In their influential assessment of the general tenets of feminist theory, feminist sociologists Acker, Barry, and Esseveld (1983) summarized three major points that became a rallying cry for feminist family science: First, feminism embodies the belief that women are exploited and oppressed as subordinates in a hierarchical social system that affords privilege to elite White males. Second, feminism is committed to the empowerment of women and to improving the conditions of their lives. Finally, feminism emphasizes that women's experiences, values, and activities are meaningful and valued. As we describe throughout this book, it is important to recognize the origin of our key theoretical ideas as rooted in differential gendered experiences as well as how they have evolved over time to include diversity and differences across individuals, families, and society.

Feminist family scholars have used feminist theory to name unequal power arrangements in families that persist by generation and gender, as exemplified in the nuclear family structure of only two generations (Allen et al., 2013; Ferree, 1990; Thorne, 1982; Walker, 1999). Further, the pursuit of gender equality continues to be relevant today because gender inequality is still prevalent around the globe. Consider the following examples. The COVID-19 pandemic has exacerbated ways in which mothers and wives, in particular, have to compromise more than other family members. In a qualitative study of 15 professional married couples from Israel, Waismel-Manor et al. (2021) were guided by critical feminist theory and found that men's workspace in the home was prioritized, but women's workspace and time were more fragmented and diffused throughout the day. Haselschwerdt and Hardesty (2017) studied intimate partner violence across all income spectrums in the United States, exposing the myth that affluent women are not subjected to wife abuse. Instead, they found that a culture of affluence surrounds wealthy families, where practices, such as maintaining family secrets and pursuing perfectionism, place women at risk of isolation and lack of support. Sexual assault is rampant on college campuses, implicating the male-dominated party culture of the mostly White Greek system in universities (Jozkowski & Wiersma-Mosley, 2017). The sexist double standard inherent in much of parent–child communication about sex, which promotes greater sexual permissiveness in sons and passivity in daughters, contributes to acceptance of rape myths and relationship violence (Weiser et al., 2021). Even more traumatic on a global scale, conservative governments in some countries are banning girls from school and women from the work force. Access to education for women and girls is now severely restricted in Afghanistan (Blue & Zucchino, 2021).

Feminist theory brings to the forefront family issues that are grounded in gender inequality, such as cultural prescriptions that deter or stereotype men who are stay-at-home parents (Liong, 2017), that all women have an instinct to be mothers (Allen et al., 2009), or that the gender a person is assigned at birth is fixed and unchangeable (Diamond, 2020). Feminist theory explains how individuals "do gender" in families (West & Zimmerman, 1987). Important are the ways in which systems of oppression and privilege, such as White patriarchal power (Collins, 1990) and intersectionality (Few-Demo et al., 2022), operate to structure opportunities in individual and family life. We will return to these concepts throughout the chapter.

History and Origins

Because feminist theory is linked to feminist activism, the theory is always under scrutiny, particularly in terms of how well feminism has led to real changes and improvements in society. After all, feminism is both a theory and a social movement that leads to significant social and political changes (Risman, 2018). As we describe throughout the chapter, feminist theory is one of the theories most open to critique and revision as feminist priorities are refined and changed, especially as feminism has become a global phenomenon (Bermudez et al., 2016; Ferguson, 2017; Srinivasan, 2021). There are many variations of feminist theory as it has evolved over time. Feminists have used various metaphors to characterize the history of feminist theory and activism over the past two centuries, including concepts such as waves (Aikau et al., 2007), generations (Reger, 2017), and tapestries (Lewis & Marine, 2015). All of these frameworks for assessing feminist theorizing have their strengths and limitations. Given the widespread use of the wave metaphor, we rely on the concept of **waves of feminism** in this book to present this history. At the same time, although thinking about feminist theory and activism in terms of waves is useful (see Figure 8.1), remember that these waves overlap, and the time frames we identify are only estimates and, therefore, debatable. On balance, by examining this history over time, we can see the effectiveness of feminist thinking on changing and improving the lives of women and families.

First-Wave Feminism

Current feminist theory is rooted in the 19th and early 20th centuries and was spurred by White women's efforts to gain the right to vote as well as their involvement in the Abolitionist movement to end slavery in America. This first wave was roughly a 70-year period, dating from 1848 with the Women's Rights Convention in Seneca Falls, New York, calling for women's suffrage and culminating in the passage of the 19th Amendment to the United States Constitution in 1920, guaranteeing women the right to vote. During this time, feminist leaders, including Susan B. Anthony, Elizabeth Cady

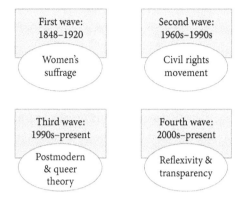

FIGURE 8.1. Four Waves of Feminism

Stanton, Sojourner Truth, and many others, organized around issues we simply take for granted today, including women's voting rights, married women's rights to inheritance and divorce, the end of slavery for African Americans, and contraceptive availability (Freedman, 2002). In an early statement that sparked today's critical race feminist theory, the former slave, abolitionist, and feminist Sojourner Truth gave a speech in 1851, in which she bared her muscled arm and asked the White women leading the convention, "Ain't I a Woman, too?" (Wing, 2003, p. 8).

Charlotte Perkins Gilman was another first-wave feminist who focused on issues that were arguably ahead of her time; Gilman advocated for mothers' access to public day care and cooperative kitchens, so they could free themselves of domestic duties and focus on careers. However, given that women were not afforded federal protections against job discrimination based on sex until much later, Gilman was not accepted as an established author until after her death (Lemert, 2008). In fact, for much of U.S. history, women were not first-class citizens; they were not allowed to vote, and married women did not own their own property. Their legal rights were dependent upon the will of their fathers or husbands. The rights we take for granted today came many years later, after much struggle and many setbacks. After women secured the right to vote in the United States in 1920, feminism went underground as a topic of national attention. Instead, the Great Depression, World War II, and the postwar period of the 1950s consumed national attention.

Second-Wave Feminism

Second-wave feminism took root in the midst of the social upheaval of the Civil Rights Movement for African Americans, the antiwar movement against the Vietnam War, and the radical New Left student movement of the 1960s. Several influential books that addressed the status of women set the stage for the second wave of feminism that emerged in the late 1960s–1970s. In her 1949 book, de Beauvoir explained how women are socially constructed as "other," objectified, and stereotyped as secondary to men. Her ideas about women's treatment in a male-constructed patriarchy were highly controversial because they critiqued the status quo as oppressive to women and led the way to challenging other forms of oppression. Another defining moment was Betty Friedan's 1963 book, *The Feminine Mystique*. Friedan reignited a national women's movement by analyzing the emptiness of married life for middle-class White mothers, most of whom did not work outside the home and were expected to find fulfillment in caring for others. Friedan called this "the problem that has no name" and wrote about it in a way that spoke to millions of women. Through Friedan's book, many women came to understand that their second-class status was due to political injustice affecting all women, not personal failings inherent to them as individuals (Coontz, 2011).

As social and political unrest was intensifying in the 1960s, women began to mobilize for their own civil rights. Radical feminists met in consciousness-raising groups to speak out against repression of their bodies, lack of educational and occupational opportunities, confinement to the home, and physical and sexual abuse with the goal of working toward legal and political reform (Snitow, 2015). As Allen (2022) explains in her analysis of five decades of feminist thought, many family and sociological feminist scholars came of age during second wave feminism. Their sense of being limited and sexualized as a female in a man's world, combined with the emerging understanding of social injustice in the broader society, sparked their feminist consciousness and commitment to social change. Known by the slogan "the personal is political," the recognition that gender inequality is structured into the very fabric of society inspired a lifelong feminist activism in academic and in personal life. Thus, **radical feminism** offered a major challenge to the pervasiveness of patriarchy by seeking to uncover the root cause of the mechanisms of women's oppression and men's privilege with the goal of creating massive social change (Morgan, 1970). Radical feminist theory critiqued the ways all social institutions (e.g., law, education, family, and military) conspired to oppress women and elevate men. One of the first analyses of the devaluation of women's labor with a call for radical change was Oakley's (1974) analysis of housework among middle- and working-class women in Britain. Oakley applied critical concepts of gender, power, social stratification, and deviance to understand why women's work in the home was unpaid, invisible, devalued, and monotonous, yet essential to the maintenance of families. She made visible the hidden intersections of gender, class, and power.

Second wave feminism was a time in which **liberal feminism**, probably the most common type, proliferated. Liberal feminism pushed for women's equality with men (Okin, 1989). Women were going after their "equal share of the pie." Liberal feminism spoke primarily to middle-class White women who sought to use their educations in a career and achieve financial parity with men. They emphasized affirmative action (which benefitted primarily cisgender White women without fulfilling its promise for people of color) in the workforce and gender neutral socialization of children in the home and school (Lorber, 2012).

Socialist feminism, rooted in Marxist class theory (see conflict theory, Chapter 3), posited that capitalism and its relation to **patriarchy** (the system of male dominance) were responsible for women's second-class citizenship (Mitchell, 1971). Marxist thought was foundational for the feminist critique of racialized, gendered, patriarchal, and liberal capitalism. Socialist feminists turned their attention to previously overlooked groups of women, such as working-class women who did not have the financial security that middle-class White women experienced. Working-class women from all backgrounds often worked in jobs that were physically exhausting, where they had little control over their time. Another concern was for the caring and domestic labor that women of color, in particular, performed. These analyses generated new ideas about the invisible aspects of the work typically performed by women as productive and reproductive laborers (Glenn, 1985; Hartmann, 1981).

The variations on feminist theorizing continued to ripple. Major challenges to liberal feminist thought in the second wave came from women whose experiences were not represented by the singular concept of gender. Gender, they argued, was not the only cause of women's oppression, and the experiences of White, middle-class, heterosexual feminists did not reflect all women's experiences. **Womanist feminism** was developed by women of color (Walker, 1983) and is the forerunner of intersectional feminist theory because it reflects the dual consciousness of women of color, who felt an allegiance to both their racialized experiences and to gender (Lewis, 2009). They were among the first to challenge the liberal paradigm, arguing that race, gender, and class cannot be separated, introducing intersectional analyses (Combahee River Collective, 1982). Black women, for example, have had very different experiences of work, given the frequent necessity to be both providers and caregivers for their own children and, historically, other women's children (Collins, 1990; Dill, 1988)—a tension about paid and unpaid labor among women today (Dow, 2016). Another major challenge to second wave feminism came from lesbian standpoint theory. **Lesbian feminism** combined sexual orientation and gender theory by critiquing the concept of "compulsory heterosexuality" (Rich, 1980), which is the idea that all women were presumed to be heterosexual, and those who were not heterosexual were considered deviant.

These feminist critiques about the variations in diverse women's experiences went hand in hand with changes in family life. As more middle-class White women were returning to the paid labor force, issues such as the lack of childcare, women's double burden of work at home and in the labor market, and the invisibility of housework were exposed. Feminist activism took on issues that no one else had conceptualized: abortion, rape, sexual harassment, wife abuse, child abuse, and pornography (Freedman, 2002). In family science, feminist theory began to explain how power impacted family members in hierarchical ways, based on gender (i.e., male and female) and generation (i.e., fathers/mothers and sons/daughters; Osmond & Thorne, 1993; Walker & Thompson, 1984). Thorne (1982) summarized how the feminist critique of mainstream family theory opened the way to reclaiming "the family" for more critical analysis, rather than thinking about family roles and relationships as natural. First, feminists challenged traditional family theories as presuming that "The Family" always referred to one type: a monolithic structure of an unchanging entity associated with nuclear relationships, the home, and bonds of love (see Chapter 1). All other forms were labeled as deviant. Second, Thorne (1982) described how, although the family appears to be embedded in the most natural and biological of relationships (e.g., birth, sickness, and death), feminists have argued that the family should be analyzed by "emphasizing the social organization of sexuality, reproduction, motherhood, the sexual division of labor, and the division of gender itself" (p. 6). Third, feminists critiqued family theory as functionalist (Chapter 2), which is the idea that the gendered division of labor became translated into a language of roles, which thereby "glosses over the complexity of behavior in actual families and falsely assumes that expressive and instrumental activities are mutually exclusive" (Thorne, p. 8). These early insights led to future analyses of the social construction of gender and the concepts that are now accepted as "doing gender" (West & Zimmerman, 1987) and "doing family" in diverse kinds of families (see Nelson, 2006; Tasker & Lavender-Stott, 2020). In this context "doing" means that gender is a social construction, not a natural or biological given.

Thus, feminist theorists, activists, and critics in the second wave demonstrated the necessity of full economic, reproductive, and sexual justice for women through social activism. Emerging challenges that led to a new movement included the necessity of looking beyond Western borders to the understanding of feminisms on a global scale (transnational feminism), the ways in which young women did and did not resonate with feminist ideas and practice, men's experiences (men's studies), critical race theory (see Chapter 12; Burton et al., 2010; Few-Demo, 2014), and the questioning of the very utility of feminist theory itself (Elam & Wiegman, 1995).

Third-Wave Feminism

The second wave faded through the challenges of women whose lives did not fit the dominant culture's mandate of being heterosexual, cisgender, White, first world, young, able-bodied, and, thus, as close to men's privilege as possible. Third-wave feminism acknowledged that no singular version of feminism can reflect all women's experiences or needs for legal justice and social change in terms of economic disadvantage, race, sexual orientation, ability, age, nationality, and other major forms of social difference. In other words, there can be no universal sisterhood, as the radical feminists of the second wave wanted, because there is no universal experience of gender or womanhood (Snitow, 2015). In an essay entitled *Age, race, class, and sex: Women redefining difference*, Audre Lorde (1984) wrote eloquently about her experiences as "a forty-nine-year-old Black lesbian feminist socialist mother of two, including one boy, and a member of an interracial couple" (p. 114) and how these identities were inseparable. The **politics of difference** was one of the main lessons learned from second-wave feminism that was carried forth into the third wave: Feminist theory is not a unified body of knowledge but is particular to the situation at hand (De Reus et al., 2005). That is, a single woman in an executive position raising a child on her own is likely to have paid help; a single woman without financial resources is likely to rely on family networks, if they are available, or to face difficult choices between work and childcare.

Two of the major theoretical modifications that emerged during the third wave are postmodern feminism and queer theory. **Postmodern feminism** deconstructs gender systems and the practices that uphold them, through challenging and exposing what has come to be seen and accepted as normal and natural (Baber, 2009). This theory suggests ways to "undo gender" (Butler, 2004). For example, a postmodern approach to women's reproductive lives challenges the motherhood mandate, which assumes that all women want to reproduce. This approach also challenges the belief that motherhood is the most satisfying of any role a woman could have; to the contrary, many families are childfree by choice (Blackstone, 2019). Postmodern feminism questions these taken-for-granted assumptions because they are not true for everyone.

Second, **queer theory** (see Chapter 13) calls attention to the social construction of sexual orientation and gender identity, rather than regarding them as a mental illness, a medical issue, or an essential identity category. Instead of focusing on how lesbian, gay, bisexual, transgender, or queer (LGBTQ+) individuals deviate from society's norms, queer theory questions the very foundation of heterosexuality as being normal and, thus, "queers" the concepts of identity, sexual orientation, and family (Oswald et al., 2005). Queer theory challenges the presumption that everyone is and should be heterosexual, and it exposes how social institutions maintain heteronormativity through pressures to conform. For example, rituals associated with major family events are designed to reinforce heteronormative expectations. Think about the greeting card section of any major store. What kinds of cards are there? Who is depicted in the cards—straight couples, gay couples, or mixed orientation/identity couples? There are sections for "husband" and "wife," and each card is filled with humor embedded in the assumption that all people identify as heterosexual and **cisgender** (when gender identity matches sex assigned at birth). Queer theory helps us see the injustice in the heterosexist and cisgendered realities of our everyday lives and offers creative new ways for doing research about LGBTQ+ individuals and their allies (Blair & Hoskin, 2019; van Eeden-Moorefield & Proulx, 2009).

Another contribution of third-wave feminism has been the insistence on including international perspectives, or global feminisms. Now, feminist theorizing is stretching beyond representations of women as a universal group to recognizing that women's experiences are socially created and vastly different depending upon geography and national origin. In many African countries, for example, same-sex relationships are illegal, allied with strong sanctions, such as imprisonment. This enforces silence and hiding among gay, lesbian, and trans individuals, rendering their families invisible. Yet the way in which individuals combine gender, sexual orientation, and economic circumstances in families does not typically resemble Western patterns. Woman-to-woman marriage exists in Southern African countries, but it is often not labeled as lesbian for fear of societal intolerance and violence against nonheterosexual people (Breshears & Lubbe-De Beer, 2016). Whereas less controversial topics, such as women's friendships or educational parity with men, might be a topic of study in the United States, female infanticide or illiteracy may be more salient in a developing country. This trend toward international feminisms that attempts to fully integrate the voices and experiences of transnational authors begs the question, "What is feminism?"

Fourth-Wave Feminism

Fourth-wave feminism grew out of the recognition by contemporary young women that women's quest for full personhood, though improved, still has a long way to go. Younger women realized that the societal belief that they could "have it all" was not working. There were still many barriers to key issues, such as equity in marriage and parenthood, lesbian rights, and economic advancement. These recognitions were born of young women's reflection on their own experience of the persistence of the **glass ceiling**, despite the many battles that had already been won. The glass ceiling refers to the invisible barrier that keeps women and other minoritized group members in lower-level positions by denying them the same opportunities for career advancement as White, privileged men. The glass ceiling metaphor calls attention to how the barrier is not overtly acknowledged, thus making it difficult to challenge and change.

Additionally, fourth-wave feminism has emerged in recent years to address a renewed interest among young people in intersectional feminist research and activism in digital spaces (Chamberlain, 2017), as exemplified by hashtag activism, particularly to call out racialized and sexualized violence against Black women (Jackson et al., 2020; see Chapter 12). Young feminists who are digital natives, having been born into the current era of the ubiquitous use of digital technology (e.g., smartphones and the internet), are accustomed to online social interaction (Lee, 2021) and have pioneered the cyberfeminist movement. They are reviving bolder integrations of what was once called (in second-wave feminism) the "personal is political." For example, the online magazine *Everyday Feminism* provides definitions of basic feminist theory and terms, such as patriarchal intersectionality, and articles on self-worth, sex, love, body image, violence, work, and the like. In our case study, Jules identifies as a fourth-wave feminist, and recognizes that he still holds privilege in society. He does not take his own privilege for granted, as if it was a birthright simply by being male.

Related to the new feminist theorizing among young scholars and activists is a more explicit use of autoethnography and self-reflection in research and writing (see Christensen, 2015; Hoskin, 2021; Magalhães &

Cerqueira, 2015), which is referred to as **reflexivity**. In family science, feminist theory is one of the original frameworks that values the use of personal experience in understanding the research process. Reflexivity refers to the conscious, reflexive practice of applying feminist knowledge to one's own life and scholarship (Allen, 2000; 2022). Feminist reflexive practice helps to keep the researcher honest by constantly recognizing the tension between sameness and difference in studying gender and its intersections with other systems of domination. Feminists have broken new ground in many areas by recognizing the connection between the oppression they were experiencing in their own lives and how it connected to macro institutions. As an example, Slater (2013) incorporates her own experiences with growing up, graduating, and moving into adult roles as a college teacher into her research on disabled youth. Rather than distancing themselves as researchers, feminist thinkers are critically engaging their own process of how feminism affects them. They are changing the ways in which we can utilize feminist principles of repression and revolt. In family science, theorizing by including personal reflections on the research process, though supported by some intersectional feminist scholars (e.g., Allen & Craven, 2020; Bell-Scott et al., 1991; Gabb, 2018; Sollie & Leslie, 1994), is still rare but growing. This transparency is helpful in understanding why the researcher has a vested interest in the issues they study.

Key Concepts

As we have discussed, some of the major areas of feminist theorizing include gender equality, power, privilege, oppression, and intersectionality. Now, we address how these concepts are defined and utilized in both feminist theory and family science. We build on and add to feminist historian Estelle Freedman's (2002) four overarching principles of the nature of feminism, as both a theory and a praxis: "Feminism is a belief that women and men are inherently of equal worth. Because most societies privilege men as a group, social movements are necessary to achieve equality between women and men, with the understanding that gender always intersects with other social hierarchies" (p. 7).

Equal Worth

Women's experiences in the home and the workplace are as valuable as men's. The idea of equal worth challenges the view that men's ways of knowing, living, and being in the world are superior, and thus, women are expected to aspire to be the same as and equal to men. Instead, the assumption of equal worth is that whatever work women have been engaged in, including traditional female activities, such as childbearing, child-rearing, parent care, or teaching, is just as valuable as the work that has historically been done by men (Freedman, 2002). Valuing women's and other minoritized individuals' experience means that men's lives—specifically White, cisgender, heterosexual, wealthy, educated, employed, married men—are *not* the gold standard for measuring worth in social and political life.

Privilege

Some individuals and groups have more advantages than others. **Privilege** refers to the taken-for-granted rights, both legal and informal, that certain people have in society by virtue of their gender, race, class, sexual orientation, age, and other ways in which society structures and regulates human relations. Peggy McIntosh (2020) observed that male privilege, just like White privilege and heterosexual privilege, is an invisible knapsack of benefits that one takes along the road of life. In the family realm, male privilege includes the greater value placed on male children, as expressed in the parental preference for boys in many cultures, which can be traced back to rules of inheritance that may no longer be relevant in contemporary society. These invisible privileges also include men's formal rights, such as the right to vote or hold political office, which did not become a reality for women in the United States until 1920. While it may seem that women can run for elected office just as easily as men, think about the scrutiny we place on women who run for offices such as president and vice president of the United States. Do we ask the same questions of men and women running for the same office? Do men have to tell us how they will juggle their emotions or taking care of children with their job in the Senate? Conversely, do we place more scrutiny on women for wanting to take on such a prestigious job?

Another way to consider the invisible knapsack is to assess how physical labor is divided in the household. Who does the "inside" chores, and who usually performs the "outside" chores? Women traditionally do cooking, cleaning, laundry, and primary childcare. Each of these duties has to be completed every day; families usually eat three meals a day, and everyone wears clothing that needs laundering at least once a week. Cleaning—or at the very least, picking up—needs to be done every day (e.g., making beds and doing dishes are both daily activities). Men, on the other hand, are usually responsible for "outdoor" duties (e.g., mowing the lawn, shoveling the snow, and, perhaps, taking out the trash). These tasks are *not* completed every day; mowing is not only a weekly task, but it is only necessary during certain seasons. Trash usually does not need to be taken out every day but, perhaps, twice or three times a week. Think about your own family life. How does gender play out in the expectations for who does the household chores? Without analyzing these differences in the gendered division of labor, we are reproducing privilege. Privilege is invisible because it occurs without anyone even thinking about it. We go about our daily lives thinking that we are just "doing what's always been done," when in reality, we are recreating advantage and disadvantage without thinking twice. This taken-for-granted quality is what makes privilege so powerful; we have to stop and think to really see it.

Social Movements

When individuals start to become aware of the differential treatment and unearned privileges operating at the personal, familial, and societal levels, they are developing a **critical consciousness** about privilege and oppression (Allen, 2022; Collins & Bilge, 2017; hooks, 1994). Consciousness-raising at the individual level has sparked the national and international feminist movements. The Women's Liberation Movement that took shape in the 1960s explicitly addressed justice for women as a primary concern (Freedman, 2002). A social movement involves the collective activism toward social change that is essential to feminism. Activist involvement includes individual participation, such as taking a gender studies class during college, providing your child with gender-neutral toys, registering people to vote, or reaching out on social media to promote local and national marches for equality and civil rights (Lorber, 2012; Risman, 2018). It can also involve participating in nationalist or global movements that work toward women's human rights and full citizenship in developing countries or those that still bar women from full participation in society, including the right to education and paid employment (Naples, 2013; Trask, 2014). Yet while individuals may participate in a variety of social movements, including ecology, socialism, and religious fundamentalism, these movements are not feminist if they overlook or affirm patriarchal authority. A social movement is feminist when it is rooted in the critique of patriarchy (i.e., male rule) and centers the improvement of women's lives (Freedman, 2002). Furthermore, involvement in a social movement like feminism requires all of us to be critically aware of our own tendencies toward injustice. As feminist scholar and activist Sara Ahmed (2017) cautions, "We have to hesitate, to temper the strength of our tendencies with doubt; to waver when we are sure, or even because we are sure" (p. 6–7).

Social Hierarchy

So far, we have primarily addressed feminism as a critique of gender differences (men versus women). However, the most important lesson of the past several decades of feminist theory and feminist activism is the recognition that gender is integrally related to other social identities and structural locations, especially those based on class, race, sexuality, culture, and ability status. The deconstruction of the universal concept of "woman," in which gender is essentialized, has occurred because of the critiques by women of color; lesbians; bisexual women; transgender and nonbinary individuals; poor and working-class women; transnational women; multiracial and multicultural men and women; and individuals with disabilities, among others, as we noted previously. Freedman (2002) states,

> Despite the prevalence of hierarchies that privilege men, in every culture some women (such as elites or citizens) enjoy greater opportunities than many other women (such as workers or immigrants). Some women always have higher status than many men. If we ignore these intersecting hierarchies and create a feminism that serves only the interests of women who have more privilege, we reinforce other social inequalities that disadvantage both women and men in the name of improving women's opportunities. (p. 8)

Freedman is referring to the ways in which multiple statuses can intersect to create advantage or disadvantage, opening up feminist theory to a broader understanding of these multiple statuses. For example, how gender operates in families is contextual. Gender is complicated by differences across the racial experiences and social and economic resources individuals bring to families. Gender matters in many different ways within families and across families, which leads us to the current focus on intersectional feminism.

Intersectionality and Systems of Oppression

As we noted in the history of feminist thought over the past decades, now in its fourth wave, feminist theory has expanded to go beyond gender hierarchy and incorporate multiple systems of oppression. Systems of oppression are the interlocking hierarchies that stratify and objectify individuals in society (Collins, 1990). Critical race legal scholar Kimberlé Crenshaw (1991) introduced the term intersectionality as "a provisional concept linking contemporary politics with postmodern theory" (p. 1244) because both feminist discourses and antiracist discourses failed (on their own) to explain the *intersecting* identities of women of color. She explained how three types of intersectionality render lived experience and political outcomes for White women and women of color differentially. First, **structural intersectionality** includes "the ways in which the location of women of color at the intersection of race and gender makes our actual experience of domestic violence, rape, and remedial reform qualitatively different than that of white women" (Crenshaw, p. 1245). Second, **political intersectionality** means that women of color "are situated within at least two subordinated groups that frequently pursue conflicting political agendas" (Crenshaw, p. 1253). Third, **representational intersectionality** includes how "the production of images of women of color and the contestations over those images tend to ignore the intersectional interests of women of color" (Crenshaw, p. 1283). Thus, Crenshaw's theorizing about intersectionality reveals the "multiple and diverse ways in which oppression is experienced, maintained, and reproduced in social relationships, belief systems, and institutions" (Few-Demo & Allen, 2020, p. 335).

As a result of hierarchical stratification, certain groups are defined by the dominant society as subordinate. As we described in Chapter 3 on conflict theory and in Chapter 12 on critical race theory, members of the elite have greater access to opportunities and rewards. They have the power to define experience, create meaning, establish the rules, and dole out sanctions (Collins, 2019; Few-Demo et al., 2022). Individuals and families who are minoritized in society experience a doubling or tripling of disadvantage. For example, Collins (2005) explains how the intersections of racism, sexism, and heterosexism are used to reinforce the color line in American culture, disproportionately affecting African American lives, relationships, and interactions with social institutions, including families, education, employment, violence, prison, health, mass media, and popular culture.

Social locations such as race, class, gender, sexuality, religion, and nationality mutually construct one another (Collins, 1990; Mahler et al., 2015). **Intersectionality** is embodied diversity (Ahmed, 2017) and the politics of location, wherein each of us simultaneously experiences privilege and disadvantage (Few-Demo, 2014; McCall, 2005). As depicted in the inequality track (Chapter 3), privilege means that to the degree that a person occupies more highly valued social positions (e.g., a wealthy, White, cisgender man), they have more doors opening with less effort. A person with privilege is less likely to be stopped by the police, more likely to get into a prestigious school, and more likely to find a suitable mate. However, every person does not live up to the "ideal" of "having it all." So this means that some social positions are less valued than others. Being a gay man, compared to being a heterosexual man, has more challenges. A wealthy White man who is gay deals with those intersections: he is privileged because of his gender, race, and class status but disadvantaged and marginalized because of his sexual orientation (Goldberg et al., 2020). This has consequences for gay men's experiences with fatherhood. It is more difficult for gay men to have children and navigate parenting culture, given the stereotypes and stigma against them. However, gay men with financial resources are able to pay for surrogacy arrangements—a function of how class intersects with gender, sexual orientation, and race in impacting family life (Berkowitz, 2020).

Hegemonic Masculinity

Patriarchy—defined earlier as a system of male dominance—is enforced through **hegemonic masculinity**, which is the "practice that defines men's roles, expectations, and identities as superior to women" (Connell & Messerschmidt, 2005, p. 832). Hegemonic masculinity is fairly easy to achieve for some, but definitely not all, men. The ideal of hegemonic masculinity includes being successful, heterosexual, married or in a relationship with a cisgender woman, aggressive, dominant, strong, wealthy, and powerful.

Historically, feminist analyses of masculinity have focused on the societal prescriptions for how men should behave. More modern interpretations of masculinity offer hope instead of simply identifying the toxic aspects of

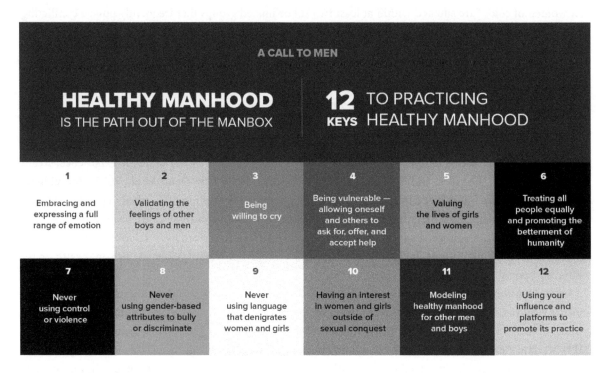

HEALTHY MANHOOD
IS THE PATH OUT OF THE MANBOX

12 KEYS TO PRACTICING HEALTHY MANHOOD

1	2	3	4	5	6
Embracing and expressing a full range of emotion	Validating the feelings of other boys and men	Being willing to cry	Being vulnerable — allowing oneself and others to ask for, offer, and accept help	Valuing the lives of girls and women	Treating all people equally and promoting the betterment of humanity

7	8	9	10	11	12
Never using control or violence	Never using gender-based attributes to bully or discriminate	Never using language that denigrates women and girls	Having an interest in women and girls outside of sexual conquest	Modeling healthy manhood for other men and boys	Using your influence and platforms to promote its practice

FIGURE 8.2. Masculinity: Updated and Hopeful

hegemonic masculinity. Figure 8.2 builds off the original idea of the "man box," a term coined by Tony Porter of A Call to Men, which illustrates the limited ways in which society has allowed men and boys to "do" gender (Porter, 2016). This original man box illustration held descriptors inside a box to signal the *acceptable* ways in which men are supposed to behave (e.g., strong, wealthy, virile, provider, and having no emotions) with oppositional phrases outside the box to signal derogatory terms men and boys are called when they fail to live up to the standards inside (e.g., bitch, pussy, or gay). Clearly, the original "man box" illustration provides a powerful way to help us understand the social construction of gender and the gender binary, but this modern update moves us beyond the dismal illustration and offers hope for moving forward.

This approach to celebrating healthy masculinity instead of simply focusing on the toxic aspects is fairly new in modern culture. Historically, scholars and practitioners have focused on the ways in which hegemonic hypermasculinity is damaging to all in society because it is based on a zero-sum game; for men to be powerful and functional, this version of masculinity needs women to emphasize feminine traits. This ideology has helped maintain the dichotomized ideas of how to "do" gender in our society. Together, hegemonic masculinity and emphasized femininity have set the standard by which all members of society are evaluated. Yet as we discuss in this chapter and in Chapter 13 (queer theory), modern critiques of the gender binary have thankfully upended the cultural discussions and practices of the past, replacing it with a new approach, as highlighted in Figure 8.2.

BOX 8.2. FEMINIST THEORY IN MODERN CULTURE: *MAID*

Maid is a television miniseries drama based on a memoir written by Stephanie Land (2019), entitled *Maid: Hard Work, Low Pay, and a Mother's Will to Survive*. The story follows main character Alex as she navigates leaving her alcoholic, abusive partner with their toddler daughter, Maddy. Alex faces hurdle after hurdle in her journey, followed by small victories and then setbacks. Many of the setbacks have to do with bureaucratic requirements that, unless you experience yourself, you might never know exist for individuals trying to leave an abusive situation. The story highlights not only Alex's struggle to find freedom but also her family of origin dynamics that prevent her from having the consistent support she needs from her parents.

Part of the story also focuses on Alex's relationship with her employer, Regina, as it blossoms from a hostile client–employee relationship to an intimate friendship. Other storylines situate Alex in precarious and complicated situations as she decides how to live on her own, without help from a new romantic interest or by rekindling her relationship with her ex. Overall, this show does a good job of illustrating the complex layers of intersectionality; Alex is White, straight, cisgender, and from low social class. Yet because of her status as a woman, a domestic abuse survivor, and someone with a poor safety net because of her family background, she suffers from distinct disadvantage. Her employer, Regina, is a Black woman with significant financial privilege, which also provokes an analysis of intersectionality.

Throughout the show, viewers are reminded of how complex identity can be, particularly when navigating significant emotional trauma. For example, Alex struggles to view herself as a victim of domestic violence because her ex never actually struck her during his outbursts. The closest he came was to punching a hole in the wall next to where she stood during a fight. Because of this, she has a hard time accepting help, including from a domestic violence safe house. Her perceived "privilege" of not having physical bruises, broken bones, or visible scars of the abuse serves as a disadvantage because she cannot identify herself as worthy of help. We encourage readers to consider other ways where privilege intersects with disadvantage throughout the show and how important it is to understand the nuance of the widespread and toxic nature of gender-based violence.

Evaluating Feminist Theory

Strengths of Feminist Theory

Feminist family theorizing has many strengths. It is one of the most dynamic, exciting, adaptable, and controversial of all the theories. Because of its variability—that there are so many versions of feminist theory—it can also be a challenge in trying to use it. As we have discussed throughout this chapter, feminist theory is full of complexity, contradiction, and possibility.

Critique of Power Dynamics in Families

Feminist theory is the original family science perspective that directly challenges inequality, privilege, and power dynamics *within* relationships, marriages, and families and seeks to enact private and public social change. Feminist theory began with critiquing the normative family structure of the separation of gendered family roles. Feminists challenged this ideology by uncovering issues such as invisible labor, family violence, unequal distribution of power in families (Walker & Thompson, 1984). Feminist theory allowed us to "rethink the family" and ask new questions about how gender is reproduced in families and how it can be deconstructed to disrupt power inequities (Thorne, 1982). By decentering patriarchy, feminist theory offers possibilities for reconstructing families from women's experiences (Baber & Allen, 1992). Today, intersectional feminist theory requires scholars to name and address the multiple axes of oppression and privilege (Allen et al., 2022; Few-Demo et al., 2022).

Valuing and Hearing Women's and Minoritized Voices in Families

Another major strength of feminist theory is that it takes the voices of the people it studies seriously. A good deal of the family research guided by feminist theory has used qualitative methods to go straight to the source and document the experiences of those who have been oppressed—in their own words. We first learned about the gendered nature of housework—invisible, unappreciated, unpaid, and delegated to women—by interviewing women about their responsibilities in the home (Lopata, 1971; Oakley, 1974), and we learned to critique the privilege of White women who hire women of color to provide domestic labor and family care, so they could pursue careers (Collins, 1990; Dill, 1988; Glenn, 1985). New insights are gleaned by investigating unexamined topics, listening to women and their family members, and paying attention to their experiences. In another example, MacTavish (2007) examined family and community life for low-income parents and children living in a rural mobile home park. By taking the perspective of the people she studied, MacTavish was able to uncover not only their feelings of exclusion but also to support it with evidence of class-segregated schooling, exclusionary recreation programs, and social stigma. Listening to the voices of diverse women and their families and taking them seriously is a hallmark and strength of feminist theory that has revolutionized family science.

Adaptable to Change

A third strength is that feminist theory is constantly being revised in light of new knowledge, social changes, and the reflexive quality of feminist scholars to critique themselves and each other, as Ahmed (2017) so cogently observed. Feminism is a dynamic and fluid theory that is not satisfied with the status quo; it is a contentious theory that challenges scholars and activists to not settle for outdated concepts or neoliberal solutions, like just securing your own piece of the pie (Allen, 2022; Sharp & Weaver, 2015). Thus, feminists have studied gender in families, first from the perspective of biological sex roles and gender roles, and after critiquing their own ideas, feminist theory has contributed new ideas that shed light on the limitations of sex and role as theoretical concepts. Instead, gender as a set of relations, about how individuals "do gender" replaced earlier and more static ideas about sex or gender roles (Risman, 2004; West & Zimmerman, 1987). The influence of intersectionality on feminist theory has reinvigorated feminist research, and scholars now understand the importance of studying how gender intersects with race, class, sexuality, family, and the like (Crenshaw, 1989; Collins & Bilge, 2016; McCormick-Huhn et al., 2019). No doubt, as we write these words, there are new ideas about feminist theory that will replace them.

Weaknesses of Feminist Theory

Just as there are many strengths to feminist theory, there are also many criticisms. Sometimes the strengths of a theory can also be its weaknesses. Feminist theory attempts to deal with very complex social and personal issues and ground them in a political context for the purpose of social change. This leads to debates about its usefulness as a way to look at the world from an intellectual standpoint.

Is It a Theory or an Ideology?

A common criticism among those who do not support feminist theory is that it is not a theory but an ideology. What this means is that concerns over gender inequality are part of a perspective, or way of looking at the world, but without "testable" propositions like other theories. As an example, structural functionalist theory (Chapter 2) would suggest that the reason that nearly 50% of marriages end in divorce is because the family has outsourced needs that were previously met *inside* the family. Therefore, if you were to examine this phenomenon using functionalist theory, you would measure family members' use of external social institutions, such as going to a therapist for emotional support, compared to when family members used to stay inside the private realm of the family to get those needs met. Prior to the Industrial Revolution that began in Western countries several centuries ago, family members worked at home, educated children at home, received religious teachings from the patriarch (father) of the household, and grew and prepared all of their food at home. Each member of the family had a specific "job," which is very different from how a contemporary family functions. The testable proposition using structural functionalist theory would be: "Divorce rates have increased since the Industrial Revolution because of modern society's reliance on external social institutions." Using feminist theory, on the other hand, you would examine the ways in which gendered ideologies have shifted over time and how women's and men's roles have changed as a result. Critics who argue that feminism is not a theory suggest that while examining gender roles in the family is important, it is not specific enough to be testable. Instead, they suggest that feminism is more of a political ideology. It is important to point out, however, that the same argument has been made in an attempt to dismiss or disparage conflict theory (Chapter 3) and critical race theory (Chapter 12), which presupposes that all social order is determined by access to wealth and power or that race structures lived experience, respectively. These are underlying processes that affect and predict how families operate and are undoubtedly important to examine.

Does It Have to Be Explicitly Feminist to Be a Feminist Theory?

One challenge in identifying feminist theory in family science is that authors often do not name their work explicitly as feminist. Several studies over the past four decades have challenged the impact that feminist theory and research have made in family science (Ferree, 2010; Thompson & Walker, 1995; Walker, 2009; Wills & Risman, 2006). Part of this issue has to do with the fact that scholars often use concepts of power, gender, and intersectionality, which are derived from feminist theory, but do not name them as such. Not giving credit where credit is due is akin to saying, "I'm not a feminist, but. ..." The very fact that some people do not want to identify their work as feminist, but have benefited by the changes created by feminist scholars and activists, is an indication of its controversial nature. It also indicates the relevance of feminist theory for challenging the status quo that all individuals are equal in society. In their recommendations for feminist family science going forward, Few-Demo and Allen (2020) urge scholars to explicitly name their feminist research on social justice as *feminist*.

Difficulty of Measuring Intersectionality

Intersectionality is an exciting and innovative theoretical concept, acknowledging that gender or race alone are not complex enough to measure privilege, opportunity, and oppression in people's lives (Crenshaw, 1991). Rather, our lives are shaped by how gender, race, social class, and sexuality intersect with other forms of social stratification. Intersectionality, as an academic concept, is relatively easy to understand. Methodologically, however, it is challenging to measure, particularly in quantitative research (Bowleg, 2008; McCall, 2005). Ferree (2010), as we discuss in the section entitled "Feminist Theory Today," suggests ways of conceptualizing intersectionality as either locational or relational, and these definitions offer suggestions for how to measure intersectionality in ways that retain the benefits of its theoretical complexity.

An Alternative Theory App: Functionalist Theory

In this chapter, we have laid out the origins, key concepts, applications, and strengths and weaknesses of feminist theory. For most students, at first glance, feminist theory stands in stark contrast to functionalist theory. However, it is still useful to consider how we would "switch" apps to explain the same phenomenon from perspectives that are seemingly polar opposites.

Think back to Chapter 2, when you learned about functionalists Talcott Parsons and Robert Merton. Parsons's theory of social change argued that change occurs slowly, over time, and that perfect equilibrium among all systems is a goal but is rarely achieved. Merton extended this line of thought and argued that not all individuals in a society can "fit" into the preexisting social institutions, which naturally produces deviance. Think about this in relation to how feminist thought has evolved over time. The first wave focused on giving women legal rights, the second wave on questioning stay-at-home motherhood mandates and giving voice to women of color, and the third and fourth waves expanded to include LGBTQ+ voices, pushing the boundaries of traditional notions of feminism in academia, and online activism among younger feminists around the globe. Each of these changes would not have been possible without considering the functionality of "deviant" voices and how, over time, the cultural system adapts to include new perspectives. There is a place in society for the "other" voices—to disrupt and evoke change in a preexisting system. Therefore, the functionalist model of social deviance and social change helps us understand how feminism has come to be what it is today.

Next, it is important to understand how feminist theory applies to the study of families at the international level. In box 8.3, we present an example of the impact large-scale military operations have on the well-being of women and children globally.

Working With Feminist Theory: Integrating Research and Practice

Feminist Theory Today

Given the complexity of intersectionality as a theoretical and methodological concept, Myra Marx Ferree (2010) provided two ways to conceptualize it. The first type, **locational intersectionality**, is concerned with the identities and social positions of disadvantaged groups, such as those who are poor, members of a minoritized

BOX 8.3. GLOBAL COMPARISONS: WOMEN AND GIRLS IN AFGHANISTAN

In 2021, the United States decided to pull troops from Afghanistan after what President Joe Biden deemed the "longest war" in U.S. history. As the allied troops were removed, Taliban troops immediately began removing women from positions of relative privilege, such as jobs in banks (Jain, 2021) and educational institutions. This signals a fatal return to widespread gender-based oppression, misogyny, and violence for women and girls. The shift toward empowering women and girls in this part of the world was quickly reversed as the Taliban regained control for the first time since 1996.

Because of such rapid social change and corresponding civil unrest, over 100,000 Afghanis have been evacuated, and roughly half of those have been issued Special Immigrant Visa applicants, which includes their families (Webb, 2021). Additionally, around 300 unaccompanied Afghan children were evacuated. Not only does this raise significant concern about the impact of such traumatic change on families but, even moreso, on the unaccompanied children. In the few months following the removal of U.S. troops, instances of child marriages and sex abuse have already been reported (Webb, 2021). Human traffickers notoriously try to capitalize on such rapid social change, which leaves large swaths of the population discarded and vulnerable. This tragic reality is an example of how macro-level forces related to military presence have a trickle-down effect on the world's most vulnerable.

Source: https://www.whitehouse.gov/briefing-room/speeches-remarks/2021/08/31/remarks-by-president-biden-on-the-end-of-the-war-in-afghanistan/

group, LGBTQ+, old, or disabled. This perspective gives voice to individuals with multiple oppressed social locations and helps others understand how people with those multiple intersections actually experience such disadvantages. For example, in Nelson's (2006) qualitative study of single mothers, the women created their families in a way that conformed to the idealized traditional family model, even though they had not been able to achieve this ideal family in their own lives. They created this by having their mothers serve as placeholders for the husbands they did not currently have but hoped to secure in the future. They relied on their mothers to provide housing, financial security, and child-rearing support, so they could complete the dream of becoming a traditional family. Nelson's study is an exemplar of a locational intersectional analysis by revealing how a woman's social locations of being a divorced, single mother reflect societal-level institutional constraints, such as the risk of poverty.

The second type, **relational intersectionality**, theorizes that intersectionality affects every person, not just those who are oppressed and marginalized. It moves beyond locational intersectionality to examine the institutional practices and social processes that produce patterns of inequality for all individuals (Ferree, 2010). Identity, then, is not static, but shifts with changing cultural discourses and social institutions. In their study of how poor women of color dealt with the welfare system, Dodson and Schmalzbauer (2005) used the relational approach to interpret their "habits of hiding" to exercise caution when interacting with social work professionals who had the power to exert control over them by denying them needed resources.

Collins (2015) reminds us of the definitional dilemmas of intersectionality as a knowledge project, which she defines as "the critical insight that race, class, gender, sexuality, ethnicity, nation, ability, and age operate not as unitary, mutually exclusive entities, but as reciprocally constructing phenomena that in turn shape complex social inequalities" (p. 2). Thus, intersectionality can be used as a theory, a concept, a methodology, an analytic device, and a praxis, and like feminism itself, it does not need to be tied down to a strict definition. Collins concludes that intersectionality can retain its critical edge with creativity across theory, method, and praxis, stating, "Holding fast to the creativity of this dynamic area of inquiry and practice yet finding a common language that will be useful to its practitioners is the cutting-edge definitional dilemma for intersectionality" (p. 17). The value of this creative, critical approach is found in the Black feminist disability framework Bailey and Mobley (2019) use to articulate the intersections of race, gender, and disability—rather than how these ideas are typically siloed in separate analyses—toward a more complex and nuanced understanding of their own lived experience.

Feminist Theory in Research

Feminist theory helps us understand how gender and its intersections with race, class, sexuality, nationality, and other hierarchical systems structure family life. In this qualitative study of 28 young women attending university in the Gulf country of Qatar, James-Hawkins et al. (2021) conducted interviews (in Arabic, then translated into English) about how gendered power operates in their lives. Although Qatar is a country that is experiencing significant reforms for women, encouraging their opportunities for higher education, it is still a highly patriarchal society in which men and women must keep physically separate, thereby limiting women's educational and occupational experiences. The authors asked the women about their aspirations and experiences regarding marriage and family, education, and employment.

James-Hawkins et al. (2021) relied on Komter's (1989) feminist theory of hidden power in marriage to analyze their findings but translated it from a European context to an Arab context. Qatari women experienced *manifest power,* or overt restrictions on their behavior and aspirations, imposed on them by their parents, particularly in the type of major they chose (avoiding medicine and law, for example) or in not being allowed to travel or study abroad. Even more common were examples of *latent power*, which are the self-limitations that the young women imposed on themselves, thereby anticipating what they thought their parents or their future husbands would want them to do. Surprisingly, their concern about their future husbands' perception of what is an acceptable career path for Qatari women is a finding that has not appeared as strongly in Western studies of young women's aspirations about marriage and career. Examples of *invisible power*, which is the internalization of social norms—in this case, that women should be primarily wives, mothers, and homemakers—was also evident among the Qatari women. Finally, there were ways that the women resisted these highly segregated gender norms. They navigated support for their educational and career aspirations with their parents, using dialogue and negotiation practices. They also contested the structural constraints and limitations imposed on them, pushing against them and agentically seeking to break barriers wherever they could find an opening.

Feminist Theory in Practice

There are several ways in which educators, practitioners, and family policymakers can apply feminist theory in their work with individuals and families. One of the most important places this theory can be applied is in examining how men embody feminist principles in broad cultural spaces to shift the narrative toward gender equity. While it is easy to paint a broad brush to condemn men for harms caused by the patriarchy, it is nihilistic. Instead, we turn to organizations in which men lead in a variety of ways to turn feminist principles into practice and offer hope for this and future generations.

One of the very first organizations dedicated to challenging misogynistic culture is A Call to Men, founded in 2002 by Tony Porter, an author, educator, and activist. A Call to Men is widely known as a leader in the fight against gender-based violence and promoting "healthy, respectful manhood" (www.acalltomen.org). Porter is well-respected for his approach to dismantling the patriarchy by emphasizing "the intersections of oppression, diversity, equity, and inclusion, white supremacy culture and anti-Blackness, and promoting gender and racial equity" (www.acalltomen.org). This group has had far-reaching influence, having provided training to professional sports leagues well-known for historically embodying hypermasculinity, including the National Football League (NFL) and others. Porter has also trained branches of the military.

Other organizations have ventured more explicitly into broad cultural spaces. The Man Enough movement (www.manenough.com) takes a feminist approach in attempting to dismantle toxic masculinity and redefine masculinity in general through several mediums. This effort is being led by influencer, actor, and author Justin Baldoni; journalist, author, and producer Liz Plank; and musician Jamey Heath. This movement is gaining momentum in mainstream culture via books (Baldoni, 2021; Plank, 2019), a TED Talk (Baldoni, 2017), and a popular podcast hosted by Baldoni, Heath, and Plank. Heath and Baldoni discuss relevant issues they face as fathers, partners, and men, centering Plank's critiques and insights as part of their conversations, effectively problematizing the traditional ways in which the dominant culture has prescribed masculinity for over a century. The ethos of Man Enough holds that by "undefining traditional roles and traits of masculinity, men will be able to realize their potential as humans and their capacity for connection" (www.manenough.com). This practical application of a feminist perspective is arguably more far-reaching than academic research conducted within the confines of an ivory tower and contributes to a growing movement that brings conversations about masculinity to bear in spaces predominantly occupied by men.

Other organizations directly confront men who are contributing to the objectification and victimization of marginalized individuals. EPIK Project (www.epikproject.org) furthers gender equity by promoting **generative masculinity**, which encapsulates the responsibility and desire to give back, be comfortable with oneself, and be willing to confront and critique gender inequality (Badaszewski, 2014). This organization, founded in 2013, embraces a radical feminist approach to holding men accountable for the demand that drives the commercial sex market, a major contributor to the victimization of marginalized bodies in sex trafficking. Nearly 250 men across North America meet monthly to disrupt other men's attempts to purchase sex from online escort advertisements, but on a broad scale EPIK also promotes generative masculinity as the antithesis to toxic masculinity, emphasizing its destructive qualities. In contrast, EPIK holds that men who manifest generative qualities have a "life-giving" impact on the world around them.

BOX 8.4. VOICES FROM LIVED EXPERIENCE

Meg is a former student of Angie's, and she reached out after graduation to thank Angie for the impact her courses had, particularly in boosting her confidence to have conversations with feminist roots. Below is an excerpt of one note:

My roommates and I hosted a nacho "party" with my new boyfriend, a few friends, and their boyfriends. We were sitting outside and someone cracked an offensive porn comment ... Ugh I couldn't resist saying something! The burden you hold when you're just full of empowerment and feminist knowledge! I had to say something that may have slightly dampened the mood, but it was totally worth it. I said something along the lines of "well, actually ..." and proceeded to explain why what they said was in fact incorrect and perpetuating the patriarchy and misogynist thinking. Now, my roommates already knew this was coming because they had listened to my rant about all the unbelievable things I had learned in class like the "man box" or that there is literally an industry for "sex tourism"! I spent the next 30 or so minutes explaining the dangers and misconceptions about porn, and to my surprise answered a lot of questions from my friends. They wanted to know more, and I was honestly shocked and nervous because I began dating a wonderful man and of course "YIKES!" popped into my head because I started to realize I'm becoming that girl that can't shut up about the patriarchy and feels inclined to educate men on feminism. But truthfully, being so candid about the realities of the patriarchy in front of someone I liked and my friends felt even more empowering. The response from my friends was amazing; in fact one guy told me he never knew anything about porn, other than the obvious ... but that's the funny thing, it isn't so obvious, and he had no idea PornHub allows all sorts of videos to be uploaded, from child pornography to rape, and that it perpetuates horrific racist tropes, or even how just watching porn from a young age can develop misconceptions about what sex will be like with a real-life partner. Even my partner looked at me in the car one day after we discussed sex and porn, and suddenly he looked at me—and I will never forget this—and he told me how I had completely changed his views on sex and porn, realizing his own problematic understandings of mainstream sex. Now, I never set out with the intention of trying to change or fix people, but then I realized, it wasn't because I was trying to change him that he had this epiphany, but instead, through our discussion over these topics, he actually developed his own ideas and understandings and was able to conclude that perhaps some of his existing views were maybe damaging and offensive, especially to women. I realized that it's not about being the preacher of feminist theory, it is simply about open, candid, and honest discussion that gets people to listen and understand what feminism is. It has always been that simple, but it wasn't until taking my classes with Dr. Henderson, and the help of my wonderful therapist, that I found my feminist voice, which to me gave me a sort of unknown power and confidence, and now? Well, now I happily interrupt a misogynistic conversation, and I'll never stop!

Conclusion

Feminist theory has contributed many innovative ideas that allow family researchers and practitioners to utilize its theoretical concepts in the real world. From its beginnings as a way to describe gender oppression and privilege, specifically related to women's rights, feminist theory has evolved to consider how race, class, sexual orientation, age, nationality, and disability, among other social locations, intersect to create differential experiences. Ultimately, feminist theory offers a critique of the status quo and provides pathways for transformative change in the lives of families and society.

Multimedia Suggestions

www.hrc.org

This is the website for the Human Rights Campaign (HRC), the most influential civil rights organization for lesbian, gay, bisexual, transgender, and queer equality. The website offers a wealth of information about state-by-state laws and policies that affect LGBTQ+ people and their families in the United States; the coming out process; religious issues; health and aging; state, federal, and global advocacy; education and employment; communities of color; and how allies can be a support system and a force for amplifying LGBTQ+ voices. The resources link contains a compilation of facts and maps about all of these issues. Because of the volatile nature of LGBTQ+ issues, the website is constantly updated to reflect changes in laws and resources.

Activate your theory app: Now that all American citizens have legal access to marriage regardless of sexual orientation, what issues are at the forefront of the HRC? And what issues regarding marriage equality are not yet "over"?

www.socwomen.org

This is the official website for Sociologists for Women in Society (SWS), a nonprofit scientific and educational organization of sociologists and others dedicated to issues, such as encouraging the development of sociological feminist theory and scholarship; promoting social justice through local, national, and international activism; and transforming academia through feminist leadership, career development, and institutional diversity. SWS publishes the journal, *Gender & Society*. Many excellent teaching and activist resources are also shared on the website.

Activate your theory app: Browse this organization's "Career Advice" section. Sometimes it is useful to really "see" the power of advice by imagining what the advice would sound like if it were directed at someone who already had privilege. As you read through the comments, take note of how reimagining that advice from the perspective of privilege helps point out some of the invisible power of gender inequality.

Tough Guise (1999)

Jackson Katz, a leading gender violence prevention trainer, has produced two documentaries to critique contemporary notions of masculinity in America. *Tough Guise* and *Tough Guise 2* examine rates of domestic violence and the stunning statistic that men commit over 90% of violent crimes in society. Yet until recently, we have not examined

Image 8.2 A Scene From *Tough Guise*, 1999

the social construction of masculinity (the "tough guise") with a critical eye. Katz illustrates how hegemonic masculinity has developed over the past 60 years and gives a particularly poignant example of the size of boys' action figures. Since the toy G.I. Joe was first created in 1963, his biceps have been steadily enlarged.

Activate your theory app: Identify some practical ways Katz's message can be applied to improve the lives of not only men and boys but all humans. Further, given that this documentary first aired in 1999, consider what has changed since then. Are boys still encouraged to bottle up emotions and to fit inside the "man box"? What about the variety of toys available to young children? Are they still highly gendered?

Hacks (2021)

Image 8.3 A Scene From *Hacks*, 2021

This television show centers on the professional relationship between Deborah, a legendary Las Vegas stand-up comedienne (a diva) and Ava, a 20ish, bisexual comedy writer who has been "cancelled" for an insensitive tweet. Now, the only job Ava can get is to write jokes for Deborah, an older woman she considers a "hack." The series depicts the intergenerational feminist antagonisms between baby boomers and Gen Z. It also reveals the tremendous odds against women performers in the cutthroat entertainment business. Despite the fact that Deborah and Ava have vastly different areas of competence and prestige in terms of their respective wealth (Deborah) and social media savvy (Ava), they do have a lot in common, especially in their lack of trust for other people. Both are relatively estranged from their families, and both have experienced devastating losses. Although a comedy, the show provides a great deal of insight into how women's lives are shortchanged, sexualized, and criticized and what they need to do to "make it," despite these odds.

Activate your theory app: Think about your own intergenerational relationships. Do you identify more with Deborah or with Ava? Were there moments in your life when you felt criticized and held back in the ways that Deborah and Ava do, regardless of age? How does this show reveal a feminist message?

Further Reading

Allen, K. R., & Goldberg, A. E. (2020). Lesbian women disrupting gendered, heteronormative discourses of motherhood, marriage, and divorce. *Journal of Lesbian Studies, 24*(1), 12–24. https://doi.org/10.1080/10894160.2019.1615356 Despite the freedom they found from living outside traditional heterosexual marriage, lesbian women must still confront the gendered, heteronormative dictates that guide all women as mothers and wives, regardless of sexuality. In this feminist, qualitative study of 17 White lesbian adoptive mothers who were in the process of dissolving their partnerships with another woman, Allen and Goldberg found that the women deployed five cultural discourses that infiltrated their own understanding of separation, divorce, and motherhood. These discourses, pulled from larger cultural narratives about what constitutes a "good family" regardless of the parent's sexual orientation, both aided and harmed these mothers as they worked through the relational dissolution process. The discourses were (a) the ideology of the good mother, (b) divorce is bad for kids, (c) marriage is the ideal way to live, (d) couples should stay together for the sake of the children, and (e) lesbians should remain friends with their ex-lovers. Ultimately, the prevalence of these discourses revealed the feminist tenet that oppression and agency comingle for women, despite leaving behind some aspects of patriarchal oppression.

Calasanti, T., & King, N. (2007). Taking 'women's work' 'like a man': Husbands' experiences of care work. *Gerontologist, 47*(4), 516–527. https://doi.org/10.1093/geront/47.4.516 Calasanti and King interviewed older, White husbands caring for their wives during various stages of Alzheimer's disease. In this study, they utilized a feminist structural approach, which means that they not only analyzed how the men constructed masculinity with relation to caregiving, but they took their social class backgrounds (i.e., structured inequality) into account as well, comparing men from working- to upper-middle-class occupations. They found that these men tended to approach caregiving in ways that reflective masculine ideas of "exerting force, focusing on tasks, blocking emotions, minimizing disruption, distracting attention, and self-medicating" (p. 516). This study has important implications for theory development and family policy because men's experiences of masculinity vary significantly by race and class, which should inform intervention development and strategies for supporting caregivers.

Gerson, K. (2009). *The unfinished revolution: How a new generation is reshaping family, work, and gender in America*. Oxford University Press. In this in-depth interview study of 120 young men and women between the ages of 18 and 32 from diverse social classes and racial or ethnic groups, sociologist Kathleen Gerson found that 95% of her participants wanted a lifelong bond with one partner, and most also wanted an equal partnership. Still, many of these young adults worried that a dual earner marriage that allowed for personal autonomy would not be possible. They still did not see the signs of broader social change that indicated these ideals were in reach. They faced time-demanding jobs, with few childcare and family-leave options that would support gender equality in marriage. The fallback position, that women opt out of paid work for stay-at-home motherhood, was less and less attractive for many of the women, who were less likely to settle, instead preferring to postpone marriage and view it as optional and reversible. The men, however, were more likely to fall back on traditional, though somewhat modified, unequal marital relationships. A majority of the men felt that equal sharing in marriage, though appealing, was too costly. These contrasting views of young men and women reveal an emerging gender divide that is challenging a new generation of parents, partners, and employees. Gerson revealed how gender informs the dilemmas they face and suggested the need for flexible social and economic supports to help new generations realize their goal of equally blending work and family.

Miller, C. (2019). *Know my name: A memoir*. Viking. In this award-winning autobiography, Chanel Miller describes her experiences coming to terms with the college campus and court system after she was sexually assaulted by a male student at Stanford University. Her initial victim impact statement, submitted anonymously as "Emily Doe," went viral after it was read aloud at the perpetrator's sentencing hearing. Published online by BuzzFeed, her statement was read 11 million times in just a few days. In this memoir, Miller reveals her identity as a Chinese-American woman, a writer, and an artist. She powerfully describes family, friend, community, and national reactions to her experience, testimony, treatment, and the courageous ways she has rebuilt her life and reclaimed her identity.

Oluo, I. (2020). *Mediocre: The dangerous legacy of white male America*. Hachette. In this important follow up to her bestselling book, *So You Want to Talk About Race*, Ijeoma Oluo describes the toxic nature of white patriarchy and the "white dudes," whose prominence in the social institutions of the United States keep others from having a voice or a seat at the table of power. In addition to showing how "white male identity is in a very dark place" in which White men are caught up in cycles of fear and violence (pp. 273–274), Oluo also reveals how those who do not occupy such positions have a stake in upholding

White, middle-class male dominance. Among her many points for change, Oluo says we "must imagine a white manhood that is not based in the oppression of others" (p. 275), and we "must stop confusing bullies with leaders" (p. 276). Instead, she states, "We must break free. We must start making better and more informed choices—with our votes, our wallets, our media, our societal expectations" (p. 276).

Questions for Students

Discussion Questions

1. What is a "gender perspective"? How does it differ from the earlier concept of "gender roles as separate spheres"?

2. Describe how status quo definitions of family, gender, and power have challenged the feminist call for social change and family justice.

3. What trends do you notice in the different waves of feminist thinking over time? If we were to have a "fifth wave," what do you think it would involve?

4. Do you believe we can finish the gender revolution without turning back the clock? How do *you* deal with resistant institutions and the contradictory pressures facing you as a gendered being today?

5. Define the concept of intersectionality. How do you see it expanding upon and improving a feminist perspective?

6. From an international perspective, give examples of how the concept of patriarchy is still relevant today. Give examples of how it may not be relevant.

Your Turn!

Find an article in which the authors have used feminist theory to study families as a framework for their research. What aspects of feminist theory did the research utilize? How did the researchers locate themselves in the study, if at all? Is there another theory the research could have utilized? What are the strengths and weaknesses of the article? What would you do differently if you were in charge of the research?

Personal Reflection Questions

1. How will you manage the gender divide in your own family and work life? What aspects of gender difference do you find useful? What aspects do you find difficult to deal with?

2. In what ways have you been an activist in your own life? What social movements do you follow? What is the difference you want to see and help create in the world?

3. What versions of feminist theory can you most relate to? What concepts are the hardest for you to relate to?

4. How does the concept of intersectionality play out in your own life? In what ways do gender, race, class, sexual orientation, age, dis/ability, and other forms of social stratification structure your opportunities and experiences?

5. When was the first time you noticed gender in your life? How old were you? What were you doing? How did those around you encourage or discourage gender roles?

6. Thinking about the concept of privilege, what are the privileges you are carrying around in your "invisible knapsack"?

References

Acker, J., Barry, K., & Esseveld, J. (1983). Objectivity and truth: Problems in doing feminist research. *Women's Studies International Forum, 6*(4), 423–435. https://doi.org/10.1016/0277-5395(83)90035-3

Acosta, K. L. (2018). Queering family scholarship: Theorizing from the borderlands. *Journal of Family Theory & Review, 10*(2), 406–418. https://doi.org/10.1111/jftr.12263

Ahmed, S. (2017). *Living a feminist life.* Duke University Press.

Aikau, H. K., Erickson, K. A., & Pierce, J. L. (Eds.). (2007). *Feminist waves, feminist generations: Life stories from the academy.* University of Minnesota Press.

Allen, K. R. (2000). A conscious and inclusive family studies. *Journal of Marriage and the Family, 62*(1), 4–17. https://doi.org/10.1111/j.1741-3737.2000.00004.x

Allen, K. R. (2022). Feminist theory, method, and praxis: Toward a critical consciousness for family and close relationship scholars. *Journal of Social and Personal Relationships.* Advance online publication. https://doi.org/10.1177/02654075211065779

Allen, K. R., & Craven, C. C. (2020). Losing a child: Death and hidden losses in LGBTQ-parent families. In A. E. Goldberg & K. R. Allen (Eds.), *LGBTQ-parent families: Innovations in research and implications for practice* (2nd ed., pp. 349–362). Springer.

Allen, K. R., Goldberg, A. E., & Jaramillo-Sierra, A. L. (2022). Feminist theories: Knowledge, method, and practice. In K. Adamsons, A. L. Few-Demo, C. Proulx, & K. Roy (Eds.). *Sourcebook of family theories and methodologies.* Springer.

Allen, K. R. & Henderson, A. C. (2022). Family theorizing for social justice: A critical praxis. *Journal of Family Theory & Review.* Advance online publication. https://doi.org/10.1111/jftr.12450

Allen, K. R., Lloyd, S. A., & Few, A. L. (2009). Reclaiming feminist theory, method, and praxis for family studies. In S. A. Lloyd, A. L. Few, & K. R. Allen (Eds.), *Handbook of feminist family studies* (pp. 3–17). SAGE Publications.

Allen, K. R., Walker, A. J., & McCann, B. R. (2013). Feminism and families. In G. W. Peterson & K. R. Bush (Eds.), *Handbook of marriage and the family* (3rd ed., pp. 139–158). Springer.

Anzaldua, G. (Ed.). (1990). *Making face, making soul = Haciendo caras: Creative and critical perspectives by feminists of color.* Aunt Lute Books.

Baber, K. M. (2009). Postmodern feminist perspectives and families. In S. A. Lloyd, A. L. Few & K. R. Allen (Eds.), *Handbook of feminist family studies* (pp. 56–68). SAGE Publications.

Baber, K. M., & Allen, K. R. (1992). *Women and families: Feminist reconstructions.* Guilford Press.

Badaszewski, P. D. (2014). *Beyond the binary: How college men construct positive masculinity* [Unpublished doctoral dissertation]. University of Georgia.

Bailey, M., & Mobley, I. A. (2019). Work in the intersections: A black feminist disability framework. *Gender & Society, 33*(1), 19–40. https://doi.org/10.1177/0891243218801523

Baldoni, J. (2017). *Why I'm done trying to be 'man enough'* [Video]. TED Talk. https://www.ted.com/talks/justin_baldoni_why_i_m_done_trying_to_be_man_enough?language=en

Baldoni, J. (2021). *Man enough: Undefining my masculinity.* HarperCollins.

Bell-Scott, P., Guy-Sheftall, B., Royster, J. J., Sims-Wood, J., DeCosta-Willis, M., & Fultz, L. (Eds.). (1991). *Double stitch: Black women write about mothers and daughters.* Beacon Press.

Berkowitz, D. (2020). Gay men and surrogacy. In A. E. Goldberg & K. R. Allen (Eds.), *LGBTQ-parent families: Innovations in research and implications for practice* (2nd ed., pp. 143–160). Springer.

Bermudez, J. M., Muruthi, B. A., & Jordan, L. S. (2016). Decolonizing research methods for family science: Creating space at the center. *Journal of Family Theory & Review, 8*(2), 191–206. https://doi.org/10.1111/jftr.12139

Blackstone, A. (2019). *Childfree by choice: The movement redefining family and creating a new age of independence.* Dutton.

Blair, K. L., & Hoskin, R. A. (2019). Transgender exclusion from the world of dating: Patterns of acceptance and rejection of hypothetical trans dating partners as a function of sexual and gender identity. *Journal of Social and Personal Relationships, 36*(7), 2074–2095. https://doi.org/10.1177/0265407518779139

Blue, V. J., & Zucchino, D. (2021, September 20). A harsh new reality for Afghan women and girls in Taliban-run schools. *The New York Times.* https://www.nytimes.com/2021/09/20/world/asia/afghan-girls-schools-taliban.html

Bowleg, L. (2008). When Black + lesbian + woman ≠ Black lesbian woman: The methodological challenges of qualitative and quantitative intersectionality research. *Sex Roles, 59*(5–6), 312–325. https://doi.org/10.1007/slll99-008-9400-z

Breshears, D., & Lubbe-De Beer, C. (2016). Same-sex parented families' negotiation of minority social identity in South Africa. *Journal of GLBT Family Studies, 12*(4), 346–364. https://doi.org/10/1080/1550428X.2015.1080134

Burton, L. M., Bonilla-Silva, E., Ray, V., Buckelew, R., & Freeman, E. H. (2010). Critical race theories, Colorism, and the decade's research on families of color. *Journal of Marriage and Family, 72*(3), 440–459. https://doi.org/10.111l/j.1741-3737.2010.00712.x

Butler, J. (2004). *Undoing gender.* Routledge.

Chamberlain, P. (2017). *The feminist fourth wave: Affective temporality.* Palgrave.

Christensen, M. C. (2015). New tools: Young feminism in the rural west. *Feminism and Psychology, 25*(1), 45–49. https://doi.org/10.1177/0959353514565219

Collins, P. H. (1990). *Black feminist thought: Knowledge, consciousness, and the politics of empowerment.* Unwin Hyman.

Collins, P. H. (2005). *Black sexual politics: African Americans, gender, and the new racism.* Routledge.

Collins, P. H. (2015). Intersectionality's definitional dilemmas. *Annual Review of Sociology, 41*(1), 1–20. https://doi.org/10.1146/annurev-soc-073014-112142

Collins, P. H. (2019). *Intersectionality as critical social theory.* Duke University Press.

Collins, P. H., & Bilge, S. (2016). *Intersectionality.* Polity.

Combahee River Collective (1982). The Combahee River Collective statement, 1977. In G. T. Hull, P. B. Scott, & B. Smith (Eds.), *All the women are White, all the Blacks are men, but some of us are brave: Black women's studies* (pp. 13–22). Feminist Press.

Connell, R. W., & Messerschmidt, J. W. (2005). Hegemonic masculinity: Rethinking the concept. *Gender & Society, 19*(6), 829–859. https://doi.org/10.1177/0891243205278639

Coontz, S. (2011). *A strange stirring: The Feminine Mystique and American women at the dawn of the 1960s.* Basic Books.

Crenshaw, K. (1989). Demarginalizing the intersection of race and sex: A Black feminist critique of antidiscrimination doctrine, feminist theory and antiracist politics. *University of Chicago Legal Forum, 1989*(1), Article 8. https://chicagounbound.uchicago.edu/uclf/vol1989/iss1/8

Crenshaw, K. (1991). Mapping the margins: Intersectionality, identity politics, and violence against women of color. *Stanford Law Review, 43,* 1241–1299. https://doi.org/10.2307/1229039

de Beauvoir, S. (2011). *The second sex* (C. Borde & S. Malovany-Chevallier, Trans.). Vintage. (Original work published 1949)

De Reus, L., Few, A. L., & Blume, L. B. (2005). Multicultural and critical race feminisms: Theorizing families in the third wave. In V. L. Bengtson, A. C. Acock, K. R. Allen, P. Dilworth-Anderson, & D. M. Klein (Eds.), *Sourcebook of family theory and research* (pp. 447–468). SAGE Publications.

Diamond, L. M. (2020). Gender fluidity and nonbinary gender identities among children and adolescents. *Child Development Perspectives, 14*(2), 110–115. https://doi.org/10.1111/cdep.12366

Dill, B. T. (1988). Our mothers' grief: Racial ethnic women and the maintenance of families. *Journal of Family History, 13*(4), 415–431. https://doi.org/10.1177/03631990881300125

Dodson, L., & Schmalzbauer, L. (2005). Poor mothers and habits of hiding: Participatory methods in poverty research. *Journal of Marriage and Family, 67*(4), 949–959. https://doi.org/10.1111/j.1741-3737.2005.00186.x

Dow, D. M. (2016). Integrated motherhood: Beyond hegemonic ideologies of motherhood. *Journal of Marriage and Family, 78*(1), 180–196. https://doi.org/10.1111/jomf.12264

Elam, D., & Wiegman, R. (1995). Contingencies. In D. Elam & R. Wiegman (Eds.), *Feminism beside itself* (pp. 1–8). Routledge.

Ferguson, K. (2017). Feminist theory today. *Annual Review of Political Science, 20*(1), 269–286. https://doi.org/10.1146/annurev-polisci-052715-111648

Ferree, M. M. (1990). Beyond separate spheres: Feminism and family research. *Journal of Marriage and the Family, 52*(4), 866–884. https://doi.org/10.2307/353307

Ferree, M. M. (2010). Filling the glass: Gender perspectives on families. *Journal of Marriage and Family, 72*(3), 420–439. https://doi.org/10.1111/j.1741-3737.2010.00711.x

Few-Demo, A. L. (2014). Intersectionality as the "new" critical approach in feminist family studies: Evolving racial/ethnic feminisms and critical race theories. *Journal of Family Theory & Review, 6*(2), 169–183. https://doi.org/10.1111/jftr.12039

Few-Demo, A. L., & Allen, K. R. (2020). Gender, feminist, and intersectional perspectives on families: A decade in review. *Journal of Marriage and Family, 82*(1), 326–345. https://doi.org/10.1111/jomf.12638

Few-Demo, A. L., Hunter, A. G., & Muruthi, B. A. (2022). Intersectionality theory: A critical theory pushing family science forward. In K. Adamsons, A. L. Few-Demo, C. Proulx, & K. Roy (Eds.), *Sourcebook of family theories and methodologies.* Springer.

Freedman, E. B. (2002). *No turning back: The history of feminism and the future of women.* Ballantine.

Friedan, B. (1963). *The feminine mystique.* Dell.

Gabb, J. (2018). Unsettling lesbian motherhood: Critical reflections over a generation (1990–2015). *Sexualities, 21*(7), 1002–1020. https://doi.org/10.1177/1363460717718510

Glenn, E. N. (1985). Racial ethnic women's labor: The intersection of race, gender and class oppression. *Review of Radical Political Economics, 17*(3), 86–109. https://doi.org/10.1177/048661348501700306

Goldberg, A. E., Allen, K. R., & Carroll, M. (2020). "We don't exactly fit in, but we can't opt out": Gay fathers' experiences navigating parent communities in schools. *Journal of Marriage and Family, 82*(5), 1655–1676. https://doi.org/10.1111/jomf.12695

Hartmann, H. (1981). The family as the locus of gender, class, and political struggle: The example of housework. *Signs, 6*(3), 366–394. https://www.jstor.org/stable/3173752

Haselschwerdt, M. L., & Hardesty, J. L. (2017). Managing secrecy and disclosure of domestic violence in affluent communities. *Journal of Marriage and Family, 79*(2), 556–570. https://doi.org/10.1111/jomf.12345

hooks, b. (1994). *Teaching to transgress: Education as the practice of freedom.* Routledge.

Hoskin, R. A. (2021). Can femme be theory? Exploring the epistemological and methodological possibilities of femme. *Journal of Lesbian Studies, 25*(1), 1–17. https://doi.org/10.1080/10894160.2019.1702288

Jackson, S. J., Bailey, M., & Welles, B. F. (2020). *#HashtagActivism: Networks of race and gender justice.* MIT Press.

Jain, R. (2021). *Afghan women forced from banking jobs as Taliban take control.* Reuters. https://www.reuters.com/world/asia-pacific/afghan-women-bankers-forced-roles-taliban-takes-control-2021-08-13/?fbclid=IwAR3UBrKPaT5_UszLl-jV-UAwlc-j68oIVVQvnmdB9eFUZjyYlRGcyoQaYMWk

James-Hawkins, L., Al-Attar, G., & Yount, K. M. (2021). Young adult women's aspirations for education and career in Qatar: Active resistance to gendered power. *Sex Roles, 85*(5–6), 271–286. https://doi.org/10.1007/s11199-020-01220-3

Jozkowski, K. N., & Wiersma-Mosley, J. D. (2017). The Greek system: How gender inequality and class privilege perpetuate rape culture. *Family Relations, 66*(1), 89–103. https://doi.org/10.1111/fare.12229

Komter, A. (1989). Hidden power in marriage. *Gender & Society, 3*(2), 187–216. https://doi.org/10.1177/089124389003002003

Lee, M. (2021). Feminist scholarship on the global digital divide: A critique of international organizations and information companies. In D. Y. Jin (Ed.), *The Routledge handbook of digital media and globalization* (pp. 66–76). Routledge.

Lemert, C. (2008). Charlotte Perkins Gilman. In G. Ritzer (Ed.), *The Blackwell companion to major classical social theorists* (pp. 267–289). Blackwell.

Lewis, E. A. (2009). Group- versus individual-based intersectionality and praxis in feminist and womynist research foundations. In S. A. Lloyd, A. L. Few, & K. R. Allen (Eds.), *Handbook of feminist family studies* (pp. 304–315). SAGE Publications.

Lewis, R., & Marine, S. (2015). Weaving a tapestry, compassionately: Toward an understand of young women's feminisms. *Feminist Formations, 27*(1), 118–140. https://doi.org/10.1353/ff.2015.0002

Liong, M. (2017). Sacrifice for the family: Representation and practice of stay-at-home fathers in the intersection of masculinity and class in Hong Kong. *Journal of Gender Studies, 26*(4), 402–417. https://doi.org/10.1080/09589236.2015.1111200

Lopata, H. Z. (1971). *Occupation: Housewife.* Greenwood Press.

Lorber, J. (2012). *Gender inequality: Feminist theories and politics* (5th ed.). Oxford University Press.

Lorde, A. (1984). *Sister outsider: Essays and speeches.* Crossing Press.

MacTavish, K. A. (2007). The wrong side of the tracks: Social inequality and mobile home park residence. *Community Development, 38*(1), 74–91. https://doi.org/10.1080/15575330709490186

Magalhães, S. I., & Cerqueira, C. (2015). Our place in history: Young feminists at the margins. *Feminism and Psychology, 25*(1), 39–44. https://doi.org/10.1177/0959353514563093

Mahler, S. J., Chaudhuri, M., & Patil, V. (2015). Scaling intersectionality: Advancing feminist analysis of transnational families. *Sex Roles, 73*(3-4), 100–112. https://doi.org/10.1007/si1199-015-0506-9

McCall, L. (2005). The complexity of intersectionality. *Signs, 30*(3), 1771–1800. https://doi.org/10.1086/426800

McCormick-Huhn, K., Warner, L. R., Settles, I. H., & Shields, S. A. (2019). What if psychology took intersectionality seriously? Changing how psychologists think about participants. *Psychology of Women Quarterly, 43*(4), 445–456. https://doi.org/10.1177/0361684319866430

McIntosh, P. (2020). *On privilege, fraudulence, and teaching as learning: Selected essays 1981–2019.* Taylor & Francis.

Mitchell, J. (1971). *Woman's estate.* Pantheon.

Morgan, R. (1970). *Sisterhood is powerful.* Random House.

Naples, N. A. (2013). Sustaining democracy: Localization, globalization and feminist praxis. *Sociological Forum, 28*(4), 657–681. https://doi.org/10.1111/socf.12054

Nelson, M. K. (2006). Single mothers "do" family. *Journal of Marriage and Family, 68*(4), 781–795. https://doi.org/10.1111/j.1741-3737.2006.00292.x

Oakley, A. (1974). *The sociology of housework.* Martin Robertson.

Okin, S. M. (1989). *Justice, gender and the family.* Basic Books.

Osmond, M. W., & Thorne, B. (1993). Feminist theories. In P. G. Boss, W. J. Doherty, R. LaRossa, W. R. Schumm, & S. K. Steinmetz (Eds.), *Sourcebook of family theories and methods* (pp. 591–623). Plenum.

Oswald, R. F., Blume, L.B., & Marks, S. R. (2005). Decentering heteronormativity: A model for family studies. In V. L. Bengtson, A. C. Acock, K. R. Allen, P. Dilworth-Anderson, & D. M. Klein (Eds.), *Sourcebook of family theory and research* (pp. 143–165). SAGE Publications.

Oswald, R. F., Kuvalanka, K. A., Blume, L. B., & Berkowitz, D. (2009). Queering "The Family". In S. A. Lloyd, A. L. Few, & K. R. Allen (Eds.), *Handbook of feminist family studies* (pp. 43–55). SAGE Publications.

Pfeffer, C. A. (2017). *Queering families: The postmodern partnerships of cisgender women and transgender men.* Oxford University Press.

Plank, L. (2019). *For the love of men: From toxic to a more mindful masculinity.* St. Martin's Press.

Porter, T. (2016). *Breaking out of the "man box": The next generation of manhood.* Skyhorse.

Reger, J. (2017). Finding a place in history: The discursive legacy of the wave metaphor and contemporary feminism. *Feminist Studies, 43*(1), 193–221. https://www.jstor.org/stable/10.15767/feministstudies.43.1.0193

Rich, A. (1980). Compulsory heterosexuality and lesbian existence. *Signs, 5*(4), 631–660. https://doi.org/10.1086/493756

Risman, B. J. (2004). Gender as a social structure: Theory wrestling with activism. *Gender & Society, 18*(4), 429–450. https://doi.org/10.1177/0891243204265349

Risman, B. J. (2018). *Where the millennials will take us: A new generation wrestles with the gender structure.* Oxford University Press.

Sharp, E. A., & Weaver, S. E. (2015). Feeling like feminist frauds: Theorizing feminist accountability in feminist family studies research in a neoliberal, postfeminist context. *Journal of Family Theory & Review, 7*(3), 299–320. https://doi.org/10.1111/jftr.12080

Slater, J. (2013). Research with dis/abled youth: Taking a critical disability, "critically young" positionality. In K. Runswick-Cole & T. Curran (Eds.), *Disabled children's childhood studies: Critical approaches in a global context* (pp. 180–195). Palgrave.

Snitow, A. (2015). *The feminism of uncertainty: A gender diary.* Duke University Press.

Sollie, D., & Leslie, L. (Eds.). (1994). *Gender, families, and close relationships: Feminist research journeys.* SAGE Publications.

Srinivasan, A. (2021). *The right to sex: Feminism in the twenty-first century.* Macmillan.

Tasker, F., & Lavender-Stott, E. S. (2013). LGBTQ parenting post-heterosexual relationship dissolution. In A. E. Goldberg & K. R. Allen (Eds.), *LGBTQ-parent families: Innovations in research and implications for practice* (2nd ed., pp. 3–23). Springer.

Thompson, L., & Walker, A. J. (1995). The place of feminism in family *studies. Journal of Marriage and the Family, 57*(4), 847–865. https://doi.org/10.2307/353407

Thorne, B. (1982). Feminist rethinking of the family: An overview. In B. Thorne with M. Yalom (Eds.), *Rethinking the family: Some feminist questions* (pp. 1–24). Longman.

Trask, B. S. (2014). *Women, work, and globalization: Challenges and opportunities*. Routledge.

van Eeden-Moorefield, B., & Proulx, C. M. (2009). Doing feminist research on gay men in cyberspace. In S. A. Lloyd, A. L. Few, & K. R. Allen (Eds.), *Handbook of feminist family studies* (pp. 220–233). SAGE Publications.

Waismel-Manor, R., Wasserman, V., & Shamir-Balderman, O. (2021). No room of her own: Married couples' negotiation of workspace at home during COVID-19. *Sex Roles, 85*(11–12), 636–649. https://doi.org/10.1007/s11199-021-01246-1

Walker, A. (1983). *In search of our mothers' gardens: Womanist prose*. Harvest.

Walker, A. J. (1999). Gender and family relationships. In M. Sussman, S. K. Steinmetz, & G. W. Peterson (Eds.), *Handbook of marriage and the family* (2nd ed., pp. 439–474). Plenum.

Walker, A. J. (2009). A feminist critique of family studies. In S. A. Lloyd, A. L. Few, & K. R. Allen (Eds.), *Handbook of feminist family studies* (pp. 18–27). SAGE Publications.

Walker, A. J., & Thompson, L. (1984). Feminism and family studies. *Journal of Family Issues, 5*(4), 545–570. https://doi.org/10.1177/019251384005004010

Webb, J. (2021). Afghan refugees 'particularly vulnerable' to human trafficking, DoD IG says. *Military Times*. https://www.militarytimes.com/news/pentagon-congress/2021/09/24/afghan-refugees-particularly-vulnerable-to-human-trafficking-dod-ig-says/

Weiser, D. A., Lieway, M., Brown, R. D., Shrout, M. R., Russell, K. N., Weigel, D. J., & Evans, W. P. (2021). Parent communication about sexual and relationship violence: Promoting healthy relationships or reinforcing gender stereotypes. *Family Relations, 71*(1), 181–200. https://doi.org/10.1111/fare.12598

West, C., & Zimmerman, D. H. (1987). Doing gender. *Gender & Society, 1*(2), 125–151. https://doi.org/10.1177/0891243287001002002

Wills, J. B., & Risman, B. J. (2006). The visibility of feminist thought in family studies. *Journal of Marriage and Family, 68*(3), 690–700. https://doi.org/10.1111/j.1741-3737.2006. 00283.x

Wing, A. K. (2003). Introduction. In A. K. Wing (Ed.), *Critical race feminism: A reader* (pp. 1–19). New York University Press.

Image Credits

Life Course Theory

D o your grades as a high school student really matter when you are 35 years old? Does being an only child impact your life differently when you are 6 years old compared to when you are 60? Does the place where and age at which you lose your virginity play a role in how you experience intimacy and family life when you are age 46? How about age 86?

Questions about how time and culture influence families have plagued social scientists for decades. Life course theory is an exciting integrative theory because with it researchers have developed methods to track the influence of both culture and change over time. Now, we can begin to answer some of these complex questions. For this reason, life course theory is an alternative to functionalist theory (Chapter 2) and family developmental theory (Chapter 5) in that its focus is on the contexts of time, culture, and context. Every family, and every individual, develops within a certain place and time. First, we set the stage for the study of life course theory with a story about the diversity and complexity of family life over time.

Case Study

Carrie is at her computer on the home page of her local community college, trying to decide if she should attempt to finish her degree. She is a 24-year-old cisgender, heterosexual single mother to Baylee, her 3-year-old little girl. They live with Carrie's grandmother in a small town in rural, mountainous Kentucky. Carrie has about two years' worth of college credits from the University of Kentucky, where she had a full scholarship after high school. She dropped out of the university because she was unable to fit in with the other kids there. When she came back home she moved in with her grandmother and mother and got a job at a grocery store, where she met Baylee's father. Since Baylee was born, Carrie's boyfriend has been arrested and sent to prison on drug-related convictions. Later, Carrie's mother was killed in a tragic car accident. Carrie knows the name of her biological father, but he has never been involved in her life in any way. She has some friends but often feels alone and frustrated and wants a different life for Baylee. If it wasn't for her grandmother, Carrie doesn't know what she would do.

BOX 9.1. AT A GLANCE: LIFE COURSE THEORY

- **Life span development:** Human development and aging are lifelong processes.
- **Agency:** Individuals construct their own life course through the choices and actions they take within the opportunities and constraints of history and social circumstance.
- **Time and place:** The life course of individuals is embedded and shaped by the historical times and places they experience over their lifetime.
- **Timing:** The developmental antecedents and consequences of life transitions, events, and behavioral patterns vary according to their timing in a person's life.
- **Transition:** A short life change that can occur in the individual or family life course.
- **Trajectory:** A change that begins when a person transitions into a new role (e.g., becomes a parent) and continues over a substantial period of time, linking behavior in several life stages.
- **Linked lives:** Lives are lived interdependently, and sociohistorical influences are expressed through this network of shared relationships.

What do you notice about Carrie's life course? Who are the important players in her life? How are her experiences linked to theirs? Is Carrie able to make choices that will help her live a life of autonomy and freedom? How does her environment play a role in her life? All these questions point to important principles and assumptions in life course theory, which we describe in Box 9.1.

What Is Life Course Theory?

Life course theory is a theoretical framework researchers use when they want to understand the ways in which time, culture, context, and the interdependence of family relationships influence people's lives. Life course theory is complex, and family scientists can use it in many ways, but a common goal of life course researchers is to look at individual and family development over time and across ever-changing and diverse sociohistorical contexts.

History and Origins

Before the 1960s, research that took into account both time (longitudinal) and social context did not exist in the social sciences (Elder & Giele, 2009). Most survey research was cross sectional, and case studies typically looked at individual lives out of the context of broader society or family life. Then, beginning in the 1960s, with the advent of federal funding in the United States and advanced research methods, social scientists became increasingly interested in ways to capture change over time and change in the context of families and cultures (Elder et al., 2003). For example, Norman Ryder's (1965) concept of **cohort** focused on the ways in which groups of people of a similar age experienced or produced social events. We sometimes also refer to this as a **generation**, such as the baby boom generation (born in the post-World War II era). However, it is important to remember that generation and cohort are two very different things when it comes to life course theory: Generations span more than one decade, and cohorts are smaller, more specific groups who experience a larger social event at a particular point in time. For example, a cohort of individuals born from 1980 to 1985 no doubt experienced the Iraq War differently than a cohort of individuals born from 1960 to 1965. The 1980–1985 birth cohort was likely to have more members serving in the war or have partners in the war, whereas the 1960–1965 cohort was more likely to include parents of Iraq War soldiers. Further, the concept of cohort is a more precise term for measuring change than generation because generation is so loosely connected to historical time (Elder et al., 2003) and often refers to a very wide range of individuals. As we saw in Chapter 8 in the discussion of the generations of feminist activism, the concept of generation is a much less precise term than cohort, both in terms of the number of years it refers to and in terms of its meaning and application.

Because life course theory developed in conjunction with more sophisticated research methods, researchers have been able to benefit from insights from earlier theories, such as symbolic interactionism (Chapter 4) and family developmental theory (Chapter 5). From its very beginning, the life course perspective, as applied to families, emerged from multiple intellectual traditions and disciplines on individual and family development (e.g., human development, family studies, history, psychology, and sociology; see Bengtson & Allen, 1993; Elder, 1981). Early stage models of individual development, particularly Erikson's (1950, 1975) eight stages of psychosocial development that included childhood, adolescence, and young, middle, and late adulthood proposed normative models of individual change, where one stage emerges naturally from the previous stage, like the unfolding of a flower. However, theories of individual development primarily from psychology (e.g., Baltes, 1987; Erikson, 1950) did not emphasize the *family* context of development.

Life course theory also improved on earlier developmental models by showing sociohistorical variations. For example, rather than mutually exclusive gender roles portrayed in the static life cycle models, where women stayed home and cared for families while men went out to work, sociohistorical studies revealed much greater variation than a one-size-fits-all model that we described in Chapter 1 as the Standard North American Family (SNAF) model (Smith, 1993). Think back to the case study from the beginning of this chapter; could we apply the earlier life cycle model to Carrie? Would Erikson's (1950) model of individual development take into account the varying dynamics of Carrie's life? No, an individual perspective on the life cycle would not; life cycle theory, in particular, does not "fit" Carrie's experiences because she is not married and cannot fulfill the expectations of that theory (e.g., traditional gender roles). Life course theory makes it possible to take into account all of the forces guiding Carrie's movement through various life course stages, including her cohort, social class expectations and barriers, and her status as a single mother. A family life course framework is much more flexible in its pairing with perspectives that emphasize a range of diverse ways of experiencing family life and, in particular, that account for the pervasive inequalities that many families experience nationally and globally, without certain privileges associated with race, ethnicity, wealth, gender, and the like (Roy & Settersten, 2022; Trask, 2018).

Life course theory allows us to take a panoramic view when we gather and analyze data; we are able to see the whole picture and how different disciplines (e.g., sociology, psychology, history, family science) can contribute to a more complex understanding of what it is we are studying. Because of this, life course theory has been posited as a theory that is emerging from new historical scholarship that has stressed (a) the complexity of social life, and (b) the continued influence of the past. For example, Elder (1981) noted that early theorizing about American family life relied on oversimplified ideas about change. Although many families might have aspired to the SNAF ideal, only some families, primarily White, middle class families, could afford this arrangement (McGhee, 2021). Likewise, scholars who have developed life course theory realized that rather than creating an overarching grand theory of the family, such as functionalism or conflict theory, they needed a theory that provided concepts both to measure and to understand family complexity and diversity over time (Bengtson & Allen, 1993; Elder, 1981; Hareven, 1978). For example, in his groundbreaking study of individuals who grew up during the Great Depression, Elder (1974) ignited scholarly interest in measuring how social-historical events effect individual and family trajectories over time. Elder traced the impact of relative degrees of economic hardship resulting from different birth cohorts' experiences in the 1930s from their childhood to middle-age years, examining the impact on their family relationships, careers, and other life course features. Over time, scholars expanded life course analysis to directly address the interdependence of individuals' lives in the family context, and most importantly by turning to those formerly left out of normative family structure models (Roy & Settersten, 2022).

Assumptions of Life Course Theory

Life course theory is built around the ideas of time, context, interdependence, and agency (Demo et al., 2005). One of the major assumptions in life course theory is that there are **multiple timeclocks** affecting families (Bengtson & Allen, 1993). Figure 9.1 provides an illustration of timeclocks. One timeclock is individual time, or the emphasis on the biological and psychological development of particular individuals. A second timeclock is family time, or an emphasis on the familial roles and trajectories in family systems. A third timeclock is historical time, or an emphasis on the events and changes particular birth cohorts (e.g., Baby Boomers or Gen X) experience together. Notice that Carrie's individual timeclock for becoming a mother and attending college is different from the norm for middle-class young adults, who are expected to complete their studies, then marry, and then have children. Because she has a strong family identity, her individual and family timeclocks are closely interlinked. Carrie did not find much satisfaction in having a full scholarship to a major university. She wanted to be close to her family and add to it by finding a partner and having her own children. As for historical time, Carrie is a part of a cohort from rural America, where it is becoming increasingly normative for young people to be involved in the drug trade to make extra money, which can lead to devastating results (Welch, 2020). Where, once, farming and coal mining were enough to sustain families of Carrie's parents' and grandparents' generations, changes in the environment and economy have severely limited her generation's prospects for supporting a family.

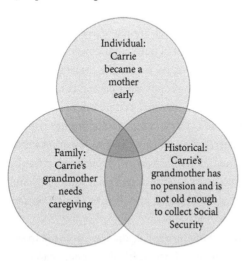

FIGURE 9.1. Individual, Family, and Historical Timeclocks

Just as there are multiple timeclocks of development, there are also **multiple social contexts** (Bengtson & Allen, 1993). Some scholars refer to this as the social ecology of families, a similar idea to the ones covered in Chapter 10 when we discuss family ecological theory. Social contexts refer to things such as one's social position in terms of gender, race, class, age, sexual orientation, and so on. Carrie is a young, able-bodied, heterosexual, working-class, White mother. In her own rural culture, Carrie is somewhat privileged. She does not have much money, but she has status as a mother and as a woman attached to a man (despite the fact that he is incarcerated). In both her local culture and the larger U.S. culture, she has status as someone who is White, young, and able-bodied. However, in other contexts, Carrie may face stigma and be categorized as a "poor, uneducated, unmarried mother."

A third assumption, similar to symbolic interactionist theory (Chapter 4), is that human beings create meaning within social contexts (Bengtson & Allen, 1993). That is, a fundamental aspect of being human is that we attribute meaning to events in our lives. **Meaning-making** may happen at an individual level, but culture plays a crucial role. Consider, for example, that the meaning attributed to and the rituals marking important life events, such as marriage, death, and birth, typically varies between cultures. In Carrie's case, maintaining her family identity is the most important factor in how she makes meaning about her life.

Key Concepts

Life course theory utilizes many concepts to guide both qualitative and quantitative research on families. We review seven of the main concepts used in this theory: (a) timing, (b) social context, (c) linked lives, (d) transitions and turning points, (e) trajectories and pathways, (f) agency, and (g) generations. Note that the concepts are interrelated and often overlap because individual and family lives, after all, are intertwined. They are also dynamic, in that they must change and adapt to social and historic forces. As we define each of the concepts, we apply them to the case study from the beginning of the chapter to help illustrate the tenets of life course theory.

Timing

Timing refers to the temporal distinctions of individual, generational, and sociohistorical time that segment or divide up the life course. Each individual family member has their own unique psychological and physical development. Besides this view of time, they also hold a certain position in the family based on their time of entry into it. That is, each member belongs to a generation in the family, such as the oldest generation, the middle generation, or the youngest generation. Broadening the scope, each individual is also born into a unique sociohistorical context, or as part of a cohort. Think back to Carrie from earlier in the chapter; Carrie is a member of a cohort that is *expected* to go to college. Her parents and grandparents, on the other hand, came of age in a time when they could secure well-paying jobs without a bachelor's degree. In contrast, Carrie's goal of becoming a manager at the local bank necessitates a college degree. Looking even further down the road, her daughter Baylee may grow up in a time when a master's degree is a required credential for most well-paying jobs. Timing also refers to historical events that can impact life course transitions: Carrie is reconsidering getting her bachelor's degree during an economic recession, which sent many who were left unemployed back to college.

In life course theory, timing also refers to the degree to which people experience major life events as expected, or whether they are "on time" or "off time." When we say that a couple's life turned out as expected, we are referring to many ways of timing as well as historical period. For example, in 1950, it was expected that couples would get married fairly soon after high school. Today, however, it is expected that couples wait until they are finished with not only college but sometimes graduate school before they marry. After that, they are expected to get stable jobs before they have children; therefore, some may not marry or have children until well into their thirties. And for many others, marriage is out of the question, and they may never experience this particular transition (Cherlin, 2020). In 1950, this would have been considered "off-time."

Social Contexts of Development

As noted previously, social contexts refer to the broadest level of social institutions that shape people's opportunities and relationships. The term "social institutions" can have a variety of meanings, but it typically refers to entities such as schools, families, religious groups, medical facilities, the economic system, the media, the prison system, and the military. Laws and cultural norms govern social institutions. This is where social location comes into play: There are norms and laws that regulate the behavior of individuals on the basis of their race, class, gender, sexual orientation, age, and so forth. For example, as we describe in Chapter 13 in the discussion of queer theory, in the United States people of the same sex were unable to legally marry in all 50 states until federal legislation passed in 2015 after the social context began changing.

Related is the idea of social pathways (Elder et al., 2003). Social pathways develop through the intersection of "historical forces" and "social institutions." Think about Carrie's daughter, Baylee. She is being raised in a historical context in which same-sex relationships are increasingly accepted (the cultural norm), which has led to legalizing same-sex marriage (the laws that govern us). Because of these changing historical forces, Baylee will most likely have a variety of pathways in front of her as she moves through adolescence into young adulthood. She may have several friends and classmates who are nonbinary, queer, gay, lesbian, bisexual, or transgender. She may see several queer couples at her high school prom and be invited to just as many gay or lesbian weddings as heterosexual weddings when she is a young adult. Those pathways—gays' and lesbians' legal rights to marry—are opened up because historical forces shifted. Baylee's life course will consist of varying pathways because norms and laws change over time. Therefore, new pathways open with changes in social institutions, particularly with changes in laws and governmental policies.

Linked Lives

The concept of **linked lives** refers to the way in which significant others' lives are mutually interlocking (Bengtson & Allen, 1993; Elder et al., 2003). When something happens to one member of the family, the lives of other family members are also changed. For example, when Carrie's mother died in the car accident, both Carrie's life and her grandmother's life were affected in significant ways. Carrie lost her mother, and her grandmother lost her adult child. These losses changed the ways in which the two women relate to one another. Carrie's grandmother took on the mothering role, just as Carrie provided the kind of help an adult daughter would give an aging mother.

There is a saying that parents never stop worrying about their children, and research on relationships between aging parents and adult children bears that out. How one's children turn out once they are grown is a source of stress to parents, particularly if the adult children's lives are marked by substance abuse, legal trouble, lack of educational and economic success, and other nonnormative experiences (Greenfield & Marks, 2006). Interestingly, recent research reveals new complexities in the parent–child relationship in adulthood. In one study, researchers found that older mothers can and do favor their adult children who committed deviant acts earlier in life (Kincaid et al., 2021). This return to favoritism has to do with how the once-deviant adult children emphasize familism (having a family orientation) after chaotic, rebellious behavior and also how these children experience increased reliance on their mothers, which, in turn, strengthens the mother–child dynamic. In another study, adult children of LGBTQ+ parents expressed the pressure to present themselves as well-adjusted to legitimate their queer family experiences (Garwood & Lewis, 2019). Taken together, much research has highlighted the importance of the quality and meaning of relationships adult children have on parental well-being, lending credence to the analysis of linked lives in families.

Transitions and Turning Points

Transitions and turning points typically involve a short life change in identity as well as circumstances and can occur at both the individual and family level (Bengtson & Allen, 1993). Important individual transitions would include the transition of Carrie taking on the role of mother. Carrie became a mother after she left college, transitioning away from the role of student and into the role of wage earner and then mother. This influences her view of herself; she no longer is only responsible for just her own needs. She has a commitment to provide for her daughter and a commitment to her place of employment to be able to keep her job. As you might imagine, this transition can be difficult for women who are not necessarily expecting to enter the role of mother, and the transition is unexpected. A change in identity may be a more difficult transition than the actual work involved. When Carrie had Baylee, her normal daily routines changed, but her view of herself changed even more. Her body changed after pregnancy and childbirth, making her feel like she is no longer young and feminine. Instead of going out at night with her friends, she is stuck at home with her daughter. She cannot spend extra money on herself for new clothes; any extra income goes straight to diapers, formula, and baby clothes. Her identity change is much more difficult than the changes in her daily routine.

Typical **family transitions** involve a change in the family system, such as entry into school, marriage, parenthood, launching, and widowhood—these are normative family life cycle events that we discussed in Chapter 5 (Duvall, 1957; Hill & Rodgers, 1964). **Turning points** are a type of transition. Typically they are very personal and may not be recognized by an outsider as particularly significant. For instance, consider Carrie's decision to go to college. This decision was a turning point in her relationships with her family of origin, none of whom had gone on past high school. The values she developed as a young adult in the social context of college set her apart from her siblings and her parents. In another example, coming out as a lesbian, gay, bisexual, nonbinary, or transgender person also can be seen as both a normative transition and a turning point. It may be that, in certain contexts, a person first has to come out to themselves (Brumbaugh-Johnson & Hull, 2019; Savin-Williams, 2001). Think about Carrie's small hometown in rural Kentucky; we could surmise that if one of her male classmates "came out" in a fairly conservative area, he might not only have to first become aware of his sexual orientation, but he would also most likely struggle with self-acceptance in a culture that can be hostile to gay men. On the other hand, coming out to others is a more normative transition for people in less conservative areas and, undoubtedly, as legal codes are changing (e.g., marriage equality for same-sex couples) and the process becomes more socially scripted on television and in the news media (see The Trevor Project, 2019).

Trajectories and Pathways

From each new transition emerges a **trajectory** defined as the continuity of roles and identities. Trajectories are marked by change over a substantial time period in which two or more life stages are intertwined (Bengtson & Allen, 1993). For example, when Carrie had Baylee, she began her trajectory as a mother. Trajectories continue throughout our lives. **Social pathways** are conceptually similar but typically have longer durations and are made up of a confluence of trajectories. That is, trajectories flow into one another, creating pathways, just as a river is made up of and shaped by streams along a landscape (see Figure 9.2).

Whereas trajectories are defined by how they begin (i.e., with a transition into a particular role, such as becoming a spouse or a parent), pathways are defined by an outcome (e.g., mental health in late life or sexual decision-making in early adulthood). For example, to illustrate how trajectories form a particular social pathway, the principle of cumulative (dis)advantage (CDA) describes how experiences in early life persist across one's lifetime (Dannefer, 2020; Gilligan et al., 2018; Willson et al., 2007). When considering how some people end up in old age with multiple health problems and relatively impoverished, while others come to late life knowledgeable about and able to afford preventive health practices, we see that multiple trajectories over the course of one's

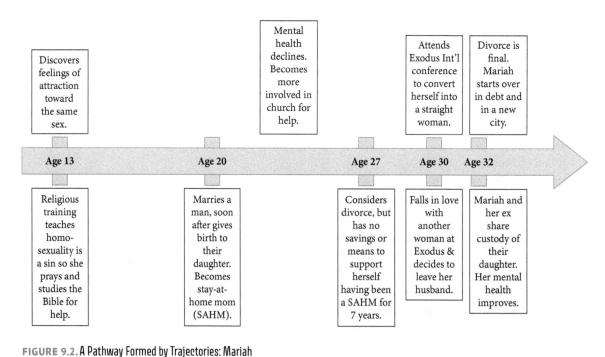

FIGURE 9.2. A Pathway Formed by Trajectories: Mariah

life have built a pathway of **cumulative disadvantage or advantage** (O'Rand, 2002). Sociologist Robert Merton (1988) first described cumulative disadvantage as "the ways in which initial comparative advantage of trained capacity, structural location, and available resources make for successive increments of advantage such that the gaps between the haves and the have-nots ... widen" (p. 606). An example can be seen in Figure 9.2, where Mariah does not accumulate advantage during her marriage, which leaves her restricted when she decides she can no longer stay married. She ends up in debt and without any recent employment history.

In other words, characteristics such as race, wealth, health, and social status intersect, resulting in either accumulated advantage or disadvantage over time. For example, Umberson (2017) found that racial disparities are evident in the loss of family ties, where Black families are more likely than White families to experience the death of a child, sibling, parent, or spouse and that these losses accumulate over the life course, thereby impacting health and well-being. In another example, educational trajectories that begin in early childhood are an obvious confluent factor that shapes opportunities throughout the life course (Serido et al., 2020). Getting a high school degree is necessary to enter college; obtaining a college degree increases one's earning potential as an adult. Still another example can be seen using Carrie's circumstances; right now, she is a single mom without a college degree. She is not a homeowner, so she is not building capital to hand down to her daughter like she would if she lived in her own home. Her opportunity to move up the social class ladder is limited by this lack of capital and savings; if she decides to go back to school to finish her degree, she will accumulate student loan debt at the cost of increasing her earning potential with a college degree. Additionally, she will have to find childcare for Baylee, so she can go to classes while she continues to work to pay bills. The likelihood that Carrie accumulates disadvantage is higher than it would be for one of her peers coming from a different social class background; that is, someone whose parents are paying for college with an inheritance or savings, who plan on helping their child buy their first home and car. This person would be accumulating *advantage* instead of disadvantage.

It is important to keep in mind that cumulative disadvantage or advantage (CDA) is a complex process; on the surface, it appears to be an individualistic problem, as expressed in the adage "the poor get poorer" and "the rich get richer" (Alexander et al., 2001), when in reality, larger, structural forces are at play. What this means is that CDA takes into account the fact that, for example, every choice we make over our life course is tempered by the choices available to us. Carrie's choice to stop attending college and have a baby before both marriage and a steady career is complicated; she grew up in a part of the country where it was not that uncommon to have children earlier than the national average. Taken together, it would be simple to blame Carrie, the individual, for her disadvantages. However, the timing of the series of events is important; she dropped out of college because she did not fit in with her peers. This is probably due to the fact that she grew up in a rural part of Kentucky, where education levels are below the national average (U.S. Census Bureau, 2019). We also do not know if she intended to get pregnant or if it was accidental. However, research suggests that some women in dire circumstances choose to get pregnant, so they can turn their lives around and have something to live for (Cox et al., 2021; Edin & Kefalas, 2011). In addition, two very important life course events occurred completely out of Carrie's control: the tragic death of her mother and the incarceration of her baby's father. To an outsider, Carrie's life course and accumulated disadvantage may appear like an individual-level problem of making the wrong choices. However, CDA would suggest that there are more complex factors contributing to Carrie's trajectories in life.

Another example of the relationship between trajectories and pathways is Carpenter's (2010) theory of gendered sexuality over the life course. Carpenter argued that the intertwining of sexual and gender trajectories creates pathways of gendered sexuality and explains variation in sexual agency over the life course. One example Carpenter gave is how the transition of virginity loss or, conversely, involuntary celibacy on people's sexual trajectory is linked with people's gender trajectory. Depending on their gender trajectory, Carpenter found that the young people she interviewed may see virginity loss in terms of a gift, a stigma, or a normative transition toward adulthood. Furthermore, people's virginity loss experience shaped their future sexual decision-making, showing that earlier life course decisions have a cumulative effect on later life course experiences. More recent research has utilized Carpenter's framework by examining how sexuality is perceived as part of a qualitative study of 23 older adults living in the Czech Republic. Participants indicated that events earlier in life undoubtedly had an impact on sexuality, relationship functioning, and the accumulation of disadvantageous experiences later in life, such as the fear of loneliness in the absence of a sexual partner (Ševčíková & Sedláková, 2020).

Agency

In life course theory, **agency** is a complex social-psychological process that goes beyond "a vague sense of human freedom or individual volition" (Hitlin & Elder, 2007, p. 171). Although it has been difficult for scholars to define, agency generally refers to one's ability and desire to make choices within the constraints of social institutions. Agency can be thought of as "purposive, directed action" (Wong, 2018, p. 126).

Life course theorists have said that early social and historical scholarship was focused too much on the structured nature of social life. That is, families were thought to be determined by social structures, such as economic and legal constraints. In this view, it was assumed that family life in the past was relatively stable because divorce was not granted except in extreme circumstances. In contrast, Elder (1981) stated that newer historical scholarship positioned families as agents, that is, "actors in structured circumstance" (p. 494). In this view, a new question posed by life course theory is, given that divorce was unavailable for most people (structured circumstance), how did couples (actors with agency) deal with marital conflict, betrayal, and abuse while staying married?

Consider all the choices Carrie has made and will make over the years. Will she finish college and increase her earning potential? Will she marry and have other children? Will she have to care for her grandmother in the near future? Although broader social structures channel the kinds of choices individuals can make, agency means we do have some control over the direction our lives will take (Hitlin & Elder, 2007). Thus, we do not simply follow societal expectations, we are also empowered to make choices on our own behalf, despite the constraints that society imposes (Connidis, 2020). The most important time for exercising agency is at the fork in the road of life—the transition point. Carrie, for example, in considering the community college courses she might take to finish her degree, is in the process of exercising agency. The direction she decides to take regarding her education is in part dependent on how she envisions her future: How does she make meaning of the difference a college education will bring in her life and in the lives of those she cares about?

Generations

One of the advantages of using life course theory is the ability to analyze how different generations of individuals experience life course events (Fingerman et al., 2020). Though researchers have not established universally agreed-upon date cutoffs, there are general characteristics that define each generation. These characteristics are based on similarities in experience and context because members of specific generations move through the life course during similar historical time frames. The Pew Research Center (2015) identified four generations with a rough estimate of the span of birth years, the Silent Generation (1925–1945), Baby Boomers (1946–1964), Generation X (1965–1980), and Millennials (1981–1997), and indicated major social, historical, and technological events associated with each generation. For example, the Millennial Generation (born in the last two decades of the 20th century) experienced adolescence and young adulthood with unprecedented access to technologies like iPhones, YouTube, Facebook, and text messaging. This access to technology and social media fundamentally changed how this generation learned how to communicate—with friends, family, and society in general. Therefore, the combination of generational membership coincides with period, or historical time, to create differential life course experiences.

Understanding generational differences is important to the study of family; after all, members of one generation typically raise members of an entirely different generation. Baby Boomers raised Gen Xers, and Gen Xers raised Millennials. Considering these generational differences is useful when explaining intrafamily dynamics as well as issues of linked lives, timeclocks, pathways, and trajectories. The different generations, as currently defined (and note that the years may vary depending upon the source), include the following characteristics.

First, the *Silent Generation*, born roughly between 1925 and 1945, emphasizes duty, sacrifice, and loyalty to family and work. They are called "silent" because they tend to be quieter and less rebellious than the Baby Boomers. Further, they are not discussed as much, when compared to other generations (Deal, 2007). For the most part, members of this generation experienced family life as male-dominated, with the father as the head of the household, and the mother as a domesticated, stay-at-home parent (as characterized by family developmental theory; see Chapter 5). They have great faith in America's institutions (Deal, 2007), view quality over quantity, and tend to willingly follow rules.

Second, members of the *Baby Boom Generation*, born between 1946 and 1964, are referred to as "the baby boomers" because of their sheer size—77 million. They were raised by parents who largely subscribed to Dr. Spock's approach to parenting. Dr. Benjamin Spock was a pediatrician who wrote a best-selling book on baby and childcare (first published in 1946, with many subsequent revised editions), which promoted a more flexible and affectionate style of parenting. His techniques were not critiqued heavily until the 1970s, for allegedly promoting instant gratification. Interestingly, the Baby Boomers are sometimes referred to as one of the first "me" generations because cultural trends of the time stressed individuality and developing into a more "whole" person (Strauss & Howe, 1997). Formative events for this generation included the Civil Rights Movement, the assassinations of John F. 7Kennedy and Martin Luther King, Jr., the Vietnam War, the Woodstock festival, the Women's Liberation Movement, and the Gay Liberation Movement.

Third, members of *Generation X*, born roughly between 1965 and 1980, are referred to as "latch-key kids" because their mothers went back to work in such large numbers, leaving them home alone after school until their parents came home from work. As children, Gen Xers experienced divorce and blended families in unprecedented numbers. This generation tends to be very family-oriented, highly educated, and skeptical of social institutions (Miller, 2011). As parents, they are very involved in their children's lives and have high expectations for their future. They are likely contributing to the "helicopter parenting" trend identified in the early 21st century, where parents "hover" too much in their children's lives (LeMoyne & Buchanan, 2011).

BOX 9.2. LIFE COURSE THEORY IN MODERN CULTURE: *DOWNTON ABBEY*

Image 9.1. A Scene From *Downton Abbey: A New Era,* 2022

The stories of the Crawley family were first featured in a television series and later in two films (*Downtown Abbey* in 2019 and *Downtown Abbey: A New Era* in 2022). The stories are centered on an aristocratic British family and set in the early 1900s. Here we describe the relationships between several main characters and how we can apply concepts from life course theory to the show.

Violet Crawley, Dowager Countess of Grantham, is one of the show's matriarchal characters. She is the grandmother of the three Crawley daughters and tends to have a very stoic attitude, reminiscent of tradition and honor. She often clashes views with another matriarchal character in the show, Isobel Crawley, connected to Violet by the marriage of Violet's granddaughter, Mary, and Isobel's son, Matthew (a distant cousin and the unexpected heir presumptive to Lord Grantham). Even though Matthew died in the television show, the two women remained connected through family gatherings and a shared great-grandson/grandson. Isobel was a trained nurse, so when Violet became very ill, Isobel spent several days by Violet's bedside, caring for her both physically and psychologically. This relationship—though it could have been severed by the death of Matthew—illustrates the concept of linked lives.

Another example of linked lives is Lady Mary Crawley and Tom Branson; both are widowed and are charged with caring for the estate together. Tom is Lady Mary's brother-in-law and could decide to leave the estate at any time because he was not a member of the aristocratic class before he married Lady Sybil Crawley (Mary's sister). Yet he and the family's lives are linked because of the emotional bonds forged during his marriage to Lady Sybil and the birth of their daughter. In addition, because he and Lady Sybil married, Tom's trajectory changed dramatically; he went from being the Crawley's chauffeur to being a member of their aristocratic family. If he chooses to stay as one of the managers of the estate, this trajectory could lead to a successful pathway of wealth and inheritance.

Life course theory also takes historical time and important events into account, which definitely influence the choices main characters Lady Mary and Lady Edith make. During the early and mid-1900s, women's rights movements were gaining strength, and this opened up new opportunities for the two sisters. Lady Edith broke away from the aristocratic ideals for women by learning how to drive, becoming a regular writer for a London newspaper, and giving birth to a baby out of wedlock. Lady Mary also benefited from the changing political landscape, having been left in charge of her late husband's share of Downton Abbey. Her father hesitated to let her help make important decisions about the estate but, finally, gives in, and Lady Mary becomes an active manager of Downton.

There are also several important turning points in this television series. One of the daughters, Lady Sybil, dies after childbirth, leaving Tom Branson feeling like he no longer belongs in this aristocratic world he acquired by marrying her. The series also takes us through World War I, and there are important historical shifts during and after the war. During the war, Downton Abbey was turned into a makeshift hospital, where wounded soldiers came to recover. They were cared for by Lady Sybil and Lady Edith, women of the aristocracy who would never have had to care for anyone before the war, much less wounded soldiers from a very different social class background than their own. This indicates a turning point in the sociohistorical context of the series: What were once well-defined roles based on social class were no longer as relevant because of the shifting needs of members of society.

Fourth, the *Millennial Generation*, born roughly between 1981 and 1997, emerged at a time when children were recast as special, giving birth to the "baby on board" signs seen in cars and a renewed focus on cultivating a child's special talents. This should be no surprise, given the parenting trends of Gen Xers. As a result, Millennials are criticized for being too coddled, and in fact, Twenge and Campbell (2009) have argued that this generation contributed to a "narcissism epidemic" in our country. Their parents—Gen Xers—are criticized for not letting their children experience disappointment, therefore contributing to a rising sense of entitlement. The technological revolution is also noted for contributing to an increase in narcissism; consider the invention of the "selfie" (taking a self-portrait and posting it on social media). Recent research has documented the negative impact social media images—often airbrushed, touched-up, or filtered—have on social media users' self-esteem and body image (de Valle et al., 2021). It is likely, however, that the negative effects of social media use have impacted *Gen Z* the most, which is the fifth generation we present in this book.

Gen Z consists of individuals born after 1997 and those who came of age during some of the most tumultuous political times in recent history. According to Pew Research Center, Gen Z has been particularly hit hard by the coronavirus pandemic, which makes sense given that the historical time of the pandemic and subsequent lockdowns coincided with this generation's "emerging adulthood" stage (Parker & Igielnik, 2020). Individuals in this period of life—18 to 25 years old—are overrepresented in service industry jobs, most of which were drastically reduced or cut altogether during the widespread lockdown orders in early 2020. This generation is also one of the most racially and ethnically diverse of any previous generation and, arguably, more racially conscious as well. Key historic moments, including the murder of George Floyd, a Black Minneapolis man killed by city police while he was being detained, have rapidly brought awareness to widespread racial injustice issues that have been plaguing not only the United States but also the world as a whole. This generation is also on track to be the most highly educated ever.

Even as we write this, new ideas about the generations emerge as time marches on. For example, the youngest group of Gen Z are referred to as Generation Alpha, born in 2012 and beyond. They were probably the first generation to have "their ultrasound picture posted on Facebook" (Rogers-Whitehead, 2021, p. 33) and, thus, are in an entirely unprecedented social, historical, and technological environment. As we can see, the sociohistorical context in which each generation moves through important life course stages is vital to understanding trends in family dynamics and experiences.

Evaluating Life Course Theory

Strengths of Life Course Theory

Like the other theories in this book, life course theory has several strengths. As we describe next, key strengths include the incorporation of context, the ability to be combined with other theories, and the utility with both quantitative and qualitative research methods.

A Contextual Approach

As we have described throughout this chapter, some of the most impressive features about life course theory include the use of multiple social timeclocks (individual, family, and social-historical time); the use of multiple disciplines to shed light on individual, social, economic, historical, cultural, and biological experiences; and the importance of understanding lives in context—how what happens to one person has a mutual influence on others in the family (e.g., linked lives). For example, Walker et al. (2005) conceptualize sibling relationships across central adulthood. In more traditional family theories, such as the family developmental perspective (Chapter 5), with an emphasis on the vertical ties of parents and children (intergenerational) and the horizontal ties of married heterosexual adults (intragenerational), sibling ties are ignored or excluded. But life course theory, with its emphasis on the timing of transitions, experiences, and linked lives, allows us to take the focus away from the static roles of individuals and look, instead, at the social relationships of how kin members relate to one another over time (Furstenberg, 2020). As we explain in Chapter 6, the sibling relationship is the longest tie that one can have, starting in early childhood (and for younger siblings at birth) and extending for many into old age. Walker et al., however, point out that life course theory in and of itself does not go far enough in conceptualizing the links between aging and social structure; hence, it is important to integrate other frameworks to shore up these deficits. The power of an interdisciplinary and flexible life course framework is that it is easily combined with other theories that do shore up any holes. Thus, Walker et al. integrate a feminist perspective on inequality in social relationships, a social constructionist framework about the partiality of knowledge, and the concept of sociological ambivalence. The concept of sociological ambivalence names the contradiction of expectations for different cohorts that are created by social structures (e.g., the legal system and gender relations) and the mixed emotions that it sets up for different family members (Connidis & McMullin, 2002).

An Integrative Theory

Another key strength of life course theory is how well it adapts to integration with other theories. For example, Roy and Allen (2022) reconceptualize our understanding of masculinity in family science by integrating three theories—life course, family systems, and queer—to address intergenerational and family-level processes, impacting the diversity of men's lives over time.

In another example, Roberto et al. (2013, 2019) integrate concepts from life course theory, symbolic interactionist theory, and stress process theory in their research on the care trajectories in families when one partner is diagnosed with mild cognitive impairment (MCI; nonnormative memory or cognitive problems that are not severe enough to be characterized as dementia). In one study, Roberto et al. (2013) analyzed how married couples adjusted to changes in their relationships after a diagnosis of MCI for one of the partners. This study is a good example of how life course theory allows researchers to take several theoretical propositions into account; the authors looked at the identity hierarchies of each spouse and how they changed both over time (i.e., a trajectory) because of the transition of one partner developing MCI. In this analysis, the concept of trajectories from life course theory combined with the concept of identity hierarchies from symbolic interactionist theory (Chapter 4) guided the interpretation of the data. The four trajectories were developed from examining changes in husbands' and wives' spousal identities over time as MCI stabilized or progressed into dementia.

Useful With Both Quantitative and Qualitative Research Methods

Although life course theory was originally developed to be used with quantitative, longitudinal data sets, it has also proven to be useful in **qualitative life history interview studies**. A qualitative approach adds the kind of insider depth from participants that help us to understand how they perceive and experience the major changes that occur throughout their lives. The experiences of singlehood has been relatively neglected in family science, with its emphasis on marriage and parenthood. Thus, pioneering efforts to understand the experience of singlehood for generations of women, in particular, have benefitted from life course theorizing that utilizes qualitative methods. For example, in a qualitative study built upon the key assumptions of life course theory, Allen (1989) found that older women who had never married or had children reflected upon going through family life transitions when they were unexpected. One older woman, for instance, reported that she did not start dating until after her parents died, when she was in her sixties. Her reflections upon life course transitions and trajectories could not be captured in a demographic survey, but they are all the more important because they were described and interpreted from her firsthand insider account. Similarly, Sharp and Ganong (2007) combined life course theory with a phenomenological methodology to study the reflections of young adult women (ages 28 to 34) on the life pathway of singlehood. Their stories revealed the uncertainty many felt about the future of their family relationships as well as their reflections on the "missed" transition related to marriage. In another example, Lavender-Stott and Allen (2022) were informed by life course and feminist theories and conducted qualitative life history interviews with single sexual minority women of the baby boom to understand how these individuals experiences family life outside heteronormativity.

Weaknesses of Life Course Theory

As we discussed in Chapter 1, no theory holds all the keys. Despite the numerous strengths of life course theory, there are some challenges in applying this perspective in family science. These challenges are discussed in the following sections.

Difficulty in Obtaining and Measuring Family Level Data

Imagine you want to study the ways in which families cope when an older family member is diagnosed with cancer. Which individuals in a family would you need to sample? In Carrie's situation, imagine that her grandmother had been diagnosed with cancer. To understand how the family would deal with her needs, whose perspective would you need from the family? Surely, you want to talk to Carrie, since she lives with her grandmother. Probably, you would want to talk with other close relatives (e.g., siblings, children) who may be helpful in providing care during her grandmother's treatment and recovery. Do you think all these people would agree to speak with you about their family lives? Do you think all these people would agree to speak with you multiple times? Suppose you were able to recruit three key members (e.g., Carrie, her grandmother, and her grandmother's sister) from 50 families. You would be very fortunate if all three members in each of the families met with you each year over three years to share the changes they were experiencing. In addition to the difficulties of recruitment, the cost of doing the interviews increases exponentially with each additional family member and wave of data collection. These very issues are important in research that is attempting to understand linked lives, or the interdependence among family members. A case in point is in studying complex life course issues associated with military family members, including ways in which the individual experiences of veterans intersect with other members in their social networks, including spouses and adult children (Monk et al., 2020). At the very least, research that is guided by life course theory can be complex, time-consuming, and costly.

Obtaining Consistent Longitudinal Data

Life course theorists are often challenged by the difficulty of modeling the complexity of individual and family lives over time (Bernardi et al., 2019). Many times the questions asked at one point in time may not be relevant decades later, as society changes. Further, because of funding constraints, it is not possible to know how long a study will continue (Elder et al., 2003). For instance, beginning in 1957, the Wisconsin Longitudinal Study began with data from all high school seniors in Wisconsin with the purpose of tracking the choices students made after high school (Hauser, 2009). Although the researchers planned to collect multiple waves of data, the study has unexpectedly been continued for decades, so now, the participants are entering late life. Questions important now, such as pathways to retirement and health trajectories, were not conceivable during the early years of the study. Thus, some important data related to health and money practices are missing from the early periods of data collection.

Easily Confused With Other Perspectives Using Family Time

Students often ask: How does life course theory differ from the family life cycle concept used in family development theory (Chapter 5)? Both family development and life course are interdisciplinary theories, relying on concepts from diverse perspectives, including demography, economics, history, and psychology, among others. But a closer look at the two theories reveals important differences and a shift in how social life is conceptualized. A good example is the way "trajectory" (from life course theory) is defined, compared to the way "career" (from family development theory) is defined. Both of these concepts share a similar origin and meaning, in that they refer to a life pathway over time. The difference, however, is that family developmental theory has a greater focus on normative structure and fixed family roles. As we learned in Chapter 5, by using the concept of career, we are looking at "the marital career" or "the work career" as if there was just one prototype. By using the concept of trajectory from life course theory, however, the focus shifts to process, social context, variation, and complexity in an individual's life (Aldous, 1990). Chapter 5 on family developmental theory includes other differences between these two theories.

An Alternative Theory App: Family Stress and Resilience Theory

In this chapter, we have laid out the key concepts, assumptions, origins, and modern applications as well as the strengths and weaknesses of life course theory. As you have learned, life course theory has the capability to take historical time and agency into account to understand trajectories of families and family members. Family stress and resilience theory (Chapter 11) has similar strengths, giving insight into a family's past, present, and future. Here we compare these two theories closely, so you can easily switch your "app" between these two perspectives.

Family stress and resilience theory addresses the fact that life is full of risks that threaten both individual and family well-being. At the heart of this theory is an analysis of the ways in which families deal with stressors. At the same time, this theory is built on the assumption that not all stress leads to negative outcomes—thus, the theory's focus on both stress *and* resilience. One way to compare this perspective to life course theory is to consider

BOX 9.3. GLOBAL COMPARISONS: EMERGING ADULTHOOD

One of the life course stages that has recently made its way into the research spotlight is the developmental period between the ages of 18 and 25, referred to as emerging adulthood. This period is more common in industrialized countries, where most young people are expected to obtain a post-secondary education before moving into parenthood or marriage/partnership. This period is an interesting time for researchers because three quarters of a century ago in the United States, high school graduates typically married and entered into stable, enduring adult roles (Arnett, 2004; Arnett & Eisenberg, 2007). More recently, emerging adulthood has become a time of identity explorations, self-focus, feeling in-between, instability, and possibilities or optimism (Arnett & Mitra, 2020). While the concept was first introduced in the United States, researchers have also found evidence of young adults experiencing this life course stage around the world in different ways. As we can see from the following examples, this relatively new stage of the life course, emerging adulthood, is highly dependent on culture and social norms:

- **Sweden** is a Nordic country, where overall, young adults leave home the earliest, most likely due to the financial support they receive from the government to encourage them to be autonomous from their families of origin to explore education, jobs, and relationships (Douglass, 2007; Olofsson et al., 2020). The support comes in the forms of housing allowances and unemployment compensation. These young adults finish college later and postpone childbearing. In addition, over half of all births are outside of marriage (usually in a cohabiting relationship).
- **Spain** is characterized by a strong reliance on the family for support. Spanish parents assume that their children will live at home into their thirties or until they get married (Douglass, 2005; Parra et al., 2019). In fact, in 2016, 80% of Spanish young people between 16 and 29 lived with their parents. Spain has high unemployment rates for this age group as well a difficult housing market.
- **Russia** has a cultural expectation that women should prioritize childbearing due to their low fertility rate (Borgen Project, 2020). Because of a widespread (false) belief that strenuous jobs pose a threat to women's ability to become pregnant, the government has barred women from certain occupations.
- **Chinese** culture has ideological roots in Confucianism, which stresses social order and harmony and suppresses personal needs and desires for the benefit of the entire group (Nelson & Chen, 2007). Only slightly over half of Chinese young adults are able to attend college (Statista, 2021). In the 1970s, China instituted a one-child policy to address population control; this policy has contributed to a gender imbalance (120 males to every 100 females; Hudson & Den Boer, 2002). The policy was in effect until October 2015, when the government announced it would now allow married couples to have two children (Buckley, 2015). The college and university system in China does not allow students to change majors (Nelson & Chen, 2007). Additionally, the sense of obligation to care for aging parents is high in China, so children rarely move far away from their parents.

how the two frameworks are complementary. Given how broad life course theory is, and how well it focuses on timing, events, and trajectories, we could easily argue that family stress and resilience theory fits well within the scope of life course theory. In fact, a life course theorist may be able to utilize family stress and resilience theory's propositions to repeatedly analyze family life in order to better understand how, for instance, advantage or disadvantage accumulate over time. Family stress and resilience theory provides an in-depth look at how families adapt and contributes nicely to providing a life course theorist with information that helps provide context for understanding families over a longer period of time, including how family adaptation from one stressor helps predict family (and individual) adaptation later in life as well as across generations.

Next, it is important to highlight how life course theory is applicable to the study of families across the globe. How individuals move through the life course differs greatly, depending on the country's culture, geography, and history. Why do you think this is? How would life course theorists explain the differences between the countries we highlight in Box 9.3? We challenge you to consider these global applications of the theory.

Working With Life Course Theory: Integrating Research and Practice

Now that we have described the historical background, assumptions, concepts, and strengths and weaknesses of life course theory, we turn to how the theory can be used in practice. First, we provide an example of one new direction of life course theorizing, which is the way that the experience of being old has been reconceptualized by life course scholars. We then analyze an empirical study that was guided by life course theory to see how scholars put the theory to work in a research project. Finally, we present ideas about how the theory informs the practice of family life education.

Life Course Theory Today

As we have discussed, life course theorists have proposed new ways of understanding young, middle, and old age, particularly in light of the changing demographics of society we identified in Chapter 1. These demographic changes include the fact that there is greater variability in adult life course trajectories due to the fact that most people are living longer; that lives differ according to gender, race, class, sexual orientation, age, national origin and the like; and that the occurrence or sequencing of marriage and family roles is not a predictable set of stages, as posited by other family theories.

One current area of life course theorizing is the experience of being old. The older years were initially described, in family developmental theory (Chapter 5), as the key transitions of retirement, widowhood, and eventual death. As a result of life course theory, old age has been transformed into early and later phases (e.g., the young old, the old old, and the centenarians; Poon et al., 2000; Teixeira et al., 2017). Changes in the way old age is experienced at the personal and societal levels lead life course theorists to ask new theoretical questions. Now that individuals are living well past their eighth decade, Settersten and Trauten (2009) ask, "How are these decades to be filled? Is it that there are no scripts for old age, few scripts, or new scripts that are in the process of being developed?" (p. 457). In the past, there were no, or few scripts for how to live in old age, in part because so few people survived to old age. Yet today, new scripts are constantly being constructed, as the life course lengthens and older adults create multiple intimate pathways (e.g., getting a divorce, dating, remaining single, or remarrying following widowhood). Thus, from a life course perspective, we can shed light on how old age is experienced by first considering how older adults lived in their young and middle adult years and who they "count" as family (Connidis 2020). That is, how individuals in later life identify who is "family" requires a multilevel approach that transcends micro-level contexts: Who someone will call family matters at the micro, meso, and macro levels (Connidis, 2020), an important consideration addressed by the historical time that life course theory takes into account. Taken together, the quality and extent of family relationships, one's educational and occupational achievements, their health outcomes and access to care, and the quality of their lives from the past will position them to respond to the opportunities and risks they face in their later years. Individual-level choice is impacted greatly by the larger social systems that are shaped by political shifts that confine who we are allowed to define as family.

Life Course Theory in Research

Life course theory is particularly suited for guiding research as well as for incorporating multiple theoretical perspectives (Giele & Elder, 1998). In a study of how Chilean lesbians navigate motherhood in the context of traditional familistic and Christian culture, Figueroa and Tasker (2020) take a multi-level, life course approach to unpacking the complexity of sexuality, religion, and family.

Life course theory provides a unique lens through which these researchers addressed longitudinal narratives of self and identity as confined by the dominant cultural scripts in a South American country strongly rooted in family and tradition, both of which sharply contrast with lesbian identity. Indeed, Figueroa and Tasker (2020) describe this narrative as squarely "lesbophobic," due to the culture's widespread rejection of lesbianism, signified by their legal policies as well. In surrounding South American countries, same-sex marriage and adoption have been legalized, but Chile's progression on these issues has been slow. Public opinion remains divided on issues of same-sex marriage and adoption as well.

Using in-depth interviews with eight Chilean women, the researchers conducted a structural narrative analysis of participants' stories framed with life course theory. Participants revealed that they initially conformed to cultural expectations about family and tradition, first getting married to a heterosexual man and starting a family. Over time, many women stifled their true identity because of lesbophobic societal pressure but began questioning their identity and relationship with their child(ren)'s father during the initial transition to parenthood.

One participant in particular was impacted by seeing media portrayals of lesbians on television, which signified another important turning point. From a life course perspective, the intersection of historical time (e.g., producers choosing lesbian characters for a television show or broadcasters licensing the show and distributing it to a general audience) made an impact for these participants. The macro-level forces and larger culture situated women in this study on a trajectory that led to all but one having taken the next step of ending the heterosexual relationship at the time of the interview. Interestingly, the majority of women in the study transitioned away from Catholicism (or organized religion) as they identified as lesbians; only three women identified as Catholic both during childhood and as adults. Generationally, the children of these mothers were even farther removed from Catholic or other faiths; only 50% of the children were identified as Catholic, and one teenage child identified as Buddhist.

Life course theory allows researchers to capture these multi-level intersections of family life as people move throughout their lives as individuals, family members, partners, and the like. Factors like sexuality, gender identity, religion, and family structure can all be accounted for using this versatile theoretical framework.

Life Course Theory in Practice

There are several ways in which family science practitioners can apply life course theory in their work with individuals and families. Recent research has focused on the COVID-19 pandemic and how families are facing unique challenges providing intergenerational care with some opportunity to strengthen family solidarity (Gilligan et al., 2020). Specifically, practitioners have had to adapt during the pandemic to help families navigate basic daily tasks like housework and caregiving as well as financial and emotional exchanges between and within families.

Family life educators could be instrumental in applying life course theory to help families understand and find resources regarding the complex dynamics associated with the rapid social changes created by the COVID-19 pandemic. Gilligan et al. (2020) found that during the early stages of the pandemic, parents and adult children who lived in close proximity to one another faced challenges when deciding if, when, or how to continue caring for one another. Combining life course theory with social exchange theory (see Chapter 7) is useful for these dilemmas because family members had to weigh the costs and benefits associated with these in-person exchanges to avoid spreading serious illness to loved ones. Additionally, because coronavirus has been shown to leave lasting, sometimes debilitating, side effects, the pandemic also likely contributed to family members needing long-term care as a result of having contracted the virus.

Using the Intergenerational Solidarity Model, researchers and practitioners acknowledge the possibility that "the COVID-19 pandemic may concomitantly promote and challenge multigenerational cohesion" (Gilligan et al., 2020, p. 432). Family solidarity could increase as a result of new digital technologies that families have begun to rely on as a result of being unable to spend time together in person. It is also true that in times of need, families have been shown to rely more heavily on intergenerational exchange as children, grandchildren, parents, and grandparents have experienced increased need during such a monumental, stressful time in history.

On the other hand, families have also experienced strain associated with dissimilar values regarding the pandemic, how it spreads, and how to stay safe. Family members may strongly disagree about safety precautions, creating the potential to sever relationships due to mounting tension and seemingly unresolvable conflict. Indeed, conflict about something that has fatal consequences could very well cause lasting trauma, which, unfortunately, could intersect with grief not only over the loss of a relationship but also over the loss of life. The potential for tragic, devastating loss is immense, leaving lasting damage to families and their members for generations.

As a result of each of these new trends, demand for mental health professionals is at an all-time high (American Psychological Association, 2021). Mental health professionals have seen an increase specifically in service requests for individuals struggling with anxiety and depressive disorders as well as sleep–wake disorders, obsessive–compulsive and related disorders, and substance-related and addictive disorders. Many practitioners are offering telehealth appointments as a result of the pandemic to meet the needs of their clients and to stay safe while still providing mental health services (Maier et al., 2021). Moving forward, it is also important to consider how many individuals who engaged in their first mental health treatment during the pandemic will continue to use services over their life course, sporadically or not. The COVID-19 pandemic presents a conundrum; it is remarkable that demand has increased as mental health and well-being become part of our overall health and wellness considerations, yet it will be imperative to meet those demands with a well-trained, trauma-informed supply of mental health professionals for years to come, a point we return to in Chapter 11 about family stress and resilience.

BOX 9.4. VOICES FROM LIVED EXPERIENCE

Candy is a first-generation college student and a doctoral candidate in family science. She was raised in a working-class family in northern Appalachia, where her father was an electrician in the coal-mining industry. Her maternal grandfather, also a coal miner, dropped out of school at the age of 12 to help financially support his family. Religion is her family's backbone. Her story reveals the power of life course theory to understand concepts, such as linked lives over time:

> Writing about the social mobility of a poor kid from Appalachia is not popular in family science. Little has been written about working-and lower-class Whites, but cumulative experiences in my life have taught me the importance of speaking up about topics others want to silence. Like many families in Appalachia, my family struggles with addiction, and my mother's addiction to religion supports her emotional avoidance. When I was 6 years old, my maternal aunt died at the age of 25 from cardiac arrest. My mother was with her. The months following my aunt's death were silent. My mother was emotionally absent, and my father, who never engaged in an emotional role as a parent was equally unavailable. Like many small Appalachian towns, the church pastor doubled as the town's therapist, so faith played a sole role in my mother's grief recovery, while my sister and I were left to deal with our grief and confusion alone. I was told only that my aunt's death was God's will. What I learned from the silence and the explanation of God's will was to not question things, accept tragedy, and avoid emotional responses. Emotions and questions meant that I did not have enough faith.

> Life choices throughout my adolescence aligned with the ways of navigating the world that my mother modeled. I continued to remain silent and accept hardship. In high school I fell for a boy who abused his power. Like the good religious girl I was socialized to be, I continually forgave him, internalizing the idea that I was "too much." I began struggling with anorexia nervosa my senior year. My mother took me to our pastor, who told me that eating disorders are a sin of vanity. Once again, I learned to silence my pain, quiet my desires, and stay emotionally and physically small. I learned to stop taking up space. I was no longer living the perfect existence that my family needed for me. At a time when I was to be primed to become a wife and a mother, I was seeking a way out.

> I found my way to college then New York City to study for my master's degree. Through these decisions, I became the "other" and was no longer understood or celebrated by my family. My timing was off. I was 27 and writing a master's thesis instead of getting married and making babies.

> Soon after my 35th birthday, I gave birth to my only child. While I was supposed to be elated, I instead felt intense anxiety. My desire to be more than a mother and my mourning for the life I

(continued)

once had triggered guilt and shame. This role was the one my family had been waiting for me to take on. Wanting a life outside of mothering also triggered memories of my aunt's death. My grandmother lost a child, and here I was questioning my role as a mother, not fully sure that I was equipped to continue. At this juncture, I finally found a way to process my grief of my aunt's death—something that was put off because of my family's lack of awareness of mental health and my mom's addiction to religion.

For 5 years, I embodied the role of the dedicated good mother. Knowing I needed more, I could no longer quiet the desire to study for my PhD. While the fear of saying too much still resides within me, I am finding myself more driven by authenticity than fear.

Conclusion

Life course theory has provided important ideas that allow researchers and practitioners to put the theory to use beyond the conceptual level. Life course theory is easily translated into concepts that can be applied to empirical research, as we have seen in our examples. Further, life course theory, with its emphasis on change over time and multiple individual and family pathways, provides rich resources from which family life practitioners can draw in order to educate and help families.

Multimedia Suggestions

www.ssea.org

This is the homepage of the Society for the Study of Emerging Adulthood, a professional association that sponsors a yearly conference and a scholarly journal, *Emerging Adulthood*. The website provides helpful resources for understanding social and psychological aspects of the post-adolescent period of ages 18–25.

Activate your theory app: Consider this age range as it relates to history. As life expectancy increases in developed countries, will emerging adulthood happen around the same ages as today, or will it extend to accommodate the longer life span?

www.aarp.org

This is the homepage for AARP, begun as the American Association of Retired Persons, founded in 1956. It is the leading organization for those aged 50 and older. With a membership of 47 million members (as of 2021), AARP has a tremendous amount of political clout. They offer a comprehensive array of practical information (e.g., health care, caregiving, and employment), discounts on insurance and recreational activities, as well as many other resources and opportunities.

Activate your theory app: Imagine how this website might change to be relevant to your generation when you hit retirement age. What unique characteristics does your generation have that analysts at AARP would have to take into account to better tailor the services offered on the site?

Wonder Years (2021–present)

This show is considered a "remake" of a popular television show of the same name that aired in the 1990s on mainstream television. The difference between the two shows, however, is that the modern version follows a Black family, the Williamses, through the same time period, highlighting how historical time, including the Civil Rights Movement, impacts them much differently than the Arnold family, from the first version of the show. Aspects of life course theory are evident throughout, especially compared to

Image 9.2 A Scene From *The Wonder Years*, 2021

the original. Each family has different turning points and transitions, and because of their race, they experience the impact of broader social norms as well as major historical events much differently.

Activate your app: Consider widely popular television shows, like *Friends*. How could a show focused on cisgender, heterosexual, able-bodied characters be remade to highlight diversity and social justice issues in a more effective way? What aspect of life course theory would best be used to describe the importance of remaking old content with a new spin to reflect cultural shifts?

Forrest Gump (1994)

This award winning film follows Forrest Gump over several decades of his life, displaying how some of the important historical events of the 20th century define the ways in which Forrest moves through his life course stages. This story also provides a look into Forrest's family relationships, specifically with his mother, his childhood sweetheart, Jenny, and his best friend, Bubba.

Image 9.3 A Scene From *Forrest Gump*, 1994

Activate your theory app: What examples can you see in this film of the importance of historical time and place as well as linked lives?

Further Reading

Arnett, J. J. (2018). *Adolescence and emerging adulthood: A cultural approach* (6th ed.). Pearson. This comprehensive textbook is written from a global cultural perspective and extends the developmental period of adolescence into emerging adulthood (ages 18–25). Although a psychologist, Arnett, a leading expert on emerging adulthood, takes an interdisciplinary, sociohistorical approach. This book is especially helpful for college students in exploring the self-discovery context in relation to the scientific literature.

Newman, K. (2003). *A different shade of gray: Midlife and beyond in the inner city*. New Press. Newman gathered qualitative data through in-depth life history interviews with 100 ethnically diverse New Yorkers. Her research paints the picture of growing old in the inner city and contrasts it to the historical landscape that situated the families in her book on a life course trajectory that often was not of their own making. Families faced White flight, children with serious illnesses, and caregiving for extended kin and grandchildren. Each of these structural forces contributed to the families' accumulating disadvantage over their life courses, in sharp contrast to where they started their lives in the beautiful boroughs of New York in the 1940s and 1950s. This text illustrates nearly every concept of the life course perspective and should be useful to all students interested in diverse family lives over time.

Notter, M. L., MacTavish, K. A., & Shamah, D. (2008). Pathways toward resilience among women in rural trailer parks. *Family Relations, 57*(5), 613–624. https://doi.org/10.1111/j.l741-3729.2008.00527.x In this article, the authors describe how resilience is a process that must be negotiated and achieved throughout the life course. Women, and their children, who live in trailer parks in rural areas must deal with, at the very least, hardships derived from the intersection of social class, gender, and geographic location. The authors document the multiple turning points in rural women's lives, in terms of how they live in relative poverty, face many intergenerational risks, and have little or no formal or informal support, but still manage to work toward family survival and strength in often harsh surroundings.

Pillemer, K. (2015). *30 lessons for loving: Advice from the wisest Americans on love, relationships, and marriage*. Avery. In this collection of stories from the oldest Americans (a sample of 700 older adults aged 65 and above), social gerontologist Karl Pillemer has analyzed in-depth interviews with an eye for the most important lessons participants had about creating and sustaining a happy relationship over time. The result of Pillemer's translation of scholarship into practical advice yields 30 excellent insights about the value of good communication, the understanding that a marriage entails more than just the members of a couple, the importance of friendship and sharing household labor, and the beauty of humor, acceptance, and lightening up in relation to one another. This is a book to share across the generations, whether one is just starting a relationship or has sustained a marriage for many years.

Settersten, R. A., Jr., Elder, G. H., Jr., & Pearce, L. D. (2021). *Living on the edge: An American generation's journey through the 20th century*. University of Chicago Press. Prominent life course theorists Settersten, Elder, and Pearce tell the story of members of the 1900 generation of individuals born from 1885 to 1908 as they endured the ups and downs of the 20th century. The authors reveal how the participants' life chances and outcomes were often predicated upon their socioeconomic and ethnic diversity. They trace the impact of major sociohistorical events and transitions, such as immigration, World War I, the economic hardships of the Great Depression, the devastation of World War II, the new opportunities of the post-war period, and the social movements for civil rights of the 1960 and 1970s. Reading this book, it is clear that the authors are also telling the story of the life course perspective—how it got started, what it covers, and how it can be applied to the challenging and ever-changing world of the 21st century. The book reveals the intellectual legacy of life course giants in generating a framework for measuring and understanding the complexity of families undergoing social change.

Questions for Students

Discussion Questions

1. Think about the "big picture" of life course theory. How has this theory responded to shifts in family realities? How might life course theory be applied if we tried to situate it in 1900? Consider the diversity of families back then and what this theory might add to the analysis. Would it work?

2. Looking ahead, is life course theory the type of perspective that lends itself to being adapted to adjust to even more changes in the diversity of families as time goes on? What types of changes might not "fit" into this theory? Which ones would?

3. Compare and contrast the issues of cumulative advantage and cumulative disadvantage. Are they mutually exclusive? Why, or why not?

4. What state or federal policies could benefit from an understanding of life course theory? Are there concepts that are more important to point out to policymakers than others?

5. Some researchers suggest that life course theory *needs* to be supplemented by another major theoretical framework. What do you think? Does life course theory stand alone, or is it best used in combination with other theories?

6. What types of research methods have been applied with life course theory? Is it possible to use qualitative, quantitative, and mixed methods to study life course concepts? Which do you think is most appropriate, and why?

Your Turn!

Find an article in which the authors have used life course theory as a framework for their empirical research. What aspects of the theory did the research utilize? Is there another theory the research could have utilized? What are the strengths and weaknesses of the article? What would you do differently if you were conducting the research?

Personal Reflection Questions

1. To what birth cohort do you belong? What are some of the characteristics of your cohort? In what ways do you, or don't you, identify with your cohort?

2. What birth cohort do your parents and grandparents belong to? Describe the similarities and/or differences you have noticed due to cohort membership.

3. To illustrate the concept of linked lives, give an example of how an event in a family member's life has affected your own life in dramatic ways.

4. How important have broader sociohistorical events been in shaping your own life course? Consider the most recent major event: the COVID-19 pandemic. How has this event in particular changed your own life course and those in your family?

5. Give an example of a way in which you, or a member of your family, has experienced a major life event "off time," from a life course perspective.

6. Compose a letter to your local state representative, arguing for a policy change using life course theory. Frame your letter as though you are writing for a specific policy change, and ground your argument in an issue that would be more fully understood if only our state representatives used life course theory when considering policy.

References

Aldous, J. (1990). Family development and the life course: Two perspectives on family change. *Journal of Marriage and the Family, 52*(3), 571–583. https://doi.org/10.2307/352924

Alexander, K. L., Entwisle, D. R., & Olson, L. S. (2001). Schools, achievement, and inequality: A seasonal perspective. *Educational Evaluation and Policy Analysis, 23*(2), 171–191. https://doi.org/10.3102/01623737023002171

Allen, K. R. (1989). *Single women/family ties: Life histories of older women.* SAGE Publications.

American Psychological Association. (2021). *Demand for mental health treatment continues to increase, say psychologists.* https://www.apa.org/news/press/releases/2021/10/mental-health-treatment-demand

Arnett, J. J. (2004). *Emerging adulthood: The winding road from the late teens through the twenties.* Oxford University Press.

Arnett, J. J., & Eisenberg, N. (2007). Introduction to the special section: Emerging adulthood around the world. *Child Development Perspectives, 1*(2), 66–67. https://doi.org/10.1111/j.1750-8606.2007.00015.x

Arnett, J. J., & Mitra, D. (2020). Are the features of emerging adulthood developmentally distinctive? A comparison of ages 18–60 in the United States. *Emerging Adulthood, 8*(5), 412–419. https://doi.org/10.1177/2167696818810073

Baltes, P. B. (1987). Theoretical propositions of life-span developmental psychology: On the dynamics between growth and decline. *Developmental Psychology, 23*(5), 611–626. https://doi.org/10.1037/0012-1649.23.5.611

Bengtson, V. L., & Allen, K. R. (1993). The life course perspective applied to families over time. In P. Boss, W. Doherty, R. LaRossa, W. Schumm, & S. Steinmetz (Eds.), *Sourcebook of family theories and methods: A contextual approach* (pp. 469–499). Plenum.

Bernardi, L., Huinink, J., & Settersten, R. A., Jr. (2019). The life course cube: A tool for studying lives. *Advances in Life Course Research, 41,* Article e100258. https://doi.org/10.1016/j.alcr.2018.11.004

Borgen Project. (2020). *5 facts about women's rights in Russia.* https://borgenproject.org/womens-rights-in-russia/

Brumbaugh-Johnson, S. M., & Hull, K. E. (2019). Coming out as transgender: Navigating the social implications of a transgender identity. *Journal of Homosexuality, 66*(8), 1148–1177. https://doi.org/10.1080/00918369.2018.1493253

Buckley, C. (2015, October 30). China ends one-child policy, allowing families two children. *New York Times.* www.nytimes.com/2015/10/30/world/asia/china-end-one-child-policy.html

Carpenter, L. M. (2010). Gendered sexuality over the life course: A conceptual framework. *Sociological Perspective, 53*(2), 155–178. https://doi.org/10.1525/sop.2010.53.2.155

Cherlin, A. J. (2020). Degrees of change: An assessment of the deinstitutionalization of marriage thesis. *Journal of Marriage and Family, 82*(1), 62–80. https://doi.org/10.1111/jomf.12605

Connidis, I. A. (2020). Who counts as family later in life? Following theoretical leads. *Journal of Family Theory & Review, 12*(2), 164-179. https://doi.org/10.1111/jftr.12367

Connidis, I. A., & McMullin, J. A. (2002). Sociological ambivalence and family ties: A critical perspective. *Journal of Marriage and Family, 64*(3), 558–567. https://doi.org/10.1111/j.1741-3737.2002.00558.x

Cox, S. M., Lashley, C. O., Henson, L. G., Medina, N. Y., & Hans, S. L. (2021). Making meaning of motherhood: Self and life transitions among African American adolescent mothers. *American Journal of Orthopsychiatry, 91*(1), 120–131. http://dx.doi.org/10.1037/ort0000521

Dannefer, D. (2020). Systemic and reflexive: Foundations of cumulative dis/advantage and life-course processes. *The Journals of Gerontology: Series B: Psychological Sciences and Social Sciences, 75*(6), 1249–1263. https://doi.org/10.1093/geronb/gby118

Deal, J. J. (2007). *Retiring the generation gap. How employees young and old can find common ground.* Jossey-Bass.

Demo, D. H., Aquilino, W. S., & Fine, M. A. (2005). Family compositions and family transitions. In V. Bengtson, A. C. Acock, K. R. Allen, P. Dilworth-Anderson, & D. M. Klein (Eds.), *Sourcebook of family theory and research* (pp. 119–142). SAGE Publications.

de Valle, M. K., Gallego-García, M., Williamson, P., & Wade, T. D. (2021). Social media, body image, and the question of causation: Meta-analyses of experimental and longitudinal evidence. *Body Image, 39*, 276–292. https://doi.org/10.1016/j.bodyim.2021.10.001

Douglass, C. B. (2005). "We're fine at home": Young people, family and low fertility in Spain. In C. B. Douglass (Ed.), *Barren states: The population "implosion" in Europe* (pp. 183–206). Berg.

Douglass, C. B. (2007). From duty to desire: Emerging adulthood in Europe and its consequences. *Child Development Perspectives, 1*(2), 101–108. https://doi.org/10.1111/j.1750-8606.2007.00023.x

Duvall, E. (1957). *Family development.* J. B. Lippincott.

Edin, K., & Kefalas, M. (2011). *Promises I can keep: Why poor women put motherhood before marriage.* University of California Press.

Elder, G. H., Jr. (1974). *Children of the Great Depression.* University of Chicago Press.

Elder, G. H., Jr. (1981). History and the family: The discovery of complexity. *Journal of Marriage and the Family, 43*(3), 489–519. https://doi.org/10.2307/351752

Elder, G. H., Jr., & Giele, J. Z. (2009). Life course studies: An evolving field. In G. H. Elder, Jr. & J. Z. Giele (Eds.), *The craft of life course research* (pp. 1–24). Guilford Press.

Elder, G. H., Jr., Johnson, M. K., & Crosnoe, R. (2003). The emergence and development of life course theory. In J. T. Mortimer & M. J. Shanahan (Eds.), *Handbook of the life course* (pp. 3–19). Kluwer.

Erikson, E. H. (1950). *Childhood and society.* W. W. Norton.

Erikson, E. H. (1975). *Life history and the historical moment.* W. W. Norton.

Figueroa, V., & Tasker, F. (2020). Familismo, lesbophobia, and religious beliefs in the life course narratives of Chilean lesbian mothers. *Frontiers in Psychology, 11*, article 516471. https://doi.org/10.3389/fpsyg.2020.516471

Fingerman, K. L., Huo, M., & Birditt, K. S. (2020). A decade of research on intergenerational ties: Technological, economic, political, and demographic changes. *Journal of Marriage and Family, 82*(1), 383–403. https://doi.org/10.1111/jomf.12604

Furstenberg, F. F. (2020). Kinship reconsidered: Research on a neglected topic. *Journal of Marriage and Family, 82*(1), 364–382. https://doi.org/10.1111/jomf.12628

Garwood, E., & Lewis, N. M. (2019). Where are the adult children of LGBTQ parents? A critical review. *Journal of Family Theory & Review, 11*(4), 592–610. https://doi.org/10.1111/jftr.12348

Giele, J. Z., & Elder, G. H., Jr. (Eds.). (1998). *Methods of life course research: Qualitative and quantitative approaches.* SAGE Publications.

Gilligan, M., Karraker, A., & Jasper, A. (2018). Linked lives and cumulative inequality: A multigenerational family life course framework. *Journal of Family Theory & Review, 10*(1), 111–125. https://doi.org/10.1111/jftr.12244

Gilligan, M., Suitor, J. J., Rurka, M., & Silverstein, M. (2020). Multigenerational social support in the face of the COVID-19 pandemic. *Journal of Family Theory & Review, 12*(4), 431–447. https://doi.org/10.1111/jftr.12397

Greenfield, E. A., & Marks, N. E. (2006). Linked lives: Adult children's problems and their parents' psychological and relational well-being. *Journal of Marriage and Family, 68*(2), 442–454. https://doi.org/10.1111/j.1741-3737.2006.00263x

Hareven, T. K. (Ed.). (1978). *Transitions: The family and the life course in historical perspective.* Academic Press.

Hauser, R. M. (2009). The Wisconsin Longitudinal Study: Designing a study of the life course. In G. H. Elder, Jr. & J. Z. Giele (Eds.), *The craft of life course research* (pp. 1–24). Guilford Press.

Hill, R., & Rodgers, R. H. (1964). The developmental approach. In H. T. Christensen (Ed.), *Handbook of marriage and the family* (pp. 171–211). Rand McNally.

Hitlin, S., & Elder, G. H., Jr. (2007). Time, self, and the curiously abstract concept of agency. *Sociological Theory, 25*(2), 170–191. https://doi.org/10.1111/j.1467-9558.2007.00303.x

Hudson, V. M., & Den Boer, A. (2002). A surplus of men, a deficit of peace: Security and sex ratios in Asia's largest states. *International Security, 26*(4), 5–39. https://doi.org/10.1162/016228802753696753

Kincaid, R., Rurka, M., Suitor, J. J., Gilligan, M., Pillemer, K., Mohebbi, L., & Mundell, N. (2021). Prodigal children: Why older mothers favor their once-deviant adult children. *The Journals of Gerontology: Series B: Psychological Sciences and Social Sciences.* Advance online publication. https://doi.org/10.1093/geronb/gbab075

Lavender-Stott, E. S., & Allen, K. R. (2022). Not alone: Family experiences across the life course of single baby boom sexual minority women. *Family Relations.* Advance online publication. https://doi.org/10.1111/fare.12721

LeMoyne, T., & Buchanan, T. (2011). Does "hovering" matter? Helicopter parenting and its effect on well-being. *Sociological Spectrum, 31*(4), 399–418. https://doi.org/10.1080/02732173.2011.574038

Maier, C. A., Riger, D., & Morgan-Sowada, H. (2021). "It's splendid once you grow into it:" Client experiences of relational tele-therapy in the era of COVID-19. *Journal of Marital and Family Therapy, 47*(2), 304–319. https://doi.org/10.1111/jmft.1250

McGhee, H. (2021). *The sum of us: What racism costs everyone and how we can prosper together.* One World.

Merton, R. K. (1988). The Matthew effect in science, II: Cumulative advantage and the symbolism of intellectual property. *Isis, 79*(4), 606–623. https://doi.org/10.1086/354848

Miller, J. D. (2011). Active, balanced and happy: These young Americans are not bowling alone. *The Generation X Report: A Quarterly Research Report From the Longitudinal Study of American Youth, 1*(1), 1–8.

Monk, J. K., Proulx, C., Marini, C., & Fiori, K. (2020). Advancing research and theory on aging military veterans in a relational context. *Journal of Family Theory & Review, 12*(2), 180–199. https://doi.org/10.1111/jftr.12378

Nelson, L. J., & Chen, X. (2007). Emerging adulthood in China: The role of social and cultural factors. *Child Development Perspectives, 1*(2), 86–91. https://doi.org/10.1111/j.l750-8606.2007.00020.x

Olofsson, J., Sandow, E., Findlay, A., & Malmberg, G. (2020). Boomerang behaviour and emerging adulthood: Moving back to the parental home and the parental neighbourhood in Sweden. *European Journal of Population, 36*(5), 919–945. https://doi.org/10.1007/s10680-020-09557-x

O'Rand, A. M. (2002). Cumulative advantages theory in life course research. In S. Crystal & D. Shea (Eds.), *Annual Review of Gerontology and Geriatrics* (Vol. 22, pp. 14–30). Springer.

Parker, K., & Igielnik, R. (2020, May 14). *On the cusp of adulthood and facing an uncertain future: What we know about Gen Z so far.* Pew Research Center. https://www.pewresearch.org/social-trends/2020/05/14/on-the-cusp-of-adulthood-and-facing-an-uncertain-future-what-we-know-about-gen-z-so-far-2/

Parra, Á., Sánchez-Queija, I., García-Mendoza, M. D. C., Coimbra, S., Egídio Oliveira, J., & Díez, M. (2019). Perceived parenting styles and adjustment during emerging adulthood: A cross-national perspective. *International Journal of Environmental Research and Public Health, 16*(15), 2757. https://doi.org/10.3390/ijerph16152757.

Pew Research Center. (2015, September 3). *The whys and hows of generation research.* https://www.pewresearch.org/politics/2015/09/03/the-whys-and-hows-of-generations-research/

Poon, L. W., Johnson, M. A., Davey, A., Dawson, D. V., Siegler, I. C., & Martin, P. (2000). Psycho-social predictors of survival among centenarians. In P. Martin, C. Rott, B. Hagberg, & K. Morgan (Eds.), *Centenarians: Autonomy versus dependence in the oldest old* (pp. 77–89). Springer.

Roberto, K. A., McCann, B. R., & Blieszner, R. (2013). Trajectories of care: Spouses coping with changes related to MCI. *Dementia: International Journal of Social Research and Practice, 12*(1), 45–62. https://doi.org/10.1177/1471301211421233

Roberto, K. A., McCann, B. R., Blieszner, R., & Savla, J. (2019). A long and winding road: Dementia caregiving with grit and grace. *Innovation in Aging, 3*(3), 1–12. https://doi.org/10.1093/geroni/igz021

Rogers-Whitehead, C. (2021). *Becoming a digital parent: A practical guide to help families navigate technology.* Routledge.

Roy, K., & Allen, S. H. (2022). Men, families, and the reconceptualization of masculinities. *Journal of Family Theory & Review, 14*(1), 28–43. https://doi.org/10.1111/jftr.12441

Roy, K., & Settersten, R. A., Jr. (2022). The family life course framework: Perspectives on interdependent lives and inequality. In K. Adamsons, A. L. Few-Demo, C. Proulx, & K. Roy (Eds.), *Sourcebook of family theories and methodologies.* Springer.

Ryder, N. B. (1965). The cohort as a concept in the study of social change. *American Sociological Review, 30*(6), 843–861. https://doi.org/10.2307/2090964

Savin-Williams, R. C. (2001). *Mom, Dad, I'm gay: How families negotiate coming out.* American Psychological Association.

Serido, J., LeBaron, A. B., Li, L., Parrott, E., & Shim, S. (2020). The lengthening transition to adulthood: Financial parenting and recentering during the college-to-career transition. *Journal of Family Issues, 41*(9), 1626–1648. https://doi.org/10.1177/0192513X19894662

Settersten, R. A., Jr, & Trauten, M. E. (2009). The new terrain of old age: Hallmarks, freedoms, and risks. In V. L. Bengtson, D. Gans, N. M. Putney, & M. Silverstein (Eds.), *Handbook of theories of aging* (2nd ed., pp. 455–469). Springer.

Ševčíková, A. & Sedláková, T. (2020). The role of sexual activity from the perspective of older adults: A qualitative study. *Archives of Sexual Behavior, 49*(2), 969–981. https://doi.org/ 10.1007/s10508-019-01617-6

Sharp, E. A., & Ganong, L. (2007). Living in the gray: Women's experiences of missing the marital transition. *Journal of Marriage and Family, 69*(3), 831–844. https://doi.org/10.1111/j.l741-3737.2007.00408.x

Smith, D. E. (1993). The Standard North American Family: SNAF as an ideological code. *Journal of Family Issues, 14*(1), 50–65. https://doi.org/10.1177/0192513X93014001005

Spock, B. (1946). *The common sense book of baby and child care.* Dutton.

Statista. (2021, July 21). *Number of students enrolled in tertiary education in China 1990–2020.* https://www.statista.com/statistics/1114979/china-enrolled-student-number-in-tertiary-education/

Strauss, W., & Howe, N. (1997). *The fourth turning: An American prophecy. What the cycles of history tell us about America's next rendezvous with destiny.* Broadway.

Teixeira, L., Araujo, L., Jopp, D., & Ribeiro, O. (2017). Centenarians in Europe. *Maturitas, 104*, 90–95. https://doi.org/10.1016/j.maturitas.2017.08.005

Trask, B. S. (2018). Integrating life course, globalization, and the study of racial and ethnic families. *Journal of Family Theory & Review, 10*(2), 451–466. https://doi.org/10.1111/jftr.12259

The Trevor Project. (2019). *Coming out: A handbook for LGBTQ young people.* https://www.thetrevorproject.org/resources/guide/the-coming-out-handbook/

Twenge, J. M., & Campbell, W. K. (2009). *The narcissism epidemic: Living in the age of entitlement.* Free Press.

Umberson, D. (2017). Black deaths matter: Race, relationship loss, and effects on survivors. *Journal of Health and Social Behavior, 58*(4), 405–420. https://doi.org/10.1177/0022146517739317

U.S. Census Bureau. (2019). *QuickFacts: Kentucky*. https://www.census.gov/quickfacts/KY

Walker, A. J., Allen, K. R., & Connidis, I. A. (2005). Theorizing and studying sibling ties in adulthood. In V. Bengtson, A. C. Acock, K. R. Allen, P. Dilworth-Anderson, & D. M. Klein (Eds.), *Sourcebook of family theory and research* (pp. 167–190). SAGE Publications.

Welch, W. (Ed.). (2020). *From the front lines of the Appalachian addiction crisis: Healthcare providers discuss opioids, meth and recovery*. McFarland.

Willson, A. E., Shuey, K. M., & Elder, G. H., Jr. (2007). Cumulative advantage processes as mechanisms of inequality in life course health. *American Journal of Sociology, 112*(6), 1886–1924. https://doi.org/10.1086/512712

Wong, J. S. (2018). Toward a theory of gendered projectivity and linked lives in the transition to adulthood. *Journal of Family Theory & Review, 10*(1), 126–140. https://doi.org/10.1111/jftr.12253

Image Credits

Family Ecological Theory

Have you ever been in a relationship with someone, and after several months, you discover something about them that is both surprising and yet makes so much sense? Perhaps, the person you have been dating revealed that they had been sexually assaulted previously but never reported it to law enforcement or sought out help from counseling professionals or support groups. As a loved one, you might feel conflicted—both angry and compassionate at the same time. Angry at the perpetrator of the assault, and angry because you wish your loved one had reported it and served justice. Yet you feel sad and want to be comforting and supportive of your loved one in whatever way they need.

Imagine the complexities associated with a sexual assault; this case can be examined on many levels, each one important in different ways to understanding families and their members. First, you imagine your loved one's family—what prevented her from telling her parents? You know the family does not have very good health insurance, and your loved one mentioned that by calling 911 she feared she would have to pay for expensive ambulance services and transportation, as well as costly hospital examinations and tests, and draw attention to her family's home with all the police and emergency vehicles that would arrive. She also has seen how law enforcement officials treat rape victims on TV; the fear of the same thing happening to her felt overwhelming. As long as she avoided the perpetrator, she could protect herself without involving anyone else. Given how close she was to graduating high school and heading off to college, she figured starting a new chapter in life would provide a chance to start over anyway.

Each of the layers to this story represents a different level of system that family ecological theory addresses. As we explain in this chapter, there are several levels of analysis that family ecological theory uses to understand families, including the microsystem, mesosystem, exosystem, macrosystem, and chronosystem. Each of these levels represents a different way of examining the interaction that families and their members have with their larger communities (e.g., neighborhoods, peers, and school), social institutions (e.g., religion and the criminal justice system), and cultural ideals (e.g., dominant values and norms) as well as how these change over time. Each of these systems will be described in detail later in this chapter, but given the comprehensiveness of this framework, it should be no surprise that this theory, though unique, has ties to many other theories, in particular family developmental (Chapter 5), family systems (Chapter 6), social exchange (Chapter 7), and life course (Chapter 9). This theory allows researchers and practitioners the chance to take into account all the forces that contribute to family interactions both internally and externally. This provides scholars and practitioners with a more complex understanding of families, including the roles that larger social institutions play in family life as well as larger cultural forces that determine what is "right," "wrong," or even "normal" for families. Further, this theory is, perhaps, the most committed to ensuring the well-being of individuals and their families. Below, we elaborate on the topic of sexual assault to provide a multifaceted look at how such an event can impact not only the woman but also her family, long after it happened.

Case Study

Nina, an Afro–Latina, cisgender woman, and James, a White, cisgender man, have been married for 12 years and have two children together. About two months after they married, James took a job 1,000 miles away and had to relocate before Nina was able to follow, leaving them living in separate states for about a month. One night after James had moved, a serial rapist broke into Nina and James's home and raped Nina, who was one of three women attacked in a three-month span. All three women reported the assaults, which provided police with DNA and the arrest of the perpetrator who was already in "the system" for similar crimes. After a jury trial, the perpetrator was sentenced to 317 years in prison.

As a result of this event, Nina and James began a long journey of interacting with social institutions on several levels. First, Nina sought out medical treatment immediately, getting tested for sexually transmitted diseases and possible pregnancy, and she also was prescribed medication to help her sleep at night and manage recurring panic attacks. She immediately connected with psychological services by establishing weekly appointments with a professional counselor, a psychiatrist, and a support group of survivors. In addition, she and James began couples counseling to help them navigate the murky complexities associated with sexual assault, marital communication, and healthy relationship building.

Over the three years following the attack, James and Nina became very familiar with how the criminal justice system processes cases like this. Nina had weekly interactions with the victim's assistance advocate, the district attorney, and investigators on the case. She testified at both the jury trial and at the sentencing hearing. In processing each step with her own counselor and her support group, she also was exposed to aspects of the larger culture that she never really had to think about before, such as the stigma associated with rape, the perception of victims who have been assaulted by strangers versus relatives or acquaintances, and the barriers women face when deciding whether or not to report sexual assault. Additionally, these experiences impacted Nina's view of herself and her sexuality as well as the relationship she built with her children, who came along after the conviction and imprisonment of the perpetrator. How would she explain what happened to her to her children? Would she raise her son differently than her daughter, given the experiences she had as a result of the sexual assault? How does the ever changing cultural discussion of sexual assault and the oppression of women inform both Nina's parenting decisions as well as her relationship with her spouse? Furthermore, what were the ripple effects that reached back to her own nuclear family, particularly her relationships with her mother, father, and two brothers? Undoubtedly, their own well-being and perceptions of these issues were also affected.

Finally, think about how women's rights have changed significantly even in the last 50 years, making discussions of sexual victimization more prominent than they were in the past. This aspect—time—made it possible for Nina not only to report the crime but to also seek professional psychological assistance because society has evolved to include positions such as a "victim's advocate" within the district attorney's office. The sociohistorical context played a huge role in the choices available to Nina and her family. Family ecological theory captures these complexities, including how they affect and are affected by systems outside families as well as how they change over time.

What Is Family Ecological Theory?

Family ecological theory helps us understand the ways in which these experiences intersect for Nina on the individual, familial, social, and cultural levels, which allows us to bring in multiple sources of information when explaining family life. This theory thoroughly captures the intersectionality of the multiple layers and how they influence and are influenced by families and their members. It takes into account complexities that families experience in their daily lives *because of* their interactions with various social systems. As we see throughout this chapter, family ecological theory has great potential for describing, explaining, and intervening in the kinds of topics that family scholars are increasingly called on to understand and ameliorate, such as intimate partner violence and victimization against children in global contexts (Hardesty & Ogolsky, 2020; Yount et al., 2017).

Think about family ecological theory in this way: Imagine a traditional wedding cake but without a couple at the top. The figure at the top is just one person; imagine it being you! The very top of the cake, where you stand, represents the individual characteristics of the family member. By examining the figure at the top, you can identify age, race and/or ethnicity, and gender, among a host of other individual-level characteristics. The layer you stand on represents the **microsystem**, or the immediate family or peers that you rely closely on and come in contact with regularly.

The next layer, the **mesosystem**, has tiny plastic stairs that lead to the wider layers below; this represents how the microsystem interconnects with the two outer layers of the cake—the exosystem and macrosystem. Think about how the economy (an exosystem), for instance, affects families differently. How does an economic recession or a widespread pandemic affect families in the working class, middle class, or upper class? The mesosystem is like a channel through which the two outer systems reach the inner microsystems. The important thing to remember is that meso separates families from systems *external* to them—forces that, for the most part, are outside of their control. What resources does your family have access to outside of your microsystem? How can you access those resources via the mesosystem to be "protected" by outer layers of the ecosystem? Consider the widespread lockdowns during the COVID-19 pandemic that sent children home from school to complete remote learning (Goldberg et al., 2022). Parents who also were able to work remotely had a much less difficult time adjusting to the change, compared to parents who worked in manual labor jobs that could not be completed remotely. Many in the service industry were laid off during the pandemic as well, which exacerbated stresses at home. The mesosystem serves as a sturdy buffer to external forces (e.g., remote work for parents and remote learning for children) *or* it can do little to protect microsystems (e.g., manual labor working parents and unsupervised children left at home for remote learning). Indeed, Lawson et al. (2020) found that children whose parents suffered job loss during the pandemic experienced negative consequences on behalf of their unemployed parents.

The next layer is the first of the three external systems. The **exosystem** can include social institutions, such as the economy, the media, industry, or the criminal justice system. How did Nina's interactions with the criminal justice system differ from that of the perpetrator? The perpetrator and his family had very different interactions with the system than Nina and her family. He had previously been "in the system" for similar crimes and was estranged from his mother and immediate nuclear family. He had extended family that had also been incarcerated, and inevitably, this affects his view of the system. Nina, on the other hand, hopes that her interactions with the criminal justice system are long behind her; she had never been in trouble with the law or victimized prior to the rape. She hopes that the three years through the assault, arrest, investigation, trial, and sentencing represent the entirety of her interactions with the criminal justice system for the rest of her life.

The largest layer, the **macrosystem**, represents cultural ideologies, ways of thinking, and attitudes that exist at a broader level. How do the societal expectations guide what you think, believe, or perceive in life? Nina had no idea how stigmatized rape victims are until she had to experience it firsthand and hear her support group members talk about it. She is now hyperaware of cultural beliefs surrounding rape, gender inequality, and victim blaming. Given the seriousness of this event in Nina's life, her interactions with the macrosystem will undoubtedly affect members of her family of origin as well as her nuclear family for generations to come.

Finally, the "invisible" system, the **chronosystem**, represents the influence of time on each layer. Imagine you are sitting atop the aforementioned wedding cake as a toddler, then as an adolescent, a young adult, and then as an older adult. Clearly, age and historical time are going to influence not only the individual but also the composition of the layers of the cake surrounding you. Exosystems and macrosystems change over time: The economy is always subject to upturns and recessions and cultural ideals not only about family life but also about broader ideologies are constantly in flux at the macro level. As such, each layer of the cake is dependent on the other, and together, they build a foundation for you to stand on. If you look too closely at the person at the top, you are missing the entirety of the cake and all the layers that are holding it up. Family ecological theory allows us to really cut into each of those layers and examine the foundation of individuals and their families, from the large bottom layer all the way up to the top. Thus, family ecological theory is one of the most comprehensive and adaptable frameworks currently in use today.

History and Origins

As we have pointed out throughout this book, it is important to examine the historical context in which a theory was developed in order to appreciate the ways in which the theory can help us to understand the issues we study. As we will see, family ecological theory has ties to many other theories. Further, it lends itself to creative pairings, as in combination with social exchange theory (Sabatelli et al., 2018), and for use in the integration of indigenous and Western ways of knowing to study marginalized and indigenous communities from a perspective of resilience (Sanchez et al., 2019). Family ecological theory has roots in two primary disciplines: human ecology (formerly called home economics) and developmental psychology.

Family Ecology

Let's start by discussing how the family ecology movement evolved out of the discipline of home economics (Faust et al., 2014; Hook & Paolucci, 1970). Now called "family and consumer sciences," home economics was the original discipline employing female scholars in the early 20th century, when women were almost exclusively barred from academic appointments in the male-dominated disciplines of sociology, psychology, biology, chemistry, and others, and most male scholars ignored issues of home and family (Thompson, 1988). The discipline has evolved over time to its current emphasis on the integration of individual well-being, family strengths, and community vitality to meet basic human needs in the context of ever-changing human ecosystems (Nickols et al., 2009).

Though a German biologist named Ernst Haeckel first coined the term "ecology" in 1873, it was Ellen Swallow Richards who adapted more general ideas about ecological science to a "science of the environment focused on home and family" (Bubolz & Sontag, 1993, p. 420). Richards, the first woman admitted to the Massachusetts Institute of Technology (MIT), used her training as an industrial and environmental chemist to study the family's interaction with the natural, biological environment. Early in her career as a scientist, Richards studied the effects of industrialization on water quality, which eventually led to the establishment of water quality standards across the United States. As she uncovered the impact of environment on families and well-being, she began to acknowledge the importance of educating the largest group of consumers: women. She envisioned a science of household management, referred to as "oekology" early on. This term stems from the Greek *oikos,* which means "place of residence." Richards viewed the family as the primary location for the foundation of life and developed a theory linking the physical environment with the social context of individual and family development. Her studies of how families operated within their environments laid the groundwork for what we know as family ecological theory today. These foundational ideas in the field of home

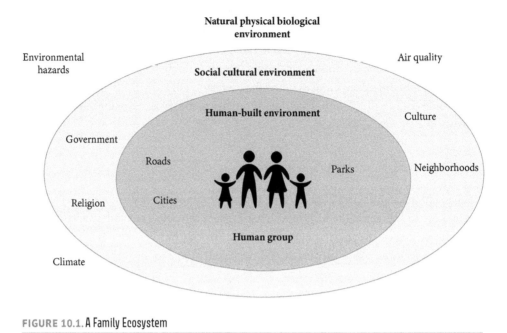

FIGURE 10.1. A Family Ecosystem

economics were concerned with the intersection of human beings in their natural or physical and human-built environments. Thus, this model considered the broader social context in which families lived and interacted every day (Bubolz & Sontag, 1993). The family ecological framework elaborated upon context, environment, interdependence, adaptation, and ecosystem. Figure 10.1 presents an ecological model from the family environmental perspective.

You can see in the figure that the family is the central focal point of the model. Families must be understood in the context of other, nonhuman groups that surround it. The environments are nested, or embedded, within one another. The natural physical–biological environment represents the largest force that encompasses every other environment. It should be easy to see why this was the first model of family ecology, given Richards's emphasis on the importance of the link between a family and its physical environment. Using this early model of family ecology, theorists, researchers, and practitioners could identify, for instance, the importance of the availability of nutritious foods, clean water, and clean air where families live. The relevance of this linkage is increasingly clear as we understand the connection among environmental racism, climate change, poor health, and toxic neighborhood quality disproportionately impacting Black, Indigenous, and people of color (BIPOC) communities (Salas, 2021). Indeed, professionals who work with families need to be aware of the dangers to children's well-being from toxic environmental conditions (Koester et al., 2021). The quality of the outermost environment is directly related to the social–cultural environment, which includes social institutions like schools. Let's look at this issue in more depth to illustrate this model of family ecology.

First, it is important to consider that not all families include children. However, for families with children, the presence of children contributes to the likelihood that a family will interact with certain social institutions. Would

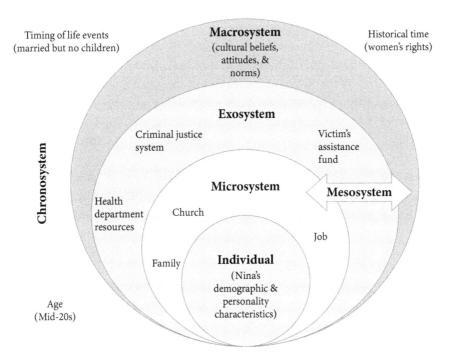

FIGURE 10.2. Bronfenbrenner's Ecological Model Applied to Nina

a family without children be as concerned about the air quality near the local school compared to a family with school-aged kids? It is important to consider these differences when taking a family ecological approach because, as you can see in Figure 10.2, the two-directional arrows suggest that the human group influences the outer environment, and vice versa. Depending on family structure, some institutions may or may not be integral to a family's well-being.

Now, thinking back to what you learned from conflict theory (Chapter 3), you should remember that schools are often directly impacted by the immediate environment and economic well-being of one's community. If poor communities have low air quality, low water quality, and limited access to nutritious foods, this inevitably affects the quality of the schools, which in turn affects the children and families who interact with the schools. Will schoolchildren be able to play outside at recess if an industrial waste site is nearby, compromising the air quality? Will that same school have regular access to clean water? Further, what human-built environments will serve as a buffer between the outer environments and the human group, or family? Consider schools that are situated in middle- or upper-class neighborhoods; the buildings and roads leading to schools are likely safe, attractive, and well-maintained. On the other hand, schools in lower-income communities are not only directly impacted by the air and water but also the safety and security surrounding the buildings and routes to school. Consider whether or not children have to cross busy highways to get to school from residential areas; in some communities, there may be a "buffer" that protects the family (and children) from the external environments. Each of these factors can be taken into account using a family environmental model.

Human Ecology

As the other major influence on an ecological model, we turn now to the field of psychology. From the perspective of ecological psychology, Barker (1968) examined the impact of the environment on individual behavior. Later, Uric Bronfenbrenner (1979), from Cornell University, articulated an individual perspective on human development by positing that nested systems of the biological, psychological, and social spheres influence the development of the individual. His ecological theory of human development was informed by the German American psychologist Kurt Lewin, who is considered a pioneer of social, organizational, and applied psychology (Bronfenbrenner, 1978). Lewin is credited with the classic statement, "there is nothing so practical as a good theory" (Bronfenbrenner, 2005, p. 43).

Bronfenbrenner's (2005) bioecological theory portrays development as an interconnected system of ever-widening layers, much like that of nested Russian dolls. Like several other theories we have examined, ecological theory emphasizes interdependence across the layers in the system (Tudge et al., 2016). Bronfenbrenner's model is also similar to the model put forth by Bubolz and Sontag (1993) in that the layers are nested and interdependent, but the two models differ in terms of the primary unit of analysis: Bubolz and Sontag's model begins by theorizing about the family, whereas Bronfenbrenner's model begins by theorizing about the individual. Indeed, Bronfenbrenner amended his framework from ecological theory to bioecological theory to emphasize the focus on human developmental (Tudge et al., 2016). Bronfenbrenner's theory includes (a) the individual family members in the microsystem; (b) the connections between microsystems, such as between families and schools, in the mesosystem; (c) the influences from larger social systems that provide the immediate context for families, such as neighborhoods, in the exosystem; (d) the largest social contexts and levels of influence, such as politics, religion, cultural, and legal institutions in the macrosystem; and (e) the timing and patterning of events over the life course in the chronosystem (Bush & Peterson, 2013).

More recent adaptations of the theory include a combination of prior versions, which, as we have seen throughout this text, is very common when it comes to theoretical development. In the field of family sociology, prior versions of family ecological theory have evolved with the influence of life course theorists (Chapter 9). In particular, Glen Elder (1974) worked with Bronfenbrenner at Cornell University, and their perspectives on individual, family, and social development over time were mutually influential (Tudge et al., 2016). In conceptualizing various dimensions of time over the individual's life (e.g., the chronosystem), the life course framework was helpful in showing the dynamic ways that different dimensions of time (i.e., individual, family, and historical) shape developmental change. Recent theoretical work has further expanded ecological theory to address the importance of cultural processes and communities on human development—not just as macrosystems but also for their microsystemic level importance in the daily interactional processes (e.g., through language and communication) impacting individuals and families (Velez-Agosto et al., 2017). Thus, the combination of human ecology and developmental theories into family ecological theory has allowed us to go beyond individual development and toward the interactions of families with their near and external environments. Figure 10.2 illustrates a contemporary version of family ecological theory that includes the chronosystem, applied to our case study involving Nina.

Further, the family ecological perspective has been a forerunner in understanding family diversity, with variations in family structure, race and ethnicity, life stage, and socioeconomic status (Bubolz & Sontag, 1993; McAdoo et al., 2005), and the focus on family diversity continues in research today—for example, emphasizing new ways to understand biological and social fathering among Afro–Caribbean fathers (Green & Chuang, 2021).

Returning to the origins of studying diversity in ecological context, Harriette McAdoo (1993; 1999) and John McAdoo (1988), who were professors in the Department of Family Ecology at Michigan State University, were among the major theorists who expanded the family ecology model to include the ecology of Black families. This framework was one of the first in our field to address the intersections of race, ethnicity, and family in an overt way. Harriette McAdoo (1993) explained that "persons of color often have a greater reliance on the social network than families who are more readily accepted within the context of our society or who have greater resources within their control" (p. 299). A more comprehensive understanding of the ecological contexts of minoritized families requires a stronger look at the mesosystemic layer, which helps us see that the differential treatment and reliance upon kin is necessary given the unequal access to opportunities and resources available to members of society who experience greater prejudice and discrimination overall. In this regard, family ecological theory has ties to the description of added stressors faced by minoritized families (see Chapter 11 on family stress and resilience theory) and the layers of resilience and adaptation that result (Anderson, 2019; Peters & Massey, 1983).

Key Concepts

Now that we have described some of the history of the development of family ecological theory, we turn to definitions of key concepts in this theory. These concepts are increasingly used in the social and behavioral sciences, including family science, psychology, sociology, and public and community health, because they cover the interconnections among individuals, families, institutions, and time.

Ecosystem

The concept of ecosystem is used in various biological and environmental sciences. It can be commonly defined as a community of living organisms that interacts with its surrounding environment (Bubolz & Sontag, 1993). Therefore, the term "ecosystem" can be used in almost any discipline that studies living organisms that affect and are affected by their environments; examples include a marine ecosystem or a desert ecosystem. A human ecosystem is a type of living system comprised of humans interactive with their environment. A **family ecosystem** is a subset of a human ecosystem that involves the interaction between families and their environment. Some of the major assumptions about human–environment relations are:

> (1) Social and physical environments are interdependent and influence human behavior, development, and quality of life; (2) Environment is a source of available resources; (3) We can choose, design, or modify resources and environments to improve life and well-being, and we should do so. Implicit in these assumptions is the worldview that humans can exert some control over their lives and the environment. (Bubolz & Sontag, 1993, p. 421)

As seen in this description, it is clear that the ecological perspective is a very dynamic one, and it has an activist component. That is, it is not enough to describe the biological–environmental connection—it is also important to protect and improve it.

Nested Ecological Levels

One of the major assumptions family ecological theory rests on is that the family is a system that is synergistically nested within larger systems (Bronfenbrenner, 1979, 2005; Bubolz & Sontag, 1993; Mercon-Vargas et al., 2020). Each system operates on a specific level, ranging from the smallest (microsystem) to the largest (macrosystem). The smallest systems are nested within the larger systems, and each level can be determined by the proximity to the individual psychologically, physically, or socially. As we move outward from the individual at the center of each model of family ecology, there is a corresponding increase in distance. That is, individuals are closer to and interact more with family members regularly than they do with laws or government.

Think back to the case study; for 24 years of her life before the assault, Nina did not have to interact with the legal or criminal justice system. She also did not have to consider cultural ideologies surrounding the objectification of women or the socialization of boys and men in society. Now, her son and daughter will be raised with unique views on power, sex, sexual assault, and what some researchers refer to as a "crisis of masculinity" in the United States (see Chapter 8 on feminist theory for a more detailed discussion of issues associated with masculinity). Nina, as an individual, is nested within (a) her nuclear family as well as her family of origin; (b) larger social institutions, which contribute to socialization of boys and men (e.g., education and mass media); and (c) the larger cultural system that perpetuates ideologies about the hypersexualization of women and the hypermasculinity and dominance of men.

Adaptation

The concept of adaptation, which emerged from systems theories, refers to the fact that individuals and families are dynamic and capable of changing their beliefs and behaviors to adapt to their environments. There is a give and take in how **adaptation** occurs. Humans are affected and changed by their environments, but given the feedback and communication processes we studied in Chapter 6 (family systems theory), humans also directly modify their environments. Adapting to inevitable changes from their near and far environments, families must learn to replace one set of rules with another (Bubolz & Sontag, 1993). For example, in various studies on the quality of the relationships of lesbian, gay, and heterosexual couples across the transition to adoptive parenthood, Goldberg and colleagues (2010, 2019) have shown that the process of adoption is linked to intersecting ecological layers. These layers include the ways parents adjust in light of intrapersonal factors (e.g., experiencing depression), relationship quality (e.g., experiencing friction and other negative emotions related to one's partner), and the broader social contexts (e.g., satisfaction with the adoption agency) that occur across time, particularly in the current digital era.

Values

Values are present on every level of the ecological model; all families have values that guide their decisions and actions. Understanding the values of individuals and their families (whether they are compatible or not) is vital to family ecological theory: "When studying a family ecosystem, one must make explicit the values and goals that each individual holds, those that are shared by the family as a unit, as well as those operative in the social-cultural environment" (Bubolz & Sontag, 1993, p. 436). A **value** reflects the belief systems of the individual, family, and society about important ideals, such as what is pragmatically useful, economically profitable, and morally correct. For example, in Green and Chuang's (2021) qualitative study of Afro-Caribbean fathers, which was guided by ecological theory, they found that these Jamaican men saw their roles as father beyond a biological one. In addition to biological children, they also incorporated social children, in their capacities as stepfathers, community members, family friends, informal foster fathers, godfathers, uncles, teachers, and mentors. Key to their experience was a spiritual component, in that they highly valued their own participation in spiritual traditions and in imparting them to the children they guided.

Family ecological theory ascribes to the value of **human betterment**, which is the goal to which humans should individually and collectively strive. In this model, there are four "great virtues" that contribute to the common good. The first is economic adequacy, to ensure adequate nourishment, housing, health care, and other essentials of life. The second is justice, to ensure equality in work, education, and health. The third is freedom, in contrast to coercion and confinement. The fourth is peacefulness, in contrast to conflict and warfare (Bubolz & Sontag, 1993). We see these values enacted in current research as well, particularly in the emphasis on family diversity and social justice that we address throughout this book.

Bioecology of Human Development

Bronfenbrenner (2005) developed a theory that identifies the complex interactions among several layers of experience. Consider his definition:

> Development is defined as the phenomenon of continuity and change in the biopsychological characteristics of human beings both as individuals and as groups. The phenomenon extends over the life course across successive generations and through historical time, both past and present. (p. 3)

There are five layers, or systems, in this model that locate individual and family development at the micro, meso, exo, macro, and chrono levels. For example, the microsystem begins with the developing child and the setting into which the child is born. The overall circumstance of a child's birth is the first context in which life chances are formed, but it is by no means a "life sentence." Given the subsequent outer layering of other systems, individual lives are constantly changing and taking new directions. For example, the neighborhood in which a child grows up impacts the kind of social and material resources available to the child and their family. Neighborhoods with convenient shopping centers, public transportation, adequate housing, local doctors, and good schools provide an adaptive environment in which children and families are supported. Yet neighborhoods with few grocery stores, inadequate schools, lack of transportation, and entrenched crime set up extra hurdles and limitations that impact family well-being. On the basis of such neighborhood deficits, Bronfenbrenner was one of the leaders in creating Head Start, a federally funded program started in 1965 to provide a support system for children in disadvantaged communities at the local level. Head Start is a good example of bolstering the mesosystem through the involvement of children, parents, teachers, and the whole community to turn around the effects of poverty and poor resources to give young children a better beginning. Half a century after its inception, Head Start remains a significant contribution to children's interest in science later in life.

> In the 1970s, Bronfenbrenner and colleagues conducted research with 276 families, each with a preschool child, in Syracuse, New York. From the beginning, their research incorporated the ways in which environmental stresses and supports associated with mass societal changes have impacted children's lives and public policies. Bronfenbrenner and Weiss (1983) describe two environmental

principles of development, both of which undergirded Bronfenbrenner's ecological paradigm: Proposition 1 states that for a child to develop well, they need the enduring involvement of one or more adults in their care. In other words, "somebody has to be crazy about that kid," meaning that "someone has to *be there,* and to be *doing something*—not alone, but together *with* the child" (p. 398). Proposition 2 is that public policies and practices must provide "Opportunity, status, resources, encouragement, stability, example, and above all, time for parenthood … both within and outside the home" (p. 398). Though seemingly self-evident, this advice is even more relevant today, as the nature of parenting and family life continues to change dramatically, and the amount of public support for marginalized children and families continues to shrink. (Gerde et al., 2021)

Another key aspect of Bronfenbrenner's theory is the macrosystem. Family policy scholars have developed and analyzed programs and policies that affect families, for better or worse, and as a result have developed models for effective work with policymakers at the broadest levels of society (Day et al., 2019). At the macro level, public policies reflect and also influence a society's cultural values (Bogenschneider, 1996). In the United States and other countries around the world, attitudes and practices regarding what constitutes a family, as well as which families "deserve" financial, health care, and other support that is underwritten by the government, are constantly changing. For example, The Defense of Marriage Act was instituted in the United States in 1996 to define marriage as a union between one man and one woman, barring same-sex marriage and all of its entitlements at state and federal levels (Bogenschneider, 2000). Yet in 2015, this act was overturned when the U.S. Supreme Court ruled in *Obergefell v. Hodges* that same-sex couples have a constitutional right to marry, in light of vast and rapid changes in the public attitudes toward marriage rights for members of the lesbian, gay, bisexual, transgender or queer (LGBTQ) population (Berger & Carlson, 2020). Society, then, must adapt to these social shifts and institute new laws, institutions, and policies to accommodate broad institutional changes.

Process-Person-Context-Time (PPCT) Model

One of Bronfenbrenner's (2005) enduring concerns has been with creating a theory and method dynamic enough to analyze individuals and families as they interact with their multiple intersecting environments—**the process–person–context–time model**. The PPCT model is the result of many decades of work in trying to specify the most comprehensive way of studying human development in an environmental context. Bronfenbrenner and colleagues identified and critiqued the **social address model** as the most simplistic way of understanding human and family development. "Social address" means that we look at only one influence from a person's environment. An example of the social address model is reducing the complexity of life to whether a child lives in a rural versus an urban environment. The social address model only captures one environmental label with no attention to "what the environment is like, what people are living there, what they are doing, or how the activities taking place could affect the child" (Bronfenbrenner, 1986, p. 724).

To advance beyond the social address model, Bronfenbrenner and colleagues proposed a more rigorous model for understanding the dynamic, interdependent, and comprehensive nature of human development. The PPCT model is based on the premise that all persons in a family respond differently to outside environmental influences. It is important to take into account the various spheres of influence: (a) the context in which development is taking place, (b) the personal characteristics of the individuals present in that context, and (c) the process

BOX 10.2. FAMILY ECOLOGICAL THEORY IN MODERN CULTURE: *POSE*

Pose is an American television show that highlights the unique "vogue" or "ballroom culture" scene in the 1980s and 1990s in New York City, consisting of African American and Latinx LGBTQ+ as well as gender-nonconforming individuals. This show is praised not only for its complex and important storylines but also for featuring openly gay actors and transgender actresses. Billy Porter won an Emmy as the first openly gay Black lead actor in 2019, and in 2021, Mj Rodriguez was the first trans lead actress to be Emmy nominated for outstanding lead actress in a drama series. This show made huge strides culturally and has much relevance when it comes to illustrating aspects of family ecological theory as well.

In the family subculture featured in *Pose*, individuals otherwise socially rejected by both families of origin and society at large live and work together in chosen families. These families live in "houses," led by older members of the community who are typically drag queens, gay men, or transgender women (Bailey, 2011). Within each house, typical family "roles" are loosely followed and members use traditional phrases like children, siblings, mothers, and fathers to refer to one another (Bailey, 2011).

Pose showcases how these subcultures interact with larger social systems—including the chronosystem—which illustrates how the human immunodeficiency virus (HIV) epidemic spiked during the decades in which this show is set. Microsystems, such as characters' immediate families, are also featured as they impact access to resources for someone like Damon, who is wholly rejected by his parents at age 17 because he is gay and becomes homeless as a result. Blanca, the main character who identifies as the "mother" of House Evangelista, brushes up against exosystems throughout the show's three seasons and access to resources becomes clear as issues surrounding homophobia, racism, and sexism permeate each level of the ballroom ecosystem. She also faces difficulties in relationships with her own family of origin as well as her chosen family. Another main character, Elektra, struggles with how her identity and gender confirmation procedures impact not only her well-being but the well-being of House Abundance. After her procedure, her access to resources is threatened, which impacts her entire house. This mesosystem—or access to financial and residential stability—is impacted by her individual-level choices, which strains her (and others') well-being. As a result, she has to move between houses and struggles to find belonging in a microsystem.

Interestingly, this show also showcases the chronosystem between seasons one and two, as it highlights the popularity of Madonna's song "Vogue," which serves to push this subculture into the mainstream more than ever before, with both positive and negative repercussions. The interactions between multiple levels of systems in this show seem endless, and it is a valuable cultural artifact that signifies an important shift in how theory can be applied to stories that are not commonly told.

through which their development is elicited. Further, the interaction among at least two of these spheres must be considered (e.g., the person-context and the process-context) as well as the influence of past and present time. The contextual nature of development, as put forth in the concept of proximal processes, is one of Bronfenbrenner's key contributions (Mercon Vargas et al., 2020).

Evaluating Family Ecological Theory

Strengths of Family Ecological Theory

Like all of the theories we describe in this book, family ecological theory has both strengths and weaknesses. The strengths include the wide popularity, applicability, and utility of this comprehensive theory of individual development in the context of family and society.

Comprehensive View of Individuals, Families, Communities, and Societies

Family ecological theory is one of the most comprehensive in use today because it weds the genetic and psychological development of the individual with the ever widening social environments to which the individual must adapt. This theory also takes family into account as a set of relationships *and* as a social institution, which enhances the original understanding of children as being influenced by biology and psychology. Although many family theories examine the individual, relational, and societal levels of influence on families (e.g., family developmental in Chapter 5 and life course in Chapter 9), family ecological theory is very useful in zeroing in on how the microsystem and the macrosystem interact via the mesosystem. The mesosystem describes the processes that operate between two or more of the person's behavior systems in mediating the biological, familial, and social. This comprehensive view gets at the mechanisms of how individuals and families function and change and allows us to analyze how the biological, familial, and social aspects of a person's life are always interacting.

Addresses the Nature Versus Nurture Question

One of the greatest contributions of family ecological theory is that it links the genetic heritage of individuals with multiple social and cultural environmental contexts. In doing so, it reveals that biology (nature) *and* environment (nurture) are both important and that nature/nurture is not an either/or question. This theory asserts that it is the interaction of nature and nurture that influences an individual's life, and the interaction between the individual and the family is especially important in the process of how humans develop and the circumstances of their lives. For example, as we describe in Chapter 13 (on queer theory), Diamond (2021) reveals how critical it is to examine the dynamic interplay between genetic and environmental factors for new understandings of sexual fluidity and its implications for same-gender sexuality.

Highly Applicable to Practice

Family ecological theory is very useful to apply across social service and health care practices. Social work, for example, is a profession intent on helping children, families, and communities deal with traumatic experiences, such as the aftermath of natural and technological disasters and the trauma of terrorist acts, during a time in which it feels as if "the world falls apart." Rosenfeld et al. (2004) approach the experience of trauma in families' near and far environments using ecological frameworks that are also integrated with cognitive and behavioral, developmental, resilience, and systems theories. An ecosystems approach is applicable across all helping professions, including human services, teaching, medicine, nursing, and counseling.

In particular, family ecological theory helps researchers and educators translate theory into practice to work with and improve the lives of clients in critical ways. For example, Bronfenbrenner originally developed this theory to address the need for enhancing formal and informal support for children at risk for educational delays, as in the Head Start program. Ann Hartman (1979), a family therapist and social worker, adapted ecological theory for use with clients in family therapy. She developed the concept of the **ecomap**, which works similarly to the genogram we described in Chapter 6 (family systems theory). The ecomap consists of the family unit in the center circle, with outer circles connected by various types of solid or dotted lines. Each line represents the energy flow to and from the client's micro to macro contexts. The ecomap has been applied to a variety of practical contexts, including work with very young children and their families (McCormick et al., 2008). In another example, Karimi et al. (2014) utilized an ecological approach to address the therapeutic value of intergenerational relationships between older adults and youth who are not related to one another.

Weaknesses of Family Ecological Theory

Despite its strengths, family ecological theory is not without its weaknesses. As we have found in most of the family theories, some of its strengths also reflect its weaknesses. For example, the adaptability of family ecological theory to multiple fields of study can also be viewed as a weakness as well as other ideas we describe next.

Difficulty of Translating Such a Comprehensive Theory Into Research

A theory with such wide appeal and applicability to many different contexts remains difficult to translate into empirical research, and scholars have been critical of superficial applications of the theory (Marcon-Vargas et al., 2020; Tudge et al., 2016). Indeed, from the beginning, Bronfenbrenner and colleagues set out to develop propositions, hypotheses, and experimental methods that would address this issue of advancing the science of ecological theory by testing it quantitatively. They sought to go beyond the typical question asked in ecological theory, "How much do heredity and environment contribute to development," which is only descriptive and, thus, to expand it to a question that allows the study of process, such as, "How do they contribute? What are the proximal mechanisms through which genotypes are transformed into phenotypes?" (Bronfenbrenner & Ceci, 1993, p. 313). Yet the experimental approach, with its benefit of predicting behavior rather than reflecting on the outcomes after the fact, has been slow to develop, despite recent scientific progress in fields of behavioral genetics and human development. It is difficult to implement the conceptual benefits of the interaction among the multiple environments that impact individual and family lives. In their analysis of theories of child maltreatment, Del Vecchio and colleagues (2013) stated that although ecological theory has been popular for many years, it remains limited because researchers have not found many ways to test hypotheses derived from the theory as a whole. Family ecological theory is a good example of how challenging it is to merge multiple fields and so many broad concepts into a theoretical whole.

Too Much Focus on the Developing Child Rather Than the Family

A major critique of ecological theory, in general, is that its focus is primarily on the developing child and the individual level of analysis, while the focus on the *family system* lags behind. This is, in part, because of the difficulty of studying families as more than just a singular unit, without attention to all of the variability that comes from studying the interaction among family members. This is a unit of analysis problem: When the model was developed with the individual child in the center of analysis, the ability to deal with the intersecting lives of family members was compromised. Other theories, such as family developmental theory (Chapter 5) and life course theory (Chapter 9), have also struggled with moving beyond the individual level to handle multiple family members over time. Certainly, advances in quantitative dyadic methods, multilevel modeling techniques, and panel designs are helping researchers deal with dependent data among family members, which is important for understanding the connections regarding major areas of study in family science, including the interface of work and family (Perry-Jenkins & MacDermid Wadsworth, 2017).

Inattention to the Social Inequalities of Race and Gender Systems

The ecological model, as proposed by Bronfenbrenner (1979) and advanced within many disciplines, primarily addresses the individual's connections to the economic system (e.g., social class) because it was originally developed to address the inadequacies of education, health, and housing for children and their families that accompany poverty. The original version of ecological theory did not adequately identify racism and sexism as matters that also affect individual and family life (Uttal, 2009). With exceptions, such as the work of McAdoo et al. (2005) and Peters and Massey (1983), noted previously, attention to other systems of oppression and privilege and their intersections have only slowly developed over time, as we see from current research that is broadening the intersectional reach of ecological theory (e.g., Green & Chuang, 2021; Sanchez et al., 2019). We look to conflict theory (Chapter 3), feminist theory (Chapter 8), critical race theory (Chapter 12), and queer theory (Chapter 13) to address the intersections of race, class, gender, sexual orientation, age, and other systems of social stratification.

An Alternative Theory App: Conflict Theory

In this chapter, we have laid out the key concepts, origins, modern applications, and strengths and weaknesses of family ecological theory. As you have learned, family ecological theory addresses the complexities associated with both individual-level and societal-level forces that affect families. As we pointed out above, it is useful to consider how conflict theory (Chapter 3) can pick up where family ecological theory leaves off.

Conflict theory assesses the ways in which access to power and conflict over resources affect family dynamics. Think back to the inequality track described in Chapter 3; how would family ecological theory explain the complexities associated with each lane, including the barriers, advantages, and unequal access to resources that exist for each competitor? Conflict theory allows researchers to examine the sometimes invisible privileges that situate some families onto very different trajectories than other families. Conflict theory directly examines access to wealth and social capital that can cushion the trauma of job loss or a failed investment. Other families that do not have access to these privileges not only lack those buffers, but they also could face additional stressors, such as discrimination based on race, ethnicity, sexual orientation, or gender identity. Conflict theory addresses these struggles by zeroing in on how conflict over resources affects families on both a micro and a macro level.

Most countries require some kind of education for children; however, the ages of compulsory, or required, education varies significantly between countries (UNESCO, 2016). Additionally, the COVID-19 pandemic has presented significant challenges to keeping children engaged in remote learning, as many children do not have reliable access to the internet—not to mention the challenges associated with keeping children's attention during a virtual school day (UNICEF, 2020).

Each of these factors affects the relationship between families (the microsystem) and the educational system (the exosystem). In some countries, like the United States, parents are allowed to homeschool their children. Imagine how each country's cultural and legal norms—undoubtedly a part of the macrosystem—affect both the social institutions of education as well as families in society. Here we describe various national policies regarding compulsory education to illustrate how each of the systems in family ecological theory might be affected, depending on the broader context (UNESCO, 2009):

- **Spain:** Children in Spain are required to attend school from ages 6 to 16, but some families do not send their children to school. In most cases, these families are left to raise their children outside a formal educational system. For the rest of the children, the school day lasts from 9 a.m. to noon, then 3 p.m. to 5 p.m. The midday siesta (an afternoon rest or nap) is typical in Spanish culture. Schools care for children younger than age 12 during the siesta. There is no siesta break for secondary students.
- **Germany:** Children in Germany attend elementary school, and after fourth grade, they enter one of three "tracks": (a) Hauptschule (similar to a vocational school) generally attracts students with average grades or below and goes to grade 9; (b) Realschule (has strict entrance requirements; all students learn one foreign language and choose between extended education in technology, home economics, and a second foreign language) and goes to grade 10; or (c) Gymnasium (students learn classical language, modern language, mathematics, and natural science), which lasts until grades 12 or 13 and ends with a qualifying examination for admission to the university. One other option is for children to attend Gesamtschule, which is only found in some states in Germany, has no entrance requirements, and goes to grade 10. This school is comprehensive and includes students from all backgrounds. In terms of prestige, the "best" students complete Gymnasium, followed by Realschule and Hauptschule.
- **India:** Children in India are required to attend school from ages 6 to 14. India also has a large private school system, where approximately a third of students receive their education (Joshua, 2014). Since India has been separated by a caste system of prestige and status, some affirmative action policies have secured spots in the school system for historically disadvantaged groups.

Now, let's consider how family ecological theory is applicable to the study of families across the globe. In Box 10.3, we present information from three different countries regarding their ages of compulsory education, which occurs at the interface between family and school. Each country has its own macrosystem, which contributes to the laws and norms that govern expectations for educating children.

Working With Family Ecological Theory: Integrating Research and Practice

Now that we have described family ecological theory, we turn to how the theory can be used in theory, research, and practice. We provide an example of current theorizing, present an article that uses the theory in research, and describe how the theory informs the practice of violence prevention.

Family Ecological Theory Today

Focusing on a cultural perspective of ecological theory, Garcia Coll and colleagues (1996) developed a model to understand identity formation among monoethnic minority youth (that is, those whose parents are both from the same ethnic background). Gonzales-Backen (2013) expanded the model to ethnic identity formation among biethnic adolescents. The cultural ecological model has commonalities with theoretical perspectives we note in family stress and resilience theory (Chapter 11), regarding Meyer's (2013) minority stress theory and its applications to LGBTQ+ individuals and families and Peters and Massey's (1983) theory of double socialization for Black children. These now classic perspectives have shed light on how families that experience racial marginalization and discrimination must prepare their children for both challenges and successes.

Gonzales-Backen's (2013) theory, then, guides scholars in understanding even more complex identity formations. Biethnic youth have parents from different ethnic backgrounds, typically where one parent is a member of the White ethnic majority, and the other parent is a member of an ethnic minority (e.g., Asian American, Latino, African American, and others). In her theoretical expansion, Gonzales-Backen (2013) focused on the rapidly increasing size of the biethnic population in the United States and internationally. She took into account the ecological nests of individual development in multicultural family contexts and the interactions with the broader social contexts and climates of ethnicity, peer influence, racism, and the like.

As we are seeing in many family theories, scholars must be cognizant of the fact that our society is increasingly multiethnic, multiracial, and multicultural, and new research is uncovering the complexity of identity issues that biracial, multiracial, and multiethnic youth, in particular, are dealing with (Durrant & Gillum, 2021; Meca et al., 2020; Nishina & Witkow, 2019; Robinson-Wood et al., 2021). Although, as Uttal (2009) pointed out, one of the weaknesses of the original ecological theory is that it did not take an intersectional approach, now we are seeing a change in how society is recognizing and accepting the diversity of individuals and families. For example, it is no longer accurate to speak exclusively in the binaries of Black/White, male/female, gay/straight, or rich/poor. As we point out in regard to feminist theory (Chapter 8) and critical race theory (Chapter 12), we must account for difference and intersectionality. The Gonzales-Backen (2013) study offers a way into this diversity by understanding the genetic and socioenvironmental factors associated with mixed racial and ethnic experiences.

Gonzales-Backen (2013) theorizes how several cultural ecological concepts can be extended to examine issues faced by biethnic youth. These concepts include social position; discrimination; segregation; promoting or inhibiting environments; child characteristics (e.g., physical appearance and child's cognitive development); and the family context (e.g., familial ethnic socialization and parent–adolescent relationship quality). Let's consider how the first concept, social position, can be used to expand family ecological theory to consider biracial identity. Social position refers to the impact of having one ethnic minority and one ethnic majority parent on a child's ethnic identity development, where the individual belongs to two different kinds of groups: one with a marginalized status and the other with greater social power. Their mixed social positions are reduced, however, to a monoethnic identity, as explained by the one-drop rule. U.S. society has a history of reducing individuals with any ethnic or racial minority background, regardless of White heritage, to being non-White, and thus, biracial or biethnic individuals are often forced to ignore their other racial identity and heritage (Root, 1999). Living in a society that is still "not there yet" in terms of recognizing mixed heritages (in ecological terms, it is the most distal, or far-reaching, factor) can make accepting and integrating their biethnic backgrounds into their identity more difficult. Thus, the expansion of an ecological framework is helpful to scholars to gain a more complete look at the processes associated with diversity, especially in adolescent identity formation.

Family Ecological Theory in Research

It is clear that family ecological theory is very useful across many fields of study. This theory is particularly useful when considering the impact the COVID-19 pandemic has had on all levels of society—both directly and indirectly—on individuals, families, and social institutions from varying racial and ethnic backgrounds. Below, we detail this theory's utility in understanding the disproportionate impact of this public health crisis on African American families and their pervasive vaccine hesitancy.

In an effort to better contextualize African Americans' vaccine hesitancy, Jones (2021) combined Bronfenbrenner's ecological theory with the health belief model. While this article does not gather empirical data, it makes sound suggestions to help us better understand the disparities in vaccination, laying the foundation for theory testing and data collection for other researchers. This approach is very appropriate given the topic is so recent, and research on COVID and its social implications is still in infancy.

To lay the groundwork for this topic, Jones (2021) details how African Americans' beliefs about COVID-19 and vaccination are communicated and reinforced at each level of the ecological framework. Racial socialization inside families—the microsystem—is one mechanism by which parents serve as a buffer and between their children and larger society, which, as detailed in Chapter 12 (critical race theory), poses disproportionate risk to African Americans, based on their skin color. Racial socialization encapsulates parents' messaging, modeling behaviors and practices, and contextualizing racialized experiences for children. An example offered in the multimedia suggestions section of Chapter 12 illustrates racial socialization in a video of Black parents giving their children specific instructions on how to interact with police to reduce the likelihood of being murdered during a routine traffic stop. Other ideas about health and disease emerge out of firsthand experiences African Americans have with Western medicine in interactions with doctors that can be and often are racially loaded.

At the level of the exosystem, it is important to take into account how African Americans have been dispro-portionately arrested for violating public health orders associated with social distancing and masking during the widespread lockdown in 2020. The majority of these arrests took place at Black Lives Matter protests (pre-dominantly comprised of people of color), as opposed to stay-at-home order protests that were carried out by predominantly White Americans (Jones, 2021). It should be no surprise that this racial targeting of non-White Americans for violating health orders would contribute to negative beliefs about the U.S. government's ability to serve and protect. Additionally, several sources of misinformation and conspiracy theories online targeted African American communities, perpetuating distrust and vaccine avoidance.

At the macro level, historical systematic racism against African Americans, including the Tuskegee Experiment, must be considered. Similarly, the chronosystem takes into account the timing of the COVID-19 pandemic and the concomitant uprising of the Black Lives Matter movement for racial justice. Given the ways in which health beliefs are impacted by each of these systems, Jones (2021) suggests the addition of the **nanosystem**, which would allow the ecological model to capture the "internal/psychological catalyst of behavior(s)" and the individual's perceptions of each system (p. 8). By measuring beliefs at the nano level, researchers would be "better able to weigh the impact(s) that each system has on the individual or group to allow for more targeted intervention and additional research" (Jones, p. 8).

In sum, the ecological theoretical framework can and should be used when trying to measure individual beliefs and behaviors by taking into account family racial socialization and widespread social injustice. As Jones (2021) suggests, researchers might just uncover that African Americans are more passionate about and perceive more serious threats from unresolved social injustice and racism than they do from coronavirus.

Family Ecological Theory in Practice

There are many areas in which family ecological theory can be applied in practice; in fact, this theoretical perspective may be one of the most versatile when it comes to its application across disciplines. We now elaborate on how this model can be used to understand how research is turned into action when it comes to family science.

While it seems intuitive that policies impacting families and society should be informed by research, the truth is not so simple. Bogenschneider (2020) elaborates on the unfortunate reality that much policy is driven by "hyper partisan and interest-driven politics" (p. 629), instead of research conducted by academicians using objective scientific methods. In an effort to rectify this, Bogenschneider lays out specific suggestions to bridge the research-to-policy divide in an effort to truly tackle social problems. Bogenschneider reviews efforts taken on by the University of Wisconsin via Family Impact Seminars, which include a "series of pre-sentations, discussion sessions and briefing reports that communicate high-quality and non-partisan research to state policymakers on timely topics" (p. 629). Universities are uniquely positioned as knowledge brokers, bridging the gap between knowledge producers (researchers) and knowledge consumers (policymakers). Bogenschneider identifies how universities become honest knowledge brokers using (a) know-why (action is required); (b) know-about (barriers to research utilization in policymaking); (c) know-what (policy issue is timely and research is relevant); (d) know-who (to target); and (e) know-how (to effectively communicate research to policymakers) (p. 629).

BOX 10.4. VOICES FROM LIVED EXPERIENCE

Owen is a 16-year-old White, cisgender, heterosexual, able-bodied boy. Below, he reflects on how the COVID-19 pandemic impacted him on multiple levels—the most powerful on his immediate family. His narrative is a clear reflection of how macro, meso, micro, and other systems interact with the family ecologically.

In March of 2020, every aspect of my life changed. My life as an individual was impacted, as well as my family, my school and sports groups, and the entire world around me. I was in eighth grade, and I lived at home with my brother, sister, and mom and dad. We all went into mandatory lockdown to help slow the spread of COVID-19, which was the beginning of some huge changes in my life.

I was no longer able to go to school and see my friends because we all had to learn online for the rest of the spring 2020 semester. We were not allowed to socialize with any friends, and sports seasons were cancelled. I did not have an eighth-grade graduation. My little sister did not have an 8th birthday party. Instead, we all loaded up in the car and drove her around to her friends' houses and they decorated their driveways and made signs and waved at us. At the time, she said it was the best birthday she ever had, probably because it was so different from anything else she'd ever experienced. Now looking back at it, we made the most of it but it's sad to think about.

Over the summer, my parents started having more conflict. The tension at home was pretty high, and I started to wonder if they were going to get a divorce because they hadn't ever fought like that before. They both went to therapy but it was stressful.

My first year of high school in fall of 2020 was really hard. I did not know anyone there and had no way to really make any social connections. I only attended in person twice a week, and we all wore masks and were encouraged not to socialize or eat together. We didn't have lockers; we had to carry everything we needed with us. We were not allowed to leave campus to go get lunch. There were no sports seasons, again. It was in-person isolation.

My dad's alcohol addiction got worse during the pandemic, and he went to rehab. When he got out, he was diagnosed as bipolar. He and my mom fought a lot and, eventually, separated. Two years after the initial widespread lockdowns, they are finally divorced.

My aunt also died—she was 43 years old and also an alcoholic. She had been hospitalized for liver issues and the doctors told her to stop drinking, but she didn't. My cousin, who is 8 years old, found her and could not wake her up.

I know the pandemic did not directly cause all of these problems, but I also am aware of how society and its ecosystems impact people and families indirectly. Every level of my life was affected by the pandemic and continues to be. As I write this two years after the initial lockdown, I for the first time tested positive for COVID-19. The virus finally directly impacted my individual body, after two years of long-lasting indirect impacts on every other level of my life.

Know-why refers to using the research at the center of every policy suggestion. Policymakers often struggle to find knowledge brokers who are honest or not agenda-driven with political interest. Policymakers often make suggestions for change that are not based on objective research or needs assessment or program evaluations; the know-why alleviates this problem because it emerges out of objective, value-free research (to the largest extent possible; much social science research is grounded in social justice—see Chapters 8 and 12).

Know-about identifies any barriers that exist to bridging the research-to-policy gap. This involves making sure that research is not laden with discipline-specific terminology and gets to the point in a practical way. At the same time, policymakers are used to engaging in long-winded presentations and debates grounded in persuasion instead of the rigor of the data. Both parties need to take a page from the other's manuals to find common ground and effectuate meaningful change.

Know-what means researchers need to know what is timely and what is relevant research to be conducted and presented to policymakers in the first place. Interestingly, this means researchers ask legislators or interested parties what *they* are needing; what topics need more research and fact-based assessment to inform policy? This can be uncomfortable for researchers, who are used to being steeped in the literature and their own interests. This component requires being patient and stepping outside of typical "expert" comfort zones to build longer-lasting relationships with individuals outside the academy.

Know-who is bidirectional; as mentioned above, it is vital for both researchers and policymakers to learn to be a little more like the other. Demand for science can only come if researchers think more like policymakers and policymakers think more like researchers. Indeed, whenever Angie, a researcher and teacher, serves on a master's or dissertation committee, she undoubtedly asks the student researcher, "So what? Why does this research matter to the layperson? How will it make the world a better place?" This approach is not always popular in academia but has been the cornerstone of doing meaningful, applied research that impacts and heals, as Angie has found in her work on behalf of survivors of commercial sexual exploitation (Tucker, 2021).

Finally, Bogenschneider (2020) points out that know-how refers to the ability to effectively communicate research to policymakers. The two soft skills researchers need for this kind of communication include persistence and hope. The legislative process is long and unwieldy; contrary to how researchers experience study design and data collection, much is out of the researcher's control during the policymaking, passing, and enforcing process. What's more, even though a law is passed, it means nothing if it is not enforced. This can seem overwhelming and pointless to researchers; yet they need to hold out hope that awareness raising and education will bridge the gap between policy and practice.

Conclusion

Since its origination in the field of home economics and its elaboration in the field of developmental psychology, family ecological theory continues to evolve. Now, it is one of the primary theories used to guide research in the family, social, behavioral, and health sciences. Indeed, the Centers for Disease Control (CDC, 2015) provides a social-ecological model as a framework for prevention of violence. This ecological model was developed by researchers associated with the World Health Organization and is applied to violence occurrence and prevention around the globe. Family ecological theory offers a rich metaphor for understanding the complex interconnections among the ever widening layers of the individual, family, community, and society, over time. Yet there are still many challenges, as in most theories, for expanding upon this theoretical foundation to investigate how these multiple, interdependent layers influence one another. Given the track record of scholars and practitioners to date, we have every confidence that this theory will continue to have a strong influence in studying and helping diverse families.

Multimedia Suggestions

www.acf.hhs.gov/ohs

This is the official website of the Office of Head Start, funded by the Administration for Children and Families of the U.S. Department of Health and Human Services. Head Start was established in 1965 as part of President Lyndon Johnson's War on Poverty campaign. The aim of this program was to provide comprehensive community-based child development services and education for disadvantaged preschool children. Among the many innovative features of Head Start is that, from the beginning, it has included bilingual and bicultural programs. The official Head Start website provides continuously updated information for parents and teachers, technical assistance to Head Start centers, implications for policies, and governmental funding opportunities. Their motto is "Head Start: Educating kids, empowering families, changing communities." Clearly, Head Start is grounded in a family ecological perspective.

Activate your theory app: What other family theories could we use to apply to the Head Start program? Choose at least two other theories from this text, and determine whether other theories "fit" this program and the families it serves.

www.ajol.info/index.php/jfecs

The *Journal of Consumer Sciences* is the official publication of the South African Association of Family Ecology and Consumer Sciences (SAAFECS). The journal publishes scholarly papers related to home economics; family studies; and consumer science, rights, and behaviors. They also examine the impact of environmental, community, and sustainability issues, particularly on the African continent. Recent articles address youth unemployment and food insecurity among youth and families.

Activate your theory app: Browse any of the recent articles, and look for both implicit and explicit applications of family ecological theory.

Divergent (2014)

Divergent is the first novel of a trilogy by Veronica Roth and was adapted as a film in 2014. In the story, we can see evidence of family ecological theory throughout many of the main characters' lives. The story is set in postapocalyptic Chicago, where individuals are divided into five "factions" based on their psychological dispositions: Abnegation (for the selfless), Amity (for the peaceful), Candor (for the honest), Dauntless (for the brave), and Erudite (for the intellectual). When society members turn 16 years old, they are psychologically tested to determine which faction they are best suited for. This process of dividing people by their individual attributes into factions of similar-minded people is a prime example of family ecological theory's micro-level systems. Each faction's immediate peers, families, and day-to-day lives are impacted by an individual's aptitude for fitting into that particular group. This pressure to "go where you are best suited" is a part of the macro-level system, or the cultural ideologies and

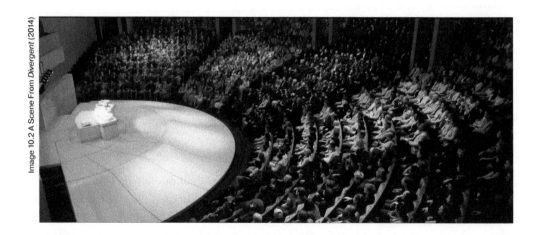

Image 10.2 A Scene From *Divergent* (2014)

expectations for all societal members. Throughout the film, viewers see how microsystems affect interactions with the exosystem, and Tris's determination to actively change not only the exosystem (the factions) but also the cultural ideologies, which present factions as the only way for a society to function.

Activate your theory app: Besides the systems mentioned above, what other examples of family ecological theory concepts do you see in this film? Does this film account for systems of inequality inherent in the storyline?

Game of Thrones (2011–2019)

Image 10.3 A Scene From *Game of Thrones* (2019)

This HBO television series was based on three storylines from *A Song of Ice and Fire* by George R. R. Martin. The show is fantasy based, and the setting for the series is thousands of years ago. It features the violent struggle between the realm's noble families for control of the Iron Throne. One of the most important themes early in the series is the motto of the Stark family: "Winter is coming." This phrase is both literal and metaphorical. The literal meaning of the phrase refers to the winter season, which lasts for years and is extremely harsh, so the phrase is one of warning.

The metaphorical meaning foreshadows the dark period that falls upon the Stark family as they are torn between the family's duty to serve the king, protecting their own, and doing what is right. There are layers upon layers involved in the storyline of both the television show and the books, and family ecological theory can be applied to almost any aspect of this story.

Activate your theory app: What examples of the different levels of family ecological theory can you find in this series? How does the early storyline in the series differ from the later storylines? Do the systems and levels change as the storyline changes?

Further Reading

Dreilinger, D. (2021). *The secret history of home economics: How trailblazing women harnessed the power of home and changed the way we live.* W. W. Norton. In this fresh and riveting history of the field of home economics, Dreilinger focuses the attention that this woman-centric field deserves. She sidesteps the sexism aimed at trivializing "home ec" and, instead, focuses on the intellectual, feminist, and activist traditions inherent in what truly began as domestic science, which sought to educate women and uplift families when opportunities were lacking. The founders of home economics were the progressives of their time and wanted to ameliorate poverty, racism, unemployment, and other social injustices impacting all but the wealthy elite. Dreilinger makes a case for why the science and practice of home economics needs to return to education for all.

Francis, L. A., McHale, S. M., King, V., & Glick, J. E. (Eds.). (2021). *Families, food, and parenting: Integrating research, practice, and policy.* Springer. This edited collection of research from multidisciplinary experts addresses food access and consumption in families from a family ecological lens. The authors examine the family ecologies of food insecurity, eating behaviors, and obesity, addressing a range of individual, familial, and societal contexts. The chapters approach issues around families and food, such as hunger, weight, emotions, eating patterns, parenting practices, and geography, from micro to macro levels. Empirically grounded recommendations for public policy changes and interventions are provided to address issues of dysregulated eating patterns as well as food insecurity and hunger.

Garbarino, J. (2007). *See Jane hit: Why girls are growing more violent and what we can do about it.* Penguin. This book, about the increasing incidence of physical aggression among girls, is one of many by James Garbarino, a renowned scholar of the social ecology of child and adolescent development, whose mentor was Urie Bronfenbrenner. In *See Jane Hit,* he explains that girls are just as likely as boys to "get physical" by participating in physically demanding activities, such as martial arts and competitive sports. Garbarino says that girls are moving away from the cultural dictate that "girls don't hit" and embracing the new cultural dictate that "girls kick ass." Female aggression is increasingly portrayed in movies, books, and television as heroic, competitive, and even violent. Examples of aggressive females include the confident and heroic female character, Hermione, who punched Malfoy in the movie *Harry Potter and the Prisoner of Azkaban,* to the deceitful and cruel teens in the film *Mean Girls,* who play a vicious game of lacrosse.

Samuels, G. M. (2009). "Being raised by White people": Navigating racial difference among adopted multiracial adults. *Journal of Marriage and Family, 71*(1), 80–94. https://doi.org/10.1111/j.1741-3737.2008.00581.x This article addresses the normative ecological context of racial discrimination in which children of color develop. When a child of mixed race is adopted, the child must be socialized from both the perspective of their adoptive family and the perspective of their own racial backgrounds. Navigating racial differences is a growing issue because multiracial children comprise a dominant (though hidden) group of transracially adopted children in the United Kingdom and the United States. One of the major experiences transracially adopted children must deal with is constantly being asked questions such as "Who are you?" and "Is that your mother?" In this qualitative interview study of 22 young adults with Black and White heritage who were adopted as infants by White families, Samuels found that they often dealt with difficult issues, such as their parents endorsing colorblindness and, thus, not preparing them for the racism they would face as children of color. This made it difficult for them to manage societal perceptions of multiracial adoption and the reinforcement of difference in being both adopted and of "mixed" race. The participants and Samuels emphasize the importance of families building connections with the members of the broader community of those who share their racial heritage, as a way to "experience their multiracial family systems and heritages as both unique and shared" (p. 93).

Song, J., Mailick, M. R., & Greenberg, J. S. (2014). Work and health of parents of adult children with serious mental illness. *Family Relations, 63*(1), 122–134. https://doi.org/10.1111/fare.l2043 This article deals with the mesosystemic context of the interface between several family microsystems. The authors are researchers at the University of Wisconsin—Madison's Waisman Center, which is "dedicated to the advancement of knowledge about human development, developmental disabilities, and neurodegenerative diseases" (www.waisman.wisc.edu). In this paper, they focus on the negative spillover from work to family and how it affects the health of mothers and fathers who have adult children with a serious mental illness (SMI). They found that work stress and the lack of work schedule flexibility could lead to greater work–family conflict. They suggest that practitioners should offer parents psychoeducation about the nature of their child's illness and ways to cope with and manage their stress over their child's behavior problems and need for assistance. At the level of public policy, they suggest greater flexibility over one's time at work, particularly for parents of a dependent adult child with SMI.

Questions for Students

Discussion Questions

1. Compare and contrast family ecological theory with life course theory (Chapter 9). How do these two theories address human development, families, social context, and time?

2. In what ways do Bronfenbrenner's and Bubolz and Sontag's ecological models differ?

3. Now that you have read about ecological theory, how do you understand the nature–nurture debate about how humans develop and are socialized?

4. In addition to biethnic and biracial identity formation, what are other important individual and family contexts to which family ecological theory can be adapted?

5. Investigate other applications of ecological theory. How is this theory applied in disciplines, such as biology and earth science?

6. Choose another theory described in this book, and show how it complements family ecological theory. Describe how these two theories can work together to explain a wider range of family behavior and process.

Your Turn!

Bogenschneider (1996) proposes ecological risk/protective theory as a supportive model for creating prevention programs and public policies to help youth at risk for substance abuse, dropping out of school, criminal behavior, and early unprotected sexual activity. Take this model, and apply it to another population often at risk, such as victims of elder abuse or veterans returning from war. How can you use the components of risk and protective factors at each of the ecological levels to promote more positive prevention programs and policies to support the population you choose?

Personal Reflection Questions

1. Thinking about your life today in relation to family ecological theory, describe events and relationships in your life that are reflected in the interrelated layers of micro-, meso-, macro-, exo-, and chronosystems.

2. If you plan to enter into an educational or health related career, how do you think you can apply an ecological perspective to your work?

3. How do the values expressed in your family reflect those values held by the various groups with whom you identify (e.g., religious, economic, ethnic, and the like)?

4. What do you believe about the relative importance of the individual, family, or social environment in terms of a person's ability to succeed and thrive in the world?

5. Draw your own ecomap by placing yourself and your family in the center circle. Now, draw the outer circles, and assess the energy flows across your ecological family system.

6. Think about your own "digital ecologies" and the communities and relationships you develop online (Bjork-James, 2015). Read Bjork-James's article, and consider in which of the ecological layers you would place your online communities. For example, do you position them at the micro level, macro level, or both?

References

Anderson, L. A. (2019). Rethinking resilience theory in African American families: Fostering positive adaptations and transformative social justice. *Journal of Family Theory & Review, 11*(3), 385–397. https://doi.org/10.1111/jftr.12343

Bailey, M. M. (2011). Gender/racial realness: Theorizing the gender system in ballroom culture. *Feminist Studies*, *37*(2), 365–386. https://doi.org/10.1353/fem.2011.0016

Barker, R. G. (1968). *Ecological psychology: Concepts and methods for studying the environment of human behavior.* Stanford University Press.

Berger, L. M., & Carlson, M. J. (2020). Family policy and complex contemporary families: A decade in review and implications for the next decade of research and policy practice. *Journal of Marriage and Family, 82*(1), 478–507. https://doi.org/10.1111.jomf.12650

Bjork-James, S. (2015). Feminist ethnography in cyberspace: Imagining families in the cloud. *Sex Roles, 73*(3–4), 113–124. https://doi.org/10.1007/slll99-015-0507-8

Bogenschneider, K. (1996). An ecological risk/protective theory for building prevention programs, policies, and community capacity to support youth. *Family Relations, 45*(2), 127–138. https://doi.org/10.2307/585283

Bogenschneider, K. (2000). Has family policy come of age? A decade review of the state of U.S. family policy in the 1990s. *Journal of Marriage and the Family, 62*(4), 1136–1159. https://doi.org/10.1111/j.l741-3737, 2000.01136.x

Bogenschneider, K. (2020). Positioning universities as honest knowledge brokers: Best practices for communicating research to policymakers. *Family Relations, 69*(3), 628–643. https://doi.org/10.1111/fare.12339

Bronfenbrenner, U. (1978). Lewinian space and ecological substance. *Journal of Social Issues, 33*(4), 199–212. https://doi.org/10.1111/j.1540–4560.1977. tb02533.x

Bronfenbrenner, U. (1979). *The ecology of human development: Experiments by nature and design.* Harvard University Press.

Bronfenbrenner, U. (1986). Ecology of the family as a context for human development: Research perspectives. *Developmental Psychology, 22*(6), 723–742. https://doi.org/10.1037/0012-1649.22.6.723

Bronfenbrenner, U. (Ed.) (2005). *Making human beings human: Bioecological perspectives on human development.* SAGE Publications.

Bronfenbrenner, U., & Ceci, S. J. (1993). Heredity, environment and the question "how": A first approximation. In R. Plomin & G. E. McClearn (Eds.), *Nature, nurture, and psychology* (pp. 313–323). American Psychological Association.

Bronfenbrenner, U., & Weiss, H. (1983). Beyond polices without people: An ecological perspective on child and family policy. In E. F. Zigler, S. L. Kagan, & E. Klugman (Eds.), *Children, families, and government* (pp. 393-414). Cambridge University Press.

Bubolz, M. M., & Sontag, M. S. (1993). Human ecology theory. In P. Boss, W. J. Doherty, R. LaRossa, W. Schumm, & S. K. Steinmetz (Eds.), *Sourcebook of family theories and methods: A contextual approach* (pp. 419–448). Plenum.

Bush, K. R, & Peterson, G. W. (2013). Parent–child relationships in diverse contexts. In G. W Peterson & K. R. Bush (Eds.), *Handbook of marriage and the family* (3rd ed., pp. 275–302). Springer.

Centers for Disease Control and Prevention (CDC). (2015). *The social–ecological model: A framework for prevention.* http://www.cdc.gov/ViolencePrevention/overview/ social-ecologicalmodel.html

Day, E., MacDermid Wadsworth, S., Bogenschneider, K., & Thomas-Miller, J. (2019). When university researchers connect with policy: A framework for whether, when, and how to engage. *Journal of Family Theory & Review, 11*(1), 165–180. https://doi.org/10.1111/jftr.12306

Del Vecchio, T., Erlanger, A. C., & Slep, A. M. S. (2013). Theories of child abuse. In M. A. Fine & F. D. Fincham (Eds.), *Handbook of family theories: A content-based approach* (pp. 208–227). Routledge.

Diamond, L. M. (2021). The new genetic evidence on same-gender sexuality: Implications for sexual fluidity and multiple forms of sexual diversity. *Journal of Sex Research, 58*(7), 818–837. https://doi.org/10.1080/00224499.2021.1879721

Durrant, L., & Gillum, N. L. (2021). White fathers' concerns for their biological Black and White biracial sons. *Family Relations, 70*(4), 993–1008. https://doi.org/10.1111/fare.12578

Elder, G. H., Jr. (1974). *Children of the Great Depression: Social change in life experience.* University of Chicago Press.

Faust, V., Jasper, C. R., Kaufman, A., & Nellis, M. J. (2014). Cooperative inquiry in human ecology: Historical roots and future applications. *Family and Consumer Sciences Research Journal, 42*(1), 267–277. https://doi.org/10.1111/fcsr.l2060

Garcia Coll, C., Crnic, K., Lamberty, G., Wasik, B. H., Jenkins, R., Garcia, H. V., & McAdoo, H. P. (1996). An integrative model for the study of developmental competences in minority children. *Child Development, 67*(5), 1891–1914. https://doi.org/10.2307/l 131600

Gerde, H. K., Pikus, A. E., Lee, K., Van Egeren, L. A., & Huber, M. S. Q. (2021). Head Start children's science experiences in the home and community. *Early Childhood Research Quarterly, 54*, 179–193. https://doi.org/10.1016/j.ecresq.2020.09.004

Goldberg, A. E. (2019). Open adoption and diverse families: *Complex relationships in the digital age.* Oxford University Press.

Goldberg, A. E., McCormick, N., & Virginia, H. (2022). School-age adopted children's early responses to remote schooling during COVID-19. *Family Relations, 71*(1), 68–89. https://doi.org/10.1111/fare.12612

Goldberg, A. E., Smith, J. Z., & Kashy, D. A. (2010). Preadoptive factors predicting lesbian, gay, and heterosexual couples' relationship quality across the transition to adoptive parenthood. *Journal of Family Psychology, 24*(3), 221–232. https://doi.org/10.1037/a0019615

Gonzales-Backen, M. A. (2013). An application of ecological theory to ethnic identity formation among biethnic adolescents. *Family Relations, 62*(1), 92–108. https://doi.org/10.1111/j.l741-3729.2012.00749.x

Green, D. S., & Chuang, S. S. (2021). A critical exploration of biological and social fathering among Afro–Caribbean fathers. *Family Relations, 70*(1), 282–296. https://doi.org/10.1111/fare.12479

Hardesty, J. L., & Ogolsky, B. G. (2020). A socioecological perspective on intimate partner violence research: A decade in review. *Journal of Marriage and Family, 82*(1), 454–477. https://doi.org/10.1111/jomf.12652

Hartman, A. (1979). *Finding families: An ecological approach to family assessment in adoption.* SAGE Publications.

Hook, N., & Paolucci, B. (1970). The family as an ecosystem. *Journal of Home Economics, 62,* 315–318.

Jones, W. D. (2021). *Social Work in Public Health.* Advance online publication. https://doi.org/10.1080/19371918.2021.2020200

Joshua, A. (2014, January 16). Over a quarter of enrolments in rural India are in private schools. *The Hindu.* www.thehindu.com/features/education/school/over-a-quarter-of-enrolments-in-rural-india-are-in-private-schools/article5580441.ece

Karimi, H., Jarrott, S. E., & O'Hora, K. (2014). Therapists working in new *and* old ways: An integrative ecological framework for non-familial intergenerational relationships. *Australian and New Zealand Journal of Family Therapy, 35*(3), 207–222. https://doi.org/10.1002/anzf, 1061

Koester, B. D., Sloane, S., Fujimoto, E. M., Fiese, B. H., & Su, L. Y. (2021). What do childcare providers know about environmental influences on children's health? Implications for environmental health literacy efforts. *International Journal of Environmental Research and Public Health, 18*(10), Article 5489. https://doi.org/10.3390/ijerph18105489

Lawson, M., Piel, M. H., & Simon, M. (2020). Child maltreatment during the COVID-19 pandemic: Consequences of parental job loss on psychological and physical abuse towards children. *Child Abuse & Neglect, 110*, Article 104709. https://doi.org/10.1016/j.chiabu.2020.104709

McAdoo, H. P. (1993). The social cultural contexts of ecological developmental family models. In P. Boss, W. J. Doherty, R. LaRossa, W. Schumm, & S. K. Steinmetz (Eds.), *Sourcebook of family theories and methods: A contextual approach* (pp. 298–301). Plenum.

McAdoo, H. P. (Ed.). (1999). Fa*mily ethnicity: Strength in diversity* (2nd ed.). SAGE Publications.

McAdoo, H. P., Martinez, E. A., & Hughes, H. (2005). Ecological changes in ethnic families of color. In V. L. Bengtson, A. C. Acock, K. R. Allen, P. Dilworth-Anderson, & D. M. Klein (Eds.), *Sourcebook of family theory and research* (pp. 191–212). SAGE Publications.

McAdoo, J. L. (1988). The roles of Black fathers in the socialization of Black children. In H. P. McAdoo (Ed.), *Black families* (2nd ed., pp. 257–269). SAGE Publications.

McCormick, K. M., Sticklin, S., Nowak, T. M., & Rous, B. (2008). Using eco-mapping to understand family strengths and resources. *Young Exceptional Children, 11*(2), 17–28. https://doi.org/10.1177/1096250607311932

Meca, A., Gonzales-Backen, M. A., Davis, R. J., Hassell, T., & Rodil, J. (2020). Development of the United States Identity Scale: Unpacking exploration, resolution, and affirmation. *Journal of Latinx Psychology, 8*(2), 127–141. https://doi.org/10.1037/lat0000135

Mercon-Vargas, E. A., Lima, R. F. F., Rosa, E. M., & Tudge, J. (2020). Processing proximal processes: What Bronfenbrenner meant, what he didn't mean, and what he should have meant. *Journal of Family Theory & Review, 12*(3), 321–334. https://doi.org/10.1111/jftr.12373

Meyer, I. H. (2013). Prejudice, social stress, and mental health in lesbian, gay, and bisexual populations: Conceptual issues and research evidence. *Psychology of Sexual Orientation and Gender Diversity, 1*(S), 3–26. https://doi.org/10.1037/2329-0382.1.S.3

Nickols, S. Y., Ralston, P. A., Anderson, C., Browne, L., Schroeder, G., Thomas, S., & Wild, P. (2009). The family and consumer sciences body of knowledge and the cultural kaleidoscope: Research opportunities and challenges. *Journal of Family and Consumer Sciences, 37*(3), 266–283. https://doi.org/10.1177/1077727X08329561

Nishina, A., & Witkow, M. R. (2019). Why developmental researchers should care about biracial, multiracial, and multiethnic youth. *Child Development Perspectives, 14*(1), 21–27. https://doi.org/10.1111/cdep.12350

Perry-Jenkins, M., & MacDermid Wadsworth, S. (2017). Work and family research and theory: Review and analysis from an ecological perspective. *Journal of Family Theory & Review, 9*(2), 219–237. https://doi.org/10.1111/jftr.12188

Peters, M. F., & Massey, G. (1983). Mundane extreme environmental stress in family stress theories: The case of Black families in White America. *Marriage and Family Review, 6*(1–2), 193–218. https://doi.org/10.1300/J002v06n01_10

Robinson-Wood, T., Muse, C., Hewett, R., Balogun-Mwangi, O., Elrahman, J., Nordling, A., Abdulkerim, N., & Matsumoto, A. (2021). Regular White people things: The presence of white fragility in interracial families. *Family Relations, 70*(4), 973–992. https://doi.org/10.1111/fare.12549

Root, M. P. P. (1999). The biracial baby boom: Understanding ecological constructions of racial identity in the 21st century. In M. H. Sheets (Ed.), *Racial and ethnic identity in school practices: Aspects of human development* (pp. 67–89). Lawrence Erlbaum Associates.

Rosenfeld, L. B., Caye, J. S., Mooli, L., & Gurwitch, R. H. (2004). *When their worlds fall apart: Helping families and children manage the effects of disasters* (2nd ed.). NASW Press.

Sabatelli, R. M., Lee, H., & Ripoll-Núñez, K. (2018). Placing the social exchange framework in an ecological context. *Journal of Family Theory & Review, 10*(1), 32–48. https://doi.org/10.1111/jftr.12254

Salas, R. N. (2021). Environmental racism and climate change—Missed diagnoses. *New England Journal of Medicine, 385*(11), 967–969. https://doi.org/10.1056/NEJMp2109160

Sanchez, R. O., Letiecq, B. L., & Ginsberg, M. R. (2019). An integrated model of family strengths and resilience: Theorizing at the intersection of Indigenous and Western paradigms. *Journal of Family Theory & Review, 11*(4), 561–575. https://doi.org/10.1111jftr.12351

Thompson, P. J. (1988). *Home economics and feminism: The Hestian synthesis.* UPE1 Publishing Collective.

Tucker, J. H. (2021, August 4). The unlikely story of a sex trafficking survivor and the Instagram account that saved her life. *ELLE.* https://www.elle.com/culture/a36898189/0086-0088-megan-s-account-august-2021/

Tudge, J. R. H., Payir, A., Mercon-Vargas, E., Cao, H., Liang, Y., Li, Jiayao, & O'Brien, L. (2016). Still misused after all these years? A reevaluation of the uses of Bronfenbrenner's bioecological theory of human development. *Journal of Family Theory & Review, 8*(4), 427–445. https://doi.org/10.1111/jftr.12165

UNESCO. (2009). *Global education digest 2009: Comparing education statistics across the world.* UNESCO Institute for Statistics. http://unesdoc.unesco.org/images/ 0018/001832/183249e.pdf

UNESCO. (2016, July). *Leaving no one behind: How far on the way to universal primary and secondary education?* UNESCO Institute for Statistics. https://unesdoc.unesco.org/ark:/48223/pf0000245238

UNICEF. (2020, September). *Education and COVID-19.* https://data.unicef.org/topic/education/covid-19/

Uttal, L. (2009). (Re)visioning family ties to communities and contexts. In S. A. Lloyd, A. L. Few, & K. R. Allen (Eds.), *Handbook of feminist family studies* (pp. 134–146). SAGE Publications.

Velez-Agosto, N. M., Soto-Crespo, J. G., Vizcarrondo-Oppenheimer, M., Veja-Molina, S., & Garcia Coll, C. (2017). Bronfenbrenner's bioecological theory revision: Moving culture from the macro into the micro. *Perspectives on Psychological Science, 12*(5), 900–910. https://doi.org/10.1177/1745691617704397

Yount, K. M, Krause, K. H., & Miedema, S. S. (2017). Preventing gender-based violence victimization in adolescent girls in lower-income countries: Systematic review of reviews. *Social Science & Medicine, 192*, 1–13. https://doi.org/10.1016/j.socscimed.2017.08.038

Image Credits

Family Stress and Resilience Theory

You may be familiar with the one phone call people who are arrested are allowed once they are taken to jail. Have you ever had to use that one phone call? If not, who *would* you call if you were ever arrested? Would it be a family member or someone else? The one answer to this very simple question can tell us so much about how you manage stress and resilience, and by extension, how your family deals with stress and resilience. Think about how your answer to the phone call question relates to your family. If you choose to call a family member, which one would it be? A sibling; an aunt or uncle; or a parent, stepparent, or guardian? Why? Some may choose to avoid calling a parent for fear of retribution or punishment. Others may automatically default to calling one parent over the other because their relationship with one is closer than the other. Or perhaps, you have seen a family member go through the same thing, and you remember what happened to them and how their arrest put the entire family dynamic in jeopardy. Sometimes you think the family never truly recovered from that experience, and it would be much worse if you were to repeat their same mistakes.

It is also interesting to imagine that *you* are the one receiving the phone call. How do you deal with it? Does it matter who the person is on the other end? Would you view it differently if it were your mother, your sibling, your own adult child, or your roommate? How would you react to the stress of being "the one" who was called?

Family stress and resilience theory is actually a combination of several theories that address the fact that all individuals experience vulnerabilities, stressors, and crises that challenge their ability to cope (Boss, 1987; Henry et al., 2015; Masten 2018). From a family sciences perspective, the family unit itself is a resource that can help us stay healthy and grow even in the face of adversity (Patterson, 2002). This theory builds upon earlier work in family stress theory (ABCX model) by Hill (1958), where A is the stressful event; B is the family resources or strengths; and C is the family's perception of the event, or how they define or attribute meaning to the event. If the event or stressor is such that the family cannot immediately figure out how to solve the problem, this will lead to crisis, the X component of the model (McCubbin et al., 1980). The other contributing perspective to family stress and resilience theory, as it is used in family science today is risk and resilience (Demo et al., 2005). This added perspective brings into focus how families react to experiences that can produce negative outcomes (risks) as well as the ability to overcome life challenges and grow stronger (resilience). Taken together, family stress and resilience theory addresses the "whole picture" of how families are prepared for, deal with, and learn from stressful events. To put it into perspective, think about your own family. How well is your family prepared to deal with external stressors? How closely integrated are you, as a family? How adaptable are family members who would be affected by the stressor? Imagine how your family would deal with your arrest, depending on how serious the offense is. Would you need to hire a lawyer or possibly face a jury trial? Would your family be able to afford such an expense? Perhaps, your family relies on shared spiritual beliefs that would provide a source of strength during such an event. Or would the family's social support network help the family adapt and become stronger because of it?

As you consider those questions, keep in mind that family stress and resilience theory takes into account the type of stressor (e.g., internal or external) and qualities like family closeness, history, and adaptability. Each of these factors helps to set the stage for interactions that can lead to positive or negative outcomes. Families provide a sense of history and understanding that help them heal, particularly through the use of shared rituals, spirituality, and cultural and ethnic traditions from their various communities (Walsh, 2016). Each of these factors makes up a family's "repertoire" for coping with problems and crises; they can provide protection against negative outcomes, leading to family resilience. Strong families are a protective factor in the face of adversity and risk. How strong is your own family? What about your friends' families? Below, we provide a case study to help you understand how the theory can apply to very complex, interrelated issues that families face in their daily lives.

Case Study

Eliza's father, Joe, has just lost his driver's license because of repeated driving under the influence (DUI) offenses. Joe, a cisgender, White, able-bodied man, was facing a jail sentence, but the family decided to pay a lawyer to get his sentence suspended. The lawyer was very expensive, and the money that went to pay for her father's legal fees was the money earmarked for Eliza's second semester tuition at college. Because of that, Eliza, a cisgendered, White, bisexual woman, had to take a leave of absence from school and get a job to once again save money for college. Her mother also took on another job to help support the family financially.

Because Joe had lost his license, he could not drive to work, so he ended up losing his job. Fortunately, the 500 hours of community service he was assigned was done at the local library, which was within walking distance. Eliza and her mother sought out support by attending Al-Anon, a self-help organization that provides support and information about living with a family member who has an addiction. One of the issues they worked on in the group was the shame that every member in the family felt about the addict's chronic alcoholism. Over time, the social support provided by this group and the move toward financial stability, along with the social capital Joe built by working at the local library, helped the family to get back on their feet. Their ability to talk with one another about the father's addiction, his willingness to get help, and the mother's and daughter's willingness to face their own feelings all contributed to the family pulling together. Shame, fear, and anger are strong feelings that can accompany addiction in families, but these feelings often coexist with the sense of hope about how individuals can change and families can restabilize, creating new rituals and positive experiences to help deal with difficulty.

What were some of the stressors Eliza and her family faced? How did they experience stress in relation to their own lives and in terms of the family as a system? What relationship processes did family members activate to help the family as a whole cope with the devastating causes and consequences of a serious and chronic condition, such as an addiction? How did Eliza, in particular, balance both risk and resilience to accept and act for positive change in the face of such adversity? What does this family's past tell us about their future? Family stress and resilience theory helps us understand the multiplicity of stressors, including how one stress can and often does lead to another, like what happened to Eliza and her family. However, this theory does not stop at just examining how stress affects individuals and families; it also takes a look at the whole picture, examining how families can become more resilient in the face of stressors, which inevitably affects how they deal with similar situations in the future. Conversely, this theory also takes into account how families may ignore or avoid challenges, which may lead to the family or its members never learning how to deal with difficulties. In this sense, family stress and resilience theory provides a unique look at families, allowing us to focus on the past, present, and future within one framework.

What Is Family Stress and Resilience Theory?

Family stress and resilience theory addresses the fact that life is full of risks that threaten both individual and family well-being. As you have learned throughout other chapters, when something happens to one individual, their family members are inevitably affected, and vice versa. Stressors are a natural occurrence in daily life, and as such, they can pile up and intensify. Stressors can also be traumatic and involve multiple losses, such as those that occur through devastating or catastrophic events. Whatever its origin, family stress disrupts how individuals and families function and adapt over time. However, stress is not the only side of the story; individuals and families also have strengths and are resilient. Resilience is the "capacity to overcome adversity, or to thrive despite challenges or trauma" (Power et al., 2016, p. 66).

One of the ways that families demonstrate resilience is in their ability to mobilize personal and community resources and, thus, cope with everyday stress and unanticipated trauma. Indeed, family resilience refers to the fact that families become stronger by coping and learning from whatever life throws their way. Family stress and resilience theory allows family scholars and practitioners to analyze reactions to present stressors by accounting for how the family has dealt with stress in the past, either making the family stronger or, perhaps, weaker. Each of these factors helps predict how the family will adapt (or not) in the present and even the future. Think back to your "one phone call"—if you considered how your arrest would impinge upon the family, you are taking history into account because you may have an idea of how an event like this was received by your family in the past. Perhaps, your family is exceptionally skilled at pretending things do not happen and brushing difficulties "under the rug," so to speak. This knowledge would inform your decision to call your favorite aunt, who you can trust not to tell your parents and disrupt the family dynamic. Right there, in that moment when you are deciding who to call, we can catch a glimpse of your family's history, how that impacts your present-day decision, and, perhaps, what you (and your family) will do again in the future. In the words of family therapist Froma Walsh (2012), family stress and resilience theory shows us how family strength is forged (or not) through adversity.

As we will see in this chapter, there is an infinite supply of stressors that impinge on families, all of which are made more pronounced with the advent of global health pandemics (APA, 2020; Chaney, 2020; Kanter et al., 2021; Thomeer et al., 2020). In addition to the everyday hassles (Patterson, 2002), such as a flat tire or an unwanted bird flying around your house, or oversleeping and thus missing a parent-teacher conference at a child's school, some stressors are more unexpected, prolonged, and severe. Examples of more severe stressors include growing up with a father who is physically violent toward your mother (Haselschwerdt et al., 2020), having a parent who has a mental illness (Power et al., 2016), the legacy of child physical and sexual abuse in adulthood (van der Kolk, 2015), the destabilizing effects of parental incarceration on child outcomes (Dallaire, 2007), and women's increased chance of drug use when their partners are incarcerated (Bruns & Lee, 2020). Stressors can also include homelessness (Distefano et al., 2022), chronic poverty (Buehler, 2020; Cooper & Pugh, 2020), major disruptions and losses to life and home caused by a fire (Jones et al., 2012), and the distress caused by periodic separation from parents due to military deployment (Huebner et al., 2007). Now, more than ever, we are aware of the stressors associated with the stigmas of minoritized identities (Meyer, 2013), such as sexuality, gender, and race, in particular (Murry et al., 2018; Oswald, 2002; Russell et al., 2014; Toomey, 2021). Severe stressors also include major catastrophes, such as war, terrorism, and natural disasters that can shatter even the most invulnerable families (Walsh, 2016). Farm families, for example, must deal with extraordinary stress and intergenerational tensions, due to the economic downturn in the agriculture industry and extreme weather related disasters linked to climate change (Braun, 2019).

History and Origins

Family stress and resilience theory began with a question about why some families, when compared to others, are able to make it through a crisis, despite going through an event that they perceive as very stressful. That is, how are some families relatively invulnerable to stress, but others are unable to cope? Some of the earliest work, however, treated families as a "one size fits all" without taking into account the ways that structural issues built in to most societies, such as pervasive racism, heterosexism, and cisgenderism, have impacted minoritized families (Came & Griffith, 2018; Tsfati & Nadan, 2021). These are topics we also address in Chapter 12 (on critical race theory) and Chapter 13 (on queer theory).

Since its inception, theorists have tried to explain the ways families, in general, marshal their resources to cope with stress. One of the key strategies used has been to join individual level theories, typically developed by psychologists, of resilience in the face of hardship, such as how a child survives and thrives in the face of parental abandonment (Rutter, 1987), with family stress theory, initially developed by sociologists (Hill, 1949, 1958) to come up with a more complex and nuanced perspective on family resilience in the context of adversity. Henry et al. (2015) describe these developments in terms of waves, with Wave 1 dealing with the origination of family stress theory, and Wave 2 expanding the theory and incorporating time, multiple pileups and the family's sense of meaning and cohesion. Wave 3 is emerging and further develops the ideas of family resilience that integrate multi-level systems and a multidisciplinary approach. Thus, the combining of family stress theory and family resilience theory has progressed over time into a multifaceted, comprehensive framework that allows us to understand the vulnerabilities and strengths of individual members, the family unit as an entity, and various community processes and policies affecting how families deal with every day and traumatic stressors and crises.

ABCX Model

Reuben Hill (1949) developed family stress theory to explain family adjustment after a crisis. His original formulation of the theory was based on the "dismemberment of a family through conscription of the husband-father into the armed services" during World War II (Hill, 1958, p. 140). He termed this theory the **ABCX model**, by conceptualizing family stress as a process that consisted of three main variables and a crisis:

a. The A factor is the **stressor,** which is the crisis-precipitating event. A stressor becomes a crisis when the family has little or no prior preparation for dealing with it.

b. The B factor is the psychosocial **resources** or strengths the family has at the time of the event.

c. The C factor is the definition of the event as stressful. This refers to the **meaning of the event** that the family (individually and collectively) attaches to it. This is also referred to as the family's perception of the situation to which they must respond.

d. The X factor is the stress or **crisis** that causes the disruption in family dynamics and leads to the family's reorganization.

Pauline Boss (1987) further developed the ABCX model as a way to help therapists and other practitioners intervene in stressful situations and to help researchers measure the ways that families define their perceptions of the crisis situation. Boss et al. (2017) combined research on stress from medical, sociological, and psychological research and devised a definition of family stress as a pressure, tension, or disturbance in the family system. The reason for this revision was that a family's definition of a situation (the C factor) is the most important factor in their recovery from stress. As Hill (1958) originally noted, no stressor event, or its interpretation, is the same for every family. You probably remember that the "definition of the situation" is also a concept developed first in symbolic interactionist theory (Chapter 4).

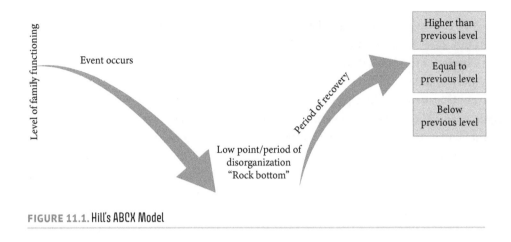

Level of family functioning

Event occurs

Period of recovery

Low point/period of
disorganization
"Rock bottom"

Higher than
previous level

Equal to
previous level

Below
previous level

FIGURE 11.1. Hill's ABCX Model

A crisis perspective on family stress and adaptation has been likened to a roller coaster (Boss, 1987; Hill, 1958). The roller coaster begins with the family being at a particular level of functioning. Then, the stressor occurs, and the family experiences a **period of disorganization**, wherein their prior ways of coping and interacting with one another are inadequate or blocked. In other words, their usual ways of dealing with family issues no longer apply because those coping mechanisms cannot meet the demands of the new stressor in addition to the other aspects of family life. Third, depending on the family's varying vulnerability to stress, they reverse this process of disorganization and activate their ability to reorganize, which is referred to as the **period of recovery**. Finally, they reach a new level of **reorganization** that is characterized by the ability, or inability, to develop new ways of interacting with each other and handling stress. One of three levels of organization usually occurs following this process: Families can reach a new level of organization that is (a) below the previous level of functioning prior to the stressor event; (b) equal to the previous level of functioning prior to the stressor event; or (c) at a higher level of functioning than prior to the stressor event (Boss, 1987; Hill 1949). The reorganization level can be an outcome that increases, decreases, or does not affect the family's ability to cope with stress. To help illustrate how this works, Figure 11.1 presents Hill's ABCX model.

Although Hill (1949) originally developed the ABCX model to account for men leaving for war and then reuniting with their families as a major stressor event, there are countless other contexts linked to military family stress for which this model applies. Current research has found issues of lingering stress and relational turbulence among the members of military families, including active duty military, veterans, and their spouses and children (Monk et al., 2020). In a study of nine wives of Israeli veterans with posttraumatic stress disorder (PTSD), for example, Dekel et al. (2005) used family stress theory to understand how women married to men with a chronic emotional illness stay in their marriages, despite living with a husband who is no longer like the one they married. This study extended family stress theory by finding ways in which the women tried to deal with their own suffering and that of their husbands. Through therapeutic change, they reframed the meaning of the most negative situation in their married life as something positive. One of the major challenges the women faced was that they felt they were losing their own sense of self, as they had to cope with their husbands' ongoing symptoms of trauma. The women lost their personal space because they had to attend to the emotional and physical needs of their husbands. Their own loss included having to deal with the physical presence of their husbands in the face of their husband's psychological absence, what we described in family systems theory (Chapter 6) as the concept of ambiguous loss (Boss, 2006). Further, although the women considered separation and divorce, they defined it as "the impossible path," saying that their husbands threatened suicide if their wives left them. Finally, all of the women found ways to move away from seeing their situations in strictly negative terms; they purposely sought out the positive aspects of their situations and found ways to view their husbands as strong and empowering, despite the new demands that living with PTSD placed on the marriage.

Double ABCX Model

Given the enduring value of the ABCX model, other scholars have offered important additions and revisions. One of the major revisions is the **Double ABCX model**, in which McCubbin and Patterson (1983) devised a way to account for how families deal with multiple stressors over time (see Figure 11.2 for an illustration). The factor of family transformation over time explored in Chapter 5 about family developmental theory helps us to understand the cumulative **pile-up of stressors** and the ability of families to effectively reorganize. The Double ABCX model became a way to address the fact that there can be multiple stressors happening in the life of the family (McCubbin et al., 1980). This addition to the theory is very relevant when we think back to Eliza's experience. Stressors in her life inevitably piled up: (a) her father's legal fees ate up her college savings; (b) he lost his driver's license and, thus, his job; (c) her mother had to take on an additional job to help pay bills; and (d) her father had to complete 500 hours of community service as a part of his court-mandated arrangement. Therefore, the Double

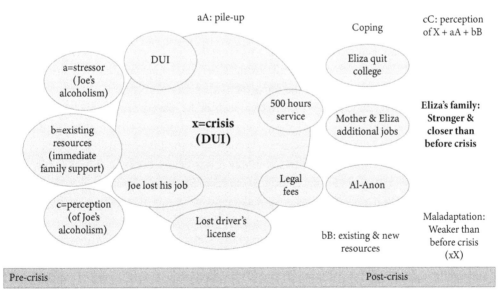

FIGURE 11.2. Double ABCX Model Applied to Eliza

ABCX model attempts to account for the multiple contributing factors that can add to and exacerbate the stress. As Lavee et al. (1985) explain, the Double ABCX model of family stress and adaptation

> redefines precrisis variables and adds postcrisis variables in an effort to describe (a) the additional life stressors and strains, prior to or following the crisis-producing event, which result in a pile-up of demands; (b) the range of outcome of family processes in response to this pile-up of stressors (maladaptation to bonadaptation); and (c) the intervening factors that shape the course of adaptation: family resources, coherence and meaning, and the related coping strategies. (p. 812)

In this model, theorists added the additional variables right into the model, identifying them with "aA," "bB," "cC," and "xX." An aA factor is the pile-up of demands and their cumulative effect over time. In the case of Eliza's family, this could describe the practical demands of transportation independence, the financial demands of paying legal fees and losing an income, and the emotional demands of living with a family member struggling with addiction.

The bB factor refers to the family adaptive resources that exist and then are expanded upon or changed when the crisis occurs. There are three types of resources that can be accessed: personal, as in family members' self-esteem and skills that are available to the family system; systemic, which include family unit cohesion and communication skills; and social support, which are the institutions and people that the family can draw upon to help them deal with their situation. For example, Eliza and her mother were able to access social support through Al-Anon and use that support to adapt to the stress.

The cC factor refers to the family's perception of the stressor that led to the crisis, or cC = perception of X + aA + bB. When the cC factor is positive, family members are better able to cope. As an example, some families swear by the adage, "What does not kill us only makes us stronger." If that perception holds true for families experiencing crisis, they will likely have a positive perception of the crisis and adapt accordingly. Thinking back to Eliza, her family could have perceived the crisis as a blessing that her father lost his license and his job, so he could go to rehab and get better, making the family stronger. Perhaps, some families view similar situations as a perfect opportunity to address the problem and move forward as a unit, stronger for having gone through it.

Finally, the xX factor refers to the postcrisis variables, such as the pile-up of stressors on the initial stressor. Thus, there is more to deal with after the crisis because factors throughout were multiplied. This is a major contribution to the original ABCX model because it accounts for the interconnected aspects of the Double ABCX model. That is, the family cannot return to the way it was before the crisis. Eliza's family has adapted to the crisis, but their lives are inevitably different now compared to before, which makes returning to "business as usual" impossible. Postcrisis, families must make new meanings of their lives to help them adapt to difficult circumstances.

It is also important to note that how the family adapts to stressful situations depends upon a number of factors. These factors include: (a) the severity of the crisis; (b) the severity of the pile-up of stressors; (c) the amount of personal and family resources and social support; and (d) the level of the family's sense of coherence of the total situation—that is, how they utilize their capabilities and strengths to handle the demands of the crisis (Lavee et al., 1985; McCubbin & Patterson, 1983).

FAAR Model

An important addition to the Double ABCX model is the **family adjustment and adaptation response (FAAR) model** (Patterson & Garwick, 1994). This model further develops the adaptive part of the stress process and focuses on how families make meaning of the stressful situation. There are two levels of meaning. The first level, situational meanings, deals with the family members' subjective definitions of their needs and capacities in dealing with the stress. The second level, global meanings, refers to the ways families transcend a situation and develop more stable cognitive beliefs about their relationships, both within the family and in relation to the larger community. As Boss (1987) noted, the level of meaning is the most difficult to understand and measure. Boss went on to develop the concept of boundary ambiguity in the contextual model of family stress. Boundary ambiguity refers to the psychological limbo when family members are uncertain about who is in their family and who is not. This concept, developed as the theory of ambiguous loss (Boss, 2006), is very useful for helping families come to terms with the various combinations of psychological and physical presence or absence of members. Boundary ambiguity can produce a great deal of stress, and its management and resolution is necessary for healing and moving forward in life.

McCubbin and McCubbin (1988) also emphasized family strengths. They borrowed from individual resiliency theory and combined it with family stress and coping theory to develop the definition of resilient families as hardy, adaptable, and able to find meaning in adversity. Thus, they acknowledged that, although a family stressor is not perceived or experienced in the same way by every family, there are some characteristics of families who are strong and resilient that are common across families. These ideas about family strengths and resilience are highly scalable across levels of analysis (from the individual level to the societal level) as well as disciplines (e.g., ecology, engineering, and family science), as Masten (2018) observed.

Still, the FAAR model requires ongoing amendments to help family scholars understand the stress, coping, adaptation, and resilience of families of color, in general, and Black families, in particular (Chaney, 2020; Murry et al., 2018; Smith & Landor, 2018). Given the history of slavery, Jim Crow laws and other forms of overt and covert racist beliefs and practices impacting Black families, the particular contexts of marginalization and strength that affect their lives must be addressed (Murry et al., 2018). At the same time, it is important to acknowledge that even for families who face extreme stress, such as the systemic racism Black Americans experience, not all are affected to the same degree (Smith & Landor, 2018). Again, when studying families, we must take into account the variations in what families bring to bear on stressful situations, how they respond, and how things turn out.

Toward a Consolidated Theory of Family Resilience

Henry et al. (2015) explain that the second wave of family stress and resilience theory began with recognition of multiple ways to conceptualize how families face hardships, express strengths, and continue to grow and change. The concept of family resilience grew out of several theories that include family stress theory (Boss et al., 2016), individual resilience theories (Masten, 2018; Masten & Monn, 2015), family systems theory (Chapter 6), and family ecological theory (Chapter 10).

Major conceptual advances have led to a more refined view of **family resilience**, what Henry et al. (2015) refer to as Wave 3. Patterson (2002) elaborated upon the nature of life as a risky venture, placing families in vulnerable positions but thereby giving families the ability to protect themselves against such risk and to make further adaptations. Another advance was the introduction of family protective factors that can be applied to any family stressor, from the ordinary hassles of daily living (e.g., forgetting that you had a doctor's appointment) to situations that involve significant risk (e.g., driving while intoxicated or without a license). Family protective factors include basic needs, such as adequate housing, nutrition, and health care, and strong interpersonal relationships between parents and children, adult partners, and their extended support networks (Buehler, 2020). For example, just having a regular routine, such as shared family meals, was shown to have protective benefits for a diverse group of young adults' emotional well-being and dietary health during the COVID-19 pandemic in the United States (Berge et al., 2021). Zartler et al. (2022) also found that parents in Austria placed a high priority on preparing nutritious meals, though some children were distressed from gaining weight during lockdown. Parents reported working overtime to help their children cope with and adapt to the changes wrought by the pandemic.

Creating balance in life, through practices such as family rituals that allow family members to rely on one another and build cohesion, helps families to cope with the stress of chronic problems. For example, in an Australian study of 11 adults who grew up with a parent with a mental illness, the stress accompanying having a parent with a chronic illness, such as depression or bipolar disorder had a severe impact on children as they grew to adulthood, yet they also found ways to cope. Power et al. (2016) examined this situation from a resilience perspective, in which families create a balance between stress/distress and optimism/strength. They found that these adult children were able to balance hope against hopelessness, even in the face of family turmoil and uncertainty. Thus, this is a highly adaptable framework and is always under revision. For example, new research suggests that positive responses to stressors typically occur in relation to feeling vulnerable, thereby disrupting the idea that families are *either* vulnerable *or* resilient. Instead, Tsfati and Nadan (2021), in their study of Israeli parents of transgender youth, found that parents described their experiences as a dialectical relationship between feelings of *both* vulnerability *and* resilience.

Key Concepts

Now that we have described some of the major features of the development of family stress and resilience theory, we turn to definitions of key concepts in this theory. These concepts include some that have been used since its inception (e.g., stressor events) and others that have developed over time and continue to show potential today (i.e., resilience).

Stress

As noted earlier in the chapter, Hill (1949) provided the formative definition and description of family stress as the process of dealing with crisis as (A) an event and related hardships; interacting with (B), the family's crisis-meeting resources; interacting with (C), the definition the family makes of the event; that may combine to produce the crisis (X). Boss (1987) also described stress as,

> An upset in the steady state of the family. It may be as mild as a bat flying around the house or as severe as a holocaust; it includes anything that may disturb the family, cause uneasiness, or exert pressure on the family system. (p. 695)

Coping

Coping refers to the fact that not all families become stressed when a crisis occurs. Many families are able to avoid a stressor becoming a crisis by holding the degree of stress to a tolerable level, thereby demonstrating their ability to cope with stress (Boss, 1987). A major way that families cope is by relying on their extended kin and friendship networks, which we understand primarily from studying how families of color, and Black families, in particular, have survived through racial, ethnic, and immigrant histories of trauma and discrimination (Bryant et al., 2010; Peters & Massey, 1983; Yosso, 2005). Traditionally, kin and friendship networks have been very helpful when families lived in close proximity to one another. For example, imagine that Eliza's older sister, Esther, just gave birth to a baby prematurely, and the baby needs to stay in the neonatal unit at the hospital until he is stronger. Esther also has two other young children at home, and her husband works two jobs to support the family. Esther has no choice but to rely upon relatives and neighbors to take care of the other children, while she goes back and forth to the hospital. Eliza and her mother take shifts to help Esther and her family cope with the current crisis. They are able to tolerate the level of stress they are experiencing, but it takes the whole family, as well as members of their community, pulling together, in spite of the many adversities they face.

In Indigenous communities, family resilience incorporates open communication, respect for tribal cultural traditions, and inclusion of broader community systems (Allen et al., 2022; McKinley & Lilly, 2022). Strengths of Indigenous families include the value placed on caring for members of one's clan, which is a reflection of a relational, holistic worldview and a deep spirituality that emphasizes connectedness (Allen et al., 2022). Indeed, among Native womxn survivors of sexual assault, a key component of healing that contributed to their resilience was the sacred act of telling their story and making their collective stories available to other survivors (Baker et al., 2021). A trauma-informed approach that is sensitive to the historical roots of extreme racism and colonialism as well as the culturally relevant strengths and resilience patterns of Indigenous individuals and families is recommended in providing care for those with severe illness (Schure et al., 2020).

Family Resilience

As we noted earlier, the concept of family resilience places a stronger emphasis on the ways a family positively adapts to and rebounds from stressful situations. Hawley and DeHaan (1996) combine the various strands in the individual and family resilience literatures, described above, and offer an integrated definition:

> Family resilience describes the path a family follows as it adapts and prospers in the face of stress, both in the present and over time. Resilient families respond positively to these conditions in unique ways, depending on the context, developmental level, the interactive combination of risk and protective factors, and the family's shared outlook. (p. 293)

Family resilience is not the same for every family, as Smith and Landor (2018) point out, but there are common characteristics that some families demonstrate that allow them to confront, cope, and rebound from what might hinder other families who are unable to regroup after a major stressor occurs. Consider again Eliza's family. One of their strengths is the ability to seek out social support during a crisis. Another factor is that they live near each other and can rely on one another for physical care and transportation. Yet what if Esther lived in another city or away from her family of origin and was unable to rely on them for daily help in caring for her other children? Esther and her family could still have the resources to cope with the situation—perhaps, they already provide emotional support daily through telephone calls, Zoom, and social media exchanges. Another resource is Caring Bridge, one of the many online support systems in which you can post updates about your loved one's illness and recovery and receive words of comfort and encouragement from friends, family, and even acquaintances. There may be neighbors and members of their spiritual community who fill in when family are not in close physical proximity. And even if Eliza didn't live near Esther, she could still organize a website to keep track of offers from Esther's local support group members who have volunteered to provide meals, babysitting, and other kinds of support. In all of these ways, Eliza and Esther and their wider support networks show the strength of emotional bonds that help families stay strong in the face of a crisis or multiple crises.

Trauma

Walsh (2007) explains that "[t]he word trauma comes from the Latin word for wound. With traumatic experiences, the body, mind, spirit, and relationships with others can be wounded" (p. 207). **Trauma** is associated with extreme stress, often coming from major disasters and other types of catastrophic events individuals, families, and communities are not prepared to deal with or deter. Some of the extremely traumatic events affecting families are (a) untimely, sudden, or violent deaths; (b) physical illness, harm or disability; (c) abduction, torture, incarceration, or persecution; (d) relationship dissolution; (e) job loss; (f) migration or relocation; (g) violence and/or sexual abuse; and (h) terrorism, war, genocide, and refugee experiences (Walsh, 2007).

Complex trauma is a relatively new concept in which it is recognized that past and present traumas that occur in a family context can intersect to revictimize individuals. In particular, complex trauma goes beyond the concept of posttraumatic stress disorder by including the role of interpersonal trauma linked to child abuse (van der Kolk, 2015). Flemke et al. (2014) reviewed the emerging research on complex trauma and intimate partner violence (IPV) and found that women's perpetration of IPV was linked to having a history of experiencing one or more forms of child abuse, particularly physical abuse, sexual abuse, or observing another family member being abused. The complex trauma lens reveals there is a critical interpersonal factor that must be taken into account when examining the intersection between individual and family stress. This concept helps us understand women's violent actions against their own partner by linking them to the family context, suggesting that when women commit acts of IPV, their earlier childhood traumas may have been triggered by some interaction with their current intimate partner. Trauma doesn't simply occur to one individual; it has a family context that in some cases has lasting or intergenerational consequences. The concept of complex trauma provides a bridge between individual-level and family-level theories of stress and resilience, particularly in an area (child abuse and IPV in the family) that is so difficult to understand, prevent, and intervene in.

Evaluating Family Stress and Resilience Theory

Strengths of Family Stress and Resilience Theory

Like all of the theories we describe in this book, family stress and resilience theory has both strengths and weaknesses. This theory is highly adaptable; gives insight into a family's past, present, and future; and addresses the very real problems and stressors families face on a daily basis, no matter how big or small. We elaborate on these strengths here.

BOX 11.2. FAMILY STRESS AND RESILIENCE THEORY IN MODERN CULTURE: *THE QUEEN'S GAMBIT*

The Queen's Gambit is an award-winning series based on a true story set in the 1950s and 1960s, which tells the story of a young girl who learns to play chess and becomes so skilled at it that she eventually becomes a world champion. The story begins with Beth growing up in an orphanage after her mother died in a car accident. She and the other children in the orphanage are given tranquilizers to make them more compliant, and this early exposure to addictive substances sets Beth on a trajectory of rather severe drug and alcohol addiction early in life.

Beth learns how to play chess in the orphanage under the tutelage of the custodian, Mr. Shaibel, who quickly observes her talent and continues to coach her in secret. Unfortunately, her abuse of the tranquilizers contributes to her mastery of chess, as she is able to visualize the correct pieces to move and begins to rely on the drugs in order to win competitions.

Throughout the series, Beth struggles in her relationship with her adoptive mother, Alma, who also suffers from addiction. They become somewhat close as they travel to tournaments together, but Alma's addiction does nothing to help Beth recover from her own issues. When Alma dies from hepatitis, Beth is understandably upset.

This show is a unique one to use for illustrating family stress and resilience theory because, technically, there is no "family" unit for Beth after the crises. Yet the interactions between Beth and her estranged father Allston (who abandons her and then tries to evict her from his late wife's home) are interesting to consider, given that her remaining "family" *adds to* her crises. She ends up purchasing the house from him and then sinks into a days-long alcoholic binge and misses her first chess tournament. Clearly, the stressors pile up for Beth in this episode.

Without spoiling the ending of the show, there is hope for Beth, and she recovers from her addiction, and according to family stress and resilience theory, *she* ends up stronger and more resilient than before. She began the show as an orphan, and ends the show without family. Yet she is more resilient than ever and found strength in her chosen kin network to help her through hard times. Her chosen family were there during her reorganization, and she is able to confidently move past many of the difficult times in her younger life at the end of the show.

Positive Perspective on Family Change and Growth

By incorporating the concept of resilience, family stress theory now includes a necessary corrective to the original focus on loss and crisis. In addition, there are positive aspects to coping, even to the extent that people can grow and even thrive in the face of such challenges to well-being and daily functioning, as Hone (2017) describes in her practical guidelines for grieving after loss to promote habits of resilience. Family bonds can also be strengthened by the processes of communication and caring that are needed to get on the other side of a stressful event or a family transition. By taking a salutary (positive) approach, family strengths are also emphasized (McCubbin et al., 1980). For example, taking a salutogenic approach to examining the strengths of happy, enduring African American marriages, Marks et al. (2008) conducted an in-depth interview study on 30 couples that was inspired by college students who wanted to read research on Black families that did not take a deficit view. The findings revealed how the couples coped with the family and work–life challenges that are often brought about by racism. They developed resilient strategies to enable them to pull together and find tremendous satisfaction with their marriage. They leaned on each other and their faith and resolved marital conflicts as they arose, rather than allowing tension and anger to fester. They believed in unity and teamwork and practiced this through their commitment to the biblical concept of being "equally yoked" in the eyes of God. Recently, Marks and colleagues (2020) focused on how three positive dimensions of religious systems—belief in God, the practice of prayer, and faith communities as a support system—sustained and contributed to Black family stability and strength, thereby demonstrating positive elements of family change and growth.

Extends Earlier Family Theories by "Normalizing" the Inevitability of Stress

Family stress and resilience theory is grounded in family developmental theory (Chapter 5), which makes sense, as Reuben Hill is also the founder of that theory. Family stress and resilience theory is also grounded in a family systems approach (Chapter 6) that emphasizes boundaries, communication, and process. Each of these theories can be considered foundational theories of the family and, thus, have roots in functionalist theory (Chapter 2) with the emphasis on normative family processes (Allen & Henderson, 2022). But family stress and resilience theory does not stop at the door of the negative or the deviant; it emphasizes that stress is a normal, naturally occurring dynamic in any family, and it can lead to positive outcomes. In fact, a new colloquialism, referred to as "adulting" and often used as a hashtag on social media, speaks directly to the ways in which moving through developmental stages (Chapter 5) and life course passages (Chapter 9) inevitably involves stress. #Adulting refers to the ways in which young adults begin to take responsibility for their own well-being and take on paying their own bills, including a mortgage, building savings, getting a full-time job, and understanding the importance of retirement and health benefits, among other things (Mitchell & Lennox, 2020). Each of these new experiences inevitably brings stress and individuals learn to cope, or else the stressors pile up. Stress and coping as well as crisis and reorganization, among other concepts, are important to consider and to keep in balance as we examine individual development after leaving the family of origin as well as the inner workings of families. Individuals and families inevitably deal with the things that make them grow: both problems and their solutions. Family stress and resilience theory, then, builds upon and extends other foundational theories we have described in this book.

Conceptualizing Family Stressors According to Severity

The concept of putting family stress, coping, and resilience into perspective as a continuum of severity is important for understanding different layers of stressor events and different levels of family resources to cope with family stress. There is a big difference between being late for a meeting because you cannot find a parking space compared to losing your home in a disaster like a flood or fire. Further, having one's house burn down is a catastrophic event for any family, but it still may be more devastating to some families than others (Jones et al., 2012). Compare, for example, the varying circumstances of a family dealing with the aftermath of a fire. How might a family's circumstances differ if they have extended kin or friends who offer their home temporarily or if they own another property that they can move into while their damaged home is being rebuilt? What about a family that lacks resources and must turn to their car or a homeless shelter for housing? How the family makes meaning of the stressor, in the context of their available resources, affects and is affected by the severity of the precipitating event.

Weaknesses of Family Stress and Resilience Theory

Despite its strengths, family stress and resilience theory is not without its weaknesses. As with other theories, we could argue that its very strengths—adaptability, for instance—can also be viewed as a weakness. We outline each of these arguments.

The Challenge of Simultaneously Focusing on Both Stress and Resilience

As Power et al. (2016) point out, emphasizing resilience alone cannot capture the ways that people also experience the stress and difficulties of family life. This is one of the reasons that the concept of family stress must be combined with the concept of family resilience. Family stress theorists say that resilience is what results from the family's ability to cope with stress. Remember Walsh's (2012) insight that resilience is forged through adversity. Thus, both are essential to understanding families. As family stress theory has evolved into family resilience theory (see the waves identified by Henry et al., 2015), it is important not to forget that how they deal with stress and the pile-up of stressors is what makes a family become resilient. This is why we position family stress and resilience theory together; the movement toward resilience theory does not capture the whole picture or process of how stress and resilience work together and must include the dialectics of stress and resilience (Meyer, 2015; Tsfati & Nadan, 2021; Walsh, 2007). For example, in a study of how adult foster care providers handle the stressors of running a business in which they are providing a "family-like" home for older and disabled adults, providers described the dialectics of gains and losses, which include both struggles and sustainability (Munly et al., 2018).

Do Normative Family Stressors and Catastrophic Traumas Simply Differ by Severity?

On the one hand, as we noted under the strengths of this theory, the concept of "severity" is helpful for putting into context differences in degrees of stress in terms of what happens to a family. But is stress and its severity really the same thing with the differences in stressful events merely running from bad to worse along a severity continuum? That is, how similar are the following events: a car accident, losing one's home, getting a divorce, becoming a refugee in another country, and the death of many family members? Do these experiences go from bad to worse, simply represent a quantitative difference between stressors, or are they qualitatively different, and thus not really comparable? This question is important in terms of helping families cope with stress and trauma. Does the same theory of stress, such as the ABCX model, work in the same way when one is dealing with the normative transition to parenthood outlined in family developmental theory (Chapter 5), as when one is dealing with a devastating loss such as the sudden death of a child? In the first instance, families can expect that the birth of a child is part of the expected family life cycle, whereas no one expects or yearns for the early death of a child. Society treats the first instance with celebration, gifts, and hope but often ignores and stigmatizes the second instance. What is important to consider is that sometimes there is more at stake than simply where a stressor falls on a continuum; birth, death, catastrophe, or trauma each are accompanied by specific societal expectations, including gendered expectations. For example, suffering from PTSD as a rape survivor is not the same as suffering as a war veteran; untangling gender from such experiences is difficult to do, even when a theory is as adaptable as family stress and resilience.

Can Individual Stressors be Resolved if the Family is the Cause?

The origins of family stress theory come from perspectives on the traumatic events that happen to individuals. As is sometimes the case when a traumatic event occurs to an individual, the family can react with denial or scapegoating (Boss et al., 2017), taking on an attitude that, "If only Dad wasn't an alcoholic, we would all be fine." Or, "If my son didn't get arrested and sentenced to prison, our family wouldn't have to cope with such stress, shame, and stigma." Thus, most family stressors occur at the individual level but families are not always equipped to cope with these challenges by addressing them at the family level. Can the individual level and the family level really be combined, or are we always just dealing with the so-called family stressor as if it was just an individual one?

An Alternative Theory App: Family Developmental Theory

In this chapter, we have laid out the key concepts, origins, modern applications, and the strengths and weaknesses of family stress and resilience theory. As you have learned, this theory addresses the complexities associated with facing experiences that can result in negative outcomes as well as positive outcomes, such as resilience, in families. As a result, this theoretical perspective allows a very close look at how families respond to external experiences to predict how they might respond again if faced with another crisis in the future.

Another theory that complements this perspective is family developmental theory. You may recall from Chapter 5 how family developmental theory suggests that each family progresses through specific "stages" with accompanying developmental milestones. Similarly, family stress and resilience theory looks at how families move through the stages of dealing with stressors that they face. This theoretical perspective builds on and enhances family developmental theory. Consider how a married or partnered couple deals with the new addition of a family member; this is an often stressful and life-changing event. Family developmental theorists suggest that families will experience struggles (e.g., sleep deprivation or anxiety) similar to other families in the same stage. However, what family stress and resilience theory adds to this understanding is a more specific *family-level* understanding of how the couple has addressed similar transitions in the past. Do they have one or more children? Did they transition from one to two children smoothly? How does that knowledge help us understand the shift from two to three children? While family developmental theory provides a general understanding of what "most" families may experience during times of transition, family stress and resilience theory gives more information about the family itself, which provides much more family-specific context when trying to understand and explain why we do what we do.

Now, let's consider how family stress and resilience theory is applicable to the study of families across the globe. In Box 11.3, we summarize the prevalence of intimate partner violence (IPV) worldwide. The United Nations is referring to the global increase in IPV against women as a "shadow pandemic" (Murray, 2021). Clearly, violence against women is regarded as a worldwide human rights issue and not just a personal issue. The National Council on Family Relations (NCFR) provided a series of articles featuring a strengths-based approach to intimate partner violence worldwide, which is needed now more than ever. In the introductory article, Asay and colleagues (2014) describe various strengths that can be used to deal with and understand family violence from an international

BOX 11.3. GLOBAL COMPARISONS: INTIMATE PARTNER VIOLENCE

Intimate partner violence is not just a private family affair, and awareness surrounding IPV has increased in recent years as communities, researchers, practitioners, and policymakers have raised concerns about the rising prevalence of IPV during the widespread COVID-19 lockdowns (Murray, 2021). Other contributing factors to IPV have historically included generational violence, alcoholism, substance abuse, and male dominance. Increasingly, many countries are finding culturally sensitive ways to prevent and intervene in the trauma of IPV:

- **Kenya:** Kenya is a society in transition. International calls to action have led to new programs, social policies, and legal advances. However, the incidence of women experiencing IPV is on the rise. According to the UN Women's Global Database on Violence Against Women (n.d.), 40% of all Kenyan women will experience IPV in their lifetimes. Efforts are underway to educate Kenyans about the illegality of IPV and to empower women and girls and help them achieve economic independence, so they can leave abusive relationships.
- **Mexico:** In 2020, emergency calls received to report intimate partner violence against women in Mexico rose 30%, indicating that the widespread lockdowns and associated confinement at home had an alarming impact on families (Murray, 2021). These results indicate the need to deal with IPV in Mexico from a multifaceted, legal, and family strengths approach.
- **Turkey:** The Turkish Federation of Women's Association (a nonprofit, non-governmental organization) reported an 80% increase in physical violence cases between March 2019 and March 2020 (Kalaylıoğlu et al., 2020). It is important to point out that the Turkish government reported a *decrease* in violence against women during this same time period, leaving the actual prevalence undetermined. Around 70% of women reported knowing where to go in case they experienced domestic violence. Yet the disparity between what a nongovernmental organization reports and what the government reports is concerning.
- **United States:** Approximately 1 in 4 women in the United States have experienced sexual or physical violence or stalking, and about a third of women have experienced psychological intimate partner violence (Robinson et al., 2021). Despite the relative advantages of a more wealthy society, IPV is still a severe problem in the United States and in need of public and governmental support for prevention and intervention programs.

perspective. Individual strengths include women's ability to think through the options available to them and seek help. Family strengths include ways family members protect and care for one another in the face of a violent member or intergenerational patterns of violence that involve multiple members. Community strengths include the coordinated efforts of public and private agencies to inform the public and push for social change. Cultural strengths are linked to the national context in which family violence and intimate partner violence occur. Global awareness helps to modify and change cultures where violence is considered a private affair and is justified by male dominance. Global women's groups, as well, are helpful in changing cultures by using an international platform to raise awareness and seek legal sanction against countries that tolerate IPV.

Working With Family Stress and Resilience Theory: Integrating Research and Practice

Now that we have defined family stress and resilience theory, described the historical origins and key concepts, and pointed out its strengths and weaknesses, we turn to how the theory can be used in research and practice. We provide an example of current theorizing, analyze an empirical study that was guided by family stress and resilience theory, and describe how the theory informs the practice of family therapy and family policy.

Family Stress and Resilience Theory Today

Meyer (2013) developed **minority stress theory** to recognize there are specific forms of social prejudice that impact individuals and families from minority groups. Although this framework is rooted in an individualistic, psychological perspective, it is highly adaptable to studies of family stress. More recently, Meyer (2015) has highlighted how resilience is an inherent partner to the study of stress, and when considering LGBTQ+ populations both individual and community based resilience must be recognized. Minority stress theory explains how "stigma, prejudice, and discrimination create a hostile and stressful social environment that causes mental health problems" (Meyer, 2013, p. 4). Being a member of a minoritized group is linked to alienation and problems with self-acceptance (e.g., internalized homophobia, racism, or sexism), and at the same time, minoritized groups have developed ways of coping that strengthen families and demonstrate resilience (e.g., Anderson, 2019; Baker et al., 2021).

Versions of minority stress theory have a strong history in family studies, particularly among scholars of Black family stress and resilience (Smith & Landor, 2018). For a classic example that set the stage for critical studies of racism and families, Peters and Massey (1983) identified a theory of racial discrimination against Black families, addressing the added stressors put upon those coping with the daily stressors of prejudice and institutionalized racism. They found that one of the ways Black families coped with this chronic stress was to socialize their children with a double consciousness about race. Children needed to understand the values and pressures associated with minoritized status as well as the expectations associated with living in the broader society. This framework helps to explain both the strengths of Black families and the unique stressors that impinge on their lives, which can also take a toll and strain resilient capacity (Anderson, 2019).

Minority stress theory has also been useful in studies of LGBTQ+ families (van Eeden-Moorefield et al., 2018). It is also highly relevant for addressing the stress that older lesbian, gay, bisexual, transgender, or queer (LGBTQ) adults experience (Allen & Roberto, 2016). Older LGBTQ+ individuals experience a unique form of minority stress, through the pile-ups of microaggressions associated with ageism and homophobia, often compounded by racism, sexism, and classism, among others. A study by Wight and colleagues (2012) was guided by minority stress theory to examine if same-sex marriage is a protective factor against the combined effects of sexual minority stress and aging-related stress. The authors analyzed a sample of gay married men (age range of 44–75 years with a mean age of 57 years) to examine the intersection of minority stress and aging related stress on their lives. They found that legal marriage among HIV-negative and HIV-positive older gay men was a protective factor that may offset the mental health issues associated with being gay and growing old. In these studies, then, minority stress theory was applied to the family context in order to incorporate the intersections of gender, race, class, sexual orientation, age, and other systems of stratification, a topic addressed as part of feminist theory (Chapter 8), critical race theory (Chapter 12), and queer theory (Chapter 13).

Family Stress and Resilience Theory in Research

In the contemporary economy in which the COVID-19 pandemic looms large, economic and employment insecurity has increased, with low-income jobs becoming more precarious, leading diverse families to experience more disruptions and transitions (Cooper & Pugh, 2020; Kanter et al., 2021). Yoon et al. (2015) examined the role of dinnertime rituals as a protective factor for parents and children when a family is under financial and parenting stress. Building on Fiese's (2006) definition of family ritual as a regular routine that contributes to predictability in family life for the benefit of children's well-being, the authors examined the importance of establishing the routine of eating together at dinnertime. Family stress is especially likely to happen when both parents work outside the home and even more so for parents who hold working-class jobs. Working-class jobs, such as factory work, often involve low wages, mandatory overtime, inflexible work hours, stressful working conditions, and minimal sick leave—and the absence of the kinds of paid family leave that are offered by more middle-class professions.

Yoon and colleagues (2015) conducted family interviews with 93 families, consisting of mothers, fathers, and children. The families were part of a longitudinal study that began during the transition to parenthood and followed them through the oldest child's transition to first grade. The parents were employed in working class positions, and their challenges included both financial stress and having limited resources to help them manage family life transitions. Yoon et al. describe how the transition to school is a "developmentally sensitive period when children may have positive or negative transitional experiences" (p. 95). Family routines are often disrupted during such transition periods, and it is increasingly difficult to maintain them.

One of the most intriguing findings of this study was the gender-specific affects. Fathers and daughters benefited the most from dinnertime rituals. Yoon et al. (2015) suggest that, perhaps, fathers are compensating for the fact that they tend to spend more time doing things with their sons and that dinnertime is an opportunity for fathers to connect with their daughters. Both fathers and daughters in this study found that family rituals were especially meaningful as a context in which positive emotional interactions occurred. The authors also explain why family mealtime is not as effective in buffering daily parenting stress for mothers. Mothers are typically the parents who organize, prepare, and facilitate meals, so there is nothing that makes dinnertime unique for mothers compared to any other activity of parenting. Instead, mothers typically seek the opportunity to have positive interactions with their children whenever and wherever they can. As such, dinnertime rituals may be more stressful for mothers than fathers. Nevertheless, the enhanced interaction and connection between fathers and daughters can be "a protective and stabilizing mechanism in family life" (Yoon et al., p. 105) that can benefit the family unit as a whole.

Family Stress and Resilience Theory in Practice

There are several ways in which educators, therapists, practitioners, and family policy makers can apply family stress and resilience theory in their work with individuals, families, and communities, particularly when families are faced with a catastrophe that pushes them beyond the brink of their resources and ability to cope. When families experience extreme trauma and disaster, family practitioners need to utilize "multisystemic approaches to recovery and resilience" to support individuals, families, and communities in dealing with such difficulties (Walsh, 2007, p. 219). Situations such as the World Trade Center terrorism attack on the United States in 2001, Hurricane Katrina in 2005, the COVID-19 global pandemic, and the displacement of refugee communities and societies through war that are rampant today, requiring a comprehensive approach to addressing adjustment, bereavement, and inevitable losses. Family life educators, social workers, and aid workers must understand that such catastrophic events shatter the very foundations of our lives. Families could be faced with the loss of their homes, their economic livelihood, the death of family members, and their faith in the future, all of which inevitably affect mental health. Yet Walsh (2016) holds that instead of conceptualizing family responses to acute stress as "bouncing back," family life educators and others should shift perspective to instead focus on when and how families move forward from the stressor(s).

Building on Walsh's original concepts, Myers-Walls (2020) offers suggestions for family life educators (FLEs) who work with families facing acute stress. First, family life educators "must assess their own readiness to do this work" (Myers-Walls, p. 666). FLEs should also practice mindfulness, especially when overwhelmed with concern for their own children and families; spillover acute stress can wreak havoc on individuals (and their families) in the helping professions. It is important to network and lean on other professionals in the same profession to, perhaps, alternate responsibilities, build a sense of belonging and solidarity, and learn and grow from one another's experiences.

Though this next suggestion seems intuitive, it is important for family life educators to be able to identify what is actually an acute stress event. Myers-Walls (2020) offers an important reminder: "Stress is a reaction, not an event" (p. 667). What this means is that it is not the FLE's job to diagnose acute stress; some families may respond to a seeming crisis with acute stress, and some may not. FLEs must be able to identify and predict what is needed by centering and listening directly to the family in a crisis. Offering the family choices and options when dealing with potentially stressful situations is key.

Other suggestions for FLEs include reuniting families, caregivers, or central figures with their children as soon as possible following an acute stress event, taking safety into account along the way. Widespread lockdowns that resulted from COVID-19 revealed that not all families are safe for their members. For example, getting a separation or divorce during the pandemic lockdowns was stalled for some families, who were forced to stay together due to financial, housing, and childcare challenges as well as the shutdown of certain government services, such as the courts (Allen & Goldberg, 2021). Further, an increased risk of intimate partner violence, stress due to financial instability and confinement-related stress have been widely reported (Prime et al., 2020). Thus, it is important to fully assess reunification options with these increased risk factors in mind.

The final suggestion for FLEs includes teaching families about stress and coping skills. This can include modeling calming relaxation techniques, helping families set smaller goals with clear, achievable steps to build self-efficacy, and fostering a sense of connectedness, safety, and, ultimately, hope. Each of these approaches can be used in a multitude of disciplines and careers even beyond family life educators; social workers, case managers, health professionals, and community care navigators can all utilize these techniques in their work with families.

All of us are vulnerable to stress and crises, and our families provide the resources and modeling for how to cope with the adversity that comes our way. As we learned throughout this book, we do not have to be biologically related to someone to consider them part of our family. Here is a story about how Zuri developed a sense of kinship with someone who is in prison, mostly through occasional visits and weekly letters:

Since the COVID-19 pandemic began in March 2020, I have written to a young man in a state prison once a week. This young man is the son of one of my closest friends, and for several years before the pandemic, I visited him once every few months. I saw firsthand the toll of incarceration on individuals and their families, from the lengthy car ride to get to the prison to the rules around visitation and contact and much more. Once the pandemic began and the prisons were closed to visitors, I wanted to keep up our connection, so I began a letter writing exchange that I have engaged in now for more than two years. At first, I just sent cards I had on hand and wrote about the weather, my garden, and taking walks with my dog. I also asked questions about my friend's life experiences and activities. Soon, I found myself looking forward to starting each Monday morning with a letter to my friend, and I was thrilled whenever he wrote back. I've worried that we had little in common—me, a recent retiree, and him, a young man in his 20s, but the very real human exchange of "how's your day going" and "I just read a book I think you will like" between two people isolated by the pandemic has led to a friendship that is very important to me. I am humbled by my own need for human connection across the generations. As I reflect on this process of writing to a young person who is far removed from me, I realize how much he has given me in this connection and how developing a friendship across vast differences of privilege, life experience, and circumstances can invite profound changes in our lives. Indeed, our connection is a source of resilience for me, and I hope it is for him as well. Visitations are starting up again, and I have recently been to the prison to see him. But we will continue our weekly correspondence. I am grateful for this life-changing connection.

Conclusion

Family stress and resilience theory has contributed major ideas to the understanding of how families experience and possibly recover from difficult circumstances, whether they involve the loss of a family member through divorce or death or the loss of a family's entire way of life through disaster and catastrophe. This theory has brought to our vocabulary necessary descriptions of stressors, crises, pile-ups, coping, vulnerability, and resilience. It has also helped us understand that not all families can be viewed as perceiving and responding to stress and disaster in the same way. Family perspectives differ according to the history of trauma in their past, the nature of resources available to them, and the community support they can muster to help them cope with and reorganize in the face of change.

Multimedia Suggestions

www.mfri.purdue.edu

The Military Family Research Institute (MFRI) at Purdue University provides research and outreach with the goal of improving the lives of individuals in military service and their families. MFRI lists five strategic goals that guide their work: (a) support the military infrastructure that supports families; (b) strengthen the motivation and capacity of civilian communities to support military families; (c) generate important new knowledge about military families; (d) influence policies, programs, and practices supporting military families; and (e) create and sustain vibrant learning organizations.

Activate your theory app: How could family stress and resilience theory be used to study military families? Are there other theories in the text that would be useful as well?

www.theaverycenter.org

The Avery Center for Research & Services is a nationally-serving nonprofit based in northern Colorado. The organization serves victims and survivors of sex trafficking as well as those involved in prostitution. Cofounders Angie Henderson and Megan Lundstrom center the voices of those with lived experience in the commercial sex trade, and every facet of programming is informed by survivors. The organization's mission statement is "lived experience must inform change," which means that the organization flips the script compared to most nonprofits. Eighty percent of full- and part-time employees and contractors are survivors, and the organization offers in-person and virtual support groups, an economic empowerment employment program, a financial wellness curriculum, a care package program, a scattered site housing program, and licensed mental health professionals for individual therapy. Because of the bonds the staff share due to their lived experience, many consider one another "family" and use familial language—"sister" and "brother"—to refer to one another.

Activate your theory app: While family stress and resilience theory focuses on the family as the unit of analysis, how does the Avery Center step in and provide social support for survivors dealing with crises? In some cases, survivors of sex trafficking are either trafficked by their families or become estranged during their exploitation. How do nonprofits fill these gaps?

A Theory of Everything (2014)

Image 11.2 A Scene From A Theory of Everything, 2014

In this Academy Award winning film, the concepts of family stress, coping, and resilience forged through adversity are dramatically revealed. The main characters are Stephen Hawking, the world-renowned physicist, and his former wife Jane Hawking, the author of the book *Travelling to Infinity: My Life with Stephen* (2007), from which the movie was adapted. In the beginning of the film, Stephen's life is shown as one of great promise and accomplishment. He came from a loving and supportive family, his brilliant career was unfolding, and he found the perfect partner in Jane. However, he discovers he has motor neurone disease, which will affect his ability to walk, talk, swallow, and move most of the other parts of his body. He is also told that he has only two years to live. Despite his challenging circumstances, Jane is determined to stay by his side. They marry, begin their family, and appear to be the perfect couple. As Stephen's ability to care for himself or contribute to raising his children worsens, the stress on their relationship takes its toll. Yet over and over again, Stephen and Jane find ways to reinvest in their marriage and family life. One of the ways they keep their family on track is enlisting the help of a young widower, Jonathan, who becomes a close friend of everyone in the family. Their relationships are all tested, however, when Jonathan and Jane become close and fall in love.

Activate your theory app: How do the challenges of debilitating illness and disability impact a family's dynamics? Did the family in this film emerge stronger, or weaker, than before?

Wild (2014)

This film was based on Cheryl Strayed's (2012) memoir, titled *Wild: From Lost to Found on the Pacific Crest Trail.* In the film, we learn about Cheryl's chaotic life leading up to her journey hiking over 1,000 miles of the Pacific Crest Trail. Scenes of Cheryl hiking the trail are paralleled with flashbacks to Cheryl's earlier life, as a child, teenager, and young adult, interacting with her mother,

Image 11.3 A Scene From *Wild*, 2014

brother, and ex-husband. Stressors in Cheryl's life could easily fit into the ABCX or Double ABCX model; her mother left a physically abusive relationship when Cheryl and her siblings were young. Cheryl married young and admits to having affairs throughout her marriage. When Cheryl's mother was diagnosed with cancer, Cheryl's crumbling marriage soon fell apart. Each of these events, including her stint with heroin leading up to her hike, can be linked to family stress and resilience theory and the way Cheryl's past coping skills predict her present and future. Hiking the Pacific Crest Trail was a major turning point in her life, when she truly began to face the reality of her past life of devastation. The long, grueling hike helped Cheryl move beyond her former life of destruction, arming her with coping skills, strength, and resilience.

Activate your theory app: Which of the models described in this chapter could be used to describe how Cheryl Strayed dealt with life's stressors?

Further Reading

Arditti, J. A. (Ed.). (2015). *Family problems: Stress, risk, and resilience.* Wiley. This edited collection of interdisciplinary research on family stressors examines multiple perspectives on the complex circumstances many families face. Stress and trauma are balanced by a social justice perspective in which broader issues of legal and social reform are incorporated as well as therapy and interpersonal changes at the individual and family level. In the first chapter, Arditti offers a comprehensive overview of family stress, risk, and resilience theories. Additional chapters focus on micro and macro stressors and traumas that challenge individual and family wellbeing yet also draw upon resilience and coping. The chapter authors examine important contemporary issues, such as parental incarceration, military families, same-sex marriage, war, substance abuse, family violence, intergenerational caregiving, and social inequality.

Dollahite, D. C., & Marks, L. D. (Eds.). (2020). *Strengths of diverse families of faith: Exploring religious differences*. Routledge. Faith is a primary way that many individuals and families cope with stressful experiences, whether they occur routinely in the course of a day or through more traumatic and tragic circumstances. In this edited volume, Dollahite, Marks, and the chapter authors have analyzed in-depth interviews to gather the stories of eight different religious communities: Asian American Christian, Black Christian, Catholic and Orthodox Christian, Evangelical Christian, Jewish, Latter-Day Saint, Mainline Protestant, and Muslim. They offer this work as a way to promote greater understanding across two primary divisions in society today: that of religion and race/ethnicity. They address the resources and strengths evident in families who are members of religious–ethnic communities to promote new insights into how diverse people engage with the sacred and express their faith in marriage, parenting, and broader family relationships.

Feigelman, W., Jordan, J. R., McIntosh, J. L., & Feigelman, B. (2012). *Devastating losses: How parents cope with the death of a child to suicide or drugs*. Springer. Written by a sociologist, a psychologist, a suicidologist, and a social worker, respectively, these authors studied 575 parents who are living in the wake of their own child's traumatic death. Although 80% of the parents lost their child to suicide, other traumatic deaths of children included drug overdose deaths, accidental deaths (such as drowning and auto accidents), natural deaths, and death by homicide. The book offers a guide for parents and practitioners who have been down the "most treacherous area of bereavement, the loss of a child to suicide" (p. xiii). Following the death of their son, Jesse, by suicide, William and Beverly Feigelman participated in survivor support groups as both participants and facilitators. They and their colleagues examine the experiences of parents who have dealt with the despair and other intense emotions that parents feel and that ultimately affect their relationships with one another. Parents reported not only debilitating and overwhelming grief and marital discord but also shame, guilt, depression, blame, and the ongoing trauma of stigmatization and insensitivity of others regarding the loss of a child in a violent or taboo way. Through therapeutic intervention, in-person and internet support groups, spirituality, social activism on behalf of educating the public about suicide, and a commitment to personal posttraumatic growth, many parents were able to cope with the loss and move forward with their lives.

Helms, H. M., Postler, K. B., & Demo, D. H. (2021). Everyday hassles and family stress. In K. R. Bush & C. A. Price (Eds.), *Families and change: Coping with stressful events and transitions* (pp. 27–54). SAGE Publications. This chapter expands upon the vulnerability–stress–adaptation (VSA) model developed by Karney and Bradbury (1995) to examine everyday hassles that cause family stress. Departing from a focus on major life crises and trauma, everyday hassles refer to the common, yet unexpected, annoyances of life. These daily hassles are distinct from major life events, such as divorce, job loss, and death of a loved one. Instead, everyday hassles include commuting to work, chauffeuring children, working extended hours over holidays, and arguing with a spouse. Such hassles also include getting a phone call in the midst of a busy workday that one's child is sick and has to be picked up at day care. Over time, these seemingly minor issues pile up, creating tensions and vulnerabilities that affect individual well-being and the family's cohesion. Family-friendly workplace policies and practices (e.g., giving workers more control over their time to address family needs; increasing worker benefits; and creating a more supportive and egalitarian workplace culture) are one of the "fixes" recommended for alleviating the influence of daily hassles.

Ladau, E. (2021). *Demystifying disability: What to know, what to say, and how to be an ally*. Ten Speed Press. In this truly accessible, intersectional book written by disability rights advocate Emily Ladau as a "101 on certain aspects of disability for anyone seeking to deepen their understanding and be a stronger ally" (p. 4), Ladau offers a primer on what it means to be disabled and shares a vision on disability, an experience that impacts 15% of the global population. She offers frank discussion about seeing the whole person, disability history, ableism and accessibility, disability etiquette, and how disability is handled in the media, where disabled people are often on display as tragic ("pity porn"), yet politically and socially erased. The final chapter, "Calling All Allies and Accomplices" provides helpful insights for making a more meaningful commitment to working alongside communities, including (a) to think of allyship as a journey, not a destination; (b) pass the microphone; and (c) keep learning.

Questions for Students

Discussion Questions

1. In what ways has Hill's original conceptualization of stress theory changed over time?

2. Compare and contrast family stress and resilience theory with conflict theory (Chapter 3). How do these two theories address crisis, change, and growth?

3. Describe ways you believe young children are resilient. What about older adults?

4. Considering all of the stressors and traumas presented in this chapter, is it possible to rank them according to severity? Why, or why not?

5. What is the grieving process for those who have lost a family member or close friend to death? Research some of the grieving practices in other countries, and examine how they are similar to or different from those in the United States.

6. Consider the needs of refugee families and children from around the world. How should family practitioners prepare to work with refugee families? Would family stress and resilience theory be applicable, or might the combination of two or more theories be better?

Your Turn!

Research best practices for helping refugee families adapt to their new country. Are there refugee communities nearby where you live? Where is the closest refugee community, and what community resources are in place? Research more than one ethnic or cultural group, and consider how community resources should be adapted to meet the needs of such unique populations.

Personal Reflection Questions

1. In what ways are you a resilient person? In what ways is your family resilient?

2. What are the most difficult challenges you and your family have faced? What resources did you rely upon to deal with the changes that these challenges brought?

3. What are the protective factors from your family that have helped you stay in college?

4. Aside from college, have you ever lived apart (e.g., study abroad, long-term hospitalization, or foster care) from your family of origin (e.g., your parents or your siblings) for a significant length of time? What was difficult about being away from home? What were strengths you discovered in yourself as a result of this experience?

5. What "everyday hassles" are you currently experiencing? How are they affecting your ability to cope with your responsibilities? What do you do to ease the tension they bring?

6. Who is your role model for dealing with life's stressors and challenges? What if you wrote them a letter describing the ways in which they inspire you? What would you say?

References

Allen, K. R., & Goldberg, A. E. (2021). Apart, but still together: Separated parents living in limbo during COVID-19. *Journal of Marital and Family Therapy*. Advance online publication. https://doi.org/10.1111/jmft.12556

Allen, K. R., & Henderson, A. C. (2022). Family theorizing for social justice: A critical praxis. *Journal of Family Theory & Review*. Advance online publication. https://doi.org/10.1111/jftr.12450

Allen, K. R., & Roberto, K. A. (2016). Family relationships of older LGBT adults. In D. A. Harley & P. B. Teaster (Eds.), *Handbook of LGBT elders: An interdisciplinary approach to principles, practices, and policies* (pp. 43–64). Springer.

Allen, S., Perrote, D. D., & Feinman, S. (2022). Family life education with Indigenous families. In S. M. Ballard & A. C. Taylor (Eds.), *Family life education with diverse populations* (2nd ed., pp. 263–307). Cognella Academic Publishing.

American Psychological Association. (2020). *Stress in America™ 2020: Stress in the time of COVID-19, vol. one.* www.apa.org/news/press/releases/stress/2020/report

Anderson, L. A. (2019). Rethinking resilience theory in African American families: Fostering positive adaptations and transformative social justice. *Journal of Family Theory & Review, 11*(3), 385–397. https://doi.org/10.1111/jftr.12343

Asay, S. M., DeFrain, J., Metzger, M., & Moyer, B. (2014). Intimate partner violence worldwide: A strengths-based approach. *NCFR Report: International Intimate Partner Violence, FF61*, 1–4.

Baker, L., Goforth-Ward, M., May, K., & Echo-Hawk, A. (2021). *Supporting the sacred: Womxn of resilience.* Urban Indian Health Institute, Seattle Indian Health Board. https://www.uihi.org/resources/supporting-the-sacred-womxn-of-resilience/

Berge, J. M., Hazzard, V. M. Larson, N., Hahn, S. L., Emery, R. L., & Neumark-Sztainer, D. (2021). Are there protective associations between family/shared meal routines during COVID-19 and dietary health and emotional well-being in diverse young adults? *Preventive Medicine Reports, 24*, Article 101575. https://doi.org/10.1016/j.pmedr.2021.101575

Boss, P. (1987). Family stress. In M. B. Sussman & S. K. Steinmetz (Eds.), *Handbook of marriage and the family* (pp. 695–723). Plenum.

Boss, P. (2006). *Loss, trauma, and resilience: Therapeutic work with ambiguous loss.* W. W. Norton.

Boss, P., Bryant, C. M., & Mancini, J. A. (2017). *Family stress management: A contextual approach* (3rd ed.). SAGE Publications.

Braun, B. (2019, September). Farm family stressors: Private problems, public issue. *National Council on Family Relations Policy Brief, 4*(2), 1–6. https://www.ncfr.org/policy/research-and-policy-briefs

Bruns, A., & Lee, H. (2020). Partner incarceration and women's substance use. *Journal of Marriage and Family, 82*(4), 1178–1196. https://doi.org/10.1111/jomf.12659

Bryant, C. M., Wickrama, K. A. S., Bolland, J., Bryant, B. M., Cutrona, C. E., & Stanik, C. E. (2010). Race matters, even in marriage: Identifying factors linked to marital outcomes for African Americans. *Journal of Family Theory & Review, 2*(3), 157–174. https://doi.org/10.1111/j.1756-2589.2010.00051.x

Buehler, C. (2020). Family processes and children's and adolescents' well-being. *Journal of Marriage and Family, 82*(1), 145–174. https://doi.org/10/1111/jomf.12637

Came, H., & Griffith, D. (2018). Tackling racism as a "wicked" public health problem: Enabling allies in anti-racism praxis. *Social Science & Medicine, 199*, 181–188. https://doi.org/10.1016/j.socscimed.2017.03.028

Chaney, C. (2020). Family stress and coping among African Americans in the age of COVID-19. *Journal of Comparative Family Studies, 51*(3–4), 254–273. https://doi.org/10.3138/jcfs.51.3-4.003

Cooper, M., & Pugh, A. J. (2020). Families across the income spectrum: A decade in review. *Journal of Marriage and Family, 82*(1), 272–299. https://doi.org/10.1111/jomf.12623

Dallaire, D. H. (2007). Incarcerated mothers and fathers: A comparison of risks for children and families. *Family Relations, 56*(5), 440–453. https://doi.org/10.1111/j.1741-3729. 2007.00472.x

Dekel, R., Goldblatt, H., Keidar, M., Solomon, Z., & Polliack, M. (2005). Being a wife of a veteran with posttraumatic stress disorder. *Family Relations, 54*(1), 24–36. https://doi.org/10.1111/j.0197-6664.2005.00003.x

Demo, D. H., Aquilino, W. S., & Fine, M. A. (2005). Family composition and family transitions. In V. L. Bengtson, A. C. Acock, K. R. Allen, P. Dilworth-Anderson, & D. M. Klein (Eds.), *Sourcebook of family theory and research* (pp. 119–142). SAGE Publications.

Distefano, R., Nelson, K. M., & Masten, A. S. (2022). A qualitative analysis of autonomy-supportive parenting in families experiencing homelessness. *Family Relations, 71*(1), 147–162. https://doi.org/10.1111/fare.12626

Fiese, B. H. (2006). *Family routines and rituals.* Yale University Press.

Flemke, K. R., Underwood, J., & Allen, K. R. (2014). Childhood abuse and women's use of intimate partner violence: Exploring the role of complex trauma. *Partner Abuse: New Directions in Research, Intervention, and Policy, 5*(1), 98–112. https://doi.org/10.1891/1946-6560.5.1.98

Haselschwerdt, M. L., Maddox, L., & Hlavaty, L. (2020). Young adult women's perceptions of their maritally violent fathers. *Family Relations, 69*(2), 335–350. https://doi.org/10.1111/fare.12406

Hawking, J. (2007). *Travelling to infinity: My life with Stephen.* Alma.

Hawley, D. R., & DeHaan, L. (1996). Toward a definition of family resilience: Integrating life-span and family perspectives. *Family Process, 35*(3), 283–298. https://doi.org/10.1111/j.1545-5300.1996.00283.x

Henry, C. S., Morris, A. H., & Harrist, A. W (2015). Family resilience: Moving into the third wave. *Family Relations, 64*(1), 22–43. https://doi.org/10.1111/fare.l2106

Hill, R. (1949). *Families under stress: Adjustment to the crises of war separation and reunion.* Harper.

Hill, R. (1958). Generic features of families under stress. *Social Casework, 49*(2–3), 139–150. https://doi.org/10.1177/1044389458039002-318

Hone, L. (2017). *Resilient grieving: Finding strength and embracing life after a loss that changes everything.* The Experiment.

Huebner, A. J., Mancini, J. A., Wilcox, R. M., Grass, S. R., & Grass, G. A. (2007). Parental deployment and youth in military families: Exploring uncertainty and ambiguous loss. *Family Relations, 56*(2), 112–122. https://doi.org/10.1111/j.1741-3729.2007.00445.x

Jones, R. T., Ollendick, T. H., Mathai, C. M., Allen, K. R., Hadder, J. M., Chapman, S., & Woods, O. (2012). "When I came home ... everything was gone." The impact of residential fires on children. *Fire Technology, 48*(4), 927–943. https://doi.org/10.1007/sl0694-012-0252-2

Kanter, J. B., Williams, D. T., & Rauer, A. J. (2021). Strengthening lower-income families: Lessons learned from policy responses to the COVID-19 pandemic. *Family Process, 60*(4), 1389–1402. https://doi.org/10.1111/famp.12716

Karney, B. R., & Bradbury, T. N. (1995). The longitudinal course of marital quality and stability: A review of theory, method, and research. *Psychological Bulletin, 118*(1), 3–34. https://doi.org/l0.1037/0033-2909.118.1.3

Kalaylıoğlu, Y., Öztürk, A. M., & Eker, G. B. (2020). *The economic and social impact of COVID-19 on women and men: Rapid gender assessment of COVID-19 implications in Turkey.* UN Women. https://eca.unwomen.org/sites/default/files/Field%20Office%20ECA/Attachments/Publications/2020/06/Rapid%20Gender%20Assessment%20Report%20Turkey.pdf

Lavee, Y., McCubbin, H. I., & Patterson, J. M. (1985). The double ABCX model of family stress and adaptation: An empirical test by analysis of structural equations with latent variables. *Journal of Marriage and the Family, 47*(4), 811–825. https://doi.org/10.2307/352326

Marks, L. D., Hopkins, K., Chaney, C., Monroe, P. A., Nesteruk, O., & Sasser, D. D. (2008). "Together, we are strong": A qualitative study of happy, enduring African American marriages. *Family Relations, 57*(2), 172–185. https://doi.org/10.1111/j.1741-3729.2008.00492.x

Marks, L. D., Moore, T. J., Skipper, A., & Rose, A. (2020). Black families and religious beliefs, practices, and communities. In A. G. James, Jr. (Ed.), *Black families: A systems approach* (pp. 34–43). Cognella Academic Publishing.

Masten, A. S. (2018). Resilience theory and research on children and families: Past, present, and promise. *Journal of Family Theory & Review, 10*(1), 12–31. https://doi.org/10.1111/jftr.12255

Masten, A. S., & Monn, A. R. (2015). Child and family resilience: A call for integrated science, practice, and professional training. *Family Relations, 64*(1), 5–21. https://doi.org/10.1111/fare.12103

McCubbin, H. I., Joy, C. B., Cauble, A. E., Comeau, J. K., Patterson, J. M., & Needle, R. H. (1980). Family stress and coping: A decade review. *Journal of Marriage and the Family, 42*(4), 855–871. https://doi.org/10.2307/351829

McCubbin, H., & McCubbin, M. (1988). Typologies of resilient families: Emerging roles of social class and ethnicity. *Family Relations, 37*(3), 247–254. https://doi.org/10.2307/584557

McCubbin, H. I., & Patterson, J. M. (1983). The family stress process: The Double ABCX model of adjustment and adaptation. *Marriage and Family Review, 6*(1–2), 7–37. https://doi.org/10.1300/j002v06n01_02

McKinley, C. E., & Lilly, J. (2022). "It's in the family circle": Communication promoting indigenous family resilience. *Family Relations, 71*(1), 108–129. https://doi.org/10.1111/fare.12600

Meyer, I. H. (2013). Prejudice, social stress, and mental health in lesbian, gay, and bisexual populations: Conceptual issues and research evidence. *Psychology of Sexual Orientation and Gender Diversity, 1*(S), 3–26. https://doi.org/10.1037/2329-0382.1.S.3

Meyer, I. H. (2015). Resilience in the study of minority stress and health of sexual and gender minorities. *Psychology of Sexual Orientation and Gender Diversity, 2*(3), 209–213. https://doi.org/10.1037/sgd0000132

Mitchell, B. A., & Lennox, R. (2020). "You gotta be able to pay your own way": Canadian news media discourse and young adults' subjectivities of "successful" adulting. *Canadian Journal of Sociology, 45*(3), 213–238.

Monk, K., Basinger, E. D., & Abendschein, B. (2020). Relational turbulence and psychological distress in romantic relationships in the military. *Journal of Social and Personal Relationships, 37*(3), 942–964. https://doi.org/10.1177/0265407519883701

Munly, K., Roberto, K. A., & Allen, K. R. (2018). Understanding resilience of adult foster care providers. In B. Resnick, L. P. Gwyther, & K. A. Roberto (Eds.), *Resilience in aging: Concepts, research, and outcomes* (2nd ed., pp. 367–383). Springer.

Murray, C. (2021, January 26). *Mexico's emergency calls on violence against women spiked in 2020.* https://www.globalcitizen.org/en/content/mexico-violence-women-emergency-calls/

Murry, V. M., Butler-Barnes, S. T., Mayo-Gamble, T. L., & Inniss-Thompson, M. N. (2018). Excavating new constructs for family stress theories in the context of everyday life experiences of Black American families. *Journal of Family Theory & Review, 10*(2), 384–405. https://doi.org/10.1111/jftr.12256

Myers-Walls, J. A. (2020). Family life education for families facing acute stress: Best practices and recommendations. *Family Relations, 69*(3), 662–676. https://doi.org/10.1111/fare.12452

Oswald, R. F. (2002). Resilience within the family networks of lesbians and gay men: Intentionality and redefinition. *Journal of Marriage and Family, 64*(2), 374–383. https://doi.org/10.1111/j.1741-3737.2002.00374.x

Patterson, J. M. (2002). Integrating family resilience and family stress theory. *Journal of Marriage and Family, 64*(2), 349–360. https://doi.org/10.1111/j.1741-3737.2002.00349.x

Patterson, J. M., & Garwick, A. (1994). Levels of meaning in family stress theory. *Family Process, 33*(3), 287–304. https://doi.org/10.1111/j.1545-5300.1994.00287.x

Peters, M. F., & Massey, G. (1983). Mundane extreme environmental stress in family stress theories: The case of Black families in White America. *Marriage and Family Review, 6*(1–2), 193–218. https://doi.org/10.1300/J002v06n 01_10

Power, J., Goodyear, M., Maybery, D., Reupert, A., O'Hanlon, B., Cuff, R., & Perlesz, A. (2016). Family resilience in families where a parent has a mental illness. *Journal of Social Work, 16*(1), 66–82. https://doi.org/10.1177/1468017314568081

Prime, H., Wade, M., & Browne, D. T. (2020). Risk and resilience in family well-being during the COVID-19 pandemic. *American Psychologist, 75*(5), 631–643. http://dx.doi.org/10.1037/amp0000660

Robinson, S. R., Ravi, K., & Voth Schrag, R. J. (2021). A systematic review of barriers to formal help seeking for adult survivors of IPV in the United States, 2005–2019. *Trauma, Violence, & Abuse, 22*(5), 1279–1295. https://doi.org/10.1177/1524838020916254

Russell, S. T., Toomey, R. B., Ryan, C., & Diaz, R. M. (2014). Being out at school: The implications of school victimization and young adult adjustment. *American Journal of Orthopsychiatry, 84*(6), 635–643. https://doi.org/10.1037/ort0000037

Rutter, M. (1987). Psychosocial resilience and protective mechanisms. *American Journal of Orthopsychiatry, 57*(3), 316–331. https://doi.org/10.1111/j.1939-0025.1987.tb03541.x

Schure, M., Allen, S., Trottier, C., McCormick, A., Other Medicine, L., Castille, D., & Held, S. (2020). Daasachchuchik: A trauma-informed approach to developing a chronic illness self-management program for the Apsáalooke people. *The Journal of Health Care for the Poor and Underserved, 31*(2), 992–1006. https://doi.org/10.1353/hpu.2020.0073

Smith, S. M., & Landor, A. M. (2018). Toward a better understanding of African American families: Development of the sociocultural family stress model. *Journal of Family Theory & Review, 10*(2), 434–450. https://doi.org/10.1111/jftr.12260

Strayed, C. (2010). *Wild: From lost to found on the Pacific Crest Trail.* Knopf.

Thomeer, M. B., Yahirun, J., & Colon-Lopez, A. (2020). How families matter for health inequality during the COVID-19 pandemic. *Journal of Family Theory & Review, 12*(4), 448–463. https://doi.org/10.1111/jftr.12398

Toomey, R. B. (2021). Advancing research on minority stress and resilience in trans children and adolescents in the 21st century. *Child Development Perspectives, 15*(2), 96–102. https://doi.org/10.1111/cdep.12405

Tsfati, M., & Nadan, Y. (2021). Between vulnerability and resilience: Parents of transgender young adults. *Family Process.* Advance online publication. https://doi.org/10.1111/famp.12678

UN Women's Global Database on Violence Against Women. (n.d.). https://evaw-global-database.unwomen.org/en/countries/africa/kenya

van der Kolk, B. A. (2015). *The body keeps the score: Brain, mind, and body in the healing of trauma.* Penguin.

van Eeden-Moorefield, B., Few-Demo, A. L., Benson, K., Bible, J., & Lummer, S. (2018). A content analysis of LGBT research in top family journals 2000–2015. *Journal of Family Issues, 39*(5), 1374–1395. https://doi.org/10.1177/019251X17710284

Walsh, F. (2007). Traumatic loss and major disasters: Strengthening family and community resilience. *Family Process, 46*(2), 207–227. https://doi.org/10.1111/j.l545-5300.2007. 00205.x

Walsh, F. (2012). Family resilience: Strengths forged through adversity. In F. Walsh (Ed.), *Normal family processes: Growing diversity and complexity* (4th ed., pp. 399–427). Guilford Press.

Walsh, F. (2016). *Strengthening family resilience* (3rd ed.). Guilford Press.

Wight, R. G., LeBlanc, A. J., de Vries, B., & Detels, R. (2012). Stress and mental health among midlife and older gay-identified men. *American Journal of Public Health, 102*(3), 503–510. https://doi.org/10.2105/AJPH.2011.300384

Yoon, Y., Newkirk, K., & Perry-Jenkins, M. (2015). Parenting stress, dinnertime rituals, and child well-being in working-class families. *Family Relations, 64*(1), 93–107. https://doi.org/10.1111/fare.12107

Yosso, T. J. (2005). Whose culture has capital? A critical race theory discussion of community cultural wealth. *Race, Ethnicity and Education, 8*(1), 69–91. https://doi.org/10.1080/1361332052000341006

Zartler, U., Dafert, V., & Dirnberger, P. (2022). What will the coronavirus do to our kids? Parents in Austria dealing with the effects of the COVID-19 pandemic on their children. *Journal of Family Research, 34*(1), 367–393. https://doi.org/10.20377/jfr-713

Image Credits

Critical Race Theory

ritical theories are, at the core, theories of pure curiosity. As a child, when a parent or caregiver told you what to do or established a rule, do you remember asking "Why?" and having your parent or caregiver respond with "Because I said so"? If you did, and if you got frustrated at that answer like most children, you should be able to easily understand critical theories. Critical theories do not accept the status quo; instead, they reject the "Because I said so" explanation because it provides no under-standing of the power dynamics behind the decision. On the other hand, the type of authentic curiosity that critical theorists use motivates us to wonder about why the rules are the way they are. Ultimately, critical theories are about an analysis of power (theory) and the promotion of social justice (action). The curiosity that drives critical theory seeks to pull the proverbial curtain back to examine the power dynamics inherent in individual, family, and societal systems.

In the study of families, scholars use many critical ways of theorizing, including conflict (see Chapter 3); feminist, intersectional, and critical disability theories (Chapter 8); as well as queer theory (see Chapter 13). All of these perspectives challenge the idea that there is a "normal" or "right" way to interact with one another, to live in families, to earn a living, and to be a respectable citizen. Instead, they point out that the hierarchical power structure that upholds society gives more privileges to people from the dominant group (e.g., White, middle and upper class, male, able-bodied, heterosexual, and cisgender) and renders the lives of those from more marginalized groups less valuable. These issues are particularly salient for families on a macro level because one of the main ways privilege is socially reproduced is within families. In the study of families, critical theories seek to unmask the oppressive conditions of society to deconstruct the belief that families do and should adhere to a "normal" status quo and to dismantle the belief that families are not political (Few-Demo & Allen, 2020; Osmond, 1987).

Does your family fit the status quo? Would you ever have had the opportunity growing up to ask critical questions about family structures, race, gender, religion, privilege, and power? If you did, you probably started practicing critical theorizing much earlier than, perhaps, your classmates. Out of all the theories we present in this text, critical theories are arguably the most applicable because, by defi-nition, they require both questioning existing knowledge *and* taking action to address contradictions and inequalities. As we learned in the feminist theory chapter, critical theories work the intersections among a critical social analysis of ideas and personal experience, through praxis (Allen, 2022). **Praxis** is the translation of theory into social action that tries to improve the life circumstances of people who are directly oppressed at micro, meso and macro levels. In this chapter, we take up a particular form of critical theory—critical race theory—to address the historical racism in most societies and to allow us to consider both the strengths and vulnerabilities impacting families of color in a society that privileges and protects White families.

Case Study

Macey and Tyra are the individuals in our case study. In their sociological theory course during the chapter on critical race theory, the professor asked the students to participate in a "privilege walk," based on McIntosh's (2020) work on White privilege. Participation was optional, but all 15 students, a mix of racial and ethnic identities, gender identities, and sexual orientations, lined up to complete the activity.

At first, as Macey (a White, cisgender, heterosexual woman) was listening to the professor describe the activity, she was certain she'd end up somewhere in the middle of the pack. She grew up in a middle-class family, has a brother who is incarcerated with a felony, and has had to work her entire adult life. She struggled through her first couple of semesters of college but has worked hard to raise her graduating GPA up to a 3.6, of which she is so proud.

Tyra, on the other hand, knew right away where she'd end up. As a Black cisgender heterosexual woman, she fully expected to be toward the back of the room. She knew she had some privilege, namely being in college, but based on her personal experiences the first 20 years of her life, she knew what it was like to be minoritized in a predominantly White state, city, and campus.

As the professor read off the statements, students were asked to take one step forward if each statement was true for them and one step back if the statement was false. Statements ranged from measuring social capital (e.g., Have you ever been offered a good job because of your connections?) to representation and belonging (e.g., When you look around your classes on campus, do you feel like you belong? Do you have any professors whose identities are similar to you?).

By the end of the exercise, Macey was at the front of the room, and Tyra was in the back. The students at the front of the room were instructed to turn around to see where everyone in the class ended up. When Macey and Colby, two White, cisgender, heterosexual students turned around, they saw their Black, Brown, nonbinary, transgender, lesbian, and gay classmates behind them. The results of the activity, the professor said, mirrored how White privilege functions in broader society. Each statement the professor read measured belonging, stigma, gender inequality, individual and institutional discrimination, and racism.

Macey felt awful. Some of her closest friends, who she'd been in a cohort with her entire time in college, were at the back of the room. She'd heard them participate in class discussions about their experiences related to racial injustice and Black Lives Matter, among other things. But it was not until the privilege walk that she truly saw how these otherwise invisible inequalities actually manifest into oppression that physically separated them from one another.

Macey also heard other classmates describe the privilege of "White passing" from students with mixed heritages, as in those who were Lebanese and White or Mexican and White. They described feeling strange when the statement asked them to take a step forward if they'd never been followed in a retail store by someone who suspected they'd shoplift. They said they knew skin color mattered and it felt strange to have that small amount of privilege awarded to them, while simultaneously knowing they were oppressed in other areas of their lives.

Tyra, on the other hand, was quiet during discussion. She had no "Aha!" moments to share; she was well aware of her lived experience as a Black woman. She appreciated how her classmates did not get defensive but, instead, modeled the types of discussions she wished occurred in other classes. At the end of the privilege walk, the class gathered together to learn about antiracism, and Tyra listened to her White classmates come up with ways to actively fight against racist ideologies, policies, and structures. Many of the students discussed how they simply were not encouraged to consider race, much less antiracism, growing up. Some students shared how their families openly espoused racist ideas, and it was not until college that these students were able to challenge their familial perspectives. Tyra thought about her own family and how she had absolutely no choice but to experience racism and **misogynoir** (i.e., specific prejudice against Black women; Bailey, 2010, 2021), as did her family members. Her uncle was killed by police during a traffic stop when she was a small child. She vividly remembers the day her parents sat her down at age 6 to discuss what to do if she were ever in the car and police pulled them over (in fact, we explore this issue in more depth in Multimedia Suggestions at the end of the chapter). She remembers feeling sad, frustrated, and confused about the entire discussion. Even at such a young age, it did not take long for her to start picking up on what her parents referenced during that talk. During the classroom discussion, Tyra didn't share any of this. She didn't need to; she stayed quiet, and she was not called on to "speak for all Black folks" like some of her other professors had done.

What can we learn from an in-person visual activity that takes a classroom of students, who have been building community all semester, and asks them to reflect and be vulnerable in a discussion around White privilege? Would this same activity work in a room of strangers? How can we, as a society, commit to antiracist actions? And what role do families play in all of this?

BOX 12.1. AT A GLANCE: CRITICAL RACE THEORY

- **Race:** A master category used as a major form of social inequality, stratification, and cultural marginalization; a social construction, not a biological given.
- **Racism:** Policies and ideas that produce and normalize racial inequalities.
- **Antiracism:** Actively calling out and upending racist policies, ideas, and practices.
- **Inequality:** The hierarchy of groups from the most to the least privileged on the basis of various master statuses, such as race, gender, and social class, created by society with real effects on an individual's lived experience.
- **Colorism:** Rooted in societal caste systems, where lighter skin is valued more highly than darker skin tones.
- **White privilege:** Unearned assets that provide overt and covert advantages for White people.
- **White supremacy:** The belief and practice that White people are superior to all other minoritized groups in society.

What Is Critical Race Theory?

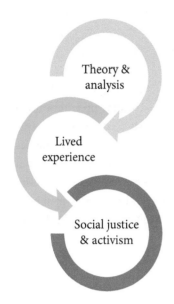

FIGURE 12.1. Interlocking Aspects of Critical Race Theory

[Figure labels: Theory & analysis; Lived experience; Social justice & activism]

Critical race theory (CRT) is first and foremost concerned with race, racism, and power (Delgado & Stefancic, 2017). Race is a primary way in which society is organized, both at the institutional level and at the individual level. Race, and racial–ethnic identity, are social constructions, not biological givens or fixed categories (Omi & Winant, 2014). Racism and racist practices are both embedded and culturally varied within and across individuals, families, communities, and societies, which are all implicated in perpetuating racialized beliefs and practices (Burton et al., 2010). Critical race theory points to how racial stratification is structured into the very fabric of society and, thus, supported by the **legal system**; indeed, it was developed as a dialectical engagement with the liberal framing of so-called color-blind legal theory (Crenshaw, 2002). Rather than posit CRT as a disembodied theoretical framework, apart from the lived experience of racism, CRT from the beginning attempted to name and challenge racial oppression by interweaving scholarship with activism and, thus, blurring the lines between theory and societal transformation (Delgado & Stefancic, 2017). As one of CRT's founders, Derrick Bell (1992) said, "we are attempting to sing a new scholarly song, even if to some listeners our style is strange, our lyrics unseemly" (p. 144). To end these racist conditions, laws, and practices, intentional steps must be taken. Hence, critical race theory is about the merger of theoretical analysis, the lived experience of people of color, and social justice and activism (Collins, 2019).

Because the historical foundations upon which our society was built were established and designed to benefit the White, wealthy men who held power and privilege over others, society continues to perpetuate and be organized according to various stratification systems (e.g., race, social class, and gender), which establish social inequality among diverse groups of people (Grusky, 2001). Racial stratification renders a racial majority as dominant, and better, and other races as not only different from the majority but also inferior (Bell, 1992; Kendi, 2019; Omi & Winant, 2014). European colonizers came to what is now North and South America in a major land grab, killing and displacing Indigenous people, a classic case of "imperialism and a particular form of colonialism—settler colonialism" (Dunbar-Ortiz, 2014, p. 2). The colonies introduced Black–White racial stratification in 1619, when enslaved Africans were first brought to what is now the United States, setting up a permanent legacy of racial inequality and racial injustice for Black and African American individuals and families (Cooke et al., 2022). There are serious and even permanent consequences of racial stratification, evidenced by the rates of incarceration for Black, Indigenous, and People of Color (BIPOC), the disproportionate number of police killings of Black men compared to White men, families living in poverty, immigration issues, mental and physical health disparities for non-White individuals, the disproportionate lack of control over work schedules for BIPOC individuals compared to White individuals, among many other indicators (Brown, 2003; Burton et al., 2013; Ray, 2019; Watson et al., 2020).

History and Origins

Critical race theory is rooted in the critique that society is marred by enduring racism, and the experience of living with racist inequality leads to a **double consciousness** for those who are oppressed (Bell, 1992; Du Bois, 1903/1996). Initially revealed in the treatment of African Americans, who came to the United States as enslaved persons four centuries ago, there has been progress for many. Yet the system of institutionalized racism persists, long after the passage of the 13th Amendment to the U.S. Constitution, which abolished slavery, decades of incremental improvements in civil rights, and the resurgence of Black radical politics (Kelley, 2002; Kendi, 2019). Enduring racism is evident in every institution of society, including economics, education, the family, health, the law, and the military (Bell, 1992). Indeed, the dehumanization of Black communities can be found in mass incarceration and aggressive policing that disproportionately affects Black Americans (Alexander, 2020; Watson et al., 2020) and Black populations around the globe (Lowe, 2022). One of the most damaging impacts of permanent systemic racism occurs for Black families, where joblessness and incarceration also disproportionately affect Black men, which consequentially means that Black fathers are increasingly less likely to live with their children and "often contend with numerous political and structural barriers that undermine their role as fathers" (Lemmons & Johnson, 2019, p. 96). While these harsh realities are fairly well-known in discourses on racially-motivated police brutality against Black men, legal scholar and activist Kimberlé Crenshaw (2016) brought attention to police violence against Black women using #sayhername. In her now-famous TED Talk, Crenshaw delivers a powerful message that illustrates how murdered Black women's names have been all but left out of the discourse on police violence against Black Americans. Ignoring or minimizing violence against Black women has significant impacts on not only Black girls, women, and families but society in general.

The history of oppressed people of color—often barred from publishing and speaking in White-dominated venues—has been passed down through storytelling, personal narrative, and family history and includes the use of parables, narratives, and counter stories to the dominant group's version of history as a form of cultural resistance (Bell, 1992; Collins, 1990; Kelley, 2002; Menakem, 2021). Indeed, in this era of "hashtagging" that we described in Chapter 8 about feminist activism in the fourth wave, now, political activism on social media allows voices previously excluded from the White-dominated media to tell their personal histories in emotional, political, and compelling ways (Jackson et al., 2020).

Resmaa Menakem (2021) wrote about how trauma is stored in our bodies and experienced from generation to generation, specifically in White and Black people as well as those who work in law enforcement. In *My Grandmother's Hands*, Menakem presents an alternative, critical approach to understanding how racism is perpetuated within and between generations and families. The following is an excerpt from the book in which he describes his own grandmother's hands:

> When I was a boy I used to watch television with my grandmother. I would sit in the middle of the sofa and she would stretch out over two seats, resting her legs in my lap. She often felt pain in her hands, and she'd ask me to rub them in mine. When I did, her fingers would relax, and she'd smile. Sometimes she'd start to hum melodically, and her voice would make a vibration that reminded me of a cat's purr.

She wasn't a large woman, but her hands were surprisingly stout, with broad fingers and thick pads below each thumb. One day I asked her, "Grandma, why are your hands like that? They ain't the same as mine."

My grandmother turned from the television and looked at me. "Boy," she said slowly. "That's from picking cotton. They been that way since long before I was your age. I started working in the fields sharecroppin' when I was four."

I didn't understand. I'd helped plant things in the garden a few times, but my own hands were bony and my fingers were narrow. I held up my hands next to hers and stared at the difference.

"Umm hmm," she said. "The cotton plant has pointed burrs in it. When you reach your hand in, the burrs rip it up. When I first started picking, my hands were all torn and bloody. When I got older, they got thicker and thicker, until I could reach in and pull out the cotton without them bleeding."

My grandmother died last year. Sometimes I can still feel her warm, thick hands in mine. (p. 4)

Throughout the book, Menakem details how generational trauma differentially impacts Black and White individuals and is facilitated within and between families. Like Menakem, many notable African American practitioners, scholars, and activists have championed critical race theory as a form of narrating and embodying an alternative reality than the dominant storyline. They offer a unique perspective rooted in experiential knowledge of living with oppression and trauma (Kolivoski et al., 2014). Indeed, one of the most powerful concepts from critical race theory is that of double consciousness, first described by W. E. B. Du Bois (1903/1996) in his classic book, *The Souls of Black Folk*, as a feeling of twoness—experienced by individuals who have been subjected to repeated oppression and abuses of power:

It is a peculiar sensation, this double-consciousness, this sense of always looking at one's self through the eyes of others, of measuring one's soul by the tape of a world that looks on in amused contempt and pity. One ever feels his two-ness, an American, a Negro; two souls, two thoughts, two unreconciled strivings; two warring ideals in one dark body, whose dogged strength alone keeps it from being torn asunder. (p. 5)

What Du Bois identified is a common experience for BIPOC individuals; as Tyra described in the case study, she remembers vividly being taught how to act if she had an encounter with police. Her double consciousness was born the day she realized she would be subject to violence just because her skin was darker.

Following the U.S. Civil Rights Movement of the 1950s and 1960s, leading to the landmark civil rights legislation signed into law by President Lyndon Johnson in 1965, critical race theory, in the 1970s, began to move away from the slow step-by-step "color blind" progressivism promoted by such a more liberal discourse of "civil rights" toward a more critical, feisty, and forceful approach for immediate social change in the life conditions of racialized and ethnic minoritized groups (Delgado & Stefancic, 2017). In recent decades, as U.S. society has become more racially and ethnically diverse, a more contemporary discourse has emerged that begins with an explicit social justice framework (Burton et al., 2010). The confluence of enduring racism, the social justice orientation in critical race theory, and massive social movements, such as Black Lives Matter, have brought us to the present time where calls for permanent social change in racial equality and racial justice are urgently expressed (Collins, 2019; Crenshaw, 2016; Kendi, 2019; Kelly et al., 2020; Watson et al., 2020).

Current ideas about critical race theory have grown out of the work of legal scholars (Bell, 1992; Crenshaw, 1991; Wing, 2003), historians (Kendi, 2019), social scientists who study racial stratification (Bonilla-Silva, 2017; 2019), and Black feminist and radical women of color scholars who pioneered the understanding that gender, race, and class, at the very least, differentially construct oppressive conditions (Collins, 1990; Davis, 1981; Lorde, 1984; Moraga & Anzaldúa, 1983; Morrison, 1992), among many others. Critical race theories can be found in analyses addressing groups of various heritages, including Asian (e.g., Curammeng et al., 2017), Latinx (e.g., Pérez Huber, 2010), and Muslim (e.g., Wheeler, 2020) individuals and families. All of these authors advocate political and practical changes to dismantle systemic racism and its intersections with other systems of social stratification and move toward the fulfillment of the promise of justice for all, regardless of race, ethnicity, national origin, and the like (Delgado & Stefancic, 2017).

Assumptions of Critical Race Theory

Delgado and Stefancic (2017) identify several basic assumptions that critical race theories share. As discussed in Chapter 1, assumptions that are specific in nature help us understand the taken-for-granted ideas that lay the groundwork for theory building. Remember at the beginning of the chapter we framed CRT as a theory of curiosity? As a result, this theory's assumptions directly question what we typically accept as truth. Each of the assumptions that guide critical race theory's different theoretical perspective are detailed below.

The first assumption of CRT is that racism is "ordinary, not aberrational," which means that it is embedded across social institutions (Delgado & Stefancic, 2017, p. 8). Though modern notions of racism can conjure up ideas surrounding events, such as the Black Lives Matter movement, it is critical to discuss how these assumptions impact *all* minoritized groups. As an example, it is important to remember how White privilege and supremacy has been sustained since the "discovery" of the Americas. Within days of invading, Christopher Columbus ordered natives, who he referred to as Indians, to become his servants. That was only the beginning; since then, over 8,000,000 people have been killed due to violence, disease, or despair (Stannard, 1993). This context is important because it helps us understand how racism has stood the test of time; it is ordinary because it is both internalized and institutionalized (Jones, 2000), and it has been for centuries.

The second assumption guiding CRT is that the privileging of the White race over other races provides both psychic and material benefits to the favored race. The advantages accruing to what a society deems as the dominant race can be seen in the privilege walk in our case study (Delgado & Stefancic, 2017).

The third assumption is that race is a societal invention, a social construction, not an objective, inherent, fixed, biological, or genetic reality (Delgado & Stefancic, 2017). This is evident when considering major historical events like the terrorist attacks on the World Trade Center and Pentagon on September 11, 2001. Much research since that event has focused on racial profiling of Arab Americans in airports and various other venues (Baker, 2002). This treatment creates a hostile environment that ignores the vast religious, ethnic, and geographic diversity among Arab individuals and families and reduces their experiences to stereotypes (Beitin et al., 2010). What this tells us as a society is that, no matter what, the dominant race in power can rearrange the racial hierarchy very easily and to their benefit. The social construction of who occupies which status in the hierarchy is determined by and large by the ruling (White) race in the Western World. In other parts of the world, different racial/ethnic groups have dominance. In China, the Han Chinese are considered to be the superior group and are often compared to the ways White people hold power in the West. Han Chinese dominance "is historically contingent: constructed, performed and institutionalized within the specific cultural framework of ethnic difference in Chinese tradition" (Leibold, 2010, p. 542).

The fourth assumption of CRT goes hand in hand with the above example. This theoretical tenet holds that racialized images and stereotypes of various minoritized groups change over time, and "everyone has potentially conflicting, overlapping identities, loyalties, and allegiances" (Delgado & Stefancic, 2017, p. 11).

Finally, the fifth assumption is based on the reality that people of color have a distinctive voice that is born of their oppression (Delgado & Stefancic, 2017). As evidenced in Box 12.2: Theory in Modern Culture, Latinx voices and experiences are the focus of an award-winning musical-turned-film *In the Heights*. Embedded in the writing of both the book and screenplays are minoritized Latinx voices that cannot be replicated by other racial and ethnic groups. The distinctive voices are at the center of the artistic process and are vital because BIPOC individuals have a certain knowledge and ability to communicate that knowledge that those in the White majority group do not know and could never comprehend firsthand.

Key Concepts

Race

According to Omi and Winant (2015), "race is a master category—a fundamental concept that has profoundly shaped, and continues to shape the history, polity, economic structure, and culture of the United States" (p. 106). Along with gender, class, sexual orientation, and other axes of inequality and difference, race is a form of social stratification and cultural marginalization. Race is a social construction, not a biological given or a form of difference that can be quantified among humans (Collins, 1990). Although race, when used as a variable, often serves as a "rough proxy" for social class, culture, and genes, "it precisely captures the social classification of people in a race-conscious society such as the United States" (Jones, 2000, p. 1212).

Inequality

Societies create a hierarchy of groups from the most to the least privileged on the basis of various master statuses, such as race, gender, and social class. Audre Lorde (1984) brilliantly described the Western European tradition of seeing "human differences in simplistic opposition to each other: dominant/subordinate, good/bad, up/down, superior/inferior" (p. 114). Thus, in mainstream thinking, inequalities are often expressed as binaries, with the "better" side on the left and the "lesser" side on the right, as in White/Black, male/female, straight/gay, young/old, rich/poor, cisgender/transgender and the like. In reality, as we described in Chapter 8, these are false binaries and do not capture the complexities of human lives.

Family Ethnic-Racial Socialization

Families are essential in helping children and adolescents learn to navigate and resist stratifications in society that are shaped by structural racism. Parents of children from minoritized groups must prepare their children for pride in their family histories but also engage in a dual socialization process in which they anticipate possible harm and prejudice based on racial oppression, as Marie Peters (1985) classically noted. Family ethnic–racial socialization refers to the cultural values, traditions, and practices associated with the family's ethnic–racial group, as well as the family's strategies for helping their children understand and cope with the potential threats based upon their ethnicity and race. In a comprehensive review of studies from 2010–2018, Umana-Taylor and Hill (2020) built on the earlier work of Hughes et al. (2006) and described four aspects of family ethnic–racial socialization: (a) cultural socialization, in which parents pass on cultural values and customs; (b) preparation for bias, in which parents teach their children that they will face societal prejudice and they need to learn ways to cope with it; (c) promotion of mistrust, which occurs when parents teach—advertently or inadvertently—their children to be wary of others outside their own ethnic–racial group; and (d) egalitarianism, in which parents teach their children about the value of diversity across groups and the need to develop intergroup relationships.

The burden of preparing children for racial prejudice falls on families of color. There is an emerging body of scholarship on critical race parenting, particularly in the education field, that is documenting this (DePouw & Matias, 2016). In a recent study about the racial socialization practices of both Black and White parents, Sullivan et al. (2021) sampled about 1,000 parents and found that White parents were relatively silent on the topics of race, racial inequality, and racial identity with their children. Black parents, on the other hand, especially after the racialized events of 2020, were increasingly likely to talk to their children about racial inequality. Furthermore, Black parents, compared to White parents, were far more worried about whether their children would be targets of bias. White parents tended to promote a discourse of colorblindness, even after the George Floyd killing, a strategy that Sullivan et al. suggested was ineffective and could also "backfire by reducing children's ability to identify and combat racial inequality" (p. 3). Implications of this research reveal that all parents require education and support for learning how to have effective conversations about race, racism, and inequality, and the time is now.

Racism

Kendi (2019) defines racism as "a marriage of racist policies and racist ideas that produces and normalizes racial inequalities" (p. 18). At the heart of this definition are policies and ideas—the conduits of racism. Policies are the "written and unwritten laws, rules, procedures, processes, regulations, and guidelines that govern people" (p. 18), and racial ideas suggest that "one racial group is inferior or superior to another racial group in any way" (p. 20). In practice, this means that BIPOC individuals continue to receive systemic disadvantages in resources across societal institutions and within interpersonal exchanges due to policies, practices, cultural ideologies, norms, and implicit standards that favor those perceived as White (Delgado & Stefancic, 2017). This concept was evident in the privilege walk presented in the case study, as Macey's eyes were opened to just how the privileges she enjoys in her life are directly tied to the experiences of others who are treated unfairly. Both Macey and Tyra exist in the same society, city, and state and are students at the same university in the same class. But the same systems treat them in vastly differing ways, whether they are overt (written) or covert (unwritten). In fact, some race scholars suggest that covert racism is much more difficult to identify, which makes it equally difficult to combat (Coates, 2011).

Antiracism

Compared to racism, **antiracism** involves activism that directly upends racist policies, actions, expressions, and ideas (Kendi, 2019). Kendi does not conceptualize antiracism as a state or destination. Instead, he argues that we "strive to be [antiracist]. Like fighting an addiction, being an antiracist requires persistent self-awareness, constant self-criticism, and regular self-examination" (p. 23). Essentially, this means that individuals with privilege must be willing to put that privilege on the line—risk it being taken away—to make progress toward racial reconciliation. Examples from White students are presented in Box 12.4: Voices From Lived Experience.

Colorism

Colorism refers to how societies value lighter skin compared to darker skin and confers greater privilege to individuals whose skin tone more closely approximates a White phenotype (Burton et al., 2010). Colorism operates in all racial and ethnic groups, such that lighter skinned individuals within and across race divisions are typically viewed more favorably, even by members of their own racial and ethnic groups (Bonilla-Silva, 2017; Golash-Boza & Darity, 2008). As Wilkerson (2020) wrote about caste systems in the United States, India, and Nazi Germany, "With few other outlets for control and power, people on the bottom rung may put down others of their own caste to lift themselves up in the eyes of the dominant" (p. 239).

Furthermore, greater privilege is afforded to individuals whose hair texture and facial features more closely resemble White (Burton et al., 2010). Our relationship to the social construction of skin tone, hair texture, eye shape, and other markers of racial identity is complicated. Banks (2000) described the complex relationship that Black women have with their hair. In her ethnography of over 60 Black women from their teens to their seventies, Banks found the great significance in how women's hair "styles" (e.g., relaxed, natural, tightly coiled, braids, dreadlocks, weaves, and extensions) construct their experience with and perceptions of race, gender, class, sexuality, images of beauty, and power, for themselves and other women.

The Racial Color Line

Racial division is the "fundamental schism in U.S. society," reinforcing "white supremacy as the master category of racial domination" (Omi & Winant, 2015, p. 131). For years, the racial color line was a Black/White divide, consisting of a large White majority and a small Black minority, as first described by W. E. B. Du Bois (Lee & Bean, 2004). However, over the course of the late 20th century, with recent waves of immigration, intermarriage across racial and ethnic groups, and new patterns of multiracial identification, U.S. society has become increasingly diverse in terms of both race and ethnicity (Lee & Bean, 2004), leading to a sizable increase in the multiracial population. By the year 2050, one in five individuals could identify as multiracial (Lee & Bean, 2004). The road to "becoming White" has widened, then, for some ethnic groups, but racial identification and stratification complicate this process. Ethnic groups, during the large waves of immigration (e.g., Irish, Italian, and Eastern European Jews) to the United States in the 19th and early-20th centuries, were originally considered to be non-White, and they eventually "became White" by distinguishing themselves from U.S. Blacks (Jacobson, 1998). Current immigrant groups, including those of Asian and Latinx backgrounds, can convert ancestry (ethnicity) more easily in the process of eroding the color line to becoming White (Lee & Bean, 2004). Thus, the color line (from non-White to White) fades more quickly for individuals of certain ethnic groups than it does for individuals who are Black, given the stubborn history of racism against Black individuals in the United States. A new type of color line—Black/non-Black—has emerged in the 21st century, revealing the persistence of this racism.

White Privilege

White privilege is as an invisible knapsack (McIntosh, 2020) that White individuals in Western societies enjoy and BIPOC individuals do not. Inside the invisible knapsack are what McIntosh refers to as unearned assets that provide both overt and covert advantages that White people often do not have an easy time understanding, much less acknowledging in order to dismantle the systems that keep it in place. When it comes to families, White privilege is a concept that comes into play when we consider how families reproduce ideas about Whiteness, privilege, and race through their daily interactions and the ways they express racialized belief systems within the privacy of their home (Few-Demo & Allen, 2020; Letiecq, 2019). As an example, White families insulate their members from experiencing racial bias, discrimination, hate crimes, and systemic injustices. These privileges do not become obvious until a family member is forced to reckon with them, often outside their family of origin's immediate socialization circle, such as with the Black Lives Matter (BLM) protests that were amplified after George Floyd was murdered by police officer Derek Chauvin in 2020.

Colorblind Racism

Related to the concept of White privilege is the idea of colorblind racism. This term describes a learned behavior wherein people pretend they do not notice race, and CRT scholar Bonilla-Silva (2017) argues this is simply another way for dominant groups to avoid addressing and discussing issues of race and racism. Families play a critical role in teaching children and family members about how damaging these perspectives are; thus, the ability to suggest race can be ignored is, in itself, a privilege for those who are members of the dominant racial group. Minoritized groups cannot and have never been able to ignore race and racism. Mellody Hobson (2014) discusses this in a TED Talk and encourages viewers to be **color brave**, which means having proactive, difficult conversations with children about these topics to model bravery instead of ignorance.

White Supremacy

The concept of White supremacy holds that White people are superior to all other minoritized groups in society, including BIPOC individuals, those who do not identify as cisgender and heterosexual, and people with religious affiliations other than Christian (Kendi, 2019). White supremacy, though commonly associated with politically based White nationalists groups like the Ku Klux Klan, is embedded in all settings in U.S. society:

> [By] "white supremacy" I do not mean to allude only to the self-conscious racism of white supremacist hate groups. I refer instead to a political, economic, and cultural system in which whites overwhelmingly control power and material resources, conscious and unconscious ideas of white superiority and entitlement are widespread, and relations of white dominance and non-white subordination are daily reenacted across a broad array of institutions and social settings. (Ansley, 1997, p. 592)

Because of these important factors, critical race feminist bell hooks (1995) suggested it is more important to use the phrase "white supremacy" as opposed to "racism/racists" to describe systems of racial oppression because white supremacy includes capitalism and patriarchy, all of which she argues need to be dismantled together. Similarly, sociological theorist C. Wright Mills (2003) suggested that White people mostly control power in the major societal institutions and set the "ideal" cultural standards, which becomes embedded in our social systems. The family, as one of the foundational social systems in all cultures, is no exception.

Whiteness Studies

Whiteness studies is a component of CRT, as it shifts the focus away from studying marginalized individuals as part of racial scholarship but instead highlights and problematizes Whiteness. Essentially, this body of work looks at the historical social construction of racial superiority by interrogating how sociopolitical and cultural structures have systematically privileged White individuals and disadvantaged BIPOC individuals. According to Frankenberg (1993), Whiteness is a location of structural advantage of race privilege and a standpoint from which White people look at themselves and others. Both racist and antiracist ideologies are perpetuated throughout social institutions in society, and families are no different. The main premise of this body of work centers around how, historically, Whiteness has been considered "invisible" because it is typically unnamed and unmarked (Delgado & Stefancic, 2017). As a result, White individuals have historically existed inside insulated environments of racial privilege, so when confronted with ideas of racism or White privilege, White people exhibit defensive reactions to protect themselves from race-based stress: anger, fear, guilt, silence, and the like. By their defensiveness and silence, White people perpetuate a racialized society that maintains social inequality for individuals who are not White (Blume & De Reus, 2009). Whiteness studies acknowledges that White racism is ultimately a problem for White people, and the burden for interrupting it belongs to White people (DiAngelo, 2018).

Power and Empowerment

Though sociologists have yet to agree on uniform definitions of power, we utilize Black feminist sociologist Patricia Hill Collins's (1990) work on domination and oppression because she takes into account power *and* empowerment. Critical theorists are focused on intentionally dismantling systems of domination and oppression, where an analysis of power relations and the political activism they engender is key (Collins, 2019). For Collins, it is not enough to emphasize that some groups use power over others to meet their own needs, and it is equally important to understand empowerment, or how oppressed individuals resist "power over" and create the results of social change. Empowerment involves choosing one's self-definition over a societal definition about one's personhood (Collins, 1990). When thinking about how this relates to families, we can begin to understand how important nuclear and extended families are when it comes to modeling empowerment *within* families and as well as *between* families. This occurs when families rely on others outside their immediate circle as they build social capital (discussed in Chapter 3 on Conflict Theory) to empower and be empowered by other BIPOC individuals.

From a family perspective, it is also important to understand how power and empowerment are passed from generation to generation (Allen & Lloyd, 2011; Burton et al., 2010; Few-Demo & Allen, 2020) as well as through educational systems (Freire, 1970/1997). Collins's (1990) ideas surrounding empowerment reveal how power can be used to lift others up in an effort to effectuate change. There are many examples of using power to uplift. Collins's (1990) early work addressed ways to empower Black women, specifically, creatively using the power of knowledge, critical consciousness, and agency to contribute to the advancement of one's community.

BOX 12.2. CRITICAL RACE THEORY IN MODERN CULTURE: *IN THE HEIGHTS*

Image 12.1 A Scene From *In the Heights*, 2021

In the Heights is a musical and a film based on a 2005 book by Quiara Alegría Hudes. The story takes place in a largely Dominican neighborhood of Washington Heights in New York City and follows Usnavi de la Vega, the owner of a small bodega in Washington Heights. Significant family relationships are formed and developed throughout the story, including Usnavi's relationship with matriarch Abuela Claudia, who took on the role of raising many children in the neighborhood as if they were her own. Lin-Manuel Miranda is both a writer and an actor in the film, and the story highlights families living in the neighborhood as they navigate heartbreak, loss, failure, all set in the rich background of Latinx culture, music, and art.

One of the main characters, Nina, experiences racial profiling when she goes away to college in a predominantly White institution. Additionally, removed from the insularity of her Dominican community, she clearly felt like an outsider during her time in college, which led to her dropping out. Her father was incredibly disappointed, and it creates a rift in the family. Though we do not know the backstory leading up to her decision to leave the neighborhood, it is possible her father did not prepare her using their traditional family ethnic–racial socialization.

Overall, the musical decenters White experiences in favor of celebrating Latinx stories, heritage, culture, art, and music. This musical features only BIPOC cast members and tells the story that is not often told in mainstream cinema—the legacy of Latinx families in New York and the importance of community, belonging, and family.

Evaluating Critical Race Theory

Strengths of Critical Race Theory

Like all of the theories we describe in this book, critical race theory has both strengths and weaknesses. Critical race theory is very much at the center of contemporary public and academic debate and often generates great controversy, which can be seen as both a strength and a weakness, yet we note that few other theories today in the academic canon have fired up more students than this one. Now, we turn specifically to three of the major strengths of CRT.

The Importance of Voice

One of the main reasons critical race theory is so impactful is that it centers the stories of BIPOC individuals with lived experience. This shifts the power of any one theoretical perspective significantly because it decolonizes the dominant narrative that has been written by, for, and about White lives. As an example, many BIPOC racial and ethnic groups have utilized storytelling for centuries because their stories were not recorded and accepted as part of any educational canon. By listening to the voices of those whose family experiences have been marginalized, we counter the dominant hegemonic narratives and make room for multiple lived realities to be heard, amplified, and preserved (Cole, 2009).

Decentering Binary Thinking and Oppositional Categories

Just as critical race theory decenters the mythical norm of only telling the story of White, middle class Americans as the standard bearer for all experience, CRT also upsets the binary of seeing human and social experience as a set of opposites (Lorde, 1984), wherein there is a winner and a loser. CRT calls attention to the ways in which one side of the opposition disqualifies and dehumanizes "the other" (Weiner, 2012). In place of racist, oppositional categories, there is now room for understanding, valuing, and critiquing the range of individual, family, community, and national experience, which is so necessary in an international, globalized world.

Practical Relevance to Real Social Change

As we've discussed throughout this chapter, CRT is a beautiful marriage of scholarly, analytical thought and practical application that promotes activism and change. Most theories never see outside the walls of the "ivory tower," but CRT is at once an account of ongoing racial strife and empowers those who engage with it to make real, lasting change (Crenshaw, 2002). Related to that is the idea that Kendi (2019) and others claim that no matter how hard we try, we will never "achieve" antiracism. It is a constant, ongoing process and battle for justice, equity, diversity, and inclusion.

Weaknesses of Critical Race Theory

Despite its great importance to issues facing family theorizing today as well as its relevance to broader issues of social justice and change, critical race theory has generated its detractors. Next, we describe some of the perceived weaknesses of critical race theory.

Controversies and Antagonisms in Popular and Academic Discourse

The dialectical engagement between theory and activism in critical race theory (Crenshaw, 2002) has generated antagonisms from supporters of CRT and detractors on both the political left and the political right (Warminton, 2020). In the field of higher education, some critical theorists, who are supportive of CRT's intellectual critique of racial oppression, are less enthusiastic about the oppositional politics and activism that CRT engenders and argue for a stronger framework from which to theorize race, racism, and hegemonic Whiteness (Cabrera, 2018). At the other end of the political spectrum, activists on the political right decry CRT as an extremist condemnation of all that is good in American society (Cabrera, 2018). One flashpoint is opposition to the Pulitzer Prize–winning *1619 Project*, which examines the role of slavery in shaping America's history and current race relations, which has been attacked by political conservatives (Serwer, 2021).

Collapsing the New Color Line

The Black/non-Black color line we described earlier can be problematic for critical race theories that collapse all racial–ethnic groups into one comparison to Whites, as race continues to matter in a society upon which the very foundation is racial stratification and inequity. The critique is that scholars cannot merge all racial and ethnic groups under one CRT framework, given the variations among diverse racial–ethnic group experiences and pathways to assimilation (Lee & Bean, 2004). Indeed, Roshanravan (2018) argues for a "racial third space of Asian America to understand the voiced frustrations of Asian Americans about our sense of racial invisibility as US subjects of color" (p. 269) and the racial ambiguity of maneuvering against the Black/White binary.

Religion Cannot Be Collapsed Into Race

Just as it is difficult to combine multiple racial and ethnic identities under one CRT umbrella, there are difficulties in separating out race from other stratification systems, such as religion. For example, Islamaphobia is a type of racism directed against "Muslimness" and individuals perceived as being Muslim (Gholami, 2021). In the context of writing about the educational disadvantages faced by Muslim university students in the United Kingdom, Gholami (2021) says that racial *and* religious disadvantages must be considered as both distinct (race; religion) and intersectional (race + religion) concepts. The danger of equating racism and Islamaphobia is that making these two concepts nearly synonymous weakens their theoretical and practical value. Equating them has the effect of reducing all disadvantages associated with race, ethnicity, and religious minority status to a general category of racial minority status. Gholami recommends two theoretical strategies to understand the complexity of race and religion: (a) racialization, as explained by CRT, and (b) religification. Thus, in addition to being racialized, Muslim individuals have also been religified, defined as a strong sense of belonging to one's religion, especially in a Western cultural context in which one's religion is maligned, leading Muslims to "become entangled in an endless web of defending, putting right, resisting, denouncing, attacking, crying, apologizing, being diplomatic ... all of which unfolds in a noxious socio-political environment" (Gholami, p. 330).

An Alternative Theory App: Symbolic Interactionism

As we do in each chapter, it is useful to compare theories to readily identify the differences between the two. Next, we show you how to switch your "app" at any time by offering an additional theory that contrasts to the one you just learned.

Symbolic interactionist theory (Chapter 4) is perceived as being both similar to and different from critical race theory. A primary way that symbolic interactionism and CRT are similar is the focus on meaning. A primary way they differ is that symbolic interactionism is largely focused on a micro level of analysis. In contrast, CRT integrates multiple levels of analysis, centering voices from lived experience on a micro level as well as critiquing the macro: the institutionalized nature of racism in society. Again, as a micro perspective, critical race theory shares with symbolic interactionism how social change allows for individuals to create and recreate new meanings and symbols as a result of the influence of broader social movements, but critical race theory has a far more wide-reaching critique of social institutions and the structural stubbornness of racism and White privilege.

Next, in Box 12.3, we consider how CRT is applicable to theorizing about families in a global context. Examples from different continents reveal that the issues we discussed in this chapter—racism, caste, and

BOX 12.3. GLOBAL COMPARISONS OF WORLD CASTE SYSTEMS

Isabel Wilkerson (2020), author of the groundbreaking book *Caste: The Origins of Our Discontents*, describes the nature of caste systems as structures that provide the fixed, underlying, and invisible scaffolding—based upon what people like like—that divide individuals and keep them in their place. She distinguishes between caste and race, saying that "caste is the bones, race the skin" (p. 19). Wilkerson explains the origins of the word caste is based upon the Portuguese term *casta*, "a Renaissance-era word for 'race' or 'breed'" (p. 67). When the Portuguese traded in South Asia and observed Hindu social divisions, they applied the term "casta" to the people of India; "thus, a word we now ascribe to India actually arose from Europeans' interpretations of what they saw; it sprang from the Western culture that created America" (Wilkerson, p. 67). Many countries include caste systems. Consider these contemporary examples:

- **China:** In China, citizens are categorized as either urban or rural at birth, and this practice is called hukou. This home registration system means that rural citizens are not given access to social welfare systems like subsidized housing, disability, health care, or education (Wu, 2020). The intent of the program was to prevent mass migration to urban centers and maintain steady agricultural production. The result is that holders of rural hukou are discriminated against, ostracized, and forced to take jobs that are dangerous and earn 40% less income than their urban counterparts. While this caste system is not based on race specifically, it clearly demonstrates power, privilege, and how social constructions of an entire population have lasting, tangible effects.
- **India:** Though subcaste systems were abolished when India became a republic in 1950, the caste system is still informally practiced. Family name is an indicator of which caste you are a member of in India; the Dalit caste occupies the lowest status in the hierarchy. Dalit were historically referred to as "untouchable" because their mere physical touch was believed to contaminate those from other (higher) castes (Jadhav, 2007).
- **United States:** While the caste system is not normally associated with the United States, anthropologists, activists like Martin Luther King, Jr., and other critical race scholars have argued that a caste system is alive and well in the United States. As a race-based hierarchy, the U.S. caste system is reinforced by White privilege and intersects with sex, social class, and systemic discrimination that has a major impact on families. Wilkerson (2020) likens the caste system in the United States to a house in the following passage from her book:

> We in the developed world are like homeowners who inherited a house on a piece of land that is beautiful on the outside but whose soil is unstable loam and rock, heaving and contracting over generations, cracks patched but the deeper ruptures waved away for decades, centuries even. Many people may rightly say: *"I had nothing to do with how this all started. I have nothing to do with the sins of the past. My ancestors never attacked Indigenous people, never owned slaves."* And, yes. Not one of us was here when this house was built. Our immediate ancestors may have had nothing to do with it, but here we are, the current occupants of a property with stress cracks and bowed walls and fissures in the foundation. We are the heirs to whatever is right or wrong with it. We did not erect the uneven pillars or joists, but they are ours to deal with now. (p. 16)

privilege—continue to be used as cornerstones of social organization. We challenge you to build upon these three examples in your own research and also find ways that societies are working to dismantle the systems of caste that scar social experience.

Working With Critical Race Theory: Integrating Research and Practice

Now that we have described the assumptions, history, concepts, strengths, and weaknesses of critical race theory, we turn to the empirical and practical applications of the theory. We provide a variation of the theory in usage today and showcase a research study that was guided by the theory. We conclude this section with how family therapists have applied this theory to study internal family dynamics—notably, the experience of shame in race relations.

Critical Race Theory Today

Critical race theory has adapted over time and is being applied across disciplines to include various intersections with race, class, gender, sexuality, and the like (Delgado & Stefancic, 2017). Critical race feminist theory, in particular, has emerged as one of the most prominent and useful forms of CRT (De Reus et al., 2005; Few-Demo, 2014). By bringing a feminist analysis to CRT, at least two key social stratifications, race and gender, can be simultaneously analyzed (Collins, 2019). Critical race feminism began with an understanding of Black women's lives, decentering the privileging of White, Western, male, middle-class, heterosexual experiences (Collins, 1990; Few, 2007). Women of color are disproportionately last in every social indicator, and this has led to their exclusion, invisibility, and, thus, the emphasis on social justice (Wing, 2003).

In family science, Shih, Chang, and Chen (2019) applied critical race feminist theory to their analysis of Asian Americans, critiquing the idea that Asian Americans comprise a "model minority," deconstructing this notion as a harmful myth. In place of the myth of Asian Americans as a model minority, which implies that racism is no longer a problem for them, Shih et al. instead provide a social justice framework for understanding the great variation among Asian Americans and, thus, emphasize the persistence of racism that still plagues this diverse population. Indeed, during the COVID-19 pandemic, racist violence against Asian Americans became rampant (https://stopaapihate.org).

The model minority myth is an ideological framework that "creates tremendous pressure for Asian Americans to have to assimilate to a White-dominated culture and conform to White-defined images of themselves" (Shih et al., p. 415). One of the key stereotypes that harms Asian Americans is their presumed educational superiority. Yet there are at least 30 ethnic subgroups comprising Asian Americans (AAPI Data), and although a few of these subgroups have risen to the top of the educational tier (e.g., Taiwanese and Asian Indian), many others, especially among groups most recently arriving in the United States (e.g., Hmong and Bhutanese) have not. Furthermore, despite the educational advantage some Asian American groups experience, Shih et al. (2019) point out that this advantage does not transfer to advances in employment; Asian Americans, especially women, are still markedly "underrepresented in the leadership ranks of law firms, government, and academic" (p. 416). Critical race feminist theory helps to explain a paradox that Asian American women face:

On the one hand, they are expected to behave according to stereotypical images of the "china doll" or "lotus blossom"—hyperfeminine, passive, weak, quiet, obedient, and submissive. On the other hand, there are images of the "dragon lady" who is fierce, dominant, and powerful. In addition, popular culture has fetishized Asian American women as sexual objects who are exotic and seductive. Taken together, these images have created a set of expectations for how others perceive and interact with Asian American women as well as how Asian American women view themselves. (p. 419)

Among the consequences of the myth of the model minority are the fact that for many AAPI individuals, this expectation of high achievement can create a "pressure-cooker environment" that leads to great emotional distress, self-doubt, and shame (Shih et al., 2019). Again, it is important to remember that the myth is promoting a "one size fits all," and there is tremendous variation among AAPI individuals and families. This can create hostilities across racial ethnic groups by pitting one group against another. It can also impact those with multiple or competing identities, wherein a person from an Asian country is dealing with the contradiction of being a "foreigner" and a "privileged model."

A **social justice perspective**, rooted in critical race feminist theory, recommends that professionals become more conscious about how structural racism against Asians creates systemic barriers. This consciousness raising is intended to "uncover diversity and nuance in educational, psychological, social, and economic outcomes of Asian Americans" and to provide culturally sensitive and appropriate mental health support for individuals and families in dealing with the stigma, prejudice, and difficulties AAPI groups experience (Shih et al., 2019, p. 424).

Critical Race Theory in Research

Grounded in CRT, Masta (2018) conducted a qualitative critical ethnographic study of Native American students in the 8th grade in a public middle school to study how they both accommodated mainstream culture and resisted it to maintain their identification as Native Americans. The particular version of CRT was Tribal Critical Race Theory (TribalCrit), using an indigenous methodological framework. Participants in the study included not only the five children but also Native American parents and elders who gave permission to conduct the study, three school personnel, and the researcher herself, an Indigenous scholar (Masta's positionality is as a member of the Sault Ste. Marie Band of Chippewa Indians). Masta observed that there are over 535 federally recognized Native American tribes in the United States and cautioned against reducing all Native Americans into a fixed race group. CRT is well-suited for understanding racialized cultural phenomena because of its perspective-taking approach to starting with the participants' reflections on their own lived experience.

One of the goals of this critical ethnographic study was to examine the tension between Indigenous and dominant cultural experience, family, and education. The study is grounded in the history of sending Native American children to off-reservation boarding schools in a societal effort to force children to assimilate into the dominant culture by erasing their Native American heritage and language, which resulted in devastating consequences, both in the United States and Canada (Rose, 2018). The impetus for this assimilation effort was the belief that Native children were deficient intellectually and academically and, thus, needed to be oriented to European-American society (Masta, 2018). Given this history of enforced assimilation policies in the previous two centuries, the educational system is an ideal way to examine the intersecting influences of race, culture, and other systems of stratification.

Masta conducted multiple interviews and spent 250 hours observing the children in their school environment. The data analysis process resulted in two different narratives, which she used CRT to help interpret. The first narrative concerned the feelings that the students had about their own Native American identity in a mainstream school environment. For example, the five students felt pride and uniqueness in being Native American, but they also felt like an outsider at the school, and some tried to hide their Native identity. The second narrative was about the students' interactions with their classmates. They were at ease interacting with one another, given their shared language and heritage (e.g., going to powwows and life on the reservation), and this was a source of support and fun in the school environment. On the other hand, their interactions with White peers was complicated, as it was common for White students to refer to Native American students with the derogatory term "apples—red on the outside, white on the inside" (p. 29). Despite this tension between students of different races, the Native students still engaged with White students, though they kept their guard up by, for example, sometimes withholding information from White students, unsure if they could be trusted.

Masta (2018) concluded that the Native American middle schoolers were engaged in a process of accommodation as both a survival strategy and an act of resistance. Some of their accommodation is a place of "inbetweenness" (p. 31) because the mainstream school setting did not fully accommodate to embrace the Native American students. Hiding parts of their identity meant they were still positioned as outsiders in the classroom among their White teachers and peers. At the same time, revealing their Native American identity was an act of resistance because they knew that being open about their families, their language, and their life on the reservation could bring negative attention and stereotypes. The students, at a young age, were learning how to navigate their sense of inbetweenness (or twoness), by both accommodating and resisting. The mainstream school system still had a long way to go to live up to its commitment to "diversity" by more fully validating the experience of its Native American students.

Critical Race Theory in Practice

Family scientists, therapists, social workers, and other professionals point to the importance of overcoming the historic effects of the dehumanization and brutality of diverse racial groups resulting in intergenerational racial trauma (Watson et al., 2020). Mental health issues linked to racial stratification include (a) nihilistic tendencies, (b) internalized antiself feelings as a person of color, (c) suppressed anger expression, (d) hypervigilance that can lead to delusional denial tendencies, and (e) extreme racial paranoia about people of color among Whites (Brown, 2003). Living with racial trauma—in one's own life and over the generations—can be a form of terrorism that requires intervention to overcome (Brown, 2003). Just being trained to be culturally competent (Kolivoski et al., 2014) and aware of multiculturalism and diversity (Kendall, 2013) is not enough. There is an urgent need for a major social movement to promote healing in the form of societal as well as psychological interventions.

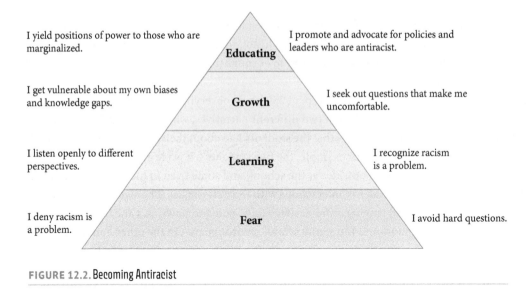

FIGURE 12.2. Becoming Antiracist

Family therapists Watson, Turner, and Hines (2020) suggest that this healing can be accomplished through the process of **restorative justice**, which is both a guiding principle of the Black Lives Matter movement and was first introduced as a concept to deal with incarceration in the criminal justice system. Restorative justice practices are communal, a two-way street to encourage relational repair between the offender and the victim of a crime. Watson et al. suggest that restorative justice can have equally powerful effects in repairing racial offenses against people of color if Black and White people purposefully work together, "but first white people must feel a human connection to Black people that then bolsters their sense of accountability and desire to repair racial harm, such as white people's assumption of an active role in Black Lives Matter protests" (p. 1369).

Another important tenet of critical race theory in practice is for White people, who have historically benefitted from White supremacy and White privilege, to do the work of deconstructing their racial privilege and taking up the mantle of antiracist work by going beyond "the professed tolerance for multiculturalism and diversity" (Watson et al., 2020, p. 1370). A place for White people to begin is to learn to unpack their White privilege through self-reflection and critical humility, practices which require that one remain humble about what one does not know (Allen & Lloyd, 2011). This type of consciously humble self-reflection is associated with a chronic discomfort that provides the emotional acuteness to sharpen one's understanding of both privilege and oppression (Allen, 2000, 2022; Smith, 1999).

One of the major issues White people face is their own shame in not interrogating or reflecting upon the role of race—and White supremacy—in their own lives (Watson, 2019), and it is important for White people to learn how to confront and dialogue with others—whether they are students, clients, or family and friends—about how they have benefitted from being members of the dominant group. This in depth understanding can help lead them to conscious action by becoming an ally. As Kendall (2013) noted in her book about authentic allyship, becoming an ally is an intentional choice "to be a change agent at both the personal and institutional levels" (p. 142). An illustration of what it looks like to move toward antiracism is depicted in Figure 12.2. The bottom section of the pyramid is

BOX 12.4. VOICES FROM LIVED EXPERIENCE

The excerpts included here emerged out of a classroom activity with Angie's sociological theory students. During the class period where students engaged in the *Privilege Walk*, she asked the students to discuss ways they could be more antiracist in their daily lives. The students each granted permission for these excerpts to be shared.

What are some ways for White folks to be antiracist?

- "Every time my partner and I see someone pulled over by police, we stop. And record it, and make sure that they know what we're there. We just hang around, because we both present as like, 'Hello, we're white women,' we're here with our cameras out. And, even though it's uncomfortable, especially with my former interactions with police that have been traumatizing. But it's still something that we do because we have the privilege, we're less likely to be brutalized because of the way that they view us." (Tonia, a White, non-binary, gay, Jewish college student)
- "Getting out of that social desirability place with your friends, and instead getting into that uncomfortable space of saying like 'hey, you said something messed up, that's wrong … and you need to reflect on that. That's an uncomfortable thing to do and you're risking their perception of you, maybe the friendship." (Chase, a White, male, cisgender, heterosexual college student)
- "One thing you can do is vote. Because you can vote for a lot of things that don't personally benefit you. The state I'm from is one of the first to give priority access to (COVID-19) vaccinations to minoritized groups. I don't know how that was decided, but if that was on a ballot, voting for something like that—I would vote for it because it's something that would mean it would take longer for me to get vaccinated but it's important to me to bridge that gap." (Bethany, a White, cisgender, heterosexual college student)

where most people start, before they learn about the consequences of race in a society. As they learn and grow, they move up the pyramid, ultimately landing at the top where they are able to practice antiracism by educating others.

Conclusion

Critical race theory exposes how racial stratification is structured into the very core of society. This is a highly dynamic framework that deftly employs theoretical analysis, new examinations of legal and historical understandings, and the voices of individuals and families on the margins of society to upend the status quo of White supremacy and privilege. CRT is both a challenge and an opportunity to reconsider the dialectics of power across micro to macro levels of society, thus giving scholars and activists new possibilities for describing, explaining, and understanding previously unexamined and misunderstood family experiences. By purposefully blurring the lines between theory and social action, CRT speaks with the voice of lived experience and generates solutions to social dilemmas that are grounded in how we actually live.

Multimedia Suggestions

www.bu.edu/antiracism-center

This is the website for the Boston University Center for Antiracism Research. Dr. Ibram Kendi is the founder. The mission of the Boston University Center for Antiracist Research is to "convene researchers and practitioners from various disciplines to figure out novel and practical ways to understand, explain, and solve seemingly intractable problems of racial inequity and injustice." By conducting research on race and antiracism that informs policy recommendations, the center is focused on leading the shift in narrative surrounding racism, equity, and justice.

Activate your theory app: After viewing this website, revisit Box 12.4: Voices From Lived Experience and Figure 12.2 and consider places in your own life where you could become antiracist or where you could further develop you antiracist approach. Was your family of origin engaged in antiracist activism? Do you foresee your future family engaged in such activism?

native-land.ca

Native Land Digital is a website that strives to create and foster conversations about the history of colonialism, Indigenous ways of knowing and settler–Indigenous relations, through educational resources such as our map and Territory Acknowledgement Guide. Their goal is to go beyond old ways of talking about Indigenous people and to develop a platform where Indigenous communities can represent themselves and their histories on their own terms. In doing so, Native Land Digital creates spaces where non-Indigenous people can be invited and challenged to learn more about the lands they inhabit, the history of those lands, and how to actively be part of a better future going forward together.

Activate your theory app: Use the education resources provided on the website to look more closely at the land you live, work, and recreate on. What concepts from critical race theory are illustrated with this resource? What did you learn by exploring the history of the land you occupy? What can we learn about Indigenous families and the important and overlooked histories from this resource?

Image 12.2 A Scene From *Hamilton*, 2021

Hamilton (2016–current) Broadway Musical

Hamilton is an award-winning musical that features an all-BIPOC cast in a musical by Lin-Manuel Miranda. As one of the first musicals to feature musical genres ranging from traditional show tunes to hip hop, R&B, and rapping, this performance tells the story of American Founding Father Alexander Hamilton. Many writers have touted the show's commitment to a diverse cast, which is the point. The casting of the show is intentional and has made a powerful statement about the impact a script can have by infusing it with nondominant cultures and featuring talented individuals who might never have been cast all in the same show. The casting and writing are intentionally antiracist.

Activate your theory app: This Broadway musical has both a traditional soundtrack and a "Hamilton mixtape." The mixtape includes songs by contemporary performers that add a creative twist to the original scores. Pay particular attention to the part in the musical where Lafayette says the line, "Immigrants, we get the job done!" and then listen to this song on the mixtape. Think about how this musical, and especially this song, illustrate CRT concepts, particularly as they have to do with family dynamics among immigrant families.

Black Parents Explain How to Deal With the Police
www.youtube.com/watch?v=coryt8lZ-DE

Trigger warning: Intense discussions about racial profiling and police violence.

Image 12.3 A Scene From Black Parents Explain How to Deal with the Police, 2017

This video, produced by *Cut,* shows the harsh realities of what Black families have to prepare their children for living in the United States: the likelihood of racial profiling and police violence during a routine traffic stop. In this video, parents discuss with their young children the safest things to say and do during police interaction to protect themselves from police violence.

Activate your theory app: Consider the content of this video and revisit the case study in which Tyra describes remembering being told similar tactics as a child. How does this change the family dynamic? How does this introduce strain and external threats to a family system that are next to impossible to mitigate?

Further Reading

Burke, T., & Brown, B. (Eds.). (2021). *You are your best thing: Vulnerability, shame resilience, and the Black experience: An anthology.* Random House. Building on their friendship, the authors Tarana Burke (a founder of the MeToo movement) and Brene Brown (whose TED talk is one of the most viewed in the world) have put together this anthology of works by Black writers, actors, and activists to share their stories of facing and overcoming race-related shame and vulnerability. Each contributing author in this anthology is a person of color, including essays by LaVerne Cox and Austin Channing Brown, because as Brown said in the video introducing the book, "lived experience always trumps academic experience".

Coates, T.-N. (2015). *Between the world and me.* Spiegel & Grau. In this powerful personal narrative, which won the National Book Award for Nonfiction in 2015, written as a letter to his adolescent son, Coates, an award-winning journalist, takes on the myths and damages of race and the painful, devastating implications of slavery, segregation, and incarceration, especially for the bodies of Black men, like his own. He defines racism as "the need to ascribe bone-deep features to people and then humiliate reduce, and destroy them" (p. 7). Through his stories of his family, including his mother, a teacher; his father, who was a Black Panther; his friend, who was shot and killed by police; and many prominent African Americans, he creates a visceral narrative of the personal impact of historical events and institutional racism that inspires a call to action for radical social change.

Idliby, R. T. (2019). *Burqas, baseball, and apple pie: Being Muslim in America*. St. Martin's Press. This memoir describes the story of how an American Muslim family navigates the socially-constructed contradictions between being American *and* Muslim. Idliby describes her own life growing up and how early experiences frame the ways in which she raises her own children. Hostility, confusion, healing, and family dynamics are all highlighted in this work, which is particularly compelling for unpacking what it means to hold multiple, warring identities in a society filled with vitriol toward Muslims.

Kendi, I. X. (2020). *Be anti-racist: A journal for awareness, reflection, and action*. Random House. Billed as "the official workbook for the international bestseller, *How to be an Antiracist*," Kendi prepared this journal "for you" to use as your own confessional in examining *your* ideas about race, racism, and antiracism. In this journal, Kendi guides the reader along with questions and prompts to reflect on and write about their own experiences and beliefs, addressing the key topics in his *How to be an Antiracist* book, including power, biology, ethnicity, the body, culture, behavior, Whiteness, Blackness, class, space, gender, and sexual orientation. This type of journal can be used in reading and discussion groups, as well, to provide a shared structure for confronting, reflecting upon, and overcoming our individual and societal shame of racism as we journey together on the path to an antiracist society that is "governed by curiosity and love and hope, honoring humanity in all its fullness."

Santiago, E. (1993). *When I was Puerto Rican*. Da Capo Press. This memoir takes readers to rural Puerto Rico to witness Esmeralda's childhood and issues her family navigated together through domestic strife, poverty, and several moves. This deep dive into Puerto Rican culture immerses readers into beautiful descriptions of the physical and emotional environments that Esmeralda navigated as she came of age. After immigrating to New York, Esmeralda describes not only the culture shock but also the new family dynamics she navigates as the eldest child of 10. This text touches on many issues facing immigrant families learning a new language, which often requires children to become language brokers (translators) for their parents.

Questions for Students

Discussion Questions

1. Define White supremacy. Give examples of how you see it operating at the individual, familial, and societal levels.

2. How does critical race theory compare to feminist theory and conflict theory, which are also critical perspectives?

3. What societal level actions are needed to address the racial divide and its outcomes?

4. In what ways does colorism contribute to within-group racism?

5. Thinking about social justice issues today, as influenced by the Black Lives Matter movement, what are some of the most positive changes occurring in terms of individuals, families, and society moving toward antiracism?

6. How is power used and abused? In what ways does empowerment matter, from a critical race theory perspective?

Your Turn!

Ask an adult from a different generation from you about what the fight for civil rights was like in the past. Which era did they live through? What were their perspectives on the activism at the time and their perspectives on activism of today? Have you ever participated in a civil rights protest together?

Personal Reflection Questions

1. When were you first aware that society distinguishes individuals by race? What is your first awareness of yourself as having a race?

2. How does your experience of race compare to your experience of gender? How about age, sexual orientation, nationality, and other systems of social stratification?

3. What were you taught about racism as a child? Who were your first teachers? How did what you learned in your family compare to what you learned in school?

4. Describe your friend group. How do the people you are close to identify by race and ethnicity? Is this something you talk with one another about?

5. Have you ever had an experience of "double consciousness," wherein you feel your "twoness"?

6. What are the ways in which you and your family are privileged?

References

Alexander, M. (2020). *The new Jim Crow: Mass incarceration in the age of colorblindness* (10th anniversary ed.). The New Press.

Allen, K. R. (2000). A conscious and inclusive family studies. *Journal of Marriage and the Family, 62*(1), 4–17. https://doi.org/10.1111/j.1741-3737.2000.00004.x

Allen, K. R. (2022). Feminist theory, method, and praxis: Toward a critical consciousness for family and close relationship scholars. *Journal of Social and Personal Relationships.* Advance online publication. https://doi.org/10.1177/02654075211065779

Allen, K. R., & Lloyd, S. A. (2011). Engaging, claiming, and changing white privilege: Educational practices for teaching and learning about intersectionalities. In L. B. Blume & L. A. De Reus (Eds.), *Social, economic, and environmental justice: Speaking out and standing up for families* (Vol. 1; pp. 173–203). University of Michigan Press.

Ansley, F. L. (1997). White supremacy (and what we should do about it). In R. Delgado & J. Stefancic (Eds.), *Critical white studies: Looking behind the mirror* (pp. 59–595). Temple University Press.

Bailey, M. (2010, March 14). They aren't talking about me. *Crunk Feminist Collective.* http://www.crunkfeministcollective.com/2010/03/14/they-arent-talking-about-me/

Bailey, M. (2021). *Misogynoir transformed: Black women's digital resistance.* New York University Press.

Baker, E. (2002). Flying while Arab-Racial profiling and air travel security. *Journal of Air Law & Commerce, 67*(4), 1375–1405. https://scholar.smu.edu/jalc/vol67/iss4/9

Banks, I. (2000). *Hair matters: Beauty, power, and Black women's consciousness.* New York University Press.

Beitin, B. K., Allen, K. R., & Bekheet, M. (2010). A critical analysis of Western perspectives on families of Arab descent. *Journal of Family Issues, 31*(2), 211–233. https://doi.org/10.1177/0192513X09345480

Bell, D. (1992). *Faces at the bottom of the well: The permanence of racism.* Basic Books.

Blume, L. B., & De Reus, L. A. (2009). Resisting whiteness: Autoethnography and the dialectics of ethnicity and privilege. In S. A. Lloyd, A. L. Few, & K. R. Allen (Eds.), *Handbook of feminist family studies* (pp. 205–219). SAGE Publications.

Bonilla-Silva, E. (2017). *Racism without racists: Color-blind racism and the persistence of racial inequality in America* (5th ed.). Rowman & Littlefield.

Bonilla-Silva, E. (2019). Feeling race: Theorizing the racial economy of emotions. *American Sociological Review, 84*(1), 1–25. https://doi.org/10.1177/0003122418816958

Brown, T. N. (2003). Critical race theory speaks to the sociology of mental health: Mental health problems produced by racial stratification. *Journal of Health and Social Behavior, 44*(3), 292–301. https://doi.org/10.2307/1519780

Burton, L. M., Bonilla-Silva, E., Ray, V., Buckelew, R., & Freeman, E. H. (2010). Critical race theories, colorism, and the decades research on families of color. *Journal of Marriage and Family, 72*(3), 440–459. https://doi.org/10.1111/j.1741-3737.2010.00712.x

Burton, L. M., Lichter, D. T., Baker, R. S., & Eason, J. M. (2013). Inequality, family processes, and health in the "new" rural America. *American Behavioral Scientist, 57*(8), 1128–1151. https://doi.org/10.1177/0002764213487348

Cabrera, N. L. (2018). Where is the racial theory in critical race theory? A constructive criticism of the crits. *The Review of Higher Education, 42*(1), 209–233. https://doi.org/10.1353/rhe.2018.0038

Coates, R. D. (2011). *Covert racism: Theories, institutions, and experiences.* Brill.

Cole, M. (2009). The color-line and the class struggle: A Marxist response to critical race theory in education as it arrives in the United Kingdom. *Power and Education, 1*(1), 111–124. https://doi.org/10.2304/power.2009.1.1.111

Collins, P. H. (1990). *Black feminist thought: Knowledge, consciousness, and the politics of empowerment.* Unwin Hyman.

Collins, P. H. (2019). *Intersectionality as critical social theory.* Duke University Press.

Cooke, B. G., Nichols, E. J., Webb, S. C., Jones, S. J., & Williams, N. N. (2022). Historical overview of the Black struggle. In K. Cokley (Ed.), *Making Black lives matter: Confronting anti-Black racism* (pp. 3–26). Cognella.

Crenshaw, K. (1991). Mapping the margins: Intersectionality, identity politics, and violence against women of color. *Stanford Law Review, 43*(6), 1241–1299. https://doi.org/10.2307/1229039

Crenshaw, K. W. (2002). The first decade: Critical reflections, or "A foot in the closing door". *UCLA Law Review, 49*(5), 1343–1372.

Crenshaw, K. (2016, October). *The urgency of intersectionality* [Video]. TEDWomen 2016. https://www.ted.com/talks/kimberle_crenshaw_the_urgency_of_intersectionality?language=en

Curammeng, E. R., Buenavista, T. L., & Cariaga, S. (2017, June). Asian American critical race theory: Origins, directions, and praxis. *Center for Critical Race Studies at UCLA, Research Briefs, 9*, 1–4. www.ccrs.ucla.gseis.edu

Davis, A. (1981). *Women, race and class.* Random House.

Delgado, R., & Stefancic, J. (2017). *Critical race theory: An introduction* (3rd ed.). New York University Press.

DePouw, C., & Matias, C. (2016). Critical race parenting: Understanding scholarship/activism in parenting our children. *Educational Studies, 52*(3), 237–259. https://doi.org/10.1080/00131946.2016.1169182

De Reus, L., Few, A. L., & Blume, L. B. (2005). Multicultural and critical race feminisms: Theorizing families in the third wave. In V. L. Bengtson, A. C. Acock, K. R. Allen, P. Dilworth-Anderson, & D. M. Klein (Eds.), *Sourcebook of family theory and research* (pp. 447–468). SAGE Publications.

DiAngelo, R. (2018). *White fragility: Why it's so hard for white people to talk about racism.* Beacon Press.

Du Bois, W. E. B. (1996). *The souls of black folk.* Penguin. (Original work published 1903)

Dunbar-Ortiz, R. (2014). *An indigenous people's history of the United States.* Beacon Press.

Few, A. L. (2007). Integrating black consciousness and critical race feminism into family studies research. *Journal of Family Issues, 28*(4), 452–473. https://doi.org/10.1177/0192513X06297330

Few-Demo, A. L. (2014). Intersectionality as the "new" critical approach in feminist family studies: Evolving racial/ethnic feminisms and critical race theories. *Journal of Family Theory & Review, 6*(2), 169–183. https://doi.org/10.1111/jftr.12039

Few-Demo, A. L., & Allen, K. R. (2020). Gender, feminist, and intersectional perspectives on families: A decade in review. *Journal of Marriage and Family, 82*(1), 326–345. https://doi.org/10.1111/jomf.12638

Frankenberg, R. (1993). *The social construction of whiteness: White women, race matters.* University of Minnesota Press.

Freire, P. (1997). *Pedagogy of the oppressed* (M. B. Ramos, Trans.; new rev. ed.). Continuum. (Original work published 1970)

Gholami, R. (2021). Critical race theory and Islamophobia: Challenging inequity in higher education. *Race Ethnicity and Education, 24*(3), 319–337. https://doi.org/10.1080/13613324.2021.1879770

Golash-Boza, T., & Darity, W., Jr. (2008). Latino racial choices: The effects of skin colour and discrimination on Latinos' and Latinas' racial self-identifications. *Ethnic and Racial Studies, 31*(5), 899–934. https://doi.org/10.1080/01419870701568858

Grusky, D. B. (2001). The past, present, and future of social inequality. In D. B. Grusky (Ed.), *Social stratification: Class, race, & gender in sociological perspective* (2nd ed., pp. 1–51). Westview.

Hobson, M. (2014, March) *Color blind or color brave?* [Video]. TED2014 Conference. https://www.ted.com/talks/mellody_hobson_color_blind_or_color_brave

hooks, b. (1995). *Killing rage: Ending racism.* Henry Holt.

Hughes, D., Rodriguez, J., Smith, E. P., Johnson, D. J., Stevenson, H. C., & Spicer, P. (2006). Parents' ethnic–racial socialization practices: A review of research and directions for future study. *Developmental Psychology, 42*(5), 747–770. https://doi.org/10.1037/0012-1649.42.5.747

Jackson, S. J., Bailey, M., & Welles, B. F. (2020). *#HashtagActivism: Networks of race and gender justice.* MIT Press.

Jacobson, M. R. (1998). *Whiteness of a different color: European immigrants and the alchemy of race.* Harvard University Press.

Jadhav, N. (2007). *Untouchables: My family's triumphant escape from India's caste system.* University of California Press.

Jones, C. P. (2000). Levels of racism: A theoretic framework and a gardener's tale. *American Journal of Public Health, 90*(8), 1212–1215. https://doi.org/10.2105/ajph.90.8.1212

Kelley, R. D. G. (2002). *Freedom dreams: The Black radical imagination.* Beacon Press.

Kelly, S., Jeremie-Brink, G., Chambers, A. L., & Smith-Bynum, M. A. (2020). The Black Lives Matter movement: A call to action for couple and family therapists. *Family Process, 59*(4), 1353–1957. https://doi.org/10.1111/famp.12614

Kendall, F. E. (2013). *Understanding white privilege: Creating pathways to authentic relationships to race* (2nd ed.). Routledge.

Kendi, I. X. (2019). *How to be an antiracist.* One World.

Kolivoski, K. M., Weaver, A., & Constance-Huggins, M. (2014). Critical race theory: Opportunities for application in social work practice and policy. *Families in Society: The Journal of Contemporary Social Services, 95*(4), 269–276. https://doi.org/10.1606/1044-3894.2014.95.36

Lee, J., & Bean, F. D. (2004). America's changing color lines: Immigration, race/ethnicity, and multiracial identification. *Annual Review of Sociology, 30*(1), 221–242. https://doi.org/10.1146/annurev.soc.30.012703.110519

Leibold, J. (2010). More than a category: Han supremacism on the Chinese Internet. *The China Quarterly, 203*(1), 539–559. https://doi.org/10.1017/S0305741010000585

Lemmons, B. P., & Johnson, W. E. (2019). Game changers: A critical race theory analysis of the economic, social, and political factors impacting Black fatherhood and family formation. *Social Work in Public Health, 34*(1), 86–101. https://doi.org/10.1177/019394599802000206

Letiecq, B. L. (2019). Surfacing family privilege and supremacy in family science: Toward justice for all. *Journal of Family Theory & Review, 11*(3), 398–411. https://doi.org/10.1111/jftr.12338

Lorde, A. (1984). Age, race, class, and sex: Women redefining difference. In *Sister outsider: Essays and speeches* (pp. 114-123). Crossing Press.

Lowe, R. H., Jr. (2022). Policing the Black diaspora: Colonial histories and global inequities in policing and carceral punishment. In K. Cokley (Ed.), *Making Black lives matter: Confronting anti-Black racism* (pp. 109–125). Cognella Academic Publishing.

Masta, S. (2018). Strategy and resistance: How Native American students engage in accommodation in mainstream schools. *Anthropology & Education Quarterly, 49*(1), 21–35. https://doi.org/10.1111/aeq.12231

McIntosh, P. (2020). *On privilege, fraudulence, and teaching as learning: Selected essays 1981–2019.* Taylor & Francis.

Menakem, R. (2021). *My grandmother's hands: Racialized trauma and the pathway to mending our hearts and bodies.* Penguin.

Mills, C. W. (2003). White supremacy as a sociopolitical system: A philosophical perspective. In A. Doane & E. Bonilla-Silva (Eds.), *White out: The continual significance of racism* (pp. 35–48). Routledge.

Moraga, C., & Anzaldúa, G. (Eds.). (1983). *This bridge called my back: Writings by radical women of color.* Kitchen Table: Women of Color Press.

Morrison, T. (Ed.). (1992). *Race-ing justice, en-gendering power: Essays on Anita Hill, Clarence Thomas, and the construction of social reality.* Pantheon Books.

Omi, M., & Winant, H. (2014). *Racial formation in the United States* (3rd ed.). Routledge.

Osmond, M. W. (1987). Radical-critical theories. In M. B. Sussman & S. K. Steinmetz (Eds.), *Handbook of marriage and the family* (pp. 103–124). Plenum.

Pérez Huber, L. (2010). Using Latina/o critical race theory (LatCrit) and racist nativism to explore intersectionality in the educational experiences of undocumented Chicana college students. *Educational Foundations, 24*(1–2), 77–96.

Peters, M. F. (1985). Racial socialization of young Black children. In H. P. McAdoo & J. L. McAdoo (Eds.), *Black children: Social, environmental, and parental environments* (pp. 159–175). SAGE Publications.

Ray, V. (2019). A theory of racialized organizations. *American Sociological Review, 84*(1), 26–53. https://doi.org/10.1177/0003122418822335

Rose, H. A. (2018). "I didn't get to say good-bye … didn't get to pet my dogs or nothing": Bioecological theory and the Indian residential school experience in Canada. *Journal of Family Theory & Review, 10*(2), 348–366. https://doi.org/10.1111/jftr.12261

Roshanravan, S. (2018). Weaponizing our (in)visibility: Asian American feminist ruptures of the model-minority optic. In L. Fujiwara & S. Roshanravan (Eds.), *Asian American feminisms and women of color politics* (pp. 261–281). University of Washington Press.

Serwer, A. (2021, May 21). Why conservatives want to cancel the 1619 project. *The Atlantic.* https://www.theatlantic.com/ideas/archive/2021/05/why-conservatives-want-cancel-1619-project/618952/

Shih, K. Y., Chang, T.-F., & Chen, S.-Y. (2019). Impacts of the model minority myth on Asian American individuals and families: Social justice and critical race feminist perspectives. *Journal of Family Theory & Review, 11*(3), 412–428. https://doi.org/10.1111/jftr.12342

Smith, D. E. (1999). *Writing the social: Critique, theory, and investigations.* University of Toronto Press.

Stannard, D. E. (1993). *American holocaust: The conquest of the new world*. Oxford University Press.

Sullivan, J. N., Eberhardt, J. L., & Roberts, S. O. (2021). Conversations about race in Black and White US families: Before and after George Floyd's death. *PNAS, 118*(38), e2106366118. https://doi.org/10.1073/pnas.2106366118

Umana-Taylor, A. J., & Hill, N. E. (2020). Ethnic-racial socialization in the family: A decade's advance on precursors and outcomes. *Journal of Marriage and Family, 82*(1), 244–271. https://doi.org/10.1111/jomf.12622

Warmington, P. (2020). Critical race theory in England: Impact and opposition. *Global Studies in Culture and Power, 27*(1), 20–37. https://doi.org/10.1080/1070289X.2019.1587907

Watson, M. F. (2019). Social justice and race in the United States: Key issues and challenges for couple and family therapy. *Family Process, 58*(1), 23–33. https://doi.org/10.1111/famp.12427

Watson, M. F., Turner, W. L., Hines, P. M. (2020). Black lives matter: We are in the same storm but we are not in the same boat. *Family Process, 59*(4), 1362–1373. https://doi.org/10.1111/famp.12613

Weiner, M. F. (2012). Towards a critical global race theory. *Sociology Compass, 6*(4), 332–350. https://doi.org/10.1111/j.1751-9020.2012.00457.x

Wheeler, K. R. (2020, February 5). On centering Black Muslim women in critical race theory. *Maydan*. https://themaydan.com/2020/02/on-centering-black-muslim-women-in-critical-race-theory/

Wilkerson, I. (2020). *Caste: The origins of our discontents*. Random House.

Wing, A. K. (2003). Introduction. In A. K. Wing (Ed.), *Critical race feminism: A reader* (2nd ed., pp. 1–19). New York University Press.

Wu, Q. M. (2021). Social stratification and housing inequality in transitional urban China. *Contemporary Social Science, 16*(3), 384–399. https://doi.org/10.1080/21582041.2020.1797148

Image Credits

Queer Theory

When we hear the word "queer," many of us might experience anxiety or discomfort, given the phrase's sociological history. The word "queer" used to denote "odd," "perverted," or "sick." The phrase was used as a derogatory slur, referring at its core to individuals who were not heterosexual; men and boys living outside the "man box" (see Chapter 8 on feminist theory) were referred to as queer for not adhering to hegemonic masculinity. Yet for the past 30 years, activists and scholars both from family science and many other disciplines in the humanities and social and behavioral sciences have done the work of reclaiming the term to capture the ways in which difference is celebrated, and instead, "normal" is problematized. As queer feminist scholar Sara Ahmed (2006) explains in her essay on queer phenomenology, the root of the word "queer" comes from the Greek word for cross and is used to explain "what is oblique or off-line or even just plain wonky" (p. 565). Queer theory is counter-normative and employs queering practices to disturb the compulsory nature of heterosexuality, cisgenderism, Whiteness, capitalism, and other hegemonic social, cultural, and political systems.

In family science, queer theory takes up the issues of heteronormativity, sexuality, gender, identity, and family, encouraging family theorists to question, "what normal is." The answers to that question come back something like this: Well, that depends on who is in the family, how they partner and relate to one another, their pathways to parenting, and many other issues and questions. Queer theory moves us away from the default assumption that there is any such entity as a "normal family," challenging the heteronormative ideology of "the family" as consisting of mother, father, sister, and brother, in which the married cisgender heterosexual parents have cisgender heterosexual biological children and rear them to adulthood, when the children form their own families and the cycle starts all over again. We learned about this foundational assumption to family theorizing in earlier theories of the family, such as functionalist (Chapter 2) and family developmental (Chapter 5). Queer theory, instead, enables us to "queer the family" by deconstructing the very essence of heteronormativity and the rigid gender, sexuality, and family binary categories of "either/or" that have gone into creating and reproducing our ideas about who and what counts as a family (Oswald et al., 2005).

In this chapter, we dismantle the rigid binaries associated with gender, sexuality, and family that have been used to construct our understanding of families in the past and that continue to dictate what is considered normal in the present. Male/female, gay/straight, trans/cisgender, married/single, monogamous/polyamorous, sexual/asexual, passive/active, and nature/nurture are among the binaries that are deconstructed using queer theory, allowing for new family forms, identities, meanings, and structures to emerge and be seen. As with other forms of radical (to break at the root) and critical (to challenge the status quo) theorizing, which we learned about in feminist theory (Chapter 8) and critical race theory (Chapter 12), the goal of queer theory is to provide alternative concepts and analyses of families that reflect the ways individuals, in all of their evolving and fluid diversity, actually live and relate to one another.

Case Study

Delilah is a nonbinary (she/they pronouns), asexual woman with a background in the foster care system. At a young age, Delilah was exposed to significant traumas, and as a result, she developed a disorganized attachment style. At 16, she ran away from her foster home and began engaging in survival sex, so she could get her basic needs met. Her mother had sold sex, and her sister still was. Because Delilah was asexual, she did not view these transactions in a negative light; they were simply transactions. She engaged in survival sex for 10 years.

During the first month of the COVID-19 lockdown, she knew she had to stop living the fast life once and for all. She had tried to find stability many times before and learned something new each attempt. This time she made a plan and exited for good, beginning the long journey of healing with complex PTSD (posttraumatic stress disorder). Now that she has exited the sex trade and is processing her traumas, she has a lot of questions for herself and her family of origin. Why did she think her sexual identity would protect her from the harms and severe trauma of the sex trade? And how did the foster care system fail her? She remembers one foster family in particular with fondness; they were so kind and provided her with love and support when she lived with them. Yet her early childhood traumas and early attachment style had a significant impact on her behavior. She felt drawn back to her family of origin, even though it was clear they were not the best role models.

As Delilah heals, she wants to know why her family had normalized being involved in the sex trade, which she feels is the main reason she got involved. Delilah harbors both anger and love toward her family of origin, but she has questions. Why did her family—her blood relatives—support her being involved in the commercial sex trade? Why did they encourage it? Why did they not try to get her out?

Today, Delilah has begun the process of healing with a new, chosen family. She has written almost every member of her biological family out of her life and is starting anew. What "family" means to Delilah is changing, yet questions about her past linger. How can she simultaneously feel drawn to her family of origin for answers, while building new relationships with people she loves and wants to spend forever with?

What Is Queer Theory?

Queer theory emerged from feminist, critical, and social constructionist ideas that took issue with gender and sexuality as fixed, binary categories (Sedgwick, 1990). Oswald, Blume, and Marks (2005) first introduced queer theory to family science theorizing as a way to challenge the taken-for-granted assumptions that only certain aspects of gender, sexuality, and family were biological, natural, and essential. In their groundbreaking analysis, Oswald et al. put heteronormativity in the spotlight by critiquing three binary categories—gender ideology, sexual ideology, and family ideology—that position certain identities and behaviors as "real" or "genuine" (e.g., cisgender, heterosexual, nuclear families) and their opposites as "deviant" or "pseudo" (e.g., LGBTQ+ identities and families). Since that time, queer theory has gained widespread popularity as a critical form of theorizing

BOX 13.1. AT A GLANCE: QUEER THEORY

- **Binary opposition:** Viewing identity as an either/or, without any gradation; "binary" means "two" or a pair of opposites.
- **Heteronormativity:** Viewing heterosexuality as the normal mode of sexual behavior, binary gender roles (masculine/feminine) as natural and all other forms of sexual and gender identity and behavior as devalued or deviant.
- **Cisnormativity:** The assumption that all individuals are cisgender, or identify with their gender assigned at birth.
- **Queering the family:** Deconstructing the primacy of heteronormativity by analyzing the interdependence of gender, sexuality, and family.
- **LGBTQ+:** Lesbian, gay, bisexual, transgender, queer/questioning, and other sexual and gender minoritized identities.
- **Queer:** Individuals whose sexual and/or gender identity do not conform to heteronormative expectations. To queer or to be queer is an empowering statement of one's difference from what is considered normative.
- **Gender nonbinary:** Viewing one's gender as outside the strict binary of male or female.
- **Sexual minority:** Individuals whose sexual identity, attraction, or behavior does not correspond with heterosexuality. This includes individuals who are lesbian, gay, bisexual, and queer, among others.
- **Gender minority:** Individuals whose gender identity does not correspond with normative gender expectations associated with male/female. This includes transgender, nonbinary, genderqueer, and gender nonconforming, among others.
- **Cisgender:** When one's gender identity corresponds with the sex assigned at birth.
- **Transgender:** When one's gender identity is different from the gender assigned at birth.
- **Asexuality:** An absence of sexual attraction to individuals of any gender.
- **Polyamory:** Openly negotiated nonmonogamous relationships among individuals of diverse sexual or gender orientations.

---

with great potential to understand the more invisible, emergent aspects of gender, sexuality, and family experiences (Allen & Henderson, 2022; Allen & Mendez, 2018; Few-Demo & Allen, 2020; McGuire, 2022; Oswald et al., 2009). Queer theory is a fluid, creative process of generating new conceptualizations that are responsive to the diversity of families and kinship systems in which sexual orientation and gender identity are queered. Queer theory is credited with spawning, for example, new theoretical approaches to understand nonbinary/trans experiences, such as transfamily theory (McGuire et al., 2016), transgender emergence (Lev, 2004), and postmodern queer family theory as applied to the relationships among cisgender women and transgender men (Pfeffer, 2017).

History and Origins

The origins of queer theory are in lesbian feminism, women's studies, and gay and lesbian studies, the last of which is now typically referred to as queer studies (Garber, 2006; Marinucci, 2016). These origins harken back to the groundbreaking work on compulsory heterosexuality by lesbian feminist scholar Adrienne Rich (1980) and the intersectional depiction of "Age, race, class, and sex: Women redefining difference" by Black feminist scholar Audre

Lorde (1984, pp. 114–123), which we described in Chapter 8 on feminist theory. Lorde and Rich were lifelong, passionate friends who shared academic and activist roots in the complex issues of the day, including feminism, politics, poetry, and a woman-centered life (Holladay, 2020).

From the start, queer theory challenged the "essentialist" position that sex and gender are preordained conditions. Instead, the focus is on experiences that foundational theories had called "deviant," such as male homosexuality, lesbian sexuality, and the very nature of gender itself. French philosopher Michel Foucault (1990) was an early influence on the rapidly evolving field of queer theory, owing to the publication of *The History of Sexuality* in 1977. Foucault theorized about the relationship between power and knowledge and how social institutions legitimate, enforce, and repress certain behaviors in the service of maintaining social control. Indeed, society creates discursive categories to reflect deviance, such as sexual minority, homosexual, and perversion and contrasts them with their "opposites" of what is valued (e.g., heterosexual, monogamous, and married) as a means of social control.

Judith Butler (1993) was another major innovator in queer theory. She, too, was critical of "institutionalized heterosexuality" (Butler, 1990, p. 25) and developed a performative theory of gender by deconstructing the very idea of "woman" and showing how gender is a category for the social regulation of bodies:

> If there is something right in Beauvoir's claim that one is not born, but rather *becomes* a woman, it follows that *woman* itself is a term in process, a becoming, a constructing that cannot rightfully be said to originate or to end. As an ongoing discursive practice, it is open to intervention and resignification. Even when gender seems to congeal into the most reified forms, the "congealing" is itself an insistent and insidious practice, sustained and regulated by various social means. ... Gender is the repeated stylization of the body, a set of repeated acts within a highly rigid regulatory frame that congeal over time to produce the appearance of substance, of a natural sort of being. (p. 33)

Butler helps us to understand that gender is not a being but a doing, an act, a **performance**. Gender is stylized, and thus, it is mutable. Gender performance, sexuality, family, and the like change over time, along with ever-evolving social, political, and historical contexts.

In family science and related disciplines, interest in studying about gay and lesbian families—the forerunner of queer family science—was evident by the end of the 20th century. There was a small but prolific body of research starting to build, which included the pioneering research about gay fathers, their homosexual identity, and their relationships with their children (e.g., Bigner & Bozett, 1989), lesbian mothers and the motherhood hierarchy (e.g., DiLapi, 1989), children's well-being in gay and lesbian families (e.g., Patterson, 1992), relationship quality among gay and lesbian cohabiting partners (e.g., Kurdek, 1989), and chosen kinship where gay men and lesbians created families from friend networks, particularly in light of rejection by biological family members (Weston, 1991).

Allen and Demo (1995) then conducted the first comprehensive systematic review of the family studies, sociology, and related literatures and found that between 1980 and 1993 only a trace number of articles (among the more than 8,000 analyzed) included topics with an explicit reference to same-sex orientation (e.g., bisexual, gay, heterosexism, homophobia, homosexuality, lesbian, or sexual orientation). Allen and Demo challenged the heterosexist bias this dearth of research revealed about the family literature, identifying its connection to racism, sexism, and classism that as "a form of institutional oppression [is] designed to ridicule, limit, or silence alternative discourses about identity and behavior" (p. 122). They called the study of lesbian and gay families a "new frontier" in family research, pointing to emergent and existing theories (e.g., standpoint, feminist, ecological, and life course) that could be mined for ways to create a more robust understanding of family diversity and chosen kin relationships.

Key Concepts

The 21st century has ushered in an exciting time for queer family theorizing and research. Consider the vast changes that have occurred in the study of "coming out." **Coming out** refers to the development of self-understanding about one's own gender/sexual identity and the act of sharing it with others. It is a nonlinear process of self-naming that disrupts the heteronormative mandate. In each new social situation, a person must come out over and over again (Allen, 1995; Denes & Afifi, 2014; McLean, 2008; Rust, 1993). Much of the earliest family research about LGBTQ+ individuals and families centered on this coming out process, charting the secrecy of "the closet" and the invisibility of individuals and families who did not fit the normative model. The empirical literature on coming out is very interesting to study because much of society, in general, has come a long way in just 30 years toward greater acceptance of LGBTQ+ individuals and families, rendering coming out less of an issue today than it was even in the recent past (Alonzo & Buttitta, 2019). Still, coming out can be challenging depending on the context. Coming out has been studied primarily from a White, middle class perspective, and in certain families and communities there may be more or less acceptance of LGBTQ+ identities, leading to the need for studying religious diversity in families and families of color from an insider lens (e.g., Barrow & Kuvalanka, 2011; Brooks, 2016; Moore, 2011). In recent studies of minoritized youth, it has been found that siblings often act as shields or scaffolds for one another, rendering the coming out process less stressful with such support (Grafsky et al., 2018; Jhang, 2018).

The research on coming out isn't the only way in which the study of gay and lesbian families has exploded to include the vast diversity hiding beneath the surface of the monolithic family norm, as three decades of empirical reviews published in the *Journal of Marriage and Family* have revealed (i.e., Patterson, 2000; Biblarz & Savci, 2010; Reczek, 2020). In just these few decades, we have progressed from conceptualizing "homosexuality and the family" to "gay and lesbian families" to "queer family scholarship." Now, there is a scholarly journal devoted specifically to LGBTQ+ family scholarship (*Journal of GLBT Family Studies*, founded by Jerry Bigner). In 2018, a special issue of the journal *Family Relations* was devoted to understanding queer families and their intersections with other social locations, giving attention to a much fuller range of LGBTQ+ family experiences, ensuring that transgender experiences in families and queer families of color are explicitly present (van Eeden-Moorefield, 2018). The tentacles of queer family theorizing extend to the application of queer theory to transformational pedagogy by truly integrating LGBTQ+ family experiences into academic coursework (e.g., Few-Demo & Glass, 2020; Few-Demo et al., 2016; Goldberg & Allen, 2018) as well as the new possibilities of queering research methods to gain a deeper understanding of how queer families challenge and redefine normative family studies (e.g., Fish & Russell, 2018; McGuire, 2022). It is important to remember that "queering" exists in a tension between playful, provocative dismantling of what is considered normative and the persistent violence and phobic reactions to those LGBTQ+ individuals who do queer our families and society (Harris et al., 2018).

Decentering Heteronormativity

In family science, Oswald et al. (2005) defined **heteronormativity** as an ideology and practice that position "gender conventionality, heterosexuality, and family traditionalism as the correct way for people to be" (p. 143). This critique of heteronormativity offered a new understanding of family diversity that led to challenging and expanding the assumptions of the primacy of heterosexuality and cisgenderism. **Heterosexuality** refers to feeling sexually attracted only or primarily to individuals of a different sex (e.g., straight), and **cisnormativity** refers to the assumption that everyone's gender identity matches the sex and gender assigned at birth (typically male or female; McGeorge et al., 2021; Reczek, 2020). Another way to think about these concepts is to reflect on your own thoughts and perceptions coming into this class. Did you expect that the case studies in nearly every chapter would include such a diversity of identities, genders, sexualities, and the like? Were you exposed to queer individuals and families growing up, or are you used to seeing them portrayed in popular media? Chances are, the answer is no. That is because our society is predicated on heteronormativity. We hope that by this chapter (you're almost to the end of the book!), it has become second nature to read and learn about such a diversity of individuals and families.

Queer theory accommodates the unveiling of multiple sexualities and multiple genders. Regarding sexuality, rather than just envisioning the binary of heterosexuality/homosexuality, there are many ways in which individuals experience their sexual identity and express themselves sexually. As we described in Table 1.1 in Chapter 1, other sexualities include **bisexual**, in which a person feels attracted to their own gender and to other genders, as well as **pansexual**, where a person feels attracted to any gender. Further, queer theory moves us beyond the normative assumption of cisgender and opens the door to multiple genders, identities, and expressions. For example, **transgender** refers to having a gender identity different from the sex one is assigned at birth, and **gender nonbinary** refers to a person who does not fit within the traditional binary of "male/female," but instead, they "may see themselves as both male and female, or as part male and part female" (Patterson et al., 2021, p. 8). In Figure 13.1, we

FIGURE 13.1. The Gender Unicorn

present the "Gender Unicorn" to illustrate a clearer understanding of gender, sex, identity, expression, attraction, sexual orientation, and the relationship between each concept to human beings. This illustration is key to helping people figure out how to conceptualize the social construction of gender, anatomical sex (assigned at birth), gender expression (e.g., performance, clothing, and presentation), and attraction.

You will notice that this figure provides a unique way to look at gender. It makes sense that a unicorn is used to signify how unique each human being is when it comes to gender, which directly disrupts the notion of a gender binary. The image, created by trans youth at Trans Student Educational Resources, expands thinking beyond how cisgender, straight people see gender and, instead, views gender from the lens of queer and trans people. The rainbow signifies the spectrum of gender identity, and the DNA represents sex assigned at birth, distinct from identity, expression, and attraction. Arrows are used to signify how the concepts exist on a spectrum, and dots are used to signify concepts that are fixed (e.g., sex assigned at birth). Taken together, this illustration is a more comprehensive, yet nuanced, way to understand the different ways that sex, identity, attraction, and expression may manifest for individuals. It not only teaches the concepts associated with gender effectively, but it also serves as a tool to help individuals navigate these issues for themselves—a great example of praxis!

Queering the Family

To queer the family is to challenge—sometimes beyond recognition—the normative understanding of gender and sexual identity, the family socialization processes that reinforce them, and the intimate relationships, including parenting and partnering, that comprise them. Queer theory questions the taken-for-granted assumption of what is considered the "best," most normal, and natural way to live, shaking the very foundation of heteronormativity. Instead of viewing people who are lesbian, gay, bisexual, transgender, or queer (LGBTQ+) as deviating from social norms, queer theory challenges—that is, "queers,"—the concepts of identity, sexual orientation, and family (Oswald et al., 2005). To "queer" is to parody (Butler, 1990), to disrupt, and to provoke (de Lauretis, 1991). Marinucci (2016) explains what queering means:

> Used as a verb, "queer" refers to the process of directing attention toward rather than away from the inconsistencies within the ideas, expectations, and attitudes associated with the hegemonic binary. To disrupt the hegemonic binary, even in very small ways, serves to "queer" the paradigm. (p. 105)

Further, writing from the perspective of quare theory, which is African American vernacular for queer, Johnson (2001) says to queer is to "act up" by committing to the struggle against all types of oppression. Thus, queer theory begins with the idea that sexuality and gender vary across individuals and that we are missing out on possibilities for understanding and benefitting from the great diversity of family life if we do not face the reality that not everyone is, wants to be, or should be heterosexual or cisgendered or live in a conventional family.

The possibilities for queer family theorizing are endless. Queer theory is a useful framework to understand families of choice in international perspective, as Mizielinska and Stasinska (2018) found in applying it to queer families in Poland, a family-centered nation in which marriage is legitimized by the Catholic Church and the government, yet where same-sex couples are still rearing children. Nakamura (2020) builds on her own experience as a U.S. citizen in a same-sex binational marriage. She details the challenges faced by LGBTQ+-parent families who do not fit the assumption that immigrant families are cisgender and heterosexual, leading to the invisibility and xenophobia they face. **Xenophobia** refers to the prejudice, even hatred, of "foreigners" or people from other countries.

In another example, we can apply queer theory to understanding families in which there are several generations of LGBTQ+ family members, a concept that was practically unimaginable a generation ago. Kuvalanka and colleagues have documented the ways LGBTQ+ youth with LGBTQ+ parents have queered the family, using the concept of second generation diversity, in their work of sexual minority mothers who have queer (Kuvalanka & Goldberg, 2009), trans, and gender diverse children (Kuvalanka et al., 2018). In all of these ways, we see that queering can be both a playful *and* a profoundly subversive way of challenging and struggling against the hegemonic assumptions that benefit the privileged few in society—a topic we take up next.

Hegemonic Heteronormativity

Queer theorizing about families has already evolved significantly since queer theory was brought into the family science canon by Oswald et al. in 2005. Samuel Allen and Shawn Mendez (2018) expanded the original theorizing on decentering heteronormativity to one of **hegemonic heteronormativity** by integrating additional contexts in which lives are structured and constrained. To gender, sexuality, and family, Allen and Mendez added five more contexts: race, class, ability, ethnicity, and nationality. As we learned in Chapter 8 about a feminist approach to hegemonic masculinity, **hegemony** refers to the power and dominance that certain identities and institutions have in society. Another major type of hegemonic power in the United States is hegemonic Whiteness and the construction of white racial identity (Hughey, 2010). Global capitalism is another type of hegemonic power around the world (Harris, 2021).

Allen and Mendez's (2018) theoretical innovation is a reminder of how quickly "unconventional" family lives can change, and thus, there is a need for ongoing theorization. Many unprecedented and rapid changes in social and political institutions have occurred recently. For example, landmark decisions at the federal level have changed the social acceptance for LGBTQ+ individuals and families, including the advent of legal marriage and divorce for same-sex partners ushered in by the United States Supreme Court's 2015 decision in *Obergefell v. Hodges* (Knauer, 2019) and the repeal in 2011 of the U.S. Military's "don't ask, don't tell" policy that banned LGBTQ+ service members (Human Rights Campaign, n.d.). There are many consequences to increased social acceptance. Greater acceptance of more diverse types of individuals and families can have the ironic outcome that these formerly "deviant" queer identities are now subsumed under the hegemonic heteronormative umbrella. This includes married lesbians who fit within the notion of monogamy, as well as trans men and women who have changed their bodies to be congruent with their gender (Allen & Mendez, 2018). What this means is that now, certain types of individuals who used to be considered "queer" are now seen as "normative," given changes in laws and customs toward greater acceptance of some LGBTQ+ individuals. Hegemonic heteronormativity, then, has not been eradicated, only expanded to include more diverse types that still uphold the heteronormative system that privileges adherents and continues to render as deviant those other queer individuals and families who do not conform. A new form of normativity—**homonormativity**—has emerged to expand the category of who counts as a "real family" under the LGBTQ+-family umbrella (Duggan, 2002), in which certain kinds of LGBTQ+ individuals and families, those that most closely mirror heteronormative White, middle-class monogamous culture, are privileged over more "queer" groups (Berkowitz, 2009). The key point is that hegemonic heteronormativity is persistent and difficult to eradicate. We see this in the uncomfortable difference with which society still labels those who are gender nonbinary, polyqueer, nonmonogamous, asexual, and the like. As Allen and Mendez (2018) assert, cisnormativity, mononormativity, and homonormativity are now the new versions of heteronormative acceptability:

> Gays and lesbians (normative sexualities) and trans individuals who are socially recognizable as their gender identity (normative genders) can now create (hetero-, homo-, mono-, or cis-) normative families—families that do not appear structurally or functionally different from traditionally heteronormative families, thus maintaining a family hegemony. (p. 76)

In sum, it is now possible for certain formerly "queer" individuals and families to actually live within hegemonic heteronormativity in their own lives. Yet we are still concerned with those whose lives are not normalized and, thus, who are still oppressed by hegemonic heteronormativity. For example, youth and adults who are genderqueer or genderfluid, who continue to transgress the gender normative pole by not identifying as either male or female, are more vulnerable and at greater risk to stereotyping and harm than those who identify with and conform to the heteronormative idea of masculine men and feminine women (Hammack et al., 2019; Russell & Fish, 2019; Worthen, 2021). This is particularly alarming for nonbinary, trans, and genderqueer children and youth, who are among the most at risk for negative health effects (Reczek, 2020), which we discuss below.

Again, let's return to our case study. Clearly, Delilah experienced intersections of disadvantage. Her early childhood trauma situated her on a trajectory that would require significant therapeutic intervention to heal, yet she did not have access to resources or a supportive family structure for that to be made possible. She participated, through her involvement in the sex trade, in hegemonic heteronormativity, though her individual identity bristled at sex and attraction. Men who purchased her body did so for a variety of reasons, but in general, sex buying and objectification of gender minorities' bodies is normalized, or a hegemonic ideal, for men seeking power, sexual excitement, or instant gratification. This narrative is traumatizing for individuals involved in the sex trade without true choice in the matter; further, it exacerbated Delilah's already-existing trauma and resulted in a debilitating condition, complex posttraumatic stress disorder, which occurs when someone is traumatized for a prolonged period instead of in a single instance. This dominant narrative of hegemonic masculinity *should* be queered because of the significant damage it causes not only to participating men but also to marginalized individuals most impacted by its ethos.

Another way to think about hegemonic heteronormativity is to consider the taken-for-granted aspects of our daily lives in which queer individuals are underrepresented, if not completely invisible. In Chapter 8, we mentioned how greeting cards represent the "normative" individual, or family/relationship. Do you notice any greeting cards tailored specifically for polyamorous relationships? Or for queer individuals or couples? This stark reality illustrates just how omnipresent hegemonic heteronormativity is in our culture. Another example that provides interesting insight is all of the separate awareness-raising days, weeks, and months that are not very well known in the broader society but do exist. To illustrate, we generated Figure 13.2 to highlight all of the times of year that celebrate or bring awareness to LGBTQ+ individuals that arise in this chapter. Will these all be on mass-produced calendars someday? Some may be better known to you than others; think about which ones and why you may have heard of them before.

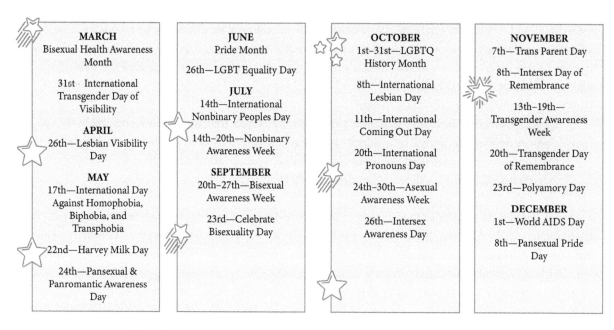

FIGURE 13.2. Queering the Calendar

Queer Intimacies

Just as in other areas of family life, intimate and sexual relationships are diverse and do not fit a normative, binary configuration. Hammack et al. (2019) introduced "queering intimacies" as a new paradigm to the study of relationships, suggesting that intimacy may occur in a variety of settings. One such configuration could be polyamory, wherein openly negotiated nonmonogamous relationships occur among individuals of diverse sexual or gender orientations. Sheff (2020) identified the ways in which consensual nonmonogamies (CNMs), like polyamory, are labeled as deviant, when in fact CNM arrangements are inherently built on open and honest communication, allow women access to multiple partners, and dismantle the ideology of the standard heterosexual nuclear family. Each of these realities for polyamorous relationships upends traditional patriarchal notions of family and, thus, assigns much more power to women in CNMs.

Intimacy and sexual attraction can also occur between individuals of any gender identity, which is referred to as pansexual (which denotes sexual attraction) or panromantic (which does not need to include sexual attraction). Panromantic individuals may also experience asexuality, when individuals do not experience sexual desire or attraction (Carroll, 2020). Asexuality is a highly invisible and, thus, marginalized identity, and it queers the very foundation of sexual expression that is seen as the impetus for forming a family (e.g., reproduction). Delilah, from our case study, identified as asexual, which she thought would make her time in the commercial sex trade easier. After she began healing from that trauma, she also decided to move toward a chosen family configuration, seeking out support and love from those who she feels truly "see" her and her true identity, loving her to her core. This type of family model can include any of the above sexual identities, can involve any gender identity configuration, and may or may not include sexual relationships at all. Because the foundation of these types of relationships is grounded in choice and, for Delilah, the need to feel truly seen and loved (trauma and all), chosen families could arguably be the "queerest of the queer," since it turns the entire traditional, hegemonic idea of family on its head. In this way, families are built from the ground up with intentionality and a commitment to creating bonds that are arguably more meaningful than those we are born with.

Gender Fluidity

The number of gender minority youth, including transgender, nonbinary, gender fluid, and genderqueer children, is growing. Although fluid notions of gender identity are prevalent cross-culturally and historically (e.g., two-spirit and hijra), as anthropologist Herdt (1997) has charted, psychologists have found that within the past few years, there is a new understanding and familiarity with the notion of gender fluidity (Diamond, 2020). Despite the increasing attention, of grave concern is that gender minority youth are at greater risk for a host of problems, including family conflict, mental health concerns, substance use, and suicidality (Catalpa & McGuire, 2018; Kaestle et al., 2020; Reczek, 2020). For example, Ryan et al. (2009) studied sexual and gender minority adolescents and found that youth who felt rejected by their families were far more likely to report high levels of depression, suicide attempts, illegal drug use, and unprotected sexual intercourse.

Scholars and activists are working to create access to and use of affirmative health care resources for the increasing number of transgender and nonbinary youth (Toomey, 2021). As Diamond (2020) points out, gender dysphoria

BOX 13.2. QUEER THEORY IN MODERN CULTURE: *SEX EDUCATION* (2019–2021)

Image 13.1 A Scene From *Sex Education*, 2021

Sex Education is a British television series that follows the lives of teenagers navigating adolescence, including sexual exploration, love, and relationships with families of origin. We selected this show in particular to highlight for the queer theory chapter because it truly "queers" mainstream television by featuring characters from very diverse backgrounds, including nonbinary, queer, gay, lesbian, neurodivergent, and disabled individuals. There is no "one-size-fits-all" narrative that most television shows promote; main characters confront commonly stigmatized sexual dynamics, turning the dominant storyline often presented in mainstream television shows on its head. This show also champions the awkwardness of learning about sex, instead of featuring gratuitous, polished sex scenes. In season two, one of the main characters, Aimee, experiences sexual assault in a public bus. Though hesitant to define it as such at the outset, her friend group rallies around her in an authentic and empowering way to help her face the fear and anxiety she was burying as a result of the trauma. Many of the other characters work through issues with their parents and model for the audience what it can look like to have healthy conflict and resolution. This show highlights very real, difficult issues facing teenagers and endorses approaching family dynamics in critical, important ways that result in impressive character development.

(the clinical diagnosis of feeling psychological distress because the difference between one's sense of gender identity and expression and the gender one is assigned at birth) for transgender individuals can be resolved by altering one's body with hormones or surgery or through changes in appearance and dress. Yet far less is known about gendered experiences and identities for nonbinary youth. They may not identify with any of the established social categories and, instead, may be trying to construct their own gender identity, as Ishii (2018) found in her study of the families of Japanese transgender children. Educating the public, including parents, teachers, and communities, about how gender identity develops in childhood as well as helping to dismantle rigid gender roles is essential for promoting positive development for all youth (Lavender-Stott et al., 2018; Russell et al., 2020). As Diamond (2020) concludes, "Whether a child identifies as male, female, transgender, gender fluid, or nonbinary, environments that foster self-acceptance, validation, openness, broadmindedness, and support regarding gender expression will yield lasting benefits" (p. 114). We must not forget that parents of transgender and nonbinary children also have new stories to tell, as they are dealing with their children's transitions as well as rewriting their own life histories (Ishii, 2018).

Evaluating Queer Theory

Strengths of Queer Theory

Queer theory is a very exciting perspective that is galvanizing the study of families. It has many strengths, which we now consider: the challenge to normativity, transdisciplinarity, and the embodied analysis from queer scholars themselves.

Innovating Family Science by Opposing the "Norm"

The most unique and innovative aspect of queer theory is its opposition to the "norm." This means that, over time, as society changes and adapts, this theoretical framework holds endless possibilities to configure and reconfigure its critique of not only any binary field but also the status quo as a whole. In this way, the concept of "what is normal" is continuously questioned, taking away the power of a standard by which to measure all individuals and family types. This allows researchers, practitioners, and students alike to understand and champion difference as opposed to measuring one another against a standard that is unrealistic and damaging. Thus, queer theory will always remain committed to social justice and committed to equity and fairness for every individual and family.

Queer Theory Is Truly Transdisciplinary

With its original roots in both the humanities and social sciences, queer theory began as a truly transdisciplinary effort. Psychologists and other sexuality researchers, in particular, have extended the transdisciplinary reach of concepts that queer traditional ways of viewing human experience in their pivoting between biology and social behavior. The queer concept of deconstructing the gender binary is one that spans many disciplines and is often confounding when trying to assess the relative contributions of biology compared to social and environmental factors linked to sexual identity and expression. For example, Diamond (2021) addresses the implications of new genetic research on sexual fluidity, which she defines as a person's capacity for situational variability in sexual responsiveness and sexual orientation, which is a person's sexual predisposition for one or both genders. It is commonly assumed that women's sexuality is more fluid than men's, but the new genetic work raises important questions about the biological/social link. Further, in an article about "the future of sex and gender in psychology," Hyde et al. (2019) upend taken-for-granted assumptions about the immutability of the sexual dimorphism of the human brain. They address assumptions from biology and neuroscience, which emphasize, for example, the role of genetics in regulating hormonal systems. Then, they turn to developmental research in psychology that reveals how the gender and sex binaries are more culturally and socially determined and, thereby, much more malleable than previous biological views predicted. Efforts, then, to queer science across disciplines have led to exciting new inroads into our understanding of sexual and gender diversity.

Potential for Deepening Family Scholarship Through Embodied Analysis

Silenced for so long, many family scholars have taken the reflexive turn in coming out about their queer identities and used their own experiences to inform family science theorizing from the particular to the general (Adams & Manning, 2015; Allen, 2022; Gabb, 2018; Hoskin, 2022). A queerer family scholarship, as Acosta (2018) argues, from her intersectional perspective as a Latinx, lesbian mother, allows her to theorize from the flesh and the borderlands, thereby connecting race, ethnicity, sexuality, gender, and other realities in her scholarship. She begins her analysis of queering family scholarship by sharing a personal reflection about disrupting a physician's presumption that she was the biological mother of her child, after the doctor walked into the room when she was nursing the baby, and said, "She looks just like you." Acosta explained her awkwardness in telling the doctor about her daughter's parentage, stating, "My daughter was conceived using my wife's eggs and donor sperm. I am her gestational parent and carried her to term" (p. 406). Thus, at a very personal level, she was queering the family—not only in the ways that her family came to exist but also in terms of dismantling the doctor's assumptions about gestational and biological parenting. Even more complex, Acosta describes how her child's genetic parentage is from one White parent and one Black parent, though Acosta herself does not share this mixed-race ancestry but is Latinx. Queering family scholarship, then, through this use of "theory in the flesh" (a phrase from the classic feminist work by Moraga & Anzaldua, 2015), is especially pronounced when it is embodied in the lives and reflections of the scholars creating the theory and analysis. Telling our own embodied stories is a way to enliven family science and create innovative pathways toward new, formerly invisible forms of scholarship.

Weaknesses of Queer Theory

Queer theory has great potential for revolutionizing family theory, as we have just described, yet it is not without its critics. Next, we describe a three of the perceived weaknesses of queer theory in family science.

Why Do We Need Queer Theory If We Have Feminist Theory?

Some would argue that queer theory is not necessary because the family science canon already has adequate theoretical tools to "queer the family." For example, symbolic interactionist theory (Chapter 4) supplies the concepts to understand how individuals create meaning through social interaction, and thus, queering the family can be understood by examining the way individuals subjectively define the circumstances of their lives. In another example, feminist theory, which is one of the origins of queer theory (Marinucci, 2016), was among the first to bring the viewpoints and missing voices of LGBTQ+ individuals and their intimate relationships to the study of families. This very argument—that theories already exist, and we don't need new ones—was once employed to challenge the necessity of feminist family theorizing because one of the original theories—conflict theory—described in Chapter 3, already provides the groundwork for critical theorizing. Yet queer theory does offer something new. In assessing the value of queer theory, Oswald et al. (2009) responded that yes, feminist theory and symbolic interactionist theory, among others, do provide their own unique contributions, but so does queer theory because no other theory can do justice to understanding and examining "how heteronormativity is reproduced and resisted by everyone" (p. 49).

Queer of Color Critique

Many intersectional feminist scholars of color have described the difficulty of embracing queer theory, given the history of both their own marginalization as well as the derogatory history of the term "queer," which was used to insult and constrain people who did not present as heterosexual. Sociologist Mignon Moore (2011), for example, in describing the identities of the Black lesbians in her study, said that many preferred to be identified as "gay," "gay woman," or "in the life" (p. 17), rather than by the term "queer": "While the term *queer* is used by some scholars and activists to describe the LGBT community, as well as in reference to queer theory, it has not been embraced by the women in my study, and I do not use it in this work" (p. 17).

The critiques by queer scholars of color have, however, made significant inroads with the conscious goal of becoming more inclusive in diverse queer theorizing building on performativity and intersectionality, as in E. Patrick Johnson's (2001) articulation of "quare theory" (noted above), which reveals the intersections among race, sexuality, and gender. In another example, Charlene Carruthers's 2019 book, *Unapologetic: A Black, Queer, and Feminist Mandate for Radical Movements*, incorporates multiple sources of the social justice movement, demonstrating how cross-group alliances are needed to create lasting and transformative social change.

When Queer Theory Is Not for Everyone

In their analysis of Oswald et al.'s (2005) model for decentering heteronormativity, Allen and Mendez (2018) found a great deal of support for the use of this model in sparking new research and interpreting findings from empirical studies of diverse families. However, they also pointed out that a few sources that cited this work had "rejected Oswald et al.'s mode and the use of queer theories in the field of family studies" (p. 71). Despite its power to diversify and innovate within family science and across disciplines in the humanities and the natural and social sciences, queer theory is contentious and politicized. Like feminist theory (Chapter 8) and critical race theory (Chapter 12), these radical frameworks may be perceived as too far out of the mainstream and, thus, can be rejected, denigrated, or not seriously considered, particularly by scholars and practitioners who promote a normative version of the family.

At the same time, some of the earliest proponents of queer theory fought against the very normalization that crystalizing the queering process into a theory or a scholarly discipline (e.g., queer studies) would beget. David Halperin (2003), cofounder of the journal *GLQ: A Journal of Lesbian and Gay Studies* warns about not losing the cutting edge of queer theory to radicalize the study of sexuality and gender fluidity by rushing to normalize it:

> If queer theory is going to have the sort of future worth cherishing, we will have to find ways of renewing its radical potential—and by that I mean not devising some new and more avant-garde theoretical formulation of it but, quite concretely, reinventing its capacity to startle, to surprise, to help us think what has not yet been thought. (p. 343)

An Alternative Theory App: Life Course Theory

As we have described in each chapter, we addressed the history and modern origins, key concepts, and strengths and weaknesses of queer theory. It is helpful to consider some of the issues covered in this chapter on queer theory, which is a newer approach, from a different theory in wider use. Now, we switch "apps" to explain issues addressed in queer theory from life course theory (Chapter 9), which offers a framework that scholars use when they want to understand how time, culture, context, and the interdependence of family relationships influence individuals' lives. The consideration of temporal dimensions—individual, family, historical—is a strength of life course theory. In considering issues of sexual or gender identity development over time, from a life course perspective, it is clear that families are constantly interacting about the transitions that individuals experience as they grow and change (Allen & Mendez, 2018; Demo & Allen, 1996; Few-Demo et al., 2016). Further, individual experiences happening for one person also overlap with those they are in relationship with, as explained by the concept of linked lives, from family member to family member. Consider a parent's gender transition from male to female. For years, their children have identified them as "father," and now not only is the parent undergoing a change, but their children are also going through a transition as they come to consider their parent's new identity. Thus, life course theory allows for this type of analysis, examining how identities, roles, and family relationships shift over time, reverberating from one family member to another because an event and transition in one life course impacts the other members' experiences as well.

Next, we want to understand how queer theory applies to the study of families in global perspective. In Box 13.3, we present an example of how three different cultures have, for centuries, not only acknowledged the existence of more than two gender expressions but, in some cases, worshipped the thought.

BOX 13.3. GLOBAL COMPARISONS: QUEERING ACROSS THE GLOBE

One of the ways we know that gender, sex, and sexuality are social constructs is by looking cross-culturally to see how other countries and cultures frame them, if at all. Below, we highlight different cultures that approach these issues in a variety of ways. By doing so, we hope that it becomes clear that the binary way of thinking that has dominated the discussion around these in many cultures is relative to the social conditions in which it was constructed:

- **Nepal:** A third gender exists in Nepal and is referred to as "meti." This term describes an indigenous group from the Himalayan region, who are born as males but present in feminine ways (e.g., clothing, hair, and makeup).
- **The American Southwest (Zuni):** Two-spiritedness is phrasing used to describe individuals who live as both genders simultaneously. In the Zuni tradition, this is called *lhamana*, and these individuals engage in both "traditional" men's and women's work (as constructed by larger society, that is).
- **Peru:** In Peru, Incas historically worshipped and honored a dual-gendered god by wearing androgynous clothing. Honoring this "third space" was a ritual that resembled not only the continuum of masculine and feminine gender but also other metaphorical spaces (e.g., the past and the present, living and dead). This practice effectively queered many different ethereal spaces in worship.

Source: https://www.pbs.org/independentlens/content/two-spirits_map-html/

Queer Theory Today

Becoming a queer scholar is rooted in multidisciplinary origins. Many queer scholars of the family have roots not only in their home discipline but also in feminist, intersectional, and critical studies, as we have written about throughout this book. In a provocative analysis blending psychological theorizing with queer theorizing, Carr and colleagues (2017) address the classic, revolutionizing work of Sandra Bem, a feminist scholar whose research on gender, sexuality, and androgyny made key contributions to psychology and, in particular, child development. Bem's (1981) gender schema theory is part of the educational foundation for studying children's lives, and no doubt you have read about her work in one of your classes. Her ideas linked cognitive development to social institutions and revealed how sex and gender stereotyping is transmitted through schools, families, mass media, and the like. In addition, Bem's husband, Darryl, also a psychologist, came out as transgender after many years of an otherwise highly egalitarian, feminist marriage. She wrote a feminist memoir about her ideas, her marriage, and her husband's transition, further queering her own theoretical models (Bem, 1998).

In their theoretical analysis of "Queering Bem," Carr et al. (2017) take up the issue of studying psychological theory and queer theory and reveal "the existence of powerful synergy when theories are integrated across disciplines and even across epistemologies" (p. 666). Carr et al. point out both similarities and differences in how a psychologist, guided by more of a postpositivist or scientific epistemology (a way of knowing), approaches gender and sexuality, compared to queer theorists, whose primary roots are in the humanities and, thus, more critical and constructivist. For example, Bem decried the gender polarization of traditional sex roles into masculine versus feminine, which runs parallel to queer theory's deconstruction of the gender binary. Bem's critique of **androcentrism** (which privileges men and masculinity as the dominant group and the universal standard) is similar to the critique of hegemonic masculinity and heteronormativity found among feminist, intersectional, and queer scholars. In addition to these similarities, Carr et al. point out ways that Bem's work differs from yet complements queer theory. For example, queer theories of performativity do not typically assess interior, psychological processes. In this way, Bem's theorizing of the intrapsychic processes that underlie external behavior can extend queer theory's ideas about gender and sexuality as socially stylized actions.

Queer Theory in Research

Manley and Goldberg (2021) were guided by queer theory in their study of how 70 U.S. parents, who practice consensually nonmonogamous (CNM) relationships, navigated parenting during COVID-19, when they were negotiating how to maintain partner contact and intimacy against the risk of viral transmission. They studied relationships that consisted of polyamorous parents who were partnered with individuals with whom they were not biologically or legally connected and often did not live together. Their sample was diverse in terms of race and ethnicity (e.g., 67% White; 19% Black; 6% Hispanic or Latinx; 4% Asian or South Asian; 3% multiethnic; and 1% Middle Eastern); parental sexual identity (e.g., bisexual, queer, gay, lesbian, heterosexual, pansexual, and other); and gender of partner(s) (e.g., cis women; cis men; nonbinary; and other). Type of relationship structure and approaches to CNM varied considerably across the sample, including polyamory and open relationships, swinging, "monogamish" relationships, currently closed relationships, and an array of combinations of all of these types.

Despite the many challenges of parenting in CNM relationships during a pandemic, Manley and Goldberg found that these families innovated in their caregiving arrangements, thereby queering the family in new and surprising ways. Three main themes were generated through the qualitative analysis. First, although they spent less time with nonresidential partners due to restrictions imposed by the pandemic and often spoke of the emotional hardship in not seeing their significant others in person, they still managed to find ways to connect across the distance. They used technology to innovate their time with nonhousehold partners, sending flirtatious texts or having sexual video calls to maintain contact despite the need to quarantine at home. It wasn't an ideal situation, as they had to balance their romantic and sexual relationships with their parenting roles and relationships with children, while also trying to tend to their own emotional and physical well-being. Second, less time in the workplace or with other partners meant more time at home with children and coparents, which posed both new opportunities for relating as well as new challenges. The family home became very crowded for some when partners moved in together, leading to a longing for "one's own space." Others created multi-household quarantine pods, which especially queered the family by engaging in "intentional and collaborative construction of small communities" (Manley & Goldberg, p. 11). These pods contained partners, children, neighbors, other relatives, housemates, and friends, clearly departing from the image of the two generational nuclear family. Finally, these families required a tremendous amount of conversation to communicate about and negotiate the potential risks involved in their partnering and parenting relationships. As CNM practitioners, they were both used to and adept at having these challenging conversations without them becoming conflictual, but on occasion, tensions did come to the forefront. A few parents reported that their own needs to affiliate with their partners were at odds with their coparents' and children's needs, and this reality required intense negotiation. Overall, parents, partners, and children adapted to the challenges of the pandemic and found ways to maintain or even enhance their connections with one another.

Queer Theory in Practice

Family therapists and counselors of all backgrounds are often on the front lines, working with clients as they undergo their own transitions to identities they claim, rather than feeling imposed on them. In this important study, family therapists McGeorge, Coburn, and Walsdorf (2021) take on the issue of helping therapists move closer to the goal of becoming an affirmative therapist for transgender and nonbinary clients. This work builds on previous efforts to become an affirmative therapist for lesbian, gay, and bisexual clients (McGeorge & Carlson, 2011), revealing how queer theory in family scholarship and therapeutic practice have been evolving over the past 10 years.

The goal to become an affirmative therapist for all one's clients is a lifelong process of becoming, rather than a destination at which one can magically arrive (McGeorge et al., 2021). Therapists must confront cisnormative and transnormative assumptions, which include ascribing legitimacy only to individuals who conform to the gender binary of male or female (cisnormative) or expecting that transgender and nonbinary people are going to medically transition. Therapists also have to deal with the institutional cisgenderism and cisgender privilege that marginalize and denigrate those who do not conform. Institutional barriers include the societal policies and actions by governments, health care systems, universities, and the like that exclude or discriminate against transgender and nonbinary individuals or render their lives invisible (McGeorge et al., 2021). For example, public bathrooms, residence halls, and health care clinics are typically designed for only those who conform to the gender binary. These personal and institutional practices can increase the physical, mental, and emotional risk and trauma experienced by transgender and nonbinary individuals.

The process of becoming an affirmative ally for transgender and nonbinary individuals involves a three-step critical self-of-the-therapist exploration process. The three steps in this model are (a) exploring binary normative assumptions, (b) exploring cisgender privilege and binary advantage, and (c) exploring cisgender identity development. Similar to other privilege exercises that turn the privilege around, McGeorge et al. offer self-reflection questions to help therapists explore these ideas, including the following. Here are a few examples of questions that McGeorge and colleagues pose for therapists to reflect upon in order to develop an affirmative ally stance regarding transgender and nonbinary individuals (p. 792–794):

Step 1: A Selection of Self-Reflection Questions to Explore Cisnormative and Transgender Assumptions:

a. What did my family of origin teach me about gender identity?

b. What are my beliefs about why I did not develop a transgender identity?

c. When I meet someone new, do I feel a desire to know if that person is a man or a woman? Do I ask new parents, "Is your baby a boy or a girl?" (p. 792).

d. What is my initial reaction when I see someone whose gender expression does not fit societal expectations for masculinity and femininity?

e. What expectations do I hold about medical procedures for people who do not identify as cisgender?

Step 2: A Selection of Self-Reflection Questions to Explore Cisgender Privilege:

a. How has your cisgender identity been encouraged, rewarded, acknowledged, and supported by your family, friends, and society?

b. Have you ever had to explain or educate others about your gender identity?

c. Have you ever worried that you might be outed as a cisgender person?

d. Have you ever struggled to find a safe restroom facility while in public?

e. Have you ever thought through how you would share your name and/or pronouns with people or who you should share your name and/or pronouns with?

BOX 13.4. VOICES FROM LIVED EXPERIENCE

Erin, a queer, intersectional feminist family science professor, reflects on her deepening understanding of gender, sexuality, time, and relationships:

> During COVID lockdown, as many people did, I really had a deep chance to evaluate my lived experience without the noise of societal influences. I came away with even greater acknowledgment and understanding how my entire life has been and is queer. Queer theory can be used as an analysis of heteronormativity though is also useful in problematizing traditional labels or ways of relating, and acknowledging the fluidity of social categories and broadly challenging normativities.

Queering Gender and Sexuality

While the word "queer" has many connotations for people, it is often used solely around sexuality. For me, my queerness is not simply about sexuality, though can encompass that aspect of being. I never had a negative connotation associated with the word, though acknowledge for some they do. And in my current community, it is not an often-used word. So, I live with the fluidity for myself and use terms people understand in their own context when required to use labels or place myself in categories. For example, when participating in an event in my town, when they asked for demographics I mentioned that for our town, gay is a word more people would understand, even though I prefer the flexibility and umbrella-nature of "queer." Similarly around gender, having the flexibility and non-fixed categories fits well with my lived experiences. I was assigned female at birth and identify as a woman. However, I have always been gender non-conforming. With radical feminist parents and surrounded by other feminist parents growing up and other non-conforming friends, even though I was aware I didn't quite "fit" the norms, I did fit and was accepted without question. Through all of my schooling this was the case and I never spent much time questioning my roles or fit in society, until I moved to my current town. Here there are strict gender role expectations and in transgressing those role expectations, people have told me they "don't know what to do with me."

Queering Time and Relationships

People in my town not knowing what to do with me is even more profound by being queer in my relationship and family structure. By legal standards and most social standards I am single. I am also late in young adulthood childfree. From a heteronormative and even homonormative framework, I am without family. Rather I have, and was raised in, a mix of family of origin and voluntary kin relationships. My queer family structure and queer timing of relations challenges normativities, including chrononormativities and what is considered success in the life course (Halberstam, 2005).

Step 3: A Selection of Self-Reflection Questions to Explore Cisgender Identity:

a. When did you learn that you were a girl or boy? How did you know? How did you first become aware of your gender identity?

b. How did other identities you hold, such as race, socioeconomic status, and ability/disability, shape your understanding of your gender identity?

c. What life experiences helped to shape your gender identity?

d. What did you learn about being a girl or boy from media sources?

e. How would you explain how you developed your gender identity?

Conclusion

Queer theory, the most recent theory to make a splash in family science, has the potential to radicalize our understanding of the great diversity found in families today. Queering the family has progressed in a few short decades from the heteronormative critique and the accumulation of new ideas and research about lesbian and gay sexuality and family issues to understanding the complexity of family experiences as it varies by sexuality, gender, and their intersections with other systems of oppression and privilege. The cutting edge of queer theory, like all family theories, is to continue to move beyond the hegemonic understanding of family diversity and take into account variations by race and ethnicity, social class, national origin, ability status, and the like and to continually incorporate new and emerging ways in which gender and sexuality are deconstructed and reconstructed, forever queering the family.

Multimedia Suggestions

www.thetrevorproject.com

The Trevor Project was founded in 1998 and initially focused on suicide prevention among LGBTQ+ youth. This project is named after *Trevor* (1994), a film about a gay 13-year-old boy who attempted suicide. Over time, the organization has evolved to provide youth access to trained counselors using a variety of outreach modalities, including a confidential chat line, phone line, text messaging, and an online space (TrevorSpace) to build community. The overarching goal of the Trevor Project is to provide free, confidential services and resources for youth in crisis, as well as guidance not only for LGBTQ+ youth but also for their families and friends.

Activate your theory app: Had you heard of the Trevor Project prior to reading about it here? Imagine a world where something like this resource is so well-known that all youth learned about it in school? What about if it was as common as TikTok or Snapchat?

www.nativejustice.org/twospirit

This website, sponsored by the Native Justice Coalition, provides a thorough discussion of how important it is to dismantle the gender binary. This organization is committed to "decolonizing gender roles and identities within our Native and First Nations communities [by] honoring the entire gender spectrum that exists in our communities." This work is made possible by centering storytelling, talking circles and building community so that families and their members who need a safe space to explore these topics have one. The social justice mission of this organization comes into play by acknowledging the reality that the gender binary, homophobia, the social construction of gender identity, gender expression, as well as sexual orientation were introduced to Natives during colonization. Thus, the organization is committed to de-colonizing the ways gender, sexuality, and identity are discussed on a large scale as a way to reclaim cultural representations of gender that are *truly* native.

Activate your theory app: Browse the website, and consider all the information presented; do you see gender-based activism? How are the issues presented here different from more mainstream "battles" for gender equity (such as those presented in Chapter 8 on feminist theory)?

Nuclear Family (2021)

Image 13.2 A Scene From *Nuclear Family*, 2021

This American documentary miniseries is directed by filmmaker Ry Russo-Young and tells the story of her own family—two lesbian mothers and a gay sperm donor father (Tom)—and how they dealt with deciding *who* was a member of their family, including what role the sperm donor, Tom, would play. After Tom sues for parental rights, the story unravels and Ry looks back through her own home movies, including those Tom made to tell her his side of the story.

Activate your theory app: Why do you think this film is titled *Nuclear Family*? Is it the director's way of un-queering family? By including such an interesting story of diversity in a documentary series with that name, does it help destigmatize queer families and normalize what it means to be a "nuclear" family?

Together Together (2021)

Image 13.3 A Scene From *Together Together*, 2021

This film follows the relationship between Matt, a single, White man in his 40s, who wants to have children but does not want to get married. He hires Anna as a surrogate, and the film features how they navigate the experience, including discussions about boundaries, expectations, and intimacy. Not your typical rom-com, this film undoubtedly queers parenthood, relationships, and everything in between.

Activate your theory app: What intersecting identities are important in this film? How do privilege, race, and sexual identity and orientation impact the story? How much different would this story be if it were told about people of color?

Further Reading

Berry, K., Gillotti, C. M., & Adams, T. E. (Eds.). (2020). *Living sexuality: Stories of LGBTQ relationships, identities, desires*. Brill. This book contains a collection of autoethnographic stories, which are told in the first person, of how LGBTQ+ individuals experience their sexuality, in the context of family relationships, friendships, and changing identities over time. Richly descriptive, especially of the emotional vulnerability that is revealed when communicating about the most intimate details—ranging from joy to challenges—of one's life, the chapters describe what is mostly invisible in traditional teaching and learning about sexuality in diverse contexts. Chapters cover issues such as gender identities, sexual relationships, the closet, monogamy, and relational endings, from both personal and theoretical perspectives.

Fabbre, V. D., Jen, S., & Fredriksen-Goldsen, K. (2019). The state of theory in LGBTQ aging: Implications for gerontological scholarship. *Research on Aging, 41*(5), 495–518. https://doi.org/10.1177/0164027518822814 This article is one of the first to examine theory use in the study of LGBTQ+ aging. In general, the field of gerontology, once described as underdeveloped in terms of theory use, has seen a rise in the use of theory to explain empirical findings from research. To assess if that trend toward greater theory use is applicable to gerontological research on older LGBTQ+ adults, Fabbre et al. conducted a systematic review of empirical articles from 2009 to 2017. They found that 52% of the studies they examined applied theory consistently, 23% applied theory partially, and 25% presented their research without a theoretical framing. Of note is that there is a growing trend to use critical perspectives, such as queer theory, intersectionality, and feminist theory, in aging research. The authors note that the emergence of queer theorizing in gerontology is a new trend and that it is useful "to understand the ways in which heteronormative social forces influence the aging experiences and well-being of LGBTQ older adults" (p. 509).

Faye, S. (2021). *The transgender issue: An argument for justice*. Allen Lane. Shon Faye, trained as a lawyer, is a British trans activist and writer. In this empowering book, Faye takes on transphobic society in Britain and writes a breathtaking manifesto for "seeing" trans individuals in all of their humanity and complexity. Faye begins with the critical perspective that trans individuals are typically reduced to mere talking points in toxic, polarized debates in the media and especially on talk shows. Instead, Faye replaces stereotypes and distortions with the realities of living as a transindividual—in families, from youth to old age, at work, dealing with healthcare, incarceration, and other social institutions. This book is a call for trans liberation, which will benefit not only transindividuals but all marginalized and minoritized people in service of a more socially just society.

Kafer, A. (2013). *Feminist, queer, crip*. Indian University Press. This critical analysis provides a new way to theorize about disability, building on queer and feminist intersectional theories. Kafer deconstructs the able/disabled binary, wherein disabilities are seen as a set of discrete categories that one either does or does not have. She blurs the disabled/nondisabled boundary by focusing on collective affinities, using the language of relationality to reimagine what is currently encased in the language of physical, sensory, cognitive, and psychiatric illness and impairment. A feminist queer crip theory for the future does not simply focus on cure or rehabilitation but, instead, dismantles the push toward normalcy contained in the mandate of "compulsory able-bodiedness and able-mindedness" (which is akin to the queer concept of "compulsory heterosexuality" by lesbian–feminist Adrienne Rich that we described in Chapter 8). Instead, Kafer values the innovations and alternative experiences of those whose lives are deeply informed by living with a vast array of physical, cognitive, and emotional experiences that are typically reduced to the limitations of disability.

Loulan, J. (1984) *Lesbian sex*. Spinsters/Aunt Lute. When this book was first published, in 1984, it was a revelation. The explicit focus on lesbian identity, relationships, and fantasies, politicized in the context of the homophobia and sexism of the late-20th century, was groundbreaking. The book also covers topics such as the physiology of women's sexual response, the actual sexual behaviors that can bring women pleasure, "the tyranny of orgasm," dilemmas of sexual addiction, and sex and disability, all of which provided a "tell it like it is" approach for women who had only experienced sex education as a "one-size-fits-all" experience. Loulan takes on the heterosexist patriarchal view of sex as for men's pleasure only and, instead, writes for a wide range of lesbian experience: "This book was written with a specific intent in mind: to help you achieve the kind of sex life you want" (p. xi). The book is augmented by photographs, drawings of the sexual response cycle and women's genitalia, quotations from lesbians who had taken Loulan's sexuality workshops, and homework exercises to help women discover and experience their full sexuality. In the days before the internet, Loulan's book and the workshops it encouraged provided one of the only safe spaces for lesbians to discover, explore, and enhance their sexuality.

Questions for Students

Discussion Questions

1. What does it mean to "queer the family"?

2. In what ways are queer theory and feminist theory intertwined? How are they different?

3. How is cisgenderism reinforced throughout society?

4. "Queer" has a derogatory history, though many LGBTQ+ individuals have reclaimed it. What is the history of the term "queer"? In what ways does it offer a useful umbrella framework to understand the history and current innovations of "queering the family"?

5. What are the possibilities for expanding our understanding of family diversity, when using queer theory? What are the drawbacks to dismantling the normative view of families?

6. Considering Figure 13.2: Queering the Calendar, what are some of the latest critical identity awareness days you are familiar with that do not yet appear on this calendar? How do you understand and explain this ever-evolving understanding of queer diversity?

Your Turn!

Think about your first experience understanding what "family" meant. How old were you? What image did you have in your head of "family"? Next, consider how it has changed over time, if at all. When were you first introduced to families that were different from yours? What was it like to figure out that other families were different? Which families did you define as "odd" or "strange"? If you grew up in a queer family, at what point did you realize not all families were alike, and vice versa?

Personal Reflection Questions

1. When were you first aware of your own gender identity? How old were you?

2. What were some of your favorite toys and games as a child? How did they represent, or transgress, heteronormativity?

3. How do your gender identity and your sexuality intersect? In what ways have you experienced your various identities as fluid?

4. What are the pronouns that describe your own identity? How do you share those pronouns?

5. In what ways do you "queer" the family in your own life? What social locations and intersections do you consider?

6. How would you explain concepts like "homonormativity," "hegemonic heteronormativity," and "queering the family" in plain language? In what ways might you change the words you use, depending on the individuals or groups you are conversing with?

References

Acosta, K. L. (2018). Queering family scholarship: Theorizing from the borderlands. *Journal of Family Theory & Review, 10*(2), 406–418. https://doi.org/10.1111/jftr.12263

Adams, T. E., & Manning, J. (2015). Autoethnography and family research. *Journal of Family Theory & Review, 7*(4), 350–366. https://doi.org/10.1111/jftr.12116

Ahmed, S. (2006). Orientations: Toward a queer phenomenology. *Journal of Lesbian and Gay Studies, 12*(4), 543–574. https://doi.org/10.1215/10642684-2006-002

Allen, K. R. (1995). Opening the classroom closet: Sexual orientation and self-disclosure. *Family Relations, 44*(2), 136–141. https://doi.org/10.2307/584799

Allen, K. R. (2022). Feminist theory, method, and praxis: Toward a critical consciousness for family and close relationship scholars. *Journal of Social and Personal Relationships*. Advance online publication. https://doi.org/10.1177/02654075211065779

Allen, K. R., & Demo, D. H. (1995). The families of lesbians and gay men: A new frontier in family research. *Journal of Marriage and the Family, 57*(1), 111–127. https://doi.org/10.2307/353821

Allen, K. R., & Henderson, A. C. (2022). Family theorizing for social justice: A critical praxis. *Journal of Family Theory & Review*. Advance online publication. https://doi.org/10.1111/jftr.12450

Allen, S. H., & Mendez, S. N. (2018). Hegemonic heteronormativity: Toward a new era of queer family theory. *Journal of Family Theory & Review, 10*(1), 70–86. https://doi.org/10.1111/jftr.12241

Alonzo, D. J., & Buttitta, D. J. (2019). Is "coming out" still relevant? Social justice implications for LGB-membered families. *Journal of Family Theory & Review, 11*(3), 354–366. https://doi.org/10.1111/jftr.12333

Barrow, K. M., & Kuvalanka, K. A. (2011). Exploration of religion, sexual identity, and familial relationships. *Journal of GLBT Family Studies, 7*(5), 470–492. https://doi.org/10.1080/1550428X.2011.623980

Bem, S. L. (1981). Gender schema theory: A cognitive account of sex typing. *Psychological Review, 88*(4), 354–364. https://doi.org/10.1037/0033-295X.88.4.354

Bem, S. L. (1998). *An unconventional family*. Yale University Press.

Berkowitz, D. (2009). Theorizing lesbian and gay parenting: Past, present, and future scholarship. *Journal of Family Theory & Review, 9*(1), 117–132. https://10.1111/j.1756-2589.2009.00017.x

Biblarz, T. J., & Savci, E. (2010). Lesbian, gay, bisexual, and transgender families. *Journal of Marriage and Family, 72*(3), 480–497. https://doi.org/10.1111/j.1741-3737.2010.000714.x

Bigner, J. J., & Bozett, F. W. (1989). Parenting by gay fathers. *Marriage & Family Review, 14*(3/4), 155–175. https://doi.org/10.1300/J002v14n03_08

Brooks, S. (2016). Staying in the hood: Black lesbian and transgender women and identity management in North Philadelphia. *Journal of Homosexuality, 63*(12), 1573–1593. https://doi.org/10.1080/00918369.2016.1158008

Butler, J. (1990). *Gender trouble: Feminism and the subversion of identity*. Routledge.

Butler, J. (1993). Critically queer. *GLQ: A Journal of Lesbian and Gay Studies, 1*(1), 17–32. https://doi.org/10.1215/10642684-1-1-17

Carr, B. B., Hagai, E. B., & Zurbriggen, E. L. (2017). Queering Bem: Theoretical intersections between Sandra Bem's scholarship and queer theory. *Sex Roles, 76*(11–12), 655–668. https://doi.org/10.1007/s11199-015-0546-1

Carroll, M. (2020). Asexuality and its implications for LGBTQ-parent families. In A. E. Goldberg & K. R. Allen (Eds.), *LGBTQ-parent families: Innovations in research and implications for practice* (2nd ed., pp. 185–198). Springer.

Carruthers, C. (2019). *Unapologetic: A Black, queer, and feminist mandate for radical movements*. Beacon Press.

Catalpa, J. M., & McGuire, J. K. (2018). Family boundary ambiguity among transgender youth. *Family Relations, 67*(1), 88–103. https://doi.org/10.1111/fare.12304

de Lauretis, T. (1991). Queer theory. Lesbian and gay sexualities: An introduction. *differences: A Journal of Feminist Cultural Studies, 3*(2), iii–xvii.

Demo, D. H., & Allen, K. R. (1996). Diversity within lesbian and gay families: Challenges and implications for family theory and research. *Journal of Social and Personal Relationships, 13*(3), 417–436. https://doi.org/10.1177/026540759613307

Denes, A., & Afifi, T. D. (2014). Coming out again: Exploring GLBQ individuals' communication with their parents after the first coming out. *Journal of GLBT Family Studies, 10*(3), 298–325. https://doi.org/10.1080/1550428X.2013.838150

Diamond, L. M. (2020). Gender fluidity and nonbinary gender identities among children and adolescents. *Child Development Perspectives, 14*(2), 110–115. https://doi.org/10.1111/cdep.12366

Diamond, L. M. (2021). The new genetic evidence on same-gender sexuality: Implications for sexual fluidity and multiple forms of sexual diversity. *Journal of Sex Research, 58*(7), 818–837. https://doi.org/10.1080/00224499.2021.1879721

DiLapi, E. M. (1989). Lesbian mothers and the motherhood hierarchy. *Journal of Homosexuality, 18*(1/2), 101–121. https://doi.org/10.4324/9781315864150

Duggan, L. (2002). The new homonormativity: The sexual politics of neoliberalism. In R. Castronovo & D. D. Nelson (Eds.), *Materializing democracy: Toward a revitalized cultural politics* (pp. 175–194). Duke University Press.

Few-Demo, A. L., & Allen, K. R. (2020). Gender, feminist, and intersectional perspectives on families: A decade in review. *Journal of Marriage and Family, 82*(1), 326–345. https://doi.org/10.1111/jomf.12638

Few-Demo, A. L., & Glass, V. Q. (2020). Reflectivity, reactivity, and reinventing: Themes from the pedagogical literature on LGBTQ-parent families in the classroom and communities. In A. E. Goldberg & K. R. Allen (Eds.), *LGBTQ-parent families: Innovations in research and implications for practice* (2nd ed., pp. 431–448). Springer.

Few-Demo, A. L., Humble, A. M., Curran, M. A., & Lloyd, S. A. (2016). Queer theory, intersectionality, and LGBT-parent families: Transformative critical pedagogy in family theory. *Journal of Family Theory & Review, 8*(1), 74–94. https://doi.org/10.1111/jftr.12127

Fish, J. N., & Russell, S. T. (2018). Queering methodologies to understand queer families. *Family Relations, 67*(1), 12–25. https://doi.org/10.1111/fare.12297

Foucault, M. (1990). *The history of sexuality, Volume 1: An introduction* (R. Hurley, Trans.). Vintage. (Original work published 1976)

Gabb, J. (2018). Unsettling lesbian motherhood: Critical reflections over a generation (1990–2015). *Sexualities, 21*(7), 1002–1020. https://doi.org/10.1177/1363460717718510

Garber, L. (2006). On the evolution of queer studies: Lesbian feminism, queer theory and globalization. In D. Richardson, J. McLaughlin, & M. E. Casey (Eds.), *Intersections between feminist and queer theory* (pp. 78–96). Palgrave.

Goldberg, A. E., & Allen, K. R. (2018). Teaching undergraduates about LGBTQ identities, families, and intersectionality. *Family Relations, 67*(1), 176–191. https://doi.org/10.1111/fare.12224

Grafsky, E. L., Hickey, K., Nguyen, H. N., & Wall, J. D. (2018). Youth disclosure of sexual orientation to siblings and extended family. *Family Relations, 67*(1), 147–160. https://doi.org/10.1111/fare.12299

Halberstam, J. (2005). *In a queer time and place.* New York University Press.

Halperin, D. M. (2003). The normalization of queer theory. *Journal of Homosexuality, 45*(2/3/4), 339–343. https://doi.org/10.1300/J082v45n02_17

Hammack, P. L., Frost, D. M., & Hughes, S. M. (2019) Queer intimacies: A new paradigm for the study of relationship diversity. *Journal of Sex Research*, 56(4–5), 556–592, https://doi.org/10.1080/00224499.2018.1531281

Harris, A. M., Jones, S. H., Faulkner, S. L., & Brook, E. D. (Eds.). (2018). *Queering families, schooling publics.* Routledge.

Harris, J. (2021). Global capitalism and the battle for hegemony. *Science & Society, 85*(3), 332–350. https://doi.org/10.1521/siso.2021.85.3.332

Herdt, G. (1997). *Same sex, different cultures: Gays and lesbians across cultures.* Westview Press.

Holladay, H. (2020). *The power of Adrienne Rich: A biography.* Nan A. Talese/Doubleday.

Hoskin, R. A. (2022). The complexities of passing: Dual realities of a queer crip white femme of Jewish descent. *Journal of Autoethnography, 3*(2), 207–211. https://doi.org/10.1525/joae.2022.3.2.207

Hughey, J. W. (2019). The (dis)similarities of white racial identities: The conceptual framework of 'hegemonic whiteness'. *Ethnic and Racial Studies, 33*(8), 1289–1309. https://doi.org/10.1080/01419870903125069

Human Rights Campaign. (n.d.). *Repeal of "don't ask, don't tell".* https://www.hrc.org/our-work/stories/repeal-of-dont-ask-dont-tell

Hyde, J. S., Bigler, R. S., Joel, D., Tate, C. C., & van Anders, S. M. (2019). The future of sex and gender in psychology: Five challenges to the gender binary. *American Psychologist, 74*(2), 171–193. https://dx.doi.org/10.1037/amp0000307

Ishii, Y. (2018). Rebuilding relationships in a transgender family: The stories of parents of Japanese transgender children. *Journal of GLBT Family Studies, 14*(3), 2130–237. https://doi.org/10.1080/1550428X.2017.1326015

Jhang, J. (2018). Scaffolding in family relationships: A grounded theory of coming out to family. *Family Relations, 67*(1), 161–175. https://doi.org/10.1111/fare.12302

Johnson, E. P. (2001). "Quare" studies, or (almost) everything I know about queer studies I learned from my grandmother. *Text and Performance Quarterly, 21*(1), 1–15. https://doi.org/10.1080/10462930128119

Kaestle, C. E., Allen, K. R., Wesche, R., & Grafsky, E. L. (2021). Adolescent sexual development: A family perspective. *Journal of Sex Research, 58*(7), 874–890. https://doi.org/10.1080/00224499.2021.1924605

Knauer, N. (2019). Implications of *Obergefell* for same-sex marriage, divorce, and parental rights. In A. E. Goldberg & A. P. Romero (Eds.), *LGBTQ divorce and relational dissolution* (pp. 7–30). Oxford University Press.

Kurdek, L. A. (1989). Relationship quality in gay and lesbian cohabiting couples: A 1-year follow-up study. *Journal of Social and Personal Relationships, 6*(1), 39–59. https://doi.org/10.1177/026540758900600103

Kuvalanka, K. A., Allen, S. H., Munroe, C., Goldberg, A. E., & Weiner, J. L. (2018). The experiences of sexual minority mothers with trans* children. *Family Relations, 67*(1), 70–87. https://doi.org/10.1177/13634607211019356

Kuvalanka, K. A., & Goldberg A. E. (2009). "Second generation" voices: Queer youth with lesbian/bisexual mothers. *Journal of Youth and Adolescence, 38*(7), 904–919. https://doi.org/10.1007/s10964-008-9327-2

Lavender-Stott, E. S., Grafsky, E. L., Nguyen, H. N., Wacker, E., & Steelman, S. M. (2018). Challenges and strategies of sexual minority youth research in Southwest Virginia. *Journal of Homosexuality, 65*(6), 691–704. https://doi.org/10.1080/00918369.2017.1364104

Lev, A. I. (2004). *Transgender emergence: Therapeutic guidelines for working with gender-variant people and their families.* Routledge.

Lorde, A. (1984). *Sister outsider: Essays and speeches.* Crossing Press.

Manley, M. H., & Goldberg, A. E. (2021). Consensually nonmonogamous parent relationships during COVID-19. *Sexualities.* Advance online publication. https://doi.org/10.1177/13634607211019356

Marinucci, M. (2016). *Feminism is queer: The intimate connection between queer and feminist theory* (2nd ed.). Zed Books.

McGeorge, C. R., & Carlson, T. S. (2011). Deconstructing heterosexism: Becoming an LGB affirmative heterosexual couple and family therapist. *Journal of Marital and Family Therapy, 37*(1), 14–26. https://doi.org/10.1111/j.1752-0606.2009.00149.x

McGeorge, C. R., Coburn, K. O., Walsdorf, A. A. (2021). Deconstructing cissexism: The journey of becoming an affirmative family therapist for transgender and nonbinary clients. *Journal of Marital and Family Therapy, 47*(3), 785–802. https://doi.org/10.1111/jmft.12481

McGuire, J. (2022). Queer theory. In K. Adamsons, A. L. Few-Demo, C. Proulx, & K. Roy (Eds.), *Sourcebook of family theories and methodologies.* Springer.

McGuire, J. K., Catalpa, J. M., Lacey, V., & Kuvalanka, K. A. (2016). Ambiguous loss as a framework for interpreting gender transitions in families. *Journal of Family Theory & Review, 8*(3), 373–385. https://doi.org/10.1111/jftr.12159

McLean, K. (2008). "Coming out, again": Boundaries, identities and spaces of belonging. *Australian Geographer, 39*(3), 303–313. https://doi.org/10.1080/000491802270507

Mizielinska, J., & Stasinska, A. (2018). Beyond the Western gaze: Families of choice in Poland. *Sexualities, 21*(7), 983–1001. https://doi.org/10.1177/1363460717718508

Moore, M. R. (2011). *Invisible families: Gay identities, relationships, and motherhood among Black women.* University of California Press.

Moraga, C., & Anzaldua, G. (Eds.). (2015). *This bridge called my back: Writings by radical women of color* (4th ed.). State University of New York Press.

Nakamura, N. (2020). LGBTQ-parent immigrant families: We're here, we're queer, we're invisible. In A. E. Goldberg & K. R. Allen (Eds.), *LGBTQ-parent families: Innovations in research and implications for practice* (2nd ed., pp. 229–240). Springer.

Oswald, R. F., Blume, L. B., & Marks, S. R. (2005). Decentering heteronormativity: A model for family studies. In V. L. Bengtson, A. C. Acock, K. R. Allen, P. Dilworth-Anderson, & D. M. Klein (Eds.), *Sourcebook of family theory and research* (pp. 143–165). SAGE Publications.

Oswald, R., Kuvalanka, K., Blume, L., & Berkowitz, D. (2009). Queering "The Family." In S. A. Lloyd, A. L. Few, & K. R. Allen (Eds.), *Handbook of feminist family studies* (pp. 43–55). SAGE Publications.

Patterson, C. J. (1992). Children of lesbian and gay parents. *Child Development, 63*(5), 1025–1042. https://doi.org/10.2307/1131517

Patterson, C. J. (2000). Family relationships of lesbians and gay men. *Journal of Marriage and the Family, 62*(4), 1052–1069. https://doi.org/10.1111/j.1741-3737.2000.01052.x

Patterson, C. J., Farr, R. H., & Goldberg, A. E. (2021, October). LGBTQ+ parents and their children. *National Council on Family Relations Policy Brief, 6*(3), 1–6. ncfr.org/resources/research-and-policy-briefs

Pfeffer, C. A. (2017). *Queering families: The postmodern partnerships of cisgender women and transgender men.* Oxford University Press.

Reczek, C. (2020). Sexual- and gender-minority families: A 2010–2020 decade in review. *Journal of Marriage and Family, 82*(1), 300–325. https://doi.org/10.1111/jomf.12607

Rich, A. (1980). Compulsory heterosexuality and lesbian experience. *Signs, 5*(4), 631–660. https://doi.org/10.1086/493756

Russell, S. T., & Fish, J. N. (2019). Sexual minority youth, social change, and health: A developmental collision. *Research in Human Development, 16*(1), 5–20. https://doi.org/10.1080/15427609.2018.1537772

Russell, S. T., Mallory, A. B., Bishop, M. D., & Dorri, A. A. (2020). Innovation and integration of sexuality in family life education. *Family Relations, 69*(3), 595–613. https://doi.org/10.1111fare.12462

Rust, P. (1993). "Coming out" in the age of social constructionism: Sexual identity formation among lesbian and bisexual women. *Gender & Society, 7*(1), 50–77. https://doi.org/10.1177/089124393007001004

Ryan, C., Huebner, D., Diaz, R. M., & Sanchez, J. (2009). Family rejection as a predictor of negative health outcomes in white and Latino lesbian, gay, and bisexual young adults. *Pediatrics, 123*(1), 346–352. https://doi.org/10.1542/peds.2007-3524

Sedgwick, E. K. (1990). *Epistemology of the closet.* University of California Press.

Sheff, E. (2020) Polyamory is deviant—But not for the reasons you may think. *Deviant Behavior, 41*(7), 882–892. https://doi.org/10.1080/01639625.2020.1737353

Toomey, R. B. (2021). Advancing research on minority stress and resilience in trans children and adolescents in the 21st century. *Child Development Perspectives, 15*(2), 96–102. https://doi.org/10.1111/cdep.12405

van Eeden-Moorefield, B. (2018). Introduction to the special issue: Intersectional variations in the experiences of queer families. *Family Relations, 67*(1), 7–11. https://doi.org/10.1111/fare.12305

Weston, K. (1991). *Families we choose: Lesbians, gays, kinship.* Columbia University Press.

Worthen, M. G. F. (2021). Why can't you just pick one? The stigmatization of non-binary/genderqueer people by cis and trans men and women: An empirical test of norm-centered stigma theory. *Sex Roles, 85*(5–6), 343–356. https://doi.org/10.1007/s11199-020-01216-z

Image Credits

Conclusion

We started this book with a discussion of theory as an application that you can use to problem solve as a family researcher and practitioner. By now, your theoretical mind should be actively engaged as you move through both your personal life and academic studies. One of the goals of theory is to fundamentally change the way you see the world around you. When you interact with loved ones, family members, or classmates, you should be seeing theory. When you watch a movie or a YouTube video or use Snapchat, Instagram, Twitter, or Facebook, you should notice concepts from this book that you cannot ignore. Your theoretical mind has been ignited, and theorizing about the world around you should be second nature by now.

Even more importantly, your theoretical insights have likely provided you with the academic toolkit you will need to pursue your professional goals, whether it is furthering your education, working directly with families and children, or even in a health care or business setting. The case study we present in this final chapter asks you to consider what life beyond this class will look like: What will you take away from a more thorough understanding of theories? How will you use what you have learned beyond the classroom, when you are working as a professional in your chosen field? A. J., the subject of our case study, is reviewing applications for a guidance counselor position in their school district serving several small schools in the area. We understand that not all of our readers may be interested in pursuing this type of career, but the case study should illustrate ways in which you can utilize your newly acquired theoretical "app" in any profession you seek.

Case Study

A. J., a nonbinary, bisexual, middle-class principal at a local school, has been reviewing applicants' resumes, cover letters, and references for a guidance counselor position in his school district. Many of the applicants have similar qualifications—the requisite bachelor's and master's degrees. Some have completed internships in places like group homes, and others have experience working in health care settings. A. J. and their search committee have narrowed the applicant pool from 55 applicants down to two final candidates. The committee gathered together to conduct telephone interviews in one afternoon, with eight questions prepared for the interviewees:

1. How did you get interested in this profession?

2. What do you think is the most important aspect of your formal education that will help you in this position?

3. What is the counseling theory or approach that you most closely follow?

4. What is the role of the school counselor in relation to teachers, parents, administrators, and other counselors?

5. What is the most difficult situation you have been faced with in your current position? How did you address it?

6. How would you handle an irate parent?

7. What is your stance on teaching critical race theory in high school?

8. What is something new you could bring to this program?

We want to note here that we do not provide identity details for the job candidates and use androgynous names. Though this is in sharp contrast to the previous chapters in the book, we take this approach for several reasons. First, we acknowledge the inherent bias in hiring practices based on gender, race, age, and appearance, among others. We did not want the case study to be clouded with any of these mitigating assumptions. We also want to avoid the mistake of tokenizing one candidate over the other in this fictional setting by insinuating that a person of color would automatically be hired for the position because of the question about critical race theory. Additionally, we wanted to avoid the assumption that the committee would prefer hiring a man over a woman, or vice versa (since the school counselor position is stereotypically seen as "expressive" and, thus, more appropriate for a woman to fill). Thus, read the following case study with as much androgyny and openness as you can! Hiring committees are expected to evaluate the candidate's qualifications—not their identity characteristics or demographics—when interviewing.

The first applicant, Shawn, held a bachelor's degree in human development and family science and a master's in school psychology from a prestigious university with a strong reputation for producing well-trained students. Shawn also had relevant work experience and an impressive list of work-related references. However, Shawn answered the interview questions tentatively and based their answers on experiences growing up in their own family and dealing with conflict across generations, between siblings, and distant relatives. The committee felt lukewarm about Shawn's responses, sensing that the experiences working at a group home—a private residence for children or young people who cannot live with their families—might have skewed their responses. The responses, for the most part, were about work experience at a group home and were based solidly on the perspective that boundaries are important between clients and counselors. The theory Shawn said they most closely followed was conflict theory (Chapter 3), based on the fact that the entire workday at Shawn's current job was spent "putting out fires." One of the committee members shook their head during the interview, knowing full well that Shawn's interpretation of conflict theory was inaccurate. Given the misapplication of the theory early on in the interview, the rest of Shawn's answers to the questions unfortunately kept referring back to this mistake, and Shawn missed opportunities to show the committee the ability to think outside the box or look at a problem from several different angles. Shawn made the mistake of basing answers only on anecdotes instead of documented trends and research in the field. In response to the question about difficult situations, Shawn said that bullying is an issue on all school campuses, and the best way to handle it is to escalate punishment for the bully and expel them from school. Shawn also said that bullying was prevalent at the group home and that the most effective way to handle it was to remove the bully from the premises permanently. Committee members were surprised that Shawn did not outline the major differences between group homes and elementary and secondary school campuses. When one committee member asked a follow-up question about how this policy would work in a school, Shawn quickly said that it could be done, no matter what the barriers.

Shawn had not learned critical race theory in college and had to ask clarifying questions about that particular question. Shawn was not familiar with important issues of social justice, antiracism, or diversity, equity, and inclusion. Shawn told the committee they would "read up on it" to be prepared to address all of these issues, if hired.

The second applicant, Charlie, has the same degrees as Shawn but from a university that the committee was not as familiar with. Charlie had strong letters of recommendation from professors, who commented on Charlie's intellect, work ethic, and ability to synthesize material at a much higher level than most of their classmates. In the telephone interview, Charlie was very impressive to the committee. The question about how formal education would help in the position was well answered; Charlie said that coursework taught them to rely on researching an issue—including what others have established works and *does not* work—before analyzing a problem. Further, Charlie said it is of utmost importance to work together as a team when serving the needs of families of children and that a school counselor is just one piece in a complex puzzle that students and families navigate within the school system. When asked about how to deal with an irate parent, Charlie cited both family ecological theory (Chapter 10) and family systems theory (Chapter 6), stressing the importance of understanding the "big picture" before developing a plan to put the student's needs first to help students grow and thrive in the best possible way. One of the most important jobs of a school counselor, Charlie said, was to listen. By listening, we can identify the heart of the problem and work together to come up with an exchange that is mutually beneficial to both parties. As an example, Charlie discussed a previous conversation with their father during their freshman year of college. Charlie was complaining about a coworker's poor attitude, shaken by how people could be so negative all the time. Charlie's father responded: "There are difficult people everywhere. They will have different faces and different names. You will come across them for the rest of your life. You just need to learn how to deal with it." Charlie cited that conversation as one of the most memorable because it taught a very important lesson in adaptation and diplomacy. When difficult interactions arise, it is best to wait until emotions have simmered so productive communication can occur.

While Charlie had limited work experience in a counseling setting, they made up for it with their thoughtful answers. Charlie viewed the role of school counselor as that of a "facilitator of success," which meant meeting students on whatever level they were on and helping them achieve their goals. This involves helping students from varying social class and racial backgrounds and those who may struggle with societal gender expectations or gender identity and identifying how students can be resilient by changing and growing over the course of their careers in school. Charlie skillfully addressed the issue about critical race theory in a thoughtful way, noting their educational training on the important issues of antiracism, social justice, equity, and inclusion. Charlie outlined the ways that they identify and work toward antiracism personally and ways to integrate that approach as a counselor. Clearly, Charlie answered the interview questions with a thorough understanding of the importance of using multiple angles to problem-solve and paying attention to timely, relevant theoretical issues facing schools and society at large.

While the two candidates presented in this case study are not meant to be representative of all hiring scenarios, there are several important aspects to note as you think about preparing for your own career. First, consider why these two candidates were chosen for telephone interviews. Shawn's cultural capital set them above the rest of the applicants because of the educational credentials from a prestigious university with a solid reputation. Charlie also had social capital working in their favor but in a very different way: Professors raved about Charlie's academic abilities, they strongly supported the job application, and each reference stated that Charlie would make an outstanding school counselor. On paper, both candidates were impressive and brought different qualities to the table.

When it came to the interview, Shawn did not have nearly as much depth to the answers as Charlie. In addition, Shawn's work experience actually worked against them; Shawn incorrectly described conflict theory and came off as inflexible when answering questions about how to deal with difficult situations. To use the analogy we have carried throughout this book, Shawn was not able to rely on a theory "app" to think quickly and answer with insight and thoughtful theoretical consideration. Shawn did not mention the precedent set by researchers in the area of school bullying and was unable to see outside of their own immediate experiences working in a group home. This concerned the committee members because they all feel it is imperative to work as a team in a school setting; Shawn's answers came off as inflexible and, thus, implying they may not be the most adaptable coworker. Shawn acknowledged the lack of understanding on issues of critical race and antiracism, which was a healthy way to address a shortcoming in an interview. However, they also could have been far more prepared for that question, given the ongoing debates about these important issues, especially in secondary education.

Charlie, on the other hand, used a theory "app" like it was second nature. Charlie's answers were thoughtful, grounded in research and practice, and showed maturity and dedication to the field. When discussing epistemological orientation to the field of school counseling, Charlie presented as firm but also flexible to be able to work as a team member. Charlie saw the "bigger picture"—even without having experience in a counseling setting—by discussing issues on both a macro level (e.g., gendered cultural norms, racism, and social class backgrounds) and a micro level (e.g., gender identity and resiliency). Many of the committee members identified with Charlie's humility and the story about learning from their father's wisdom, while also presenting as knowledgeable and well-informed. Importantly, Charlie had prepared a thoughtful stance on issues regarding race, racism, and equity.

By now it is probably clear who the committee chose to hire for this position. While both candidates had assets and liabilities, Charlie was able to "think theoretically" and bring a level of intellectual maturity to the position that the committee felt was very important. As the principal, A. J. also felt strongly about finding a candidate who would be adaptable and able to see things from multiple perspectives and utilize available resources to make well-informed decisions.

Having your theory "app" activated and well-tuned can only help you as you traverse the rest of your academic journey and begin your professional career. Before you move to the next section in this chapter, go back to the list of interview questions we posed in the case study, and consider the career path you are seeking. For instance, edit the question about the role of a school counselor with a similar question about a social worker, program director, therapist, educator, policy analyst, or health care provider; in addition, exchange the word "student" with "client." How would you answer these questions? Even if the hiring committee may not ask specifically about your "theoretical approach," how might your theory app be used in a more subtle way? To use theoretical terms, how might your theory "app" develop with you as you move through the life course and add more experience to your professional repertoire? Are you gravitating toward one theory over the other because it resonates with your own personal experience? How do you think that might change over time?

Functionalist
Macro (families are social institutions) and Micro (who fulfills roles within families)

Family Systems
Macro (family system & subsystems) and Micro (interdependent individuals) are needed to understand how families seek equilibrium

Family Developmental
Micro (family members) progress through Macro (predictable stages)

Conflict
Macro (haves vs. have-nots) and Micro (conflict is inevitable but can be positive)

Feminist
Macro (intersecting oppressions) and Micro (personal is political)

Critical Race
Macro (systemic racism inherent in social and cultural systems) and Micro (choosing to be antiracist & doing the social justice & activism work)

Queer
Macro (hegemonic heteronormativity, cisnormativity) and Micro (gender performance, identity)

Life Course
Macro (historical timing, cohort membership) and Micro (agency)

Family Ecological
Macro (physical & cultural environment) and Micro (family & individual-level characteristics)

Family Stress & Resilience
Micro (family vulnerability & resilience) and Macro (external stressors)

Social Exchange
Micro (individuals make decisions about relationships by maximizing benefits & minimizing costs) based on Macro (resources available to them)

Symbolic Interactionist
Macro (meanings associated with symbols & labels) helps us understand Macro (socially embedded identities & the generalized other)

FIGURE 14.1. A Theory Map for Your Theory App!

Clearly, your theoretical app can be engaged on a micro level, helping you select and identify which framework best matches your own epistemology as you move forward through the life course. However, it is also important as a professional to keep the other frameworks close at hand because just one theory will not fit all the problems you will face in the workforce. Later in this chapter, we outline ways you can utilize several theoretical lenses at once to address issues facing families in the local community. But first, let's consider *all* of the differences and similarities between the theories we have covered in this text. We have presented the 12 theories in the chronological order in which they emerged within the disciplines of human development and family science, psychology, and sociology. In each chapter, we also highlighted each theory's unique perspective when it comes to explaining family dynamics, structures, and contexts. While it may be challenging to keep the complexities of each perspective in mind at all times, we hope Figure 14.1 can serve as a handy reference when you need to quickly compare and contrast the theories and their basic propositions.

As you can see, we do not categorize any theory as strictly micro or macro level. In fact, all of the theories covered in this book can be adapted to include both micro- and macro-level analyses. While we presented the theories chronologically in this text, we group them in this "theory map" in a way that illustrates that there are similarities and differences in how each theory conceptualizes individuals, families, and society.

As an example, notice the first group of three. Functionalist, family systems, and family developmental theories are near to each other because they are similar in orientation: They examine family behavior as it relates to norms, systems, and institutions surrounding families in society. Functionalist theorists and family systems theorists may approach studying the family in similar ways; they may analyze what part of a system is not functioning as it should. Similarly, family developmental theorists would analyze the progression of family members through predictable "stages" in life and analyze family issues in the context of those developmental norms and expectations.

Conflict, feminist, critical race, and queer theories are also similar in orientation to each other because they approach the study of families from a structural standpoint. As an example, conflict, feminist, and critical race theorists critique the unequal distribution of power in society. They would ask: How can we explain family dynamics by examining who has access to power and who does not? Queer theory critiques the dominant, heterosexist narrative that situates all other experiences and identities as "other" or "deviant." This messaging emerges out of cultural discourses at the macro level. Thus, these theories are grouped together.

Life course theory and family ecological theory are together because they take aspects of both the previous understandings into account. It should be no surprise that such contemporary perspectives have had the opportunity to build on earlier theories, resulting in the opportunity to analyze complex relationships over time. Both of these theories allow researchers to account for individual-level factors (e.g., agency in decision-making) as well broad social forces, such as historical time, cultural norms, and environmental influences that impact families.

Family stress and resilience theory, another relatively new perspective to family science, is on its own to represent its focus on the family as the unit of analysis as well as this theory's ability to look at a family's response to past stressors to predict future outcomes (similar to life course theory). Family stress and resilience theorists are able to capture micro-level processes in response to both stressors. This theory contrasts with other theories that are primarily macro level in analysis, however, because it allows researchers to study diverse family forms, such as LGBTQ+ families, families or color, and blended families with complex structural histories. This theory also posits that stress is a normal part of family life and that positive change often results from confronting and handling adversity with resilience. It all depends on how family members respond.

Finally, social exchange theory and symbolic interactionist theory are together because they offer primarily micro-level perspectives, though each takes macro-level forces into account. Social exchange theory analyzes how individuals calculate costs and benefits when, for instance, deciding whether or not to become involved in a relationship. Macro-level forces are at play during this decision-making process, especially when considering what available alternatives one may have and what resources exist when calculating an important decision. Similarly, symbolic interactionist theory argues that individual actors are undoubtedly influenced by symbols, labels, and preexisting generalizations when deciphering meaning from individual-level interactions. In fact, this perspective suggests that the meaning derived out of those individual-level interactions is both dependent on and interacts with larger, more macro-level forces, like culturally embedded stereotypes and expectations about family and relationships. Thus, while this theory focuses on micro processes that some other theories overlook, it is still in the same "family" (pun intended) as macro-level theories because structure is very important to this perspective as well.

BOX 14.1. THEORETICAL ANALYSIS OF FAMILIES AND SOCIAL MEDIA

Image 14.1a–d

Using social media is one of the most common ways that people communicate in modern society. As a family researcher and practitioner, it is important to consider how social media has affected family life, for better or for worse. Here, we theoretically analyze family use of social media with a few of the theories we have presented in this text. Let's begin with more macro-level theories.

From a functionalist perspective (Chapter 2), social media can serve an important purpose for families. Parents and children can communicate and keep updated on life events both big and small via social media, and this is especially important when families are separated by geographical distance. Thus, the manifest function of social media, which keeps people connected, is relevant for families. At the same time, there could be several latent functions; Facebook has been shown to increase feelings of jealousy in romantic relationships (Imperato et al., 2021; Muise et al., 2009) and also increase rates of depression among its users (Forchuk et al., 2021).

Life course theorists (Chapter 9) might be interested in how different generations in the family respond to the rapidity with which interactive technologies are evolving and changing. For example, parents are introducing infants and toddlers to interactive technologies, and professionals report an urgency to help parents learn how to scaffold young children in their technology use (Archer et al., 2021). Youth and emerging adults are among the most adept and invested consumers of technology (Vaterlaus et al., 2019), yet the posts of preadolescents and adolescents on social media can affect them later on in their adult lives (Palfrey et al., 2010). Inappropriate posts, messages, videos, or pictures can pop up later in life and put reputations at risk, even if one has outgrown immature behaviors. These issues are important for families to consider as parents help children navigate social media. Additionally, the intersection of social media use and the COVID-19 pandemic, including misinformation about the public health crisis, would also be of interest to a life course theory researcher (Puri et al., 2020).

From a conflict perspective (Chapter 3), social media can increase (or decrease) families' social capital. Parents often post on social media to ask for parenting advice or advice related to purchases for their families. This is called crowdsourcing: "asking for advice on social media provides a quick way of getting a lot of opinions and ideas at one time" (Wallace, 2015). By capturing these responses, Facebook users are able to literally capitalize on their social networks and make a more informed decision about what approach might work best. Social and cultural capital can both be strengthened on social media (Poecze & Strauss, 2020).

In a similar way, social media gives us insights into how families operate using more micro-level theories as well. Symbolic interactionist theory (Chapter 4), particularly Goffman's (1959) concepts of "presentation of self," can be applied to various social media sites like Facebook,

(continued)

Instagram, Twitter, Snapchat, and Pinterest. Pinterest is a website where members can save "pins" to categorized boards, ranging from craft ideas for children to recipes and ideas for hairstyles, outfits, and travel destinations, and it is often used in teaching and learning around the globe (Schoper, 2015). It should be no surprise that women outnumber men as Pinterest users 18 to 1 (Ottoni et al., 2013), which provides a tool for women to surveil themselves, as well as other women, by following what women post and save on the site. Research has examined mothers' use of Pinterest and the so-called "mompetition" that can occur on such sites (Griffin, 2014). Pins that mothers choose to save to their boards can serve as a presentation of self that mothers idealize and aspire to, reminiscent of Hays's (1996) conceptualization of intensive motherhood. At the same time, behavior on sites like this contributes easily to studying Goffman's presentation of self and impression management because pins are often based on how people want others to perceive them (Griffin, 2014).

From a family stress and resilience perspective (Chapter 11), we recognize that contemporary family life has been described as a time of rising anxiety and "heightened conditions of risk, uncertainty, and rapid social change" (Livingstone & Blum-Ross, 2020, p. 17). While there are risks associated with increased technological use, any of the social media sites—Facebook, Pinterest, Twitter, Snapchat, or Instagram—can also be used to communicate to friends and followers that a family crisis or stressor is occurring. Now, families can augment their use of verbal and nonverbal communication strategies with the use of emoticons on social media sites (Hertlein & Twist, 2019). On Facebook and Twitter, for example, users can choose an emotion when they update their status, such as feeling pained, drained, emotional, sad, or broken, to name a few. This alerts friends and family members to a stressful time or crisis in someone's life, which can serve the purpose of drawing on potential resources for dealing with the crisis as well as initiating the coping process.

There are endless possibilities for applying the theories presented in this book to social media. Consider your own experiences with social media, and think about ways in which you have witnessed one or more theories "in action" on Facebook, Snapchat, Pinterest, YouTube, Instagram, or any other medium worth analyzing. How do you think theories of family will adapt to these new forms of communication in the future? What other aspects of social media should be considered when applying theory to a very complex (and new!) set of social norms and expectations about how to use social media?

Using the Theories

Now that you have learned the ins and outs of all the theories presented in this book, you are most likely finding yourself preferring one or two theories over others. Below, we outline how to use multiple perspectives at once to come to a solution you or others may face in your profession someday. Indeed, it is increasingly common for family scholars to combine theories, offering a hybrid approach to how studies are guided and research is interpreted (Allen & Henderson, 2022). The scenario we present asks you to bring your theoretical "app to the table" to help partners in the community address the needs of local individuals and families.

Representatives from the United Way (a nonprofit community service organization), the County Department of Public Health, the community services board, the local school district, the local university, a local behavioral health organization, and the city's neighborhood resource office manager have all come together at a meeting to address how to best support low-income families in need of affordable child care, so they can manage working the 12-hour day shifts at a local factory. The purpose of their meeting is to gather information about available resources in the community and come up with a plan to disseminate the information to families in need.

From a family ecological standpoint (Chapter 10), there are several considerations that need to be made when pooling together a list of solutions. First, the macrosystem should be analyzed to account for the diversity and complexity of the families who are in need of childcare. The neighborhood resource office manager presents a map of the city to outline where the majority of plant workers and their families live, the available public transportation, and schools and childcare centers that are open before and after the 12-hour day shift. By doing this, the manager is factoring in the mesosystem (connections between the micro family system and greater society) as well. From this map and discussion, the group identifies several social institutions that should be included in the "network of help" they have begun to outline for families and children in the area.

Several nonprofit organizations in the area have been known to offer services that may have been helpful in the past, but the group is not sure if those services are presently available. The group decides to reach out to employees at the city-operated community center to see if they could transport children after school to their facility to provide programming free of charge like they do for residents in nearby neighborhoods. You begin to notice that the conversation surrounding this issue sounds a lot like social exchange theory (Chapter 7); someone mentions that the community center may be eligible for an increase in both grant money and city funding if they can prove that the needs of children in the surrounding areas outweigh the available resources. The school district official volunteers to contact the community center to see if they might be willing to front a few resources to help this cause, in exchange for the documentation of need to increase the resources they receive. Hopefully, these two community partners can pool their resources to improve both the services offered and families reached by this one organization.

Finally, the university researcher present at the meeting suggests gathering data on the families in the targeted area to establish exactly what developmental stage they are in. For instance, some of the workers at the factory may be in the preschool family stage, and therefore, may not need afterschool care; they may just need childcare with an emphasis on early childhood education. Conversely, it could be that a sizable proportion of families are in the middle years and, perhaps, part of the "sandwich generation," wherein they are caught between caring for teenage or young adult children and their own parents, who need caregiving (Hämäläinen & Tanskanen, 2021; Miller, 1981). It is important to know exactly what the needs are of this group of workers, so the community partners can come together with solutions that make sense for the families in need. During this discussion, you hear aspects of both family developmental theory (Chapter 5) and life course theory (Chapter 9). You are also quick to make the link between theory and research, noting that both are equally important as you try to assess the needs of families and come up with solutions that can be flexible and pragmatic.

As you can see throughout this chapter, we are constantly connecting theories we covered throughout the book to help fine-tune your "app." Now that we have addressed what that might look like during a job interview and in the workforce, we move to another modern culture example in Box 14.2 to remind you that theories—whether you like it or not—are everywhere!

BOX 14.2. FAMILY THEORY IN MODERN CULTURE: *OZARK*

Image 14.2 A Scene From *Ozark*, 2022

Ozark is an American drama that follows the Byrde family as they relocate to the Lake of the Ozarks from a posh suburb of Chicago to set up a money-laundering scheme for the Mexican cartel. The opening episode features mom/wife Wendy Byrde having an affair, and at the behest of her lover, she attempts to leave her husband Marty for him. However, as fate would have it, she is unable to leave as circumstances surrounding Marty's money laundering scheme spiral out of control and he and his family have to face the consequences. They flee to the Ozarks and try to do what they can to survive.

Though the show does not touch on all 12 theories presented in this book, a few stand out. Conflict theory (Chapter 3) at both the micro and macro levels is evident throughout the storylines that make clear that the Byrde family has a particular type of social capital at the beginning of the show, which evolves over time to include a diversity of characters they come to count on. At the micro level, the Byrde family experiences significant conflict, some of which is resolved, some is managed, and quite a bit is left to unfold over the three seasons of the show.

Another theory illustrated in this show is symbolic interactionism (Chapter 4). Both Marty and Wendy are on the verge of splitting up at the beginning of the show, and because of the impending crisis and threats on their lives, they are forced to partner together to avoid being murdered by their pursuers. As a result, their bond strengthens temporarily, and the meaning associated with being a "family" quickly shifts from any semblance of normalcy to all four of the family members, including a teenage daughter and an adolescent son, playing a role in the money laundering schemes just to stay alive.

One final theory that is evident in this show is family stress and resilience (Chapter 11). The Byrde family does not experience a singular stressful event; because of their criminal involvement, stressors pile up and pile up, and the family stays in perpetual crisis. They do reorganize, as mentioned earlier, but they remain in crisis mode even after the reorganization. The children become engaged in their own criminal activity, and soon their entire daily lives revolve around chaotic criminal activity with other local Ozark families. Their "new normal" is anything but, and unfortunately, the show does not provide an example of what their family looks like postcrisis; their lives are one big crisis, day after day.

Future of Family Theories

In Chapter 1, "What Is Theory?" we described several assumptions that all family theories make about the inner workings of families and the broader structures that constrain and support them: (a) the *developmental* assumption that families change over time; (b) the *diversity* assumption that families vary in their composition and structure; (c) the *systemic* assumption that families are systems; and (d) the *processual* assumption that families are dynamic. As we reflect back on these core ideas of change, diversity, systems, and dynamics that all family theories address, we cannot ignore the role that technology increasingly plays in the future development of family theories. Family

BOX 14.3. GLOBAL COMPARISONS: CELL PHONE AND SOCIAL MEDIA USE

Consider the use of cell phones, the internet, and social media as ways that families now communicate and stay connected. How does this trend apply to various destinations around the world? A 2021 report from the Pew Research Center (2021a) found that 97% of Americans have a cell phone, and many developing nations (such as South Africa and Brazil) are rapidly catching up to cell phone use patterns similar to the United States. Other countries, such as Pakistan and Mexico, however, lag behind the United States, with approximately 50–60% of their populations having a cell phone (Sava, 2022). On balance, though, the trend for the vast majority of citizens of most countries to own a cell phone is likely to rise because many developing nations have "skipped landline technology and moved straight to mobile" (Rainie & Poushter, 2014).

The Pew Research Center (2021b) also reports on technology and global trends in social media use. Americans are most likely to have access to and use the internet (93%). A different pattern has been found in some other countries, particularly emerging nations. Although emerging countries include a smaller share of adults who actually use the internet, those who do are very active social media users. Compared to the United States, where 72% of internet users are also social networking site users, figures are much higher in the United Arab Emirates (99%), South Korea (89%), and the Netherlands (88%).

Consider how access to and use of new technologies affects family mobility. We could argue by using functionalist theory (Chapter 2) that some family members may outsource their needs—such as romance, affection, and love—by using (or abusing) the internet to form extramarital relationships. Additionally, think about the increase in awareness about feminist activism, racial injustice, and issues facing LGBTQ+ communities, and the like, that we addressed in Chapters 8, 12, and 13. Social media and new modes of communication have played a significant role in raising awareness and helping activists organize around important, emerging issues (Jackson et al., 2020). Digital connections with like-minded people have contributed to individuals engaging in chosen families and seeking social support online as well (Saud et al., 2020). On the whole, and particularly during the COVID-19 pandemic, technology connects families across a distance like never before. How have your own family and relationships with loved ones benefited from technology? On the flip side, what have the downsides been? Keep tuned in to your theoretical "app" as you work through these personal experiences to help name some of the pros, cons, and unexpected outcomes of technology use in families.

mobility, communication, stress and resilience, development, and relationships have all been revolutionized by technology. Now, all family theories must also incorporate the assumption that *technology* is infused throughout family life, regardless of social location and nationality. Therefore, we hope that we have connected you with theories of family in the same way that your technologies connect you with ways of thinking, knowing, doing, and learning. Additionally, while technology does change rapidly, we hope we have communicated that the family is an enduring institution that has proven capable of adaptation and transformation over time, and you are now equipped with the ability to follow these changes with your theoretical "app"! We look forward to observing and explaining how technological innovation will intersect with the assumptions we have identified in continuing to change the nature of family theory and family theorizing in the future.

Multimedia Suggestions

The websites are listed here to familiarize you with the occupations that family science students are most likely to pursue after graduation. While this list is not exhaustive, it should provide an overview of what fields you could consider for yourself, as a budding family theorist!

- Family science: https://www.ncfr.org/
- School counselors: https://www.schoolcounselor.org/
- International Association for Counseling: http://www.iac-irtac.org/
- World Federation of Occupational Therapists: http://www.wfot.org/
- Social work: https://www.socialworkers.org
- Nonprofit work: http://www.idealist.org/
- Community health workers/educators: http://explorehealthcareers.org
- Adoption work: https://www.nationalcenteronadoptionandpermanency.net/

Activate your theory app: Rank the occupations above in terms of your level of interest, and map out how your experiences both inside and outside the classroom will help prepare you for each field. Have at least one "backup" plan in mind.

Harry Potter (1997–2007)

Image 14.3 A scene From *Harry Potter and the Sorcerer's Stone, 2001*

Harry Potter is arguably an "empire" based on seven novels written by British author J. K. Rowling. The books were first turned into films, then video games, and even an amusement park owned by Universal Studios and Warner Brothers, opened in 2014. The premise of the story is centered on a young boy, Harry, as he develops into a wizard at Hogwarts School of Witchcraft and Wizardry. Harry is orphaned as a baby because the dark wizard Voldemort murdered his parents. The adventures of the series pit Harry against Voldemort, and several themes and plots can be analyzed using *any* theory presented in this book. To list a few: (a) family stress and resilience (Chapter 11) can be used to analyze Harry's relationship with his guardians, the Dursleys; (b) symbolic interactionist theory (Chapter 4) can be used to analyze the meaning associated with the four houses of Hogwarts; (c) feminist theory (Chapter 8) can be used to analyze the role Hermione plays in the fight against evil; and (d) family systems theory (Chapter 6) can be applied to the Weasleys.

Activate your theory app: Compare the Harry Potter series to another popular trilogy or film series that has been produced during an older family member's lifetime. Apply theory to the two, and contrast them, paying attention to how cultural and social expectations affect each.

The Wizard of Oz (1939)

Though this film was made over 80 years ago, it remains one of the best known musicals of all time. It is also a great movie to apply theories of family to! The main character, Dorothy, "dreams" of visiting the "Land of Oz," arguably because she was experiencing considerable stress after an interaction with a mean neighbor, a fortune teller, and then a tornado on her family's farm in Kansas. Social exchange theory (Chapter 7) is evident when Dorothy needs to present the Wizard of Oz with the Wicked Witch of the West's broom in exchange for a brain (for Scarecrow), a heart (for

Image 14.4 A Scene From *The Wizard of Oz*, 1939

Tin Man), courage (for Lion), and a return trip home for Dorothy. From a family systems perspective (Chapter 6), we could also analyze the subsystems in Dorothy's family: she has close kin-like relationships with the farmhands as well as her guardians. The power surrounding the Wizard of Oz could also be analyzed through the lens of conflict theory (Chapter 3), as the fantasy world seemingly operates with one individual (Oz) profiting off the backs of many (the Munchkins).

Activate your theory app: You may also be familiar with the story *Wicked,* which is a "prequel" to the *Wizard of Oz* that includes both a novel and Broadway musical. Consider how we could theoretically analyze the story of Elphaba as it relates to the *Wizard of Oz.*

Further Reading

Gorman, A. (2021). *Call us what we carry*: *Poems*. Viking. This is a collection of poetry by Amanda Gorman, who is a *New York Times* bestselling author and Presidential inaugural poet. This collection features poetry from a variety of different styles, including the poem delivered at President Biden's inauguration in 2021, "The Hill We Climb." The poems included not only carry variety in form but also cover a wide range of topics, including history, language, and identity, all in the midst of a global pandemic. Readers would be hard-pressed to not find material relevant to critical race theory, feminist theory and intersectionality, conflict theory, among many others. The collection also offers what Gorman became so well-known for touching on in the inaugural poem: hope for a better tomorrow.

Kendall, M. (2020). *Hood feminism: Notes from the women that a movement forgot*. Penguin. This collection of essays by Mikki Kendall drives home the reality that the feminism we know in modern society has major flaws. Kendall clearly and undeniably details the ways in which the most marginalized voices have been overlooked, perpetuating the very thing feminism is purporting to dismantle: stark, mostly invisible inequalities. Kendall covers issues such as the hypersexualization of women of color, reproductive justice, and the over-reliance on carceral solutions and grounds each argument in intersectionality. Kendall also does readers a favor by providing clear, practical suggestions and calls to action—a great example of feminist praxis.

Mills, C. W. (1959). *The sociological imagination*. Oxford University Press. This book by C. Wright Mills is a sociological classic. No doubt this is assigned in many theory classes because it provides the grounding on which scholars learn, often as students, how to begin and hone the process of thinking theoretically. The book also teaches about the process of critique. For example, Mills provided a critique of the grand theories at the time (e.g., Parsons's structural functionalism) for attempting to be abstract and value free. Mills's insights have inspired generations of scholars to think outside the box, be creative in their theorizing, and take bold steps in conducting research that matters to those we seek to understand and assist.

Newman, B. M., & Newman, P. R. (2016) *Theories of human development* (2nd ed.). Psychology Press. This book is written for students interested in understanding the kinds of theories that are used by psychologists and human development scholars. The authors describe 10 theories from three major perspectives: (a) those that emphasize biological systems (i.e., evolutionary, psychoanalytic, and cognitive developmental); (b) those that emphasize environmental factors (i.e., learning, social role, and life course); and (c) those that emphasize a dynamic interaction between the person and the environment (i.e., psycho-social, cognitive social-historical, bioecological, and dynamic systems). This book is a good complement to the current text on family theories, especially for gaining insight into how family and human development theories overlap and differ.

Wacker, R. R., & Roberto, K. A. (2019). *Community resources for older adults: Programs and services in an era of change* (5th ed.). SAGE Publications. In this comprehensive book, gerontologists Robbyn Wacker and Karen Roberto combine theory, research, policy, and practice to help students and practitioners understand the needs of older adults, from the aging baby boomers to the oldest-old. The book is applicable to social workers, gerontologists, family practitioners, health care providers, adult services administrators, just to name a few disciplinary backgrounds, who work in private, nonprofit, and public agencies and organizations. The authors offer many practical suggestions that are grounded in a variety of theoretical frameworks that build upon and extend the theories we address in this book.

Questions for Students

Discussion Questions

1. We have presented theories of family in this book as emerging from different disciplines, such as sociology, psychology, family science, history, and economics. Compare how two of these disciplines (e.g., family science and sociology) approach studying the family. What are the main differences and similarities?

2. Consider the following research question: What predicts whether or not a couple engaged to be married *will actually* get married? Think about which theoretical framework would be best suited to answer this question and why. In contrast, which theoretical framework might not be the best to explain this research question?

3. We have described four main assumptions (development, diversity, system, and process) that all family theories seek to make and then added a fifth (technology). Now that you have read every chapter in this book (we hope!), can you think of any other assumptions that run through all or most of the theories?

4. How would you explain the ways that theory, research, and practical application work together to help family scholars intervene into family life and family problems?

5. Which of the theories you have read about seems to be the most applicable to everyday life? That is, which of these theories translates best into practices and policies that can improve family life?

6. Next time you go on a job interview, do you think you will incorporate any of these family theories into the questions your prospective employer might ask about how you work with families? Why, or why not?

Your Turn!

Using one of the theoretical frameworks from this textbook as a starting point, construct *your own* theoretical framework to be used to study families. Identify whether or not your theory will be micro, macro, or a combination of both. Create and define at least two concepts that are unique to your theory, and give examples of how those concepts are different from the theory you are starting from and what new considerations they bring to the theoretical canon.

Personal Reflection Questions

1. Revisit those five reasons people get divorced that you identified in the first personal reflection question when you read Chapter 1. Which theory or theories align with your answers? Or have your answers changed after reading this book? Try to match a theoretical framework with where you stand.

2. Which family theory, or theories, can explain most of the way you see the world? Which theoretical frameworks from this text do you most identify with? Which ones do you least identify with? Why?

3. If Katherine and Angie (the authors) asked you to help them revise this book, which of the theories would you suggest they "throw out"? Are there other theories you would like to know more about?

4. Thinking about all of the case studies we have described in this book, write up a case study, based on your own life, and show how at least two of the theories can help explain the circumstances you describe.

5. On a scale of 1 to 10, with 1 being low and 10 being high, how would you rate your understanding of theories now, compared to when you first opened this book? Why?

6. What is the last TV show or film you saw to which you found yourself applying some of the theoretical concepts in this book? In what ways?

References

Allen, K. R., & Henderson, A. C. (2022). Family theorizing for social justice: A critical praxis. *Journal of Family Theory & Review*. Advance online publication. https://doi.org/10.1111/jftr.12450

Archer, K., Wood, E., & De Pasquale, D. (2021). Examining joint parent–child interactions involving infants and toddlers when introducing mobile technology. *Infant Behavior and Development, 63*, Article 101568. https://doi.org/10.1016/j.infbeh.2021.101568

Forchuk, C. A., Plouffe, R. A., & Saklofske, D. H. (2021). Do you "like" me? The roles of Facebook reassurance seeking and attachment style on depression. *Psychology of Popular Media, 10*(2), 223–229. https://doi.org/10.1037/ppm0000312

Goffman, E. (1959). *The presentation of self in everyday life.* Doubleday.

Griffin, K. M. (2014). *Pinning motherhood: The construction of mothering identities on Pinterest* [Doctoral dissertation, University of Central Florida].

Hämäläinen, H., & Tanskanen, A. O. (2021). 'Sandwich generation': Generational transfers towards adult children and elderly parents. *Journal of Family Studies, 27*(3), 336–355. https://doi.org/10.1080/13229400.2019.1586562

Hays, S. (1996). *The cultural contradictions of motherhood.* Yale University Press.

Hertlein, K. M., & Twist, M. L. C. (2019). *The Internet family: Technology in couple and family relationships.* Routledge.

Imperato, C., Everri, M., & Mancini, T. (2021). Does Facebook 'threaten' romantic relationships? Online surveillance and couple visibility behaviours in romantic jealousy and couple relationship quality in a sample of Italian women. *Journal of Family Studies.* Advance online publication. https://doi.org/10.1080/13229400.2021.1987295

Jackson, S. J., Bailey, M., & Welles, B. F. (2020). *#HashtagActivism: Networks of race and gender justice.* MIT Press.

Livingstone, S., & Blum-Ross, A. (2020). *Parenting for a digital future: How hopes and fears about technology shape children's lives.* Oxford University Press.

Miller, D. (1981). The "sandwich generation": Adult children of the aging. *Social Work, 26*(5), 419–423. https://doi.org/10.1093/sw/26.5.419

Muise, A., Christofides, E., & Desmarais, S. (2009). More information than you ever wanted: Does Facebook bring out the green-eyed monster of jealousy? *CyberPsychology and Behavior, 12*(4), 441–444. https://doi.org/10.1089/cpb.2008.0263

Ottoni, R., Pesce, J. P., Las Casas, D., Franciscani, G., Jr., Meira, W., Jr., Kumaraguru, P., & Almeida, V. (2013). Ladies first: Analyzing gender roles and behaviors in Pinterest. *Proceedings of the International AAAI Conference on Web and Social Media, 7*(1), 457–465. https://ojs.aaai.org/index.php/ICWSM/article/view/14438

Palfrey, J. G., Gasser, U., & Boyd, D. (2010). *Response to FCC notice of inquiry 09–94: Empowering parents and protecting children in an evolving media landscape* [Harvard Public Law Working Paper 10–19]. Berkman Center Research Publication.

Pew Research Center. (2021, April 7a). *Mobile fact sheet.* https://www.pewresearch.org/internet/fact-sheet/mobile/

Pew Research Center. (2021, April 7b). *Social media fact sheet.* https://www.pewresearch.org/internet/fact-sheet/social-media/

Poecze, F., & Strauss, C. (2020). Social capital on social media—Concepts, measurement techniques and trends in operationalization. *Information, 11*, Article 515. https://doi.org/10.3390/info11110515

Puri, N., Coomes, E. A., Haghbayan, H., & Gunaratne, K. (2020). Social media and vaccine hesitancy: New updates for the era of COVID-19 and globalized infectious diseases. *Human Vaccines & Immunotherapeutics, 16*(11), 2586–2593. https://doi.org/10.1080/21645515.2020.1780846

Rainie, L., & Poushter, J. (2014, February 13). *Emerging nations catching up to U.S. on technology adoption, especially mobile and social media use.* Pew Research Center. www.pewresearch.org/fact-tank/2014/02/13/emerging-nations-catching-up-to-u-s-on-technology-adoption-especially-mobile-and-social-media-use/.

Saud, M., Mashud, M., & Ida, R. (2020). Usage of social media during the pandemic: Seeking support and awareness about COVID-19 through social media platforms. *Journal of Public Affairs, 20*(4), e2417. https://doi.org/10.1002/pa.2417

Sava, J. A. (2022, January 18). Mexico: Smartphone users as share of population 2015–2015. *Statista.* https://www.statista.com/statistics/625424/smartphone-user-penetration-in-mexico/

Schoper, S. E. (2015). Pinterest as a teaching tool. *Journal of Teaching and Learning with Technology, 4*(1), 69–72. https://doi.org/10.14434/jotlt.v4n1.13114

Vaterlaus, J. M., Berkert, T. E., & Schmitt-Wilson, S. (2019). Parent–child time together: The role of interactive technology with adolescent and young adult children. *Journal of Family Issues, 40*(15), 2179–2202. https://doi.org/10.1177/0192513X19856644

Wallace, K. (2015, January 13). *Why Facebook parenting can backfire.* CNN. http://www.cnn.com/2015/01/13/living/feat-facebook-crowdsourced-parenting/

Image Credits

IMG 14.1a: Copyright © by Meta.

IMG 14.1b: Copyright © by Snap Inc.

IMG 14.1c: Copyright © by Meta.

IMG 14.1d: Copyright © by Twitter, Inc.

IMG 14.2: Copyright © 2022 by Netflix.

IMG 14.3: Copyright © 2011 by Warner Bros. Entertainment Inc.

IMG 14.4: Copyright © 1939 by Metro-Goldwyn-Mayer Studios Inc.

Glossary

ABCX model A is the stressful event, B is the family resources or strengths, and C is the family's perception of the event. X is a crisis, when the family cannot figure out how to solve the problem.

Adaptation Individuals and families are dynamic and capable of changing their beliefs and behaviors to adapt to their environments.

Agency A complex social-psychological process referring to one's ability and desire to make choices within the constraints of social institutions.

Alienation When workers are removed from the product of their labor, from fellow workers, or from reaching their full human potential.

Androcentrism Privileging men and masculinity as the dominant group and the universal standard.

Antiracism Persistent, ongoing activism to upend racist policies, actions, expressions, and ideas.

Assumptions Ideas that scholars believe to be true about families.

Backstage Where social actors retreat from the performance.

Bargaining The rational way couples distribute resources, as described in the exchange/economic model of marriage.

Behavioral psychological approach A psychological exchange model that uses principles of learning and reinforcement that occur between a dyad of two indviduals.

Bisexual A person who feels sexually attracted to their own gender and other genders.

Blended family The family form that includes children from a previous marriage.

Boundary The various parts of a system are divided into discrete boundaries that are either permeable or impermeable.

Bourgeoisie The ruling class who own the means of production (e.g., landowners and capitalists).

Capitalists Those who profit off the labor of the working class.

Chronosystem An "invisible" system that represents the influence of time on each layer.

Cisgender When gender identity matches sex assigned at birth.

Cisnormativity The assumption that everyone's gender identity matches the sex assigned at birth.

Class consciousness Workers' awareness of their relationship to the means of production as a source of workers' oppressive conditions.

Classes Groups of people in competition for scarce resources.

Cohort Groups of people who experienced or produced social events at a specific point in time.

Collective conscience Common sense of morality that all members of the community believe in and uphold.

Color brave Having proactive, difficult conversations with children about topics such as race and racism, which models bravery instead of ignorance.

Colorism How societies value and privilege lighter skin compared to darker skin.

Coming out The development of self-understanding about one's own gender/sexual identity and the act of sharing it with others.

Comparison level (CL) A measure of relationship satisfaction by which people evaluate the rewards and costs of a relationship in terms of what they feel is deserved or obtainable.

Comparison level for alternative (CLalt) A measure of relationship stability that refers to the lowest level of relational rewards a person is willing to accept given available rewards from alternative relationships or being alone.

Concepts Terms and definitions used to explain a theory's framework based on the assumptions; the building blocks used to create the theory.

Conflict management Occurs when the conflict is addressed but does not disappear.

Conflict resolution When the conflict ends because a solution has been reached.

Consciousness When individuals start to become aware of the differential treatment and unearned privileges operating at the personal, familial, and societal levels.

Consensus The stable state needed to reach either conflict resolution or management.

Conversation of gestures Humans engage in social interaction and interpretation to make sense of the world around them.

Cost–benefit analysis Calculating the potential rewards or benefits and the costs in a relationship to decide whether or not the relationship is worth investing in.

Costs The potentially negative things about a relationship that we seek to avoid or minimize.

Crisis, the X factor The event that causes the disruption in family dynamics and leads to the family's reorganization.

Critical consciousness Developing an understanding of the differential treatment and unearned privileges operating at the personal, familial, and societal levels.

Critical epistemology What gets to count as knowledge is defined by those who are in power, and thus, the powerful members of society impose their definitions onto others.

Critical lens An approach to challenging taken-for-granted assumptions, questioning the status quo, and trying to understand social life from the perspective of those who live it, rather than the dominant group.

Cultural capital Nonmaterial forms of capital, such as aesthetic preferences, verbal skills, and levels of education, knowledge, or expertise.

Cultural lag When society evolves but aspects of culture, such as beliefs and values, take longer to change.

Cultural system The overarching system of values, norms, and symbols that guide the choices individuals make, which limit the type of interaction that could occur.

Culture What members of a family, group, or society value; provides a tool kit toward meaning and action.

Cumulative advantage or disadvantage The ways in which structural location, available resources, and opportunities accumulate over time.

Cybernetics A model for understanding the forms and patterns that steer a system and allow that system to self-regulate.

Deprivation-satiation proposition When a reward loses value because it has been given too much in the recent past to hold high value.

Differentiation of self One's sense of being an individual compared to being related to others.

Disengagement When there is low cohesion among family members; they tend to operate independently of one another.

Distributive justice Based on equity theory, the expectation that a person in an exchange relation will expect their rewards will be proportional to their costs.

Double ABCX model How families deal with multiple stressors over time. The model includes precrisis and postcrisis variables.

Double bind When a person is given two commands that contradict each other.

Double consciousness People who experience institutionalized oppression (such as systemic racism) have a feeling of twoness: one that reflects their own experience and the other that reflects the dominant narrative.

Dramaturgy Life is acted out like a stage drama or play.

Dynamic density The number of people living in any given place as well as the number of people interacting.

Dysfunction The part of a system that has broken down.

Ecomap A practical model, similar to the genogram, used in working with families, consisting of the family unit in the center circle with outer circles connected by solid or dotted lines.

Economic capital The material resources, such as wealth, land, and money, that one controls or possesses.

Economic–utilitarian framework A sociological exchange model that examines broader institutions dealing with power and inequality.

Emotion work When we attempt to change an emotion or feeling so that it is appropriate for the situation.

Emotional cutoff The extreme distancing that family members can experience as a way of coping with heightened anxiety.

Emotional labor The idea of extending emotion work into the paid labor force, existing to "sell" emotions to customers. Includes surface acting, deep acting, and genuine acting.

Enmeshment When there is high cohesion among family members, who are highly dependent upon one another and closed off to others outside the family system.

Epistemology One's orientation to answering questions about the world.

Equilibrium Seeking a balance between change (positive feedback loops) and stability (negative feedback loops).

Exosystem Social institutions such as the economy, the media, industry, or criminal justice system.

Expressive roles Showing love, care, concern, and support in the system.

Extrinsic rewards When the outcome of a relationship is more important than the emotional value (intrinsic reward) of the relationship.

Family Adjustment and Adaptation Response (FAAR) model How families make meaning of the stressful situation, including family member's subjective definitions of needs and capacities and how families transcend the situation to develop more stable cognitive beliefs about their relationships within the family and in relation to the larger community.

Family career Family dynamics over time that includes individual members, the family as a system, and the family within broader society.

Family development A longitudinal process of going through a hierarchical system of age and stage related changes, such as birth, death, marriage, and divorce.

Family developmental tasks Individuals and family units have normative goals they must accomplish to move forward to the next level of development.

Family ecosystem The human-built environment, the social-cultural environment, and the natural physical–biological environment.

Family life cycle Beginning with marriage, the normative stages and shared experiences in families as they progress over time.

Family of origin The family one is born into.

Family of procreation The family that is started when partners marry and have children.

Family resilience The ways that a family positively adapts to and rebounds from stressful situations.

Family stages Predictable phases across the family life cycle, marked by marriage, procreation, parenthood, the empty nest, grandparenthood, and widowhood.

Family system A unit of interdependent individuals.

Family transitions A change in the family system when major changes occur in individual family member's lives.

Feedback A way of capturing the interdependence function of systems, wherein individuals in a family system influence one another; feedback can either be negative or positive.

Front stage Social actors tailor their role performance for an audience.

Function The purpose each part of a system serves to contribute to the overall operation.

Gender nonbinary A person who does not identify with the traditional binary of male/female but instead may see themselves as both male and female or as part male and part female.

Generalized other An organized set of attitudes that are common in the group to which an individual belongs.

Generation Similar to a cohort, when a group of people experienced or produced social events but spanning decades.

Generative masculinity A type of responsible masculinity that seeks to give back, be comfortable with oneself, and be willing to confront and critique gender inequality.

Genogram A clinical and empirical technique for uncovering intergenerational family patterns.

Glass ceiling The invisible barrier that keeps women and members of minoritized groups in lower-level positions by denying them the same opportunities for career advancement as White, privileged men.

Hegemonic heteronormativity Understanding the ways that lives are structured and constrained by gender, sexuality, family, race, class, ability, ethnicity, and nationality.

Hegemonic masculinity Socially mandated ideas of how men should behave; can refer to strength, power, wealth, virility, aggression, and being emotionless.

Hegemony The power and dominance that certain identities and institutions have in society.

Heteronormativity An ideology and practice that position gender conventionality, heterosexuality, and family traditionalism as the correct way for people to live.

Heterosexuality Feeling sexually attracted only or primarily to individuals of a different sex.

Holism The importance of studying the whole family system.

Homeplace A self-supporting safe space wherein minority individuals can experience the safety, affection, and full acceptance not available in the wider society.

Homonormativity The new normalcy that certain kinds of LGBTQ+ individuals and families have when they most closely mirror heteronormative, White, middle-class, monogamous culture.

Human betterment The goal to which humans should individually and collectively strive.

Human capital Knowledge and skills a person acquires; less tangible than physical capital.

Identity Internalized expectations and meaning.

Identity salience Our identities are arranged in a hierarchy by order of importance.

Imbalanced exchange When one individual becomes dependent on the person with more power because they have few rewards to offer and few alternatives to turn to.

Impression management Social actors try to control or guide the impression others form.

Index person The person whose life is featured in a genogram.

Individualization The decisions individuals make for themselves affect the possibilities of forming and maintaining families.

Institutionalization When a part of the larger cultural system becomes part of a standard in society; a long-standing tradition that is embedded and identifiable.

Instrumental roles Being a leader, making important decisions, and providing material needs for the system.

Internalization When individuals adhere to the cultural norms in such a way that they become part of need-dispositions and our patterns of communication and ways of thinking.

Interpretive epistemology The view that knowledge is subjective with the goal of understanding how families make meaning of their own experiences. Explains the why of family dynamics.

Intersectionality How multiple systems of oppression, such as race, class, gender, sexuality, religion, age, and nationality, intersect to create advantage or disadvantage; the politics of location.

Intrinsic rewards The tangible and intangible things we find pleasure in and of themselves, not because they provide the means for obtaining other benefits.

Latent functions Unintended consequences of the system.

Legal system Racial stratification is structured into the very fabric of society and supported by the legal system; there is no such thing as colorblind legal theory.

Lesbian feminism Combined sexual orientation with gender theory by critiquing the concept of compulsory heterosexuality.

Liberal feminism The push for women's equality with men.

Lifetime family A type of family history, which consists of four subcareers: the sex experience career, the marital career, the parent–child career, and the adult–parent career.

Lineage family The intergenerational family life cycle that lasts through time.

Linked lives The ways in which a person's life is changed when something happens to another family member.

Locational intersectionality The identities of social positions of disadvantaged groups, such as those who are poor, members of a minoritized group, LGBTQ+, old, or disabled.

Looking-glass self How an individual's sense of self develops based on beliefs about how they are perceived by significant others.

Machismo Exaggerated male pride in some Hispanic cultures.

Macro level The analysis of the larger patterns in society that influence individual and family life.

Macrosystem The largest layer represents cultural ideologies, ways of thinking, and attitudes that exist at a broader level.

Manifest functions The intended purpose of an action.

Marxists Sociologists who utilize Marx's theories to critique the effects of capitalism on various aspects of society.

Meaning-making Attributing meaning to events in our lives.

Meaning of the event, the C factor Perception of the event or situation to which they must respond.

Mechanical solidarity Societies held together by commonalities, where members are generalists and perform similar tasks with similar responsibilities.

Mesosystem The connection between the microsystem and the exosystem.

Micro level Analyzing phenomena more closely and in smaller doses to explore meanings and experiences for individuals.

Microsystem Your immediate family or peers that you rely on closely and come in contact with regularly.

Mind Individual psychology; the mind is only intelligible in terms of social processes.

Minority stress Specific forms of social prejudice that can impact the mental and physical health of minoritized individuals and families by creating a hostile and stressful social environment.

Misogynoir The intersection of racialized and sexualized oppression experienced by Black women and girls.

Moral individualism An outlook on life based on what is good for oneself.

Multiple social contexts One has multiple social positions in terms of gender, race, class, age, sexual orientation, and so on.

Multiple timeclocks Individual time, family time, and historical time that are interrelated over the life course.

Nanosystem The individual's perception of each of the layers in the ecosystem model, used to understand the internal/psychological catalyst of behaviors and, thus, allow more targeted interventions.

Need-dispositions Types of action guided by emotion and individual drive, or representations of individuals' personal uniqueness.

Negative spaces Aspects of everyday family life that are hidden from view.

Norms Societal expectations.

Norms of reciprocity and fairness The history of equity and fairness in a relationship that strengthen feelings of trust between both parties in an exchange relationship.

Object Ideas, roles, social norms, behaviors, or actions.

Ontogenic change How an organism, such as a family or individual family members, changes and matures over time.

Organic solidarity Societies held together by difference.

Pansexual A person feels attracted to any gender.

Patriarchy A political system of male dominance.

Performance Gender is a stylized act; it is a doing, not a being.

Period of disorganization The previous ways a family coped or interacted with one another are inadequate or blocked and cannot meet the demands of the new stressor.

Period of recovery Reversing the process of disorganization and activating their ability to reorganize.

Personality system Takes individual characteristics into account, while still being embedded in the social structure.

Physical capital Resources that are tangible and observable.

Pileup of stressors When stressors accumulate over time and affect the family's ability to reorganize.

Pluralistic A heterogeneous population made up of different genders, racial or ethnic groups, religions, sexual orientations, and social classes.

Political intersectionality Women of color are within at least two subordinated groups that often pursue conflicting political agendas.

Politics of difference Feminist theory is not a unified body of knowledge; rather, it is particular to the situation at hand.

Position The location of a family member in the family system.

Positivist epistemology The view that guides the scientific method and presumes there is an objective, value-free truth that can be discovered about families through systematic research procedures.

Postmodern feminism A feminist approach that deconstructs gender systems and the practices that uphold them, primarily through challenging and exposing what has come to be seen and accepted as normal and natural.

Power In exchange theory, the probability that one actor in a relationship will carry out their own will, despite resistance from the other actor in the dyad.

Pragmatism The meaning of objects lies in their practical use.

Praxis The part of feminist theory that guides the practical or activist part of feminism.

Privilege Power differences in society create social institutions and interactions that value and advantage the elite group and create disadvantages for minoritized groups.

Process–person–context–time (PPCT) model The four components in the bioecological model that influence the developmental outcome and interaction among nested systems.

Proletariats The working class who sell their labor to the capitalist class in return for a wage.

Propositions Statements that make theories testable and are based on both assumptions and concepts we use when we "apply" theory to the study of families.

Qualitative life history interview studies In-depth interviews conducted between the researcher and the participant that address an individual's experiences over time.

Queer theory The social construction of sexual orientation as a social phenomenon, rather than a mental illness or medical issue.

Queering family Challenging the binary notion that simplistically divides families into "normative" versus "nonnormative" by more fully representing family complexity and diversity.

Radical feminism A feminist approach that seeks to uncover the root cause of mechanisms of women's oppression and men's privilege with the goal of creating massive social change.

Rational choice The assumption that individuals will act on the desire to maximize their own personal advantage by making decisions based on a cost–benefit analysis of the situation.

Reflexivity An explicit and comfortable use of self-reflection and autoethnography in research and writing.

Relational intersectionality A type of feminist theory that explains how intersectionality affects every individual, not just the most oppressed and marginalized.

Representational intersectionality The production of images of women of color and the contestations over those images that ignore the intersectional interests of women of color.

Reorganization The ability or inability to develop new ways of interacting with each other and handling stress.

Resources The tangible and intangible forms of capital that individuals have to exchange in a relationship.

Resources, the B factor Strengths to help a family be resilient. Assets the family can draw on to respond to the stress or crisis.

Restorative justice A two-way street to encourage relational repair between the offender and the victim of a crime. A guiding principle in the Black Lives Matter movement, criminal justice social change, and antiracist activism between Black and White people.

Rewards The potentially positive benefits about a relationship that we seek to maximize.

Rhetoric Messages that are aimed at persuading the audience.

Role The dynamic aspect of a position; a detailed set of obligations for interaction; behavioral expectations and meanings that are attached to positions located in the social structure.

Self The individual's emergence through social interaction.

Self-interest One of the driving forces that motivates individuals in an interdependent relationship for exchanging something of value to one another.

Significant other Humans give greater weight to the perspectives of individuals who are most important to them.

Social address model A simplistic way of understanding human and family development, based upon only one influence from a person's environment.

Social capital An individual or family's network of contacts and acquaintances that can be used to secure or advance one's position.

Social construction of reality The belief in what is real arises out of social interaction; typically considered important and valuable if seen that way by powerful members of society.

Social integration The degree to which people are tied to their social groups.

Social justice perspective Acting on a conscious approach to dismantling structural racism and other systems of oppression on behalf of minoritized individuals and families.

Social pathways A confluence of trajectories with longer durations.

Social system The level of interactions between two or more actors, wherein actors are aware of one another's ideas and intentions and their interactions are governed by shared norms or expectations.

Socialist feminism An approach to feminism that is rooted in Marxist class theory, wherein capitalism and its relation to patriarchy are responsible for women's second-class citizenship.

Socialization When individuals come to regard specific norms as binding; it occurs during the interaction of the personality and the social systems.

Standard North American Family (SNAF) The normative model of White, middle-class North Americans with married, heterosexual parents.

Stimulus proposition When an individual responds to a stimulus that provided a reward in the past.

Strain theory Societies have a set of cultural goals that all societal members are pressured to achieve, or live up to, which results in strain.

Stressor, the A factor Internal or external and are a natural occurrence in daily life, can be traumatic, and/or involve multiple losses; the crisis-precipitating event.

Structural functionalism A variation of functionalist theory that emphasizes how social systems produce shared moral codes and norms that trickle down to individuals.

Structural intersectionality The ways in which the location of women of color at the intersection of race and gender makes their experiences qualitatively different from White women's experiences.

Subjective The experiences we have with objects and how we make meaning of those experiences through social interaction.

Subsystems Smaller subcultures that are under the umbrella of a social system; also, units within the family that can be examined on their own in relation to the larger unit.

Success proposition When individuals are rewarded for their actions, they repeat them.

Symbolic capital Prestige, honor, reputation, or charisma.

Symbolic interactionism A micro-level theory that considers processes at the individual level.

The Family A term that implies there is one typical or "normal" family, rather than an acknowledgement that families are very diverse.

Theorize The process that we work through in creating or refining a theory.

Theory A set of ideas that serve as a framework for understanding the world around us. A strategy to describe, interpret, and/or explain a phenomenon.

Trajectory Emerging from each new transition, such as becoming a spouse or a parent, and marked by the continuity of roles and identities.

Transgender Having a gender identity different from the sex assigned at birth.

Transnational carework When primarily migrant women work as live-in or live-out domestic workers for families in wealthy nations.

Trauma Associated with extreme stress, often coming from major disasters or other types of catastrophic events that people are ill prepared to deal with or deter.

Triangulation When a three-person relationship occurs, and two of the members of the relationship exclude the third.

Turning points A type of transition that is very personal and may not be recognized by an outsider as significant.

Value The individual, family, and society's belief system about important ideals.

Waves of feminism A way to think about and characterize the history of feminist theory and activism over the past two centuries.

Whiteness studies Highlighting and problematizing the structural advantages of White racial privilege.

Wholism The idea that the whole family should be studied in order to understand family dynamics.

Womanist feminism A feminist approach developed by women of color to challenge the liberal paradigm, arguing that race, gender, and class cannot be separated.

Xenophobia Extreme prejudice against "foreigners" or people from other countries.

Zero-sum game Family dynamics are dependent on one another to the point that when one member of the family gains, other family members lose.

Index

third-wave, 206–207

The Feminine Mystique (Friedan), 203

feminist theory, 127, 200–202, 386
    adaptable to change, 214
    case study, 199, 200–201
    challenges, 214
    critical consciousness, 209
    criticism on, 215
    as critique of power dynamics, 214
    gender equality/inequality, 200, 202, 204, 208, 215, 219
    generative masculinity, 219
    glass ceiling, 207
    hegemonic masculinity, 200, 212–213
    intersectionality, 200, 210, 214, 216
    lesbian feminism, 205
    liberal feminism, 204
    locational intersectionality, 216–217
    machismo, 200
    man box, 212
    misogynoir, 200
    in modern culture, 212
    political intersectionality, 210
    politics of difference, 206–207
    postmodern feminism, 206
    in practice, 218
    praxis, 200, 218
    privilege and oppression, 200, 208–209
    queer theory and, 206–207, 363
    reflexivity, 200, 208
    relational intersectionality, 217
    representational intersectionality, 211
    in research, 218
    social hierarchy, 210
    socialist feminism, 204
    social movements, 208–209
    structural intersectionality, 210
    systems of oppression, 210–211
    valuing and hearing women's and minoritized voices, 214
    voices from lived experience, 220
    waves of feminism, 202–210
    womanism/womanist feminism, 200, 205

Ferree, Myra Marx, 216

Few-Demo, April, 95, 101–102, 215

Fiese, B. H., 309

Figueroa, V., 249

Fingerman, K. L., 46

Fleabag television series (2016–2019), 77

Floyd, George, 8, 243, 329

Forrest Gump film (1994), 253

Foucault, Michel, 354

France, caregiving for older adults in, 187

Freedman, Estelle, 208

Freud, Sigmund, 97, 111

Friedan, Betty, 203–204

front stage, 91

functionalism, 30, 32, 95
    dynamic density, 32
    dysfunction, 34

    mechanical solidarity, 32
    modern adaptations of, 42
    organic solidarity, 32
    social integration, 33–34

functionalist theory, 7–9, 14, 17–18, 29, 31, 48, 385
    assumptions of, 43
    case study, 30
    collective conscience, 32
    complementary roles, 36
    and critical race theory, 44–45
    cultural goals, 31, 39, 40
    cultural system, 36, 38
    deviance, 31, 39
    dynamic density, 32
    dysfunction, 34
    expressive roles, 38
    institutionalization, 37–38
    instrumental roles, 38
    internalization, 38
    latent functions, 39–40
    LSOG, 45–46
    manifest functions, 39
    mechanical solidarity, 32
    in modern culture, 41–42
    need-dispositions, 36–37
    organic solidarity, 32
    personality system, 36
    in practice, 47
    in research, 46–47
    social integration, 33–34
    socialization, 38
    social system, 36
    strain theory, 40
    strengths of, 41–42
    structural functionalism, 34–35, 39
    structure of family, 33–34
    subsystems, 35–36
    voices from lived experience, 48

G

Gambia, same-sex marriage in, 71

Game of Thrones television series (2011–2019), 284

Ganong, L., 245

Garrett-Peters, R., 95

Gavazzi, S., 122

Gay Liberation Movement, 241

gays, 3, 236
    couples' experiences with transition to parenthood, 129
    gender identity of, 359
    legal rights to marry, 236

gender, 204, 210
    equality/inequality, 200, 202, 204, 208, 215, 219
    in family subsystems, 146
    fluidity, 361–362, 364
    ideology, 352
    inattention to social inequalities of gender systems, 276
    nonbinary, 3–4, 75, 210, 359, 362, 368–369, 379
    performative theory of, 354
    schema theory, 366–367

gender-based violence (GBV), 157
gendered sexuality theory, 240
Gender Nonconforming (GNC), 3
Gender & Society journal, 221
Gender Unicorn, 355, 357
generalized other, 88–89
general systems theory (GST), 143–145
Generation Alpha, 243
generations, 232–233, 240–241
Generation X (1965–1980), 241
generative masculinity, 219
genogram, 152
Gentile, Douglas, 129–130
Gen Z, 243
Germany
    compulsory education in, 277
    family–school interface in, 278
Gholami, R., 335
G. I. Bill (federal assistance program), 14
Gilligan, M., 250
Gilman, Charlotte Perkins, 203
Glass, Valerie, 95, 101–102
glass ceiling, 207
GLQ: A Journal of Lesbian and Gay Studies, 364
Goffman, Erving, 90–91, 385–386
Goldberg, A. E., 270, 366
Gonzales-Backen, M. A., 278
Gottman, John, 154, 162
Gottman, Julie, 154, 162
grandparents
    grandparent–grandchild subsystem, 143
    raising grandchildren, 1, 16
grand theory, 76
Greece, wedding rituals in, 99
Green, D. S., 270
group–interactional dimension, 113

Hacks television show (2021), 222
Haeckel, Ernst, 265
Halperin, David, 364
Hamilton (2016–present) Broadway musical, 342–343
Hammack, P. L., 360
Hamon, R., 144
Han Chinese, 328
Hardesty, J. L., 202
Harry Potter film series (1997–2007), 390–391
Hart, Kevin, 21–22
Hartman, Ann, 275
Haselschwerdt, M. L., 202
Hawking, Jane, 312
Hawking, Stephen, 312–313
Hays, S., 386
Head Start program, 271, 275, 283
Heath, Jamey, 219
hegemonic/hegemony, 358–359
    masculinity, 200, 212–213

helicopter parenting, 38
Henderson, Angie, 312
Henry, C. S., 299
Hepp, Willis, 93
Herdt, G., 361
heteronormativity, 355, 357–359
heterosexual(ity), 206, 355
    community, 47
    couples' experiences with transition to parenthood, 129
    institutionalized, 354
Hidden Brain podcast, 191
Hill, Reuben, 114, 119, 295, 300, 304, 329
Hines, P. M., 340
historical timeclock, 234
The History of Sexuality (Foucault), 354
Hobson, Mellody, 331
Hochschild, Arlie Russell, 90, 92, 97, 99
holism family systems theory, 146
Holmes, E. K., 159–160
Homans, George, 175–176, 182, 186
homonormativity, 358
Hone, L., 303
House Joint Resolution, 66
Hughes, D., 329
Human resource (HR), 47
Human Rights Campaign (HRC), 221
Hyde, J. S., 363

Iceland, legal definitions of marriage and family in, 16
ideal family, 39, 41
imbalanced exchange, 177
Immigration and Nationality Act, 12
impression management, 90–92
index person, 152
India
    caste system in, 336
    compulsory education in, 277
    family–school interface in, 277
    wedding rituals in, 99
Indigenous peoples, 4, 324, 342
Indonesia, legal adult status in, 128
induction, 9
Industrial Revolution, 31–32
inequality/inequalities, 322, 328
    gender, 185, 202, 204, 214, 218, 221, 264
    social, 276
    into social structure, 43
    societal, 72–73
    track, 61–62, 69, 72
Instagram, 379, 386
institutionalization, 37–38
instrumental roles, 38
intergenerational ambivalence theory (IGA theory), 72
intergenerational relationships of families, 10, 146
Intergenerational Solidarity Model, 250

internalization, 38
interpretive epistemology, 6
intersectionality, 199, 200–202, 210–211, 214, 216
    in conflict theory, 70
    locational, 216–217
    political, 210–211
    relational, 216
    representational, 211
    structural, 210
intersex, 4
In the Heights film (2005), 328, 333
intimate partner violence (IPV), 189, 202, 306–307
intragenerational relationships of families, 10
irrelevant person, 148
Ishii, Y., 362
Islamaphobia, 335
Israel, women as emotional labor in, 92
Italy
    caregiving for older adults in, 187
    same-sex marriage in, 71

J

Jamaica, wedding rituals in, 99
James, A. G., 144
James, William, 86
James-Hawkins, L., 218
Japan
    legal definitions of marriage and family in, 16
    maternity and paternity leave policies, 44
Jennings, E., 188
Jensen, T. M., 43
Jim Crow laws, 299
John, Elton, 124
Johnson, E. Patrick, 357, 364
Johnson, Lyndon, 282–283, 326
Jones, W. D., 279–280
Journal of Consumer Sciences, 283
Journal of Marriage and Family, 355
justice, 270
    racial, 280
    restorative, 340
    sexual, 204
    social, 11, 214, 221, 282, 326, 334, 337

K

Karimi, H., 275
Katz, Jackson, 221–222
Kelley, Harold, 177–178
Kelly, S., 186
Kendall, F. E., 340
Kendi, Ibram, 329, 330, 336, 342
Kennedy, John F., 241
Kenya, IPV in, 307
King, Jr., Martin Luther, 40, 241, 336
Klebold, Sue, 34
Klein, David, 117
knowledge building, 9
Komter, A., 218

Ku Klux Klan, 331
Kuvalanka, K. A., 358

L

Landor, A., 187, 188
Land, Stephanie, 213
Lareau, Annette, 72–74
LaRossa, R., 95
latent functions, 39–40
latent power, 218
Latina/Latino, 4, 142, 160, 262
Latinx/Latine, 4, 70, 327, 330, 333, 363
Lavee, Y., 298
Lavender-Stott, E. S., 245
Law on Adaptation of Society to Aging, 187
legal adult status in global countries, 128
Lesbian, Bisexual, and Gay Student Association (LGBTQA), 47
lesbian, gay, bisexual, transgender, or queer individuals (LGBTQ+ individuals), 3, 67, 207, 217, 278, 353, 358–360
    awareness of, 359
    Casbah case, 36
    changes in social acceptance, 358
    deal with racism, 101
    as deviating from social norms, 357
    family research about, 355
    HRC for, 221
    minority stress theory for, 308
    safe program, 47
    voices, 216, 220
lesbian, gay, bisexual, transgender or queer (LGBTQ), 272
lesbians, 3
    couples' experiences with transition to parenthood, 129
    family life cycle, 128
    feminism, 204
    gender identity of, 359
    legal rights to marry, 236
    sexuality, 354
Leshem, Ron, 105
Levin, Daphna, 105
Lévi-Strauss, Claude, 175
Lewin, Kurt, 268
liberal feminism, 204
life course theory, 12, 117, 231, 365–366, 384
    agency, 232, 240
    assumptions of, 234–235
    career concept, 246
    case study, 231–232
    cohort concept, 232
    as contextual approach, 244
    cumulative advantage or disadvantage, 239–240
    difficulty in obtaining and measuring family level data, 245
    difficulty in obtaining consistent longitudinal data, 246
    emerging adulthood, 247
    experience of being old, 248–249

Philippines, legal definitions of marriage and family in, 16
physical capital, 179–180
Piaget, Jean, 111
Pinterest, 386
placater, 148
Plank, Liz, 219
Poland, maternity and paternity leave policies in, 44
policy development, 74
political intersectionality, 210–211
politics of difference, 206
polyamory/polyamorous families, 1, 4, 115, 353
polygyny, practice of, 115
Porter, Tony, 212
Pose television show, 273
position of family member, 116
positivism, 6, 18
positivist epistemology, 6, 18
postmodern feminism, 206
postmodern queer family theory, 353
posttraumatic stress disorder (PTSD), 296, 352
power, 176, 182, 186, 197, 300, 332
pragmatism, 86
praxis, 200, 218
"presentation of self" concepts, 385
The Presentation of Self in Everyday Life (Goffman), 91
privilege, 200, 208
process–person–context–time model (PPCT model), 272
processual assumptions of family theory, 12, 388
propositions, 9–10
psychosexual development theory, 97, 111
psychosocial development stages, 233
public health, 157, 279

Qatar, 218
qualitative life history interview studies, 245
quare theory, 364
The Queen's Gambit television show (2020), 303
queer, 2, 352, 357, 363
        of color critique, 364
        families of color, 355
        intimacies, 360
        studies, 354
queerer family scholarship, 363–364
queering
        Calendar, 359
        compassion, 12
        family, 2, 352, 357
        gender and sexuality, 369
        time and relationships, 369
Queering Bem, 366
queer theory, 186, 206–207, 351–352, 370
        androcentrism, 366
        asexuality, 360
        binary opposition, 353
        bisexual, 356
        case study, 352
        cisgender, 353, 355, 357

"coming out" concept, 355–356
        feminist theory *vs*, 363
        gender fluidity, 361–362, 364
        gender minority, 353
        gender schema theory, 366–367
        Gender Unicorn, 356–357
        heteronormativity, 353, 355, 358–361
        history and origins of, 353–354
        homonormativity, 358
        LGBTQ, 357–360
        LGBTQ+, 353
        and life course theory, 365–366
        in modern culture, 361
        normalization, 364
        opposition to "norm," 362
        pansexual, 356
        polyamory, 353
        in practice, 367–368
        queerer family scholarship, 363–364
        in research, 366–367
        rigid binaries deconstruction, 351–352
        self-of-the-therapist exploration process, 368–369
        sexual minority, 353
        transdisciplinary effort of, 362
        transgender, 353, 355–356
        voices from lived experience, 369
        xenophobia, 358
Quiara Alegría Hudes book, 333

race/racial/racism, 102, 323–325, 327–329
        colorblind, 331
        color line, 330–331
        division, 330
        global racial hierarchy, 102
        inattention to social inequalities of, 276
        intellectual critique of racial oppression, 334
        in LGBTQ+ community, 101
        living with racial trauma, 339
        racial–ethnic identity, 324
        religion and, 335
        socialization, 144, 279
racial stratification, 324
        Black–White, 324
        mental health issues linked to, 339
radical feminism, 204
radical New Left student movement, 203
Raleigh, E., 102
rapid-onset gender dysphoria (ROGD), 161
rational choice, 173, 179
reality, 85
        objective, 96–97
        social constructions of, 7, 96
        symbolic, 86
reflexivity, 200, 208
Reitzes, D. C., 95
relational intersectionality, 216
relationship science research, 185
religion and race, 335
reorganization, 296, 304

representational intersectionality, 211
research. *See* academic research
restorative justice, 340
retreaters, 40
rewards, 173, 180–181, 184
rhetoric theory, 7
Rice, Tim, 124
Rich, Adrienne, 353
Richards, Ellen Swallow, 265
Roberto, Karen, 191, 244
Roberts, R. E. L., 45
Rodgers, R. H., 115, 122, 123
roles, 116
    complementary, 36
    of emotion in human behavior, 97
    expressive, 14, 38
    in functionalist theory, 36
    of individuals in social structure, 92
    reversals in families, 155
    symbolic interactionist theory, 93
Rosenblatt, Paul, 158
Rosenfeld, L. B., 275
Roshanravan, S., 335
Roth, Veronica, 283
Rowling, J. K., 390
Roy, K., 244
Rubio, B., 129
Russia, emerging adulthood in, 247
Ryan, C., 361
Ryder, Norman, 232

S

Sabatelli, R. M., 188
safe program, 47
Safe Zone training, 37
Sami people, wedding rituals among, 99
Sanner, C., 43
Satir, Virginia, 147, 148, 156
Saudi Arabia, same-sex marriage in, 71
Scanzoni, J., 180
Schitt's Creek television show, 68
Schmalzbauer, L., 217
Scotland, legal adult status in, 128
The Second Sex (de Beauvoir), 201
self, 84, 86, 88, 90–92, 160
self-consciousness development stages, 87–90
self-esteem, 46
self-interest, 174–175, 185
self-of-the-therapist exploration process, 368–369
Senegal, legal adult status in, 128
Senior, Jennifer, 133
Settersten, R. A., Jr., 248
"severity" concept, 304
    conceptualizing family stressors according to, 304–305
    differentiation of family stressors and traumas, 305–306

Sex Education television series (2019–2021), 361
sexual assault, 202, 261–262, 270, 301
sexual attraction, 360
sexual ideology, 352
sexuality, 42, 210, 218, 240, 274, 294, 352, 358, 363, 369
Sharp, E. A., 245
Sheff, E., 360
Shih, K. Y., 337
sibling
    relationships across central adulthood, 244
    sibling–sibling relationship, 159
    subsystem, 143, 156
    ties, 43
significant others, 93, 95
Silent Generation (1925–1945), 241
single parent families, 1, 14, 74, 76
Skinner, B. F., 176
Slater, J., 208
Slater, Suzanne, 129
Snapchat, 86, 91, 379, 386
social address model, 272
social approval, 177, 181, 184
social capital, 64, 180
social change, 14, 199, 334
social constructions of reality, 7
social contexts of development, 236
social exchange theory, 70, 186, 384
    arranged marriages, 175
    bargaining, 186
    bridging gap between research and practice, 184
    caregiving for older adults, 187
    case study, 172
    comparison level for alternatives, 178
    cost–benefit analysis, 180
    costs, 172, 180
    deprivation–satiation, 176
    distributive justice, 182
    economic metaphor, 184
    economic–utilitarian framework, 176
    equity theory, 182
    extrinsic rewards, 181
    family scholarship, 185
    human capital, 180
    imbalanced exchange, 177
    intrinsic rewards, 181
    in modern culture, 183
    norms of fairness, 177
    norms of reciprocity, 180
    physical capital, 179
    power, 176, 182, 186
    in practice, 189, 191
    rational choice, 173
    in research, 188
    resources, 179–180
    rewards, 180
    self-interest, 174
    social capital, 180
    stimulus proposition, 176
    success proposition, 176
    testability in research, 184–185

Walsh, Froma, 294
Walters, T. L., 94
Wandavision television series, 41
War on Poverty campaign, 283
Watson, M. F., 340
wedding rituals, 98
Weiss, H., 271
Whitchurch, G. G., 145
White Americans, 279
White families, 14, 34, 70
White, James, 117, 126
White patriarchal power, 202
White privilege, 322, 340
white supremacy, 330, 340
Whiteness studies, 332
Wiener, Norbert, 145
Wight, R. G., 308
Wild film (2014), 313
Wild: From Lost to Found on the Pacific Crest Trail
   (Strayed), 313
Wilkerson, Isabel, 330, 336
Winant, H., 328
Wisconsin Longitudinal Study, 246
The Wizard of Oz film (1939), 391
woman, 354
   in Afghanistan, 217
   deconstruction of universal concept of, 210
   as emotional labor, 92
   emotion work of, 92

and family stress theory, 296–297
FMLA for, 74
involvement in legal profession, 7–8
middle-class White women, 205
mobilization for civil rights, 204
transnational care work, 17–18
working-class, 204
womanism/womanist feminism, 200, 205
Women's Liberation Movement, 20, 209, 241
Women's Rights Convention in Seneca Falls, New York,
   203
Wonder Years television show (2021–present), 253
Woodstock festival, 241
world caste systems, 336
World Health Organization, 282
World's Women 2020, The: Trends and Statistics, 157

X

xenophobia, 358

Y

Yellowstone drama series, 183
Yoon, Y., 309
YouTube, 241, 379

Z

Zartler, U., 300
zero-sum game, 65, 71, 212
Zhang, Y., 188–189

Milton Keynes UK
Ingram Content Group UK Ltd.
UKHW020126181123
432785UK00003B/57

9 781793 548290